SHURTER'S COMMUNICATION IN BUSINESS

SHURTER'S COMMUNICATION IN BUSINESS

FOURTH EDITION

DONALD J. LEONARD
College of Business Administration
Arizona State University

McGRAW-HILL BOOK COMPANY

New York   St. Louis   San Francisco   Auckland   Bogotá   Düsseldorf
Johannesburg   London   Madrid   Mexico   Montreal   New Delhi   Panama
Paris   São Paulo   Singapore   Sydney   Tokyo   Toronto

Library of Congress Cataloging in Publication Data

Shurter, Robert LeFevre, date
    Shurter's Communication in business.

    First-3d ed. published under title: Written communication in business.
    Includes index.
        1. Commercial correspondence. 2. Business report writing. 3. Communication in management. I. Leonard, Donald J. II. Title. III. Title: Communication in business.
HF5721.S54 1979   651.7′4   78-12775
ISBN   0-07-037183-0

SHURTER'S COMMUNICATION IN BUSINESS

    4 5 6 7 8 9 0 F G R F G R   8 3 2 1

This book was set in Century Schoolbook by Monotype Composition Company, Inc. The editors were John F. Carleo, William J. Kane, George S. Thomas, and Nancy B. Moore; the designer was Elliot Epstein; the production supervisor was Charles Hess. New drawings were done by Fine Line Illustrations, Inc. Fairfield Graphics was printer and binder.

CONTENTS

PART FOUR: NONWRITTEN ASPECTS OF WRITTEN COMMUNICATION

PREFACE

Revising Dr. Shurter's third edition of *Written Communication in Business* has been both a valued privilege and a very challenging experience. Reworking the creation of such a respected author was a job that could not be taken lightly. I must admit that I approached the task with some trepidation. The fact that I thought we shared many philosophies of business communication, however, made the assignment a little easier to undertake.

If I had to state the goals that were mentally uppermost as the fourth edition took shape, I would say they were preservation and progress. I strove to maintain the qualities of the third edition that made it such a useful teaching aid. Furthermore, I tried to make it even more useful for the 1980s by including guides, examples, and exercises that reflect the changes that have taken place in recent years in the world of business communicators.

Among the aspects of the third edition I tried to preserve was Dr. Shurter's emphasis on the importance of thinking before writing. He recognized that many people are reluctant to write because it forces them to think or, worse, exposes the fact that they have not thought. Sharing that belief, I have retained his attention to the patterns of thinking which must precede all forms of writing. These patterns are stressed in the section dealing with letters as well as in the one on reports.

Another aspect of the third edition I tried to maintain was Dr. Shurter's demonstrated appreciation for precision and propriety in the use of our language. In keeping with that appreciation, I have retained most of the reference section from the third edition. It could serve as a valuable review for students who haven't seen these rules for a while and might also prove handy for teachers who wish to use it as a grading aid.

Dr. Shurter's sense of humor lent a quality to his writing that I genuinely enjoyed and, thus, attempted to preserve. I hope that my additions to his collection of comical examples measure up to his standards of wit. Related to his humor was his esteem for creative ways of accomplishing goals through written communication. To this end, he included exercises designed to force students to think creatively. The new exercises in the fourth edition have the same objective.

One last parallel is worthy of mention here. Dr. Shurter intended the third edition for two types of readers—college students taking formal courses in the various forms of business writing, and readers who are already engaged in their business careers. Although the last section of the fourth edition has been restructured and expanded, this section, like the others, was designed with the same two types of readers in mind.

Preservation of the commendable qualities of an earlier edition, however, does not justify a revision. I believe readers will find that this fourth edition contains many new features that provide such justification.

Textbooks are revised for a number of reasons, but perhaps the most important reason is the need to keep readers abreast of developments in the field to which the book relates. Certain types of business communications have changed drastically within the last decade. Those changes have been brought about, for the most part, by federal legislation. Because much of this legislation carries stiff penalties for violations, business communicators need to know whether they are communicating legally or illegally. Corporate law staffs of large companies are usually well aware of developments in federal legislation. Thus, companies like Sears and Wards typically keep their employees up to date on the legal do's and don'ts of their business communications. People who work for smaller businesses are not so privileged and often not nearly as well informed as they might be. Because one can't assume that readers of this book will work for only large companies, the legal implications of certain types of business communications are covered where applicable. Thus far, federal intervention has concentrated on the credit and employment processes. The chapters treating these subjects are, therefore, the ones with the most frequent references to Uncle Sam's hand. Wherever such references are made, however, they are made in language that can be understood by readers who don't have a law background.

Another new characteristic of the fourth edition is its sexual neutrality. In the third edition, third person masculine pronouns were used extensively, as they traditionally have been used, in cases where one did not know whether the person addressed or referred to was male or female. In the fourth edition, however, every effort has been made to recognize the likelihood that the principals of examples and exercises could be either male or female.

Teachers who have used the third edition will notice that all the end-of-chapter exercises in the fourth edition are new. These new exercises were designed to challenge future business communicators of the 1980s to put forth their maximum creative efforts. Also new are many examples in the chapters. A large number of those examples were borrowed from actual business correspondence to give readers a realistic picture of the types of messages being sent and received in business.

That the fourth edition of this book is entitled *Shurter's Communication in Business* reflects a new fourth section of the book which provides coverage of other forms of business communication besides writing. This section is called Nonwritten Aspects of Written Communication and covers dictation (Chapter 20), the oral presentation of reports (Chapter 21), and communication reception (Chapter 22). The latter chapter examines the subjects of listening, reading, and nonverbally communicating.

The last two new elements of the fourth edition that I shall mention here have been produced with business communication teachers in mind. Both deal more with the instructor's manual than with the text. The first is the transparency masters that can be torn out of the manual and used in developing classroom teaching aids. The second is the manual's abbreviated guide to the reference section in the text. This concise listing of rules and text pages on which they appear may also be torn out of the manual. My hope is that this guide to the reference section may facilitate the teacher's job of telling students where to go (no pun intended) to further understand and then avoid the errors in their written communication.

Expressions of indebtedness must begin with my wife, Mary, and my daughter, Dawn, who gave me their patient support in this project after having just recently done the same during the completion of my dissertation.

I am, of course, also indebted to Dr. Robert L. Shurter for the meticulous efforts he put into the earlier editions of this book. I must additionally acknowledge the influence of two other authors upon me: Dr. Raymond Lesikar and Dr. Wayne Baty. I have had the privilege of working with both these men and have developed a great deal of respect for them and their work.

To Dr. Don Porterfield I give thanks for recommending that I work on this revision. My colleagues at Arizona State University also deserve a note of appreciation for their inspiring dedication to teaching written business communication. In a similar vein, the members and publications of the American Business Communication Association merit acknowledgment as constant sources of stimulation.

To Lorraine Krajewski I extend my gratitude for her very conscientious work on end-of-chapter exercises. I also thank the many editors and publishers who generously made available the example materials used in the text. Finally, I would like to thank all the students of business communication I've had in classes through the years. I hope that I'll always put forth my best effort to hear their voices when raised in criticism as well as when raised in other fashions.

Donald J. Leonard

SHURTER'S
COMMUNICATION
IN BUSINESS

ONE
PRINCIPLES OF
BUSINESS
COMMUNICATION

In a society where "machines talk to machines" and electronic gadgets bid fair to replace humans, it is comforting to remember one basic fact: like water in its natural state, communication never rises above its source. And that source is a human being. Simply stated, this means that the quality of any written message can never rise above the ability of the human being who wrote it.

At first glance, these statements appear to be so obvious as not to require repeating. But the emerging technology associated with today's communication explosion, with its array of automatic typewriters, computers, and electronic devices, has created the erroneous notion that emphasis on the medium has somehow replaced emphasis on the message. It is a little like concluding that a stupid speaker, given all the resources of television with its vast audience, will be anything but stupid, when, in fact the speaker will only be so for more listeners.

Part One of this book, as well as subsequent chapters, is based on two fundamental convictions about written communication:

1. The ability to express one's thoughts clearly and concisely in writing is one of the most sought-after skills in business—and will continue to be.

2. The quality of written communication is always a result of the writer's knowledge of the basic principles of communication.

For the student or businessperson, therefore, it would be absurd to "write off writing" for the 1970s and 1980s because of computers or mechanical devices. No evidence exists to indicate that written communication will play a less important role in the future business world than it has in the past. Plenty of evidence *does* exist, however, to indicate that it will play a changed role, brought about in part by the appalling costs of today's written word (which are discussed in Chapter 1) and in part by the electronic and mechanized devices now available.

This changed role will undoubtedly involve a technique, widely used—and taught—in the business community, called "management by exception." Under this principle, routine and repetitive situations are treated routinely by a carefully planned method of dealing with them, thus freeing executives—and writers—to concentrate on the unusual, the creative, and the original. In essence, therefore, tomorrow's business writer will require greater skill, broader knowledge, and more flexibility. As the widely quoted advertisement of IBM describes it, "Machines should work; people should think."

Today's frightened assumption that tomorrow's written business communication will involve dehumanized, impersonal interchange between machines in which English has been replaced by FORTRAN or COBOL is nonsensical. Certainly tomorrow's business writers will command the greatest arsenal of methods and techniques—computers, tapes, dictating equipment—that any communicators have ever had; and they will have the responsibility of choosing the quickest or the most appropriate or the least expensive among them, depending on the purpose. But these methods and techniques are servants which provide communicators with the time and opportunity for the challenging and interesting aspects of communication.

Finally, before we begin our discussion of the principles of business communication, we ought appropriately to make a statement which startles many students and business people:

If you are now paid (or will be paid) to write in business, you are in a very real sense a professional writer.

Most business people back away from this statement out of modesty—"Come on now. I'm no Hemingway"—or out of mild shock—"Oh, I don't write that much on the job." (Actually myriads of people in business do more writing during their careers than many novelists, if we consider simply the amount of their writing. Numerous surveys show that business executives spend the major part of the day communicating.)

The alternative to being a *professional* is to be a hack writer, turning out words just to make money without concern for ethics or principles or self-improvement. Of course there are hacks in business as in every other facet of our society. But there are professionals too—and if you are now an "apprentice" in college, you should aim at professionalism in your writing. In the chapters of this book, we have tried to emphasize professionalism by raising questions and providing exercises dealing with ethical aspects of business writing; we have tried to select as many examples of creative, original, and humorous business writing as possible to underscore the belief that writing in business does not necessarily have to be drab and stereotyped. Consider, for the moment, how to define or describe a car: it can be "more than 25,000 separate pieces of metal, plastic, rubber, and other materials assembled into . . ." or "a body placed on four wheels propelled by. . . ." But then consider this:

A car is to tie shoes on and go off to start a new life in.

A professional has left a mark here, as in the beautifully worded letter, just to cite one example, from Yeck & Yeck which is reproduced on page 88.

What is it that distinguishes professionalism in communication from hack writing? A lot of things, but the essence of professionalism is *to keep endlessly trying to improve.* This means seizing every opportunity to write; using every chance to read and to learn how other writers express themselves; and recognizing and respecting the generally accepted principles of effective writing. To scoff at these principles is to condemn yourself to an endless stream of writing frustrations where your thoughts are either misunderstood or denied their true value. Because these principles are so important, they are the subject of the following five chapters.

Chapter 1 attempts to paint a picture of the changing world of today's business writer. Even though technology is exercising considerable influence upon this world, the costs of written communication continue to be a major concern of people in business. Elements in the process of written communication are introduced and reviewed in this chapter. Finally, to set the stage for the material in Chapters 2 through 5, you are encouraged to recognize the many purposes that might be served by a written business communication.

Chapter 2 examines the most basic component of a written message, the word, and cautions readers against some of the most common word-choice abuses of business writers. Fashion, specialization, complexity, jargon, and trite and outworn expressions are treated and exemplified so that readers can avoid these pitfalls that confuse meaning and doom a message to minimal success or to failure.

In Chapter 3 we proceed one step further in the task of developing your business writing proficiency. Here we study a more involved unit of construction, the sentence. Subjects discussed are modifier placement, emphasis, parallel constructions, conciseness, sentence length, passive and active voice, and the portrayal of verbs as verbs. The stress here is on encouraging you to put words together so that they express clear units of thought.

How sentences are grouped to form clear and coherent paragraphs is the subject of Chapter 4. Here we examine how one achieves paragraph unity, logical sequence, transition, proper length, and an organization for impact so as to attain these goals of clarity and coherence. A paragraph demands more concentration from a reader than does a sentence. We should thus take care not to demand too much of our reader by developing long, involved, unrelated, and unwieldy groupings of thoughts that overtax the reader's powers of concentration.

Chapter 5 concludes this first section of the book by examining style as it relates to capturing and maintaining the reader's attention. By avoiding irrelevancies, watching your pace, keeping an appropriate tone, and being specific, you are more likely to secure your readers' attention because you are styling your message to their taste.

This first section lays a foundation for business students concerned with improving the quality of their written work. After mastering these principles, you will be in much better shape to handle the larger units of composition (letters, memos, and reports) to which the rest of the book is devoted.

1
THE INFORMATION EXPLOSION AND THE BUSINESS WRITER

The goals of this chapter are three: to familiarize the student with the circumstances surrounding and influencing business writing today, to acquaint the student with the elements involved in the process of written communication, and to make the student aware of the many purposes that can be served by written communication in business.

CONDITIONS AFFECTING TODAY'S BUSINESS WRITING

Before we go on to discuss the meaning and purposes of business writing, we ought briefly to examine the conditions which affect communication in today's business community. The phenomenon in our society conventionally labeled "the information explosion" has had a profound impact on both the form and the substance of business communication, and this leads to a logical question of "Why put it in writing?" The answer derives from two conditions which have been uniquely characteristic of the seventies and which are likely to be even more influential in the eighties:

1. Never before has the businessperson had so wide a choice of media for a message.

2. The cost of business communication has become astronomical.

Just as the Victorian-era quill pen gave way to the typewriter in the early twentieth century, today's technology provides the businessperson with a myriad of choices beyond the conventional writing it down or talking face to face. Would it be best to telephone, teletype, televise by closed circuit, use electronic taping or videotaping, or employ some other method to get a message across? The age-old dream of instantaneous communication regardless of distance has become a reality. In fact, this dream may well become a nightmare induced by the very abundance of our technical ability to communicate: one estimate, for example, of the rate at which we are adding to the existing store of knowledge in the form of reports, trade journals, letters, documents, and seminar proceedings places it at 500,000 pages per minute.

Yet though this figure may appear impressive, people in business are still communicating with one another at a snail's pace compared with the rate at which the computer allows information to be collected and processed. Sorting and processing of complex information that previously took weeks and years can now be done in minutes and seconds. Yet it still takes an average executive and secretary a good part of a morning to get relatively few pages of business correspondence on their way. And when the cost of this time-consuming task is multiplied by the total number of exchanges, the resulting figures are staggering.

The U.S. Post Office reports that 51.37 billion pieces of first-class mail were delivered in 1975.[1] For several years the figure 86 percent has been used to estimate the amount of first-class mail that is business rather than personal. If this percentage is applied to 51.37 billion, the result is 44.18 billion items of first-class business mail. The Dartnell Institute estimates that in 1975 it cost a United States company $3.79 ($4.17 in 1976) each time it sent an average business letter. What this all means is that in 1975 United States companies spent about $167 billion on first-class business correspondence only.

Shall we then conclude that business should, as one corporation suggests, "Call, don't write—not at over four dollars a letter"? The best way of handling our original question "Why put it in writing?" is, first, to consider whether some alternative medium—like the telephone—would better serve the purpose and the reader's or listener's need and, second, to pay attention to the relative costs of the potential media. While there have been tongue-in-check advertisements by manufacturers of dictating equipment and telephone companies warning that IT IS NOW VITAL THAT AMERICAN BUSINESS PEOPLE FORGET HOW TO WRITE, one needs only to recall the stagnation and inactivity of the business community at the time of the March 1970 postal strike if he or she doubts the basic necessity for writing in business.

It is realistic to assume that oral communication will probably play a larger role in future business communication than it has in the past, but writing will always be with us. Certainly the telephone is personal, immediate, and two-way, and it provides an opportunity to discuss questions or interpretations as they arise. In many instances, telephoning is less expensive than writing.

On the other hand, a written communication leaves a permanent record to be referred to; that is why, even when oral methods of communication are used, we so often conclude by saying "I wish you'd put that in writing" or "I'd like to see it in black and white." A written business communication gives its writer a

[1] U.S. Postal Service, *Annual Report of the Postmaster General*, 1974–75, p. 15.

chance to consider and to organize thoughts; it provides the chance to reread and to revise; and it offers a choice of various forms and styles in which the message can be couched. It is foolish to think, therefore, that reports or memos or letters will be replaced as integral parts of the communication process in business, and it is absurd to use the cost of the letter, for instance, as the sole reason for considering it obsolete. Instead, business is making a sensible, cost-conscious attempt to use the kind of communication best suited to the message, the purpose, and the reader or listener. And since written communication is often the most effective method, it also becomes the least expensive way of getting the job done.

Admittedly, the fantastic potential of the varying communication choices is not altogether an unmixed blessing. The fact that we can produce more words on paper more quickly does not provide any assurance that the *quality* of our communication will improve; the danger is that we may become so enamored of the techniques and media of communication that we forget the substance of communication. In a brilliant article in *Saturday Review* (March 12, 1966) the poet Stephen Spender reminds us that the capacity to speak, think, and write clearly should be at the core of all education. In his title Spender supplies us with an apt description of the dangers implicit in communication during the last third of the twentieth century—"The Age of Overwrite and Underthink."

In the rest of this chapter, we will examine the elements and purposes involved in communication. An understanding of these fundamentals is essential for business writers who want to avoid the twin dangers of thinking too little and writing too much.

THE ELEMENTS IN WRITTEN COMMUNICATION

What do we mean by "communication"? We can define it quite simply as *imparting or exchanging thoughts or information;* since we are dealing with only one form of business communication, we must add *in writing* to pay our respects to the medium of communication. But such a definition really doesn't help very much. We come closer to the fundamentals of written communication by thinking of it as a process which always includes:

1. A writer

2. The material or message—facts, ideas, information, recommendations, conclusions—which that writer wants to communicate

3. A medium of expression—which for our purposes can be generally described as typewritten words in the form of reports, memos, or letters

4. A reader or, more realistically in the case of reports, group of readers.

This analysis may be oversimplified, but it is better than the impersonal tone of our first definition because it puts human beings—a writer and reader(s)—into the process of communicating. "It takes two to speak the truth," said Thoreau; "one to speak and another to hear."

In this two-person relationship let there be no doubt about who bears the responsibility for effective communication. The responsibility rests on you, as the writer. You might as well accept this responsibility right now. It will be forced on you in business. You will have to abandon certain alibis you may have used in the past. You won't be able to blame misunderstandings on "a stupid reader"; you'll have to make every effort to write with such clarity and simplicity that your writing can be understood. You won't be able to say that your reader is stubborn, narrow-minded, pig-headed, or disagreeable. You'll instead have to use tact and persuasion and evidence to make that reader see your point of view. Of course, you may still fail to get your ideas across; it would be unrealistic to think that you can always succeed with your reader. But if you fail, you have at least done so with the knowledge that you did your best—and that is the essence of responsibility in writing, as in anything else.

Fulfilling your responsibility requires that you *think*. Think *before* you write and *when* you write—and think about how you can improve or revise *after* you have written. Writing which serves your particular purpose requires that you think the purpose through. Clear writing stems from thoughtful planning. Concise writing results from thinking your way through to essentials, eliminating the extraneous and irrelevant. And writing which is correct and appropriate in style reveals that you have thought of how the reader will react and have designed your communication to produce the reactions you want.

We can sum up these observations on thinking, and at the same time state a major theme of this book, by saying that you must have your reader always in mind. You must always be thinking of what the *reader* wants to learn, what you want the *reader* to learn, what *reader* reactions you want to produce and what you want to avoid, and how your writing can accomplish these objectives.

The more you can learn about orderly habits of thought and the logical sequence of events and ideas, the better you can organize your material. The more you can learn about psychology and human relations and people, the more you can know about your readers. These habits of thought and a broad knowledge of people are the most useful background you can have for writing in business. They will enable you to avoid the pitfalls of "thought-less" writing and accomplish the particular purposes you have in mind for a communication. You will, of course, have to supplement this background with a knowledge of the techniques of writing which are discussed in this book as they apply to the specific problems of writing letters, reports, memorandums, and other forms of business communication. But whatever the form, the fundamentals remain the same.

When business writers forget the fundamentals of the communication process and ignore the thinking behind it, a phenomenon known to electrical engineers as *noise* or *interference* occurs. In their diagrams of mechanical or electronic communication, the engineers show messages from source to destination like this:

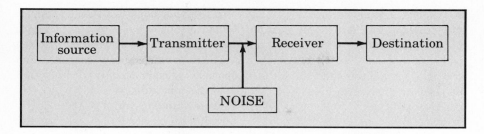

The noise here is the static on your radio, "snow" or fading on your television screen—in short, anything which blocks or impedes the transmission of sound or sight. Unfortunately, human beings are probably even more ingenious when it comes to producing noise or interference in their written communications. The noise caused by thought-lessness—whether in the form of ambiguity, tedious wordiness, inappropriate style, distracting irrelevancies, lack of concern for the way the reader might feel about the subject, or any number of other writing faults—damages the impression you are trying to plant in your reader's mind.

For the most part, good business writing is just good writing. But if your education until now has involved only nonbusiness writing—essays and short stories, for example—you may be disappointed by your first attempts at business writing. We have stressed the importance in business writing of having your purpose clearly in mind, and this, of course, applies to all writing. If you really understand the elements of good writing and are aware of the particular purposes they serve, then you will be successful whether you are writing an essay, a short story, a magazine article, a scholarly article, or a business letter or report. But if your writing experiences have not taught you the "why's" of what you have done, you may have to do some catch-up work in this area as you learn to be an effective business communicator.

Some distinctions between business and literary writing are quite apparent. The reader of a business communication is generally in much more of a hurry than is the reader of a literary work. Conciseness, brevity, and such devices as headings and summary sentences or paragraphs are more important to business than to literary writing. At the same time, the reader of a business communication is rarely looking for entertainment. Witticisms, clever allusions, and paradoxes may add much to the enjoyment of literary writing, but they are more apt to annoy the business reader.

These distinctions are rather obvious. We will explore many less obvious purposes in business writing. The materials in the five chapters of Part One are designed to relate the "how" to the "why" of business writing. The intention is not to persuade you to write in a certain way because it is *the* way to write in business, but to help you decide the purposes to be served by what you write and to learn the techniques appropriate to serving them.

One aspect of business writing that you can learn only on the job concerns the particular forms, procedures, and even writing style that have been established by the business organization you work for. Many companies have a single acceptable form for letters, for example. Some companies insist that letters and reports conform to a particular style manual, such as the *New York Times Style Book.* These details should not concern you now. It will be easy to adapt your writing to them if you understand the fundamentals of good business writing and the purposes they serve.

THE PURPOSE OF A WRITTEN COMMUNICATION

If we were to coin a slogan for this chapter, it would be "Think now; write later." Before you can begin to plan the "how" of business writing, you have to understand the "why." Until you have established just what purposes a written communication is to serve—both your own and your readers' purpose—you cannot decide what is the most appropriate form of presentation. The failure of writers to think through their purposes causes more frustration to readers than any other writing fault. Nor is this frustration lessened by the thought-less writer's stereotyped, lame excuse "I thought you wanted something different."

In all fairness, we should add that such misunderstandings frequently arise because readers or executives do not know, or do not express clearly, what they want. One executive, for example, has the irritating custom of sending the letters or memos he receives on to his subordinates with a cryptic penciled notation such as "Noodle something more on this" or "Supply more info by the fifteenth." College students who are baffled by what some of their instructors want in their assignments will understand the bewilderment which ensues. They will also recognize the "solution"—to try to include every possible purpose in a kind of shotgun approach so that they will be protected from the accusation "This isn't what I wanted."

Here are a few examples taken from both business and government of the waste generated by the failure to think about purposes or to define them sharply:

> A senior officer in the federal government complained that all the reports written for him were five or six times as long as he thought they should be, vague, and hard to read. It turned out that the people writing these reports simply did not know exactly what purposes the reports were to serve. Consequently, they tried to serve every possible purpose, writing long and largely irrelevant reports.
>
> A senior partner in a management consulting firm was considering a training program to improve the writing of the firm's engineers. The reports they were writing to the firm's clients were eliciting a lukewarm response, yet the partner knew his people were highly competent engineers. A little investigation revealed that the engineers were accustomed to writing a routine report describing the work they had done and the recommendations they had come up with. It had never occurred to them that their readers were unlikely to

adopt a recommendation that involved changing methods of operating a business unless they were shown clearly and emphatically what they had to gain by change. A client who was not "sold" on the consultant's recommendations rarely adopted them, and the reputation of the consulting firm suffered. The engineers had simply never been aware that one of the purposes of their reports was to "sell" the client on their recommendations.

A production manager was dissatisfied with the reports of an assistant, a recent graduate of a business school. The assistant had been asked to write a series of reports on the advisability of acquiring various kinds of new production equipment. The production manager intended to use these reports to justify to the top management a recommendation that the equipment be purchased. She felt the reports did a poor job of persuasion. It turned out that the assistant was not aware that the manager had already decided to recommend the purchases. He had assumed his reports were to serve as a basis for the manager's decisions; consequently, he had tried to present an objective and balanced analysis of the pros and cons.

In all three of these cases a writer was making an unsatisfactory impression simply because that writer did not understand the purpose of what was being written.

Every written communication should serve its own particular set of purposes. A letter may be designed to sell goods or services, to collect an overdue account, to obtain a job, to build goodwill by expressing appreciation, or to retain goodwill while denying a request. The point is that you must know precisely what the purposes are before you begin to write. We are going to discuss in this chapter one purpose that will be served by almost everything you write: demonstrating your business ability.

Demonstrating ability is especially important for a young and inexperienced writer who has not yet earned the confidence and respect of his or her business organization. It may not seem to you very important to convince others in business that you are able to write well. But your writing conveys more than your ability to write well. It demonstrates your ability to think, to analyze, and to make sound judgments. Most people react unfavorably to a badly written report, but relatively few are able to tell exactly what is wrong with it. If you write an inadequate report, your readers are just as likely to blame you for poor thinking as for poor writing. In fact, there is a very common belief that bad writing *always* results from bad thinking. Ineffective writing, then, can gain you a reputation for illogical thinking and bad judgment. The fact that this conclusion may be unjustified will be small consolation to you.

What you write in business may well go to people with whom you have no other contact. This provides both an opportunity and a risk. Your letters, memorandums, or reports may be passed on by a superior to people further up the line. Because of this practice, you may be able to demonstrate your ability to people who are in a position to affect your promotions and the kind of work assigned to you but who are generally inaccessible to you. Even the routine writing you do for an immediate superior may be handed on to other people without your expecting it. This means that a piece of work hastily or carelessly done, which you did not expect to go beyond a superior with whom you are already on pretty good terms, may actually reach some influential people who have no other knowledge of you. The result inevitably is that they form a low opinion of your ability.

It is obvious to college students that the principal purpose of their written work in school is to demonstrate knowledge and ability to an instructor. Yet many people forget this purpose when they start writing reports, letters, or memorandums in business. You cannot afford to forget how important your writing is to your personal success. Numerous studies have shown that business people typically rank facility in business communication at or near the top of any list of abilities needed for optimum business performance.[2] But despite this united appeal for skill in this area, we are being told that among average high school graduates, writing performance is deteriorating at an alarming rate.[3] Such an indictment is admittedly frightening; yet interpreted from a personal standpoint, it supports the idea that the employee who can write well will have a significant edge in promotability over the many who cannot.

If you remember the personal importance of your writing, you will have made a good beginning. You will next have to identify the specific purposes you should be trying to serve in any particular writing situation. For example, you may be attempting to persuade someone to do something, providing information to help someone do or decide something, or trying to build goodwill for your company. It may surprise you that anyone could have trouble identifying purposes such as these, but recall the examples quoted in this chapter. It is crucial to have the correct set of purposes in mind.

We will deal in some detail with the purposes peculiar to reports in Part Three and with the special purposes of letters in Part Two. This chapter will continue with a discussion of general purposes and principles, so that when we move to specific features of good communication it will be possible to relate these to the purposes of the communication.

Sometimes the purpose of a written communication is very clear, or seems so. A person who has bought an electrical appliance, had trouble with it, and received poor service takes up a pen to give the manufacturer some opinions about the company, its products, and its personnel. If asked for the purpose of the letter, such a reader would probably answer, "I'm going to blast this company." But is this really the purpose? On reflection, the writer may decide that what is actually wanted is a replacement for the defective appliance or, at least, adequate repairs. The satisfaction gained by "blasting" the company is less important than achieving these results.

[2] Two of the studies that draw such conclusions are James C. Bennett, "The Communication Needs of Business Executives," *Journal of Business Communication,* pp. 5–11, Spring 1971 and the Report of the Undergraduate Studies Committee of the American Business Communications Association, "How Undergraduate Business Communications Programs Can Meet the Communications Needs of Business," *The ABCA Bulletin,* pp. 1–17, June 1973.

[3] "Why Johnny Can't Write," *Newsweek,* December 8, 1975, pp. 58–65.

Passive → is being
            has been

Active → is
          was
          will

3 tomorrow
4 Wednesday
3 Thursday

Hohman & Highland
parking lot across street free

Comma —
   and, but, for, not

If the real purpose of the letter is to obtain a replacement, then the manufacturer must be made to feel that a customer has suffered unreasonably, that the company is responsible, and that it would be good business to replace the appliance. Now we are developing a rather specific set of purposes, or perhaps subpurposes, since the principal purpose is still to obtain a replacement. And now we can begin to see what content and attitude the letter requires. It must, for example, be reasonable. It may display annoyance, but it must not appear to be the letter of a crank. It should quickly convince the reader that the writer is not exaggerating the troubles, that he or she is intelligent enough to treat an electrical appliance properly, that he or she does not expect every appliance to be perfect, and that the complaint is justified. At this point the writer may decide that blasting the company would provide greater satisfaction than going to all this trouble to get a new appliance. Nevertheless, the choice of purpose should be a conscious one. Don't blast the company and then complain that they didn't replace your appliance.

Here are some questions you might ask yourself as you try to identify the purposes of any written communication:

1. Who is going to read this—one person? several? a clerk? a responsible manager?

2. What do I want this person to do, or say, or decide?

3. What sort of feeling must I produce in the reader in order to persuade him or her to do as I wish?

4. What has the reader asked for?

5. What does the recipient intend to do with what I write?

In any particular situation you can probably think of more questions, questions more specifically related to the letter, report, or whatever it is you have to write. If you can ask the right questions as to purpose and answer them, you will find that deciding on the form of your writing is easier and there will be a much greater probability of your communication accomplishing what you really want it to.

Closely related to the determination of purpose in a communication is the fundamental question of whether the communication should even be in writing. This book deals mostly with written communication, but behind every written communication lies a decision that writing, in that particular case, is more appropriate than speaking. This is a decision that should rest on the purpose of the communication and, of course, on the policies of the company.

Most of us prefer to talk rather than to write. Writing well is hard work, and a poorly written document may survive as evidence of our deficiencies. But no one expects our conversation to be as well organized and smooth-flowing as our writing. And no one remembers exactly how we spoke. This can lead to all kinds of rationalizations for choosing to speak rather than to write. The usual reason is that a speaker can adapt what is said to the listeners' reactions. A speaker can repeat when the listeners are puzzled, speed up when they show boredom, or move to another topic when they fail to respond in the manner desired. And, of course, a speaker can get a reaction to a question or a suggestion before deciding what to say next. Some purposes are certainly best served by oral communication. A coach's pep talk in writing would hardly inspire a football team, and most teachers would be out of work if education could be achieved entirely through written instruction. But before you decide that it will be easier to convey your thoughts orally, be sure your purpose is really served by oral communication.

Consider the case of an office manager who is bothered by the fact that too many employees are arriving late for work and that too much time is being spent on coffee breaks. She decides to remind all the employees that they are expected to be at their desks by 9 A.M. and that the morning and afternoon coffee breaks are limited to 15 minutes. She begins to draft a memorandum to be distributed to the employees or posted on a notice board. She grapples with the problem of how to appear firm and get results while at the same time avoiding the impression that she is treating the employees like children or, perhaps even worse, that she is participating in a sort of game in which she tries to get the employees to work hard and they try to avoid work. After starting two or three times and tearing up each draft, she begins to think it would be much better just to talk to the employees. There are too many to talk to all at once, so she speaks to groups and individuals.

A day or two later all, or almost all, have been told. There is an embarrassing incident when the manager angrily asks an employee arriving at 9:15, "Didn't I remind you just yesterday that we begin work at 9:00?" and the answer is a bewildered, "No." The manager thought she had spoken to everyone, but apparently she had missed a few. One stenographer is about to quit because the manager spoke to him alone and he concluded that he had been singled out as the only employee who came late and took too long for coffee breaks; this, he feels, was quite unfair. A few employees believe that the office is now opening earlier than it used to, others say the coffee break has been abolished, and still others say that only the afternoon break is to be done away with. Six weeks later the employees have forgotten the whole incident, and the manager is bothered by the fact that too many employees are arriving late for work and that too much time is being spent on coffee breaks.

If the manager had given adequate thought to the purpose of her communication, she might have decided that it was this: to eliminate or greatly reduce tardiness and overlong coffee breaks, to accomplish this for as long a time as possible, and to avoid confusion and resentment. In deciding how to achieve this purpose she would probably, but not necessarily, have chosen a written communication. At least she would have foreseen the dangers in an oral communication and might have taken special care to avoid them.

It is appropriate to say, in conclusion, that we have purposely kept this discussion brief so that students may concentrate on the exercises. They illustrate one fact which does not communicate well in generalities—that it is often *very* difficult to decide on the central purpose of a communication because the choice is affected and limited by a complex of personalities, alternative decisions, and unknown factors. The central purpose of the exercises is to underscore the fact that in selecting a purpose and medium there is often no one right answer.

EXERCISES

1. You are supervisor of three management trainees of the Gotham Company, a manu- facturer of residential and commercial solar energy systems. You are concerned about the trainees' attitude toward good business writing. They believe that as long as they convey the necessary technical information in their letters and memos, they are communicating successfully. The trainees do not seem to have an understanding of the four elements of effective communication. Your goal today is to develop this under- standing in them. Should you communicate orally or in writing with the trainees? What will you tell them?

2. The three management trainees of the Gotham Company have made good progress in the improvement of their writing. However, you feel that they will be even more motivated to write better if they understand the relationship between their business writing and their own personal success, for they are eager to be promoted. What will you tell the trainees to help them understand how their writing can affect their career success?

3. You have worked as a salesperson for Latham Shoppes for 15 years. Two years ago Latham was acquired by Atco Industries but continued operating under the name of Latham. You were not a member of Latham's pension plan but automatically became a participant in Atco's pension plan at the time of acquisition. You can retire in five more years but are considering the possibility of retiring at the end of the current year. You want to know what benefits, if any, you are entitled to if you choose early retirement. You are also wondering how these early retirement benefits compare with the regular retirement benefits. You have asked your store manager these questions, but he was not able to answer them.
   a. Whom do you think you should communicate with now?
   b. What medium would you choose and why?
   c. What will you say?

4. The Eckhorn Company manufactures precision electronic components for computers, the space industry, and electronic monitoring systems. Most of the employees have been with the company for over 10 years, and many have seen it grow from a 25- employee operation 20 years ago to its present 4,500-employee size. The employees feel secure in their jobs, and management has done much to foster a feeling of teamwork among the workers.
   Up until last week, that is. Because of a severe downturn in the country's economy and the loss of several government contracts, Eckhorn has been forced to lay off 2,500 employees, including management personnel. Rumors have been flying that more layoffs will be coming shortly. The high morale and spirit of teamwork among the employees still working have dropped to near zero. Not only have production rates greatly decreased, but much pilferage of small precision tools is occurring. The plant

supervisor, expressing much concern about the pilferage, has asked you to "give her a guideline as to what action to take."

a. What are the possible purposes in this situation?

b. What will your major purpose be?

c. How will you achieve your major purpose?

5. Jane Steele, a chief operator, had been with your company, Specific Statics, for 26 years. One Friday you, her superior for the last year, were informed that she was absent from work because of a bad cold. You called her residence several times that day, and again on Saturday, Sunday, and Monday, but never got an answer.

When she returned to work on Tuesday, you questioned her about her long weekend. She claimed that she had been to see her doctor on Friday and Monday and had stayed home in bed over the weekend. When you mentioned your calls and asked to speak to her doctor, she admitted that she had not been ill but had gone off to the mountains for those four days.

You conferred with your immediate superior and discovered several similar instances during Jane's long tenure with the company—four within the last five years. You, your superior, and several other company administrators decided to give her the option of retiring, quitting, or being fired. She chose retirement. The reason was to be kept confidential among higher management personnel.

Within days, however, rumors began flying around the office. Numerous theories were being offered to explain Jane's mysteriously quick departure. One such rumor suggested that she had been fired to cut off her retirement benefits. The group that offered Jane the three options has been called together for a meeting this afternoon. Keeping in mind the company image, morale, and the confidentiality agreement, what would you suggest as an appropriate course of action? How would you implement your plan?

6. Assume that the Fishmann Company has 700 employees, located in two separate buildings about 10 miles apart in the same city. The organizational hierarchy is: president and 2 vice-presidents, 4 division managers, 16 department heads, 30 section supervisors, and 647 unclassified employees. For each of the following situations, describe what purposes the communication should accomplish, what method of communication is most appropriate, and why.

a. An announcement by the payroll department that Social Security deductions have been increased by congressional order and that the next paycheck will reflect this increase.

b. A complaint from one of the word processing secretaries to his supervisor that he is being given all the tedious, lengthy jobs.

c. An announcement by the company president that the Christmas bonus will be increased this year as a result of successful employee efforts to reduce energy waste.

d. A performance appraisal report on an unclassified employee from a section supervisor to her department head.

e. A performance appraisal report from a section supervisor to the employee appraised.

f. Notification from the accounting department head to the purchasing department head about a change in the procedure for recording transactions occurring after the 20th of each month.

g. An announcement of the addition of dental insurance to the existing health insurance package, effective immediately. Although employees currently pay half the cost of their health insurance, this increase in benefits will cost employees who have been with the company for at least two years nothing additional. The company will pay for their dental benefits.

h. A request from a section supervisor to his department head for pay raises for three of his unclassified employees.

i. A request from a vice-president to the communications division manager for complete information on electronic mail.

j. Information on electronic mail in answer to the vice-president's request.

k. An announcement from a department head to a section supervisor that an unclassified employee is being transferred to the supervisor's section from another section.

l. A recommendation from a division manager to a vice-president that Enrico Montez be hired as head of the personnel department. Six people were interviewed for the position.

m. An offer from the division manager to Enrico Montez of the job as personnel department head.

n. An announcement by a section supervisor that the 15 employees she supervises will be required to work until 9 P.M. on Wednesday, September 28, because of the delay last week in the printing of the Christmas catalog.

7. The department of transportation of your state, as directed by its director, will be implementing a word processing system. The current one-to-one boss-secretary relationship will be replaced; instead, bosses will have two teams of support personnel. One team will handle all the correspondence of the department and will be located in a central communication center. Message originators either will call their messages into the center, where they will be recorded on dictation equipment, or will provide the center with handwritten or edited copy. Correspondence will then be prepared on text-editing equipment and returned to the originators for their signatures within 24 hours. The other team will be administrative assistants; they will handle telephone communications, conduct research, and perform other administrative support functions for a group of transportation specialists. The department of transportation employees must be informed of this new arrangement, which will be implemented in two weeks. The secretaries will be allowed to choose whether they want to be correspondence secretaries or administrative assistants. If they do not wish to be either, they will be transferred to another traditional secretarial position in the state government. No typewriters will be permitted anywhere except in the communications center as a way of forcing personnel to use the center. Orientation for users of the center will be scheduled by the center manager as soon as secretarial personnel are in their new positions.

Your job is to inform all employees of the word processing system. You realize that a better way to implement such a system would have been to involve personnel in the planning stages and to solicit their suggestions. You know that there will be strong resistance to the change from both the secretaries and their bosses.

a. What will be your purpose in communicating notice of the word processing implementation?

b. What method will you use to inform the 75 secretaries and the 250 transportation specialists of the change?

c. Will you notify both the secretaries and the specialists in the same communication, or will you notify them separately?

d. Compose the communication(s).

8. Because of your own education and skill in horticulture, you have been reading with much interest newspaper and magazine articles describing the many offices and banks that are moving toward the concept of "office landscaping." This concept, based on a systems approach, involves thorough planning so that the office environment conforms and is conducive to each company's special needs. Individual and department work flows, communication patterns, administrative support functions, etc., are all studied, resulting in an office designed to produce noticeable improvements in efficiency and tangible cost savings.

   An integral part of this open office concept is the use of movable panel dividers and plants to define and divide space. These plants are rented from firms which take care of watering and feeding them. Periodically plants are rotated among companies to provide variety in the office.

   You are presently working for a nursery but would like to start your own business. You have a medium-sized greenhouse at home and have many contacts among nurseries. You also have a "magic touch" with plants and can make anything grow. You know that you could be successful in the office plant business; your main problem is how to make the initial contacts. Should you use the telephone, distribute flyers, put an advertisement in the local newspaper, send a letter to selected executives, or use some other medium? Write what you would say in such an advertisement or letter. What are the advantages and disadvantages of written communication in such a situation?

2
WORDS–THEIR
USE AND ABUSE

"There's glory for you!"

"I don't know what you mean by 'glory'," Alice said.

Humpty Dumpty smiled contemptuously. "Of course you don't—till I tell you. I meant 'there's a nice knock-down argument for you'!"

"But 'glory' doesn't mean 'a nice knock-down argument'," Alice objected.

"When I use a word," Humpty Dumpty said in rather a scornful tone, "it means just what I choose it to mean, neither more nor less."

"The question is," said Alice, "whether you can *make words mean so many different things."*

"The question is," said Humpty Dumpty, "which is to be Master—that's all."

"There is magic in words properly used," says the excellent *Monthly Letter* of the Royal Bank of Canada, "and to give them this magic is the purpose of the discipline of language." The emphasis here is on *discipline,* and a younger generation of writers who insist on "telling it like it is" must sooner or later recognize the inescapable fact that accuracy and precision in language stem only from the disciplined knowledge which enables us to put "proper words in proper places with the thoughts in proper order."

As Merrill Sheils of *Newsweek* pointed out and as Carroll's quote above from *Alice in Wonderland* illustrates, only confusion can result from staunch insistence upon being masters rather than servants of language. If every new colloquialism, dialect, fashion, or jargon were to demand and get equal but limited usage, we would soon find ourselves back in Babel. The unavoidable fact is that rules and recommendations for word usage, however tedious, must exist and be adhered to if written human communication is to remain decipherable.[1]

The English language is unusually rich in words whose shades of meaning differ only slightly. We thus have at our command an extremely sensitive instrument by which to express the finest distinctions of meaning. Such delicate distinctions, however, make it very easy for the undisciplined writer to mislead and confuse readers.

Sometimes the poor choice of a word stems simply from the writer's misunderstanding of its meaning. When the author of a current text on financial management wrote, "There are several pragmatic reasons which mitigate against sharply drawn lines of distinction," he confused *mitigate,* which means to reduce the severity of, with *militate,* which means to have force or effect for or against. His mistake is perhaps less embarrassing than that of the consultant who wrote, "This is an important decision and must be approached with levity," under the impression that *levity* meant seriousness, when in fact it means frivolity.

The confusion of one word with another which resembles it in some way is labeled a *malapropism,* a name derived from Mrs. Malaprop, a character in Sheridan's *The Rivals,* who makes such outrageous errors as "an allegory on the banks of the Nile." Her misuse of words has probably never been matched— unless, perhaps, by a recent mayor of a large American city, who was reported in the press to have originated such abuses as "Together we must rise to ever higher and higher platitudes" and "I resent the insinuendos."

You can test your own sensitivity to the distinctions of meaning in words which sound alike by making the correct choice in the following sentences:

1. He (appraised, apprised) his department head of the situation.

2. She made an (illusion, allusion) to what had happened the week before.

3. We need a witness who is completely (uninterested, disinterested).

4. After hearing the evidence, we were (incredible, incredulous).

5. Because he was related to the (principal, principle), he was (accepted, excepted) from testifying.

The remedy for confusion about the word which precisely conveys your meaning is to know the meaning of the word before you use it or to look it up in a dictionary. (If you can't conveniently use a dictionary at the time, use another word the meaning of which you are sure.)

The confusion of one word with another which looks or sounds like it can at least be called "an honest mistake"; but increasingly, in our society, the use and abuse of words must be ascribed to other and less forgivable causes. Among these are the following, which we will discuss in the rest of this chapter.

[1] Merrill Sheils, "Why Johnny Can't Write," *Newsweek,* December 8, 1975, p. 65.

Showing off the latest fashion in words

Using specialized language

Making simple things sound complex

Using jargon

Using trite and outworn expressions

SHOWING OFF THE LATEST FASHION IN WORDS

As everyone knows, our language grows by coinage, by adding new words, and by joining old words in new combinations. "Splashdown," for instance, is a beautifully accurate description of the return of a space vehicle—a word with the ring of the last third of the twentieth century. By contrast, large numbers of parrotlike nonthinkers in our stereotyped society hear a word used by someone else, adopt it as their own "fashionable" expression, and use it to impress their listeners. One could list hundreds of such tired expressions of the past few years, of which these are but a few:

Viable For the past few years no one could describe a program, an economy, or a trend without calling it "viable."

Charisma This obscure term, derived from the Greek, suddenly represented the *sine qua non* of every American politician.

Dichotomy To say "a split" or "a division of opinion" is, of course, not as impressive. Since dichotomy is now worn thin, let's try a new fashion—a bifurcation of thought.

Dialogue This used to be a part of drama, but for several years no two people or groups have been able simply to talk or discuss. They must have a dialogue. It's even more *de rigueur* in socioeconomic-political contexts pertaining to ethnic differences and peer groups.

Expertise Just to know something, to be expert, is old hat in a world where only expertise can put a person in the front ranks of knowledge.

One of the most recent stimulants for the fashion-conscious verbalizer was the media coverage of the Watergate hearings. To many impressionable viewers of this investigation, "then" became "at this point in time" and "no longer operative" could be used to gloss over the fact that an earlier statement was no longer true, while "inappropriate" became an acceptable euphemism for referring to clearly illegal acts. These verbal attempts to identify with the "in" group, to follow the fad of the word-of-the-moment, mark their users as pompous and pretentious—stuffed shirts who think in clichés, which—as someone once remarked—should be "avoided like the plague."

USING SPECIALIZED LANGUAGE

We have an admirably descriptive phrase in English to denote clear, concise communication; we say of a speaker or writer, "He speaks my language." Actually, however, in a highly specialized society, most educated people speak not one language but two—the general language of their society and the specialized one of their business or profession. When metallurgist communicates with metallurgist, for example, physician with physician, educator with educator, specialist with specialist, their expertness finds expression in the finely honed words evolved by their profession.

But a speaker or writer who uses technical language to communicate with nontechnical listeners or readers might as well expect confusion and frustration from the recipient(s) of the message. For example, when a patient is told she has agrypnia instead of insomnia or cephalalgia instead of a headache, we would suggest therapy not for the patient but for the language. When a parent is told by the educator that his children should take "enrichment courses in a properly structured sequential summer program," he should ask, "Why does he have to go to summer school?" And when the taxpayer is confronted at income tax time with instructions like these, we should ask for a change *fast:*

> A detailed and contemporaneous recording of an expenditure, supported by sufficient documentary evidence, has a high degree of credibility not present with respect to a statement prepared subsequent to the incurrence of an expenditure where there may be a lack of accurate recall. Thus, the corroborative evidence required to support a noncontemporaneous statement must have a high degree of probative value to elevate such statement and evidence to the level of credibility reflected by a detailed and contemporaneous record supported by sufficient documentary evidence.

Such aborted attempts at message transmission might be avoided if we kept in mind the simple model developed by Wilbur Schramm, presented on the following page.

This model vividly depicts the fact that successful interpersonal communication occurs only when the encoder and the decoder have had similar experiences (overlapping fields) with the signals being used. When a specialist uses technical language to communicate with nontechnical people, the fields of experience do not overlap and the communication is doomed to failure.

Stephen Spender, the poet, has some words of wisdom on the subject of specialization:[2]

> Whether what scientists have to explain to us is communicable, or whether they have to explain that it is incommunicable, the fact is that the present breakdown in communication is due at least partly to the neglect of English. It is slovenly to accept without question the cliché that we cannot communicate because we live in "an age of specialization."

[2] Stephen Spender, "The Age of Overwrite and Underthink," *Saturday Review,* March 12, 1966, p. 22 Copyright © Saturday Review, Inc.

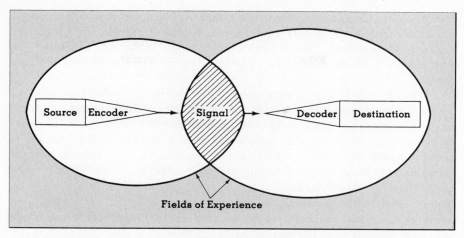

FIGURE 2-1 Schramm's Model of Interpersonal Communication. *Source:* Wilbur Schramm (ed.), *The Process and Effects of Mass Communication* (Urbana, Ill.: University of Illinois Press, 1954), p. 6. © 1954 by the Board of Trustees of the University of Illinois.

The most sensible procedure in business writing is to estimate the level of your reader's understanding and to write on that level, keeping these two points in mind:

1. If you know your readers are specialists and speak your technical language, you can communicate in your common shoptalk to your heart's content. In fact, if you do not, they may feel you are talking down to them and failing to appreciate their understanding.

2. If you are not sure of your readers' familiarity with your special language, stick to simple, everyday English. If you can't avoid technical terms, define or explain them carefully.

Words and phrases like "current ratio," "return on equity," and "standard deviation" are terms that you may feel you have earned the right to use after your college career. You may even initially resent having to simplify your vocabulary for people who are not business-educated. But if you do so, you are likely to find that you achieve your communications objectives more easily than you would have if you had allowed the technical-language semantic barrier to stand.

MAKING SIMPLE THINGS SOUND COMPLEX

One of the qualities we associate with profound thinkers is their ability to explain highly complex matters in clear, simple language. The opposite is characteristic of the shallow mind, which continually tries to make relatively simple things appear complex by the use of what can only be described as dishonest language.

Unfortunately, this fault is often manifested by young employees in business, who think that by using polysyllabic words they will impress their superiors. Similarly, they bulk out their reports and memos under the mistaken belief that long communications convey the impression of intensive work and profound thought.

The fact is that any simple process or idea can be arrayed in language that makes it seem complex and difficult, as the following actual instance shows: A consultant on communication was being escorted through the offices of a company by its vice-president when they came to the room which housed the central files of the company. Turning to a file clerk, the consultant asked, "How long do you keep things in these files?" "Normally we don't keep forms no more than three years," he said. "Then you can either tear them up yourself or give them to the janitor." The visitor turned to the vice-president. "When we get back to your office, let's see how this situation is described in the Procedures Manual," she suggested. Here is what the manual said:

> At the end of the established retention period, which is normally three years, mutilate the forms or carbons to be destroyed by tearing them into small bits or pieces or by shredding them, and dispose of the resulting waste in accordance with the procedures established for the Maintenance Department.

Whoever wrote that statement was attempting to make a relatively simple task sound impressive and complex. The words of the file clerk, despite his bad grammar, are a far more effective explanation, because he tried to express an idea rather than to impress a listener.

The sentence below was taken from an actual report. What does it mean?

> We will make a judgment on this once we have had time to crank in the intangibles.

What it really means is that the writer does not know what the answer is and is playing for time.

Here's a sentence from a young social scientist to a businessperson who wanted to know what the company could do to help improve education in the community so that better employees could be attracted by way of good schools for their children:

> Acceptance of the postulate framework and its resultant conceptualized statement diagramming the functioning of the education system within the community leads to an analysis of the system as well as of the potential impacts and implications of the consequence of the process.

Why do some people feel compelled to grasp at the most complex, and often least effective, way of saying things? Judge for yourselves which of the following versions of two thoughts are the easiest to understand.

The conclusion ascertained by the committee was predicated upon the assumption that an abundance of monetary funds would be forthcoming.

The committee made this decision because they expected to get more money.

This machine has a tendency to develop excessive and unpleasant audial symptoms when operating at elevated temperatures.

This machine may get noisy when it gets hot.

When four monkeys died in 1969 while being prepared for a 30-day earth orbit, a scientist at Cape Kennedy explained the death of one as follows:

One succumbed unexpectedly apparently as a result of an untoward response due to a change in feeding regimen.

This statement very well illustrates another danger of using abstract, complex ways of saying simple things. In addition to forcing your reader to exert extra mental effort to understand what you write, there is also the possibility that your abstraction may be so vague as to prevent this understanding. The "change in feeding regimen" above, for example, does not tell us whether the monkey died because it ate too much or too little, or because the feeding schedule had been changed, or because it had been given a different kind of food.

USING JARGON

"Jargon" is a derogatory term implying unintelligibility or the use of wordy, worn-out, often meaningless expressions peculiar to those who share the same work or way of life. It encompasses most of the faults we have thus far discussed—and more. Jargon is a form of vagueness, of loose thinking, and it is the worst enemy of clarity and conciseness. Called by various names—gobbledygook, bafflegab, and businessese—it is characterized by vague, general words instead of precise, informative ones; and its prevalence in business stems from a thoughtless reaching for words which have always been used or which everyone else uses.

The history of these expressions dates back to the fifteenth and sixteenth centuries, when commerce was finally beginning to be viewed as an acceptable profession. Developing a *special* language of business was apparently one of the ways through which people in the profession sought to remove the social stigma that had previously been attached to the practice of business. This special language took on two identifiable characteristics. First, it borrowed from the languages used by the more socially acceptable elements of society, the aristocracy and those involved in the legal system. Second, it retained sprinklings of expressions that portrayed a form of servitude or prostration of the businessperson before the client. Thus, by the late nineteenth century, jargon like the following expressions had been formalized into the official and proper language of business:

"We wish to acknowledge receipt of . . ."

"Please be advised that . . ."

"Allow me to say that . . ."

"We are awaiting your favor . . ."

"We beg to state that . . ."

During the first half of this century, strange, meaningless, trite, and pompous expressions persisted in business writing. In the past 10 to 20 years, however, there has been a great deal of progress in eliminating business jargon, thanks to the efforts of progressive teachers in our business colleges and universities. Furthermore, business people themselves have become conscious of the cost—in both dollars and unintelligibility—of language misused. Very seldom, therefore, do we find much of the jargon, exemplified above, which for so long survived as a hangover of so-called business courtesy. Such windy techniques persisted too long, however, because untrained writers sat down to write letters and reports with only the incoming correspondence and the hackneyed reports in the files to guide them.

George Orwell, author of *1984,* once compared using jargon to the process of picking up ready-made and worn-out strips of words and gluing them together as an easy way to avoid the thought required for original writing. Here are a few examples of gummed strips of business jargon, with equivalents in simple English:

Met with the approval of the Council of Executives . . .	The Executive Council approved . . .
They were able to reach a decision.	They decided.
The discussion by the committee was on the subject of the underutilization of recreational facilities.	The committee discussed why recreational facilities were used so little.
After a dialogue with the representatives of the sales department, it was decided that a dichotomy of interests would prevent implementing the policy.	After talking with people from the sales department, we found the policy would not work because of different interests.

Instead of using obsolete language, present-day jargon often reflects a desire to avoid the responsibility of making a direct and clear statement. It also reflects the muddy thinking of its users, of course. Consider that overworked word *finalize,* which purists have objected to because it contorts an adjective into a verb. But language grows by such methods, and we should not object on that score. The real objection is that the word doesn't tell us anything which can't be said more clearly by other words—*end, finish, conclude, terminate, stop,* to cite a few. When a businessperson writes that an advertisement will be *finalized* this afternoon, this may mean making a final decision on the content of the advertisement or obtaining someone else's final decision, or completing the layout of the advertisement, or placing an order for the running of the advertisement, or approving the running of the advertisement or obtaining someone else's approval, or probably any one of several other things that will complete some stage in the preparation and running of an advertisement. Instead of finding and using the term that describes precisely what is to be done, the businessperson reaches for a vague word that gives a general idea of the kind of activity planned for the afternoon.

The indiscriminate use of the suffix -*wise* is an all too obvious instance of the way jargon spreads. To tack -*wise* onto an endless number of words is to substitute mechanics for thought—to telescope a thought which could be better conveyed by well-established words. Hence we have such horrendous combinations as "prestige-wise," "customer-wise," and "sales-wise." When a businessperson says "Tax-wise, that would be a good course of action," does this mean that the action will reduce taxes, postpone them, eliminate them, cause a shift from one form of tax to another, or make it easier to pay the tax? Here we see the real objection to jargon—it does not fill any real need other than a sloppy or lazy writer's desire to avoid thinking. As one tongue-in-cheek editor wrote of a hopeless piece of "creative" writing: "Story-wise it is lacking surprise-wise." Or as a newspaper editor reprimanded a correspondent by telegram: WORDWISE "WEATHERWISE" UNWISE.

Similar poverty of language can be illustrated by too many specific examples, of which these are but a few:

make a judgment

vary the mix

hardware, software

a survey in depth

togetherness

implement a decision

the interface of the systems

I'm for it 120 percent

touch all the bases

a can of worms

Students should listen and read with careful attention to make their own lists of these modern equivalents of yesterday's women who were pretty as pictures, mails slow as molasses in January, things that look like something the cat dragged in, and—to coin a phrase—minds that are dull as dishwater.

Much jargon is simply showing off by writers who hold the mistaken notion that the longer and more obscure their words are, the more impressive they will be.

Here's a clever satire, called "Syllable Happy," by Franklin N. Turner of Shell Oil Company, which appeared in *The Wall Street Journal*.[3]

How often we've been told to write, at college age and less,
In terms as plain as Mr. Lincoln's Gettysburg Address—
Avoiding phrases erudite where simple ones are clearer,
The better to express the thought, not just impress the hearer.

Though few dispute this sound advice, inside a corporation
The common touch in writing is a victim of inflation:
The language of the office walks on stilts the long way 'round,
Discarding easy words whenever hard ones can be found.

We find the sub-executive whose eye is on advancement
Proclaiming that the net return reflected some enhancement
(A mouthful meaning neither more nor less than PROFITS ROSE,
And gaining nothing from the gilt of ostentatious prose).

To say ABOUT is frowned upon—APPROXIMATELY's better—
While LATER must be SUBSEQUENTLY in the business letter.
BEFORE is out, since PRIOR TO sounds more sophisticated,
And no one writes EXPECTED who can spell ANTICIPATED.

Disguising CAUSE as CAUSATIVE FACTOR shows one's on the move,
And words like OPTIMUM, for MOST, are really in the groove.
INAUGURATE and FINALIZE are favored, though, in truth,
BEGIN and END are more exact and not at all uncouth.

Sir Winston's famed BLOOD, SWEAT AND TEARS, that sparked the English nation,
Would never have endured with SWEAT dressed up as PERSPIRATION
So here's a plea for plain words that more clearly tell the story
Than polysyllable displays of verbal repertory.

Some well-established words are also used frequently in business writing to convey only vague, general impressions. *Problem,* for instance, is a favorite word of those who cannot be bothered to think of the right words to express their thoughts precisely. Here is an example:

In trying to increase his company's efficiency, Mr. Withers faces the problems of union opposition, what to do with employees no longer needed, not knowing how much money is available for modernization, and that after he is all through his products may be obsolete.

Problems are something we *solve.* A union's opposition is not a problem; it is an obstacle, or perhaps a difficulty that we try to *overcome.* What to do with superfluous employees is a question, something that must be *answered.* Not knowing how much money is available is probably an obstacle or difficulty, and

---

[3] Reprinted by permission of the author and *The Wall Street Journal.*

that the products may be obsolete is a risk that Mr. Withers must *run.* The following version is much more precise in thought and language:

> In trying to increase his company's efficiency, Mr. Withers faces the obstacle of union opposition and the difficulty of not knowing how much money is available for modernization; he must answer the question of what to do with employees no longer needed; and he runs the risk that after he is all through his products may be obsolete.

Phase is another word that is often used as a sort of fill-in when a writer can't think of the right word to express a meaning:

> All phases of the company are currently moving to a position of optimum efficiency, productivity, and organization.

A phase is an aspect of something whose appearance changes. A company can go through phases as its characteristics change. But here, presumably, what the writer had in mind were not different stages through which the company was moving but different parts of the company, perhaps divisions or departments. Exactly what the writer had in mind we don't know.

The word *area,* commonly used to describe a body of knowledge or a specialty, can be confusing when it is used in conjunction with a concept of space:

> In the area of plant location there is still need for planning.

"The area of plant location" suggests a physical area reserved for the location of a plant, but the rest of the sentence indicates that this is not the kind of area that the writer had in mind. The writer is referring to the topic or job of plant location.

These examples indicate the need to examine your writing constantly to see if you are taking refuge in vague, fuzzy expressions when you should be selecting precise words to tell your reader exactly what you mean. It is very easy to slip into trite generalities, but a reader who is looking for useful analysis or information will soon realize that he or she cannot find it. Like Hamlet's answer to the question "What do you read, my lord?", the result is "words, words, words" but not meaning.

For the writer who wishes to inform rather than to impress, who wants to use precise tools of thought rather than worn-out, blunted, and overworked instruments, who feels responsible for the reader's understanding, the best words on words are these four principles from H. W. Fowler's *The King's English:*

> Prefer the familiar word to the far-fetched.
>
> Prefer the concrete word to the abstract.
>
> Prefer the single word to the circumlocution.
>
> Prefer the short word to the long.

TRITE AND OUTWORN
EXPRESSIONS TO AVOID

The following is a list of the more common expressions found in business jargon. Beginning students should consider them as warnings of bad habits that writers may fall into; experienced writers may use them as a yardstick against which they can measure the effectiveness of their work.

Acknowledge receipt of   as in "We wish to acknowledge receipt of your letter." Forget it and say "Thank you for your letter."

Advise   as in "In answer to your letter of August 7, we wish to advise that shipment has been made." *Advise* is a perfectly good word, but it means "to give advice." In general, it should be replaced by *inform* when information is being conveyed; or you could be more direct and just tell the readers what they need to know, as in "The shipment about which you inquired in your August 7 letter has been made."

Allow me to   as in "Allow me to express our appreciation for. . . ." A pompous method of saying "Thank you for. . . ."

Along these lines   as in "We are carrying on research along these lines." A meaningless phrase. Make it specific.

As per   as in "As per our records," "As per your report," etc. Another barbarous mixture; say "According to."

Attached please find,
Enclosed please find   No hunting is necessary if your check or order is attached or enclosed. Say "Attached" or "Enclosed" and let it go at that.

At an early date,
At the earliest possible moment,
At your earliest convenience,
or In the near future   Say "soon" and save yourself some words; or suggest a specific date if your relationship with your reader allows you to or if there is a good, logical reason for the date.

At hand   as in "I have your letter of May 9 at hand." Omit it entirely, since "at hand" adds nothing. "Thank you for your letter of May 9" or better "Your letter of May. . . ."

At the present writing,
At this time   Overworked and roundabout jargon for "now."

Awaiting your favor — Few business people use "favor" as a synonym for "letter." Instead, say "I hope to hear from you soon" or "As soon as I receive your reply, I will. . . ."

Beg — as in "beg to inform," "beg to acknowledge," "beg to state," "beg to remain," etc. Omit "beg" entirely. Go ahead and inform, acknowledge, state, or remain; it is absurd for perfectly solvent firms to go around begging in their business letters.

For your information — Tactless and unnecessary. Everything in the report or letter is for the reader's information. Omit it.

Hand you — as in "We herewith hand you our check for $37.10." A meaningless and outworn expression—and what long arms you have, Grandma! Say "Enclosed is our check for $37.10."

I have your letter, *I have received your report* — A thought-less warm-up for starting letters or memos. Since you are answering, the reader knows you have the letter or report. Say "Thank you for your report" or "We appreciate your letter of February 15."

In receipt of — as in "We are in receipt of your check." Say "We have received your check" or "Thank you for your check."

In (or *to* or *for*) *the amount of* — as in "We enclose our check in the amount of $33.16." Simply say "for," as in "We enclose our check for $33.16."

Permit me to say — Go ahead and say it; no permission is needed. Furthermore, to ask permission and then to say it before receiving permission could be regarded as presumptuous.

Replying to yours of December 12 — A sure way to show your reader that you want to avoid thinking. Omit it and refer to the date of the letter indirectly.

Thanking you in advance — as in "Thanking you in advance for any information you may send." This phrase displays poor psychology because it antagonizes the reader by too obviously assuming that he or she is going to do what you want done. Say "We shall be grateful for any information that you may care to send."

Thank you kindly	An absurd statement. Why are you being kind in thanking him? Just say "Thank you."
The writer	as in "The writer believes" or "It is the opinion of the writer." An obvious and pompous attempt to give the impression of modesty by avoiding the use of "I" or "we." Don't be afraid to use "I believe" or "We think." The business letter is supposed to be a personal medium in which personal pronouns are the standard way of referring to the people involved.
This letter is for the purpose of requesting	Why all the preliminary? Go ahead and ask. When you write effective letters, their purpose is clear.
This will acknowledge receipt of your letter	Another wasted warm-up.
Under separate cover	as in "We are sending under separate cover. . . ." Athough this phrase might be an appropriate title for a proper sequel to the movie *Bob and Carol and Ted and Alice,* its business usage leaves something to be desired. Wherever possible, be specific, as in "We are sending . . . by parcel post" (or express or special delivery).
The undersigned	See comments on "the writer." Say "I."
Up to this writing	Say "Up to now."
We regret to inform you that we are in error.	Wordy and hackneyed. Say "We are sorry for our mistake." Another way to transmit essentially the same thought is to convey your apology indirectly by emphasizing the action being taken to correct the error.
You claim, You state, You say	Avoid these wherever possible because they antagonize the reader by implying that the statement to which you refer is not true. Recast the sentence to eliminate them.
Yours	as in "Yours of recent date." Say "Your letter" or "Your order."

These are the specters that have haunted business communication. But jargoneers have other devices to assure pompousness. Above all else, they enjoy using several words where one or two are necessary. Just as they prefer *in the amount of* to *for,* they select the following wordy expressions in the left-hand column rather than those in the right, which effective writers use.

Answer in the affirmative	*say yes*
At a later date	*later*
At the present time	*now*
Despite the fact that	*though, although*
✔Due to the fact that	*since, because*
For the purpose of	*to, for*
For the reason that	*since, because*
In accordance with your request	*as you requested*
In addition	*also*
Inasmuch as	*since*
In order that	*so*
In order to	*to*
In the event that	*if*
In the nature of	*like*
In the neighborhood of	*about*
In the normal course of our procedure	*normally*
In the very near future	*soon*
In this connection	omit
In this day and age	*today*
✓In view of the fact that	*since, because*
Of the order of magnitude of	*about*
On the grounds that	*because*
On the occasion of	*when, on*
Prior to	*before*
Pursuant to our agreement	*as we agreed*
Subsequent to	*after*
The reason is due to	*because*
Under date of	*on*
We are not in a position to	*we cannot*
Will you be kind enough to	*please*
With a view to	*to*
Without further delay	*now, immediately*
With reference to	*about*
With regard to	*about*
With respect to	*about*
With the result that	*so that*

Equally dear to the hearts of jargoneers are redundant phrases. Here are a few examples of some of the more commonly used doublets that say the same thing twice.

✓The reason is because	The reason is . . . or
	This happens because . . .
✓Absolutely complete	*complete*
Agreeable and satisfactory	just one
Anxious and eager	one or the other
Basic fundamentals	*fundamentals,* being basic, will suffice
✓Consensus of opinion	*consensus* can't be anything but opinion; say just *consensus*

Courteous and polite	one or the other, not both
Each and every one of us	*each of us, every one of us, all of us*
Exactly identical	*identical*
First and foremost	either one, not both
Full and complete	just one
Hope and trust	*hope*
If and when	either one
Insist and demand	choose one
✓My personal opinion	*my opinion;* it can't be anything but personal
Right and proper	don't say the same thing twice
Sincere and earnest	select one
Thought and consideration	only one
✓True facts	since facts are true, omit the adjective
Unique—as "the most unique," "very unique," etc.	*unique* cannot be qualified; it means one of a kind, without equal

EXERCISES

1. Words that appear similar often have subtle differences which, when ignored, can lead to ambiguity and language barbarism. Test your ability to convey meaning precisely by choosing the appropriate word in each of the following sentences.

   a. Wayne's promotion will definitely (effect, affect) the way things are done in the accounting department.

   b. Gloria could not decide (between, among) the four decorating schemes available for her office.

   c. The vice-president was impressed by the (amount, number) of people who came to the meeting that she had announced only an hour before.

   d. He is not (apt, likely) to make the decision within the next week.

   e. She (complimented, complemented) her employees on their response to her call for greater productivity.

   f. We need an arbitrator who is (uninterested, disinterested).

   g. The warehouse is (farther, further) from the factory than it should be.

   h. The personnel department promised to make (fewer, less) interruptions on the intercom between 8:00 and 10:00 A.M.

   i. Arthur (implied, inferred) from my comments that I was displeased.

   j. The (principal, principle) reason for the proposed merger is the possible obsolescence of our product in 15 to 20 years.

2. How would you explain the wording of the following excerpts from letters, considering the fact that they were written by non-business people.

   a. From an engineer to a banker:

   Pursuant to our telephonic conversation of even date, I am herewith enclosing copies, for your information, of assignments of the construction loan documents to XQRB affiliated partnerships and copies of Last International Bank's acceptance of these assignments.

b. From an applicant to the Welfare Department:

In accordance with your instructions, I have given birth to twins in the enclosed envelope.

c. From a letter by a normally very personable kindergarten teacher seeking help from business people for a school carnival:

This is to inform you that at the present time the Smith Elementary School #12 is making its preparation for its fourth annual school carnival for the purpose of purchasing additional classroom equipment.

3. Which word ought to be changed in the following sentences? What word is it confused with? Define both words.

a. George was an extremely complacent employee, and I would recommend him highly for the position in your public relations department. (complaisant)

b. Professional topography will greatly enhance the appeal of the new sales brochure. (typography)

c. I am loathe to discuss the promotion with you again, for it has already been decided. (loath)

d. Our company's magnets want a complete report on the work stoppage by Friday. (magnates)

e. Please see that this productivity report is dissipated throughout our entire organization. (disseminated)

f. The newly hired office manager showed the proper difference to the company's president when they were introduced. (deference)

g. Because of her rapport with the audience, she was able to illicit many good ideas and suggestions. (elicit)

h. The travesty of our current financial situation must not be ignored. (gravity)

i. Subordinates can be motivated by a sense of pride in their work; therefore, a superior should guard against being too hypocritical. (hypercritical)

4. What is the writer really trying to say in the following sentences? Rewrite each sentence so that the idea is stated in clear, simple words. If the original idea is vague, make it more concrete.

a. The feasibility of this tentative proposition as a viable alternative for the unquestionable solution of the situation under discussion will be deliberated upon at our succeeding assembly.

b. What is necessitated by the substantiality of the data is the supplementary addition of unprecedented dimensions to the pedagogical process.

c. A re-evaluation of our assumptions was precipitated by the overutilization of the substances of fabrication.

d. Let's acknowledge that we are inundated with a deluge of perplexities and pursue the facilitation of a resolution.

e. The vice-president put forth the conception that we adopt a more expenditure-conscious approach to our *modus operandi*.

5. Rewrite the following letters to eliminate jargon and redundancy and to make the sentences direct and forceful.

a. This is to acknowledge receipt of your letter of April 21. Please allow me to express our appreciation for your interest in our company. For your information, the Zalco

Company has been a manufacturer and producer of stereo cartridges and styli since 1960. The catalog I am sending you under separate cover will give you complete and detailed specifications about our fine products. In accordance with your request, I am also sending you a list of Zalco dealers in your area. If and when you decide to purchase a Zalco product, they will be happy to serve you. Thank you kindly for writing us.

b. Enclosed please find my check to your order in the amount of $5 for the purpose of ordering one box of your imported French soap. As per your advertisement, it is my understanding that you will pay the postage to ship the soap to me. Inasmuch as I would like to use this soap in the very near future, I would appreciate your sending this merchandise at your earliest convenience. Also, would you be good enough to send me a copy of your most recent catalog. Thanking you in advance for your kind attention.

6. Your boss, Karen Galinski, a direct, action-oriented person, has called you into her office to discuss the work of Marcia Jackson, a young woman with a bachelor's degree in business administration and a master's degree in future studies. Jackson has been hired to advise your company on forecasting and long-range planning.

"I don't know what she is talking about. And when she writes me a report, I don't know what she is saying," Galinski tells you as she reaches for one of Jackson's reports. "Listen to this:

The utilization of auxiliary methods such as the cross-impact matrix can supplement extrapolative and explanatory methods by examining the consistency of sets of independently generated forecasts.

"Look at these words: 'synergistic dynamics,' 'systematic exploitation of precursors,' 'exogenous variables.' I don't know whether I'm stupid, whether she's using these terms to impress me, or what. She came in yesterday to give me another report, and after a lot of conversation, I finally told her I didn't know what she was talking about. Now, can you suggest what to do, because we have to get our 10-year plan ready to present to the stockholders." Your job is to:

a. List all the possible reasons for this impasse between Galinski and Jackson.

b. List all the possible alternatives for solution to this situation.

c. Choose one or more of these alternatives and write a memo to Ms. Galinski which will be helpful to her.

3
SENTENCES–THEIR SENSE AND NONSENSE

As Chapter 2 demonstrated, words, when chosen with care, have the power to duplicate meaning in the mind of a receiver. Unfortunately, however, many communicators spoil this duplication process by allowing fashion, jargon, specialization, and rubber stamps to infiltrate their writing. Sentences are the second rung on the ladder of writing skill that you will climb as you attempt to develop your proficiency as a business communicator. They, like words, are subject to either the virtue of clarity or the verbal virus of confusion.

Clarity is usually assumed to be essential to all forms of communication, but occasionally there may be reasons for being deliberately unclear. Historians still disagree as to Calvin Coolidge's meaning when he uttered his famous words concerning his possible candidacy in 1928: "I do not choose to run." Were his words an outright denial of further presidential aspirations? Was he merely stating a personal preference which would change in the face of urgent demands? When we comment that "the answer is not clear," we are saying that Coolidge's six-monosyllable sentence lacks the quality which we are calling clarity.

Another incident illustrates deliberate and very effective ambiguity. There is a story to the effect that the management of a British steamship company once decided that the officers of its passenger ships should wear swords. This, the management felt, would add to the glamour of a transatlantic crossing and appeal to the passengers. But because the wearing of swords might make company personnel resemble naval officers, the management decided to request permission of the British Admiralty before making the change. The Admiralty was not enthusiastic about the idea and yet did not wish to say no. Finally a reply was drafted, saying that the Admiralty had no objection to the company's proposal provided that the swords were worn "on the right side." This put the company in a dilemma. Did the letter mean the Admiralty insisted that swords be worn on the *correct* side, which is the left side, or were the company's officers to wear their swords on the *right-hand* side, to distinguish themselves from naval officers? Too embarrassed to ask for clarification, the management dropped the whole idea, and the Admiralty achieved a quiet triumph.

You will rarely run into a situation calling for lack of clarity, that is, intentional vagueness. But it is important to think of clarity, or any other attribute of writing, as serving some purpose in a particular piece of writing, rather than as an end in itself.

Many elements of writing contribute to clarity, and we shall discuss some of them in subsequent chapters. But probably the most important aspect of clarity is coherence. Coherence refers to connections between words, sentences, or paragraphs, or between topics or ideas. In a coherent presentation each sentence is connected in some logical way with both the preceding and the following sentences. Each topic or idea appears to follow logically from the preceding topic.

Coherence usually depends upon good organization—arranging your topics and ideas in the proper sequence and linking them by logical transitions. This involves giving *structure* to your writing and a logical *sequence* to the development of your ideas. This sequence is especially important in organizing sentences, as we shall see in the next section of this chapter. That section will then be followed by discussions of several other guidelines for achieving clarity and coherence in your sentences. Proper emphasis, parallelism, conciseness, and brevity are just some of the ways of getting your reader to *see* the same relationships between ideas that you see.

PLACE MODIFIERS NEAR THE MODIFIED

SCHOOL BOARD BANS SEX BEHIND CLOSED DOORS

You have probably seen statements similar to this newspaper headline. Their humor lies in the location of a modifying phrase—in this case, "behind closed doors"—next to a noun it was never intended to modify. Readers tend to link in their minds ideas and words that are located together. Although a little thought leads to the conclusion that the writer meant to refer to a closed school board meeting, the first impression is of something quite different.

Consider this misleading modifier from a university newspaper; what is written deviates substantially from what was intended:

> SDS also attacked Blank Corporation for its "war profiteering." As the seventh leading defense contractor, SDS claims that last year 20% of its $159 million profit came from military work.

Here is a more complex example:

> He is aware that he should uphold the authority to fire workers of his supervisors who disobey orders whenever possible as a management representative.

The sentence begins fairly well but soon degenerates into an incoherent scramble of thoughts. We will try to put the writer's meaning into coherent form. First we'll isolate the satisfactory beginning: "He is aware that he should uphold the authority to fire workers." This is coherent and expresses the main thought of the sentence. *Of his supervisors* is out of place because it appears to refer to *workers* although it seems clear that the writer intended it to refer to *authority*. Otherwise there would be nothing to tell us whose authority he is talking about. So we move *of his supervisors* up to follow *authority*. Now we have:

> He is aware that he should uphold the authority of his supervisors to fire workers who disobey orders whenever possible as a management representative.

This is better: *who disobey orders* has now fallen in place after *workers,* the word to which it was evidently intended to refer, instead of seeming to refer to *supervisors.*

But *whenever possible* and *as a management representative* still seem wrongly placed. *As a management representative* seems at first glance to refer to *workers,* but it can really refer only to *he;* there is no other single person mentioned in the sentence. To make the reference quite clear, we could shift this phrase to precede or follow *he.* The expression "He, as a management representative, is aware" is correct but a little awkward, especially as the beginning of a rather long and involved sentence. "As a management representative, he is aware" is better.

We now have to decide what to do with *whenever possible.* There is genuine doubt here as to what the writer meant. Should this phrase refer to workers who disobey orders whenever possible? Probably not, because this would limit the application of the whole sentence to an insignificant number of situations. There are only three verbs in the sentence to which *whenever possible* could refer. If it doesn't refer to *disobey,* then it can refer only to *should uphold* or to *to fire.* Probably the writer intended it to refer to *should uphold.* On this assumption we rewrite the sentence as follows:

> As a management representative, he is aware that he should uphold whenever possible the authority of his supervisors to fire workers who disobey orders.

What we have done is to reconstruct the sentence so that the apparent references—apparent because of their location—are the correct ones. The reader is no longer temporarily or even permanently confused by apparent references that the writer never intended.

Clarity is probably the most important single quality that business writing can have. We can best describe it as a means of getting your ideas across so that they cannot possibly be misunderstood. As an example of unclear writing and consequent misunderstanding, *Training Manual No. 7* of the Federal Security Agency cites the following sentence, which was sent to at least 100,000 inquirers over a seven-year period:

> In order to be fully insured, an individual must have earned $50 or more in covered employment for as many quarters of coverage as half the calendar quarters elapsing between 1936 and the quarter in which he reaches age 65 or dies, whichever first occurs.

The *Manual* laconically comments that the response of one mystified citizen was "I am no longer in covered employment. I have an outside job now."

Here is a sentence sent out by the clerk of a Board of Education which particularly wanted clear reports of school activities sent to all taxpayers because a new school levy was soon to be voted upon:

> Current topics of interest are reported through films, reading, and discussion in a class made up of the combined student body from Mr. Green's and Mr. Brown's classes not included in choir or industrial arts on the day they meet.

Since it is impossible to detect what this sentence is intended to convey, we cannot correct it. Its lack of clarity and emphasis stems from trailing too many items along in haphazard order, ending with the mysterious phrase *not included,* and misusing the pronoun *they,* whose reference remains an enigma. Beyond grammatical and rhetorical technicalities, what the sentence really proves is that vague and unclear minds produce vague and unclear communications.

GIVE THOUGHT TO THE EMPHASIS DESIRED

An important element of clarity is proper emphasis. This means simply that important ideas should be emphasized, less important ones subordinated. In a paragraph or a report, position may indicate importance. The topic sentence, at the beginning of the paragraph, will introduce the central idea. Or the paragraph may lead up to the important topic, which is given an emphatic position at the end. In a report, the same rule holds true. Central ideas or recommendations should not be buried in the text, but should be given an eye-catching place at the beginning or the end.

Although the position of a thought in a sentence may have some bearing upon the emphasis that thought receives, other ways of achieving emphasis on the sentence level are likely to have greater impact. The most basic method stems from the general rule that the important point should be in the main, or independent, clause. As an example, let us look at the sentence we rewrote in the previous section.

> As a management representative he is aware that he should uphold whenever possible the authority of his supervisors to fire workers who disobey orders.

As this sentence stands, its dominant idea is *he is aware.* If we want the reader to be struck by the importance of *a management representative should uphold the authority of his supervisors,* we will have to remove this thought from its subordinate position. If we consider awareness equally important to our message, we will have to construct our sentence with two independent clauses, separated by a semicolon:

> A management representative should, whenever possible, uphold the authority
> of his supervisors to fire workers who disobey orders; he is aware of this.

Normally, readers expect the subject of the sentence to be featured, and to be followed by the action (verb) and then the receiver of the action (object). Normally, they do not want to indulge in mental gymnastics to rearrange your sentence or to locate these important parts. (We have to put our own emphasis here on "normally," since variety in sentence structure is desirable so that this reader will not be lulled into boredom by an endless succession of subject-verb-object sentences.) But notice the roundabout wordiness of the following:

> There have been developed by the local branch of the Management Association,
> seven new methods for reducing the amount of papers in company files. (Say:
> The local Management Association has developed, etc.)

> Three trips are made to the warehouse each day by our truck drivers in order
> to replace supplies. (Say: Our truck drivers make three trips daily, etc.)

A complete lack of emphasis and an undercutting of the total effect of the sentence occur when we use for the ending some unimportant comment or afterthought. Note how these sentences trail off into nothingness instead of leading up to a clear-cut ending:

> Our new computerized typewriter saves time, eliminates mistakes, and reduces
> costs, we are sure.

> Tomorrow's business will offer more opportunity for civic responsibility and
> a greater share in national problems than ever before, I think.

If these sentences let you down with a thump as you read them, you know how readers react when you use an important part of the sentence for trivia.

Another way of giving different units of thought different degrees of emphasis is by varying the length of the sentence. An item expressed in a brief, succinct statement is more likely to receive greater attention than one camouflaged in a long, involved construction. Compare, for example, the degrees of emphasis given the same thought in the following two sentences from a retailer interested in handling a manufacturer's product line:

> Do you allow the return of unsold merchandise?

> Would you please send me information on point-of-purchase displays and any
> other advertising assistance you provide, on your policy on the return of unsold
> merchandise, and on the shipping procedures you follow?

Because the thought is given the importance of an isolated entity, the first sentence gives the impression of a very pessimistic retailer who is doubtful of the product's potential. The second sentence conveys the picture of a retailer interested in all aspects of selling this manufacturer's line. We do not suggest that you overrely on long, drawn-out sentences. But remember that if you phrase a thought in a short, simple sentence, it is going to get more emphasis than it would as one of several thoughts in a longer, more involved sentence.

Our last guideline for sentence emphasis deals with a special type of sentence—the question. Although it may sound like a gross understatement to suggest that you put questions in question form, it isn't. Too many writers have the habit of completely ignoring this simple suggestion when they write inquiries. Sentence openers like "I would appreciate knowing" or "It would be nice if you could tell me" actually belabor the courtesy objective and dull the point of the sentence. A concise, direct question with that attention-getting mark at the end is much more likely to have the impact you desire—an answer. Questions like the following are not likely to be ignored:

> For how long is the Miracle Mower guaranteed?
>
> In how many colors do you make the Baker Blender?

References to appreciation in letters seeking information are usually made at the opening and/or closing. A writer shouldn't, therefore, feel abrupt about getting to the point(s) in the body of the letter.

USE PARALLEL CONSTRUCTIONS TO CONVEY PARALLEL THOUGHTS

One of the most useful devices for achieving clarity and emphasis is parallelism— *expressing parallel ideas in parallel form*. Parallelism helps readers by employing both form and substance to establish relationships. We can fall back on one of the techniques of intelligence and vocabulary tests to illustrate the discordance that results when logical relationships are violated:

> Which of these words has nothing in common with the rest?
>
> *a.* report
> *b.* memorandum
> *c.* vice-president
> *d.* letter
>
> And which of these?
>
> *a.* to write
> *b.* to speak
> *c.* to listen
> *d.* a commentator on the radio

In the first of these oversimplified examples, *vice-president* offends the logical mind because it has nothing in common with the other three words; in the second group, *a commentator on the radio* is jarring because its form is not parallel to the three infinitives. This discordant, illogical effect is what you produce in your reader when you connect facts, words, or thoughts which do not belong together (such as "vice-president"); it is equally illogical to use a parallel form to group together thoughts which have no relationship.

When you present two or more ideas and want to emphasize a similarity or a contrast to make them clear, avoid such misleading sentences as these:

> Salespeople are expected to travel at least four days a week, to send in daily reports, and must make out weekly expense-account vouchers.

> All typists are given instruction in handling office equipment and how to serve as receptionists.

> It was not only Smith's poor forecasting of market conditions but also he didn't seem to provide adequate production facilities.

> Either the executive has the ability to plan or getting things done.

By putting ideas that logically belong together in the same form, you can achieve clarity and emphasis:

> Salespeople are expected *to travel* four days a week, *to send* in daily reports, and *to make out* weekly expense-account vouchers. (Since the first two items use infinitives, the third should be an infinitive form.)

> All typists are given instruction in *handling* office equipment and in *serving* as receptionists. (*Handling* is a participle; therefore, *how to serve* should be changed to a participial form.)

> It was not only Smith's poor forecast of market conditions but also his failure to provide adequate production facilities. (A noun parallel with a noun)

> The executive has the ability either *to plan* or *to get* things done. (Parallel infinitives)

> The executive is responsible either for *planning* or for *getting* things done. (Parallel participles)

Notice that when you use connectives like *either . . . or, not only . . . but also,* you are signaling your readers that you are expressing similarities or contrasts and that they can expect parallel forms. In long sentences, you can underscore this parallelism by repeating the key word which leads into the parallel structure:

> We must teach our students everything *about* preparing for the interview with the company's representative, *about* actually meeting and greeting the person the company sends, and *about* following up the interview with a letter of thanks.

Notice how the parallelism[1] of the following sentence is doubly emphasized by repetition:

> The Widget Electric Company *offers* years of experience *but* remains at the cutting edge of research, *offers* the most precise quality control *but* always has the most competitive prices, and *offers* the fastest service in the industry *but* never sacrifices quality for speed.

In the final analysis, you should regard parallelism as a means not merely of attaining grammatical consistency but of writing clearly and emphatically. One has only to cite a few of the best-known sentences of our heritage to see how effective and memorable this device can be:

> But, in a larger sense, we cannot dedicate, we cannot consecrate, we cannot hallow this ground.
>
> —Abraham Lincoln,
> *The Gettysburg Address*

> For thine is the kingdom, and the power, and the glory, for ever.
>
> —*The Lord's Prayer*

> As Caesar loved me, I weep for him;
> As he was fortunate, I rejoice at it;
> As he was valiant, I honored him;
> But as he was ambitious, I slew him.
>
> —William Shakespeare,
> *Julius Caesar*

BE CONCISE

Good writing, says an old adage, is the art of speaking volumes without writing them. In business writing, you should write so that your reader will not only understand, but understand as quickly and easily as possible. Don't tax the attention with a sentence such as this:

> During the past two weeks, we have been wondering if you have as yet found yourself in a position to give us an indication of whether you have been able to come to a decision on our offer.

This statement uses too many words to say: "Have you decided on our offer?"

Being concise is not the same as being brief. A 37-page report can be concise, and many a one-page letter lacks conciseness. A concise piece of writing is efficient; it conveys all that the writer wishes to say and all that the reader

[1] You will find more information on parallel constructions in the reference section at the back of this book.

needs to know in the shortest, most direct way. The difference between being too brief and being concise is well illustrated by the wire a nosy and overly aggressive columnist sent to ascertain a star's age:

HOW OLD CARY GRANT?

Back came the reply:

OLD CARY GRANT FINE. HOW YOU?

Here is a sentence from a letter written in response to an inquiry as to when a very expensive piece of equipment could be delivered:

As you probably know, we just recently received approval of drawings to permit our proceeding with engineering details on this installation, and as you can understand it is difficult at this early date to determine a more definite delivery schedule than our originally quoted promise.

This obese statement is a compound of evasion, padding, and nonthinking. What it says is:

The drawings have been approved, and we can now start the actual engineering. But right now we can't give you a more specific delivery date than the one we originally quoted.

Lack of conciseness creates boredom and inattention along with the same feeling of frustration that a bright student in a group of slow learners endures.

The causes of a lack of conciseness are so numerous that they can hardly be listed; but among them are many of the things we have talked about—attempts to impress, unnecessary technical language, jargon, inability to think about purposes, and failure to consider readers. For *their* part, readers of such windy writing can fervently subscribe to George Eliot's words: "Blessed is the man who, having nothing to say, abstains from giving in words evidence of the fact."

KEEP YOUR SENTENCES SHORT

How short is "short"? No simple answer will suffice; Dr. Rudolph Flesch, who wrote *The Art of Plain Talk,* believes that an *average* sentence length of 17 words makes for high readability. Writers in business should aim at variety in both the length and the pattern of their sentences. They should occasionally check the average length of sentences in their letters and reports to see that it falls somewhere between 15 and 20 words. If it does not, they should employ a very useful device—the period—more frequently; most long sentences lend themselves logically to this chopping-up process.

> I should greatly appreciate your letting me know what your decision is so that I can send the report to Ms. Jones in our Memphis office with a request for more information which we will need to make our plans for the coming year and to encourage her to make any suggestions she may want to incorporate. (*One sentence, 57 words*)

> I would greatly appreciate your letting me know your decision. I can then send the report to Ms. Jones in our Memphis office requesting more information. We will need her suggestions for next year's plans. (*Three sentences, 35 words*)

Perhaps the best analysis of why sentences should be kept short and clear is this statement by Herbert Spencer in his *Philosophy of Style:*

> A reader or listener has at each moment but a limited amount of mental power available. To recognize and interpret the symbols presented to him requires part of this power; to arrange and combine the images suggested requires a further part; and only that part which remains can be used for realizing the thought conveyed. Hence, the more time and attention it takes to receive and understand each sentence, the less time and attention can be given to the contained idea; and the less vividly will that idea be conceived. . . .

This analysis of what happens when the reader reads is a good argument for carrying the reader along step by step. Don't force him or her to go along until breathless from the sheer length of your sentences. By doing so, you merely divert the small amount of attention that is left for comprehending.

One of the major causes of excessive sentence length in business writing stems from the techniques of dictation, which are discussed in Chapter 20. We can highlight the difficulty here by calling attention to the danger of rambling along in the oral process of dictating without sufficient regard for the length of sentences. Since you can't actually *see* how long the sentence is in this process, the transcriber or typist can help. He or she could call attention to the fact that a sentence is too long, too involved, or too cumbersome, and that it will be more effective if it is broken into shorter units.

PUT YOUR QUALIFYING IDEAS IN SEPARATE SENTENCES

Paradoxically, one of the worst attributes of business writing stems from an admirable human quality—the desire to write the exact, absolute, and final truth in a sentence. But since a sentence follows a pattern of one thought at a time, it is impossible to express all kinds of qualifications and conditions without producing a long, complex, and highly involved sentence. "And you become obscure," said Aristotle, "if, in seeking to introduce a number of details in the middle of a sentence, you do not complete the sense before you mention them." As we noted earlier, this zeal for accuracy throws ideas or information at the reader at too fast a pace. Notice this example:

The result of this study is a recommendation that our hiring policies should be changed during the coming year but it should be remembered that this recommendation may not be sound if there is an appreciable change in the labor market during that period or if changing circumstances affect our own company's level of operations so that we need to increase or decrease the total number of employees.

You can always spot this kind of long-windedness by such words as *under certain circumstances, under different conditions,* and similar phrases. They are almost inevitable in these sentences because that is just what the writer attempts to do—to take care of all the possible contingencies, conditions, or variable elements in one sentence. As we have suggested, the cause may be intellectual honesty or it may be the opposite—a desire to hedge, to avoid unequivocal commitment. Whatever the cause, don't clutter your sentences with too many qualifying ideas. Break such sentences as the one cited above like this:

The result of our study is a recommendation to change our hiring policies during the coming year. This recommendation may not be sound if the labor market changes in the next year or if unforeseen business conditions affect our company's level of operations. If that happens, we will have to change the number of employees.

The classic definition of the sentence is *a group of words to convey a single thought.* Too many writers in business err on the side of putting qualifying phrases and clauses into their sentences and hence lengthen them to a point which passeth understanding. Aim at conciseness, at clean-cut sentences, and put the qualifiers in separate sentences.

Usually we find that our refrigerators give maximum efficiency when they are stored in a very dry place until they are used, but occasionally we hear of a case where such storage has resulted in a drying out of the insulation around the door, in which case we recommend that it be treated by applying a damp cloth so that the moisture in the rubber may be replaced. (*One sentence, 68 words*)

We find that our refrigerators give maximum efficiency when they are stored in a very dry place. Occasionally, this results in drying out the insulation around the door. We then recommend applying a damp cloth to the insulation to replace the moisture in the rubber. (*Three sentences, 45 words*)

Schopenhauer expressed the reaction of most readers when he commented: "In these long sentences rich in involved parentheses, like a box of boxes within one another, and padded out like roast geese stuffed with apples, it is really the memory that is chiefly taxed."

Fundamentally, the sentence is the basic test of how clearly you think. It can be a hazy, vague, flabby collection of words or a functional, well-designed garb for a thought. The result will depend on how much thinking you have done before you write. Great writers have always recognized this link between clear thinking and effective writing. Perhaps the best illustration of this concerns Richard Brinsley Sheridan, the famous dramatist who wrote *The School for Scandal* and *The Rivals*. A friend asked him how his new play was coming along. "It's finished," said Sheridan. "When can I read the script?" asked his friend. "Oh, I haven't written a word yet," Sheridan replied. And that is where good sentences are "written" first—in your mind.

AVOID TOO MUCH USE OF THE PASSIVE VOICE

In a passive-voice sentence, the subject is being acted upon by some other entity. The opposite is the case in the active-voice sentence, where the subject is the doer of the action. Consider these two slightly different ways of expressing the same thought:

> *Passive:* The procedures used to take inventory were being studied by the new accountant.

> *Active:* The new accountant was studying the procedures used to take inventory.

Excessive use of the passive voice can easily result in wordiness, monotony, vagueness, and complete lack of vigor. The passive has its uses. You may find that older readers, and technically trained people such as engineers and accountants, prefer an impersonal, passive style because they were schooled in that tradition. The tradition, however, is breaking down. A better reason for using the passive voice is to achieve an unemphatic, impersonal style in the specific cases where this suits your purpose. Rather than point a finger of accusation, for example, you may prefer to be a little vague. Compare these two examples:

> The sales manager has permitted unauthorized expenditures on advertising.

> Unauthorized expenditures have been made on advertising.

To a reader who understands the company's organization, the two sentences may mean the same thing. The first is vigorous, very explicit, and would be recommended by most text writers. However, the second may suit your purposes better.

Note that it is all too easy to take refuge in the passive to avoid admitting your own responsibilities:

> Because sales were overestimated last year, an inventory level that is higher than normal has resulted.

> I made a bad estimate of sales last year, and now our inventory is too high.

You might prefer to write the first sentence, but a reader who understands your responsibilities will quickly see your attempt to cover up.

On the whole there is far too much use of the passive voice in business writing. Writers get into the habit of using the passive voice, perhaps because of a constant unwillingness to be specific and commit themselves emphatically, perhaps because they have read so much business and technical material written in the passive. Here is an unfortunately typical construction from a business report:

> When our employees are subjected to long work hours which are necessitated by storms, it is expected that a higher rate of accidents will prevail.

What this writer means is:

> When storms force our employees to work long hours, we can expect a higher accident rate.

Unless you have a specific need for the passive voice, stick to the active except for occasional variation. But let the passive be the variation, not the theme. Here are examples in which the active voice improves a statement:

Passive: It is believed that our employees will be benefited by this policy.

Active: We believe this policy will benefit our employees.

Passive: Consideration is being given to this matter by our sales department.

Active: Our sales department is considering this matter.

Passive: It is occasionally found that one of our customers has been unintentionally missed by our representative.

Active: Occasionally, our representative unintentionally misses one of our customers.

LET YOUR VERBS BE THEMSELVES

At one time or another most of you have probably had to make an appearance at an official social gathering attended largely by strangers or by people with whom you had very little in common. You probably dreaded going and were somewhat uncomfortable while there. Chances are that afterward you felt you didn't "come across" well, at least partly because you were expected to be something which you were not. Although verbs lack the capability of being uncomfortable, they are affected in somewhat the same manner as described above when they are employed as that which they are not (participles, infinitives, and adjectives). They don't always "come across" well.

Verbs are action words, and they most vibrantly express their action as verbs instead of as verb derivatives. The vividness of Sir Winston Churchill's writing is due in large part to his reliance on verbs and to his choice of strong, expressive verbs. Participles, infinitives, and adjectives carry much less force than active verbs. Even nouns are frequently less effective than well-chosen verbs. Notice this statement of conclusions from a report:

> It was found that by selection of the proper test conditions it was possible to duplicate the actual use of the machine by the housewife. Under these conditions, there was a definite tendency for the fan mechanism to deteriorate or to break down completely after usage which was equivalent to 3½ years of service in the home. It is believed, therefore, that it is desirable to replace the fan mechanism by substituting the larger motor, which is capable of 6 years of service under the same conditions.

These 87 words virtually stand still, but by inserting some strong verbs, and especially by replacing infinitives, we can give the paragraph both conciseness and forward movement.

> By selecting proper test conditions, we duplicated the housewife's actual use of the machine. These tests showed that the fan mechanism deteriorated or broke down after the equivalent of 3½ years of service in the home. We believe the larger motor should be used because our tests show it can give 6 years of service under the same conditions.

Notice how these sentences from letters and memorandums can be improved by putting verbs to work:

Instead of: Application of these principles is the best way for us to obtain the cooperation of our retailers.
Say: By applying these principles, we can get our retailers to cooperate.

Instead of: This sales message is something of vital concern to all our personnel.
Say: This sales message vitally concerns all our personnel.

Instead of: This contract has a requirement that it be signed by you.
Say: This contract requires your signature.

Instead of: This makes it necessary for us to refuse your request with regret.
Say: We regret that we must, therefore, refuse your request.

Instead of: This does have a direct bearing on the possibilities for future sales.
Say: This directly affects future sales.

Some of this wordiness stems from the passive; some of it comes from roundabout expressions like *is something of vital concern,* where one verb will express the idea; and some of it results from abstract words like *application,* which can usually be replaced by verbs.

Remember the advice of John Hookham Frere, an English diplomat and writer of the nineteenth century:

And don't confound the language of the nation
With long-tailed words in osity *and* ation.

You can do two things to pack more action into your sentences:

1. Change words like *requirement, selection,* and *application* to verbs: *require, select,* and *apply.*

2. Use expressions such as *it is* and *there is* sparingly.

These expressions lead to such awkward and cumbersome sentences as "It is to introduce our new products that we are sending this brochure," when you can cut out the deadwood by saying "We are sending you this brochure to introduce our new products." Wordiness inevitably results in writing which overuses these expressions:

Instead of: It is my personal opinion that . . .
      Say: I think . . .

Instead of: There are certain problems which confront us . . .
      Say: Certain problems confront us . . .

Instead of: It was our understanding that . . .
      Say: We understood that . . .

Instead of: It is the responsibility of our Production Department to see that it meets the requirements of our Sales Division. (Note that the first *it* is indefinite and the second refers to Production Department, making a very confusing sentence.)
      Say: Our Production Department must meet the requirements of our Sales Division.

Recognizing the rationale behind the suggestions made in this chapter will not automatically make you a brilliant writer. But if you are careful to structure your sentence parts in a logical fashion, if you make most of your sentences fairly short and concise, and if you use forceful and active verbs, your business writing style cannot help but improve. Try to remember that communication involves at least two people. The success of the communication process is determined by how much of the sender's meaning is duplicated in the receiver's mind. The foregoing guides are aimed at making that duplication process easier and more complete, sentence by sentence. The remaining chapters of this text will be dedicated to enhancing the duplication process for more involved units of business composition.

EXERCISES

1. Rewrite the following sentences to make them clear and emphatic.
   a. The customer service department needs to be reorganized according to the board of directors which has done an inadequate job.

    b. Decentralization of the word processing center by the report was suggested to facilitate work flow and reduce its noise.

    c. The airline must decide whether to reschedule the charter flight to Hawaii with the disabled rudder for next week.

    d. All of those reasons are good for decreased sales offered by the marketing representatives, but I don't think they understand their importance in losing money.

    e. Should we replace the data processing equipment now partially outdated on our own by spring or wait until all features are improved by top management's approval in the fall?

2. What are the main points presented in the following paragraphs? Critique the manner in which the ideas are presented. Rewrite the paragraphs in a clear, more emphatic style.

I think we might have learned a few things from our attempts to try and define the critical and important strategic issues our company will address each year. By the way, our attempts were finally successful last year which was good because the year before we had difficulty so we were pleased.

I have no doubts, of course, that we learned how easily a committee's attention can be diverted away from discussion of the future. We all know how current problems keep us locked into the present, I guess. Operating managers are uncomfortable when they speculate about the future because they feel they should know all the answers and we all know that no one can predict the future with 100 percent accuracy. Anyway, "predict" is probably the wrong word; what this is all about is forecasting, and there is a difference, you know.

Third, we learned that at the division level planning is often lacking in having a truly long-range orientation. But this could be because most, and maybe all, statements call for backing up with thorough documentation; and intuitive judgments cannot be documented too thoroughly but they are often very valid, in my opinion.

So we have learned some things about how to go about figuring out plans by defining issues that are critical and strategic. We have learned to be careful of diversions, to be sure that our plans are long range, and then being prepared to be wrong and contradicted, which I consider could be the most important thing to remember.

3. Change the following sentences to show the relative importance of the ideas and to make them more concise.

    a. The voting started at 9 A.M. and ended at 1 P.M., and Leroy won to much surprise.

    b. My new office is quite large—9 × 12 feet—with a large window overlooking the park where I can see the lake, and Ms. Harper informed me only a few minutes ago that I have an unlimited decorating budget for it.

    c. This new method of ink-jet printing is a much-needed innovation, and I have seen with my own eyes that it is 40 times faster than conventional printing.

    d. Please send me information about the colors you have available, the cost, how long it will take for delivery, and most important, if the merchandise can be safely shipped in the summertime heat.

    e. Barry started a new job this week and is glad to be working for a company that practices participative management because his new boss has already shown confidence and trust in Barry by involving him in decision making.

4. Rewrite the following sentences, using the principle of parallel construction.

  a. The treasurer planned to fly to Philadelphia, meet with the division manager, and then was returning to the home office.

  b. The new employees found the handbook useful not only in orienting themselves to company procedures but also to get acquainted with the various departments.

  c. In a word processing system secretarial duties are divided; the correspondence secretary does all the typing and the administrative assistant's job is to handle all the nontyping responsibilites.

  d. Instead of opposing the award as originally planned, the board member is to endorse it.

  e. Kate opened her own business last month and has learned a lot about dealing with customers, ordering merchandise, and how to plan an advertising campaign.

  f. Not only was the desire to achieve success a strong motive of hers, but maintaining good interpersonal relations was also a strong desire.

5. How would you change the following sentences to make them more direct and concise? Would more than one sentence be better in some instances?

  a. The decision reached as to the method of transport by which our merchandise manufactured in the southern locale of our country would be conveyed to the northern markets was that train would be a superior means of transportation as opposed to the interior shipping method by truck, especially if gas continues to increase in price, which seems very likely.

  b. The enclosed regulations were formulated with the aforethought aim of constituting a more succinct approach to the determination of which employees are eligible for leaves of absence.

  c. Since it is an expected practice for us to provide recognition of outstanding employees of our organization who have performed in a superior manner, we would like to take this opportunity to invite you to our awards assembly on May 16.

  d. The management of our store has concluded that it would be helpful to our fine customers if our establishment were to remain open later than the usual closing hours on Saturdays during the hectic Christmas shopping season, so you can shop in our store now until 9 P.M. every day except Sunday, when our store will be open from noon till 5.

  e. The accountant questioned the accounts receivable clerk about his procedure for recording transactions involving foreign currency in great detail because she seemed to feel that his way of recording such transactions was incorrect; and she wanted a thorough explanation of why he was doing it that way.

  f. The school board said they would consider the proposal to allow the conference to be held in the school as long as the organizers would guarantee that the conference would be finished by 5 P.M. because there was a sports banquet being held there that night which was honoring the boys and girls who had participated in spring sports.

  g. We appreciate your letter telling us about the success you have had with our new, improved facial cleanser since our laboratory has been working for the past two years on creating a more effective product to fit the needs of busy women like you who want a cleanser that is quick to use and which cleans thoroughly.

  h. Sales have increased by 10 percent this quarter which speaks well for our sales staff who have been putting forth a lot of extra effort to bring about such an increase, and we hope that next quarter will show similar results but, of course, much of their success depends on the economy in general and whether consumers will spend freely like they did this past quarter or hold on to their money in savings accounts.

6. Change the following sentences from passive to active voice, and where possible change the camouflaged verbs into their verb forms:

 a. Forty work-hours a week can be saved by the implementation of this new procedure.

 b. A 22 percent increase in sales is expected this month as a result of the new advertising campaign.

 c. A complete reorganization of the home office administrative staff is being effected by the new chief executive.

 d. Our new Model 30 Rader refrigerators can be ordered by you in a choice of six different colors.

 e. The strictest adherence to these rules will be enforced by the security personnel.

 f. It is demanded by the union stewards that this issue of disciplinary authority be immediately brought to the attention of top management.

7. Improve the following sentences by using action verbs:

 a. It was our belief in the discussion of the backlog of work that the creation of a new staff position would not result in a resolution of the situation.

 b. In the application of these procedures to the five branch offices, the recommendation is given that their implementation be made on a gradual basis.

 c. There is the possibility that the content of the report will be subject to different interpretations by the company officials.

 d. Because of the restriction on purchasing, our stock is low; and replacement of popular merchandise will not be an occurrence until we have our buyer's approval.

 e. It is with great pleasure that we can provide you with the information that shipment of your order will take place on Wednesday, September 8, with the provision that someone will be home to receive the furniture.

8. Can you synthesize what you have learned in this chapter and write clear, concise, emphatic sentences to express the following ideas? You will need to create additional information to make the sentences more specific and complete.

 a. Notify Phoenix branch office—they had a few costs reduced last month; overall company earnings limited by inflation.

 b. Inform management—employees are angry with a management decision; they don't really understand the decision, though.

 c. State another advantage of using electronic registers—processing of a credit transaction takes less time; customers wait less.

 d. Tell customer—order will be shipped as soon as inventory is replenished.

 e. State qualities of your new dictating machines—compact, easy to operate, excellent voice reproduction capabilities.

4
PARAGRAPHS-THEIR DEVELOPMENT AND DEMOLITION

In the last two chapters we have outlined, in stairstep fashion, guidelines for dealing with the two most basic elements of written communication, words and sentences. In Chapter 2 you were cautioned about a number of pitfalls in word usage that work against the reader's ease of comprehension. In Chapter 3 you were given several suggestions aimed at helping your sentences to make sense.

In our efforts to develop proficiency in business writing, paragraphs will be the next level of analysis subjected to our scrutiny. More specifically, we shall now examine the qualities that distinguish clear and coherent paragraphs at one extreme from incoherent, unclear ramblings of a disorganized mind at the other extreme.

Paragraphs, like sentences, demand carefully arranged sequences of topics and ideas. But paragraph construction makes two demands that rarely concern you in building sentences. A paragraph must be built around a single theme or major topic, and the ideas or minor topics that are discussed in the paragraph must be connected with each other by logical transitions. A sentence is usually short enough for every part to deal with a single topic or theme, and you rarely find so many ideas in a sentence that it is difficult to connect them.

In addition to these two subjects, unity and transition, this chapter will deal with several other guides to effective paragraph design. The length of a paragraph, for example, directly affects the effort a reader must expend to comprehend it as a unit. Although no hard and fast rule can be applied to every paragraph you construct, we can encourage you to take some precautions against demanding the impossible of a reader.

Another paragraph quality we'll consider will be its organization as related to its desired impact. A paragraph intended to persuade someone to accept a conclusion might be organized differently from one intended to convey objective, incontestable information. Treated with this coverage of order for impact will be the different ways a paragraph's design may be varied so as to emphasize or subordinate the items contained therein.

PARAGRAPH UNITY

Most writing texts will tell you that a paragraph should deal with a *single topic*. This is fine as long as you know what a single topic is. Probably the best test to use is this: Put yourself in your reader's place, read over your paragraph, and decide whether there is a central theme or major topic that runs through the entire paragraph. If there is not *some* such theme or topic, then you do not have a satisfactory paragraph. Either it should be broken into two or more paragraphs or it should be rewritten.

The first sentence of your paragraph should indicate the major topic of that paragraph. You may use a *topic sentence,* one that states the topic explicitly, or you may merely imply in your first sentence what your major topic is. In any case, your readers are going to decide on the basis of this sentence what *they* think the major topic is, and they will expect you to stick to that topic. It is this consistency that is called *unity* in a paragraph.

Unity requires that the minor topics of your paragraph—what you have to say about the major topic—all be part of the major topic or be closely related to it. To achieve this unity, once you have selected your minor topics, you must establish a logical sequence for them, as in the construction of sentences. Once the sequence is established, you must devise transitions to carry the readers' attention from one minor topic to the next in what appears to them to be a logical way.

Unity and Logical Sequence

The following excerpts are from a report to three young people planning to open a repertory theater. They had very little business experience and turned to a businessperson for advice. The report began:

> (1) I think that the idea of forming a repertory theater is excellent. However, you should consider starting the project on a smaller scale.

This seems to be a good beginning. The writer has come directly to the point and offers a specific recommendation. What do you expect will follow these two sentences? Probably a discussion of why or how the theater should be started on a smaller scale. Small-scale operation seems to be the major topic of the paragraph. Here is how the report actually progressed:

> (2) I think that the idea of forming an experimental repertory theater is excellent. However, you should consider starting the project on a smaller scale.

The statement of the general manager of a similar venture attributed its failure to inexperienced management.

The third sentence, instead of dealing with small scale, has switched to inexperience. Is there any connection between the first two sentences and the third? Perhaps, but the writer certainly hasn't told us what it is. We are left wondering whether the topic of small-scale operations has been abandoned and why inexperience has been introduced. Now we add the writer's fourth and fifth sentences:

(3) I think that the idea of forming an experimental repertory theater is excellent. However, you should consider starting the project on a small scale. The statement of the general manager of a similar venture attributed its failure to inexperienced management. The man who is to be your business manager has not the experience to operate such a large enterprise as you are planning. Besides, the rest of the group have had little theatrical experience and are not well known.

At last we know why inexperience was brought in. The writer apparently believes this group has the experience necessary to run a small operation (at least this is implied), but not a large one. But we had to read through one distracting and apparently irrelevant sentence to find this out. And even now we are not sure why that third sentence was included. Was it intended to prove that inexperience dooms a large venture but not a small one? It certainly doesn't say so. It simply tells us that the failure of another venture, which may have been large or small, has been attributed to inexperience.

The fifth sentence, too, has added a new topic. The writer says the members of the group are not well known. Is this intended to strengthen the argument for small-scale operations? Probably, but the writer doesn't tell us why. This seems to have dragged in another topic that may or may not be relevant. The writer certainly doesn't show why it is relevant.

The next two sentences, still in the same paragraph, were the following:

(4) You intend to invest $20,000 to rebuild an old factory building in a city populated by people you regard as "Philistines." As your repertoire will be experimental theater, how can you appeal to this group of people?

What has happened to the theme of small-scale operation? It seems to have been dropped completely when the writer switched to the "Philistines." The writer gives us no explanation for the switch, and in fact seems to be arguing against any theatrical venture, large or small. Probably what the writer intended to say was that a very small part of the city's population would patronize the proposed theater, and hence it should be kept small. But the report didn't say this.

We might rewrite the entire paragraph as follows, keeping to the theme of optimism but small-scale operation, which is what the writer presumably had in mind.

> I think that the idea of forming an experimental repertory theater is excellent. However, you should consider starting the project on a small scale. Your business manager does not have the experience necessary to operate the large enterprise you are planning, and the rest of the group is inexperienced as well. Lack of experience has been blamed for the failure of a venture similar to yours. Another reason for small-scale operation is the probability that only a small segment of the city's population will be interested in experimental theater. You yourselves characterize this population as "Philistine."

Notice that we have preserved the theme, or major topic, throughout the paragraph. And we have arranged the sequence of ideas so that each one seems to follow logically from the one before.

All of this may seem picayune to you. A common reaction of sloppy writer to a reader's complaint is: "But you know what I mean." And in fact we were able to deduce what the writer probably had in mind even when the paragraph seemed to be wandering hopelessly. But your job as a writer in business is not to provide guessing games for your reader. Let him or her know very quickly when you begin a paragraph what that paragraph is about. And then stick to your topic. Make sure not only that each sentence is related to your topic but also that this is obvious to your reader. The writer of the paragraph we have been discussing may have known perfectly well why a "Philistine" population indicated a small theater. But the writer didn't bother to show us why, and we had to puzzle it out.

At least we were able to puzzle out that paragraph and reconstruct it in coherent form. But can you do the same for the next three paragraphs in the report?

> (5) The general idea of your project is to fuse the American and English traditions in a repertory theater. Therefore my suggestion is the following:
>
> We know about a successful repertory theater established seven years ago in your city operating in a tiny building.
>
> As you want to stay in the city, I suggest you rent a small place there.

What do you expect after reading the first of these three paragraphs (5)? Surely you would be ready for a suggestion as to how the three people may accomplish their objective of fusing the American and English theater traditions. But what actually comes next is a statement about another theater operating in a very small building. Is there any logical connection at all? There doesn't seem to be. The writer has apparently returned to the theme of small-scale operations, pointing out that another repertory theater is successfully operating on a small scale, and concluding that this group should rent a small place too.

The first of the three paragraphs in (5) is simply incomprehensible as it stands. The author may have believed it to be relevant, but there is no clue from which we could deduce the relevance. This is writing at its most incoherent. You can probably see why a reader of this report might conclude that the writer just couldn't think clearly.

Transitions

Transitions make a paragraph "hang together." You can think of transitions in two senses, as *logical connections* among ideas or as *mechanical aids* in linking these ideas. Consider an example:

> (6) We do not have the experience necessary to operate a large theater; we shall have to be content with a small one.

There is a logical connection between the topics of lack of experience and limitation to only small-scale operations. One is the cause of the other. We can add a mechanical transition—the word *therefore*—to obtain the following:

> (7) We do not have the experience necessary to operate a large theater; therefore, we shall have to be content with a small one.

We have in fact discussed logical connections already, as part of the arrangement of topics in a logical sequence. In this section we shall be concerned with mechanical transitions.

Mechanical transitions may be words, phrases, clauses, or whole sentences. Some typical transition words and phrases are arranged below according to the functions they serve:

Listing or additions:	*Result:*
In addition	Accordingly
First, second, third, etc.	As a result
Again	Consequently
Also	Hence
Furthermore	Therefore
Finally	Thus
Moreover	For this reason

Comparisons:	*Explanation or elaboration:*
Here again	For example
Likewise	To illustrate
Similarly	For instance
In like manner	

	Summary:
Contrasts:	In other words
	In brief
On the contrary	In sum
However	On the whole
In contrast	To sum up
On the other hand	
Yet	
Still	

In addition to these fairly obvious means of connecting thoughts within paragraphs, several more subtle means of accomplishing the same purpose are available to writers. By repeating a key word, for example, the writer signals the reader that the same subject is still under discussion. Those writers who don't like to repeat too much can use a variation of this technique. They can use synonyms and pronouns to refer to a subject already mentioned. The demonstrative pronouns—this, that, these, and those—and their adjective forms are also especially helpful in tying thoughts together. Finally, words like *the former, the latter, the one,* and *the other* are also good transition devices. Can you spot any of these more subtle means of transition in this paragraph? If you can't pick out at least ten, you have not looked hard enough.

None of the expressions in the preceding list is new to you, nor is the idea of mechanical transitions. In fact, the subject is important because of the common overuse and misuse of transitions, not because of widespread failure to use them. To begin with, if your sequence of topics is not logical, so that you are placing topics with no logical connection next to one another, no mechanical transition will create a connection that seems reasonable to your reader. And even if there is a logical connection among your topics, you may find yourself using the wrong transitions, or using a transition where none is needed.

If a connection between two topics or ideas is perfectly clear, adding a transition will not contribute to a reader's understanding and will probably slow him or her down and give an impression of childish writing. Compare the following two paragraphs. Do all the transitions added in the second version serve any purpose?

(8) A large-scale operation can be successful only if it is well financed and the management is experienced. Your manager is not experienced, and you have little capital. You should limit yourselves to small-scale operation.

A large-scale operation can be successful only if it is well financed and the management is experienced. But your manager is not experienced, and second, you have little capital. Therefore, you should limit yourself to small-scale operations.

In the following example at least one transition is used in each sentence following the first. (The transitions are italicized.) Which do you think are useful in guiding a reader? Which are unnecessary because they only point out what is obvious? And which are actually false, in that they imply logical connections which do not exist?

(9) I think that the idea of forming a repertory theater is excellent. *However,* you should consider starting the project on a smaller scale. *This is because* your business manager does not have the experience necessary to operate the large enterprise you are planning. *Therefore,* he is qualified to run only a small-scale operation. *Also,* lack of experience has been blamed for the failure of a venture similar to yours. *Another* reason for small-scale operation is the probability that only a small segment of the city's population will be interested

in experimental theater. *This is because* you yourselves characterize this population as "Philistine."

However is useful in signaling a qualification to the statement made in the first sentence. Without it the second sentence may seem to contradict the first. *This is because* is probably superfluous, although it is not incorrect. *Therefore,* on the other hand, is probably incorrect. The fact that a person is not experienced enough to operate a large enterprise does not prove that he or she is qualified to run a small one. The person may or may not be.

Also is not false (it does not imply a nonexistent logical relation), but it is temporarily misleading to a reader. The reader expects *also* to be followed by another reason for small-scale operation, but instead the sentence tells why experience is important.

Another helps to bring the reader's mind back to reasons for small-scale operation after a brief digression to show why experience is important. You cannot avoid occasional digressions, and you may have to provide reminders of your principal topic.

This is because is false. The probability described in the preceding sentence is not caused by anyone's characterization. The writer's guess that certain things are probable is consistent with the readers' characterization, and this consistency may help convince the readers that the writer is correct, but there is no causal relationship involved.

Compare the example with the rewritten paragraph on page 58.

PARAGRAPHS AS READABLE UNITS

Readers in the twentieth century have become accustomed to seeing material in smaller units than those used a century ago. Advertisers, journalists, and other writers have, therefore, learned to break text into shorter and more readable units. You can test this on the basis of your own habits when you read a novel. If you are typical, the chances are that you read most of the conversation and skim over most of the description. You do this not because the conversation is necessarily more interesting than the description, but because it generally comes in shorter units of text.

When you write reports, letters, or memorandums, you should remember that long paragraphs, heavy chunks of typing or print, have an eye-repelling quality for today's reader. They should be divided into more easily comprehended bits by a technique which advertising people call "letting daylight into the copy."

No one can say authoritatively how long a paragraph should be; that will depend on how thoroughly or in how much detail you are trying to develop an idea or a topic. It will also depend on the reader, whose preferences in business writing we have already indicated. To be completely practical, however, most long paragraphs in business communication can be broken up without any loss of logic. In fact, most long paragraphs are written because writers have lost sight of their readers and the way they read.

If you are interested in a general guide, you might consider five lines to be an acceptable *average* paragraph length for business letters. Business report paragraphs, which usually deal with more involved topics, might *average* around ten lines. Keep in mind, however, that these are only general guides to which you may often find exceptions.

Letter opening and closing paragraphs are two such exceptions. Because their objectives are usually simple and few, they may not exceed two or three lines. Goals of emphasis and subordination might also justify exceptions to these general guides. A very short, one-sentence paragraph almost guarantees that the idea presented will get more attention than it would if it were sandwiched into a collection of several other thoughts. But if you don't want to give a thought undue attention—as might be the case when you are refusing some request—a longer paragraph might serve the purpose of subordinating the unpleasant idea.

In business letters, you can often disregard the literary definition of the paragraph as "a group of related sentences forming a unit of thought." Think of it, instead, as a device for making the message easier to read and as a method of dividing the message into functional parts. For instance, as we shall see later, the sales letter usually has four functions—attracting attention, creating desire for the product or service, convincing the reader, and motivating action. To each of these functions within the letter, a paragraph is devoted. The following two letters illustrate how the paragraph can contribute to the ease of reading:

Dear Mr. Potter:

We are glad to tell you, in answer to your letter of May 4, that our service department has found nothing seriously wrong with your Blank Camera, Model 12 A. A few comparatively inexpensive repairs and adjustments are needed, the chief of which are replacement of one part of the shutter mechanism and readjustment of the timing. The camera appears to have been dropped or seriously jarred. Our guarantee covers "any defect of workmanship or materials within one year of normal use," but, as you doubtless realize, it does not cover careless handling. If you will send us your check for $5.50, we will put your camera in first-class condition and renew our guarantee on workmanship and materials for another year. Just as soon as you sign and mail the enclosed, stamped, addressed post card, we'll return your camera as good as new—ready to catch that picture ahead that you'll treasure as a moment of happiness recaptured.

Sincerely yours,

Dear Mr. Potter:

We are glad to tell you, in answer to your letter of May 4, that our service department has found nothing seriously wrong with your Blank Camera, Model 12 A.

A few comparatively inexpensive repairs and adjustments are

needed, the chief of which are replacement of one part of the shutter mechanism and readjustment of the timing. The camera appears to have been dropped or seriously jarred.

Our guarantee covers "any defect of workmanship or materials within one year of normal use," but, as you doubtless realize, it does not cover careless handling. If you will send us your check for $5.50, we will put your camera in first-class condition and renew our guarantee on workmanship and materials for another year.

Just as soon as you sign and mail the enclosed, stamped, addressed post card, we'll return your camera as good as new—ready to catch that picture ahead that you'll treasure as a moment of happiness recaptured.

Sincerely yours,

A glance shows how much more inviting to the eye the second version of this letter is than the first, which repels the eye by its lack of paragraphing. Furthermore, the second letter helps the reader by using paragraphs to divide the message into its logical functions. Thus, in the four-paragraph letter above, the division is made on the following basis:

Paragraph 1: A reference to the date of the letter being answered and a statement of what this letter is about

Paragraph 2: A statement of what is wrong with the camera and why

Paragraph 3: An explanation of why the guarantee does not cover this situation and a statement of the cost

Paragraph 4: An incentive to action

To present these subdivisions of the thought in the most readable fashion, the paragraphs of the business letter should be kept short. In using paragraphs to suit such functions, we are actually returning to the original meaning and use of the word. For *paragraph* is composed of two Greek words: *graph,* from *graphein,* "to write," and *para,* "beside." At one time, a paragraph was a mark, usually ¶, written beside the text of a manuscript to mark a unit or subdivision of the text for the reader. While we have replaced the mark with indentions or arrangements of single and double spacing, the purpose of the paragraph is unchanged—to help the reader by breaking the text and to arrange clusters of sentences in logical units.

As was noted earlier, there are exceptions to every principle. William Faulkner, for instance, wrote paragraphs which extend over several pages—but for the purposes of business writing, short paragraphs are more readable. If you combine this shortness with a logical or functional grouping of the ideas expressed by the sentences within the paragraphs, you will achieve the two main purposes of the paragraph in business communication, unity and coherence.

IMPACT ORDERING

Let us now consider a special kind of paragraph design option used for special purposes and kinds of readers. When a paragraph contains a conclusion of some type and the support for that conclusion, you may want to consider two alternative arrangements of these items. The arrangements differ in the placement of the conclusion, and which you choose would depend upon your purpose and reader.

The first alternative may be called *direct* because it proceeds from an opening statement of your general conclusion to the specific supporting details. Because it gets to the main point quickly, it is the preferred and more common arrangement in business writing. In fact, a busy executive who trusts a report writer's objectivity may read the conclusions and skim over the supporting details when this arrangement is used.

The second, or *indirect,* arrangement saves the conclusion for the end of the paragraph. Although not as popular, it also has its use in business writing. The use of the indirect arrangement is usually related to a need for persuasion. If, for example, you were writing a report for a group of readers who had had no previous experience with you—as would be the case if you were working in a new job—you might want to consider this indirect approach. Since your readers would have no predetermined basis upon which to judge your objectivity, it might be wise to lead them down the path of your logic (that is, give your support) before you spring your conclusion on them.

Such an indirect approach might also be warranted if you knew your reader well enough to know that he or she held preconceived notions about the paragraph's subject that differed from your conclusion. Getting such a reader to first accept the facts behind your way of thinking might go a long way toward getting him or her to accept your final conclusion. Read the following examples of the indirect and direct arrangements, respectively, and try to decide which would be less likely to alienate a reader who already favored another choice.

> Seadale, at a population of 156,000, is 20 percent larger than Hahnville and 35 percent larger than Jamestown. Furthermore, Seadale has grown twice as fast as has either of the other two cities. Couple these figures with its projected growth trend of 7 percent annually (compared with Hahnville's 3 percent and Jamestown's 5 percent); and Seadale's choice, on the basis of population statistics, becomes obvious.

> On the basis of population statistics, Seadale is the obvious choice. Its population of 156,000 is 20 percent larger than Hahnville's and 35 percent larger than Jamestown's. Furthermore, it has grown twice as fast as has either of the other two cities. And its projected growth trend of 7 percent annually (compared with Hahnville's 3 percent and Jamestown's 5 percent) lends additional support to its choice.

The preceding discussion and examples might give you the impression that paragraph order for impact might be worthy of your attention only in reports. However, direct and indirect paragraphs are also useful in business letters. What you use in any given case will be influenced by the expected impact of the information you'll be delivering.

With good or neutral news, the direct order is likely to be the more appropriate. On the other hand, if your conclusion is likely to disappoint your reader, you would probably be wise to use either the indirect approach or a variation of it. The variation might first present the reasoning, followed by the unpleasant conclusion, which would then be followed by thoughts with a more positive ring. The objective of such an arrangement would be to subtly move your reader away from the disappointment that might result from the negative news. As illustrated by the following example, an indirect arrangement in the paragraphs and in the entire letter can help to soften the blow of a refusal.

Dear Dr. Smith:

Thank you for asking me to chair this year's United Fund Drive. The purpose of the United Fund is certainly very worthwhile, one to which citizens should devote whatever time and attention they can afford.

In this same spirit, I recently volunteered for committee work with the March of Dimes and membership on the Budget Advisory Board of our church. When I added these new responsibilities to the demands of my recent promotion and my position on the town council, however, I decided that my family would have to come before any additional commitments. I therefore must decline the offer to chair the United Fund Drive this year. I am certain that the Drive will achieve greater success with a leader who can devote the time and attention that this challenging but worthwhile task warrants.

You might want to consider John Jones, our Director of Public Relations. He is a very responsible citizen, and he has worked with fund-raising drives before. Also, his job would provide him with contacts that could help the Drive considerably. If you are interested in John, I would be happy to talk to him about chairing the drive.

Good luck in your efforts to reach your goal this year. You will certainly have my moral and financial support.

Sincerely,

This writer had the unpleasant task of declining an honor that went hand in hand with a good deal of work. A brief refusal of the "I have too many commitments" variety would have given the impression of an irresponsible writer who didn't want to be bothered. Tact, concern, and a genuine desire to help to the fullest extent possible are all writer qualities conveyed in this letter. This arrangement does call for a bit more effort than what goes into the type of letter that begins with "I regret to inform you. . . ." But writers who are interested in portraying themselves as human beings will usually find that the results of that additional effort make it worthwhile.

EXERCISES

1. Use paragraphs and any other changes to make the following memorandum clearer and more emphatic:

This is in response to your inquiry dated April 3 inquiring about the possibility of offering an in-service training program in communication for our employees. It is worthy of noting that several executives have suggested that some of the secretarial staff improve their grammar and punctuation skills. I don't know if we could require some of them to take the course and not require others. Likewise, some of the secretaries have voiced complaints that their bosses do not know how to write a clear, concise business letter and that they spend a great deal of time correcting their errors and rewriting sentences. So perhaps it would be a good idea to offer two communication courses, one for the secretarial staff and one for the executives, unless we combined them into one class. Also, oral communication could certainly stand some improvement in this organization. It seems that communication through telephone calls is replacing much of the letter writing that formerly was done before. Therefore, if we decide to improve oral communication, we should also seriously think about including the teaching of listening skills, since the process of speaking involves someone to listen to what is being said. Also, we must think about when a communication course would be offered. Would it be in the morning before work, or would employees be excused an hour early each week to attend class? A good ten sessions would probably be required to make the endeavor worthwhile, depending, of course, on what we decide should be covered. Furthermore, since summer is vacation time, the course probably shouldn't be implemented until the fall when regular schedules are in operation. We should also think about who would teach such a course. Would one of our employees who is skilled in communications be a good choice, or should we choose to hire someone from the outside, perhaps a professor from the university? Well, these are all points to consider before making the decision as to whether we should think about offering an in-service communication program. Please do not hesitate to get in touch with me for further input to this decision, for there are probably other considerations that should be thought about that I have not included in this answer to your inquiry.

2. Giving special attention to sequence and transition, how would you change the following examples to make them clearer and more coherent?

    a. In answer to your request for information about our products, I think you will be pleased to know that we sell the most portable home water distillers of any company. Therefore, you can be sure of purchasing a quality product. A home distiller enables you to have pure water for only pennies a day. Your water will be free of chemicals and impurities. It is excellent for drinking, cooking, and even washing your face with. And even though you think your city's water supply is safe, you must also consider the pipes through which the water flows. The water is tested at the treatment plant but not when it comes out of your tap. Many cities have old pipes which are too expensive to replace. Also, the pipes in your home may be old, and lead pipe and corrosive water could result in lead poisoning. Many authorities believe the fall of the Roman Empire was a direct result of lead poisoning from water pipes. Enclosed is a booklet illustrating the five different models of distillers that we sell. One is sure to fit your needs. All are guaranteed for one year. Although the initial cost might seem high, remember that you use a lot of water and that your distiller will last for many years. The price per gallon is very little. Isn't your health worth a small investment?

b. This is the report you requested a few days ago. It deals with the Cooperative Office Education (COE) students we have hired this year. The students have performed very satisfactorily. Their supervisors here have formally evaluated them twice so far. Major strengths of the students were reported as possessing good attitudes toward work, accuracy in their work, willingness to accept responsibility, and pride in their work. The teacher-coordinators have visited the students on the job and have discussed their performance with the work supervisors. We have six COE students from Central High School and four from East High School. One of the objectives of the program is to give students experience in several different departments of our company. They are rotated on a monthly basis. The COE program is a good way for the schools and businesses to cooperate with each other.

3. The following are paragraphs from a report entitled "The Future Needs of the Montvale Community Center," written for the community center's board of trustees. What changes would you make in it?

On the basis of our study, we have concluded that the future needs of the Montvale Community Center are:
1. An addition to the present building
2. More daytime activities
3. More attention to the needs of senior citizens
As you know, our community center was established five years ago, originally to provide the teenagers of the community with activities and a place to go to that they felt was theirs. With the success of the youth program, the center's activities were expanded gradually to include recreation for the entire family. These have been very successful, too.

Unfortunately, the demand for our programs is now such that we cannot serve everyone who desires to participate. An addition to the present building is needed. These rooms will be used for arts and crafts, which seems to be the area of greatest interest for our citizens.

Our definition of "future" is approximately the next 10 years, or what is sometimes referred to as the "foreseeable" future, even though it is difficult in such fast-moving times as ours to foresee a great deal.

More daytime activities will be needed for several reasons. The number of women seeking activities outside the home will probably increase. These include both recreational and educational activities. When the children are in school is a good time for the mothers to be at the community center. Several of Montvale's businesses are seriously considering the four-day work week, so more full-time employees will most likely want to use the facilities of the community center on their days off. Because of the climate here in Montvale, an increasing number of people are choosing to retire here. Several of the people we consulted in preparing this report projected an even greater increase in the senior citizen population in the next ten years. They will enjoy spending time at the community center, and we should design some activities and courses specifically for them. This doesn't mean that they should be excluded from the other activities at the center. We are merely recommending that activities be planned so that they can meet and socialize with other senior citizens because they have a lot in common and this will help to prevent loneliness in a new town.

In conclusion, the population of Montvale will continue to grow and change. Our community center is the heart of our town. We want to maintain citizen interest in Montvale, and the community center is a good way of doing this. So our recommendations should be carefully considered.

4. What changes would you make in the sequence and transitions of the following letter to give it greater clarity?

> Dear Ms. Brukowski:
>
> We are sorry to hear from your letter that you have been experiencing difficulty with your subscription to our publication, *Administrative Management News*. It seems that your copies have been arriving a few weeks late, and you never received the January issue. We are sending you today a copy of the January issue so you do not miss out on this special issue which deals with forecasts and trends for the coming year.
>
> A check of our subscription records shows that you renewed your subscription in October and that your address changed from where you were previously receiving our publication. This probably caused the issues to arrive late. Your January issue probably got lost in the mail. Address changes take about six weeks to become effective. A regular renewal would have ensured continuing service, but an address change renewal requires an update of our computerized mailing list here at our editorial offices and also a change at the office where the magazines are distributed.
>
> Your copies of *Administrative Management News* should arrive from now on the first week of each month. If they do not, please let us know and we will try to correct the matter. We appreciate your calling this to our attention.
>
> Sincerely,

5. Should either of the following paragraphs be reordered? What assumptions would support the arrangement of the second paragraph? What assumptions would suggest a change?

   a. We regret to inform you that we cannot extend the credit you applied for on June 9. Several factors are thoroughly investigated whenever a credit application is processed by our company. One of these factors is the ratio of current assets to current liabilities. We recommend a 2 to 1 ratio. Your company's ratio is 1.72 to 1. As soon as this ratio reaches the required level, we will be happy to process your application again.

   b. Our inventory is at the highest level it has ever reached. Although demand is good and market prices are high now, there is reason to believe that we may be headed for a minor slump within the next two or three months. For these reasons, and because appreciable style changes are expected in about six months, I recommend an immediate, major price-cutting promotional program.

5
STYLE–TO THE READER'S OR THE WRITER'S TASTE

We have discussed in the last four chapters the importance of thinking through the purpose of everything you write, and we have gone through the elements of clarity and correctness in word choice, sentence construction, and paragraph design. Once you know what you are doing, once your writing is clear and correct, isn't that adequate? For many purposes, it may be. But if your aim is to persuade your readers to your point of view, to make them act, to impress them with your knowledge or your reasoning powers or the effort you have put into your work, you must first capture their attention. One of the qualities in writing that compels and maintains attention is *style*.

Written communication is a two-way street. It does not do you much good to write if no one is going to read. One subject on which we need a great deal more research is how writing is read. Normally, as in this book, emphasis is placed on how good writing is written, yet the real test of its quality is how it is read. Does the message get across to the reader in the way the writer intended?

Young business writers need to be reminded that many times their readers will misunderstand them. The reasons? Conventionally—and generally quite properly—we blame such failures on incompetent writers. Nonetheless, it is perfectly true that what sometimes appears to be a clear message ends up in the reader's mind as something different from what the writer meant. *What has the reader done to it?* We need to know not only a lot more about how to get readers to understand our writing but also *why* they misunderstand. It is interesting to note that about ninety out of a hundred of our sayings on the subject of communication deal with what the writer does or should do; those that are concerned with reading tend to be in the nature of tributes to reading as a means of education, like Bacon's "Reading maketh a full man. . . ." Apparently the weight of the past is on the side of making writers responsible for misunderstanding. Nevertheless, since we want you to think, to question, and to find out about all the basic principles of communication, here are a few of these oft-repeated guides for class discussion or for your own consideration:

Attention has a narrow mouth; we must pour into it what we say very carefully, and as it were, drop by drop. —Joubert

If you want me to weep, you must grieve. —Horace

Slow beginnings put readers to sleep. —A textbook on writing

Words are like leaves; and where they most abound
Much fruit of sense beneath is rarely found. —Pope

When you don't know what you mean, use big words—that often fools little people. —Facetious comment by a speech teacher

A conversation is always going on inside your reader's head—about himself.
—Advice by a communications consultant

A picture is worth a thousand words. —Old Chinese proverb

Write the way you talk and your readers will understand.
—Advice in a letter-writing manual

Learn to write for the reader who knows less about the subject than the author, but who doesn't want to know all. —S. I. Hayakawa

Some authorities have pointed out that readers seem always to be armed with the writer's two worst enemies—lack of interest and an infinite capacity to misunderstand. It would be misleading to overemphasize this concept. As a matter of fact, in business writing it is fair to assume that what you have written *will* be read, or at least, that someone will *begin* to read it. Most of your writing will concern things your reader wants to know about.

Even though business writers can generally assume that a ready-made interest exists, they must also remember this: When we ask readers to pay too dearly for what they are getting, we not only lose their interest but we also squander their principal, the time they invest. Exorbitant demands by writers result in skimming, skipping, and frustration and reflect anything but credit on the writer.

An effective writer learns to capitalize on the reader's initial interest and to hold it thoughout the communication. To do this, the writer must understand the reader. The degree of understanding will, of course, vary in different situations. If you are writing reports and memorandums for the same people frequently, you will come to know a good deal about your readers, and you will have the added advantage of feedback—their comments on how well you are doing.

Such personal contact occurs less frequently when you write business letters. Often you will know very little about your reader, and you may never receive a reaction to your letter. But lack of familiarity with your reader is no excuse for ignoring him or her when you write. In fact, it is additional reason for thinking through carefully what a reader probably is looking for in your writing and what the probable effect of what you have written will be on most readers.

Understanding your readers does not require any elaborate feats of psychology. Except in special situations, you are probably safe in assuming that your readers think somewhat as you do: that their general intelligence is about the same, that they appreciate clarity and conciseness as much as you do, and that they would like to be able to understand your message without undue effort. Readability studies have shown that writing at a level slightly below readers' ability to comprehend is more comfortable for them.

Consider the results of these studies and the fact that many readers of your business writing won't know as much about the subject as you do, and you have two good reasons for simplifying many of your first efforts to communicate. The guidelines discussed in Chapter 2 bear repetition here. Not only should you avoid trying to impress your readers with the size of your vocabulary, but you should also give thought to aiming your message at a level slightly below what you estimate to be their actual ability to understand.

In previous chapters we discussed a number of reasons why readers often misunderstand business communications; inappropriate use of highly technical language, attempts to impress, and overindulgence in jargon are just a few. The following specific principles have a common goal of styling your writing to your readers' taste as well as to their understanding.

1. Avoid irrelevancies.

2. Watch your pace.

3. Keep your tone appropriate.

4. Be specific.

AVOID IRRELEVANCIES

In Chapter 3 you were advised to be concise in choosing words to build sentences. The opposite and major enemy of conciseness is irrelevancy. Writers almost always tend to go on at great length about the things that interest them. And most of us are vain enough to wish to display our knowledge of the subject we are discussing. The result may be that much of what is written appears quite irrelevant to the reader, whose needs do not necessarily fit the writer's interests and who has no desire to wade through a display of proficiency.

Here is a portion of an auditor's report to a comptroller on incorrect procedures discovered in a company's payroll department:

> I have discovered what is, in effect, a mishandling of funds. Employees are
> permitted to authorize payroll deductions for savings bonds, in accordance

with a decision reached during the Korean conflict, when the Board of Directors decided to encourage bond purchases as a patriotic gesture. At the end of that crisis no change was made in the policy, probably because many employees were purchasing bonds and the company likes to see them building security for emergencies and their old age. The deductions are posted to savings bond accounts and, when an employee's account is large enough, a bond is purchased for him. Some employees have discovered that the payroll is actually made up quite early in the month and that the savings bond deductions are posted at this time to the employees' savings bond accounts. It has always been company policy to permit an employee to withdraw from his account any savings bond deductions that have not yet actually been used to buy bonds. This policy was established at the insistence of the Treasurer, who has been with the company for 23 years and has worked in every one of our plants. He felt the money in the accounts was still the employees' and that they should be able to do as they like with it. The employees referred to above, who have learned of the posting procedure, withdraw amounts from their savings bond accounts as soon as the postings are made, long before payday. Thus they obtain, in effect, an advance salary payment.

It seems unlikely that the comptroller needed to know the history of the payroll deduction plan or the details of the treasurer's past life. What the comptroller did need to know was: (1) that employees were allowed to authorize payroll deductions for bond purchases, (2) that the deductions were posted to individual accounts well before payday, (3) that withdrawals were permitted as soon as postings had been made, and (4) that some employees were making these withdrawals and in effect receiving advance payments of salary. The preceding 50 words convey all that is relevant to the comptroller's needs, out of the 255-word statement. You may feel that the 50-word summary is a little too abbreviated, but you can expand it considerably without coming close to the length of the original. The trouble with the example is not merely its length but also the way in which the reader is distracted—taken away from the important findings and forced to read useless information.

WATCH YOUR PACE

Inside the doors of buses in a certain city appears this cryptic statement: "Pay enter East Pay leave West." Habitual riders are accustomed to seeing strangers to the city snarled at by bus drivers when they try to find out when to pay their fare or when, still worse, they drop it into the box at the wrong time. There is both a complete failure of communication and a ducking of responsibility by irritated drivers, who wearily point to the signs as if the instructions were simple English. What the signs really mean is: When you are on a bus going east, pay when you enter the bus; when you are going west, pay when you leave. Since strangers usually can't figure out what the signs mean and don't even know whether the buses are going east or west, utter confusion results. Contrast the statement with the sign one bus driver lettered on his fare box: "Don't fumble while others grumble. Please pay exact fare 18¢ when you get on," and you have the difference between inadequate and effective communication.

The first example is an illustration of poor pacing—trying to say too much in too few words. Whenever you see someone puzzling over how to operate a vending machine, how to follow a receptionist's instructions for getting from one office to another, or how to run an automatic elevator, poor pacing may be responsible. The instructions go too fast for the reader; they attempt to say too much in too few words, or they wrongly assume that everyone understands the short cuts in language. Occasionally, terseness and compression of several ideas in one sentence are effective changes in pace, but this sort of writing requires great skill. Here is an example from *Time:*

> In Chilliwack, B.C., Mrs. Edna Fenton walked into police headquarters and asked the desk constable how she might get herself jailed to escape her angry husband, was advised to hit a cop, did, was.

Unless you are a very able writer, you will do well to avoid trying to pack too much information into your sentences. The potential result of such tight packing is a sense of irritated frustration on the reader's part. Test your own reaction to this instruction on the changed income tax forms for 1970:

> If line 15a is under $5,000 and consisted only of wages subject to withholding and not more than $200 of dividends, and you are not claiming any adjustments on line 15b, you can have IRS figure your tax by omitting lines 16, 17, 18, 20, 21, 22, 23, 24, 25 and 26 (but complete line 19).

The "powers that be" at the IRS apparently realized that this sentence attempted to communicate too much with too few words. The 1975 version of this same set of directions—and a few additional pointers—is made up of an introductory statement and a numbered list of seven separate instructions.

The opposite fault in pacing occurs when a few meager facts or ideas are strung out on a long clothesline of words. Slow pacing occurs more frequently in business writing than fast pacing. Here's an example from a business report which moves at a snail's pace:

> Since the beginning of large-scale research programs on automatic controls, there has been a need for simple but rapid tests to evaluate these controls. These methods of evaluation must be easy to use and fast. They should also give a definite answer. What is needed is a method which says "yes" or "no" to a specific problem of using automatic controls. The current emphasis on these controls has posed a difficult problem in the field of their evaluation. We, therefore, need evidence which will give us a method of deciding when to use them.

Such slow-paced writing creates a knotty problem for the reader. A first reading gives a vague impression that the writer is actually saying something significant.

A second reading would show that 6 sentences and 95 words have been expended to express one simple idea:

> Because of the widespread use of automatic controls, we need to develop a simple, fast, and definite method of evaluating their use.

Here is another example from a text on financial management:

> Financial management is the responsibility for obtaining and effectively utilizing the funds necessary for the efficient operation of an enterprise. The finance function centers about the *management* of funds—raising and using them effectively. But the dimensions of financial management are much broader than simply obtaining funds. Planning is one of the most important activities of the financial manager.

What we have here is a fairly good definition of financial management in the first sentence. But apparently the writer was not fully satisfied with it and chose to say the same thing again, in different words, in the second sentence. Then it seems that these first two sentences were judged incomplete, because the third sentence expands on the original idea while partly recapitulating it. Finally, in the fourth sentence the definition is completed. What the whole paragraph seems to say is:

> The financial manager has the responsibility for obtaining and effectively utilizing the funds necessary for the efficient operation of an enterprise. Planning is one of his or her most important activities.

KEEP YOUR TONE APPROPRIATE

When you write, tone is particularly important. You can't convey your feeling by a smile, a gesture, or an inflection; you must rely completely on written words. And when you write in business, particularly when you write letters, the tone of your writing expresses not only your own personality but that of your company. The customer who receives a discourteous, pompous, or abrupt letter may well decide that this represents the tone of the whole company. We can give so many shades of tone to our communications—positive or negative, helpful or indifferent, courteous or impertinent—that it is impossible to discuss all of them. Only highly skilled writers have complete control over the tone of their writing, but here, too, the key is understanding the reader's point of view. Here are two examples:

> Please investigate this matter and *submit* a report as soon as possible.

> Please *do not hesitate* to call upon us if we can be of help.

The word *submit,* which has connotations of yielding, surrendering, and showing humility, is likely to arouse resentment and hostility even though the reader may not be able to identify just what it is about the request he or she doesn't like. The expression *do not hesitate* suggests that the writer is so full of self-importance as to believe the reader will pause before daring to disturb him or her. You can improve the tone of the first sentence by substituting *let me have* or *give me* for *submit*. In the second sentence, simply delete *do not hesitate to*.

Here are two sentences from the report of an accountant on what she regarded as an improper procedure in a department of her company. Each sentence is followed by a revision written by a "writing expert." The expert believed he was improving the readibility of the original without changing its meaning. Do you agree?

> Mr. Smith feels there have been no violations of any company policy in his department.

> Mr. Smith denies that anyone in his department has violated any company policies.

> I am sure you will agree that these people's actions were not within the results we desired our policies to achieve.

> I am sure you will agree that these people perverted our policies.

Test your own reactions to these sentences from letters and reports:

> Since you misunderstood the proposal in our last report, the only intelligent thing to do is to abandon the project.

> We do not handle inquiries from retail customers at the Central Office, but if you are still interested you can get in touch with our local dealer.

> You state that your contention about a late shipment is correct, but our records do not verify your contention.

> We again apologize for the dissatisfaction you had and regret our failure to correct the unfortunate error.

BE SPECIFIC

There are occasions in business when general statements are advantageous—but such occasions are comparatively rare. Just to illustrate one such situation where general language is preferable to specific, let's assume that your company's distribution committee has received a request for funds from a church in the area. Although you have considerable money available, a rigid policy has been established to support only educational and health and welfare institutions. Instead of going into the specifics, a general statement such as the following is probably better:

Dear Reverend McCullough:

You will understand, I'm sure, that each year we receive innumerable requests for funds from very worthy organizations like yours. We wish that we could support every one of them and we regret that we cannot.

We're sorry that we cannot contribute the support that you requested, and we sincerely hope that you will get it from some other source.

Sincerely yours,

Another of these rare occasions for being general instead of specific results from the need to refuse certain types of credit applicants. Some folks don't deserve credit because they have been able but not willing to pay their bills in the past. In other words, they have proved themselves to be poor moral risks. In such cases, your implication of the reason for the refusal would usually suffice. A person who has developed such a reputation would not have to see the details of what credit references reported. To harp upon the poor ratings and opinions expressed by these references would be regarded as inhumane by some people and would probably eliminate your chances of securing the applicant's cash business.

As we shall see in Chapter 9 on credit letters, an applicant who feels that a refusal is unjustified may demand additional information—the details. However, whether or not the marginally unworthy applicant is able to get this information later on, you are still advised to be general in the refusal itself. The majority of people who have firmly established poor credit reputations would probably rather not see these adverse judgments in black and white.

The principle governing both of the situations discussed above is clear: Use general words and statements where detail and specific statements are not helpful. Usually, however, readers of your business writing will want the specifics. Look at this report of an important meeting by a company secretary:

The meeting opened with a discussion of some of the company's sales and production problems. This discussion was followed by a proposal from the research staff for a considerable increase in budget for fiscal 1975. Several objections were raised to this increase, but in the long run it was approved with certain modifications.

There seems to be a reason for secrecy, because these minutes tell readers little or nothing. What are the problems connected with sales and production? What was the specific proposal of the research staff? How much was the "considerable" increase asked for? What were the specific objections, and who raised them? And after what modifications? Interested readers of these minutes are simply being tantalized by generalities which may cause them to read the worst into such nonspecific expressions.

Writing in specific terms makes your writing style more vivid and generally creates a more favorable impression on your readers. Not only are you writing in a way that is more concrete and meaningful to them, but you are also giving them evidence that you are considering their interests. Consider the following letter to a customer about an order:

> Dear Ms. Jones:
>
> Thank you for your order of July 17. We have shipped part of it today, and that part should reach you within a week.
>
> Unfortunately, several of the items you wanted were out of stock and had to be back-ordered. We shall mail them to you as soon as receive them.
>
> We appreciate your patronage and hope to hear from you again soon.
>
> Sincerely,

It is possible that the writer of this letter actually thought that it was promoting goodwill by acknowledging the customer's order. It is certainly a little better than nothing. But doesn't it leave the reader hanging in midair? Which items are being shipped? Which will be delayed? When can the reader expect to receive the back-ordered goods? Contrast that first letter with the version that follows, and judge for yourself which one a customer would prefer to receive:

> Dear Ms. Jones:
>
> Thank you for your order of July 17. The enclosed invoice lists the goods that were shipped to you today by express. You should receive them within a week.
>
> Because of an unusually high summer demand, the electric bean pots, broilers, and popcorn poppers were out of stock when your order reached us. We had already placed an emergency order for these items, and the manufacturer has assured us that they should be in by the 26th. As soon as they arrive, we shall fill the rest of your order and ship it postage-paid, fast-freight to you.
>
> The enclosed brochure describes the appliances on which we will be having special promotions in September. You'll notice that many of them would make ideal Christmas specials.
>
> Sincerely,

The details presented in this second version demonstrate concern for what the reader wants to know. As we said earlier, there may be legitimate reasons for occasionally wanting to be unspecific about a situation. In the majority of cases in business writing, however, you will be styling your messages to your readers' taste by thinking about and including specifics that are likely to be of concern to them.

EXERCISES

1. Rewrite the following, avoiding irrelevancies:
   a. Thank you for your interest in our summer camp. We are entering our twenty-fourth year of operation here in the beautiful mountains of north central Pennsylvania. Our founders, Mr. and Mrs. Kirkwood, were natives of this area who felt that more people should enjoy the peace and beauty of the area. So they started a small summer camp for children. The first few years were a financial struggle, but as the word got out, the number of campers increased. Kirkwood Camp is now operating from a solid financial base and each year must turn away over a hundred campers because all spaces have been filled. Many of our campers enroll for the next season at the end of their current stay with us, and this reduces even further the number of available places for new campers. So if you are planning on enrolling your children, we suggest you do so as soon as possible so that they will not be disappointed.

   Our staff is a well-trained, experienced one. Many of the counselors are elementary school teachers and recreation specialists, and they work well together as a team, with your child's well-being as their goal. Each child is treated as an individual as his or her social skills develop within the framework of a cooperative group.

   Enclosed is a brochure explaining more about Kirkwood Camp. We hope you will choose us to be your child's summer home.
   b. I am very dissatisfied with the clock radio manufactured by your company that I purchased two months ago from Boulevard Appliances, which I thought to be a reliable store but now I have my doubts since they have tried to repair the radio three times but have not been successful. They told me that perhaps I should write directly to you, the manufacturer, because they cannot seem to find what is wrong with the radio. I think Boulevard should have written to you, not told me to, so I don't think I will ever buy anything from them again if this is the way they treat their customers.

   The radio worked fine for a week, but then the buzzer alarm wouldn't go off when I had it set for music/alarm. The radio would come on when it was supposed to, and the buzzer was to sound ten minutes later. But it didn't. I am a sound sleeper, and usually just a radio will not wake me up. I need the buzzer, and even then sometimes it has to ring for a few minutes before it wakes me up. Boulevard repaired the alarm without charge, and it worked fine for about two weeks. But then the radio would not come on—only the buzzer would sound. What is the purpose of having a clock radio if the radio doesn't work? I like to lie in bed for a while and listen to music before getting up. Boulevard repaired the radio and it worked OK for a month. But then the same thing that happened the first time happened again—no buzzer, just music. So they repaired it again and it was good for a week. Now it is broken again—no buzzer—and I was late for work the other day because of it. When I complained to Boulevard, they said they had done everything they could. So what are you, the manufacturer, going to do about this clock radio? My confidence in your products is badly shaken.

2. a. Paying particular attention to the pace, write the directions for getting somewhere or for doing something. Then exchange what you have written with a partner. Read your partner's instructions and evaluate them on the basis of clarity and pace. Write your reactions and comments at the bottom of the page; discuss your evaluation orally with your partner.

b. Rewrite the following, with emphasis on the pace:

We appreciate the interest you showed last year by participating in the "Night in Old Denver" street fair. The prizes your company contributed enabled us to run games of chance which brought in revenue and provided the fairgoers with fun and entertainment. The "Night in Old Denver" is held annually to raise money for the preservation and restoration of old buildings in our city. The fair is a means of uniting businesses and people to foster community spirit and pride. The fun and entertainment of the fair give fairgoers an opportunity to spend money for a good cause and a good time. But unless local businesses help by contributing prizes, money, food, or items to be sold, we cannot achieve our purpose of saving Denver's historic buildings and building civic spirit. Would you be willing to contribute to this year's fair? Your support will enable us to make the fair even better than last year's. May we arrange for a volunteer to meet with you to discuss your contribution to this community venture?

3. Rewrite the following to give them a more appropriate tone:

a. After careful examination of your credit history and your financial resources, we are afraid that we cannot grant you the credit you have applied for. Because of our store's policy of providing the highest-quality merchandise at the lowest possible cost, we must be very careful to keep our expenses low. Therefore, we cannot afford to extend credit to anyone who is not a good risk. If your financial situation should improve, please feel free to reapply for an account with us. In the meantime, we welcome your cash business.

b. Enclosed is a brochure describing the data processing services our company offers. It is not realistic for us to quote you prices until we know exactly what your needs are, the size of your business, how many transactions per day you process, and other pertinent information. Therefore, why don't you contact one of our local representatives and arrange for a meeting to discuss these things.

c. The watch I purchased last month is the shoddiest piece of merchandise I have ever owned. How can your company manufacture such garbage and still remain in business? The watch ran well for a week but then started gaining about five minutes an hour. Until yesterday, that is, when it stopped running altogether. I want my money back. If you want the watch back, you are welcome to it. I am planning to smash it with a hammer and throw it in the trash can otherwise.

4. Making whatever logical assumptions are necessary and inserting additional information if needed, make the following examples more specific:

a. (From a report on a location study)

Lakeview appears to be a much better choice on several counts. It is considerably larger than Evansville or Sun City. In addition to that, its residents spend more of their income on durable goods than do the residents of the other two communities.

b. (From a sales letter)

This amazing little appliance will work its way into your heart. You'll find so many uses for it in your kitchen that you'll wonder how you ever got along without it.

c. (From a letter to a customer explaining why a claim cannot be granted because of the customer's misuse of the product)

We received your October 11 letter and your Model 246 AM-FM radio.

After examining the radio, we regret to inform you that we cannot grant your request for a refund. We suggest you refer to paragraph 3 of your warranty for the explanation. We could, however, fix your radio for the cost of materials and labor.

Please let us know your decision, and we will get the radio back to you as soon as possible.

5. For each of the following situations:
   a. Identify your reader. (Who is the reader? What does he or she already know? need to know?).
   b. Compose a good business letter, being sure to avoid irrelevancies, watch your pace, keep your tone appropriate, and be specific.
   c. Create whatever additional information you need to achieve your objectives; only the basic facts are given.
   d. Exchange your reader identification and letters with a partner. Assume the role of the reader described and evaluate each letter from that point of view. Make notes of the strong and weak points of the letters. Discuss these with your partner after all letters have been evaluated.
      (1) A letter from the admissions director of the state university to a prospective freshman granting admission on a provisional basis. Because of low scores on the math entrance exam, the student will have to enroll in a noncredit remedial math course during the first semester.
      (2) A letter from the president of the local chamber of commerce to the president of the high school Future Business Leaders of America club. The chamber of commerce president is declining an invitation to speak at the annual career day; she will be attending a national conference that week.
      (3) A letter from the credit manager of Miro's, a department store, to a customer who has owed $250 for the past two months. Usual terms of payment are 30 days. This is the first time the customer has fallen behind in payment within the past five years.
      (4) A request from the Tucson branch store of the Byte Shop, a personal computer store, to the main office. Two data recorders are needed to fill customers' orders; and since the Tucson store has none of these in stock, it would also like to have two or three extras to keep on hand.
      (5) A letter to a college student from the personnel department of a large insurance firm. The company cannot hire the student for summer work. The student's application letter was sloppy and contained misspelled words, and the data sheet did not indicate that the student's education and experience were sufficient qualifications for work with an insurance company.
      (6) An invitation to high school business teachers in your state from the state Department of Education. The teachers are being invited to attend a free Saturday workshop, "Computer Technology and Its Place in the Business Curriculum."

TWO
SPECIFIC TYPES
OF BUSINESS
LETTERS

We are now going to consider in specific terms the first of the major forms of business communication—the business letter—and the methods, principles, and problems which relate to it. One definition of the letter that is useful to keep in mind is the following: *The business letter is a message that attempts to influence its reader to take some action or attitude desired by its writer.* Similarly important are the basic qualities all letters should have— the "you" attitude; appropriate tone and personality; an effective organization; and correctness in language, form, and mechanics.

As in the last edition, this section is organized according to the purposes and functional categories of letters used by most large corporations. Since the business executive tends to think of each letter in terms of its purpose—and often to think in organizational patterns performing that purpose—the executive's language classifies it as a collection letter if its aim is the collection of a bill (by the collection department), an adjustment letter if it adjusts a claim (claims department or claims and adjustment section), and so on. This is helpful terminology for students to learn; but those who intend to become professionals, in the sense we have been describing, should be wary of jumping to the erroneous conclusion that all letters fall neatly into one pat classification or another. They do not; no textbook, therefore, can do better than to adopt one of several convenient means of classifying letters for the purpose of intelligent discussion.

As a matter of fact, Chapter 6 presents another way of looking at business letters. At the end of that chapter we discuss a popular way of approaching letters according to the news they convey. This discussion compares the strategy or organization of letters that deliver good or routine news with the strategy of those that convey disappointing or unpleasant messages to those that attempt to persuade readers to do something. These general outlines can be understood and retained for future reference for the letters we will treat as well as for the less common types that don't fall within the scope of our discussion.

Readers will note that Chapters 7 and 8 contain Letter Problems (as distinguished from the exercises at the end of the chapter). The intent of these problems is to provide specific applications of the principles discussed in the chapters and to set up topics for classroom discussion. Each letter problem has been deliberately selected to require imagination, originality, and skill in expression *in a difficult situation*. The problem in Chapter 7 allows the students to generate possible solutions, whereas the one in Chapter 8 presents alternative responses for the students to evaluate.

Unique to this revision of this text is the special emphasis given to federal legislation relevant to various types of business letters. We are living in a time when an unintended oversight or other form of slip-up could leave your business open to having thousands of dollars in penalties and/or damages assessed against it. Large corporations have legal staffs and timely policies aimed at preventing such mishaps. Smaller firms, however, are often hard pressed to learn of and keep up with the ever-increasing number of requirements of the various federal agencies and laws. One of the most significant new features of this section, therefore, is a review of recent and likely legislation that has had and might have an impact upon the specific types of letters treated.

6
BASIC QUALITIES OF BUSINESS LETTERS

The real answer to the question "How can I best accomplish the purposes I've identified?" leads us to the reader, since we accomplish our purposes only through this person. In this chapter, therefore, we shall talk about what letter writers should know about readers. We shall discuss this knowledge in terms of four basic qualities all business letters should have: the "you" attitude, a tone adapted to the reader that conveys a personality that appeals to him or her, an opening and a closing which are designed for the reader, and an overall sequence of ideas that will move the reader to agree to the legitimacy of your objectives.

THE "YOU" ATTITUDE

The past two decades have witnessed a more searching analysis than ever before of what takes place when one human being tries to persuade another to do something. We have had mathematical analyses of persuasion, studies of interpersonal communication, research on letters and advertising as "an educational factor in wish-fulfillment," and a broad variety of popular and scholarly books and articles involving the study of language as an aid to understanding human nature. In an era when people can achieve what once was impossible and go to the moon, every additional piece of research about persuasion and communication is vital. It is unfortunate, and all too symptomatic of our times, that many such studies are so specialized or esoteric that they do not communicate very effectively.

So far, no new research study has contradicted the old principle of *I–you* communication: if *I* want to persuade *you* to do something, the best way is for me to show you how and why you benefit from doing it. This principle, which we have purposely expressed in the simplest words, offers the best possible guide for writing the business letter. Nothing related to business correspondence is more important than this point of view, known for many years as the *you attitude:* we can most readily persuade others to do what we want them to do by demonstrating that it is to their advantage to do it.

At this point, mental reservations burst out into accusations—usually from students who rate hypocrisy as the one unforgivable sin. "It's just a way of manipulating people." "It's insincere and dishonest because it says the end justifies the means." "It's a phony way to sell stuff."

In Chapter 2, we mentioned the fact that language can be deliberately used for unclear or misleading purposes; now, with the you attitude, we face one aspect of the ethics of business communication as exemplified by the accusations in the preceding paragraph. There is obviously a real danger that some inexperienced correspondents will think of the concept of the you attitude as a pose or a "gimmick" which offers a short cut to achieving their purpose of manipulating people. We have to admit that many business writers will use any means to achieve an end—and the you attitude can be misused as that means.

This book reflects the belief that in the term *you attitude,* the emphasis should be placed on *attitude,* something which reflects our feelings, moods, or convictions. What then are the attitudes which we ought to reflect in our relations with others? Sincerity, truthfulness, and integrity should rank high on the list—and those are the qualities which the you attitude *ought* to reflect. Cynics will comment that the reason is "because it's good business to be sincere, truthful, and honest." So be it then. But one additional fact should be noted—readers of letters are quicker to detect insincerity than any other quality. For that reason, only arrogant and intellectually condescending people will dispute the fact that the essence of good human relations in correspondence is to avoid superficial cordiality, exaggerated claims, and cleverness in the form of distortions of the truth. Properly used, the you attitude should tell the reader honestly, truthfully, and tactfully about the benefits he or she obtains from an action or attitude implicit in the letter's purpose.

All of us are tempted to write about what we ourselves are doing or hope to do. We delude ourselves by thinking that everyone is interested in *our* problems, *our* wishes, *our* products. In letter writing it is a good principle to forget yourself and to go back to one of the fundamentals of all communication—remember your reader. Here is an example of how the you attitude can improve letters:

Dear Sir/Madam:

I need a lot of information on the way in which businesspeople react to the current crises in our colleges, and I selected you and some others to send this questionnaire to because your names were mentioned in the newspapers.

I have to have this information within two weeks, because my term paper is due then, and I hope you will help me by returning the questionnaire promptly.

Sincerely yours,

Dear Mr. Jones:

You and several other prominent businesspeople were recently quoted in *The Record* concerning the present crises in our colleges—and your comments so interested me that I decided to write my term paper on "Business's View of Today's Colleges."

Your answers to the enclosed questionnaire—all you need do is to check *yes* or *no*—will be kept completely confidential. If you wish, I will send you a summary of the results based on my survey of 50 prominent business people in this area.

You will recognize that I am attempting, in a small way, to open communication between education and business by means of a realistic survey. You can help by checking the answers and returning the questionnaire in the enclosed, self-addressed envelope.

Sincerely yours,

These letters have identical purposes—to get a questionnaire filled out and returned. But notice how the first writer talks only of *my* need, *my* deadline, and *my* hope; by contrast, the second writer stresses how easily *you* can do this, why *you* will recognize its importance, and how *you* can benefit by participating through getting a summary of results.

Here are two more examples of the different impressions created by different focuses of attention:

We are enclosing an order blank and a booklet containing illustrations and prices of the various items we carry for hi-fi equipment. After you have looked through this booklet, you will know how inexpensive these quality hi-fi components are. And when you send us your order, you will be on the way to the finest sound you have ever heard.

I happened to see your advertisement for a technical writer in this morning's paper, and I should like to have you consider me. In the first place, I am very much interested in working for you because your offices are close to a rural area where I can ski and fish. And in the second place, I have heard of the liberal attitude you have toward employees.

My four years of undergraduate study in physics at the University of Michigan and a master's degree in English from Columbia should qualify me for the position in technical writing which you advertised.

The second example above gives the impression of a rather irresponsible individual interested primarily in having fun. Furthermore, the reference to the company's "liberal attitude" suggests that this person might be a bit of an oddity who wouldn't be appreciated or tolerated by more conservative employers.

One situation to which the you attitude seems ill-adapted is collecting past due accounts; nevertheless, thousands of collection letters are sent out daily whose chief effectiveness lies in their argument that it is to debtors' own advantage to pay their bills. The following paragraph from one such letter shows how this may be done.

> As a businessperson, you certainly realize that your most valuable asset is your credit reputation. Without it, you cannot long remain in business. We know that you would not willingly lose this priceless possession for a mere $158.92, the amount of our bill. By placing your check in the mail today, you will help to keep your business on that firmest of foundations—a sound credit rating.

You need only glance through the advertising pages of any magazine to see the reader's viewpoint underscored by pointing out concrete advantages in the form of economy, utility, profit, pleasure, appearance, or enjoyment:

> Along the shore are stretches of pink-tinted beach and hidden coves, ideal for sunbathing or swimming or having picnics. An ocean of clear-blue water invites you to come on in or just to look. Take a horse-drawn carriage or a motorbike or a quaint old-fashioned car for a leisurely look at a historic land.

> This little battery-charger will save you time, money, and effort. You won't have to go dashing out for batteries for that flashlight that suddenly went dark, and you'll save the cost of the charger in six months. From then on, it's all charged to your savings account.

> A car is to go out with your girl in.

> Your family is safer on these tires than ever before, and that's the best car insurance you can buy.

> You're a man, not a mannequin—and that's why Custom Tailors were born.

> You can pay off your mortgage . . . but could your family do so?

Analyze the purpose in these statements by professionals and notice the appeals by which they attempt to reach readers through the use of the you attitude.

A TONE ADAPTED TO THE READER

In Part One we emphasized the importance of "talking the readers' language" and of writing to them as if they were human beings instead of depersonalized names. Here, for instance, is a horrible example of what not to do:

Dear Mr. Blane:

Surrender of the policy is permissible only within the days attendant the grace period on compliance with the citation relevant options accruing to the policy so we are estopped from acquiescing to a surrender prior to the policy's anniversary date. We are confident that an investigation relevant to the incorporation of this feature will substantiate that the policy is not at variance with policies of other companies.

Yours truly,

This is how the policy holder replied to that letter:

Dear Mister:

I am sorry but I don't understand your letter. If you will explain what you mean, I will try to do what you ask.

Yours truly,
Henry Blane

The use of such highly specialized language or of supposedly "impressive" terminology is one of the worse faults of business correspondence.

Admittedly, we cannot always know what kind of people our readers are, but we can make a good start by deciding that we're not going to talk over their heads or talk down to them. When President Johnson and William McChesney Martin, Jr., Chairman of the Federal Reserve Board, were in disagreement over increasing the rediscount rate, J. A. Livingston, who wrote a syndicated column on economic problems, attempted to write an explanation of the economic implications of raising the rediscount rate. As a result of his column, he received the following letter:

You are interesting, J. A. L., and often informative, but please dumb down to the mutt mind and don't use the money-boys' jabber.

What has this flap between Martin and Johnson got to do with the price of pork and our loss of gold? Come on, J. A. L., give it to us good—real plain words, short sentences, and no jargon.

Letter writers will do well not to "dumb down" or "dress up" their language but instead to keep it clear, simple, and sincere. When you are answering a letter, you do have certain clues from the correspondence itself; you should then try to form a mental image of your reader from such facts as:

The type of business the reader is in, if any

The position the reader occupies

The original reason for writing

What he or she wants to know

The kind of language used

Information in the letter itself

But even when you have no correspondence to guide you, you can keep in mind the moral pointed up in the following excellent letter from Yeck and Yeck of Dayton, Ohio, written by John and Bill Yeck:

QUEEN VICTORIA
WAS A TOUGH CUSTOMER:

If you think Congress doesn't like the President because he vetoes some of their bills, you should have talked to Prime Minister W. W. Gladstone back in Queen Victoria's day.

Every time he went in to see her on a matter of State he came out looking vetoed. He didn't seem able to convince her of anything. She was proud and haughty and dignified. She loved to say "no."

Now, when Disraeli was Prime Minister, things were different.

"The Queen was pleased"; "The Queen agreed"; "The Queen commended." Everything was peaches and cream for Dizzy.

One day someone asked the Queen, "Why?"

She thought a moment, pushed her crown back on her head, cleared the room and her throat, and said softly, "It's this way . . ."

"When Mr. Gladstone talks to us, he talks as though we were a public meeting; but when Mr. Disraeli talks to us, he talks as though we were a woman."

The Queen had something there.

When *you* want conviction, remember Queen Victoria of Great Britain and of her possessions beyond the seas, and Empress, if you please, of India . . . it paid to talk to her "man to man"—like a human being.

Yes, in advertising, in public relations . . . it helps to be human. Writing that is friendly, interesting, pleasant, is writing

to a Queen's taste.

John & Bill

Yeck and Yeck

What this classic letter has is the remarkable—and indefinable—quality we call personality. Contrary to the opinion of many letter writers—an opinion all too glaringly reflected in their letters—personality does not mean peculiarity or freakishness. The best letters are those which reflect a tone of friendly interest and warmth, as the following:

Dear Ms. Jarden:

The Chinese have a proverb which seems to me to contain a great piece of advice concerning letter writing:

> In the midst of joy do not promise to give a person anything; in the midst of great anger do not answer a person's letter.

We're neither joyful nor angry, but we are puzzled as to why we haven't had an order from you in more than six months.

If we haven't served you in the way you expect, we hope you'll let us know so that we can correct any lapses on our part. But most of all, we hope you'll drop in to see us as an old friend.

Sincerely yours,

While these aren't business letters, note how well personality and humor come through in this interchange between Sir James M. Barrie and A. E. Housman:

Dear Professor Houseman,

I am sorry about last night, when I sat next to you and did not say a word. You must have thought I was a very rude man; I am really a very shy man.

Sincerely yours,

J. M. Barrie

Professor Housman replied:

Dear Sir James Barrie,

I am sorry about last night, when I sat next to you and did not say a word. You must have thought I was a very rude man; I am really a very shy man.

Sincerely yours,

A. E. Housman

P.S. And now you've made it worse for you have spelt my name wrong.

Even a brief business letter can convey a tone of friendliness and warmth in expressing a desire to be of service:

Dear Mr. and Mrs. Edwards:

Although the telephone book calls us landscape architects, we much prefer to be known simply as people who for over 80 years have been helping folks with THEIR ideas and THEIR schemes for making their grounds more useful and attractive.

Try to visualize a capable friend working with you; that's mostly what it's like . . . and that's somewhat the manner in which we should like to be of assistance to you.

Could we possibly be of service to you?

Sincerely yours,

BEGINNING AND ENDING LETTERS

Letter openings and closings are in positions of emphasis because they create the first and last impressions the reader gets from the letter. Unfortunately, however, writers who wish to avoid rubber-stamp beginnings and endings often have the greatest difficulty starting and finishing their letters. For these reasons, the first and last paragraphs deserve our special attention.

While every letter writer likes to think that his or her message will completely absorb the reader's attention, we cannot write from that assumption. As we indicated before, we do not know enough about "how writing is read," but certain inferences about how the business letter is read seem justifiable in view of the following conditions:

1. Many business people have numerous claims on their attention and letters other than ours to read.

2. The vast increase in the number of letters in the mail probably means that the reader gives less attention to each letter received.

3. The phenomenon of "junk mail" has made letter readers increasingly skeptical, more likely to toss letters aside after a quick glance.

4. As a practical, functional form of communication, the business letter carries with it a general expectation that it will be direct, concise, and—as we say—businesslike.

We can reason, then, that the business letter will generally be read by someone who is busy and wants the message to get to the point, who first asks the question "What's this all about?"—and wants it answered, and whose attention must be aroused if the letter isn't to go in the wastepaper basket. Therefore, for this busy or skeptical or mildly interested reader, the letter *must* get off to a running start by saying something from the first word and come to a neat stop by ending without boring repetition or stale clichés.

The First Paragraph

Ideally, the first paragraph of the business letter should aim at performing some of these four functions:

1. It should get favorable attention.

2. It should indicate what the letter is about.

3. It should set a friendly and courteous tone for the whole letter.

4. It should link up with previous correspondence by a reference to date or subject.

If the opening paragraph is direct and interesting, the whole letter may be read with care; it if is not, the rest of the message may be skimmed or skipped entirely. To be effective, the first paragraph of a business letter should observe two principles:

1. It must be short.

2. It must say something.

A short first paragraph in a letter leads the reader on to the rest of the message. Regard your first paragraph as a kind of headline which will attract your reader to move to succeeding paragraphs. As a general rule, never put more than two or three sentences in your first paragraph; if you can use fewer, so much the better. The reference to the date of earlier letters or to similar details should always be subordinated. A surprising number of correspondents begin their letters with some such sentence as:

This is to answer yours of October 14.

We have received your letter of October 14.

Referring to yours of October 14. (An incomplete thought.)

The fact that a specific letter is being answered should be taken as sufficient evidence that it has been received; why waste the most important part of the letter—the equivalent of a newspaper headline—merely to tell a reader that her or his letter has been received or that it was dated October 14? The important task of the first paragraph is to announce what *this* letter is about in order to arouse the reader's interest; all else should be subordinate. Notice the effectiveness of the second method of writing each of the following opening paragraphs:

Weak and ineffective, Replying to yours of May 10, we can say that our
because the first 10 research staff has been working for a long time on
words tell the reader the problem that you mentioned and has finally
nothing he or she succeeded in solving it.
doesn't already know:

Direct and effective: Our research staff has successfully solved the problem of insulating old homes, about which you inquired in your letter of May 10.

Incomplete sentence: Acknowledging receipt of your letter of February 15 in which you asked for a copy of "Better Homes for Small Incomes." We are glad to send you a copy of this booklet.

Better: We gladly enclose "Better Homes for Small Incomes," which you requested on February 15. In it you will find the answers to your questions about design, construction costs, and financing of your new home.

Trite and ineffective: Yours of January 15 received and contents duly noted. We wish to say that we are referring your question to our sales department.

More concise and direct: Our sales department is assembling material which should prove helpful in answering your inquiry of January 15.

Good writers never begin a letter with a participial expression. Almost invariably such a beginning indicates that the writer has not thought out what to say and is merely stalling for time until an idea comes to mind. Furthermore, there is a strong possibility that this beginning will turn out to be ungrammatical. (See the Reference Section.) Don't warm up with inane expressions: "Referring to your letter of January 27"; don't rehash what your reader already knows: "Your order of March 12 has been received." Avoid all unnecessary preliminaries in your first sentence and get into your message fast. Here are some good beginnings.

You need not pay a cent to examine this new book at your leisure.

Thank you for your request for information about our reproductions of antiques.

The catalogue you requested on May 27 was mailed today.

Here is the bulletin you asked us to send.

Thank you for your helpful suggestions about our sales conference.

Congratulations on the fine progress your annual report reveals.

We are pleased to send you the material you requested.

The material on page 16 of the enclosed brochure will answer the questions in your letter of June 16.

Just as soon as we received your letter, we wired our New York office to ship your fishing tackle.

The tires which complete your order LL-138 were shipped today.

Because the first paragraph is so important, here are ways of classifying the kinds of examples we have been citing:

1. What's the letter about?—Your order for hi-fi components was shipped by Railway Express on January 15.

2. A direct question—When may we expect to receive the 27 copies of *Looking Backward* which we ordered on August 14?

3. A statement of appreciation—You were thoughtful to send the copy of your company's annual report, and I do appreciate it.

4. A mention of a name—Professor J. Ashmore Burington has suggested that I write you about (a job, some information needed, a speaking engagement, or whatever). (This beginning is no better than the significance of the name used to the reader—and courtesy and common sense dictate that you request permission to use the name.)

5. A significant time or date—Our New Year celebration we share with customers. . . . July 10 means a great deal to both of us; you started business that day, and we received our first order from you.

6. A polite request or courteous command—May I have two minutes of your time to save you hundreds of hours in the future? . . . May I ask a favor that will help both of us? Don't make one more investment until you have read this book! (The test of how effective these openings are is simple: Does the rest of the letter follow through with the implied promise? If not, the opening has merely enhanced readers' cynicism for the future.)

7. A clever or startling or unusually phrased statement—It's quite possible you owe your life to us, and it's time you let us know how you feel about what was done. (Sent as a fund drive for a hospital to previous patients, many of whom thought it too blunt.) . . . Our Aquagirls wear Swimtex—or nothing. (Sales letter from a resort hotel that had a tie-in with a swimsuit manufacturer.) People who pray together, save together. (Sales letter to church groups offering savings on group travel.) You don't owe us a cent . . . but you will after you've seen the bargains in this catalog. (These openings are effective *only* if the rest of the letter lives up to the first paragraph.)

8. A statement of fact—We serve more than half the homeowners in Garden Town. . . . Your laundry was delayed last week because we moved to our new facilities, which were built so that it won't happen again.

9. An appropriate quotation—An old Norwegian proverb says "On the path between the homes of friends, no grass grows." . . . Did you know that the reason the Chinese have a saying "One picture is worth a thousand words" is that it would take a month to write those thousand words in Chinese?

The Last Paragraph

Like today's railroads, a lot of letter writers have inadequate terminal facilities, and despite the customary advice to "end letters with a bang," they trail off into a whimper. If you've ever had guests who say "good night" and then sit down to tell one more story or experience, repeating the process a few more times, you know how annoying the technique can be. Unlike the weary host, the reader whom you weary with repetition and platitudes can—and does—quit reading. One principle governs your conduct in writing final paragraphs: *Stop when your message is complete.*

The function of the last paragraph of every letter is to make it as easy as possible for the reader to take an action or to accept a point of view that the writer wants taken. If the you attitude is properly employed, the final paragraph will show the reader how easy it is to do this thing that will benefit him or her. Hence, when a department store wants to get a customer to return some piece of merchandise which has been replaced , the last paragraph of the letter should not read:

> We hope that you will return this dress for credit as soon as possible.

It should offer some such incentive to the customer as:

> Just as soon as you return this dress, we shall gladly credit your account with $11.75.

By enclosing self-addressed envelopes or postcards and referring specifically to these enclosures in their final paragraphs, many correspondents stimulate action by making it very easy. Especially effective are such closing paragraphs as the following, which make definite suggestions and offer an easy means of taking action:

> Just sign and mail the enclosed postcard and you will receive all the news in concise, readable form for the next 52 weeks.

> Your check in the enclosed envelope will enable you to maintain that high credit reputation you have always enjoyed.

> A call—collect, of course—to our sales department will bring a trained member of our staff to give you an estimate, at no obligation to you.

A direct question constitutes a good close because it gives the reader a specific query to consider and to answer.

> May I have an interview with you at your convenience? You can reach me at my home address or at 213-4289.

> Are you willing to give Blanco Fuel a 10-day trial to let it demonstrate in your home its efficiency and economy? Your signature on the enclosed card will bring you a 10-day supply without cost. May I have ten minutes in which to substantiate these statements?

> Would you jeopardize your credit rating for so small an amount?

The most ineffective of all closes is the participial ending. It is weak, hackneyed, and incomplete in its thought, and it offers no incentive to action because it eliminates the possibility of taking the you attitude. "Thanking you in advance" and "Trusting we shall have your cooperation in this matter" are the products of the same type of mind as that which begins the letter with the incomplete "Referring to yours of October 15." Such closes can at least be changed into direct statements, as "We shall hope to hear from you soon" or "We appreciate your cooperation in this matter." But by the use of the you attitude, these closes can be further improved by transforming them into direct incentives to action or builders of goodwill such as the following:

> Mail us your check today and your order will arrive on Thursday.
>
> Just sign your name at the bottom of this letter and return it in the enclosed postage-free envelope.
>
> Will you let us know by April 14 so that we can place your order promptly?
>
> We think this brochure will answer your questions, but if you need more information, please let us know.
>
> Just fill in the card and we'll gladly send a representative to help you.

You can think of the various ways of ending a letter as generally falling into one or another of the following categories:

1. A friendly or personal expression of goodwill—All of us wish you every success with the opening of your new shop. . . . I hope you will find all the arrangements that we have made for you at the convention comfortable and convenient.

2. A polite question (usually requiring no question mark)—May we join all your other business friends in wishing you continued prosperity. . . . Would you like more information? If so, please let us know and we'll furnish it promptly.

3. A courteous command—Remember, the sooner you send in the card, the sooner your subscription starts. . . . Write us as soon as possible, please, and we'll get the information for you.

4. A statement of appreciation—Thank you very much for your cooperation. . . . We do appreciate your understanding of our problem.

5. A look forward to an event that might be of some interest to the reader— Please keep our January Clearance Sale in mind. You'll be able to take advantage of savings up to 40 percent off our regular stock of housewares. (Such endings are particularly useful for moving the reader's mind away from disappointing news that an earlier part of the letter might have conveyed.)

Whichever ending is appropriate, remember the two principles:

> Your purpose is to induce the action or attitude you want.
>
> When your message is complete, *stop.*

AN APPROPRIATE SEQUENCE OF IDEAS

The foregoing suggestions were offered to you because writers very often encounter problems in starting and ending letters. The beginning seems to create the biggest hurdle, so this section is aimed at giving you additional help in getting the letter underway. More specifically, its objective is to familiarize you with categories of letter situations and the general sequence of ideas that could be considered appropriate for each category.

The logic for discussing the categories that follow stems from a fairly humanistic view of the various purposes served by business letters. The person who believes that a business letter should simply transmit a specific meaning—such as asking for something or giving or denying something—will probably find letter writing a fairly easy task. It's the human being who recognizes the existence and importance of the human being at the other end of the communications process who will find the task a bit more challenging. We of course are talking about the goodwill or public relations objective of business letters. In very few instances will you have the option of completely ignoring this important purpose. How you handle it and your other more explicit objectives, however, will vary with the delicacy of the situation. These varying degrees of delicacy are the subjects of the paragraphs that follow.

The first category that we'll consider is by far the easiest. It calls for a frank, right-to-the-point approach, justified by the fact that you are dealing with either a very routine situation or news that will be quite well received by your reader. In such a case you are doing your reader a big favor by getting to the point as quickly as possible. If you need information, start the letter with a general or specific question. If you are granting information, give a specific or general "yes" answer in the letter opening. The following letter excerpts are examples of the ways one might start either routine letters or messages carrying good news for the reader.

> Would you please provide me with some information on the package of land you advertised in the summer issue of *Arizona Industry*. I have a client interested in a 300-acre tract for a plant location and would be interested in answers to the following specific questions.

> Is the Mammoth outdoor furniture advertised in the June issue of *Furniture World* guaranteed rust resistant? I am considering adding such a line to my stock and would appreciate your answers to this and the following questions.

> I would be happy to answer your August 23 questions about the package of land we advertised in *Arizona Industry*.

> Yes, the Mammoth outdoor furniture you saw in *Furniture World* and inquired about in your June 19 letter is guaranteed to resist rust for 10 years.

In each of these cases the writer accomplishes something at the very start of the letter. In the first and third examples, the purposes are immediately identified. The reader knows right away that the writer will ask or answer some questions.

The second and fourth illustrations go one step further in directness by asking or answering a specific question. You may feel that such a beginning is almost too direct, but notice how such an impression is minimized by the incidental inclusion of details that identify the situation for the reader.

The rest of a letter of this type would be devoted to a thorough and orderly presentation of the other questions or answers, followed by a personal goodwill close that avoids the use of rubber-stamp expressions. We shall study some specific examples of this type in Chapters 7 and 8.

The second general category of letters that we shall examine is not as easy to handle as the first. These letters deal with cases where you expect your reader's reaction to your message to be negative. Such situations typically stem from having to refuse people something they have requested. Whether the request is for information, a favor, credit, or an adjustment, saying no while getting your reader to accept your justification is not an easy task.

Try to remember asking your father for the car for a Saturday night. If Dad said no and then proceeded to list the reasons, how much attention did you give to those reasons? He had already pulled the trigger, and your mind, like a steel trap, had snapped shut to reason. A typical reader reacts to refusals in much the same way. If we spring the disappointing news in a letter's beginning, he or she is not likely to be very receptive to the reasoning that follows. But if we begin in some neutral fashion and adroitly move into the supportive information while the reader's mind is still open, we stand a much better chance of ultimately getting that reader to accept our decision as a just one. The appropriate sequence of ideas for such letters is described in the following paragraphs.

You would begin with some neutral comment related to the request that would indicate neither a yes nor a no. Ideally, the opening would also allow you to move smoothly into your explanation; that is, it would noncommittally introduce the idea behind your reasoning. Once this is done, you can more easily develop an unhurdled transition into your explanation.

When you present your reasoning, you should do so with logic and persuasion. The latter is best accomplished by using the you attitude as much as possible. Even the most negative situations can often be interpreted as benefiting the reader in some way. For example, a policy of nonreturnable sale merchandise allows a retailer to offer products at lower prices and greater savings to customers. Even a credit refusal to someone on shaky financial ground can be presented as being in the reader's interest. Such a person can more quickly solidify his or her financial standing by avoiding additional credit obligations.

After you have presented your reasoning in a logical, persuasive fashion, the next step is to refuse. The refusal should be short, clear, and as positively worded as you can make it. If you have done an adequate job up to this point, the reader should now be ready to accept the refusal as a logical outgrowth of the case you have built. That reader may still be disappointed, but at least he or she will be more likely to see the justification.

The last parts of a letter of this nature should do whatever is possible to move the reader's mind away from the disappointment of the refusal. If a counterproposal is feasible, here would be the place at which it might be introduced.

The letter on page 65 of Chapter 4 illustrates the application of the sequence of ideas described above. The following letter is another example of a well-sequenced refusal. It attempts to convince a grocer that there are good reasons why he can't deal directly with the manufacturer at wholesalers' prices. You'll see further discussion and illustrations of indirect letters in Chapters 8 and 9.

Dear Mr. Lusco:

Thank you for your February 27 order for two cases of Yippy Dog Chow. It demonstrates that you are a retailer who is interested in providing your customers with high-quality products at reasonable prices.

We at Nutritional Mills have the same objective with regard to our customers, Mr. Lusco. Through extensive research, we have developed a line of pet foods that we feel is unsurpassed in nutritional content and taste appeal.

To deliver this line to our dealerships throughout the nation, we have developed a comprehensive distribution network of jobbers. Sampson Wholesale Grocery Company, in New Orleans, is a member of this network. The personnel at Sampson have been trained to provide for your every convenience in your handling of Nutritional Mills products.

So that you might be served most efficiently and conveniently by the exclusive distributor nearest you, we have forwarded your order and check to Sampson Wholesale. Mr. Don LeBlanc, the Sampson representative for the Lock Port area, should be calling on you within a week to explain Sampson's pricing and to help you set up your Nutritional display.

While he is in your store, you might want to inquire about our newest cat food, Kitty Kome Kwickly. From all test market indications, it promises to be a strong seller.

Sincerely,

Most business letters apply some degree of persuasion toward getting a reader to accept the writer's point of view. Some letters, however, seek more than agreement and, thus, encounter more initial resistance to what the writer ultimately wants to accomplish. Consequently, messages like sales, collection, and application letters that try to get the reader to *do* something fall into a separate category.

A popular acronym used to sum up the sequence of ideas used for persuasive-style letters is AIDA. It stands for Attention, Interest, Desire, and Action and highlights the sequence of accomplishments with which a persuasive letter writer should be concerned.

BusinessWeek

1221 Avenue of the Americas
New York, New York 10020

Dear Subscriber:

> "What power does your Internal Revenue agent really
> have . . . and how much should you cooperate with
> him?"

> "What are the pros and cons of these 'total immersion
> courses'?"

> "How should you approach your Senator or Congressman
> when you have a problem—or need a favor?"

The answers to questions like these make good reading. And
they're but a small part of a 320-page book I'd like to send you
free. If, that is, you decide to renew your BUSINESS WEEK subscription now. The Guide to Personal Business has been purchased
by more than 35,000 astute businessmen for as much as $9.95. Yet
this special soft-cover edition, unabridged, can be yours free if
you renew now.

> But there's not much time left. Your subscription to
> BUSINESS WEEK expires in just three weeks, and we've
> received no renewal instructions from you.

After a year as a subscriber, you know how profitable it is to
be "in the know" about the entire spectrum of modern business.
Reading BUSINESS WEEK gives you a unique advantage: an accurate
overview of business conditions that non-subscribers can only
envy . . . while they suffer through stacks of newspapers, magazines and special reports.

When you realize the amount of information that's packed into
BUSINESS WEEK, it's hard to imagine doing without it. And if you
act quickly, there's no need to. All it takes is a moment to mark
the enclosed card.

> Please remember, only three issues are left in your
> current subscription. So the time to move is now.

Of all the decisions you make this week—or this month—renew-
ing BUSINESS WEEK is sure to be one of the more important ones. Yet
it's one of the least costly: $12.95 for one year, or $28 for three
years.

Don't risk an interruption in your subscription. Return your
BUSINESS WEEK Renewal Card to me today, or we must issue a
"stop" order to our Circulation Department in Hightstown, New
Jersey.

Cordially,

Peter W. Ware

Peter W. Ware
Circulation Director

PWW:ds
cc: Glenn Locke
    Hightstown Office

Attention is the primary goal of the opening of persuasive letters. Unless you can get the recipient to read the start of your letter, your efforts are doomed to failure. The various appropriate means of gaining the reader's attention for different types of persuasive letters are treated in detail in Chapters 10, 11, and 12. An impressive or unusual statement or a question that introduces a need are just a couple. Suffice it to say now that the major requirements for the opening of a persuasive request are that it gain the reader's attention and that it do so in an acceptable manner related to the overall subject of the letter.

Attention might be compared to a fleeting glimpse and interest to a gaze. Unless the attention you gain in the opening can be turned into interest, your cause is lost. You must, therefore, begin stimulating and nurturing your reader's interest early in the letter. You can do so by convincingly presenting the various advantages for the reader of the action you want taken. It is in such letters that the you attitude can be most effectively applied. Remember that we are all the centers of our own universe and are most readily moved by concern for our own needs and desires.

By concentrating upon the reader's interests, you hope to stimulate a desire for that which you are selling. Whether it be for a product, for making a payment (as in a collection letter), or for a job applicant, your aim is to work up a desire on the part of the reader. Once this desire is created, the close of such a letter should simply take the reader verbally through the steps necessary to acquire the object of your persuasion.

The letter on page 99 illustrates the application of the persuasive strategy. Other examples of this category of letters are presented in Chapters 10, 11, and 12.

EXERCISES

1. Put yourself into the situations described below. Write the necessary letters, concentrating on the you attitude. Use your imagination in creating whatever additional information you need.

   a. You and a friend want to spend a weekend "stepping into the past" on Smith Island, a rather isolated island in Chesapeake Bay. There are two small villages on the island, and the inhabitants make their living by crabbing in the summer and oystering in the winter. Life is very slow paced, and a real sense of community exists. You want to stay as paying guests in the home of Captain and Mrs. Edwards, whose hospitality was recommended in a travel guidebook you have. The book also praised Mrs. Edwards' sumptuous meals. Write to the Edwards inquiring about accommodations for the weekend of June 15. Although you don't know the cost of room and board, you wonder whether you should ask, for you don't want to create the impression that your main concern is money.

   b. You have read about a new stereo system utilizing a microcomputer recently developed by a brother and sister team in California. This revolutionary product is creating a lot of talk among stereo technicians and owners, and you would like to know more about the system. Also, you would like to know where you could see and hear the equipment. You are planning to buy a new stereo system, so your interest is not mere curiosity. However, the article you read mentioned that the brother is a bit eccentric and will only sell to people he likes or who will truly appreciate the quality and uniqueness of the product.

c. You owe your local department store $230 for charge account purchases. At the time you made the purchases, you were employed and planned on paying off the account in two months. Three weeks ago you were laid off from your job; you have not been successful in finding another. You feel an obligation to let your creditors know of your situation and of your intention to pay as soon as you are working again. There is no way you can pay them anything now.

d. You heard a paper presented at a solar energy symposium which you felt summarized very accurately the impediments to the acceptance of solar devices. You are preparing an oral report for your marketing class about solar energy and would like to distribute copies of Dr. Werner's paper. Can he provide you with a copy of his paper? May you reproduce it for distribution to the 40 class members? Has he done any further research in the area?

2. Exchange the four letters you wrote for Exercise 1 with a partner.
   a. Assume the role of the message receiver. What is your reaction to each letter? Write your feelings at the bottom of each letter, together with a listing of the strong and weak points of the communication.
   b. Compose a reply to each letter. Whether you respond positively or negatively is your decision. Remember to imagine who your reader is and to use the you attitude.
   c. Exchange the four reply letters with your partner. What is your reaction to each letter? Write your feelings at the bottom of each letter, together with a listing of the strong and weak points.
   d. Return all letters to their writers so that the comments can be read.

3. Compose the first paragraphs of the letters needed in the following situations:
   a. An answer to a letter dated March 10 requesting a copy of our catalog and an order blank. We are a natural foods store and organic farm. All products grown here are raised without pesticides and chemical fertilizers. We have been at this location for 40 years, and the bulk of our business is mail order.
   b. A thank you to a professor at the University of Massachusetts. We asked him for some suggestions on how to hold a Futures Fair; he had organized a similar, very successful fair three months ago. He sent us much useful information and many suggestions. Our fair, an event for local high school students, will be held in two months.
   c. A clarification of a customer's order. Her October 19 letter stated that she wanted 16 skeins of medium-weight yellow yarn and 9 skeins of lightweight orange yarn. She did not specify whether she wanted wool or Orlon fiber. The wool is $3 a skein; the Orlon, $2.40. The customer was charging this order to her account.
   d. An acknowledgement of a customer's order for 12 cassette recorders. The recorders were shipped by United Parcel Service today. The fidelity of these recorders is remarkable considering their compactness.
   e. An inquiry as to the status of the training films we ordered four weeks ago. These films are to be used in the training of our cashiers. We had originally planned to use them only to train new cashiers. Since we haven't received them yet and we have had to hire three new cashiers, we will probably show the films to all the cashiers as a "refresher" course.

f. A request that a local businessperson serve on the advisory council of the local high school. The council is a means by which business teachers and the business community can work together in developing, implementing, and evaluating the school and work programs that will best meet the needs and interests of the students and their prospective employers.

4. Compose the last paragraph of the letters written in the following situations:
   a. Your company is applying for credit with a wholesaler.
   b. You, the publisher, are acknowledging receipt of the first three chapters of a textbook a college professor is under contract to write.
   c. You are replying to a customer's complaint about a shirt being permanently wrinkled. You want your laboratory to perform tests on the shirt.
   d. You are starting a new magazine and are seeking prospective subscribers. If they subscribe now, they will receive the first issue before they are billed and may cancel their subscription at any time.
   e. You are applying for a job as a management trainee with a company in your city.
   f. You are a supplier welcoming a new store as one of your customers.

5. The public relations director of the Homestead Insurance Company received the following letter:

   I am a student at Brookline Community College and am taking a course where the teacher is requiring us to visit a local business. I am especially interested in knowing if your company has any kind of data processing setup because I think I would like to work with computers when I finish school next year. Can I arrange to visit your company as soon as possible? Our reports are due in two weeks. Even if you don't have a data processing center, I would like to visit your company because it is near my house. I will be waiting for your reply.

   a. How do you think the receiver of this letter might react? What image of the writer has been created by this letter?
   b. Would the fact that Homestead has an outstanding data processing center, one that has been written about in several national publications, evoke a different reaction than the one you have just described?
   c. Rewrite the letter, including any additional information you think is desirable.

6. Assume you are the public relations director of Exercise 5 and have just received the well-written request letter composed for that exercise.
   a. Reply favorably to the request, arranging for a tour of the data processing center and the rest of the office facilities.
   b. Reply negatively to the request. For security reasons, only employees with special clearance have access to the data processing center. However, a tour of the other office facilities can be arranged.

7. You want to cancel your membership in a book club. You think you have purchased the required number of books stated in the initial membership agreement. Write the letter making this request.

8. The book club has received your letter. A check of their records shows that you agreed to purchase six books during the past two years; however, you have only purchased five. They, therefore, cannot allow you to cancel your membership. Assuming the role of a book club employee, write the refusal letter.

9. Obtain an actual business letter, preferably one that was sent to you. Write an analysis of the letter, covering these points:
   a. What mental image of you do you think the writer had?
   b. Was the you attitude used? Where? (underline or state)
   c. Was the first paragraph successful in getting your attention? Why or why not? What other functions did the first paragraph serve?
   d. Did the last paragraph get you to feel or do what the writer wanted? How was this achieved, or why was it not achieved?
   e. Did the last paragraph stop when the message was complete?
   f. What was your overall reaction to the letter?

10. As Academic Performance Improvement Committee chairman for your local chapter of Delta Sigma Pi Professional Business Fraternity, you've decided that your fraternity should have a file of exams given by professors in the college of business. Not only would such a file help your active members, but if all the business students were given access, your fraternity's recruitment might also improve. Using your imagination, the you attitude, an appropriate tone, and the proper sequence with an effective opening and close, write the letter that will persuade these professors to contribute to such a file.

11. Last semester you wrote a term paper entitled, "Swing the Pendulum Back." Its theme was that every businessperson has a major responsibility for improving the public's image of ethics in business. It took a historical view but emphasized the most recent surge of scandals that have been uncovered.

   Because the professor commended you before the class, an older part-time student asked to read it. Today you receive a letter from that student, who happens to be affiliated with the local chamber of commerce. To your horror you read that she would like you to highlight the content of this paper at the next chamber of commerce monthly luncheon.

   Although it would be an excellent opportunity for you to meet local business people, you must decline the invitation to speak before them. The fact of the matter is that you have no public speaking experience. You are certain that you would turn to mush before such an august group. But you would be happy and honored to have a more qualified speaker talk about the content of your paper. After you kick yourself and vow to take Speech 101 next semester, write the letter declining the invitation.

7
INQUIRIES, ANSWERS TO INQUIRIES, ORDERS

Among the routine types of letters most frequently written to business firms is the letter of inquiry. This letter seeks information on a broad variety of matters such as the operation of machinery, the price of certain products, the construction of various models or the uses to which they may be put, or any one of an infinite number of similar subjects. The simplest way to classify these letters is:

1. *The solicited letter of inquiry,* which is usually a response to an advertisement inviting the reader to write in for further information to a certain department or division.

2. *The unsolicited letter of inquiry,* in which the writer takes the initiative in asking for information.

Such inquiries very often come from ultimate consumers, as well as from company representatives. It is thus important to know about them for two reasons: first, every person at one time or another writes such a letter and, second, the response of any business enterprise to such inquiries is a sensitive barometer of its efficiency and attitudes.

THE SOLICITED INQUIRY

Resulting as it does from a specific suggestion, the solicited inquiry presents no difficulties. It should be very brief, usually no longer than one or two sentences, and should state definitely and directly what is wanted. Usually, a mention of the advertising medium in which the suggestion to write appeared is appropriate. The following examples are typical:

The Equitable Life Assurance Society
1285 Avenue of the Americas
New York, N.Y. 10019

Gentlemen and Ladies:

Please send me the prospectus on Individual Annuity Contracts which was mentioned in your ad in *Time* last week.

Incidentally—and perhaps this is just idle curiosity on my part—would you please tell me why your company uses "Assurance" in its name rather than the more normal "Insurance"?

Sincerely yours,
Howard J. Bender
27 Pine Street
Columbia, South Carolina 29202

Pitney-Bowes, Inc.
1350 Pacific Street
Stamford, Connecticut 06902

Gentlemen and Ladies:

Please send me information about the features and cost of the desk model postage meter which you advertised in *Nation's Business* for July 1970.

Yours truly,
Robert Black

F. W. Dodge Corporation
119 West Fortieth Street
New York, N.Y. 10018

Gentlemen and Ladies:

As offered in *Business Week*, July 13, 1970, please send a copy of your *How to Improve Sales Effectiveness in the New Construction Market* to me at 2719 Park Street, Seattle, Washington 98114.

Sincerely yours,
Esther A. Marshall
(Mrs. Robert Marshall)

Writers of inquiry letters should remember two things that make a satisfactory reply possible:

1. Be as specific as possible about what you want.

2. Include your address if you use paper without a letterhead. Advertisers and business people testify unanimously to the large number of inquiries they can't answer because writers forgot to include their addresses.

THE UNSOLICITED INQUIRY

The unsolicited inquiry letter is more complex and detailed than is the solicited, but the direct approach is still appropriate for most letters of this type. That is, the writer should not be timid about getting to the point of the letter for two reasons. First, inquiries, solicited or unsolicited, are the most routine type of business letter written. Business people expect to send and receive many of them. They are usually not anguished at having to respond because they expect the same courtesy from others. In most inquiries, therefore, you should not feel the need to open with all sorts of persuasion or general explanation for your request. The second reason stems from the fact that many inquiries, when properly handled, result in sales. Progressive business managers recognize this and are very receptive to letters about their products and services. For one or both of these reasons, most unsolicited inquiries can be handled in a very direct manner. You can begin such letters with either a specific question (promptly followed by whatever general explanation is necessary) or a general question that asks for answers to queries contained in the body of the letter.

Even though business people expect inquiries, a writer is still asking something of another, and so one should strive beyond all else *to make the inquiry easy to answer*. This goal can be accomplished in a number of ways. First, phrase your inquiries in question form. Sentences that start with "I shall appreciate your telling me . . ." or "I would be interested in knowing . . ." are roundabout and just camouflage the question. Second, be as specific as possible. No writer of an unsolicited letter of inquiry should expect a complete stranger to spend several hours answering questions of a general nature. Third, if the inquiry is lengthy, tabulate the questions. This technique virtually guarantees that the respondent will not overlook items you ask about. If the inquiry is relatively brief and a tabulation isn't warranted, at least put your questions in separate sentences. When several questions are combined in one sentence, the chances that the respondent may overlook one are increased. Finally, for maximum ease of response, if the nature of the inquiry allows, use an arrangement in which your questions may be answered by "yes" or "no" or by checking.

Courtesy demands that a stamp or a self-addressed, stamped envelope be enclosed if the inquiry is addressed to an individual or to a small firm. If it is sent to a large firm with its own mailing department, the stamp should not be included because it will probably interfere with the regular mailing routine.

To give the reader sufficient information to allow an intelligent and easy answer, the well-planned unsolicited inquiry usually contains:

1. A clear statement of the information desired or of the problem involved. This should include:
   a. What is wanted.
   b. Who wants it.
   c. Why it is wanted.

2. A tabulation of questions or a reference to an enclosed questionnaire.

3. An expression of appreciation.

To ensure getting the maximum amount of information from the letter, the writer of an unsolicited inquiry should:

1. Ask as few questions as possible.

2. Phrase questions so that they are clear, direct, and easy to answer.

3. Where confidential information is requested, promise to keep it confidential.

4. Try to avoid sending inquiries at those seasons when the pressure of business is heaviest.

5. If possible, stress the way in which the recipient will benefit by answering the questions.

The following example shows how an unsolicited letter of inquiry may be used to obtain information:

Gentlemen and Ladies:

Have you any information concerning what hours your employees like to begin and end their work? Because of the heavy traffic peaking at the hours of 9 A.M. and 5 P.M., a number of our employees have requested a change.

To do so, we are first undertaking a survey of the practices of a number of other companies within the greater Boston area. You can help us with this survey, which goes only to companies employing more than 2,000 people, by answering these questions:

1. What are your company's present working hours:
    8–4 _____
    8:30–4:30 _____
    9–5 _____
    Other _____

2. Have your employees indicated any wish to change?
    Yes _____ No _____
    If yes, to what hours _____

3. Would you think it desirable for the 20 largest companies in our geographical area to work out a cooperative system of staggered working hours?
    Yes _____ No _____
    If yes, what would be the best means to achieve this end?

4. Since it is obvious that if all the companies decide to change, we may end up where we started, would your company be willing to participate in a program where starting hours are allocated to individual companies for the greatest convenience of all?
    Yes _____ No _____

Please help yourself and all the other companies in our congested traffic area by supplying this information by October 15. We hope to tabulate the survey responses and compile a report by early November, at which time we'll mail you a copy of the results.

Sincerely yours,

Progressive companies often use the inquiry letter for a variety of purposes such as sales, keeping mailing lists up to date, and maintaining contact with customers, as in the following example:

Dear Mr. Grantwood:

Would you please help us to make *Handy Hints to Photographers* more beneficial to you? We hope that this monthly folder has been useful to you, but now we would like to use the comments of users to make whatever improvements they think should be made.

Only a minute of your time would be necessary to answer the questions listed below. A stamped, addressed envelope is enclosed for your convenience. Your response will help us to send you the "handiest hints" we can.

Sincerely,

1. In which of the following are you most interested:
   Color ____   Black and white ____   Other ____
   Slides ____   Snapshots ____
2. Which section of *Handy Hints* has proved most useful to you:
   New equipment ____   Taking better pictures ____
   Enlarging and developing ____   Other ____
3. Would you be interested in a contest for the best picture taken by a local photographer each month?
   Yes ____   No ____
4. Is the address to which *Handy Hints* has been sent correct? If not, please list the correct address here:

ANSWERS-TO-INQUIRY LETTERS

The time has long since gone when business people regarded letters of inquiry as a nuisance or, at best, as trivial matters. A few inexperienced correspondents are still sending out the essentially thought-less responses characterized by "Here's the catalog you asked for and we hope it's useful." But the majority of business people now realize that the inquiry—solicited or unsolicited—represents an opportunity to turn requests for information into orders and goodwill.

One factor should be predominant in answering inquiries—you are writing to a reader who has already expressed an interest in a product, a bit of information, or something else. Your answer is therefore important to your reader since he or she has taken the initiative to ask for it. As one expert has said, "A letter to the company is a personal act of the writer. . . . When a woman takes up her pen to write a letter, she is . . . entering into a personal relationship with a company. . . . She hopes that she is writing to another human being like herself."

Suppose for the moment that you are Mr. Bender, whose letter to the insurance company appears on p. 106. What would be your reaction if you received the prospectus you requested along with a form letter but no answer to your question about why the word *Assurance* is used instead of *Insurance*? "Another big impersonal corporation geared to treat my letter just like everybody else's," you growl. "It wasn't really important—the question I asked—but still I'd like to know. . . ." Despite the denial, it *was* important and should have been treated accordingly.

Fortunately, in the instance of Mr. Bender's request, The Equitable Life Assurance Society *did* answer and very effectively. After a "thank you" for the request and a mention of the prospectus enclosed, the letter continued:

> Your question about the use of the term "assurance" in our company's name rather than the term "insurance" is a good one which we frequently receive.
>
> Words such as "ensurance," "assurance," and "insurance" have been, at various times, synonymous, and their usage has overlapped. In 1697, for example, Daniel Defoe spoke of "ensuring of life," in the monetary sense. In 1762, a group of Englishmen founded "The Society of Equitable Assurances of Lives and Survivorships," known since, familiarly, as "The Equitable Society of London" and "The Old Equitable." (Significantly, this company was formed on the basis of "mutual contribution," a concept that is considered the very foundation of mutual life insurance.)
>
> The term "insurance" as part of a company title vied with "assurance" in company titles at least as early 1799, so Henry B. Hyde had a choice of words when in 1859, at the age of 25, he founded a mutual life insurance company and named it The Equitable Life Assurance Society of the United States. Our historical records do not indicate why he chose the word "assurance."

The explicitness and care taken in this letter from Assistant Vice-President Bruce L. Roberts stand in welcome contrast to the ironic fact that many companies, after soliciting inquiries, do not answer them or answer them inefficiently.

Perhaps computerized responses will correct this situation, but surveys now show tardiness, sloppiness, and error-ridden answers to inquiries. Classes in written communication frequently write to companies that invite inquiries in magazines. Misspelled names, wrong addresses, delay in writing, and failure to answer at all are too often revealed in such surveys and point to four principles:

1. Answer all inquiries promptly.

2. Take special care in addressing, posting, and enclosing material.

3. Make certain that you have answered all the inquirer's questions in clear, understandable language.

4. Refer specifically in your letter to any catalogs or brochures enclosed or sent separately.

The simplest way to discuss answers to inquiries is to group them into two categories: those granting requests and those refusing requests. The discussion that follows is therefore organized in that manner.

Granting a Request

As we have said before, the letter that says "yes" is always easier to write; however, it should go beyond a mere "yes" if it is to build sales or goodwill. Since someone has already expressed interest in your company's products, methods, or operations, the letter granting a request has already passed the first hurdle of many sales situations—gaining the reader's interest—and the letter should capitalize on that fact.

Frequently, such letters involve the sending of catalogs, brochures, pamphlets, or reprints as part of answering the request. Ideally, on the basis of considerable experience, the best results are obtained when the letter and the supplementary material are sent together as one piece of mail. In actual practice, however, this has to be modified by such practical factors as mailing costs, the size and weight of the material, and the urgency of the situation. Even worse than the outmoded "Here is your catalog and we hope it is useful" letter mentioned earlier, is the letter which says "The answers to your questions are on page 197 of the catalog we are sending you," leaving the inquirer's frustration to build for two weeks until the catalog arrives. If the answering letter and supplemental materials must be sent separately, tell your reader *when* you are mailing the supplemental material (preferably "today," the same day as the letter), and give an approximation of when it can be expected to arrive—"within a few days," "next week," or whatever seems realistic.

Correspondents answering requests with enclosures would do well to organize their letters according to the following three functions:

1. State the action taken.

2. Refer specifically to the enclosure.

3. Motivate action or build goodwill.

Notice how this is done in the following example and in the letter displayed on page 113.

Dear Mr. Slobody:

We are happy to send you a copy of "Greater Efficiency in Office Layouts," which you requested.

The diagrams of typical office layouts on pages 14 to 19 should interest you. Surveys by our architects and engineers show that these arrangements can save you as much as 50 percent because they use space efficiently. The five typical installations on pages 26 to 30 show how you get more privacy and greater efficiency because the lightweight Acme Partitions are tailored to your individual needs.

Our agent, Mr. John J. Pratt, will call on you within the next three days to demonstrate how Acme Partitions can make your office a more efficient, comfortable, and economical place to work.

Sincerely,

The tone of these letters and their references to specific pages of the requested booklets make them effective sales emissaries. Their writers properly use an answer to a letter of inquiry as the first step in making a sale.

In situations where answers to inquiries do not directly involve sales, the correspondent should aim at building goodwill. Above all else, these letters should convey a tone of helpfulness and should contain sufficient information to answer the inquirer's questions. Here is an effective example:

Dear Ms. Fife:

Your letter asking about our program for executive development interested me greatly. I am glad to have an opportunity of telling you about our policies.

The answer to both of your questions is "yes." We do have a definite program for developing potential executives, and we feel that it has been very worthwhile. I am enclosing an outline of our program showing the topics which have been discussed during the past year.

We believe that the success of such a program depends largely on the method of selection by which people are admitted to it. For that reason, we have developed a very elaborate personnel appraisal sheet by which candidates for the program are rated by their superiors and their coworkers. The enclosed blank will show you the personal qualities with which we are concerned. If we can help you further, please let us know.

Sincerely yours,

This letter avoids the two main pitfalls which characterize many answers to inquiries: giving the reader a sense that she is receiving a perfunctory treatment or a brush-off and conveying an impression of answering questions grudgingly or in such general terms that the result is meaningless.

HOME BUILDERS SUPPLY COMPANY
271 LAKE AVENUE
ALLENTOWN, PENNSYLVANIA 18104

May 10, 1970

Mr. Ronald E. Thompson
76 Maple Street
Scranton, Pennsylvania 18519

Dear Mr. Thompson:

We are sending you our booklet "Modern Insulation for Older Homes." which you requested on May 8.

As the owner of a home which was not originally insulated, you will be particularly interested in the description on pages 23 and 24 of the simple technique by which Blanktex Insulation can make older homes as snug and warm as those with original insulation. You will want to read on pages 37 to 41 the unsolicited statements by satisfied users of Blanktex Insulation proving that as much as 20 percent of the annual heating cost can be saved by our modern methods.

After you have read this booklet, you will probably have questions pertaining specifically to the insulation of your home. Our heating expert in your territory is Mr. Robert Vaughan, 69 Main Street, Scranton, Pennsylvania 18505 (Phone Diamond 381-3109)

As a graduate engineer, Mr. Vaughan can give you exact figures on costs, fuel savings, and similar facts regarding your home—all without obligation on your part. A card or phone call to Mr. Vaughan can make this winter the warmest you have ever spent in your home.

Yours truly,

Allan Whitlock

Allan Whitlock
Sales Manager

AW:MR

Refusing a Request

The refusal of a request is one of the more difficult types of letters. Great tact and courtesy must be used if the reader is not to be antagonized. Many of the requests or inquiries that are made of business people are inconsiderate or unreasonable, but the answers to these requests should never be brusque, even when the request is refused. A harsh refusal may antagonize a potential customer or develop a source of ill will toward a company. Regardless of how thoughtless the request may seem, the intelligent technique is to refuse it tactfully. By doing this, good correspondents have learned that they can say "no" and still retain the reader's goodwill.

In Chapter 6 we discussed the strategy or plan of presentation that might be used to convey disappointing news to a reader. Such a strategy would suggest the following pattern for letters refusing requests:

1. A neutral statement of appreciation for the request that does not imply that you are granting it. An effusive thank you might have such an implication.

2. An explanation of why the request must be refused. Wherever possible, avoid vague terms like *company policy* or similar generalities.

3. A brief, clear, and courteous refusal of the request.

4. If possible, an inclusion in the closing paragraph of either a constructive suggestion or an offer to be of service in the future.

The individual circumstances of each request and the person who makes it will, of course, govern the amount of detail included in the refusal. In many instances there need be no elaborate explanation of the reason for refusal; in others no constructive suggestion can be included. But whatever the details of the situation, the tone of the letter should be tactful and helpful. This is especially necessary when the request comes from a friend, an acquaintance, or a good customer; the refusal of a request from such a source would follow *in detail* the outline above. To illustrate the application of this outline, let us assume that Mr. Lawrence Miller, a customer of yours, is opening a new business which is similar to yours but will not compete with you in any way. Mr. Miller has written to you asking for information concerning the basis on which you pay your salespeople, and you must refuse his request. What is the best way to refuse Mr. Miller? Notice the contrast in the point of view of the following letters:

Dear Sir:

I have your letter of April 12 asking about the basis on which we pay our salespeople.

I regret that I cannot let you have this information because confidential reports have a way of getting out. I might say that our system of remuneration has been very successful and our salespeople are completely satisfied with it.

It is my hope that you will not consider this refusal an uncooperative act on our part and that our pleasant business relationship may continue in the future.

Very truly yours,

Dear Mr. Miller:

Thank you for the interest expressed in your letter of April 12 concerning the way in which we pay our salespeople. We are flattered that you would ask our advice.

Each of our salespeople works under an individual contract. Several years ago they requested that the terms of these contracts be kept secret. Since we cannot violate their confidence, we feel that you will understand why we cannot divulge this information.

We have, however, found E. J. Smith's booklet, "Setting Up a Successful Sales Organization," to be invaluable in its practical suggestions for dealing with specific problems. It might prove useful to you.

If we can be of assistance to you in some other way, please write us. We offer you our best wishes for success in your new venture.

Sincerely,

The first letter is completely negative with its wrong emphasis, such as hoping "you will not consider this refusal an uncooperative act"; it is almost insulting in its thoughtless suggestion that the reader cannot be trusted—"confidential reports have a way of getting out"; it is irritating in its teasing tone of "our system of remuneration has been very successful"—*but* we can't divulge it. The second letter, by contrast, is tactful, sincere, and as constructive as possible. Its reader cannot help feeling that the explanation is honest.

USING INQUIRIES AND ORDERS FOR SALES-PROMOTION LETTERS

Alert people in business make use of all occasions for writing letters to promote business, and high on the list of these occasions is the receipt of inquiries or of first orders. Letters acknowledging other orders tend to be rather routine, but even so, a letter of thanks at an appropriate time is an excellent sales promotion device.

When a first order is received, goodwill can be fostered by a letter of acknowledgment; the sequence of parts can be varied, of course, but such a letter usually contains:

1. A reference to the order and a statement of appreciation

2. A statement of how the order is being shipped

3. A brief sales message on the quality of service you expect to render or an expression of interest in the customer's needs.

The following letter illustrates how this outline may be applied:

Dear Mr. Havens:

Thank you for your order of May 15. We are very happy to learn that you are planning to feature our line of Spring Weave men's suits in your store.

You will be pleased with the way these suits sell. Spring Weave is a name that men know because of our 10-year national advertising campaign.

Your order is being shipped by express today. With it, we are sending you a set of displays, keyed to our advertising campaign, which you will want to use in your shop windows.

Thank you very much for your order. If there is anything we can do to help you with the promotion of Spring Weave suits, please let us know.

Sincerely,

When a new purchasing agent is appointed in a company with which a Chicago firm does business, the following excellent letter is sent to acknowledge an order and to build goodwill with the new person:

Dear Ms. Jenks:

Thank you for your order number 862, which came in this morning. Naturally, we always appreciate orders; but this one makes us especially happy because it represents our first dealing with you.

We've done business with your firm for a number of years and have always enjoyed a friendly relationship. You may be sure that we will do our best to keep it that way.

Congratulations on your new position. If we can make your job easier or help you in any way where our products are concerned, we want to do so. Please call on us—any time.

Sincerely yours,

There is plenty of room for originality, sincerity, and occasional humor in such letters, as demonstrated in this classic exchange between a tongue-in-cheek customer and a correspondent with a sense of humor:

Gents:

Please send me one of them gasoline engines you show on page 785 and if it's any good I'll send you a check for it.

To which the company replied:

Dear Sir:

Please send us the check, and if it's any good, we'll send you the engine.

Notice how graciously this original letter performs its function of welcoming a customer's first order:

Gentlemen and Ladies:

I walked past a bookstore yesterday. It had a "going out of business" poster on the door, and in the window a sign which said

Words Failed Us

We're not going to let words fail us in acknowledging your first order. We hope we succeed in expressing our reaction when we say

We are grateful.

But even those words don't say everything we mean, which is

We want our service to deserve your business; if it doesn't live up to your expectations

We want to hear from you.

Sincerely yours,

LETTER PROBLEM 1: *Response to an Order*

You work for a highly exclusive menswear and sporting goods shop whose name is associated with absolute reliability and prestige. In a recent advertising campaign, you have featured the opportunity to try your custom-made shirts, which are usually sold (with a minimum of three in an order) at $24.95 each, by ordering just one at $15.95. "Once you have worn this one shirt, you will be our customer for life."

Implicit in your advertisement was your intention to get *new* customers to come in and be measured for one custom-made shirt so that with their measurements permanently on file they would continue to order shirts in lots of three at $24.95 each.

To the bewilderment of everyone at Dalrymple & Dalrymple, 497 Fifth

Avenue, New York, N.Y. 10019, the following letter addressed personally to Henry C. Stimple, salesperson in your Hunting and Fishing Supplies section, arrives three days after the advertisement appears:

> Dear Hank:
>
> Saw that ad of D & D's in yesterday's paper and decided I ought to try one of those custom shirts of yours. Send me one and a bill. I need the shirt for a wedding 10 days from now.
>
> I'll be down this spring because we're going to need a lot of equipment.
>
> Yours,
>
> *Josh*
>
> Josh Avery
> The Green Lodge
> Lew Ridge, New York 12831

At an informal council of war, Henry Stimple says, "He's one of our very best customers. Twice a year he comes to the city and orders thousands of dollars of hunting and fishing tackle for his guests at the lodge. I don't know whether he knows what a custom-made shirt is or whether he's pulling my leg—but I know one thing: we don't want to antagonize him and lose his business."

Someone else says, "It's a gag. He knows he can't buy custom-made shirts without being fitted and he's just having fun at our expense." Another salesperson says, "If you try explaining custom-made shirts to him, he's just going to decide that we're a bunch of city slickers looking down our noses at a country bumpkin. I know because I was brought up in the country myself. If you sound patronizing or snooty, you'll never get another order from him."

Taking all of this background into careful consideration, write the letter you would send to Mr. Avery.

■　■　■

Curiously, most businesses spend more time and effort welcoming new accounts than they devote to their old customers. This is natural, partly because human nature tends to take for granted what it already possesses, and partly because business measures success in terms of new and added sales. Progressive companies realize, however, that the steady customer is the bedrock upon which business success is built, and they write letters expressing their appreciation for such patronage. This type of letter is usually called a *business-promotion letter*. While it is often closely associated with the acknowledgment of an order, it can be effectively used on anniversaries, at year's end, on holidays, or on any other appropriate occasion.

The essence of the business-promotion letter is a statement of appreciation to a customer for that customer's business, cooperation, interest, or promptness. Highly relevant to the spirit of this type of letter is a story about Rudyard Kipling when he was at the height of his career. A group of Oxford undergraduates, upon reading that Kipling was to be paid 10 shillings a word for an article, wired him 10 shillings with the request, "Please send us one of your best words." Back came Kipling's answer, "Thanks." Correspondents who learn to use "thanks" as one of their best words will find its value beyond price. The writers of such letters certainly reap a harvest of goodwill from a very small investment by letting old customers know that their orders and patronage merit thanks. Here are some excellent examples of the way in which correspondents use letters which are basically acknowledgments of orders or inquiries as a method of promoting sales and goodwill.

Dear Mr. Bradley:

With Father's Day approaching, you may enjoy the story of the college student who sent Dad a cheap pair of cufflinks with the message:

This isn't much, but it's all you can afford.

This letter isn't much either in terms of expressing our genuine thanks for the confidence you've shown by your increased orders and prompt payments during the past year.

But we did want you to know that your continued patronage affords us the opportunity to say one very important word—THANKS.

Cordially yours,

The next letter faces up frankly to the fact that established customers are too often forgotten:

Dear Mr. Byers:

BEFORE a guy marries—
He'll send the girl flowers and take her to the theater in a taxi.

AFTER—the only "flour" she gets is Gold Medal. And she has to lug it home from the Cash and Carry in a 24-pound sack.

Business is a lot like that.

Firms spend much to make someone a customer. And then the best that customer gets is an invoice.

We believe a firm should tell customers that their trade is appreciated. And that's why we are writing you this letter to tell you how much we appreciate the steady flow of orders you've sent us during the past year.

Not to sell you—but to tell you—it's always a real pleasure to serve you.

Cordially yours.

Increasingly, a large number of business enterprises are using inquiries to rebuild sales among customers who have not used their charge accounts for a certain period, usually from three to six months. One sends out an actual bill showing a balance due of $0.00 with these words typed on the bill:

We're sorry about "nothing"!

Your account is paid in full, and we're concerned because you haven't bought anything from us lately. On the back of this bill, you'll find three questions about the service we've tried to render. You can help us by checking the answers and returning them in the enclosed envelope.

Better still, stop in and visit one of our convenient suburban branches, where we're featuring Spring sales of ladies' coats.

The following inquiry letter with a penny attached has been highly successful in reactivating accounts:

Dear Mr. Jones:

A PENNY FOR YOUR THOUGHTS—
. . . and here's cash in advance . . .

We are still trying to find out why you have not used your charge account at Rosenfield's recently. We do not wish to annoy an old friend by being too persistent. But we do want to know if anything has happened to displease you in the slightest.

It will take just a minute for you to tell us the reason, in the space below, and to let us know if you would like us to continue sending you your current credit card each month.

We have thousands of customers who find their charge account a great convenience in getting the things they want at Rosenfield's, and we sincerely hope you will use your account again. This letter is just to find our your wishes, so that we may serve you as you want to be served.

There's a postage-paid envelope enclosed which will bring your reply to my desk. And thank you very much.

Sincerely yours,

The Joseph M. Stern Company of Cleveland has had great success getting orders with what it calls a "Miniature Message for Busy Buyers":

Dear Friend:

We have some grass mats for which we need orders.

Perhaps you have some orders for which you need grass mats.

If so, we should get together. Right? Write!

Concisely yours,
The Joseph M. Stern Co.

P.S. We may be short on words but we are long on QUALITY and SERVICE. All orders for standard-size grass mats are shipped on the same day received.

In an era when the servicing of a great variety of mechanical, electrical, and electronic devices has become a necessity, one highly reputable dealer selling TV sets actually used poor service (caused by a work stoppage by builders of his new repair shop) to win back customers with this letter:

Dear Mrs. Northrup:

Someone told us about the daughter who couldn't spell and wrote her mother:

Please send me my genes.

Her mother replied:

If you don't have them now, there's nothing I can do about it.

Back in September, we decided there *was* something we could do about it—and we started a new repair shop. We were delayed, our service wasn't what we wanted it to be; but now we have the most modern and efficient TV service in the city.

Like the daughter, we say please send us your set. You'll find that there's something we can do about it quickly, honestly, and satisfactorily.

Just put the enclosed sticker with our telephone number on the back of your set to remind you where to call.

Sincerely yours,

The letter displayed on page 122 illustrates an effective acknowledgment of an order from an old customer. It expresses gratitude and builds a sound relationship for future sales.

Many a sermon has been preached on the text, "If a man asks you to go with him a mile, go with him twain." The text is applicable to the whole subject of letter writing. The letter which goes beyond routine, which goes "the second

THE GENERAL STEEL MFG. CO.

4156 EASTERN AVENUE
PITTSBURGH, PA. 15215

MYRON WOODRUFF
VICE-PRESIDENT

November 5, 1970

Mr. Charles E. Goodwin
Tool Producers Company
771 West Avenue
Milwaukee, Wisconsin 53404

Dear Mr. Goodwin:

When a friend helps us on with a coat, we smile and say "Thank
you." If we drop something and someone picks it up for us, we
practically burst with gratitude.

Strange? Not at all.

But it is strange that when we get into business, we take so
many things for granted that we forget to say "Thank you."
Take old customers like you, for instance.

You did something pretty important for us—important because
we think so much of your business that it gives us a great
deal of pleasure to see it grow.

I just wanted to write you personally, telling you how much we
appreciate your order, and saying "Thank you" for your confidence
in us.

Very truly yours,

Myron Woodruff

Myron Woodruff, Vice-President

MW:RT

mile" where others stop with the routine "first mile," is the really effective message. For that reason, these letters succeed; they reflect a policy which is designed not only to win new friends but to keep old ones.

EXERCISES

Chapter 6 of this book presents the general principles pertaining to all types of effective letters. In the exercises in this and the following chapters, you will be learning to apply these general principles to the specialized problems described. You will find your letter writing easier and more effective if you answer these questions briefly in writing before you write each letter:

1. Who is my reader?
2. What do I want to tell the reader?
3. What do I want the reader to think or do?

1. Select two advertisements from newspapers or magazines which invite readers' inquiries. Choose ads for two different products or services. Write the letters of inquiry; send the originals to the companies and submit carbon copies to your instructor.

2. When you receive the replies to the letters you wrote in Exercise 1, critique them. Point out your reaction and the strong and weak points of the letters. Turn in to your instructor the letters and analyses; perhaps the letters could also be shared with your classmates.

3. You will be graduated from the community college in your town in June and have applied for upper-division admission at the state university, 300 miles away.
   a. Write to the financial aid office, inquiring about loans, scholarships, and work-study programs. What specific questions will you ask? In what detail should you discuss your financial situation?
   b. Write to the housing director, inquiring about dormitory accommodations. What will you want to know? You are also curious about off-campus apartments. Should you ask about these in this letter, or should you wait until you hear about dorms and then ask about apartments?

4. Exchange your letters from Exercise 3 with a partner (select someone you haven't worked with before). Reply to their two letters, using factual or invented information to provide complete answers. If your partner inquired about apartments in the second letter, assume that there is a tenants' association on campus which handles all questions about off-campus housing.

5. As part of a project for your office administration class, you are surveying 50 businesses in your city to determine if they are using text-editing typewriters. You want to know what brands are used; whether they are rented, leased, or purchased; and what percentage of the total office correspondence is prepared on these typewriters. Write the letter of inquiry which you would send to these companies. Include any other questions about the typewriters or the companies that you think are necessary or pertinent.

6. Pick any product with which you are familiar and assume the role of marketing correspondent for the manufacturer of that product. Answer a request for information about that product from David Hovey, owner of Hovey's Department Store in Terre Haute, Indiana. Make whatever references you feel necessary to the brochure you will include with the letter.

7. As part of the basic psychology course required of all education majors at the local university, students must work 20 hours as volunteers in community youth programs. As coordinator of the volunteer program, it is your responsibility to find local churches, clubs, or agencies that would like to have the help of these students. The 20 hours of service may be spread out over the 15-week semester or over a shorter period of time. Two brief written reports from the activity leaders are asked for by the university. The number of student volunteers each semester is generally about 50. Write the letter of inquiry which will be sent to community youth program leaders, adding any information you think will make your letter a strong one.

8. In your 10 years with the First National Bank, you have advanced to loan department manager. Today you receive a letter from Tod Jones, professional program chairman of your alma mater's chapter of Delta Sigma Pi International Business Fraternity. Tod wants you to speak about careers in banking at a business meeting in two weeks. Because of certain organizational changes taking place at the bank over the next month, you won't have the time to prepare such a talk. Write the letter declining the invitation.

9. You are customer services representative for Johnson's Inc., a manufacturer of ladies' sweaters, and must convey some negative news to the owner-manager of Karen's Shop. After seeing several of your sweaters advertised in *Belle* magazine, Ms. Karen Naquin wrote to Johnson's asking about the possibility of handling your line. Karen's Shop is in Thibodaux, Louisiana, a city of about 18,000 people. Also in Thibodaux is Ellis Braud's Department Store, which handles your line. Because of your policy of one exclusive retail distributor of your line per 25,000 population area, you must explain why you can't do business with Ms. Naquin now. Of course, you wouldn't want to close the door on business with Karen's Shop forever; circumstances could change in the future.

10. Assume that for the last five years you have owned and managed an exclusive restaurant in your home town. From a tally that you've kept during the past two years, write a letter of appreciation to the 100 most frequent patrons of your establishment. Use your imagination to devise a way to show, as well as speak, your gratitude.

11. As a life insurance agent for the Megalaharlitan Life Insurance Company of America, write a letter to the people to whom you've sold insurance during your two years with the company. In addition to saying "thank you," try to conceive a way of opening up negotiations for additional coverage, should a customer's circumstances have changed since the first policy was purchased.

12. Your company, which sells wall murals which are applied like pre-pasted wallpaper, has just received an order from Karen Kelley, 65 Delsea Terrace, Clayton, New Jersey, a new customer. The mural, a 3×5-foot desert scene, was sent today by first-class mail. A computer check indicates that this is the first mural you have sold to anyone in Clayton or the immediate area. Acknowledge Karen's order and lay the foundation for future sales to Karen and others in her town.

8
CLAIM AND
ADJUSTMENT
LETTERS

"To err is human," according to Alexander Pope, and the number of errors committed in the routine transactions of business attest the truth of Pope's words. Orders may be filled improperly or incompletely; goods may be damaged or unsatisfactory; misunderstandings may arise over discounts, bills, credit terms, and exchanges. Or, as a lead in *The Wall Street Journal* (June 26, 1969) describes the situation more dramatically:

> Roofs leak. Shirts shrink. Toys maim. Toasters don't toast. Mowers don't mow. Kites don't fly. Radios emit no sounds, and television sets and cameras yield no pictures.

The letters written to bring these errors to the attention of those who must take the responsibility for them are known as *claim letters;* those written to take action on such claims are called *adjustment letters.*

The most recent consumer movement of the sixties and seventies has made both parties more sensitive to the existence, effects, and solutions of problems caused by business errors. Customers are less hesitant to voice their dissatisfactions, and many business representatives appear more prone to act immediately upon these expressions of dissatisfaction. Some of this heightened sensitivity of business has been encouraged by federal legislation like the Consumer Product Safety Act and the federal Truth-in-Lending Act; however, the fact remains that both sellers and buyers are more aware of the responsibilities of business to provide what it says it will provide.

To anyone acquainted with the complexities of modern business, the important fact is not that errors do occur but that the percentage of error is actually very small. The surest indication of the amateur in business is a willingness, at the one extreme, to promise that mistakes will *never* occur or, at the other, to become angry and threatening as soon as such errors are made. Before novices in business send angry or threatening adjustment letters, they should heed the advice in the following piece of anonymous doggerel:

> *Lives of great men all remind us*
> *As we o'er their pages turn*
> *That we too may leave behind us*
> *Letters that we ought to burn.*

Experienced business people develop a certain degree of tolerance toward the errors made by their own associates and by others; this is not to say that they are complacent about mistakes made by their own organizations or ready to continue doing business indefinitely with those whose blunders are too numerous. But from experience, they have learned that there is an irreducible minimum of mistakes made in business, and this knowledge prevents them from losing their tempers over the mistakes of others or from promising that they will never again let such an error occur in their own company.

THE CLAIM LETTER

The tolerant attitude just described is the correct viewpoint from which the claim letter should be written. Claim letters lacking this tone usually originate with those unfamiliar with business. A letter like the following is all too typical:

> Dear Sir:
>
> That television set your store sold me last week is a disgrace. The picture is distorted and flops around so that we can't look at it. You've sent your repairman out twice and each time the set is worse after he tinkers with it. I think you knew it was no good when you sold it to me and hoped I wouldn't have sense enough to complain. This is the last time I'll ever buy anything from your store.
>
> Yours truly,

The first and natural reaction to stupid mistakes and unreasonable blunders is anger; but, on second thought, shouldn't we realize that *we* make mistakes too? Good manners alone should prevent such explosive reactions. To write such an angry and accusing letter is simply to let one's emotions run away with reason. In fact, the worst attitude for the claim writer is nicely summed up in an old ditty:

> *In controversial moments*
> *My perception's very fine;*
> *I always see both points of view,*
> *The one that's wrong—and mine!*

A little thought before writing a claim letter will show that *it is to the writer's own advantage to be somewhat tolerant and even-tempered in the letter.* It is unlikely that the dealer who receives the vindictive letter about the television set will try to be as scrupulously fair as he might have been had the situation been described without malice. In fact, this type of letter gives the reader every excuse to write the customer off. The letter stated that "this is the last time I'll ever buy anything from your store." Doesn't the writer of this letter come across as a fairly irrational individual whose judgment might not be worthy of concern? Couldn't the dealer conclude, "Why try?"

Since people stand a greater chance of getting a reasonable adjustment by being fair, the claim letter should avoid anger, sarcasm, and accusations. In its phrasing, the claimant should shun such terms as *complaint, disgusted, dishonest, false, unfair, untrue, worthless,* and *no good.*

An analysis of the claim letter shows that four elements are usually present:

1. A straightforward explanation of what is wrong. This explanation should give exact dates, amounts, model numbers, sizes, colors, or any other specific information that will make a recheck easier for the reader.

2. A statement of the inconvenience or loss that has resulted from this error.

3. An attempt to motivate action by appealing to the reader's sense of fair play, honesty, or pride. Don't threaten loss of business at the first error.

4. A statement of what adjustment is considered fair; the writer who doesn't know what adjustment is equitable should try to stimulate prompt investigation and action.

This analysis puts a premium upon specific facts rather than emotions in the claim letter. It is predicated on the assumption that the overwhelming majority of people in business want to do the fair thing, if only because it is good business to do so; hence, an appeal to fairness or honesty is the best possible motivation. With regard to the actual adjustment, the claimant may not know exactly what he or she wants or what would constitute a fair settlement of the claim. In that event, *it is generally best to let the adjuster suggest a satisfactory settlement.* Several surveys of department stores and retail establishments have shown that when the customer has a reasonable claim and has left its settlement completely up to the store, the adjuster will usually grant more than the customer would ask. This technique will not appeal to those who believe that all business is conducted on the plane of "beat the customer before he or she beats you." But for those with a realistic background of experience in business, such a technique is the best method of writing claims. This is so because it stems from a belief on which American business is founded—that honesty in business is the best policy.

Contrast the tone of the following letters with that of the first one presented in this chapter.

Gentlemen and Ladies:

On your bill for February, I was charged $22.75 for a fishing rod and reel which I purchased in your sporting goods department on December 18.

This bill was paid on January 14 by my check on the Guaranty National Bank. This canceled check was returned with the bank statement which I received on February 2. The next day I received your bill showing this amount still unpaid.

Will you please see that my payment is credited to my account so that I am not billed again?

Sincerely yours,
John H. Middleton

Gentlemen and Ladies:

On September 15 we ordered 50 maple kneehole desks to be shipped on September 28 for delivery here on September 30 in time for the opening of our new dormitory.

When this shipment arrived on September 28, we found that it contained 25 desks, which we had ordered, and 25 maple tables. I attempted to get the cartage company which delivered the furniture from the freight station to leave the desks and return the tables to the station. They insisted they had no authority to do this and that we would have to accept the whole shipment or return all of it.

When I attempted to call you long distance, I could locate no one who knew anything about this situation. This has caused us considerable inconvenience since we were forced to open our dormitory for inspection before it was completely furnished.

We are, therefore, asking you to send the 25 desks immediately and to arrange to have the tables removed from our dormitory locker room as soon as possible because we urgently need this space for trunks and luggage.

Sincerely yours,
Henry Green
Business Manager

THE ADJUSTMENT LETTER

Typical of the proper attitude of modern business people toward handling complaints are the following comments:

It has been our invariable policy to let people know we appreciate hearing from them if they are dissatisfied in any way. We have always recognized the customer's right to expect our products to fulfill any claim we made for them in our advertising. (H. F. Jones, Vice-President, Campbell Soup Company)

I make it a rule to answer every letter of complaint that I can personally handle. If a busy schedule prevents me from doing this, an associate takes care of the letter for me; but the point is—every letter is answered. (John C. Whitaker, President, R. J. Reynolds Tobacco Company)

I think that to fail to answer an intelligent letter about one's product, flattering or the other kind, is to lose an opportunity . . . (G. H. Coppers, President, National Biscuit Company)

I certainly do welcome flattering letters . . . but I also welcome the other kind because they give me a check on what's happening from indignant sources. It's a standing rule here that each letter addressed to me, in which the writer has a gripe, comes to me personally . . . and is acknowledged at once by me. (L. A. Van Bomel, President, National Dairy Products Corporation)

These and similar comments by business and industrial leaders show that alert business people welcome comments from their customers. Actually, claim and adjustment letters offer an excellent check on the quality of service or merchandise, and many companies keep a continuous record of these letters as a control mechanism for their products and service. Furthermore, progressive business people realize that there is nothing more detrimental to good public relations than discontented or dissatisfied customers who go around telling all their friends and acquaintances that "the Blank Company is a poor place to do business." If they can be persuaded to write directly to the company and thus get their troubles "off their chests," the company has an opportunity to convert these potential liabilities into boosters who tell their friends, "The Blank Company is reliable; if they make an error or their merchandise isn't satisfactory, they'll make good every time." Of such elements is the intangible quality called *goodwill* composed—and as we have seen, *progressive* business people recognize its importance.

Unfortunately, this progressive attitude has not been universal, as shown in a comprehensive roundup titled "Caveat Emptor" by the staff of *The Wall Street Journal* (June 26, 1969). After ascribing a rising tide of complaints about inferior products and service to poor quality control and increased competition, the article ends with a story which should remind all business people to handle complaints effectively. An Iowa grandfather, angry at a national chain store which installed a leaky roof on his house years ago, now ends all his letters to his grandchildren with these words:

Love, and don't buy anything from Blank's.

Unadjusted complaints apparently leave their mark "even unto the third generation."

Even worse is the situation described by Lee Kanner, writing in the financial pages of the *New York Times* (November 12, 1967):*

---

* © 1967 by The New York Times Company. Reprinted by permission.

The age of the non-hero and the hippie freak-out has a new addition—the non-response of business, particularly in the retail industry.

The non-response has many variations. In its most elemental form, it is non-response to a letter of complaint. It is non-response that arrives weeks, sometimes months, after a letter is written, but says little or nothing, and is not acted upon.

After citing numerous specific examples of non-response to complaints, the article ends with these ominous words:

Is there a solution to the non-response problem? The stores say time and better training will overcome all difficulties. The facts say no. The non-personalized numbers game of the computers inevitably will more and more de-humanize relations between retail establishments and their customers. Apparently customers—or former customers—will all have to learn to live with this depressing fact of life.

Despite Mr. Kanner's pessimism, another solution seems possible—using the adjustment letter intelligently as a vital element in building goodwill. Here are four principles which govern its intelligent use:

1. Every complaint or claim, no matter how trivial it seems, is important to the person who makes it.

2. It therefore requires a prompt answer or acknowledgment.

3. The answer should be factual, courteous, and fair.

4. Above all else, it should not argue or take a critical attitude. Remember, instead, an old Italian proverb: One good word quenches more heat than a bucket of water.

Naturally, the adjustment letter will reflect the company's attitude toward claims. In general, there are three policies in effect concerning the granting of claims:

1. *The customer is always right;* therefore, all claims are granted. This policy is used by only a few firms at present who deal in expensive merchandise for an extremely reputable clientele.

2. *Grant adjustments wherever the claim seems fair.* This is by far the most widely used policy toward claims. It offers the advantage of letting each case be decided on its merits, and it avoids committing the company to a single policy regarding adjustments.

3. *Caveat emptor—Let the buyer beware!* He or she bought the goods and can assume the responsibility; therefore, no claims are granted. No reputable firm can afford to adopt such an unfair policy.

Unless there are peculiar problems connected with the particular business, the second policy outlined above is the most effective one.

But regardless of what the policy is, correspondents have a special obligation in handling adjustments to make the policy clear, to apply it to the situation at hand, and to emphasize its fairness and consistency. For that reason, vague statements like "company policy prevents our doing this" should be replaced by specific explanations against the broad background of a company policy which is applied impartially. A company which operates from principle rather than expediency, from policy rather than partiality, has gone a long way toward winning customer acceptance of its fairness.

Writers of adjustment letters should always realize that they are handling delicate situations. The customers are disgruntled and probably believe sincerely that they have very real grievances, whether they have or not. The aim of adjusters should be to make the readers see that they are trying to be fair. But they must steer a straight course between the two extremes of sympathizing too much with claimants (and thus making them believe that their grievances are indeed greater than they originally thought) and, on the other hand, of seeming to argue or to accuse customers of making unjust claims.

More than any other quality, the adjustment writer needs a sensitivity not only to the meanings of words but also to their connotations and overtones. The little boy who wrote home from summer camp to say "I'm glad I'm not homesick like all the boys who have dogs are" was too young to recognize that language carries unstated meanings and unspoken implications. Actually, claim letters used to be called "complaint letters," which they are, but the connotation of "complaint" is too harsh to be used in the reply. Similarly, the writer of adjustment letters ought to avoid such phraseology as *you state* or *you claim* or *we cannot understand,* because such phrases antagonize the reader; nor should the writer use such words as *failure, breakdown,* or *poor results,* because they add extra weight to the reader's belief that the product is inferior. Instead of saying, "You claim that our heater is no good," the trained adjuster will write, "Thank you for telling us of your experience with our heater."

Test your own reaction to the following negative letter:

Dear Mr. Sinclair:

We cannot comply with your claim for an adjustment on the radio you purchased from us.

In rejecting your request, we want to emphasize that we never make adjustments on merchandise after the customer has kept it three days. You state that the radio was marred when it reached you, but our final inspection showed it was in good condition when we sent it. Unfortunately our policy prohibits our making any adjustment in this case.

Sincerely yours,

Instead of this negative approach, the letter should explain in a matter-of-fact way the details of the situation. In short, it should be expository rather than argumentative in tone.

Granting the Adjustment

In trying to develop a way of thinking that should pervade letters that grant adjustments, writers would do well to remember the example set by Corning Glass Works. After manufacturing 360,000 electric coffee percolators (Model E-1210) in 1974, Corning learned that the handles on some were coming unstuck because of a faulty epoxy. The company might have tried to keep publicity about what was happening to a minimum, while hoping that its reputation wouldn't be too seriously injured. Instead, before the Consumer Product Safety Commission decided whether the percolators presented a serious hazard, Corning voluntarily launched a massive media campaign to recall the pots. The aim of the campaign was to earn consumer respect, and the overwhelmingly favorable mail received from consumers indicates that it was on the right track.

The moral of the Corning experience would go something like this: If one makes a mistake, owns up to it, and takes quick action to correct it, one will ultimately stand taller among the people who witnessed what happened.

Actually, because the letter granting an adjustment says "yes," it should be fairly easy to write. One must remember, however, that its ultimate purpose is not just to grant the adjustment but to retain the goodwill and the business of a disgruntled customer. Combine the goodwill-building objective with the fact that there doesn't appear to be any one best way of writing such a letter, and you discover a bit of challenge in writing an effective adjustment-grant letter.

Skilled adjustment correspondents disagree about both the arrangement and the content of such letters. The disagreement, however, centers around two predominant schools of thought. The first school is more positive and appears to be becoming the more popular approach. It follows this pattern:

1. Grant the adjustment.

2. Make any necessary explanation.

3. Resell the product, the service, and/or the company.

A letter following this pattern would directly present in the opening the news in which the reader is most interested. An explanation would follow, after which one would move to convince the reader that the likelihood of a recurrence is minimal. Information about a specific change in your operations or an assurance of increased vigilance are just two of the ways in which you might work toward regaining your reader's faith in your product or service and company. The logic for accentuating the positive and eliminating expressions of regrets and apologies is summed up by the old saying, "Actions speak louder than words." Telling the reader what you have done to reduce the chances of a similar mishap should be more encouraging than numerous words of sorrow. The following letters exemplify the application of this pattern to granting adjustments:

Dear Mr. Middlefield:

You're quite right in expecting merchandise from this store to be in perfect condition, and that's why we are sending you a brand new replacement for your Finetone Radio on Thursday.

Apparently some slip-up in inspection caused the problem, and you did us a favor by calling it to our attention. We have taken steps to reduce the likelihood of this happening again.

For six years you've patronized our store. We still desire to make every transaction satisfactory to you. If it isn't, we'll make it right, as you now know.

Sincerely,

The second letter responds to an irate customer who had recently purchased a range from a store but had not been able to get a defective timer replaced. As the letter unaccusingly explains, the writer and the repairperson had tried but had simply been unable to make contact with the customer.

Dear Mrs. Kotter:

A repairperson will be sent to your home as soon as you let us know when you want the repair done. Just call me personally at 965-6205 so that we may arrange a time that is convenient to you.

In the 20 years that we have done business with Tippex, we have found them to be very reliable in both product quality and dealer service. They again demonstrated this reliability by sending your new timer by express when they learned of your need. After receiving the part, our service representative stopped by your house on October 9 at 1:00 P.M. and again on October 14 at 10:30 A.M. But there was no one there. I then telephoned your home several times but was also unable to get in touch with you. Even with the best of intentions, such things will happen occasionally. However, we are now expecting your call and will dispatch a service representative as soon as we receive word from you.

On this visit the representative will also check your range completely and answer any questions you may have about its use. After this service check, it should provide you with many years of dependable service.

Sincerely,

The major difference between the first approach, exemplified in the preceding letters, and the second one that some adjusters prefer is the insertion of an apology for what happened. Proponents of this approach feel that an apology is advisable in most cases and mandatory when considerable inconvenience has resulted from the error; when we are dealing with important, perhaps confidential matters; or when a mistake is unexplainable. They write from the premise that "whenever we make a mistake, we should say that we're sorry for it, and we owe the customer a reasonably complete explanation of what happened." The following version of the letter to Mr. Middlefield and the letter on page 135 typify the writing of the second school of thought.

Dear Mr. Middlefield:

We're sorry that the radio you purchased from us was unsatisfactory. You have every right to expect merchandise from this store to be in perfect condition, and we appreciate your telling us of this experience.

Our shipping department makes every effort to see that every piece of merchandise is thoroughly inspected before it is sent out. Unfortunately, your radio was not inspected because of the negligence of one of our temporary employees.

We expect to receive another shipment of Finetone Radios tomorrow, and on Thursday we shall send you a new radio to replace the one you have.

Your patronage of our store during the past six years has been greatly appreciated. We want you to know that we value your friendship highly, and, for that reason, we wish to make each transaction satisfactory to you. If it is not, we hope you will inform us, as you did this time, so that we may make an equitable adjustment.

Yours very truly,

Probably the best resolution of the debate on what to stress in letters granting adjustments would come from a recognition of situational variables. While many cases would be suitably handled by accentuating the positive corrective measures that regain goodwill, some situations will also call for a sincere apology. But if you decide that a case warrants an apology, include it without vividly depicting the inconvenience or trouble for which you are apologizing. If you too clearly rehash the suffering experienced by the reader, your efforts to regain goodwill may backfire. Rather than overemphasizing the agony that your product or service caused in the past, try to project an optimistic look toward what it is capable of doing in the future.

Refusal of Adjustment

Much more difficult is the refusal of an adjustment, which may be defined as any letter that does not grant the original claim. A partial adjustment may be made, but if it does not comply with the request, from the customer's viewpoint, it is still a refusal of adjustment. The correspondent who is frequently called upon to refuse claims might well take as a text the Biblical injunction that "a soft answer turneth away wrath"; there is no better advice for the refusal of adjustment. If a "soft answer" is the tone to be given such a letter, its contents will usually be as follows:

THE CONTINENTAL BANK
WINCHESTER, MASSACHUSETTS 01890

January 8, 1971

Mr. Eugene Gaston
76 Pond Road
Woburn, Massachusetts 01801

Dear Mr. Gaston:

I certainly appreciate your writing to me about the fact that your last two bank statements have been sent to you in envelopes which were unsealed. I am especially sorry that this happened to one of our oldest depositors.

If there is one thing that Continental Bank insists on, it is having our employees take every precaution to see that the financial affairs of our depositors are kept absolutely confidential.

I am grateful to you for calling this matter to our attention and for your fairness concerning the situation. We have taken every precaution to see that this does not occur again.

Sincerely yours,

Seth L. Everett
Cashier

SLE:CLR

1. An attempt to get on common ground with the reader by agreeing with him or her in some way

2. A clear explanation of the situation from the adjuster's point of view

3. A complete refusal of adjustment or a statement of a partial adjustment

4. A reference to something positive that might help to maneuver the reader's mind away from the disappointment resulting from the refusal

Such a letter may require a great deal of tact and self-control from the writer. The customer may have emotionally expressed criticism of the product and the company. When we investigate the situation and find that it's not the company but the customer who is at fault, we may be tempted to write back with a "ha ha, you turkey" attitude. We must do whatever we can to suppress this temptation. No good would come from making the customer feel like a shamed, naughty child. Instead, we should proceed under the assumption that the customer didn't know something (in which case we would rationally inform him or her of whatever it is) or simply made a mistake (as all human beings are prone to do from time to time). Notice how the following letter tactfully and positively refuses to accept a returned dress that had been bought on sale.

Dear Mrs. Reynolds:

Thank you for your letter of November 12. You are right to expect a dress by Galatoi to fit perfectly. The ultimate goal at Godchaux's is to provide its clientele with the finest in fashion at reasonable prices accompanied by the best service we can offer. When a customer feels this goal hasn't been met, we want to hear about it.

Your letter noted the $169.95 sale price, which represents a $100.00 reduction from the original $269.95 at which the dress was marked. We have found that the only way we can offer such major price reductions to our customers is to eliminate the cost of returns. We attempt to communicate this policy during sales by posting it on cash registers and receipts. The best we can do in this case, therefore, is to invite you to take advantage of our expert alterations department, free of charge.

You should receive your dress, postage-paid, within three days of this letter's arrival. Then, if you can get to the store during the week of November 22 to 26, you can accomplish two objectives. You can be fitted and have your Galatoi tailored to your most exacting specifications, and you can take advantage of our Christmas-Shopping-Spree sale. This annual event offers markdowns of 20 to 30 percent off our regular stock and is advertised only by mail to our preferred customers. We hope you'll take advantage of these substantial savings.

Sincerely,

One of the most difficult situations requiring a refusal of adjustment occurs when customers take unjustified discounts on their bills. Suppose, for example, that your firm has a policy of granting a 2 percent discount for bills paid within 10 days. One of your customers has paid a $600 bill three weeks later but has taken a $12 discount and has protested angrily when you billed him for the $12. Obviously, in this situation it is not the amount, but the principle, which should count. Here is the way one correspondent handled this delicate situation:

Dear Mr. Leavengood:

Thank you for your letter of November 12. I appreciate your giving us an opportunity to explain a situation which might have led to a misunderstanding if you had not written.

As you know, we have had a long-standing policy of permitting a 2 percent discount to customers who pay their bills within 10 days of the date of their bills. We maintain this policy because it enables us to effect similar savings by paying our own bills promptly. Actually, then, we pass our savings on to our own customers as a reward for their promptness.

Since we make no savings when our customers do not pay within the prescribed time, we must adhere rigidly to our principle. Actually, the amount of $12 is not in itself a major issue, but in fairness to all our customers, we maintain a consistent policy. I think you would rightly object if we granted certain terms to other customers and different ones to you.

Now that you have the facts in this situation, I am sure that you will see the fairness of our bill for $12. We want you and all our other customers to take advantage of our discount policy, but we want to treat everybody fairly and consistently. To do so, we have to follow our principle, and I feel sure you will agree that this is the only just and equitable method of operating.

I am grateful to you for writing to me because I realize that only by frank discussion can our companies work together for their mutual benefit.

Sincerely yours,

No exact formula will solve the problem of writing effective adjustments. Whether the claim is granted entirely, partially, or not at all, correspondents must seek to:

1. Convince readers that they are being treated fairly

2. Gain their confidence in the products, services, or policies of the company

3. Retain their goodwill

It may be helpful, at this point, to review the entire process of granting or refusing a claim. We can do this best by posing another Letter Problem to which we offer specific solutions for classroom discussion. Remember, as you read the problem, that generally the policy of the company for which the correspondent works will determine whether claims are granted or refused; in this instance, so that we may illustrate both types of letters, we are assuming that company policy is sufficiently flexible so that we can say either "yes" or "no" to the claim.

LETTER PROBLEM 2: Adjusting a Claim

You are one of three adjusters for the Bleakowen Department Store, and you have received the following letter:

> Gentlemen and Ladies:
>
> On March 26, I purchased a size 14 tweed coat for my daughter in your Junior Miss Department. For this coat, which my daughter wanted for Easter, I paid $42.75.
>
> One week after Easter, you advertised this same coat on sale in the *Morning Chronicle* for $29.95. It seems to me that it is outrageous for you to charge almost thirteen dollars more for a coat just because it is purchased ten days before your sale, which I couldn't have known anything about. And anyway, we needed the coat for Easter.
>
> I expect you to send me a credit slip for the difference in price; otherwise I'll never do business with your store again.
>
> Sincerely yours,
> Amanda E. Lewis
> (Mrs. J. E. Lewis)

In the past, the store has been quite careful to avoid adjustments on merchandise purchased prior to major holidays such as Christmas and Easter, which have always been followed by major sales.

After checking on Mrs. Lewis's record, you find that she has been a good customer for nine years, has bought substantial amounts from Bleakowen's, and has paid her bills promptly.

You discuss Mrs. Lewis's letter with two other people in your department, and it becomes apparent that there is disagreement about two main points:

1. Whether to grant or refuse her request

2. How the letter should be organized to do either of these things

Here are the pros and cons of these two points as they emerge in the discussion:

1. Whether to grant or refuse the request:
   "Why should Bleakowen's risk losing a good customer for a mere $12.80, which is actually what Mrs. Lewis wants?"

   "A lot of other customers just as good as Mrs. Lewis bought coats before Easter. Just because they didn't ask for a refund, are we going to ignore them?"

   "Mrs. Lewis is just one customer. What difference does it make if we keep her happy for a mere $12.80? Tell her we've made an exception in her case, but that we'll never do it again."

   "This sets a dangerous precedent. If you grant Mrs. Lewis's request, she's going to tell all her friends her daughter got a new Easter coat at sale prices."

2. How to organize the letter:
   "When someone like Mrs. Lewis writes in to us, the first thing she wants in an answer is a direct reply to her question 'What are you going to do?'—and the letter should inform her of our decision in the first paragraph without beating about the bush."

   "The way to get her to accept a decision is to give reasons first and then the decision."

(This analysis is intended to provide insight into the variety of factors and methods which can have some bearing on just one letter-writing situation. Actually, most of these questions would be answered by well-established policy.) Your department head then tells all three of you to write the best letter possible to grant or refuse Mrs. Lewis's request.
Here are the results:

Granting Her Request

Dear Mrs. Lewis:

Since we want all our customers to know that our reputation has been built on fair dealing, we are crediting your account with $12.80, as you requested.

Your letter certainly struck a responsive note with us. You see, we disliked the price change almost as much as you did . . . but for a different reason. Our Easter coats were such an outstanding value in quality and workmanship that they were worth every cent of the pre-Easter price; but because we needed space so badly, we had to sell them fast. Hence the lower price a week later.

As you said, "we needed the coat for Easter," and Bleakowen's is pleased that you had it. For your patronage, we are truly grateful.

Sincerely,

Refusing Her Request (A matter-of-fact solution)

Dear Mrs. Lewis:

Your reaction at reading about the reduced price on your daughter's Easter coat was certainly natural. But may we explain?

Bleakowen's always offers sales after holidays such as Christmas and Easter—and always will. But customers like you who buy before the holidays have the advantage of far wider selection and of enjoying their purchases for the holiday itself. For these privileges, they pay a little more—but for your daughter to have the coat for Easter, the difference was certainly worth it.

We're sorry we can't grant your request for credit on the difference in price. To do so would be inconsistent with our policy of treating every one of our customers alike.

We hope that you will agree that being fair is an important part of providing customer satisfaction.

Sincerely,

Refusing Her Request (A more original approach)

Dear Mrs. Lewis:

When I read your letter about the Easter coat, I couldn't help but think of another time of the year when similar things happen—Christmas.

I got to thinking about how we all go out and buy a tree for five or ten or even twenty dollars from some corner lot . . . and the day after Christmas the leftover trees aren't worth a cent.

But it was worth ten or twenty dollars, wasn't it, to have that tree for Christmas Eve and Christmas Day? And I think it was the same way with your daugher's Easter coat. Don't you?

We hope so, because we want to keep you as the good customer you are . . . and we want to keep the hundreds of other customers who enjoyed their Easter coats at Easter . . . by treating all of you alike.

Fair? We try to be. Won't you see it that way too?

Sincerely yours,

Which of these letters seems to you most **appropriate** to achieve its **purpose?** On what basis would you decide that an adjustment should (should not) be made in Mrs. Lewis's case? Write the letter you would send to **grant** or **refuse** her claim.

In concluding this problem, it is fair to point out that neither of the last two letters of refusal may convince Mrs. Lewis. At best, they are what we have called "salvage operations." But they do represent honest attempts to persuade a reader in a difficult situation.

■   ■   ■

Admittedly, much of the writing procedure in handling claims and adjustments is more or less routine; but it would be a mistake to conclude that the treatment of such situations must necessarily be stereotyped. We have constantly stressed the fact that writing in business offers opportunity for originality, creativity, and humor. As an example of how these qualities can help in situations which otherwise might become tense, we close this chapter with a classic interchange between Harry Bannister of radio station WWJ Detroit and L. E. Kaffer, then on the staff of the Palmer House. If there were the equivalent of a Hall of Fame for letters, these two would be in it. The situation occurred years ago; shortly after Mr. Bannister had stayed overnight at the Palmer House, he received a letter from Mr. Kaffer telling him that "two woolen blankets, replacement value of $8 each, were missing from the room you occupied" and asking Mr. Bannister to look through his luggage when unpacking since "guests frequently, we find, in their haste inadvertently place such items in their effects and, of course, return same when discovered." Instead of losing his temper, Mr. Bannister used his sense of humor as the basis for the following rather devastating reply:

My dear Mr. Kaffer:

I am desolated to learn, after reading your very tactful letter of September 1, that you actually have guests at your hostelry who are so absent-minded as to check out and include such slight tokens of your esteem as wool blankets (replacement value of $8.00 each) when repacking the other necktie and the soiled shirt.

By the same token, I suppose that passengers on some of our leading railroads are apt to carry off a locomotive or a few hundred feet of rails when disembarking from the choo-choo on reaching their destinations. Or, a visitor to a big city zoo might might conceivably take away an elephant or a rhinoceros, concealing same in a sack of peanuts—after removing the nuts (replacement value of $.05).

In this particular case I may be of slight assistance to you in running down the recalcitrant blankets. As I had a lot of baggage with me, I needed all the drawer space you so thoughtfully provide in each room. The blankets in question occupied the bottom drawer of the dresser, and I wanted to place some white shirts (replacement value of $3.50 each) in that drawer, so I lifted said blankets and placed them on a chair. Later, the maid came in and I handed the blankets (same blankets and same replacement value) to her, telling her in nice, gentlemanly language to get them the hell out of there.

If you'll count all the blankets in your esteemed establishment, you'll find that all are present or accounted for—unless other absent-minded guests have been accommodated at your emporium in the meanwhile. That's the best I can do.

                              Very truly yours,
                              Harry Bannister

P.S. Have you counted your elevators lately?

To this, **Mr. Kaffer** replied as follows:

Dear Mr. Bannister:

I wish to thank you for one of the most delightful letters it has been my pleasure to read in my entire business career. It would take a radio executive to compose a letter that would cause Damon Runyon, Mark Hellinger, and a lot of other writers radio might hire, to blush with futile envy. My sincere congratulations to you.

Yes, Mr. Bannister, we do a lot of counting around here. I've counted the elevators—and they're right where they should be, and operating, every one of them. What I want to count now is more important to me. I want to continue counting you as a friend of the Palmer House.

You, in your executive capacity, must of necessity supervise countless counts of so-called "listening audiences," "program polls," and all the bothersome promotions that annoy countless people in the middle of their dinner, or get them out of bed on cold nights to answer telephone queries. I shall assume, therefore, that you have naturally realized that you were most unfortunately a victim of a machine-like routine made necessary by the very vastness of an organization so well managed as the Palmer House.

There are a lot of folk in this merry world that would, as you so naively put it, "carry off locomotives, hundreds of feet of rails, and pack away an elephant or a rhinoceros." Just put a few ash trays, towels, blankets, pillows, glassware, and silverware in your public studios and reception rooms and see what happens.

Twenty-five thousand dollars' worth of silverware (actual auditors' "replacement value") is carried away annually by our "absent-minded" guests. A similar total (in "replacement value") is cherished annually by sentimental guests who like our linens as a memento of their visit to the Palmer House. They even go religious on us and take along the Gideon Bibles to the number of several thousand yearly. Nothing is sacred it would seem.

And so it goes. We are sorry, Mr. Bannister, that you were bothered as a result of a maid's mistake. Her lapse of memory started a giant wheel of routine. I am, in a way, happy the incident happened, because it gave me a chance to read your letter. It was a swell missive.

As the song says, and WWJ has no doubt played it "countless" times, "Let's Call the Whole Thing Off." And there's another song you also use, "Can't We Be Friends?"

Very sincerely yours,
L. E. Kaffer

So long as letters such as these can be written within the province of claims and adjustments, there is no need for further refutation of the charge that business letters must necessarily be dull and routine. Originality, humor, and cleverness can play an important role in any letter. In closing, we might well adopt Mr. Kaffer's idea of the theme song; for claims and adjustments, our theme should certainly be, "A soft answer turneth away wrath."

EXERCISES

1. How would you have written the following claim letters?
   a. I'm sorry I ever subscribed to your magazine, *The Office*. Every month I receive the current issue at the end of the month. All other publications I get are mailed at the beginning of the month or at the end of the previous month—why isn't yours? What good is stale news? And I never even received the April issue. I hope you have a good answer for your poor service, and I hope you aren't going to say it's the Post Office's fault. They can't be blamed for everything, you know.
   b. The minicomputer we purchased from you last month has done us more harm than good. It has sent out bills to customers who owe us nothing and failed to bill customers who do. Also, we attempted to transfer some of our correspondence files to the computer's memory, just like your sales representative said we could, but with miserable results. We got the files into memory all right, but then couldn't retrieve them. Two secretaries spent their valuable time playing around with these computer files for two days when they could have been attending to their secretarial duties. At first they viewed this computer thing as a challenge, but they ended up feeling very frustrated and not wanting to ever have anything to do with the computer. And your sales representative made such a strong selling point of the fact that the secretaries would love how the computer relieved them of drudgery and was their friend! With friends like this, who needs enemies?
   c. I know that tie-dyed clothing is considered fashionable by some people, but I don't really think a white dress shirt with the tie-dyed look of blue ink down the front could be considered desirable by anyone. But that is what I have, thanks to your pen. Although I think a fountain pen writes better than a ballpoint, I guess I should have stuck with ballpoint. My new fountain pen, manufactured by your company, is responsible for my blue and white shirt. I had the pen in my pocket and somehow the ink leaked out. And the cap was on tightly. I don't want your crummy pen or my tie-dyed shirt. What I want is a refund of $10 and a new white shirt.

2. Based on the following information and on any other data you want to invent, make a list of the possible adjustments for the claims presented in Exercise 1. Write a letter for each of the three situations, using one or more of the solutions you have devised.

   a. The magazine is mailed from New York as third-class mail at the beginning of each month. First-class mailing can be provided for an additional $5 a year.

   b. A service representative was dispatched immediately to the Calrox Company. He discovered that the computer had been programmed entirely wrong. A check with the sales representative revealed that Calrox hadn't wanted to purchase the commercial software package available from the computer manufacturer. Calrox had insisted that they had an employee who knew programming and could easily get the computer working.

   c. This is the first report the pen company has had of their pen leaking. They would like to examine it, in addition to making a fair adjustment for the customer.

3. Pick a product or incident you feel justified in complaining about. Preferably this should be a recent occurrence; but if necessary, a past one will do. Write the claim letter. After your instructor has critiqued it, make any necessary revisions. Mail the letter if the claim is a current one, keeping a copy for your files.

4. Assume you are the recipient of the claim letter written for Exercise 3. Write two adjustment letters—one granting the adjustment, the other refusing the adjustment.

5. If you receive a reply to the claim letter you mailed in Exercise 3, analyze it, noting these points:

   a. How many days did you have to wait for a response?

   b. Was a full or partial adjustment made? Or was the adjustment refused?

   c. What pattern was used?

   d. What was your reaction to the letter?

6. For the following situations, write an appropriate claim letter.

   a. Three months ago you renewed your one-year subscription to *Management Today* and have your canceled check to prove it. You are still receiving renewal notices; and on the mailing label of the issue you received today, you noticed that the code indicates your subscription will expire in July. You think your one-year subscription period runs through October. Furthermore, you never received the November issue, and apparently some articles of great interest to you were in that issue.

   b. You are office manager of the Cornwall Construction Company's new Philadelphia office. This office is designed to be the company's East Coast headquarters, and you were given a free hand in furnishing it. After much investigation and product comparison, you decided to purchase all furniture and equipment from S. Webster, one of the country's leading manufacturers of office furnishings. Webster's local representative is Harmon Brothers, with whom you have been dealing directly. When the purchase contract for $65,000 was signed on February 4, Harmon's sales representative promised delivery on April 15. The products had to be special ordered, for they were in a color combination not ordinarily manufactured by Webster. On April 10 you received a telephone call from Harmon informing you that there would be a delay of five days in the delivery of your order. Three days later Harmon told you that delivery would be delayed another week—something about a backlog of orders at the plant.

(1) At this point, do you feel a claim letter might be justified? Or a telephone call?

(2) Would you contact Harmon or Webster?

The furniture finally arrives today, May 1. But it is the wrong color, and several of the desks have deep scratches. You are now very angry with Harmon for not inspecting the furniture before delivering it to you and with Webster because they are the manufacturer. After talking to Harmon on the phone, you decide to temporarily use this furniture because you have a newly hired office staff that must begin work.

(3) What attempts at a settlement of this problem will you undertake now? Who will you write to? What adjustment do you consider fair?

(4) Write the appropriate letter(s).

   c. You own a pottery business, Clay's Clay, located in a resort town. Your usual raw materials supplier is Frogel & Co., from whom you last purchased materials on January 23. On February 18 you mailed Frogel your $400 check as complete payment for this purchase. Your display at an arts and crafts fair on February 28 has resulted in a buyer from a major New York department store ordering a large quantity of pottery, contingent upon your ability to fill the order in two weeks. This means you will have to work night and day, beginning immediately. You call Frogel for a rush delivery of $700 worth of materials. The sales clerk refuses to authorize this purchase on credit, however. Their records indicate you still owe $400, and company policy does not permit account balances over $600, which yours would be with this additional purchase. Your explanation that you have already paid the $400 carries no weight; Frogel's owner is out of town, and the sales clerk has no authority to do anything about this "supposed" error. You end up purchasing the required raw materials from another supplier with whom you also have an account but whose prices are much higher than Frogel's. You are able to fill the New York order, but at much less profit than you had anticipated. What will you say in your claim letter to Frogel?

7. Your job now is to write the adjustment letters for the situations described in Exercise 6. In *a*, the facts are correct as stated by the subscriber. In *b*, Webster had been struck by its fabrication workers for two weeks. The proper color furniture had been manufactured but somehow had been shipped to the wrong customer. In *c,* a clerk at Frogel & Co. erred in not crediting Clay's Clay for the $400 payment. Handle these three situations in the fairest possible way, taking whatever action you think is reasonable and feasible. Remember, you want to keep your customers' goodwill, but you also don't want to go bankrupt doing so.

8. For the following situation, write two letters granting the adjustment. The first letter should be written according to the pattern described on page 132. The second letter should follow the second pattern described, in which an apology is inserted.

Charles Modem purchased one of our electric shavers by mail. It worked well for a month but then started making a loud buzzing noise. Now the motor is completely dead. Mr. Modem lives in a rural area and cannot bring the shaver to one of our authorized repair shops. He mentioned in his claim letter that he owns several of our other products and considers us to be manufacturers of durable, reliable products.

   a. Which pattern do you personally prefer?

   b. How would you decide which pattern to use?

9. In the following situations, you cannot grant the adjustments desired by the customers. Write the refusal letters, being as tactful and positive as you can.

   a. Your furniture store recently had its yearly clearance sale. All merchandise was advertised and marked "As is"; all sales were cash and carry and final. Prices were reduced from 50 to 75 percent to make room for new merchandise. You have just received a letter from Lawrence Fernsler in which he describes the tear in the arm of the chair he purchased at the sale. He says the tear wasn't there when he bought the item and wants his money refunded.

   b. You have received a letter from Tom Adams about our company's detergent removing not only the stain on his bright green shirt but also the color. He wants us to replace the shirt, which was "ruined by a mislabeled product which ignores the fact that many men are unfamiliar with the power of detergents." Actually, the instructions on the bottle contain step-by-step instructions, the first of which says, "Test for colorfastness by applying a small amount of Spot-Out on an inside seam."

   c. You receive a watch from Alice Lewis to be repaired under the terms of the one-year guarantee. The guarantee specifically excludes free repair of a watch that has been dropped or tampered with. The crystal of Ms. Lewis's watch has been pried off and jammed back on; therefore, you cannot repair it for free. You will, however, give her an estimate of the repair charge if she desires.

9
CREDIT LETTERS

Someone has said that "credit" is an abstract word—until you have to borrow money. Certainly this word, which derives from the Latin *credo,* "I believe," has many different connotations for economists, business people, and average citizens. Some business people kiddingly used to speak of the "three C's of credit—character, capacity, and character." Along the same lines, J. P. Morgan remarked that "credit is 99 percent character"; and Alexandre Dumas humorously referred to it as "using other people's money."

Such comments and definitions are interesting; but if we are to get a useful idea of what credit means, as applied to correspondence, we should think of it in simpler terms:

1. To the user of credit, it is a means by which he or she may have something now and pay for it later.

2. To the grantor of credit, it is an estimate of someone's ability and willingness to pay later.

These definitions, oversimplified as they may be, underscore the two salient factors relevant to credit letters—the primary importance of a sound credit reputation and the necessity of rating someone's ability to pay.

Students tend to regard the whole process of granting or refusing credit as remote from their own lives. To drive home the immediate importance of credit, we suggest thinking for a moment about the answers to these questions:

How much of your college education are you and/or your parents paying for? How is the rest paid for?

Do you now own a car? Or do you want to own one in the future? How much

147

of a down payment can you make on it? Where does the remainder of the money come from?

What is your attitude toward borrowing? Is it a "good" or a "bad" thing to do? What has determined this attitude?

The last questions are particularly pertinent because all of us have value judgments about going into or staying out of debt.

Regardless of our personal judgments, however, it is no exaggeration to say that credit has become a major element in the American economic way of life. Without it, our economic system cannot survive. One essential element must be added to this discussion of the "have now, pay later" concept—*the ability to obtain information as the basis on which credit will be granted or refused.*

In the last few years consumers have become increasingly familiar with the credit-investigating industry. Until the Fair Credit Reporting Act (FCRA) of 1970, they actually knew very little about this multimillion-dollar business that locked details of their personal lives in computer banks. Acting upon the rights guaranteed by the FCRA, however, consumers have found that the files are often incorrect or misleading.

It is not our purpose here to condemn or defend the credit-information-collection industry. We should, however, be aware of the public's attitude toward this process, the original purpose of which was to protect businesses from bad debts. Furthermore, people who are or might one day get involved in the credit-extension process should be aware of the government's past and likely future responses to public opinion.

The fact of the matter is that the public's cry of disenchantment has been loud enough to result in several recent pieces of legislation, and Uncle Sam gives no indication that business has seen the last of the federal regulation of credit. The 1974 Chapter 4 "Credit Billing" amendment to the Truth-in-Lending Act, the 1975 Privacy Act, and the 1975 Equal Credit Opportunity Act have all had explicit and implicit significance for credit-related procedures. Where these acts and the FCRA affect specific types of written business communication will be noted in this chapter and the next one as specific types are discussed. Our point now is that in order to force a few companies to recognize their responsibilities to the subjects of credit investigations, all businesses must now contend with a good deal more red tape and expense than were required a few years ago.

The reactions of people in business to these new federal ground rules for credit have been less than optimistic, to put it mildly. Many predict that the cost of adherence to these laws will ultimately have to be absorbed by the consumer. Some suggest that as the pendulum of power in the billing relationship swings to the credit user, businesses will have little choice but to make the qualifications for getting credit more stringent. Regardless of the ultimate impact of these laws upon consumers, one point remains certain for anyone in business engaged in the credit process: It is a very dynamic field that *demands* the most scrupulous behavior of its occupants and *promises* harsh penalties to those who don't adhere to the letter of the law.

THE APPLICATION

The most appropriate place to begin our two-chapter discussion of credit extension and collection procedures would be at the inception of the process—the application. And right at the start of the process, we find a federal shadow safeguarding the rights of all applicants. This shadow takes the form of the Equal Credit Opportunity Act, which became effective October 28, 1975. The general intent of this act is to ban discrimination against any applicant on the basis of sex or marital status. It is actually an amendment to the Consumer Credit Protection Act, but it applies to business as well as consumer credit. Among the things that creditors are forbidden to do are the following: assign values to sex or marital status in a credit scoring plan, ask about birth control practices or child-rearing intentions, fail to consider alimony or child support under an agreement or court decree in the same manner as other income, discount income because of sex or marital status, and end credit or impose new conditions because of a change in marital status. Since the value of more detailed coverage of this act here would be questionable, we will conclude this reference with two suggestions. First, any creditor, large or small, must become familiar with this act. Second, applicants should know their rights guaranteed by law to assure compliance by businesses with whom they might wish to deal on credit.

Given that the conscientious and/or cautious creditor is going to respect the rights of applicants, how would a person or business go about applying for credit? Because starting the engine of the credit process is one of the simplest stages, our discussion of it will be brief. Consumers simply fill out an application form in the vast majority of cases. Many businesses do likewise when applying for credit from other businesses.

On some occasions, however, a business may apply through a letter accompanied by appropriate financial statements. In such cases, the letter's organization would closely resemble the form or plan suggested for routine inquiries in Chapter 7. Since such a request is common, one should be direct and ask for credit at the start of the letter. The body of the letter would then be devoted to giving whatever information is not on the financial statements but is needed for a judgment of the applicant's creditworthiness. The close would include some goodwill-building comment that looks forward to the relationship that the writer is trying to establish through the letter. The letter that follows exemplifies this plan for requesting credit.

Gentlemen and Ladies:

Please consider opening a line of credit for my company with an initial limit of $1,000.

The enclosed recently compiled financial statements should give you an idea of our solvency. The companies listed below could serve as references to our repayment performance.

XYZ Manufacturing Company
8261 Aim Street
Krambo, California 94123

The Fahlgren Company
683 Van Ness
Filbert, California 93862

The Folse Frame Company
114 Elm Street
Thibodaux, Louisiana 70301

We are now putting together our first order, which we'll send after we hear from you.

Sincerely,

TYPES OF CREDIT AVAILABLE

Businesses offering credit to other businesses will differ in the terms of the credit agreement. Very often, however, the amount owed is due 30 days after the invoice date. Another very common part of such a business-to-business agreement is the opportunity to reduce the bill by 2 percent if the debtor pays within 10 days of the invoice date. Businesses which take advantage of this discount are, in effect, allowing their creditors to do the same on their bills.

In consumer credit there are also many different types of credit arrangements, but the four most basic types are listed below (although the terminology may vary from store to store and from place to place):

1. The regular or 30-day account. You will get statements monthly, and payment without finance charges is due within 10 to 30 days after billing.

2. The 90-day or budget account. Payable in equal installments, i.e., three equal installments in 90 days. No financing charge is made if the debt is paid within 90 days unless there is a default in any payment.

3. The revolving account. This type is a variant of the budget account which spreads out payments and new purchases over additional months, with interest charges assessed on unpaid balances.

4. Long-term installment accounts. The term usually runs 6 months in department stores and from 36 to 48 months with car dealers. Essentially, this arrangement is used for major purchases where payments (including finance charges) can be spread over a long period.

LETTERS RELATED TO THE EXTENSION OF CREDIT

Many of the interchanges of information related to the credit process are handled by phone or in person. Furthermore, credit bureaus have reduced the need for some types of letters related to extending credit. Despite these developments, however, the following four types are still used to an extent that would justify some coverage of them:

1. A letter acknowledging the customer's order or the application for credit and requesting that references or other information be sent

2. Letters requesting credit information from the references furnished

3. Letters from these references giving the credit information

4. The final letter to the customer
   a. Granting credit and explaining the terms
   b. Refusing credit

Of these four types, the first and the last are the most important; but since letters to and from credit references are still used by credit managers who want to get a thorough picture of an applicant's repayment habits, we will discuss them and their legal implications.

ACKNOWLEDGING APPLICATIONS FOR CREDIT

These acknowledgments respond to two situations: (1) when a letter requesting credit is received or (2) when an order is received from someone who has not yet established credit. In either event, the letter of acknowledgment is primarily a sales promotion letter with stress on sincere appreciation of the request for credit and on the kind of service you hope to render. Since the situation and specific company policy determine whether you get credit information direct from the customer, acknowledgments may include most or all of the following elements:

1. A statement welcoming the new customer or expressing appreciation for that first order

2. An explanation of the firm's credit policies

3. (If information is not obtained from a credit bureau) A request that credit references be sent or that an enclosed credit blank be filled out

4. (If you have requested credit information from the customer) An incentive to action emphasizing that the sooner the credit information is received, the sooner the applicant may receive the order

5. (If you have received satisfactory information from a credit bureau) A sales statement about service, quality of merchandise, or your future relationship

The first of the following letters requests credit information but also fills the first order. The second requests that a form be filled out so that the order may be shipped.

Dear Ms. Weldon:

We certainly appreciate the opportunity to do business with your firm that you have given us in your first order. Your expression of confidence is gratifying, and we will do everything in our power to live up to it.

Since you probably need this merchandise as soon as possible, we are shipping your order by express tomorrow. So that we can handle your future needs without delay, we'd appreciate your sending us your financial statement. Or if you prefer, just fill out and return the enclosed credit form.

This credit information will, of course, be kept confidential. We are looking forward to having you as a regular customer. May we have your credit information soon?

Sincerely yours,

Dear Mr. Barrett:

We greatly appreciate the order for $237.21 worth of canned goods which you placed with Mr. White, our representative in your territory.

Since this is our first transaction with you, we must ask you to fill out and return the enclosed blank from our credit department. This is part of our regular routine in handling all new accounts; the information you send us will, of course, be held in confidence.

Your account will be opened and your order will be shipped as soon as this information reaches us. It is our hope that this is the beginning of a long business relationship. We shall do our best to make it a pleasant and profitable one for you.

Sincerely yours,

The preceding discussion relates primarily to letters to businesses that have applied to other businesses for credit. Since consumers most often apply for credit by application form, it is unlikely that you'll need to request further information from them; so the first acknowledgment they would receive would be the letter that grants or refuses them credit.

REQUESTING CREDIT INFORMATION

As we mentioned earlier, requests for credit information are very often made by phone. Furthermore, credit bureaus relieve many companies of writing to other companies with whom applicants have done business. Letters, however, are still sometimes justified. Some credit executives, for example, like to know more than the simple fact that an applicant's past payment record wasn't bad enough to be reported to a credit bureau. And when an applicant has only recently moved to town, it may be less expensive to write the references than to call them.

When such letters are written, they would resemble in plan the letters of inquiry discussed in Chapter 7. Above all else they should be easy to answer. The questions asked should be specific rather than general. The customary procedure is to enclose a credit blank to be filled out. Where less detailed information is required, such a form as the following, with the credit applicant's name typed in, is used:

Gentlemen and Ladies:

We would very much appreciate your giving us the benefit of your experience with the _____ Company of _____. In applying for credit with us, they have given your name as a reference.

Please answer the questions on the form below and return this letter in the enclosed stamped envelope. Your reply will be kept confidential.

Sincerely,

How long has this company dealt with you? ....

The terms were ....

The amount now owing is $ ....

The highest credit you will extend is $ ....

The date of the last transaction is ....

Remarks ....

....

(Signed) ....

(Date) ....

GIVING CREDIT INFORMATION

The letter giving credit information should be factual and fair. In many cases forms, such as that in the preceding letter example, will obviate the need for writing a letter. However, when the inquirer hasn't included such a form, you'll need to don your composition cap and put together a response. A favorable reply to such a request for information is relatively easy to write. The following letter exemplifies the frank, concise approach that could be applied:

Gentlemen and Ladies:

Mr. Allen Eaton, 27 Broadway, Hurley, Indiana 47033, about whom you asked us on July 26, has always had a good credit rating with us. He has been a customer of ours for seven and a half years, and he has usually paid his bills on the first of the month following purchase. His credit limit with us has been $500.

Sincerely yours,
The Taft Brothers

When such a letter is generally positive with a few exceptions, try not to give the exceptions too much emphasis. Starting or ending a letter with mention of the few bad marks a person has on an otherwise good record would be giving the negative ideas more emphasis, by placement, than they deserve. Try your best to be completely fair to both parties, the subject and the recipient of your letter. Notice how the following letter concentrates on facts, subordinates the negative, and refrains from making a judgment about the applicant:

Dear Ms. Walters:

Mr. Arthur Kincade, the subject of your August 22 request for confidential information, has had an account with us for three years.

During that time, the maximum credit extended him was $500. He paid this seven-month-overdue balance in August of 1974. Since then his account has only once exceeded $400. His present balance is $85.70, currently due.

Since September of 1974, his purchases have averaged $113 per month, ranging from a low of $32 to a high of $350. His payments, during this same period, have varied from $83 to $231, averaging $116 per month. His checks have arrived regularly between the sixth and tenth of each month; and with few exceptions, he has cleared each billed amount within 30 to 40 days of the statement date.

We hope the facts provided here will help you in your evaluation of Mr. Kincade's credit. If we can provide you with other such reports in the future, let us know. We will be happy to do so.

Sincerely,

If you ever find yourself in the position of having to write a largely negative report on a credit applicant who is using your company as a reference, you'll have good reason to exercise considerable caution. Just as in the preceding examples, you'll want to be fair and report facts. You'll also, however, want to be especially careful not to make a subjective judgment about the applicant's creditworthiness or to transmit secondhand information—such as that which you might have gathered from other sources when you were considering the applicant for credit.

To do either of these things would earn you the title of "credit reporting agency" according to the Fair Credit Reporting Act of 1970. This law applies only to consumer credit and not to credit granted to businesses. As we'll see in the next section of this chapter, the title of credit reporting agency could subject you to unnecessary legal repercussions.

One final point might be made about giving credit information. Traditionally, some reference is made to the confidential nature of the information. Don't give this reference too much stress, as you would do if you made the mention of confidentiality the content of an entire sentence. Do so incidentally, with an adjective or a clause, as for example, "We are happy to provide this confidential information to you."

The following letter illustrates a cautious, objective approach to reporting negative information about an applicant. Notice how it sticks to firsthand, factual information and does not judge the subject of the letter by predicting his future credit performance.

> Dear Ms. Dupont:
>
> James Jones, the subject of your July 3 inquiry, has had an account with us for one year.
>
> His monthly purchases on credit averaged $110 during the first ten months of business with us. We are presently dealing with him on a cash basis only, because he fell behind in his payments after the first six months. Payments during the last half year have arrived an average of 2½ months after the due dates. The present balance of his account is $283.
>
> If we can provide you with such confidential information on any other applicants in the future, we will be glad to do so.
>
> Sincerely,

THE FINAL LETTER, GRANTING OR REFUSING CREDIT

Thus far, the letters we have discussed offer no very serious problems. But in the final letter, the credit manager must express, however indirectly, an estimate of the customer's willingness and capacity to pay later. If the opinion is favorable, the letter is comparatively easy to compose; but if the opinion is unfavorable and credit is refused, the most difficult of all business letters must be written. Because of the resulting difference in technique, each of these types is discussed separately.

The Letter Granting Credit

The letter granting credit is not merely a statement of terms and conditions; it is also a sales letter which tells the customer of the quality of the merchandise and of the excellence of the service the firm tries to give. It may be compared in its general tone to a note of welcome to a friend who has just arrived in the writer's city; it should welcome him or her and express the hope that the "visit" will be enjoyable and that he or she will take advantage of the many facilities the "city" offers. The general tone of welcome, of interest in the customer's welfare, and of willingness to serve is invaluable at the beginning of what the creditor hopes will be a long and pleasant business relationship. Notice the difference in cordiality in the following letters. By stressing negatives, the first appears to grant credit with apprehension and crossed fingers. The second employs a much more suitable optimistic tone.

Dear Mr. Jones:

In accordance with your request of May 11, we are granting you credit with a top limit of $500. Our bills are sent on the 16th of each month and are payable by the 10th of the next month. If you don't pay your balance by the 10th of each month, we charge 1½% interest. We hope you will enjoy shopping in our store.

Sincerely yours,

Dear Mr. Jones:

We are happy to grant your request of May 11 for a credit account with us. We welcome you as a charge customer, and we are genuinely interested in serving you in the friendly manner that has become a tradition at Portland's most modern store.

Bills, payable by the 10th of each month, are mailed on the 16th of each month and include all charges up to the 10th. Unpaid balances are subject to a finance charge of 1½% each month.

As a charge customer you will be given the opportunity to shop at all our sales before advertisements reach the general public. You will probably also want to take advantage of our shopping service, which enables you to shop by phone for the ultimate in effortless buying. A call to Miss Parker will give you this efficient service, and, of course, at no extra charge. All you need say now is, "Just charge it to my account."

The enclosed booklet will tell you of the hundreds of services offered for your convenience. We want you to use them because they will save you time and money. We hope that we may adequately express our appreciation for your patronage by being able to serve you efficiently for many years to come.

Sincerely,

The second letter is far more skillful than the first in expressing hope for the new relationship established. By indicating a determination to make it a good one, this letter goes far toward building goodwill at the very start. Usually the letter granting credit contains:

1. A granting of credit

2. A statement of terms

3. A sales talk on the type of service the company hopes to render

4. An expression of appreciation

Although the order of these parts may vary, all of them are generally present. The personality of the letter is as important as its contents; if the granting of the credit is friendly, cordial, and helpful in tone, the letter will be effective.

The Letter Refusing Credit

Correspondents customarily believe that the letter they are engaged in writing at any given time is the most difficult of all types of letters. The immediate problem before us always seems the most perplexing, but if we objectively considered what is the most difficult of all the usual types of business letters, there is little doubt that we would select the letter refusing credit. The mere refusal of the credit is not so difficult, although the implication that the applicant represents a poor risk is hardly a pleasant one. The problem in refusing credit arises from the intelligent writer's desire to make this letter something more than just a refusal. Far too many business people are content with a routine form letter starting with the unimaginative words, "This is to inform you that we are unable at this time to extend credit," and ending with a pious hope that things may be different at some indefinite time in the future.

What else should the writer try to do? The applicant has been judged so poor a risk that no credit can be granted. Why not let the whole matter end with a vague or indefinite refusal? That is obviously the easiest way out for the credit manager, but it is not the intelligent way. If the writer has thought out what he or she is trying to do in this letter, he or she is not refusing credit so much as *trying to get the applicant's business on a cash basis.*

There are perfectly sound arguments which can be used to convince customers that cash buying is to their own advantage. The credit manager can advance such incentives as a discount for cash, savings on interest charges, or the advantages of buying in small quantities for cash and thus keeping up-to-date merchandise in stock, or the pleasures of end-of-the-month freedom from bills, or the fact that cash buying over a period of time will establish a reputation so that credit may be granted in the future. Perhaps the applicant won't accept these suggestions; perhaps he or she can get credit from another source. But the alternatives for the writer of this type of letter are to refuse and stop there or to try to do something constructive. The intelligent correspondent will not be content to be negative; he or she will try to prevail upon the customer to buy for cash.

The specific content of letters refusing credit varies according to two aspects of the situation. It will vary by applicant, that is, according to whether you are refusing credit to a consumer or to another business. It will also vary according to the reason for the refusal. If you could not grant credit because of information the applicant provided, you would refuse in a manner different from that which you would use in a case where the refusal stemmed from information provided by others. Because of these distinct differences, our discussion of credit-refusal letters will be organized by customer and by reason.

CREDIT REFUSALS TO BUSINESSES

Perhaps because people in business live in a world of similar pressures and restrictions, they soon learn what actions on their part are appreciated by other business people. Mention was made earlier, for example, of the 2 percent discount which, when taken by customers, allows the creditors to do likewise on their own bills. The smart executive knows that punctuality in paying bills is the only way to keep open the lines of credit that are vital to the operation of a business in our society today. For one or both of the reasons stated above, very few businesses attempt to evade their credit obligations simply out of disinclination to pay. When we get bad credit reports or references on businesses, we'll find that most often these poor records result from the poor financial condition of the business. What this ultimately means, then, is that we can combine two of the categories above and treat them as one. In other words, we can talk about credit refusals *to businesses* as usually resulting from information *they provided*.

The preceding line of logic allows us to approach this type of refusal in a very frank manner. Since we can assume that we are not talking about the character or moral fiber of the business owner or credit executive, we can be more straightforward. Most people, business or otherwise, have found themselves, at one time or another, in a less-than-fully-desirable financial condition. To be told that this is the reason for the refusal of credit is easier to take than the idea that the business is a poor risk because of a demonstrated inclination to fudge on its obligations.

An outline of the content of such a letter, designed to refuse credit to a business while trying to secure its cash business, appears below:

1. Open on a fairly neutral note:
   a. Perhaps with an expression of appreciation for the application (being careful not to go overboard and, by so doing, imply that you will grant the credit).
   b. Perhaps with a reference to the nature of the order (if one accompanied the credit application).

2. Move into the explanation of the refusal.
   a. Try to show, through your wording and content, that you are concerned with the welfare of the applicant's firm.
   b. Try to avoid the tone of a lecture. This may be difficult, but try nonetheless.

3. Make the refusal briefly but clearly. Avoid harsh negative terms that give additional emphasis to this unpleasant part of the letter.

4. Verbally move the reader away from the refusal. Attempt to get an order on a cash basis by
   a. An offer of a cash discount, usually 2 percent.
   b. A suggestion that cash buying in smaller quantities will give a wider selection and more up-to-date stock.
   c. Talk of the extension of credit in the future when the financial condition of the applicant's company is sufficiently improved.

5. Project an optimistic look toward some aspect of the business interchange that hopefully will follow. This might be accomplished in conjunction with one of the substeps noted in step 4 above.

Notice how effectively one credit manager handled a difficult refusal, making no mention of the probable fact that Mr. Travis is a very poor credit risk because of the circumstances surrounding his new venture:

Dear Mr. Travis:

Thank you for your promptness in sending us the credit information we requested. We are glad to report that all your credit references spoke favorably of you as a businessperson.

The new store which you are opening in Bellport should eventually prosper, since yours is a thriving community. But its location within 20 miles of New York City does force you to compete with the larger stocks and lower prices of the metropolitan department stores so readily accessible to commuters from Bellport and similar communities. Because a large indebtedness might hamper your ability to meet such competition with the resources you have available, we must propose that we temporarily deal on a cash basis.

May we suggest, therefore, that you cut your order in half. Cash payment will entitle you to our 2 percent cash discount, a saving which you may pass on to your customers. By ordering frequently in small quantities, you will probably be better able to meet the competition of the New York stories because you will be keeping up-to-date merchandise on your shelves. Thus, through cash buying, you will establish your business on a sound basis that will enable you to establish lines of credit very easily.

The enclosed duplicate of your order will assist you in making your selection. Just check the items you wish and sign the order. Your merchandise will arrive C.O.D. within two days after our receipt of the order—in plenty of time for your opening sale.

Sincerely,

This credit manager took the very realistic point of view that half an order is better than none. To get it, several logical arguments were used. A comparison of the tone of this letter with that of the following letter shows how skillfully or ineptly credit can be refused.

Dear Ms. Haley:

Thank you for your order of February 16. We regret to state that our investigation of your credit standing shows that your firm is not a good credit risk.

We hope that you will understand our position in this matter, as we want your business, but we operate on so small a margin of profit that we dare not risk any credit losses.

You stated that 2,100 of our No. 14 cardboard containers would fill your needs for the next three months. In that case, we think we would be placing no hardship on you if we ask you to order C.O.D.

If you still want to place an order with us, we shall be glad to take care of it. As you know, our workmanship is better and our prices are lower than any of our competitors'.

Yours truly,

The writer of this letter appears determined to antagonize the reader with negative words like "not a good credit risk," "credit losses," and the presumptuous "we would be placing no hardship on you." The entire letter seems to be geared toward convincing the reader that the writer's company comprises people interested solely in their own welfare. Ms. Haley could quite easily conclude that she must have been crazy to have wanted to do business with them at all. This letter might serve as a reminder that even though we are refusing credit to a business, we are writing to a person. That person will make a decision as to whether there will be *any* future dealings, cash or otherwise, between that person's firm and ours. Whether you relate to that person like a human being or like a computer is therefore important.

CREDIT REFUSALS TO CONSUMERS

Refusing credit to consumers can be more difficult than refusing credit to a business. How explicit or implicit we are in the letter will depend upon the reason for the refusal. Furthermore, whether or not the refusal must meet the requirements of the Fair Credit Reporting Act depends upon the reason for the refusal. Our discussion of credit refusals to consumers, therefore, will be organized according to the reason for the refusal.

Refusals Resulting from Information the Consumer Provided

A consumer applying for credit is usually asked to indicate income and present monthly obligations on an application form. The incomes of some applicants will be insufficient to meet projected obligations and expenses during the loan period in question. These applicants must be denied credit. As with businesses on shaky financial ground, you can be forthright with these applicants because you are not reflecting negatively on their character. Rather, you are talking about what is probably a temporary condition that will be corrected in time. In fact, if you are not candid enough in conveying the reasons for the refusal, such applicants may well think that you are insulting their character.

The structure and content of refusal letters sent to these consumers will, with a few exceptions, resemble that of letters sent to businesses in weak financial condition, as outlined on pages 158 and 159. After a neutral start, you would move into your candid explanation of the refusal and then the refusal itself. The last part of the letter would then work toward securing the individual's cash business. You usually can't talk of discounts to consumers as you could to businesses, but you can talk of the general advantages of doing business with your organization. Since the applicant's financial condition is probably temporary, one could justify talking about the likelihood of credit in the future. Notice how the following letter frankly refuses credit but does so with an air of optimism and a constructive suggestion as to what the consumer might do instead of buying on credit.

Dear Ms. Hebert:

Thank you for your credit application of June 19. We are always grateful for any expression of interest in the services provided by Blanko's Department Store.

As we do with all credit applicants, we have examined the information provided on the form you completed. The comparison of your present income with your obligations and living expenses suggests that your best interests would now be served by buying in cash until your obligations are reduced. The best we can do now, therefore, is to offer you our services on a cash basis with the hope that we may be allowed to review your application later as your financial condition changes.

You may be interested in our convenient lay-a-way plan. For just 20 percent down, you can have your purchases carefully stored until you are ready for them and wish to complete payment.

We are now receiving several shipments daily of new fall fashions. We hope you will continue to keep Blanko's in mind as a source of satisfaction of all your clothing needs.

Sincerely,

In all fairness we must admit that this applicant may not be overjoyed about receiving this letter and may be able to get credit elsewhere where the standards are more relaxed. Thus, Blanko's may not get the cash business. But at least an effort was made, and the alternative suggested just may prove acceptable to this customer.

Refusals Resulting from Information Provided by Third Parties

Credit managers must sometimes refuse credit because a credit bureau and/or the applicant's references indicated that the applicant is a poor credit risk. More specifically, the applicant has built up a bad credit reputation by not honoring obligations in the past. One must exercise a certain degree of caution in writing such refusals for two reasons.

In the first place, we *are* dealing with a person's character here, and so we wouldn't want to get too concrete or specific. The person who has built up a solidly poor credit reputation knows it. There is no good reason to hit such a person over the head with all sorts of quotes about past payment habits. A writer would be wise, in such a case, to implicitly explain and refuse, that is, to tell the general nature of the reasons for the refusal.

Another reason for caution in writing these refusals is the Fair Credit Reporting Act. This act applies directly to consumer credit refusals resulting from information provided by third-party sources. The requirements of this act differ, however, according to whether the third-party source is or isn't a credit reporting agency. Remember that although the term "credit reporting agency" normally refers to credit bureaus, a bank or department store could become a credit reporting agency if it reported secondhand information or made a subjective judgment about the applicant's creditworthiness.

If credit is denied someone because of information provided by a credit reporting agency, the firm denying credit must give the applicant the name and address of the credit reporting agency. The applicant who so wishes may contact that agency and find out what is in its file. If the information is incorrect, it must be changed.

The requirements of the act differ for third parties other than credit reporting agencies. When credit is denied because of information provided by such parties, the firm refusing credit must in the letter inform the applicant of his or her right to learn the nature of the information provided within 60 days, if he or she so desires.

Notice how the following letters subtly explain the reasons for the credit refusals while fulfilling the requirements of the Fair Credit Reporting Act. The first must deny credit because of information provided by a credit reporting agency. The second must do so because of information provided by references who reported facts and did not make subjective judgments.

Dear Mr. Carpenter:

Thank you for your credit application of January 15. As soon as we received it, we began our routine credit check.

As part of this credit check, we contacted the Kerrville Credit Bureau, 717 Kent Street, zip code 82305. Because of the content of their report, we must propose that we deal on a cash basis.

Cash buying at Klineschmidt's will provide you with many savings.

The upcoming fall clearance sale is one example. During this sale, discounts of 30 to 60 percent off our regular stock will be offered throughout the store. We hope you'll take advantage of this chance to stock up on some exceptional bargains.

Sincerely,

Dear Mrs. Riggers:

Thank you for the expression of satisfaction with our ability to serve our discriminating customers evidenced in your July 2 credit application. We try to do all that we reasonably can to maintain the pleasure of patrons like you.

Because of our desire to serve you with expediency, we immediately contacted the references you provided on your application. You have a 60-day right to learn the nature of the information they gave us. The records that some of them provided indicate that it would be in your best interest for you to take advantage of our "Reserve a Trousseau" plan. For a minimal 15 percent deposit, you can fulfill all your daughter's and your wedding needs, have your preferences safely and attentively stored, and not have to remit the balance until you are ready for the apparel in October.

To assure you of the very latest and finest selections, I have enclosed six invitations to our July 14 showing of Damian's newest creations. Although he did an excellent job with Tricia's wedding, I am sure that he would excel to even greater heights for Lisette's. We are very much looking forward to seeing you at this event.

Sincerely,

Notice how the first example, with seasonal changes in the last paragraph, could be used as a form for many refusals of this type. The second letter, on the other hand, was much more personalized. As you might have gathered from the content and terminology, the second writer's store specialized in expensive merchandise and individualized attention to its clientele. Even in such cases, however, store owners find that they must deny credit to some who apply. Such tasks demand the utmost in diplomacy if one hopes to retain the cash business of such applicants.

Notice also that neither of the preceding examples spoke of, or hinted at, the extension of credit in the future. An applicant with a blemished credit reputation will need a good deal of time to clear those blemishes. Because most businesses are reluctant to accept an applicant with a poor payment record, regaining a good reputation is an uphill battle. To suggest (even with such terms as "at this time" or "temporarily") that you might judge an application differently in the near future might establish false hopes that would have to be crushed when the applicant reapplied. For this reason, it is best not to say or imply anything about credit in the future.

As we have stated before, credit refusals are probably the most difficult and least pleasant type of business writing that one might be called upon to undertake. Collection letters, the subject of Chapter 10, are probably the second most unpleasant writing task that a businessperson might face. Before moving on to collection letters, however, we might take a look at some of the more positive and profitable opportunities for business writing that stem from the credit extension process.

USING CREDIT SITUATIONS FOR BUSINESS-PROMOTION LETTERS

As we have seen in inquiries and acknowledgments of orders, modern business uses any opportunity from birthdays to New Year's greetings as an occasion to stimulate business or goodwill. These business-promotion letters can be effectively used as adjuncts to the whole process of granting credit in three situations:

1. Offering credit privileges to those who have not as yet set up credit terms

2. Attempting to revive credit accounts which, for one reason or another, have become inactive

3. Expressing thanks to customers who have fulfilled their credit obligations promptly or over a long period of time

There is room for originality, humor, and sincerity in these letters, which attempt to create new customers or cement relationships with old ones. Their pattern is comparatively simple:

1. The use of some occasion such as a holiday, a sale, or a span of time as the reason for offering credit, reviving its use, or acknowledging that it has been used with integrity

2. An explanation of the advantages of credit from the users' standpoint

3. A convenient method by which credit may be established or used or an expression of appreciation for using it well

Here are two effective letters offering credit privileges:

Dear Mrs. Greenspan:

You've been busy, we know, since the process of moving from one city to another is generally a hectic one.

The next time you have a minute, we think we can save you a lot of minutes in getting settled. The enclosed card is your passport to the Wonderful World of Wundermans Department Store. We've served Middleburg people for 88 years from a complete stock of the modern merchandise you'd expect in the city's biggest department store.

Just sign and mail the card today. From there on you can do all your shopping by telephone, conveniently and quickly.

Sincerely yours,

Dear Mrs. Blake:

Miss Rita Conway, the head of our book department, has told me of your interest in our spring book sale and has suggested that you might be interested in opening a charge account with us.

You will find such an account of the greatest convenience, for it will enable you to call Miss Conway at any time and order the books you want without the inconvenience of making long trips downtown. In this way you will be able to keep up with the latest books and still have the benefit of Miss Conway's expert advice.

With a charge account, these same privileges are available in all the 51 departments of our store. Just call any one of the departments listed in the enclosed folder, order what you wish, and say, "Charge it"; or if you are undecided about gifts for friends, our Personal Shopping Service is available without cost to charge customers. Furthermore, you will receive advance notice of our many sales in the various departments of the store.

Just sign and mail the enclosed card, which offers you carefree and convenient shopping.

Sincerely yours,

Since business people spend considerable time, money, and effort in putting new customers on their books, common sense dictates that they do what they can to keep these accounts active. Letters to revive such accounts are frequently sent in series over a period of months; ostensibly they are letters of inquiry, but actually they promote sales by making the customer feel missed and important. The following letters and the one on page 166 are examples of such volume-revival efforts:

Dear Mr. Dart:

We've just heard about a husky restaurant patron who left his expensive hat with a note:

It belongs to the heavyweight champion and I'm coming right back.

When he returned, the hat was gone and had been replaced by this note:

Taken by the world's champion long-distance runner—and I'm not coming back.

We've wondered why *you* haven't been back since you took out that

WILLIAMS TOYS AND NOVELTIES COMPANY

4726 SIXTH STREET
CINCINNATI, OHIO 45203

November 12, 1970

Mr. Eldon E. Hightower
The Children's Shop
76 West Avenue
Middletown, Ohio 45042

Dear Mr. Hightower:

We've missed you . . . .

And we're wondering if we haven't somehow slipped up without
realizing it.

Your account and your friendship are important to us, because
we like to think that we continue to deserve the confidence
and the good will of customers like you. For that reason, if
we have not rendered the kind of service you should receive,
we'd appreciate your telling us so that we can do whatever we
can to correct the situation.

We realize, of course, that you may not have needed any of our
products in the past few months. But with the holidays approaching,
we have many novelties and children's toys which will be attractive
to your customers and profitable to you.

Because we've counted it a privilege to serve you in the past,
we are looking forward to hearing from you soon.

Sincerely,

James E. Williams, President

JEW:RLS

charge account four months ago. You'll find us champions of service whose major concern is keeping customers like you.

Come right back for our Spring Sale, with savings in every department—even hats.

Sincerely yours,

Dear Mr. Alexander:

Old friends are the best friends. . . .

That's the way we feel about the old friends we've made in our 22 years of business. And when you don't see an old friend for a long time, you're naturally concerned.

That's why we're writing you. Because we're concerned that we have unintentionally done something you didn't like. If so, we want to know about it and remedy the matter.

We have valued the confidence you've placed in us for many years now. A lot of new customers have been entered on our accounts during that time, but the old friends are those we treasure most. Because we've missed you, may we hear from you soon?

Cordially yours,

An amusing indication of the nature of our modern computerized business world was supplied in response to a Texas bank's inquiry as to why a certain customer had closed her bank account. The answer:

I married Account Number 621-30157.

Finally, letters of thanks to customers who have fulfilled their credit obligations present a fine way of maintaining good customers:

Dear Mr. Wynkoop:

Every year we start anew by singing "Should old acquaintance be forgot and never brought to mind . . ."

We don't want old acquaintances like you to be forgot, particularly because you have provided us with a lot of business in twelve months and have lived up to your credit obligations promptly.

We're grateful to you. May our old acquaintance continue for years to come.

Sincerely yours,

Dear Mr. Franklin:

With a new year just around the corner, we want you to know how much we have appreciated your cooperation during the past year.

Your account has been paid promptly, and we hope that you have enjoyed doing business with us as much as we have with you.

That's why we want to say "thank you" and to wish you a happy and prosperous New Year.

Cordially yours,

These letters demonstrate that situations associated with credit can be used effectively to promote good relations with customers. One danger to be avoided is that of sounding "gushy" or insincere; but properly used, these business-promotion letters allied to the credit function offer countless opportunities for creating favorable impressions, cementing established relationships, and maintaining customers' goodwill.

EXERCISES

1. You live in a remote area of Maine and plan to open a hunting lodge in two months. You have already booked the lodge half full for the season and don't think you will have any problem booking the rest of it; the region is well known for its excellent hunting. Your food supplier, Baker & Co., is located 200 miles away, and you will be driving there every two weeks to purchase at least $400 worth of food. Write a credit application letter to Baker. You have authorized the Bangor National Bank to release your financial information to prospective creditors.

2. Your company, World Imports, has two very successful retail stores—one in Philadelphia and one in Boston. These stores sell jewelry, small gift items, and handmade clothing from 30 countries. You are planning to expand your merchandise line to include arts and crafts for the home. Write the application for credit that you will send to Burton Ltd., in London, England, a wholesaler for this type of merchandise. Burton was recommended to you by McCarthy & Beaumont, a London firm with whom you have been doing business for three years. You anticipate your initial order from Burton will be for approximately $1,000, with subsequent monthly orders averaging $500. If you think it appropriate, you may supply the names of other creditors as references.

3. Apply for credit with Casswell Art Supplies and enclose your first order for $150. You own The Art Shop, your primary customers are local university students, and you have been in business for five years.

4. Compose the following acknowledgment letters:
   a. A favorable reply to the request in Exercise 1. Establish a $1,000 line of credit, payable within 30 days of the billing date, with a 2 percent discount if paid within 10 days.

b. A reply to the request in Exercise 3, filling the order but requesting that a credit application be filled out.

5. You have received the following letter:

> Mr. Charles Shrock
> 27 Greenway
> Williamsport, PA 56832
>
> Dear Mr. Shrock:
>
> We have decided to grant you the credit you requested in your recent credit application. This will be our regular credit account, which means that you must pay the balance due within 20 days after billing or you will be charged 1½ percent a month interest on the unpaid balance. Since we are required to do so under federal law, we are enclosing a statement of our credit policies which spells out in complete, understandable detail all you will need to know about your account. If you should have any questions about our credit policies at any time, I will be glad to answer them for you.
>
> > Sincerely,

a. What is your reaction to this letter?
b. Rewrite it as you would have preferred to receive it.

6. You have received a credit order for $200 from Wenonah Appliance Center. No financial statements or references were given. Reply to their letter and request them to fill out an application form before the order can be shipped.

7. The credit request letter you received from Marshall's Pet Store gave Mivulski & Co. as a reference. Write to Mivulski requesting credit information about Marshall's.

8. Assume you work in the credit department of Mivulski & Co. and are replying to the letter of Exercise 7. Write three letters, utilizing the following information:
a. Marshall's Pet Store has been a credit customer for two years, has always paid their account within 30 days, and has a credit limit of $400.
b. Marshall's has been a customer for three years, had a four-month overdue balance of $300 last year, has paid their account within 30 days since then, currently owes $110, and has a credit limit of $250.
c. Marshall's has been a customer for 18 months, has a five-month overdue balance of $175, paid their account within 30 days the first seven months, and paid their account thereafter 10 to 20 days late. You have also heard from another pet store that a large number of Marshall's expensive fish just died, resulting in severe financial strain.

9. After receiving the credit information letter from Mivulski written for the third situation, you have decided not to grant Marshall's Pet Store the credit they requested. Compose the refusal letter.

10. You are credit manager of a department store with six branches in the Phoenix, Arizona, area. On the basis of the credit report you obtained from the Tri-City Credit

Bureau, 6420 Main Street, Mesa, Arizona, you cannot open the charge account requested by Vince Shasto. Write the refusal letter to this individual.

11. You work in the credit policies department of a large nationwide department store. You think a credit refusal form letter might be a more efficient way of handling the hundreds of refusals your department handles. You envision a letter in which the reasons for refusal would be listed; the credit manager would simply place a checkmark in front of the appropriate reason or reasons. Compose the form letter that you think would be suitable.

12. For the following situations, write business promotion letters:
   a. Custom Interiors, a drapery and carpet store, has been a cash customer of your wholesale fabric store for one year. Their monthly purchases have averaged $600, and you would like to offer them credit privileges.
   b. Albany Office Supplies has been a credit customer of your paper company for seven years. However, a check of your records indicates that they have not made any purchases during the past nine months. You would like to regain their business.
   c. You own an exclusive women's clothing store and want to express your appreciation to those people who have been steady customers since you first opened your store five years ago. What are some ways in which you can show your appreciation?

10
COLLECTION LETTERS

As pointed out in the previous chapter, the relationship between granting credit and collecting debts is a close one. When credit has been expertly managed, the work of the collection department becomes much simpler. Equally important is the relationship between the collection and sales departments. The customer who has owed money for a period of time ceases to be a customer; for if that person needs additional merchandise, he or she may turn to competitors of the firm that has carried him or her on its books.

Many collection people face up quite candidly to the fact that debtors aren't buyers in letters like the following:

Dear Mr. Johnson:

Last night the children were shrieking and pounding upstairs until I finally asked my wife, "How on earth do you stand all that noise?"

"It's when I don't hear anything that I really get worried," she said.

And that's why we're worried . . .

. . . because we haven't heard anything about that $178.42 balance in your account.

. . . because you probably won't order anything else from us until you've paid it.

This silence means that you lose sales and profits and we lose your business. Why not make a noise with that check of yours? We'll both benefit.

Yours truly,

Dear Ms. McMaster:

We send you this not just to collect the $47.52 you owe us but also *because we want you to buy from us again.*

Sincerely yours,

Another firm sends out this letter showing the amount due in very large figures in a drawing of a magnifying glass:

Dear Mr. Locke:

Little things sometimes get magnified out of all proportion.

Maybe your outstanding balance doesn't seem a "little thing" to you— but we don't want it magnified so that it affects our relations. We appreciate all the business you have given us in the past, and we want it to continue.

Won't you send us your check—in full, if you can—or a substantial payment? After all this time, you must need a number of our products . . . and we, of course, want you to have them.

Sincerely yours,

Unfortunately, the letters of many companies sound as if their collection correspondents and their sales correspondents were not speaking to one another. While the salespeople have been dealing with the customer under the theme of "how to win friends and influence people," the collection department all too often takes over with a rough, offensive tone more than likely nullifying all the sales effort. This situation can be corrected only through the closest cooperation between sales and collection policies. To do this, correspondents must remember the twofold object in collecting a past-due account—to get the money and to retain the customer's goodwill and patronage. The language and the tone of the collection letter should be carefully scrutinized on the principle that a collection letter which retains the customer's goodwill stands a better chance of collecting the amount due than one which irritates or antagonizes the customer. Try your own reaction to the following letter. It was sent by a publisher to a customer who had returned the item in question two months before this letter was sent.

Since you have not sent payment by now, I assume you don't care if you dishonor yourself and your family by having your bad debt status spread all over (the customer's city).

Our lawyer is sending your file, (the customer's name), to a local agent in your town. He will initiate a local investigation to learn all he can about your affairs. He will talk to your neighbors, your in-laws, your employer, and your local storekeepers. The information he gathers will be turned over to all local companies that extend credit to you—your electric company, your oil company, your telephone company, local charge accounts. Thereafter your credit with them will be suspended and your credit cards all revoked.

And once you've lost your credit, (the name again), you will never be able to get credit again—anywhere. We cannot prevent this unfortunate outcome unless I receive full payment on your account by return mail.

When contacted, a company representative admitted that the note was a form letter and a bluff. Nevertheless, it's efforts like this that infuriate the public and result in increased government involvement to protect individuals from the insensitivities of a few not-too-ethical businesses.

The following letter, although not as repugnant as the preceding one, still has a tone that leaves a good bit to be desired.

Dear Mr. White:

We cannot understand your failure to reply to our previous reminders about your delinquent account amounting to $47.43.

By ignoring our letters, you leave us little choice but to decide we were wrong in extending you credit. After all, you must realize that the expense of sending repeated reminders makes this a very unsatisfactory experience for us.

You can prove we were not wrong in our judgment by sending us your check, now.

Yours truly,

The needless negative emphasis of such words as *cannot understand, your failure, delinquent, ignore, wrong, unsatisfactory* certainly cancels a lot of sales-promotion effort. Without appearing soft, the correspondent can collect and still keep goodwill by being persuasive and constructive. Notice the difference in point of view and general tone of the following letter dealing with the same situation:

Dear Mr. White:

We have sent you several reminders about your past-due account for $47.43, without a response from you.

In fairness to yourself, we hope you'll consider how important an asset your credit standing is. Certainly, you would place a far higher value on it than the amount you owe us.

To protect this asset, you can write us frankly as to when you will make payment—or better still, send us your check now. By doing so, you'll get this off your mind. Use the envelope we are enclosing for your convenience—and mail it today, please.

Yours truly,

As you will see in the following section, a collection letter is usually a part of a series of messages. How much of the series a creditor must use will depend upon when the debtor feels or can be made to feel ready to pay the debt. Before we discuss the stages of the series, however, readers should be familiar with certain assumptions which underlie this discussion.

The first of these assumptions is that any business which engages regularly in the extension of credit will sooner or later find that it must put together a series of form collection efforts. Some debtors will be delinquent in payment, some slightly, some seriously. The range of reasons for delinquencies is broad, but it is nonetheless a fact of a creditor's life that overdue accounts will be encountered. And in a firm that regularly extends credit, they will be encountered often enough to justify creating a series of form messages. These forms may be "personalized" to some extent by their mechanics, as when they are individually typed, and by their content, as when parts are adapted to seasons or other circumstances. In larger firms the forms may be automatically handled by a computer that dictates which form is sent at which time. However, even though we are talking about forms, we should not lose sight of the fact that the forms represent messages from one human being to another. The dangers of impersonality and dehumanization are nicely illustrated by the following note from a customer to her bank:

Dear Machine:

You have misspelled my name again and failed to correct last month's wrong balance. If you don't make these corrections this month, I shall bend your card.

Yours truly,

The debtor is not a button which when pushed will submit the amount of the debt. Instead, we are likely to be dealing with a person who either has forgotten the bill or is experiencing problems. Essentially, the creditor's job is to seek a mutually satisfactory solution to a mutual problem.

Hopefully, the solution will be the remittance of the billed amount. In this vein of thought, most collectors envision their central purpose as persuading debtors that it is to their own advantage to pay. These collectors proceed from the assumption—and actual statistics show it to be a sound one—that most people want to pay their debts and that persuasion and perseverance are the best ways of getting them to do so. However, most creditors hold open the door for special arrangements (e.g., partial payments now) that might be necessitated by a debtor's extenuating circumstances.

Another assumption underlying our discussion of collection series relates to the types of accounts being collected. As we will explain later, a series to collect business accounts would differ from one which would be used for consumers. Furthermore, the length and content of consumer collection series will differ by type of account. Because revolving and installment accounts represent, far and away, the bulk of the consumer credit extended today, most of our discussion and illustrations will center around these types. We might keep in mind that a customer overdue in such an account faces another obligation in 30 days.

Our next assumption deals with the differences in the series resulting from the type of credit risk involved. Debtors are usually classified as good, fair, or poor credit risks on the basis of the reputation they have established in the past. Collection efforts aimed at poor risks usually get more rigorous more quickly than such efforts aimed at the other categories. Although we will recognize differences in collection series for good and fair credit risks, we will not give specific attention to collecting from poor risks. Companies that extend credit to proven poor risks usually do so knowing that they will probably have to pressure the customer into paying—very possibly at the sacrifice of a payment to another creditor. In other words, it's okay if the debtor robs Peter to pay Paul as long as I am Paul. We take the view that such a practice borders upon being unethical. A person or firm with a poor credit reputation should not be extended credit, so our treatment of the collection series will pertain to people and firms ranked as fair to good risks.

The next assumption basic to our treatment of the series deals with the methods of collection available. Students familiar with collection procedures will know that phone calls are often used in collecting accounts. In fact, for local accounts, many collection managers prefer the phone because they can thus secure some kind of commitment from the reluctant debtor. Furthermore, a few unprincipled collectors relish the use of the phone to browbeat or intimidate debtors into paying. Although we acknowledge the use of the telephone, we ask that students not let it overshadow the use of a written collection series for several reasons.

First, for distant accounts the written word is still very often the less expensive method. Second, because of the abuses of the telephone in collecting delinquent accounts, legislation is now pending that would sharply restrict its use. Third, if we remember the collection process's twofold objective of getting the money *and* retaining goodwill, we will realize that the telephone has its drawbacks. To begin with, the telephone conversation is a very vivid, concrete experience for a debtor; it singles that person out and could leave a stronger and more lasting impression of guilt than would a letter. This feeling of guilt could work against the goodwill that we would like the customer to feel toward our firm. For this reason, the phone should probably be used only after several written attempts have proven fruitless.

Another reason for our reservations about phone collections involves the people doing the collecting and the messages they convey. One can't be as meticulous and cautious in oral communication as in writing. Unless a telephone collector has been carefully selected and thoroughly trained, this person could do more to hurt than help the firm's cause.

Before we discuss the collection series itself, one final point should be made. That point is the recognition of the inherently dynamic nature of the collection process. This process is an intricate part of the overall credit process. The credit process is ingrained in contemporary business. Business and government and our society are all intimately related. Thus, as the economy fluctuates, as public opinion makes itself known, as the mood of government changes, as all these influences have their impact, the collection process must reflect these changes. In the following sections of this chapter, we will make specific references to how these factors have altered the collection process.

THE COLLECTION SERIES

Actually, there is no such thing as *the* collection letter; like troubles, collection letters "come not singly but in battalions" known as *the collection series*. This series of letters is a practical expression of the fundamental belief behind all collection procedures—*that the customer will pay if he or she is reminded regularly and with increasing insistence that payment is due.* The frequency of the reminders and the degree of insistence will depend upon a number of factors.

As we mentioned in the preceding section, the type of risk the customer is will influence the frequency and the tone of the collection messages. The upper limit of credit extended to the customer will also play a part. Likewise, whether the customer is a consumer or a business will have an effect. Perhaps because businesses appreciate and expect punctuality in dealings with each other, perhaps because business-business dealings tend to be less personal than business-consumer dealings, and perhaps because of the larger dollar figures involved, collection series for business accounts usually move faster than those used for consumers.

Furthermore, not all types of consumer accounts are collected in the same manner. The more exclusive credit card companies are usually fairly selective in opening accounts and tend to collect them somewhat slowly and tactfully. Revolving and installment accounts, on the other hand, are collected with more haste. They are the most common types of consumer accounts today, and debtors who fall delinquent in these accounts face another payment 30 days down the road. Combine these features with the unfortunate impact of inflation upon the paying habits of some credit holders, and many companies see justification for a shorter collection series that gets serious pretty quickly.

Finally, two other factors conceivably could influence the length and tone of the collection series: the state of the economy and the condition of the business. If the economy is slow and/or the business falls upon hard times, one way of at least temporarily improving the business's solvency, even if only slightly, would be to press a little harder a little earlier for payment on delinquent accounts.

The preceding factors play a part in determining the length and nature of the collection series. But regardless of all these factors, successful collection always results from a carefully thought-out plan which moves from gentle reminders to the most insistent point of informing the debtor of some sort of drastic action that will be taken to collect. This plan can best be explained by examining the assumptions underlying the steps in the plan and the manner in which each assumption contributes to the increasing insistence of the series as a whole.

1. The assumption that the customer wishes to be reminded that payment is due

This reminder may be a very brief letter or simply a statement. If a letter is sent, it is very routine, as in the following:

Dear Mr. Davis:

Just a friendly reminder of our terms, which are full payment monthly. Our account will be off your mind if you send us your check for $13.48 in the enclosed envelope.

Very truly yours,

Dear Ms. Brady:

We thought you'd appreciate a reminder that your account is past due. If you have sent us your check, please accept our thanks and disregard this notice.

Sincerely yours,

2. The assumption that the customer has forgotten to pay

Sometimes called the *follow-up reminder*, this is most often a bill or statement stamped with some such notation as "Second Notice" and sent usually to good credit risks. Many stores and companies do not use these follow-up notices or letters on the theory that one reminder is enough.

The following letters illustrate the approaches available for such second notices. Note that each contains a simple, straightforward request for payment. No major persuasive effort is thought to be necessary at this point.

Dear Mr. Graham:

We previously reminded you that your account, as shown on this statement, is past due. Since we have not yet received your payment, may we again ask that you send us your check as soon as possible?

Sincerely yours,

Dear Mr. Jewitt:

An executive whose garage delivers his car to him every day found a card on the front seat one December morning:

Merry Christmas from the boys in the garage.

Despite good intentions, he delayed doing anything about it, so the next week he found another card:

Merry Christmas, Second Notice.

This is our second notice about that $65.37 bill. Will you please send us your check today?

Very truly,

Dear Ms. Franklin:

Perhaps you overlooked it—

Possibly you forgot—

At any rate, we haven't received the monthly payment of $. . . . . . requested in our recent statement. We want to explain that Club Plan Accounts are opened with the understanding that the installments shown on the contract are to be paid each month when due.

A stamped, addressed envelope is enclosed for your convenience in remitting.

Yours truly,

3. The assumption that you need to be informed of something

The letter written under this assumption attempts to get some kind of response from a silent customer by asking if there was an error in the billing or the service. The theory is that an offer of an adjustment combined with a sales message about the kind of service you want to offer may dent a customer's silence. The chance that your company's error may have caused the delinquency is a slim one, but suggesting it allows you to work in a plea that the customer complete the terms of the contract if you fulfilled your part. The following examples show how such an approach may be taken:

Gentlemen and Ladies:

DID WE OVERLOOK SOMETHING?

Is it because of some omission on our part that we have not received your check? If so, may we please have an explanation? We'll do our part toward making any necessary adjustment.

On the other hand—if we've performed our part of the sales contract, won't you now complete yours? Your check will do the trick. And, by the way, if you need any more cups, include your order.

Cordially yours,
Universal Paper Products Co.

Gentlemen and Ladies:

A long time ago one Greek said to another, "So now you've invented a zero—and what do you have? Nothing!"

That's what we've had in response to our previous notices and letters.

If our service wasn't what you expected, tell us. If we've made any mistakes in your bill, let us know.

We'll gladly make any fair adjustment. But if there are no corrections to be made, please use the envelope enclosed to send us your check for $167.31.

Sincerely yours,

4. The assumption that more serious persuasion is necessary

Up to this point you've reminded the customer, you've asked if anything is wrong, and still you haven't heard a thing. You assume now that stronger appeals are necessary. This stage may include more than one letter, and these letters are likely to be more involved than previous efforts because your objective is more involved. The objective is to develop some sort of appeal that will move the debtor to meet an obligation. The first of these letters could still maintain a fairly positive tone while appealing to the debtor's pride in a good credit reputation. The last would be more negative, talking about the plight of one who loses credit privileges. Although compassion and empathy may be overworked words, what they stand for might still be used as a worthwhile guide to our writing efforts at this stage. The following letters apply the assumption that serious persuasion is necessary:

Dear Ms. Meyer:

From school days on, we learn the importance of "good marks." In business, for example, we all know the value of silver marked "sterling," of jewelry by Tiffany, of cars by Cadillac.

Your "mark" is your credit standing. To keep it high requires constant vigilance. We're sure that you don't want your past due account for $113.43 marked "Delinquent."

For your own sake, don't neglect this account another day. Send your check by return mail today.

Sincerely,

Dear Mr. Martin:

As a businessman you certainly realize the value of a good credit reputation. You know that it is probably your most valuable asset.

Yet your credit rating is being jeopardized for $89.26, the balance of your account with us. Surely you are being unfair to yourself to place so low an estimate on your most valuable asset.

Prompt attention to your obligations is the one way to maintain your credit reputation. Send your check today and preserve that valuable asset.

Sincerely,

5. The assumption that the customer will pay only if made to pay

In this final stage, letters often become adjuncts to other methods in modern collection practice. To impress debtors with the urgency of the situation, phone calls, telegrams, and personal interviews are being used increasingly. When letters complement these methods, they are frequently sent by registered mail or over the signature of a top executive. The motivating force here is that unless payment is received, or other terms worked out, by a specific date—usually within five or ten days—action will follow in one of various forms: reporting to the credit bureau, turning the account over to lawyers or professional collecting agencies, garnisheeing a percentage of salaries or wages (in states where that can be done), or repossessing merchandise. Where letters are used, their tone reflects a genuine reluctance to resort to this action and their content suggests that the debtor has a far more pleasant solution; but no doubt is left that the creditor intends to go through with the action necessary. Here are examples whose effectiveness readers can test by imagining that they themselves have received such messages:

Dear Mr. Jones:

We have received no payments on your $233.11 past due account for merchandise we shipped to you on August 7.

Since we have not had any reply to our previous correspondence, there seems to be no alternative for us except to place this matter in the hands of our attorneys.

For you, there is still one alternative—send us your payment in full within five days. Otherwise we shall be forced to take an action which, frankly, we dislike.

Yours truly,

Dear Ms. Bender:

Frankly, we are reluctant to report your delinquent account to our credit bureau and our collection agency. After all, without the ability to obtain credit, you simply cannot operate a business in today's world.

We are, therefore, giving you a final chance to avoid such actions.

But you must do your part. Your check for $150 and assurance that you will pay the remaining balance within two months are what we consider your part. Within the next five days, it's your move.

Sincerely yours,

Dear Mr. Miller:

Unless we receive a check from you for $182.65 within 10 days, we shall have no choice but to report you to the Blank Credit Bureau.

We don't want to do this because of the impact that such a report would have upon you. Your credit reputation would be seriously injured, and you would find it extremely difficult to get credit in the future.

These effects are not to be taken lightly, but the matter is now completely up to you. Payment within 10 days is the only way to avoid these unfortunate consequences.

Sincerely,

In summary, the collection series should be viewed as a logical *but flexible* method to be adapted to the different categories of debtors, to changing economic conditions, to types of accounts, to company policies, and to human beings. If debtors respond by telling of expenses caused by illness or by other contingencies, reputable companies are willing to temper the wind to the shorn lamb. What all this adds up to is that a *system* of collection should never make us forget that debtors are individuals, and, regardless of how we group them, they remain individual human beings.

ORIGINALITY AND HUMOR IN COLLECTION LETTERS

It was mentioned earlier that many types of letters that were formerly handled in a routine fashion have now become clever or humorous messages strong on getting attention. Such letters have been used to good effect in collecting small accounts, usually in the early stages of the collection series. An almost endless variety of devices, gadgets, and novelties are used by collection correspondents to point up the basic message, *please pay*. Typical are letters in small type (we're whispering about your bill), letters with strings attached (as a reminder to pay), or messages with bars of music across the top (we have the blues about your account). Such stunts and the use of gadgets can be carried too far, but their basic purpose of attracting the reader's attention is important. The following letters demonstrate how originality, cleverness, and humor can be used to get results:

Dear Mr. Miller:

The public utility in our area had to notify a bride: "Please pay the amount. You have been paying the date."

May we make it clear that *your* amount is $17.40, and just date the check today, please.

Very truly,

Dear Ms. Fernwood:

Someone defined a pessimist as "an optimist—after taxes."

Want to help with our definition—"an optimist is a pessimist after all bills have been paid"? It takes a mere $9.50 and we'll both feel better.

Yours truly,

dear mr. meyer:

we don't want to make a big fuss and we know you don't want us to— so could you please send us that check for $21.49 today? thanks

Sincerely yours,

Gentlemen and Ladies:

After winning an important case a lawyer wired his client:

JUSTICE HAS TRIUMPHED!

Back came the answer

APPEAL AT ONCE!

May we appeal for justice? Just $24.13 *today*.

Sincerely,

Say, Mr. Cornwall,

Are you still carrying that check for $10.50 around in your pocket?

Yours truly,

Dear Mr. George:

Your account for $216.82 is now 9½ months overdue. This means that we have carried you longer than your mother did.

We must now inform you that unless you give birth to a check and wing it to us by way of the U.S. Postal Stork within ten days, we will have no choice but to send announcements to the Franklin Credit Bureau and our lawyer.

Sincerely,

The letters which follow have, in a sense, become classics. They are probably too well known to be used with any freshness, but they are included because they illustrate what originality and humor can accomplish and because users of this book in previous editions have requested that they be included:

Dear Mr. Engel:

An effective collection letter should be:

1. Short

2. Courteous

3. Successful

This letter is short; we hope you think it's courteous. The rest is up to you.

Sincerely,

Dear Mr. Dowling:

Said Mark Twain: "Always do right. This will gratify some people—and astonish the rest."

We won't be astonished, but we'll certainly be gratified if you'll do right by your account for $87.12.

Yours truly,

The City Club of Cleveland used this to dust off delinquencies:

Dear Member:

Man is made of dust.

Dust settles.

Be a man!

Your Treasurer

Dear Mr. Millet:

A shy secretary didn't want to tell her boss the reason for her resignation, so she asked her husband to explain. He sent the following note:

"My wife's reason for leaving will soon be apparent—and so will I."

It's just as apparent to us that there must be an explanation as to why we haven't heard from you. Won't you write and explain—or better still, send us your check for $23.49?

Sincerely,

Dear Mr. Richardson:

How do you do?

Some pay when due.

> Some pay when overdue.
>
> A few never do.
>
> How do you do?
>
> Your balance is $ . . . . . .
>
> Very truly yours,

Such letters reflect creativity and originality, but the real test is whether they get results. Writers of collection letters cannot lose sight of the fact that their purpose is not entertainment but collecting bills; there is no substitute for the basic principle we have discussed in the collection series—*the best way to collect money is to keep constantly pressing delinquent accounts with a gradually increasing insistence culminating in action.* Perhaps this insistence may result in a reply such as the following, received by a Georgia firm in answer to a long series of collection letters:

> Dear Sir:
>
> Here is your money and you won't be one bit gladder to git it than I am to send it. Please don't send me no receipt for I don't want to hear from you no more.
>
> Yours truly,

But at least the debt *was* collected.

RECENT AND LIKELY DEVELOPMENTS IN CREDIT COLLECTION

That credit is becoming a more and more important force in the American business scene hardly needs to be pointed out. But with its ever-increasing significance come opportunities and problems that do need to be recognized. As people rely to a greater extent upon credit for their wherewithal, we will find that some of them overextend themselves. How a business relates to the temporary and longer-term problems of such customers used to be a more or less private matter between the two parties immediately involved. However, two factors appear to be working toward removing the shield of privacy from the collection process.

First, as was mentioned earlier, some companies have abused the collection process by completely ignoring individual human rights. Such unethical practices as repeated phone calls at unusual hours, calls to employers aimed at embarrassing the employee-debtor, threats of physical injury, and vulgar language have been used to pressure debtors into paying. In our age of consumerism, such depravity cannot long be tolerated. And it appears that it will not be, because of the second factor working toward removing the shield of privacy from the process.

This second factor is the recently emerging popularity of the occupation of "investigative reporting." As more and more monumental scandals are being unearthed, a new industry is arising. This industry is made up of people dedicated to undermining the perpetrators of evil in our American institutions. They are determined with an almost religious fervor to shed light upon the dim and seedy activities of people in public and private walks of life. When these activities directly affect individuals, the story that is publicized has even more concrete public appeal.

It is this type of publicity, though it may apply to only a few credit collectors, that promises to result in legislation which directly controls the credit collection process. As of now, only eight states and the District of Columbia have strong debt-collection laws. These laws prohibit certain specific debt-collection practices and allow consumers to file suits for violations of these laws.

At the federal level, the Fair Credit Billing Act, implemented in 1975, applies to anyone who regularly extends open-end credit with payments in more than four installments or who imposes a finance charge. The major thrust of this law is the quick correction of billing errors. It gives the consumer 60 days after the receipt of a bill to make a written claim of error. The creditor must acknowledge the complaint within 30 days of its receipt, and correct the mistake (if one is found) and inform the customer that there was or wasn't a mistake within 90 days of receiving the complaint. During that time and for 10 days after informing the customer of the complaint's resolution, the creditor cannot report the account as delinquent to anyone. Furthermore, such creditors must inform their customers of these rights either with an involved semiannual notice or with an abbreviated monthly notice.

Although the Fair Credit Billing Act goes a long way toward assuring quick responses from creditors to debtors who think they have legitimate questions, it does not deal specifically with collection methods. However, a bill now before Congress proposes to regulate these methods. The bill introduced by Representative Frank Annunzio would, if passed, sharply restrict what creditors could do to collect accounts. Only two phone calls a week could be made and only between 8:00 A.M. and 9:00 P.M. Calls to employers would be allowed only under certain circumstances. The bill would prohibit specified acts of harassment and intimidation along with false representations of the collector's identity and intended actions. Suits would be permitted, with rather heavy damages allowed for violations.

If this legislation were passed as proposed, it would apply only to collection agencies and not to companies that collect their own accounts. Apparently, the logic is that since collection agencies are only concerned with collecting money, they are the ones who need the closest supervision. Retailers who collect their own accounts should be concerned with more than simply getting money from a reluctant debtor. The distinction here allows us to reiterate an important point discussed earlier in the chapter. That point is the twofold objective of the collection process, to get the money *and* retain the customer's goodwill. If we ignore the latter, we invite the helping hand of Uncle Sam in yet another aspect of business behavior. If, on the other hand, we try to get our money while keeping in mind the dignity, as well as the future business, of the debtor, we are, at the same time, contributing something concrete toward preserving the "free" part of the free enterprise system.

EXERCISES

1. Jim Bronson, 85 Medlock Drive, Vienna, Virginia, has been a good credit customer of your clothing store for two years. Now, for the first time, however, he is two months overdue in paying his 30-day account. Write Mr. Bronson, reminding him of the $85 balance.

2. Your magazine, *Nature World,* has a continuous renewal option. Subscriptions are automatically renewed yearly, with the subscriber receiving a computerized bill. The majority of the automatic renewal subscribers remit their $12 with this first bill. However, about 20 percent need a follow-up reminder. What are the various approaches you might suggest for this second notice? Compose one.

3. As credit manager of Mike's Motorcycles, you must write a collection letter to Sharon Boerner, 1915 Payson Lane, Salt Lake City, Utah. Sharon has been paying $75 a month plus 1½ percent interest over the past four months for the purchase of a used motorcycle. She is currently two months behind in her payments. Using the assumption that you need to be informed of something, write an appropriate letter.

4. Wilderness Sports Center has owed your company $425 on their 30-day account for three months. This $425 represents their initial order; you granted them credit after receiving a favorable report from a credit bureau. Your two previous collection letters have gone unanswered, and you now assume that more serious persuasion is necessary. Write the letter or letters that you think are called for at this stage.

5. You have reached the final stage in your attempts to collect the $284 owed you by Alan McKeever for his purchase of stereo equipment. He has ignored all other collection letters and suggested payment plans. You, therefore, assume that he will pay only if he is made to.
   a. What methods might you use in addition to or instead of letter writing to persuade him to pay?
   b. What are some of the actions you might have to resort to in collecting this account?
   c. Write the letter you would send at this final stage.

6. You are the head bookkeeper for a professional association of four orthopedic surgeons. Elaine Fiore's account totaled $2,200, of which $2,000 was paid by her insurance company. She has written to you explaining her financial situation as a graduate student and that she can only afford to pay $10 a month on her outstanding balance. Reply to her letter, explaining that the $10 monthly payment will be acceptable, there will be no interest charge, and if she can possibly pay more at any time it would be appreciated.

7. Your company sold $1,200 worth of power equipment to Gettle's Metals in March. The credit terms were six installments of $200 each, plus 1½ percent interest on the unpaid balance. It is now the middle of May and you have just received the following letter from Gettle:

> Gentlemen and Ladies:
>
> We realize that our second installment on the $1,200 power tool purchase was due two weeks ago. However, we are experiencing some financial difficulty—two of our major machines broke down beyond repair, and we had to replace them.
>
> Therefore, we cannot pay all our creditors the amounts previously agreed to. Would it be possible to reduce our monthly payments to you for a few months until we are in better financial condition? Although we cannot say with certainty when that will be, we project a three-month recovery period.
>
> Sincerely,

Gettle has made substantial purchases from you in the past and always kept their financial commitments. Although you do not want to establish a precedent of altering installment contracts, you feel that special consideration is warranted in this situation. Write to Gettle explaining that you will accept $100 monthly payments with interest charges suspended for three months.

8. How do you feel about humorous collection letters? Do you think they are more difficult for *you* to write than a "straight" letter? Do you think they are more effective? Invent the circumstances calling for a collection letter and write a humorous letter.

9. The initial transaction: Randy and Maria Bauer purchased $2,600 worth of furniture from your store on a two-year, 1½ percent monthly interest installment contract on April 8.

Your position: You are the credit manager of Jeuner's Home Furnishings.

The situations: For each of the following sets of circumstances, write the appropriate letter or letters. Consider these situations to be a series of related events; your letters should be considered a *series* of well-thought-out collection letters.

a. The Bauers have made prompt payments for the first four months. However, it is now September 6 and you have not yet received their fifth payment, which was due on September 1.

b. It is now September 15 and you have not heard from the Bauers. Will you write them again now? If not, how long will you wait before contacting them?

c. It is now October 5, and the Bauers are two months overdue in their payments.

d. When will you decide that more serious persuasion is necessary? Remember that at this stage more than one letter might be necessary, with stronger appeals than were used previously.

e. It is three days after you sent the Bauers your last letter. Apparently it was effective, for they have at least responded by telephoning you. With much embarrassment and distress, Mr. Bauer explained that he had been laid off from his job, that he didn't know when he would be called back, and that he was looking for another job. He seemed very concerned about his credit rating and asked if some kind of arrangement could be worked out. You told him that you would take his situation into consideration and would write him the next day. A check with your credit bureau reveals, among other things, that the Bauers live in a well-to-do neighborhood and own two late-model, expensive cars. Inventing any other pertinent information, list several alternatives for handling Mr. Bauer's request. Select the one you consider most appropriate and present it in your letter to him.

f. The Bauers have taken no further action in settling their account. You now believe that they will do nothing unless they are made to pay. You must prepare your strongest letter to them—you are at the final stage of your series. What are your alternatives? Choose the one you consider most forceful for this concluding letter.

11
SALES LETTERS

Why use letters as a medium when selling goods or services? The debate about the merits of direct mail selling compared with magazine, newspaper, radio, or TV advertising has been going on for years. Advocates of each medium present "conclusive" evidence that theirs is the most productive or inexpensive or widest in coverage or hardest-hitting of all media.

One fact is certain—the volume of sales letters has increased tremendously over the past two decades, and this increase is likely to continue. By somewhat circular reasoning, one can conclude that if the sales letter is used increasingly, it must be effective. Almost anyone can name very profitable concerns whose business has been built up by direct mail exclusively. Of course, ample evidence is also available to show the efficacy of magazines, newspapers, radio, and television in building sales. But since a discussion of the relative advantages of various advertising media does not fall within the scope of this book, we should concern ourselves with two interrelated questions relative to the sales letter:

1. Why is it used so widely?

2. When is it most effective?

In a sense the answer to both questions is the fact that *the sales letter is the most selective of all advertising media.* It can reach almost any age group, financial class, professional group, geographical area, or occupation that may be potentially interested in a given product or service.

The reason for this selectivity is the mailing list, which sorts people into endless—and sometimes amazing—categories. Thanks to computer technology, the mailing-list industry has become very sophisticated. Officials in the industry claim that they generate about $45 billion in sales a year. They contend that they can put together a list of prime prospects for just about anything a company wants to sell. In fact, if you were to name any group of people with something in common, the chances are good that someone is selling a list of those folks for $25 to $50 per 1,000 names each time the list is used.

To the uninitiated, a glance through a catalog of mailing lists is an eye-opening experience in terms of the way it divides humans into "all sorts and conditions" of men and women. You are offered a range of choice from 28,000 owners of parakeets to 16 manufacturers of celery salt; from thousands of people who practice self-hypnosis to more thousands who buy baby chickens. You can select lists of those who want to quit smoking or those who like to make home brew, wines, and liqueurs. Literally, the lists proceed from birth to death. You can have monthly lists of babies born in all the states of the Union or in any more precise geographical subdivision, such as a county. As for death, you have your choice under "Cemeteries" of such lists as "Names of superintendents of," "Largest," "National," "Divided by states," and even "Cemeteries for pets."

The rifle-shot selectivity of such lists as these makes the sales letter the least expensive form of sales *per potential customer,* because if the list is up to date, little or no money is wasted on uninterested readers. A second advantage claimed for the sales letter is that its readers have no other items competing for their attention when they read it—as do magazine readers, for example, who probably have pictures or a story before them along with the advertising. This second advantage may indeed be theoretical, since we do not know enough about how readers go through their mail—in front of a TV set, for instance, or when they first get home and are hurrying to do something else, or at leisure giving it their full attention. Finally, sales letters will carry a heavier percentage of advertising than other media; they can concentrate on material bearing directly on the product or service being sold without wasting time or space on irrelevant entertainment or attention-arousing pictures.

These advantages may be somewhat offset by what appears to be growing resistance to "junk mail"—a term which raises hackles among direct-mail practitioners. Whether this resistance is real or confined to a highly vocal minority is debatable: the Direct Mail Advertising Association sponsored a study in the mid-sixties showing that 8 out of 10 people surveyed have no general dislike for direct mail. On the other hand, numerous newspaper and magazine articles cite rising resentment. In fact, this resentment has even resulted in suits against some of the largest companies that sell or rent these lists. The plaintiffs contend that the actions of these companies constitute both invasion of privacy and unjust enrichment to the marketers of the lists.

Thus far, these contentions have had some impact upon the industry. The 1975 Privacy Act, for example, restricts the information government agencies can collect from individuals and what they can do with that information. Furthermore, the Direct Mail/Marketing Association now advertises that it will remove the names of people from lists upon which they do not wish to have their names. It is unlikely, however, that we shall soon see any major changes legislated against this industry. Anyone who believes in the free enterprise system and recognizes the need for the marketing function must also accept the fact that merchandising by mail is a logical, economical, and timely alternative for introducing and getting some products to some prospects.

The sensible viewpoint is to agree that when sales letters are cheap, mass-mailed, corny appeals to join this or that "exclusive" club or to take advantage of some "once-in-a-lifetime" offer, they truly deserve to be called "junk mail." (It is fair to say that our era also has "junk" magazines, books, movies, products, and newspapers.) But one should not abandon perspective. A great many sales letters are honest and sincere; others are original and humorous; and many render a useful service. These are the types we will discuss from this point forward.

The advantages of the sales letter—selectivity, concentrated attention, and high percentage of sales message—must be considered in terms of specific products, services, or merchandise. In answer to our question of *when* the sales letter is most effective, we find that it is best adapted to selling products or services with a specialized appeal, with fairly high prices, or of the category "novelties." By contrast, we would find that manufacturers of toothpaste, groceries, tires, spark plugs, drugs, and tobacco products would select the medium that reaches the greatest number of people because their products are used by almost everybody. With its selectivity, the sales letter should be used where potential buyers can be picked out from many uninterested ones. Its success, in the last analysis, will depend on three factors:

1. The product or service which is being sold

2. The prospect or list of prospects to which the material is sent

3. The sales letter itself

When the product or service is attractive, the list of prospects carefully selected, and the sales letter effectively written, direct-mail selling is a highly profitable medium. Progressive business people, recognizing its flexibility and selectivity, use the sales letter for the following purposes:

1. To make direct sales

2. To obtain inquiries about services and products and to locate leads for salespeople

3. To announce and test the reaction to new services and products

4. To reach out-of-the-way prospects and to build up weak territories

5. To reinforce dealers' sales efforts and to secure new dealers

6. To build goodwill

After recognizing the purposes listed above, the sales-letter writer must be concerned with a very important question: *Why do people buy what they buy?* Thus stated, the question seems deceptively simple; yet its answer is very complex and only dimly understood. The criteria of "a fine product, a good mailing list, and an effective sales letter" work, but getting these three requisites synchronized represents the real hurdle. To fully appreciate the complexity of this task, students might candidly examine their reasons for buying whatever it is they buy.

Is it because you really need things? Or because you want to keep up with—or ahead of—the Joneses in the student body? Because of vanity, prestige, self-respect? Or pride of ownership? Or a desire to be like others? Or different from them? An honest self-appraisal of such motives should help you to appreciate the fact that buyers may behave the way they do for a multitude of reasons. Thus, it is not an easy task to acquire the right list of people who share some of the same reasons for buying what they buy. The following factual cases reveal some of the problems and the unexpected relationships inherent in the process of selecting the "right" mailing list.

> A men's magazine, traditionally aimed at hunters, fishermen, and outdoor devotees, decided that its potential circulation was limited by its "hairy-chested" image. It decided, therefore, to tone down this aggressively masculine reputation in order to acquire new readers through a mail advertising campaign.

> The problem was how to pick out lists which would offer the maximum number of potential subscribers for the "new look" in the *Outdoor Magazine* (not its real name).

> As might be expected, a list of names rented from a manufacturer of sleeping bags zeroed in with excellent results. But unexpectedly, so did two other lists—of ham radio operators and of door-to-door salespeople.

> A list of 200,000 people who sent in for a leather wallet which sported a thick sheaf of plastic windows for credit cards proved to be excellent prospects for books on travel and on business. They also turned out to be just as excellent prospects for corrugated boxes!

> Lists made up of people who sent in for a reducing pamphlet proved to include excellent prospects for inspirational magazines; several thousand people who sent in for special pillows and various sleep aids showed an abnormal interest in buying fruit cakes; and people who sent in for a widely advertised, chemically treated cleaning cloth for cars were excellent prospects for mutual funds and theater tickets.

By citing such examples, we are not trying to make sales motivation "a mystery wrapped in an enigma." But students can learn much by thinking about—and discussing—such questions as these:

> What is the possible connection between ham radio operators or door-to-door salespeople and outdoor activities like hunting and fishing? Between leather-wallet purchasers and corrugated-box buyers? Or between subscribers to

inspirational magazines or between buying fruit cakes and aids to sleep? Or between uses of car cleaning cloths and prospects for the theater or for mutual funds?

Is it possible that no logical relationship exists between such apparently disparate interests?

Is it perhaps just as well that we don't know the precise answer to these questions? Is it better for us not to know exactly the way to "manipulate" people by understanding why they buy what they buy?

To these and other questions associated with buying motives, no one "right answer" exists. In order not to compound the confusion further, we had best rely on the pragmatic answer which sums up what we *do* know: a fine product, a good mailing list, and an effective sales letter do produce sales. In the rest of the chapter we will proceed on this assumption.

THE STRUCTURE OF THE SALES LETTER

So basic is the structure of the sales letter that it can be used for almost any letter in which an attempt is made to obtain agreement or favorable action from the reader. To make anyone act or think as we want, we must first gain that person's attention, next create a desire for the product we sell, then convince him or her of the truth of what we are saying, and finally make it easy for the reader to act. The structure of the sales letter is designed to arouse these reactions in the reader. Its parts are arranged to:

1. Attract the reader's attention

2. Create a desire for the product or service

3. Convince the reader that the product or service is as good a value as we claim it to be

4. Motivate action

Frequently, the individual sales letter devotes a paragraph to each of these functions, which for brevity we shall call *attention, desire, conviction,* and *action.* Sometimes the second and third functions, desire and conviction, are approached in the same paragraph(s). In a series of sales letters, one or more of the letters may be devoted to each of them. But whether a single letter or a long series is used, the basic purposes remain the same.

One of the best methods by which the novice can learn the fundamentals of sales-letter structure is through an analysis of printed advertising to see in detail how advertising experts accomplish these four tasks. A careful reading of the advertisements in any magazine will show that the underlying structure is always the same although the details may vary considerably:

Attention	by pictures, catch phrases in large type, questions, commands, or humorous illustrations
Desire	by descriptions of pleasure, profit, utility, or economy of the product or service
Conviction	by statistics, testimonials, samples, tests, or guarantees
Action	by easy-to-follow suggestions such as "Fill in the coupon" or "Send for this pamphlet" or "Go to your neighborhood grocer today"

These four elements in the structure of a sales letter must be adapted to a viewpoint which answers one central question: Why should my readers do what I am asking them to do? The following pages of the text suggest various methods which may be used to answer this question in the four-part structure of the sales letter.

1. Attracting attention in the sales letter

As we have indicated, the vast number of sales letters mailed annually has developed a rather heavy armor of sales resistance among readers. To exaggerate this would be pointless; nonetheless, there is little doubt that many readers glance at the first paragraph of the letter and either read the rest of it or toss it aside *depending on what the first paragraph says.* If it attracts the reader's attention, the rest of the letter can capitalize on that fact; but if it does not, the whole sales letter fails. What devices can be used to attract the reader's attention?

One method employed successfully in numerous sales letters is a *pertinent question,* which has the virtue of being direct and of arousing the reader's curiosity to read further in order to discover the answer. Here's an example which at first glance seems a shocker:

Why don't you try minding your own business?

Actually this opening comes from a successful sales letter in which the readers are completely won away from their first resentment or surprise when they learn that it is a sales letter to interest them in a franchise operation in which they would own and operate their own business. After what seems a blunt and brash opening, readers are disarmed by reading the rest of the message, which they unquestionably will do.

The following questions are intended to develop a similar desire to read on:

Could you ask your boss for a raise today and get it?

Are you satisfied with the amount of money you save?

How many times have you wished that you could find time to read the best sellers that all your friends are discussing?

How about a different vacation this year? Could you enjoy two weeks of riding through sun-dappled forests, splashing through cool gurgling streams, or just sitting among blue mountains?

What power does your Internal Revenue agent *really* have . . . and how much should you cooperate with him?

Do you ever wish you had a better memory? (The opening of a letter from Career Institute, Little Falls, New Jersey)

What would it be worth to your company, in bigger profits and better working relations, if more of your employees could be made to realize that merely "good enough" is *not* enough today?

Ever get the feeling that the world is moving too fast?

Will you be ready for the new kind of boom ahead? (The opening of a letter from The Kiplinger Washington Editors, Inc.)

How much help do you give your supervisors?

How long can you afford to wait for your younger executives to discover the facts of life? (The two preceding examples are openers of two sales letters from The Economic Press, Inc. Each letter promoted a different biweekly brochure of management tips)

What is one legal document you should *not* keep in your safe deposit box? (The opening of a letter from U.S. News and World Report, Money Management Library)

A *courteous command* is another technique used frequently to open sales correspondence.

For your family's sake, don't drive on tires that are worn smooth!

Don't read this if you have all your labor troubles solved!

Take just four minutes, Mrs. Smith, to solve all your Christmas shopping problems!

If you're thoughtful enough to give a gift, you're thoughtful enough to give the *right* gift. The gift that really counts. All year. So prove it.

Stop envying people with superior memories . . . Why not develop one for yourself? (The opening of a letter from the Career Institute, Little Falls, New Jersey)

A *"split" beginning* arranged in such a way as to attract maximum attention is widely used. The following illustrates the split beginning:

Millions of people enjoy gum—
    but not in their carburetors.
      (From a letter with a stick of gum attached to sell a carburetor cleaner)

We can't make all the roofing in the world—
    so we just make the best of it!

> They canceled their order . . .
>> and we liked it.
>>> (The letter goes on to explain that the original order was canceled and replaced by an order for twice as much.)

> Very few autographs are worth $10,000 . . . but yours may be! (From a sales effort by a finance company)

> If *saving money* is your #1 priority this year—saving on food bills, saving on household costs, saving on family expenses . . .
>> If you're determined that your family is *not going to suffer through another year like the last one* . . .
>>> . . . then welcome to *Consumer Reports,* the monthly magazine that's helping almost 2 million subscribers make dollars go further. Much further.
>>> (Copyright 1977 by Consumer Union of the United States, Inc., Mount Vernon, N.Y. 10550. Excerpted by permission from Consumer Reports 1977.)

A *statement of a significant fact* or a *quotation from an eminent authority or promient individual* will arouse interest if the fact is significant or the authority is known to the reader:

> You can judge a company by the customers it keeps. Forty-nine percent of our customers have "kept company" with us for more than fifteen years.

> One out of three has it! . . . Did you know that one out of every three electric water coolers sold is a G.E.?

> Surveys show that the average executive increased his work capacity an hour a day by dictating data, correspondence, and details to an Edison Voicewriter.

> A prominent industrialist, now head of a U.S. government agency, once told an editor of *Forbes* that a single sentence in *Forbes* saved him a quarter of a million dollars!

Anecdotes are frequently used to attract attention, and they do get read. Their purpose is not to entertain the reader, however, but to promote sales; therefore, the story should have some connection with the sales message and should not be told just for the story's own sake. Your reader may be an ardent golfer, and an anecdote about golf will doubtless get his or her attention; but if the rest of the letter sells electric fans or nuts and bolts, which don't interest the reader, you'd better avoid that opening. Here are some examples which are relevant to the message which follows them:

> Mark Twain once remarked that the most dangerous place to be is in bed, because more people die there than anywhere else. (This is followed by a sales message for home accident policies showing that Twain "had a point.")

> A little boy we know wrote Santa at Christmas saying

Dear Santa:

Do you leave presemts for little boys who flunk speling? A freind of mine wants to know.

John

Yes, John, he leaves "presents" for poor spellers. (Goes on to describe a well-known dictionary as a suitable present for birthdays, graduation, and Christmas.)

I once read about a man from Illinois who scribbled down all his thoughts on tiny scraps of paper which he crammed into his hat. One began: "Four score and seven years ago . . ." (It's a true story.) (The rest of this letter then promotes a portable cassette recorder/playback system.)

The story-telling approach has been especially effective in letters seeking contributions. The following letters demonstrate how difficult it can be to resist appeals that use such an approach.

I'D LIKE TO TELL YOU A STORY ABOUT A GUY WHO ONCE DIED ON THE INSIDE!

Who is he?

Perhaps a guy from your hometown. Or, maybe a relative. It really doesn't matter.

You might find him sitting in a wheel chair in the corner of a dark living room. He may not have shaved for days and the only reason his body is clean is because his wife still loves him enough to care.

We'll call this guy Jim. But his name could just as well be Joe or Tom. For this isn't a story about one particular person. Jim is just a name for thousands of disabled American veterans you've helped us reach over the years.

A land mine in Vietnam ripped off both of Jim's legs and his right hand. But this isn't what caused Jim to die on the inside. It was coming home that did it.

For three days, Jim received a hero's welcome. People brought food . . . wished him luck . . . and marveled at how well be handled the hook on his right hand. Then they left.

On the fourth day, he started asking people for a job. That's when he stopped being a hero and started to die.

For five months Jim went anywhere that might lead to any kind of job. But people had a lot of excuses for not hiring a handicap . . . even a handicap that had given so much to his country.

It wasn't long before his savings ran out and Jim's wife had to find work. But the bills kept piling up and little by little their small world was repossessed.

Jim finally gave up. He retreated to his dark corner and even stopped taking care of himself. His fellow countrymen had broken him.

We wouldn't have reached Jim if it hadn't been for our fleet of service vans touring the country. They stop at small towns from coast to coast to help disabled veterans who are either too sick or too poor to travel several hundred miles to a VA office.

At first, Jim wasn't interested in talking to us. But he couldn't help notice that our representative was also a disabled veteran.

It took a lot of persuasion. But finally we reached something inside. He straightened up in his wheel chair and asked, "Do you really think I have a chance?"

That was all we needed!

Next, we started processing compensation claims that would provide Jim with some income. He had been totally unaware of the benefits he was entitled to receive.

Finally, we assisted Jim in finding a job. It wasn't much. Just routine work. Suddenly, he was alive again.

Where do you fit into Jim's story? Right there beside us. You and many other concerned Americans helped us reach the many disabled veterans represented in Jim's story.

There are thousands of other disabled veterans out there who need us. Both of us!

We can't give them back priceless limbs or eyesight. But we can return their confidence and respect.

Would you send five dollars to help soften the adjustment of living without legs? Would you send more, if you can afford it?

We've enclosed a set of handy address labels as a small way of saying thank you.

Please take a moment, right now, and make out your check to DAV. Share a portion of your good fortune to help men and women who gave more than any of us can ever repay.

Sincerely yours,

THE VISIONS OF CHRISTMAS . . .

How will Christmas morning be in your home? A festive table. The shimmer of tinsel and lights. Ribbon, tissues and papers scattered beneath the tree.

Now think of a small child, alone and hungry in a cold and barren room, knowing that this morning—Christmas morning—will be like all the others. Joyless, toyless, friendless.

That's how Christmas will be for many children in our own community. *Unless* you help.

Each year The Salvation Army brings the joys of the holiday season to needy families. And all through the year, we offer help and hope to the disadvantaged.

We do *for you* what you don't often have the opportunity to do on your own. Through us, you lend a helping hand to a neighbor in need.

A few dollars buys a small toy . . . or, more important, a pair of shoes. A little more means Christmas dinner and warm clothing. Contributions of $50, $100 or more spread the blessings of Christmas throughout the year.

Help us make Christmas a time of joy. Anything you give is significant. And the knowledge that you've helped someone less fortunate will surely make your Christmas even more special to you.

May God Bless You,

Another technique used to gain a reader's attention is to touch upon a *mutual experience.* Such an approach can sometimes establish a common ground between the writer and the reader that might encourage the recipient to read on. One publisher, for example, began its selling effort with a cartoon of a man paying his bills while his wife looks on over his shoulder. Her comment, in the caption, read, "I'd sure hate to be in our creditors' shoes this month."

A letter selling attitude posters to employers began in the following manner:

Employees are hard to convince . . .
Frequently the harder you try, the more skeptical and suspicious they become—the less inclined to listen and believe.

(An opening to a letter from the Economic Press, Inc.)

As you might be starting to suspect, the avenues available for getting a reader's attention are many and diverse. Some companies, for example, have used a rather bold opening that addresses possible reader objections *head-on* at the start of the letter. The following paragraph exemplifies such an opening.

It may sound strange but I'm writing to tell you about a travel club whose biggest benefit concerns the travel you and your family do to shop, to get to work, or even to play golf.

The next opener uses a bit of empathy and subtle praise to reduce the reader's possible disturbance at getting "another" such letter.

If the list upon which I found your name is any indication, this is not the first—nor will it be the last—subscription letter you receive. Quite frankly, your education and income set you apart from the general population and make you a highly-rated prospect for everything from magazines to mutual funds.[1]

Two other attention-getting techniques merit brief mention before we move to the rest of the sales letter. The first of these techniques is becoming common in selling efforts that involve long letters and brochures. In such cases, an informal note is often included, supposedly directed at readers who have decided not to take advantage of the product or service offered. The note usually expresses wonder at the reader's decision and highlights the major selling features covered in more detail in the rest of the selling effort. It is labeled an attention-getting device here because its casual appearance often causes it to be the first thing at which readers look.

The last attention-getting device we shall discuss involves the use of the envelope as an integral part of the selling effort. This device has a wide range of variations. Some envelopes contain numerous illustrations. Some contain a question designed to stimulate interest. Others contain nothing that would hint at the nature of the envelope's contents. Companies that employ the last strategy often exclude return addresses and have the recipient's name and address handwritten.

Besides the preceding, relatively ordinary methods of securing a reader's attention, the sales letter also offers opportunities for all kinds of devices and stunts with the same aim. Common is the technique of enclosing checks for the reader's time, stamps, keys, pencils, cigarettes, samples of products, and strange contraptions designed to arouse curiosity. Sales letters are printed on all shades and all shapes of stationery. The Ralph J. Bishop Co. has had excellent results by designating their best customers "honorary directors," even to the point of declaring 7¢ dividends. Enclosures, unusual letters, and offbeat designs cost money; whether they pay for themselves in terms of added business should be the criterion in deciding whether to use them. The sales letter must, as we have said, attract attention, but if the readers are merely interested in a tricky device or clever opening which does not carry them along into the remainder of the sales message, the correspondent has failed as badly as if the opening aroused no interest at all. To the sales correspondent, the attention-arousing device is a means to an end rather than an end in itself.

2. Creating desire for the product or service

One of the longest—and most inconclusive—discussions about readers centers on what is the best method of making them desire goods or services. Basically, there is the appeal to emotions or the appeal to reason, or, more frequently, a combination of the two. In a simpler era, it used to be thought that males

---

[1] Copyright 1977 by Newsweek, Inc. All rights reserved. Reprinted by permission.

responded to logic, females to emotion—but no longer. Perhaps it is an unflattering commentary on people's rational power, but a glance through the advertising in most magazines will show how much more widely the emotional appeal is used than any other form. Refrigerators, oils, automobiles, and similar workaday products are sold through advertisements that depict pretty women or humorous situations or play on our desire to keep up with the Joneses. These are frequently attention-arousing techniques, but often we are made to want some product not on its merits alone but through highly emotional appeals to snobbishness, or fear, or the need to be like (or different from) other people. A lot of insurance, for instance, is sold to supposedly logic-motivated men through an appeal to their emotions ("If you weren't here, could your wife pay off the mortgage?"; "You do want to guarantee your children a college education, don't you?").

Whether to appeal to the reader's logic by expository and rational methods or to emotions by descriptive techniques will depend on the product, the kind of reader, and the overall situation. In selling products to retailers, for example, manufacturers and wholesalers stress practical concerns like profit margins, advertising assistance, and expected or proven demand. The same products, however, are promoted to consumers on different bases. Diamond rings are often sold to customers on the basis of their aesthetic or sentimental value. Cars are frequently promoted to the buying public through appeals to appreciation of elegance or style.

Many advertisers feel that a logical appeal is best for necessities and an emotional one for luxuries or novelties. One problem arising from this dichotomy, however, is the fact that our increasingly affluent society sometimes clouds the distinction between what is a necessity and what is not. Furthermore, there are so many exceptions to this simple rule that we have to fall back on the old saw of elementary logic: "All generalizations are false—including this one."

Nonetheless, certain human desires are more or less universal, and appeals directed to them will at least reach readers. A few years ago the Direct Mail Advertising Association listed the following 25 reasons why people spend money:

To make money	To gratify curiosity
To save money	To protect family
To save time	To be in style
To avoid effort	For beautiful possessions
For comfort	To satisfy appetite
For cleanliness	To emulate others
For health	For safety in buying
To escape physical pain	To avoid criticism
For praise	To be individual
To be popular	To protect reputation
To attract the opposite sex	To take advantage of
To conserve possessions	opportunities
For enjoyment	To avoid trouble

These are at least reasonably specific, and you can test your own reasons against them. The following excerpts from sales letters show how correspondents use the you attitude in their sales appeals:

You've heard the names all your life—Tahiti, Bora Bora, Moorea—the land of Bali Ha'i, Bali, Rarotonga, and our own Hawaii—home of Waikiki and Diamond Head. Now instead of being names, they'll become real places, places you once dreamed of, shining places in your memories.

You want to keep intelligently informed about the rapidly changing world in which we live. You want to be able to talk confidently about national affairs and foreign affairs, about what is being invented, voted, written, painted, about what is being discovered in medicine and science. You want the news fully, concisely.

We have a book that you will want; your secretary will want it; your mailing department will wonder why they couldn't have had it long ago. It is a concise encyclopedia of authoritative postal knowledge compiled with the cooperation of the Postmaster General.

Wouldn't you like to have the most successful collection people in the country explain their methods to you, show you the actual letters they use, and tell you how economically they have solved their collection problems?

At sunset, the haze over the Catskills is a soft purple. You remember, of course, how much you enjoyed vacationing here in Rip Van Winkle Land last year—and it's just as peaceful and lovely this year.

3.   Convincing the reader of the merits of the products or service

Thus far, our analysis has revealed the technique of the sales letter to be chiefly descriptive, expository, or narrative. The function of the third section is to marshal support to show that the claims made for the product are true. This is the technique of argument, which may be defined as *the art of influencing others to accept our beliefs by an appeal to their reason.* Previous claims and statements must here be supported by fact or logic; otherwise, the reader will correctly assume that the claims are grandiose and the statements untrue. In general, three types of logical support may be used in sales:

Expert Testimony. This consists of statements by qualified experts concerning the product sold. Because of the widespread use of testimonials from people in no way qualified to speak about various products, the average reader became rather skeptical of this sort of support. As a result, this practice fell under federal regulation. Now the person quoted must be really qualified by education or experience to speak about the product. When such is the case, these endorsements can constitute very sound sales arguments.

Facts. Since the statements in the first part of the sales letter belong in the category of opinion (e.g., "The Colderator is the most economical refrigerator on the market today"), their truth is best shown in the third section by a solid basis of fact. Tests made by independent experts, statements about the number of sales made within a specified period, actual cost of operation of the product, mention of the number of satisfied customers, and specific data about the product under actual working conditions—all these give an objective, factual support to the claims made for the product.

Use of Logic. Since our logical faculty uses both facts and expert testimony on which to base its conclusions, this final division is somewhat arbitrary. In the sales letter, however, logic may be used to appeal favorably to readers' reasoning or to get them to draw their own conclusions. A trial offer of the product may be made with the purpose of getting the reader to conclude, "If they are willing to let me try it out, it must be pretty good." Samples and guarantees are similarly effective. A correspondence school may use analogy to show that other students have taken a given course and have gone on to great success. The conclusion, "What they have done, you can do!" is inaccurate logic, but it seems to create sales. Widely used also are causal relationships, such as "Because Pan-American coffee is packed in air-tight tins, it reaches you as fresh as the day it was roasted."

Whichever of these three types of logical support is employed, the sales correspondent should make sure that the statements used do rest on a solid foundation and that the conclusions reached are logical. The following examples show specific applications of how these methods may be used to win conviction:

> Sixty years is a long time, isn't it? And that's how long we've been serving companies like yours with the technical skill that comes only from experience.

> Just to substantiate these statements, I am enclosing a circular which contains the names of over a thousand graduates of our secretarial course who have voluntarily reported salary increases within the past year. Perhaps you may know, or know of, some of these people. Their record shows in dollars and cents the value of the Blank Secretarial Course.

> Our company has paid off its insurance claims through four wars and a half-dozen depressions. Our 80 years' experience is your guarantee that your policy is secure in spite of unsettled conditions.

> As a person who has shown interest in conservation, you should join the 35,000 subscribers to a magazine which is dedicated to conservation. For two decades, we've informed readers when natural resources were being despoiled, told them what to do, and urged them to do it. We need your subscription to be more effective; but you need us to become a member of a group which knows what's new in conservation—and *does* something about it.

> Because more than 50,000 Europeans used it, we imported it. Because our own tests showed its quality, we guaranteed it against defects in material or workmanship for one year. It costs a little more, but it's worth it. If you don't agree, you can return it after a two-week trial.

4. Motivating action

The final paragraph of the sales letter should do two things; offer a specific suggestion concerning the action the reader should take, and point out how he or she will benefit by taking this action. The easier it is for the reader to take this action, the more effective the sale message will be; hence, stamped and addressed envelopes or the more economical business-reply permit envelopes, which do not require the payment of postage unless used, are frequently enclosed, or the reader is told to call by telephone or to wire collect. Whether these devices are economically feasible depends largely upon the product being sold. The second function—pointing out the benefit to be gained by taking the proposed action—has been called a "sales whip." It involves making a brief reference to the product or service's major selling feature as you attempt to move the reader to action. The following closing paragraphs show various methods to motivate action:

> It's a practical offer for practical people . . . and we wouldn't dare to make it if we couldn't back it up. Just initial the enclosed card and drop it in the mail.

> Please take a few moments to complete your personal and Christmas gift order now, while it's on your mind. Then drop your order in the mail today . . . before the holiday rush begins.

> To try the letter for the next six months, just check and return the enclosed form with your payment . . . or ask us to bill you or your company later. Either way, the sooner you do this, the quicker you'll profit from the penetrating forecasts, judgments, and advice you'll get in each weekly issue. (The close of a letter from The Kiplinger Washington Editors, Inc.)

> The enclosed card requires only your signature to bring you 52 issues full of entertainment, information, and enjoyment.

> Wouldn't you like to see the way this new machine might aid you to reduce overhead? Just sign and mail this postcard for a demonstration.

> The coupon below will bring you a copy—without obligation. Won't you sign and mail it *today?*

> Take a moment *right now* to check the items that interest you. We'll gladly send you a sample of each.

> Your subscription expires with the next issue. Act now! Sign the enclosed blank and you won't miss a single issue.

You might have noticed that several of the preceding examples used various ways to urge immediate action. Words like "today," "right now," and "Act now!" and reasons like limited supplies or offers good for only a certain amount of time are often used in such endings to encourage readers to act fast—with good reason. If the letter is effective, readers are not likely to ever again be as stimulated to take action as they are at the letter's end. Putting the letter aside for later consideration represents almost certain failure for the selling effort. Thus, many sales correspondents encourage their readers to strike a note of commitment while the iron of temptation is hot.

Before taking a look at some examples of complete sales letters, students should be reminded of one important characteristic of sales-letter writing. This characteristic is that in no other form of business writing is creativity more highly valued. The content of such letters is admittedly partly dictated by the letters' objectives and by the essential information that must be included. There is, nonetheless, room for originality, humor, and a bit of the unusual in such efforts.

EXAMPLES OF SALES LETTERS

The sales letter can be used effectively both as an individual message—for instance, to announce a sale to individual customers before public announcement is made—or as part of a series. Such series frequently consist of an original message and three or four follow-up letters; other series, such as those sent to dealers, are never-ending.

The following sales letters show the various ways in which devices to stimulate attention, desire, conviction, and action can be incorporated into unified and coherent messages. Try to decide what motivation they appeal to, and judge their effectiveness in terms of how well they would stimulate action by the reader.

Dear Mrs. Johnson:

"The world is a book of which those who remain always at home read only one page."

Whoever wrote those words knew what travel can do to broaden mental horizons and to free us from the narrow routine of daily living.

For 27 years, we've helped thousands of people travel near and far . . . cruises to the Caribbean, escorted tours to our National Parks, group and go-it-alone trips to Europe. . . . Whatever you choose, we can make your arrangements for you, by land or sea or air.

The enclosed folder lists the various ways you can read the many pages of this book we call the world. Just check the trips that interest you and mail it back to us postage paid. We'll call you then and tell you about costs, alternate arrangements, and financing. The world is literally waiting. Don't let it wait one more day.

Sincerely yours,

Dear Mr. Peters:

We'd like to BLOW YOU UP!

Don't call the police. We just want you to send us any black and white picture and we'll blow it up to poster size—2 × 3 feet costs $3.50, 3 × 4 costs $7.50. We'll return your photo and the poster in a sturdy mailing tube.

Send your check in the enclosed envelope and in a week you'll have a perfect example of pop art, a genuine conversation piece, and a unique decorative ornament for your home.

Very truly yours,

Dear Mr. Myers:

Early this morning the white mists were lifting their curtains to reveal the blue-green Catskills in the distance.

Your summer home is at its loveliest now. Haven't you longed for those blueberries that line the winding paths around the hotel? Or for that view of the soft haze around High Point? Your four weeks at the Mountain View last summer must hold a cherished place in your memory.

Why not store up more memories to gladden your future? You'll go back to work more fit, more efficient, if you get away from it all for a while.

Mountain View offers you the same rates as last year, and if you want us to, we'll reserve the same room. Why not wire your reservation to us today?

Sincerely yours,

Do you know how much your
Social Security is worth
under the law now in
effect?

The Social Security Act has been changed repeatedly, and for some people the changes made will mean increased benefits.

But do you know what you personally may expect to receive?

At no cost to you, we will be glad to give you an estimate of your benefits, based on your own Social Security taxes and the number of your dependents who might become eligible to receive Social Security payments. This service has been very popular because most people like to know how their benefits have been affected by the changes.

In a day or two I will call and make this information available. The estimate of your benefits can, with your cooperation, be made in a few minutes.

Sincerely yours,
(From a representative of
an insurance company)

Dear Mr. Ellender:

Sincerely yours,

P.S. We have an idea that's too good for words. May we stop in and tell you about it at your convenience?

Dear Mr. Cole:

Someone has said that "brevity is the art of speaking volumes without writing them" . . . and so we'll be brief.

CONWAY, GREEN, AND MILTON

CONSULTANTS TO MANAGEMENT

FIDELITY-PHILADELPHIA BUILDING

PHILADELPHIA PA 19118

February 3, 1971

Mr. William O. Zentgraf, President
The Chemical-Industrial Corporation
The Dupont Building
Wilmington, Delaware 28032

Dear Mr. Zentgraf:

"Sculpture is very easy," said a famous sculptor. "All you do is take a block of marble and chisel off all the stone you don't want."

That's a good description of the way we can serve you as management consultants. For fifteen years, we've been aiding industry by cutting off the inefficiency and red tape that management doesn't want.

The enclosed brochure describes the many ways we can serve you—from expert time and motion studies to personnel evaluation plans. You'll be interested in the comments from our clients on pages 24-26.

Your signature on the enclosed card is all that's needed for you to arrange an interview at your convenience and, of course, at no obligation.

Sincerely yours,

Charles E. Conway
Partner

CEC:MEG

Employees Are Hard To Convince...

Frequently the harder you try, the more skeptical and suspicious they become--the less inclined to listen and believe.

That's why our new POSITIVE ATTITUDE POSTER service uses a low-pressure, humorous approach. It starts with a smile--a cartoon by Ted Key, the creator of Hazel. Then a brief statement that makes so much sense it's bound to strike home. No shouting, no finger-pointing, yet each poster plants the seed of a positive, constructive attitude toward a man's job and the company he works for.

Keeping people alert and productive is one of the never-ending problems of managing a business. Even the best of workers need occasional reminders to keep them moving ahead under a full head of steam. The management which relaxes its efforts to create and promote good employee attitudes leaves the door wide open for poor attitudes to move in and take over.

You'll find these posters a big help in your efforts to keep employees thinking constructively. Walnut-finished frames are available, if you wish, which make them just as suitable for the handsomest office as the busiest factory.

Just return the enclosed card. We'll start sending you new morale-boosting POSITIVE ATTITUDE POSTERS to display every two weeks.

Sincerely,

John L. Beckley
Publisher

pap/d

The ECONOMICS PRESS, Inc.

Tel 201-227-1224

12 DANIEL ROAD · FAIRFIELD · NEW JERSEY 07006

We've been in business for 23 years . . .

   . . . supplying commercial photographs
   . . . to more than 30,000 customers
   . . . for catalogs, house organs, sales brochures
      and presentations of all kinds.

May we discuss your photo problems with you? There's no obligation. Just mail the enclosed card and I'll call at your convenience.

Sincerely yours,

One question might be drawn from the preceding examples of sales letters: Is it more effective to use a variety of appeals or to fully develop one major appeal? Authorities differ on the answer to this question. Some suggest that to keep the sales letter down to a length that will help ensure its being read, the writer should only concentrate on one major appeal. Others profess that a variety of appeals will increase the chances of successfully touching upon an unsatisfied reader need. We take the view here that both arguments have merit, and both views can offer worthwhile guidelines. A sales-letter writer is probably wise to use more than one appeal. At the same time, however, the writer would not want to employ so many appeals that each is not developed fully or that the letter becomes unmanageably long.

EXERCISES

1. Your publishing company runs the Nu-Age Health and Vitality Book Club and is starting a campaign to increase its membership. You have obtained mailing lists from the publishers of health magazines and from mail-order vitamin companies. Write a sales letter in which you offer an introductory book for only $1, with no obligation to purchase any additional books.

2. You are in charge of the fund raising for the annual scholarship given by your university's Alumni Association. As a recent graduate of the university and a recipient of one of these Alumni Scholarships, you are very aware of the value of college experiences and of the scholarship. Compose the fund-raising letter to be sent to all Alumni Association members.

3. Obtain one or more sales letters you or friends have received.
   a. What is your overall reaction to the letter?
   b. Pick out the four structural parts of the letter. Analyze the effectiveness of these individual sections. Did the opening encourage you to read on? What specific words and sentences were used to persuade and motivate you?
   c. Did the letter achieve its purpose? Why or why not?

4. Write a sales letter to be used for each of the following purposes:
   a. To sell leather, pocket-sized appointment calendars to business executives.
   b. To attract customers to the grand opening of your new discount stereo equipment store.

    c. To inform would-be travelers of the unusual tours to places all over the world your travel agency is sponsoring. (Use your imagination!)

    d. To announce a one-day symposium on psychic phenomena to be sent to people who are known to have an interest in such things.

    e. To explain to charge customers of your department store the new gift-buying service available at no cost. Customers complete a form describing the person to whom they want to give a gift the amount they want to spend, etc., and a computer prints out a list of suggested items.

5. Your insurance agency, which prides itself on the friendly, personal service it provides community members, sends a welcoming letter to new residents. Compose the letter you think would be most appropriate.

6. The insurance agency mentioned in Exercise 5 has just opened a branch office on the west side of town. You want to inform your current customers of this new office and also get them to think about increasing their insurance coverage. In addition, you want to introduce yourself to people living on the west side who are not yet customers.
    a. Would you send the same letter to both groups? Why or why not?
    b. Compose the letter or letters you would send.

7. You are the director of the Master of Business Administration program at your university. For reasons not related to the quality of your program, the number of students enrolled has been declining over the past year. You now must recruit students for your program.
    a. What might be some of the reasons for the decline in enrollments?
    b. What are some of the selling points of your program? How will an M.B.A. benefit the student?
    c. Write the recruiting letter which will be sent to a selected list of college seniors and people working in business throughout the country.
    d. Do you have any ideas other than this recruiting letter for increasing enrollments?

8. You are planning to publish a magazine directed to a special-interest group (you pick the group, based on your own interests). You want to determine the possible market for such a publication; therefore, you are sending a letter offering a special charter membership. Charter members will receive a two-year subscription for the price of a one-year subscription ($8); and if they wish to cancel during the first year, their entire subscription fee will be refunded. Write the letter that will best motivate these potential subscribers to take a chance on a new publication.

9. You are director of the Americans for Alternative Energy, a nonprofit citizens' group which is attempting to educate Americans about the necessity of developing alternative energy sources, inform them of the availability of alternative energy and of the research and development currently being undertaken, and influence policy makers and lawmakers in favor of alternative energy. All the funding for the AAE comes from private donations. Write the letter you will send to solicit these funds.

10. Your nationwide mail-order company is starting a new sales campaign. As an inducement to new customers, you are offering a free copy of your 450-page catalog plus instant credit up to $200. You are planning to hit both city dwellers and rural folks in this campaign. Would you send the same letter to both groups? Why or why not? Prepare the letter or letters to be used.

12 LETTERS RELATED TO EMPLOYMENT

In recent years our economy has experienced several dark periods where unemployment reached double-digit peaks in many areas. During such periods many companies virtually ceased their college recruitment activities, and graduates were dramatically introduced to the importance of being able to apply in writing for a job. Actually, every individual should regard this ability not only as insurance against stormy economic weather but also as an effective means to improve one's own position. In fact, no writing that you will ever do is likely to have greater potential for affecting your life than your writing connected with the process of applying for a job. And it is worth noting that employers often attach as much importance to the *way* in which job credentials are presented to them as to the experience or education contained in those credentials.

THE PROPER POINT OF VIEW

Throughout this text, we have stressed the theme, "Think before you write." The process of applying for a job is one situation in which careful thought can pay handsome dividends. An indispensable ingredient of successful job seeking is *objective self-analysis;* and since the gift of seeing ourselves as others see us has not been universally conferred upon humans, self-appraisal is not easy. Here are some questions you ought to think about before you put anything on paper:

> What are my best qualifications for employment?
>> Education?
>> Experience?
>> Some specific skill?
>> Personality traits?

Am I seeking a specific position (i.e. secretary, salesperson, accountant, engineer, typist, receptionist, etc.) or general employment?

What is it that I really want in a job—salary, opportunity for advancement, challenge, commitment, the opportunity to serve others, or what?

What organizations offer the best opportunity for me to find what I want?

Unless you are the casual I-just-want-a-job type, you need a detached and searching look-at-yourself-in-the-mirror answer to these questions.

Later, you can check up on how well you've passed this self-examination by asking a classmate or a teacher to go over what you write about yourself in your application. But the self-analysis must come first.

After this emphasis on "I," you will have to translate the results of your thinking into a prospective employer's viewpoint and write in terms that appeal to that employer. It's all too easy for applicants to write about "how much *I* would like to work for your company" or "how much *I* dislike my present job" or "how badly *I* need work"; but after the objective I-analysis we have described, the results must be transformed to answer a reader's question: "What does the applicant offer which will prove useful or profitable to me?"

THE PURPOSE AND METHODS OF APPLYING FOR A JOB

The purpose of writing application letters is not, as many think, "to get a job" but more normally *to get an interview*. The positions which educated applicants seek are almost never given without an interview; the goal of getting one, therefore, is primary in the application process.

Although we are discussing *written* techniques only, it may prove helpful to examine briefly the other ways of seeking an interview. Why not go in person and ask for one? Or why not use the phone to arrange an interview? In other words, why *write?* The answer actually will depend on timing, distance, and various other circumstances, all adding up to the conclusion that there is no one "best" way. But if you make a personal visit unannounced, you may not see the person you want to, and if you do, you may interrupt a busy schedule. If you phone, you may not get through to the right person, and you'll be told to come in for the interview before you've had a chance to supply your background. The advantages of these two methods are, of course, that they are quick and direct and reflect your interest and willingness to get a job promptly. While the written process of application is slower, it has these advantages:

1. It gives the person responsible an opportunity to analyze your qualifications and the company's needs at his or her convenience.

2. It provides background for a constructive interview.

3. It can be put on permanent record against the time when a suitable position is available.

4. The effort it demands says more for your determination and interest.

A final aspect is worth mentioning: whether you phone or call in person, you will usually have to write anyway, since most companies have forms or questionnaires to be filled out. By using the steps in the process which are explained in the next pages, you have the chance to present your credentials in a form that *you* have chosen as the best way to present them.

THE STEPS IN APPLYING FOR A JOB IN WRITING

The following are the most widely accepted steps in writing to apply for a job:

1. A data sheet which gives all necessary details about the applicant's background under such headings as Education, Experience, Personal Details, and References.

2. A comparatively brief letter, usually three or four paragraphs, featuring the applicant's best qualifications and ending with a courteous request for an interview. In the middle paragraph(s) of this letter, an indirect reference is made to the data sheet which is enclosed.

3. A follow-up letter after the interview or (in very rare instances) a follow-up letter when there has been no response to an application letter and data sheet sent earlier. Since these letters depend heavily on varying circumstances, we shall discuss them only briefly.

The letter of application and the data sheet are, of course, the two most important steps in this process.

The advantages of the combination of letter and data sheet are fourfold. First, it enables the applicant to feature, in a letter short enough to be readable, those qualities which best fit him or her for a specific position. Second, the applicant can convey a far greater amount of information in a readable form in this combination of letter and data sheet. Third, this form of application is adaptable and sufficiently flexible so that it can be used in a variety of situations. Regardless of whether there is an immediate need for it or not, every young educated person should have a data sheet readily available, because once it is drawn up, it can be used over and over again; the letter to accompany it can be varied to meet the specific employment situation. Fourth, the data sheet presents in a concise form, which can be filed easily, all the details about an applicant and how he or she may be reached. Hence, it remains as a ready reminder of the job seeker's qualifications and availability if a vacancy does occur. These advantages suffice to make the combination of letter and data sheet the most effective technique of seeking employment by mail; the applicant who wishes to make the best presentation will certainly use it.

All of this discussion is, of course, based upon the assumption that the job seekers possess the essential qualifications to fill the positions for which they apply. It should not be necessary to say that even the best letter will not get a job for an unqualified applicant; yet a surprisingly large number of persons seem to believe that by a lucky break they can get jobs for which they are not trained. To the contrary, it is education, experience, and ability that successful job applicants must depend upon.

In the following pages we shall examine the three steps in the application process listed above. In other words, we shall first study the writing you would do in applying for a job. Afterward, we shall look at two other letters related to the job-seeking process but written by someone else. These are letters to and from references. Although some people would question the extent and value of their use today, you should still be familiar with them, should you ever be called upon to write one.

THE DATA SHEET

The data sheet will be discussed first because it is normally compiled before the application letter is written. A data sheet might be defined as a well-organized and neatly arranged concise review of the background information that qualifies you for a job. Before discussing its content and construction, we should distinguish between a data sheet and a résumé. Although the terms are often used interchangeably, there are differences between the two. These differences lie in the content and grammar of each.

The data sheet concisely reviews your qualifications. It is concise to the point that incomplete sentences are allowable and considered advisable by many. Furthermore, as mentioned above, it reviews your qualifications; it does not interpret your background in terms of the job for which you are applying. This function, interpretation, would be accomplished by the letter that accompanies the data sheet.

The résumé, on the other hand, is not normally accompanied by an application letter. It is therefore usually a more involved selling effort than a data sheet. In complete sentences, the résumé might give more details of your background than would a data sheet and might interpret that background as it relates to the job you are seeking. As an example, consider your extracurricular activities. On a data sheet, you would simply list these activities and make mention of them in the application letter. In a résumé, you would list them and make some reference to something like how such activities improved your ability to get along with and/or organize people. Having made this distinction, we can now review the makeup of the data sheet.

The greatest advantage of the data sheet is that it can be adapted to any individual's needs or experience. Certain characteristics are, however, invariably the same. Centered at the top of the sheet are the name and address of the applicant with the phone number in the upper left-hand corner and the month and year in the upper right-hand corner. This arrangement makes the information easily visible when the sheet is filed. The conventional headings for listing other information are Education, Experience, Personal Details, and References. Thus the fixed parts of such a data sheet look like this:

Telephone   John Smith   August 1970
607-213-1246   12 Main Street
                             Elmira, New York 14901

Education

Experience

Personal Details

References

Students who are interviewing near the end of their senior year may have a special problem. If they will be moving out of their dormitory or apartment at the school year's end, they might consider putting two addresses and phone numbers at the top of the page, one in each corner. These addresses and phone numbers might be entitled "temporary" and "permanent" or "until (date)" and "after (date)" The latter set of titles might be more advisable, since "permanent" could give the impression that you don't care to move from the second address.

No pains should be spared to make this personal record sheet pleasing in appearance by keeping it well balanced and uncrowded. The headings may be made to stand out by capitalizing all the letters or by underlining. These headings might be placed at the left margins, as exemplified above, or centered. The information presented below these headings might be arranged in rows or columns. If an item is long and drawn-out, it would best be arranged as a row across the page. If an item is made up of a series of shorter items, like the name, title, and address of a reference, it might be arranged in column form.

In years past, most data sheets were arranged with personal details first, followed by education, experience, and references. This order might have developed from a general feeling that a "person's" personal details introduced her or him in such a way that the other facts made more sense or were more concrete when later read. Lately, however, data sheet compilers are being told to order the parts in the way that works best for them. If education is a person's major selling feature, it should come first. In later years, after a person has built up a certain amount of work experience, that experience becomes the background aspect of greatest interest to potential employers and should be featured first. Many job seekers list their business experience in reverse order on the sound theory that a prospective employer is chiefly interested in what the applicant has done most recently. When reverse order is used for one part, such as Experience, it is a good idea to use it for other parts, such as Education.

Since the material on the data sheet need not be expressed in complete sentences, there is room for great detail and for attractive spacing. Dates of educational, military, and business experience ought always to be given; and whenever possible no gaps in the applicant's record should be left unaccounted for.

As a recent college graduate, you would include in your review of your education all high schools and colleges attended and their locations. In later years, the high school reference(s) would be dropped. Your college reference(s) would include degree(s) earned and major field studied. Whether or not you note your grade point average would depend upon whether it deserves mention. Even in these days of grade inflation, however, a 3.0-or-better average is still worthy of being mentioned. If your cumulative average doesn't measure up to that, compute your average in your general or specific major. If you are majoring in accounting, for example, your business courses average or your accounting courses average may be better than your cumulative average.

Under Experience, it is best not merely to give the title of the job but to specify what its duties were. Don't merely say clerk, salesperson, or chemical engineer, but describe what the specific duties of these positions were. Also, don't be shy about including part-time or summer jobs that *seem* unrelated to the job for which you are applying. Such jobs indirectly say certain things about you that would be of interest to employers. Finally, don't forget to indicate whether your work experiences were full-time or part-time when your list contains a mixture of the two.

The section labeled Personal Details is difficult to categorize, since personnel people don't agree as to what it should include. Furthermore, state laws affecting fair employment practices vary among states, and federal legislation varies from time to time. This section of the data sheet has generally been regarded as a miscellany containing what is not classifiable under the other headings. As such, it is still safe to include comments about your height, weight, health, and major interests and hobbies. Also, if you earned at least 25 percent of your educational expenses, you might mention it here.

In considering whether to include sex, age, race, religion, or nationality, think about whether their inclusion might help your cause. This same criterion might be used in deciding whether or not to include a picture on the data sheet. Remember that employers may be prohibited from asking for these details, but that doesn't mean they are not interested or that you are forbidden to offer such information. Furthermore, if your data sheet and application letter get you an interview, you will still have to fill out an application form. This form will ask only allowable questions and is the item that is likely to be kept in your permanent record with the company.

Personal material may be arranged in almost any fashion to suit the individual's needs. One may save space by arranging it as follows:

Personal Details

Age, 25; height, 6 feet, 1 inch; weight, 185 pounds; health, excellent; unmarried; American; veteran, USNR; hobbies—photography and stamp collecting; sports—tennis and golf.

Or if the personal record sheet seems to have too little material on it, the personal details may be listed this way:

Personal Details

Age	25	Nationality	American
Height	6 ft. 1 in.	Veteran	USNR
Weight	185 lbs.	Hobbies	Photography, stamp collecting
Health	Excellent		
Marital Status	Unmarried	Sports	Tennis, golf

Under References are placed the names and addresses of at least three people who can testify to the applicant's business experience, education, or character. Common courtesy requires that the consent of the individual used as a reference should be obtained *in advance* of the actual application. The full title and complete address of each reference ought always to be given; where the references are local, their telephone numbers may also be listed. If a reference's relation to you is not understood (by, for example, the person's academic title, or position in a company for which you worked), make it clear. You might do so with a title like "personal" or "character."

Before we illustrate acceptable data sheets, a few final comments should be given additional emphasis. Spare no pains to make the data sheet as neat as you possibly can. Commit yourself to typing it several times to produce the most eye-pleasing appearance. Remember, this effort is the first impression of you that the employer is going to receive. Also, don't panic if your data sheet exceeds one page in length. Some authorities suggest that you work hard to keep it down to one page. We take the view that if your background is varied enough to warrant more than a one-page description, more power to you. If your background is interesting and relevant, most potential employers won't mind flipping the page to read on.

The two sample data sheets that follow illustrate two different approaches that can be taken. The first example might be called a *general* data sheet. It describes the applicant's background in such a way that it could be sent to many firms in application for several different types of jobs. The accompanying letter would personalize the selling effort. This is the most popular approach because this data sheet can be economically duplicated and sent to a large number of potential employers. If, however, you find yourself primarily interested in one particular type of job with two or three companies, you might be more interested in the approach illustrated in the second example. Notice how this *personalized* data sheet includes captions and content that more explicitly and implicitly indicate a strong interest in the job for which the individual is applying.

THE LETTER TO ACCOMPANY THE DATA SHEET

This letter is used as a device to highlight the job seeker's best qualifications. It follows the structure of the sales letter, but it leaves the details to be filled in by the personal record sheet. Its contents should include:

1. An opening statement or question that gains the reader's attention and identifies the nature of the letter.

2. Amplification of the opening, stressing the qualifications that might appeal to the reader's interest.

3. A reference to the fact that complete details about the applicant are contained in the enclosed data sheet.

4. A closing request for some appropriate form of action from the reader (usually an interview).

The Opening Paragraph

Beginning the application letter is probably the most difficult part of the whole technique, as the hundreds of thousands can testify who have told their teachers, "If I could only get this letter started, the rest would be easy." Ideally, the opening paragraph should be direct; it should have the you attitude; it should feature the applicant's best quality. One of the simplest ways of attaining these qualities is by a summary beginning:

> Two years at Blank Business School have given me a training in business administration which should be useful to you.

> Because of my three years' experience as a salesman for the White Company, I feel that I can qualify for the sales position which you advertised in this morning's *Boston Herald*.

> My five years' experience in the collection department of the Black Company makes me confident that I can help solve your collection problems as you want them solved.

> Four years of college at the University of Michigan plus two summers of work with the Brown and Brown Company have given me a knowledge of the theory and practical application of engineering problems. May I put this knowledge to work for you?

Although such beginnings are not too original, they will arouse the interest of an employer who is seeking applicants. From the writer's standpoint, these summary beginnings make the transition to the second paragraph very simple because it logically should give further details about the education or experience referred to in the opening paragraph. Furthermore, the summary beginning avoids the possibility of using such negative, colorless, or completely useless openings as:

> I should like to be considered as an applicant for a position as clerk with your firm.   *No you attitude, trite, colorless*

> I happened to be reading the *Washington Star* and saw your advertisement for a secretary.   *Don't bother telling such trivial details*

Data Sheet
of
DON JONES

504-766-2231   March 1977

1025 Dalrymple Drive
Baton Rouge, Louisiana 70803

EDUCATION

May 1978: Will graduate from Louisiana State University, Baton Rouge, Louisiana, with a Bachelor of Science degree in Business Administration. GPA = 3.27

May 1974: Graduated from Edward Douglas White High School, Thibodaux, Louisiana, in top 20 percent of class. Took commerce curriculum.

Extracurricular Activities

Pi Sigma Epsilon Professional Marketing Fraternity: member from fall of 1975 to spring of 1978, correspondent from fall of 1976 to spring of 1977.

Lettered in high school track, two years. Member of high school debate team for three years.

WORK EXPERIENCE

Summer 1977: Worked as a production clerk in Olefins Unit of Union Carbide Plant in Hahnville, Louisiana. Duties included recording and graphing production of unit and refiling engineering designs.

Summer 1976: Worked as driver for Stores Department of Union Carbide Plant in Hahnville, Louisiana. Work involved delivery and pickup of tools and supplies within the plant.

Summer 1975: Employed as a carpenter's assistant for Thompson Construction Company in Thibodaux, Louisiana.

October 1972 to August 1974: Worked as shoe salesman and cashier for West Brothers Department Store in Thibodaux, Louisiana. Part-time during school and full-time during summers.

PERSONAL DETAILS

Age, 21
Height, 5'11''
Weight, 150#
Health, excellent
Marital status, single

Hobbies and Interests:
   swimming, tennis,
   reading, and traveling
Earned 50 percent of college educational expenses

REFERENCES

Mr. James C. Cooley, manager
West Brothers Department Store
Nicholls Shopping Center
Thibodaux, Louisiana 70301

Mr. Frank Murphy, Supervisor
Olefins Unit
Union Carbide
Hahnville, Louisiana 70760

Professor Leon C. Megginson
Management Department
College of Business
Louisiana State University
Baton Rouge, Louisiana 70803

Professor Jerry Wallin
Management Department
College of Business
Louisiana State University
Baton Rouge, Louisiana 70803

Preparation of
JANE R. WEEKS
for the position of
Management Trainee
with Taylor Ltd.

Address until June 5, 1977
1012 E. Lemon, #13
Tempe, Arizona 85281
Phone: 602-966-6201

Address after June 5, 1977
1816 West Coast Highway
Newport Beach, California 92662
Phone: 415-324-4632

SPECIALIZED EDUCATION IN BUSINESS MANAGEMENT

May 1977: Will have earned a Bachelor of Science degree in Management from Arizona State University, Tempe, Arizona. GPAs were:
3.46 in general, 3.69 in all business courses, and 3.82 in management coursework. Classes taken in major included:

Principles of Management
Production Management
Methods Management
Training and Development
Managerial Decision Making
Human Relations in Business

Personnel Management
Social Responsibility of
    Management
Industrial Relations and
    Collective Bargaining
Business Policies

May 1973: Graduated from Tempe Union High School in top 10 percent
of class. Majored in business.

Activities that Enhanced the Education

At Arizona State University:

Member of Sigma Iota Epsilon Honorary Management Fraternity,
two years. Member for two years and historian for one year
of Delta Sigma Pi Professional Business Fraternity. Served
as Vice President of the Business Administration Student
Council for one year.

At Tempe Union High School:

Worked on the school paper for three years as a writer and
one year as editor. Served in the Speakers Bureau for two
years.

WORK EXPERIENCES THAT ALLOWED FUNDAMENTAL APPLICATIONS

September 1975 to May 1977 (excluding summers): Employed as part-time student worker in the Department of Administrative Services, Arizona State University, Tempe, Arizona. Duties included typing, test duplication, and mail distribution.

Summers of 1974, 1975, and 1976: Worked full-time in Gift Department at Diamond's Department Store, Thomas Mall, Phoenix, Arizona. Progressed from sales clerk in 1974 to supervisor of the evening shift in 1976.

PERSONAL DETAILS

Age, 22
Height, 5'7''
Weight, 130#
Health, excellent
Marital status, single

Hobbies and Interests:
  tennis, skiing, sewing,
  and ice skating.
Earned 75 percent of col-
  lege educational expenses.

PEOPLE WHO WILL SPEAK OBJECTIVELY

Dr. Lohnie J. Boggs, Chairman
Department of Administrative
  Services
College of Business Administration
Arizona State University
Tempe, Arizona 85281

Professor Bill Werther
Department of Management
College of Business
  Administration
Arizona State University
Tempe, Arizona 85281

Ms. Mary Hultz, Supervisor
Gift Department
Diamond's Department Store
Thomas Mall
4201 East Thomas
Phoenix, Arizona 85014

Professor Heinz Weihrich
Department of Management
College of Business
  Administration
Arizona State University
Tempe, Arizona 85281

Now that business is again aggressively pushing sales, you are undoubtedly adding to your
staff. I should like you to consider my qualifications.

*Don't tell what the reader al-
ready knows as though he or
she didn't*

Applicants are usually much too concerned with the introductory section
of their letters and, consequently, spend so much time in introducing themselves
that they lose the reader's interest before the preliminaries are concluded. A
good test of an introductory paragraph is to read the letter without it; if something
important is omitted from the letter with such a reading, the opening paragraph
is important and says something direct; the three opening paragraphs above, like
the various pests in Gilbert and Sullivan, "never would be missed."

Another effective way to begin, if you have the person's permission, is the
name beginning, which mentions some business associate, friend, or customer of
the prospective employer.

Mr. James Johnson of your advertising department has told me that you will
soon need another secretary. My college education and three years as a private
secretary in a legal firm should merit your consideration.

Mr. J. J. Moore has suggested that I might be well qualified for sales work in
your International Division because of my command of four languages and my
background of travel abroad.

The ultimate value of such beginnings depends almost entirely on the name
used; but the fact that a friend, business associate, or customer is mentioned will
invariably win consideration for this type of letter.

A third method of opening is by a question intended to challenge the
reader's attention. While this type of beginning sounds rather abrupt, it has the
desirable effect of forcing the applicant to plunge into the middle of his or her
most salable qualities without any preliminaries or introduction.

Can your sales force write letters which get a minimum of 5 percent returns?
I have done that consistently and with a more highly specialized product than
yours.

Can your stenographers take dictation at the rate of 120 words a minute? I
can—and I am eager to prove that such speed does not lessen my accuracy.

Could you use a general utility infielder? A person who could fill in at any of
the positions on your staff and relieve you of the worries and delays caused
by absences of personnel?

Applicants who use this question beginning should first be absolutely certain
that their qualifications *do* answer the question which they raise; otherwise, the
letter accomplishes nothing.

Another form of opener is that which incidentally mentions some point of
knowledge about the company. This approach is related to one of the most

common complaints of college recruiters—the fact that too many college students know very little about the companies to which they apply. To many recruiters, this lack of knowledge implies lack of interest. In much the same way, the fact that you know something about the company implies a degree of interest greater than that demonstrated by applicants who canvass the market. The following openers exemplify this approach by noting an awareness of what is happening to the company:

> Now that Dixon is expanding its Western sales region, won't you need another trained and experienced salesperson to call on your new accounts? My marketing degree and four years of sales experience lead me to believe that I can fill that need.

> When Last National Bank prepares to open the doors of its two new branches, please consider allowing me to put my six years' experience as a teller to work for you at one of those branches.

The Middle Paragraph(s)

Depending upon whether the letter is a three- or four-paragraph application, the one or two middle paragraph(s) generally amplify or highlight the features you want to stress. Somewhere in this part of the letter should be a reference to the enclosed data sheet, but this reference should always be indirect. Sophisticated readers of application letters don't need to be told, "Enclosed please find a data sheet of my education and experience" as if they would have to hunt for it. Make such references indirect and casual, as follows:

> As you will see on my data sheet, I am fortunate in having my military service behind me.

> My previous education, which is listed on my data sheet, has motivated me to seek a position where I will be able to do part-time graduate study.

> My major interest is people, as the section on extracurricular activities in my data sheet shows.

The best way to regard the function of the middle paragraphs is to think of them as your chance to emphasize or select from the factual and rather impersonally presented material on the data sheet those qualities or experiences you want to stress for a specific job. Here are some examples:

> You may consider it important that I earned more than 80 percent of my college expenses doing sales work during summer vacations. As my data sheet shows, I have done door-to-door selling, worked in a booth at the State Centennial Exposition exhibiting merchandise, and served as a promotion agent for a summer camp.

> My interest in communications has increased steadily. As my data sheet

shows, the courses I selected and the activities I tried out for centered on learning how to express my ideas in speech and writing.

What I offer, actually, is a very good education combined with a limited experience in summer jobs, shown on my data sheet. But this combination makes me very eager to apply what I have learned to actual business problems. My enthusiasm to "get going" may well prove to be most useful to you.

As you will see on my data sheet, I have always moved to a position with greater responsibility and higher salary. A broad variety of experiences in middle management has prepared me for the abilities and responsibilities required at the top level of management.

My skills, which are detailed on my data sheet, include the usual ones required of a secretary. But the intangibles are hard to put down on paper the way I can quantify how many words a minute I type or take dictation—and those intangibles include the ability to work with others, to run an office which is gracious but efficient, and to relieve my boss of unnecessary detail.

One very good clue to the effectiveness of these middle paragraphs is to judge them from the reader's viewpoint—do they give an insight into the kind of person writing the letter? And reversing the perspective, the applicant can judge how well they represent him or her by asking: "Is this a clear statement of my best qualifications?" These criteria ought to be supplemented by applying the principles of unity and coherence to the middle paragraph(s); trite as it is to say so, the application letter has a beginning, middle, and ending. Thus, the choice of the opening paragraph drastically affects the middle paragraph(s). If that beginning is a summary paragraph (My four years at Blank University qualify me . . .), then the middle paragraph(s) should supply details. If the beginning uses a name (Professor Blank has suggested that I apply . . .), then the middle paragraphs ought to supply reasons why you and Professor Blank think you have the requisite training or experience. Finally, if you begin with a challenging statement or question (Could you use a general utility infielder?), your next paragraph had better supply an answer focused on the reader's question, "What makes you think you can be 'a utility infielder'?"

As in a sales letter, the body or middle paragraph(s) should work to convince the reader that the product (you) is worthwhile enough to satisfy a real or potential company need. It is here that you persuasively attempt to sell yourself. Since most college students have never before been called upon to do this, a few words about the appropriate tone to be used might be in order.

Since it is a new experience, students sometimes mistakenly go to one of two opposite extremes. To some, to speak subjectively about the personal benefits of certain experiences is akin to boasting. Because of this attitude, they stick entirely to facts: graduation dates, times of employment, etc. The letter becomes simply a repetition of certain facts from the data sheet. It makes for rather dull reading, since it employs little or no reader orientation.

Other students operate according to different assumptions. They assume that all businesses are looking for extremely confident, ultradynamic go-getters;

and they try to project themselves as such on paper. While it is true that some jobs call for a greater degree of extroversion than others, it is also true that most employers would rather receive an application from a human being than from the southern end of a northbound horse.

The appropriate tone lies somewhere between these two extremes. It is businesslike. It is objective. It is sincere. It embodies the demeanor of a salesperson who knows that a product has enough quality built in to warrant consideration by customers. This salesperson knows that with proper installation and user care, the product will perform as promised, and is therefore not embarrassed to speak of its merits. And just as this salesperson would describe the product's qualities in terms of customer satisfaction, you should not be hesitant to portray your background in terms of what it might realistically mean to potential employers.

The Closing Paragraph

The closing paragraph has primarily one function—to ask for an interview. On the theory that the application letter, like the sales letter, ought to make action easy for the reader, many applicants formerly enclosed self-addressed postcards on which the prospective employer could fill in the date and time when he or she could conveniently see the applicant; others ended by suggesting that "You may call me at 231-2897." Such closings ought to be avoided, because most intelligent readers can locate your phone number and address on your data sheet and would prefer to use their own means of getting in touch with you *if* they are interested. The following closes are effective:

> May I have an interview? I could come by your office on any weekday afternoon, at your convenience.

> Although my data sheet contains considerable detail, you doubtless have questions you want answered. May I come in for an interview at your convenience?

Notice how much more direct the preceding examples are than the following timid or colorless endings, which should be avoided:

> I trust that you will grant me an interview.

> I shall hope to hear from you soon.

> If you feel that I may be of use to your organization, please let me come in for an interview.

How should the letter close when the prospective employer is at a considerable distance from the applicant? This situation is always a difficult one to which there seems no completely correct solution. The job seeker cannot very gracefully suggest coming 600 miles to be interviewed by the prospective employer. A few employers would welcome so tangible an expression of interest in their company, but the great majority feel that it places too much responsibility on them. They fear that the applicant is likely to conclude that since he or she is not deterred from coming, he or she certainly must have excellent prospects of getting a job. The ideal way is for the applicant to be invited for an interview or, barring that, to suggest a means by which the interview can be arranged without too much difficulty. The following closes may suggest methods of handling such a situation:

> I shall be in New York from December 22 to January 3. Would it be convenient to talk to any of your staff there concerning the possibility of employment? (This is obviously a student making good use of Christmas vacation.)

> Is it possible that you or some member of your staff will be in this vicinity within the next month? A telegram to me, collect, will bring me to see you at your convenience.

> I shall be in Wilmington on May 4 and 5. May I see you on one of those days?

> (It is altogether possible that the applicant's sole reason for being in Wilmington is the chance of getting this job, but it is usually better not to tell the employer this. Many an applicant has obtained a job through being willing to take a five- or six-hundred-mile trip to "Wilmington" on his or her own responsibility.)

> You or your associates will undoubtedly be in _____ (name of the nearest large city) during the next few months. When you are there, may I have the opportunity of seeing you?

> Does a representative of your company plan to visit this school? If so, I should be grateful for an opportunity to talk with that person.

If none of the preceding approaches can be adapted to your needs, you can always close by either suggesting further correspondence or asking that the reader contact your references. At least such closes would leave the next move up to the employer while still suggesting constructive action.

The following letters show how some of these suggestions may be incorporated into complete application letters:

Mr. D. J. Wright, President
The William C. Bryan Company
3190 West Canal Street
Boston, Massachusetts 02126

Dear Mr. Wright:

Could you use a dependable secretary?

During the past two years I have been with Jennings and Sessions, Inc., of this city. Because our office was small, I performed many different duties; this gave me an excellent understanding of the routine of an office.

I can take shorthand, operate a switchboard, type rapidly and accurately, act as a receptionist, and write letters dealing with routine situations. The enclosed data sheet will give you complete details about my education and personal qualifications.

May I come in to see you at your convenience?

Sincerely yours,

Dear Mr. Stevens:

My ten years' experience as a salesperson for the Green Wholesale Grocery Company should qualify me for a position as sales manager with your company.

I have traveled in western Massachusetts for the past six years, and my wide acquaintance among grocers and food buyers in that section should be valuable to you in marketing the new line of Premex Foods which you are introducing. My record as a salesperson has been excellent, as my references will show; as a sales manager, I could use my own experience in training personnel rapidly but efficiently.

As the enclosed data sheet indicates, I am a college graduate and have taken several graduate courses in Marketing and Sales Organization. I am widely known among businesspeople in this city, since I have been active in many civic and fraternal organizations.

May I have an interview to substantiate these statements and to answer your questions? You may reach me at 106-4137.

Sincerely yours,

Since it is helpful to see how people actually handle the letter of application, here are two rather offbeat examples. Reaction to their unusual approach has tended to be strong—either very favorable or very unsympathetic. How do you react?

Dear Mr. Smith:

You have the job that I want . . . in ten or twenty years.

As president of your company, you've established a great record . . . and I think I can do the same.

This may sound like the job applicant who said, "During the five years I worked for IBM the company doubled its sales and profits" . . . but if you'll look at my data sheet, you'll find I'm more realistic.

Interested? Then I hope you'll see me. Will you?

Sincerely,

Edward Blank

Sincerely yours,

write or telephone me at 317-1004 at Blank, Ohio.
I am sure that we can arrive at a satisfactory arrangement if you will

This is the only way to get ahead.
done this all through life, and I believe that I shall continue to do so.
Well, as you can see, I am not afraid to start at the bottom. I have

firm.
afraid to start at the bottom, to become a sales representative for your
You state that you have a position open for a young man, who isn't

York Times of January 14.
I am writing this letter in response to your advertisement in the New

Gentlemen:

New York, New York 10010
2471 Park Avenue
Blank Sales Company

January 19, 1970
Blank, Ohio 44444
747 Miami Street

The following application letter could accompany the data sheet of Don Jones on page 219 as he sought one of a variety of jobs in business:

Dear _____ :

Could the _____ Company use a conscientious new employee who is knowledgeable in business fundamentals and eager to learn the basics of your business? If so, please consider the following qualifications.

A degree in business administration, to be awarded in May, has given me a broad familiarity with all the functional areas of business. As such, I could serve as a trainee in a variety of capacities. Furthermore, the varied part-time and summer work listed on the enclosed data sheet has already permitted me to apply some of that education, while earning over 50 percent of my college expenses.

In recognition of the fact that businesses thrive on people working in cooperation with other people, I actively participated in Pi Sigma Epsilon Professional Marketing Fraternity for three years. I do feel that this experience has given me additional insight into human relations within organizations.

If you now or will soon have a need for a worker with a knowledge of business basics and a proven desire to expand that knowledge, may I have an interview? I could visit your office at a time convenient to you.

Sincerely

Don Jones

Don Jones

ONE MORE LETTER

Let us suppose that you are in that blissful state in which you have worked long and well over your letter and data sheet, and your labors have had their reward in an interview. Is there anything you can do but sit and wait?

The answer is *yes:* you can write a follow-up letter *if* your best judgment based on your experience in the interview suggests that you will help your cause by writing such a letter. If, for instance, the interview terminated with anything like "Don't get in touch with us; we'll get in touch with you," no such letter should follow. If you have the slightest suspicion that any further move on your part would be considered overly aggressive, you should not write. But if in your best judgment an occasion for the follow-up letter emerges *naturally* from the interview, use it. Why? Because it will set you apart from other applicants (9 out of 10 won't use it), because it will recall you and the interview to the employer's mind, and because it will give you the satisfaction of knowing that you have done everything possible to get the job you want.

Such a follow-up letter may express thanks for the interview; it may refer to your attitude about the firm or company or job now that you know more about it; it may mention something that took place during the interview; or it may supply new information that now seems appropriate because of the interview. Frequently, during the interview, brochures, annual reports, or similar company publications are handed to applicants, and a natural response can be made after you have read them. The letter should always be brief and modest in tone and generally should be sent a day or two after the interview. Here are two examples:

Dear Mr. Moore:

I appreciate your kindness in granting me an interview yesterday. Your explanation of the problems faced by the automotive industry was very helpful to me. I hope that my past experience may entitle me to favorable consideration because the problems which you mentioned aroused my interest and I would like to aid in solving them.

Sincerely yours,

Dear Ms. Minard:

I have now read the pamphlet you gave me on "Educational Opportunities with Blank Industries." Because my most urgent wish is to continue my growth through education, I was truly impressed by the wide range of educational opportunities which are available to your employees.

Thank you for your courtesy. I do hope that my educational background will merit favorable consideration by Blank Industries.

Very truly yours,

One other form of follow-up letter is occasioned when the application letter and data sheet have been sent and no acknowledgment has been received. Discretion here dictates that (1) sufficient time has elapsed for the reply to have been made and (2) the applicant has reason to believe that his or her qualifications fit the employer's needs. Actually, any application—or indeed any letter of any kind—deserves acknowledgment, but some companies do disregard far-out or off-beat or totally unqualified job letters. Because there is always the possibility that mails are delayed or misdelivered or that the original application reached the wrong person, a follow-up letter may properly be sent. It should be regarded strictly as a letter of inquiry; it should not repeat or duplicate the information sent earlier; it should refer courteously to the job sought, the date of application, and any other items which will identify the original application. And its tone should be polite, neutral, factual. Above all else it should avoid any suggestion of being pushy or accusatory ("I sent you an application on May 19 and you never answered it.")

LETTERS RELATED TO REFERENCES

Not all the letter writing related to the employment process is done by applicants. Once an employer has received your material and has determined that there may be a place for you in the company, a check of your credentials will be in order. The extent of this checking process will vary with the employer. One practice that is not followed universally is the contacting of references.

Some personnel directors have for years taken a dim view of this practice. They regard it as at best a very subjective selection device and at worst, more often than not, a simple whitewash of the applicant about whom the reference is written. Furthermore, the Buckley-Pell Amendment to the Family Rights and Privileges Act has given support to the latter view. This amendment gives parents and 18-year-old students access to their files in public schools. Because of this act, employers now believe that college professors would not dare include anything negative in a reference about a former student for fear of legal repercussions. There is also a general apprehension in business that federal legislation giving employees access to their company files is just around the corner. Such legislation would even further reduce the credibility and value of references written by former employers. Many reference seekers and givers have turned to the telephone as a "safe" method. The telephone, however, does not provide complete safety, since telephone conversations can be quoted in court.

Admittedly, the letter of reference has always been at least partly subjective; and admittedly, the trends discussed above do work, in some cases, to reduce its effectiveness as a reliable selection device. But both these realities are indeed unfortunate, because when handled properly references can give employers a good deal of otherwise unobtainable insight into the work behavior of a potential employee. It is in recognition of this inherent value and because references are still used by some employers that we shall briefly discuss letters asking for and giving references.

The Letter Asking for a Reference

The letter from an interested employer seeking a reference from someone is relatively simple to construct. In fact, when a company employs a large number of people in one type of job (such as insurance agent), the personnel department will usually develop a form to use in seeking references. Such forms usually include questions dealing with the characteristics necessary for adequate job performance. Recipients are typically asked to rank the subject on scales and to make whatever comments they might think relevant.

When a company is small or doesn't have many people working at the job being sought, such forms may not be practical. But the letter that would instead be written need not be involved. Because it is a relatively routine situation, the writer can get to the point in the opening by asking either a specific or a general question. The next sentence would then give the reason for the request, making reference to the fact that it has been authorized.

The body of the letter would be devoted to asking other relevant questions. The questions asked would be determined by the nature of the job and the qualities that the holder of this job should possess. The writer should keep one point in mind while formulating the questions: The recipient of this letter may not be familiar with the exact nature of the job being sought by the applicant. The writer should therefore give whatever background job information is necessary for a pertinent response by the reader.

The letter might be ended by some appropriate goodwill-building comment. It might be an expression of appreciation for whatever insight the reader can give you. It might be an offer to reciprocate, if distance and the situation make the need to do so a logical likelihood. Finally, in either the close or the opening of such a letter, it is conventional to make an incidental reference to the confidentiality of the information being sought. Even though legislation might make total confidentiality doubtful, such a reference to it is nonetheless meaningful, since the writer would still protect the privacy of such information from parties without a legitimate concern.

The following letter is an example of a typical request for a reference from a past employer:

Dear Mr. Joseph:

Would you please give us the benefit of your employment experience with Mr. Richard Farris? He has applied to us for the position of sales manager of our eastern region and has given your name as a reference.

When he worked for you, was he ever given any supervisory responsibilities? As sales manager, he would oversee the work of eight salespeople and three office workers. Do you feel that he could handle the human relations part of this job adequately?

Also, was he timely and accurate in submitting required paperwork? The job for which he is applying involves a great deal of administrative detail. We are naturally interested in someone who can cope with such detail effectively and efficiently.

We will genuinely appreciate whatever answers you can give to these questions, as well as any other information you think might help us in evaluating Mr. Farris.

Sincerely,

Letters Providing References

Letters answering requests for references require the utmost in objective reporting. Writers of letters of reference too often think in terms of letters of recommendation. As such, they frequently give glowing reports on mediocre people, and sometimes even lie by omission by concealing very relevant weak points. They sometimes rationalize such misrepresentations by saying that they are giving the subject a "second chance." What they don't care to admit is that they are doing so at the expense of another party.

Reference letter writers must recognize responsibilities to two parties: the subject of the letter *and* the receiver. It is all too easy to overlook the obligation to the second party, since the writer knows the subject (applicant) well and the receiver is only an unfamiliar representative of some abstract entity. The writer must, nevertheless, face up to the responsibility to be complete and truthful to the receiver. That receiver has a very legitimate interest in information about the applicant. The writer should provide whatever *relevant* information the receiver needs to evaluate the applicant.

One point might be made about the handling of what might be called negative information. If a reference letter is largely positive with one or two pieces of negative news, it would be unfair to the applicant to begin or end the letter with the negative point(s). Negative items, by their nature, command attention. It would be unfair to the applicant to give these items the additional emphasis of such a prominent position in the letter. It would be far better to subordinate them by sandwiching them into the middle of a paragraph in the middle of the letter.

Whether the reference letter is largely positive or negative, it answers the reader's request and therefore will be favorably received. Because of this reception, it can be constructed in direct order. In other words, you can begin such a letter either by answering one of the questions asked about the applicant or by giving a general "yes" answer to indicate that you are providing the information requested. In either case, your opening should identify this letter as a response to the earlier request for information.

Depending upon whether you begin with a specific answer to a question or a general "yes" statement, the body of the letter would answer either the rest of or all the questions that were asked about the job applicant. You would answer these questions in as fair and as objective a manner as possible. If you state a personal opinion about the person, back it up with facts.

The close should attempt to build goodwill between you and the reader. It might express your willingness to have answered the questions or to provide other information if necessary. As with the letter requesting this information, it is conventional to incidentally mention the confidentiality of the information either here in the close or in the opening. Take care, however, to do so incidentally, as with a clause or adjective, not with a complete sentence. To say "We of course expect you to hold this information in strict confidence" is too strong. Giving the reference to confidentiality the emphasis of a complete sentence implies that you distrust the reader.

The following letter of reference about Mr. Richard Farris is a response to the preceding letter illustration. Notice how it subordinates the point that he was occasionally tardy with his reports.

Dear Ms. Davis:

I shall be happy to give you the information you requested about Mr. Richard Farris in your March 12 letter.

Richard joined our sales force in 1972; and by the time he left in 1976, he was third highest seller of a 20-person crew. Even though he outperformed most of his fellow workers, he got along with them very well. In fact, while I was on three-week vacations in 1975 and 1976, I left him in charge. Upon my return each time, I found that everything had gone smoothly while I was away.

Richard's reports were always very accurate. Upon occasion, perhaps 10 percent of the time, they were submitted a day late. We accepted this occasional tardiness because of his excellent performance in the other aspects of his job.

In summary, I feel that Mr. Richard Farris has good supervisory potential. I am happy to provide you with these confidential answers to your questions. If you should need additional information, please write.

EXERCISES

1. Prepare a data sheet for yourself that you could use now to apply for a variety of jobs. If you were preparing it close to the time you expect to be graduated, how would it differ from today's? If you were applying for a job five years from now, how would the data sheet be different? If you were applying for a specific kind of job, how would your data sheet differ from a general data sheet?

2. Imagine the first job you would like to have after graduation. Write a description of it. Assume that you are qualified for this job and write a letter of application.

3. Trade the job description prepared for Exercise 2 with a partner. After reading each other's descriptions, exchange your application letters. What is your reaction to the letter? Are you motivated to interview the applicant? Make a list of the strong and weak points of the letter. Discuss these with your partner.

4. Clip several help wanted ads from the newspaper. Choose one for which you qualify and write a letter of application. Choose another for which you are not totally qualified but you do have most of the stated qualifications. Apply for this position.

5. One of your professors, Dr. Charles Timly, knows that you are looking for a part-time job while you are attending school. He suggests that you write to Alice Garcia, a vice-president of the Bannon Company, to apply for any jobs that might be available. Dr. Timly does consulting work for the Bannon Company; and although he doesn't know what specific jobs might be open, he knows that they hire several business students each year. The qualifications that Bannon seems to look for are a general business educational background, flexibility, adaptability, and the desire to learn on the job. Write to Ms. Garcia.

6. It has been said that a large number of jobs that will exist 10 years from now have not yet been invented. This means, among other things, that the first people to hold these new jobs will be pioneers, creating the duties and parameters of the jobs as they go along. Project 10 years into the future and invent a list of several new jobs. Use your imagination! Then select one job and apply in writing for it. Because the job description is not very definitive, you will have to stress your general skills—those that would be applicable to many jobs. What else do you think would motivate an employer to hire you for a job that will be determined more by present and future circumstances than by past practices?

7. From reading the business section of your local newspaper, you have learned that Tracy's, a local department store, has broken ground for their third store. You are a sophomore marketing major working as a work-study student in the marketing department office of your college. You aspire to a career in retailing and would like to work part-time in a store while you are earning your degree. You visualize yourself working your way up in the store and then being offered a full-time position by that company upon graduation. Write the letter you will send to Tracy's personnel director inquiring about and applying for a job in their new store. Create any other information you need to write an effective letter.

8. Assume that you were interviewed for a job in the new Tracy's store described in Exercise 7. You feel that the interview went very well. You and William Ruppert, the personnel director, discussed several positions that you might be suited for, including retail selling, display and advertising, and working in the administrative office. The store will be opening in six months; therefore, a decision on your hiring will probably not be made immediately. You feel that a follow-up letter would be appropriate. What will you say in this letter?

9. You have interviewed Sandra Kowalski for a secretarial position in your law firm and are contacting her references. The job involves working for three lawyers, doing research in the firm's library, and getting along with six other secretaries. Top secretarial skills are, of course, a necessity, as is an understanding of the seriousness of legal work. The reference you are contacting, Walter Golden, has a one-boss office with two secretaries.
   a. What specific things do you want to know about Ms. Kowalski?
   b. What do you need to tell Golden about the job you have interviewed Ms. Kowalski for?
   c. Write the letter you will send to Golden.

10. Assume you are Walter Golden, the reference contacted in Exercise 9. Answer the letter in two different ways.
   a. Ms. Kowalski was an excellent secretary, and you reply very positively to the inquiry.
   b. Ms. Kowalski had some shortcomings (you decide what these were), and your reply cannot be entirely positive.

THREE
THE REPORT
AND
MEMORANDUM

If you are planning a career in business or industry, six words—or their equivalent—are an inevitable part of your future: "Give me a report on that." The report has become an essential means of business communication. Even the facetious statement that "It takes a ton of paper to produce a ton of product in today's business" is an acknowledgment of the importance of reports.

The report-writing function of business will unquestionably increase in importance. As companies grow larger and employ more people, the number of reports required to maintain communication increases not in an arithmetical progression of 1, 2, 3, 4, but more nearly in a geometrical progression of 2, 4, 8, 16. Added to increasing size is increasing distance, resulting from the trend toward widely separated plants and agencies and creating an attendant need for better communication through reports.

The ability to write effective reports is, therefore, one of the most useful skills you can acquire for a career in business. In Part 1 we discussed business writing as a demonstration of your ability. To a large degree, you will be judged solely on the basis of the reports you write, often by key personnel who have no other contact with you. Whether you view report-writing assignments as an opportunity or an ordeal will depend largely on how well you can learn the techniques of report writing, for we like to do the things we do well. That is why most of the complaints about the need to write reports in business come from employees who can't write them effectively. Business badly needs people who can write clear, concise, accurate, and readable reports. If you can fill this need, you'll go far. It is no exaggeration to say that in modern business a person is known by the reports he or she writes.

Of course, how successful you are in demonstrating your ability depends on how well you perceive and serve the needs of your readers. In the next chapter we will discuss the reader's purposes in requesting a report, and the succeeding chapters will deal with how to serve those purposes. This introduction will tell you, in general terms, what you should know about reports.

What is a report? This is a surprisingly difficult question to answer. Etymologically, we can derive the word from its Latin sources: *portare,* "to carry" (as in *portable, transport,* and *export*), and the prefix *re,* "back" or "again." Thus, a report is something which carries information back or again, although this definition is none too precise. We might also define it by example, citing such types of reports as progress reports, research reports, periodic reports, and a host of others. If time were our criterion, we could list weekly, monthly, quarterly, and annual reports; or, if we give our readers top billing, we would name reports to stockholders, directors, and management. All this terminology may seem confusing, but it merely reflects the actual usage of the word *report* in modern business. In fact, one basic thing to remember about the word, as you will hear it used in your business career, is that it means a great many things to a great many people.

More often than not, the terminology of business and industry stems more from local usage and company practice than from any overall and consistent system of classification; the Sales Report of one company, for example, may be the Performance Analysis Report of another. When you are asked to write a report, you will, therefore, have to apply a very loosely used word to a particular purpose, business, and reader. Your supervisor may say "Give me a report on that by tomorrow," and mean what is often called a memorandum. In fact, we might informally define a report as a memo in full dress, for the line of demarcation between the long memorandum and the report is very thin. If, on the other hand, your supervisor says "I wish you'd spend the next week at the Bartlesville substation and give me a report on why production fell off there last month," you ought to know that he or she expects something more comprehensive than what was wanted in the first instruction. And, just as obviously, your report on the Bartlesville situation will differ from the report made after three years' study by 52 engineers on "The Water Needs of Blank City for the Next Twenty-five Years."

The trend in business, however, is to use short report forms more frequently and to make them less formal; this brevity and informality have been achieved by limiting the scope of reports to a single definite subject and by breaking complex or broad subjects into clearly defined reportable elements.

Probably the best way to define a report is in terms of what it *does*. Its purpose, generally, is to provide managers with information on the basis of which they can decide or act. Professor C. A. Brown, chairman of the English department of the General Motors Institute, defined a report in this way:

> We say it as simply as we possibly can, and that is, that a report is a communication from someone who has information to someone who wants to use that information. The report may be elaborately formal, it may be a letter, or in a great many organizations it is simply a memorandum, but it is always planned for use.

The usefulness of your reports is what you must constantly keep in mind. Whether a report is good or bad generally boils down to how useful it is to its readers. Suppose James Jones, the sales manager of a manufacturing company, is considering adding a new product to his line. He wants to know how well it would sell and how it should be priced. He asks his salesmen, or perhaps a market research staff, for reports that will help him answer these questions. He needs to know the cost of production and whether the company has the necessary manufacturing facilities. He asks production people for reports which answer these questions. The decision as to whether to manufacture and sell the product will be based on the reports. When production begins, reports will tell the sales and production managers whether the costs are within the expectations and whether the quantity and quality are satisfactory. Reports will tell Jones whether sales are up to expectations, whether competition has appeared unexpectedly, whether anticipated prices can be maintained. On the basis of these later reports, plans may be changed, new research undertaken, or production or sales methods changed. A great many reports will have been written, probably by many people. Each report will have had a specific purpose or set of purposes to serve; each will have been expected to enable its readers to do or to decide something. Whether or not a particular report was successful will have depended largely on how well the writer understood the use readers expected to make of it.

At this point you may still wonder what is unique about a report, what makes it differ from a letter or memorandum. The answer will vary from company to company and even from businessperson to businessperson. But it is probably safe to say that, in general, a report, as "a communication from someone who has information to someone who wants to use that information," is marked by three characteristics:

1. It is preceded by considerable investigation or research.

2. It tends to be longer, more complex, and more detailed than the letter or memo.

3. Its scope requires more careful analysis and organization than the shorter forms of business communications.

The thoughtful reader may properly ask why reports, like letters, cannot be divided into types. After all, we have analyzed letters by types: *credit, inquiry, application,* and *sales*. Why not a similar analysis of business reports? The answer is that actual business practice makes such an analysis unrealistic. Our analysis of letters parallels actual business organization, which, if it is of considerable size, divides its functions into such units as a credit department, a sales department, and a personnel department, to mention a few. Each of these units has a reasonably precise function in letter writing.

In report writing, the function tends either to be spread around so that "everybody writes reports or memos" or to be so specialized that time would be wasted discussing it. For example, a prime function of business is getting out an annual report to shareholders, a function, incidentally, in which business has shown a remarkable degree of improvement over the past ten years. How are such reports "written"? Normally, everybody gets into the act. Each department, divison, or unit submits a report on its annual activities. Within each department, each section head has probably written a report about his or her section's activities. These reports, based on reports from individuals in the sections, are incorporated into the department's report; the departmental reports go up the line to the division heads, the executive staff members, or the vice-presidents. They then go to the president or the chairman of the board, who presumably "writes" the report for the stockholders. All along the line, material has been compressed, condensed, or deleted. This is a reasonably accurate account of the way reports ascend the business pyramid, with the important additional statement that at some point all this mass of information will generally be turned over to a specialist—to a committee, to the public relations office, to one person, or to an advertising agency—for *writing*.

The report function of modern business, then, is both so diffused and so specialized that it would be totally unrealistic to approach it from the same basis as the function of correspondence, which is reasonably clear-cut. Your business career will unquestionably involve a myriad of reporting situations; you will write reports directly to one other person, reports to groups, reports that are passed up or down through several levels of authority, reports for other people to sign, reports written with other people, reports concisely digesting other reports, and so on, ad infinitum. In this welter of types, kinds, and occasions, the only realistic preparation you can make is to learn the problems and principles of good report writing and apply them to the specific on-the-job situations which you encounter.

In preparing to do this, you should heed the importance which business executives almost unanimously attach to the ability to write effective reports. Equally significant is their increasing complaint that "too many of our recent college graduates come to us from college with no ability to express themselves logically. They have never been taught to size up a situation or a problem and to direct their report to a concise discussion of the problem, their results, and their conclusions in a readable form." As one executive has said, "The ability to write clear memos and reports lies at the foundation of all other management skills. And this ability becomes more important as one advances to more responsible managerial activities. In an age of rapidly advancing technology and increased specialization, preparation in writing reports is certainly one of the most basic aspects of education."

13
THE REPORT-WRITING PROCESS—A SPECIFIC EXAMPLE

Because the process of preparing a report or a long memorandum involves several steps in gathering, organizing, and presenting pertinent material, we are going to use this chapter for a preliminary view of the entire procedure. Naturally, individual memos and reports must be adapted to such specific conditions as, for example, whether the writer initiates the report or memo or responds to a request, or whether reports are regularly circulated to groups or are read only by the individual chiefly concerned with the problem. Such on-the-job conditions affect the form, the organization, and even the style of reports and long memos. At the outset, however, the important fact to remember is that once you understand the basic principles governing effective reports and memos, you can readily adapt these principles to differing requirements and conditions.

To that end, we will follow a report-writing situation through its various stages—from the moment a problem first materializes through the gathering of necessary information and finally to the writing of the report incorporating solutions to the problem. Each of these steps in report writing will be discussed in greater detail in subsequent chapters; our central purpose here is to show *by specific example* how you can respond effectively to the challenge labeled ". . . So you have to write a report." The topic we have selected is one that most college students are familiar with.

From now on, you are to identify yourself as Pat Boom, a member of the student council of Quidnunc College, which has an enrollment of 5,000 students equally divided between males and females. Each of the 5,000 full-time students takes five courses; and 750 students in Quidnunc's Evening Division each take one course. You and the ten other students elected to the student council are, in the council's charter, "responsible for bringing student problems and possible solutions to the attention of the college administration so that action may be taken promptly whenever it is warranted in the judgment of the appropriate member of the administration."

The council's first meeting of the second semester occurs on February 24, 1½ weeks after classes have started. The president opens the meeting by saying, "We have had a lot of complaints from students because their grades for the first semester were late. The seniors particularly are upset because they need their transcripts to apply to graduate schools or for job interviews." A rambling, unorganized discussion ensues; the following excerpts may or may not be relevant to the president's opening comments:

"I hear that the real reason grades are always late is that the dean and the registrar don't like each other and they won't cooperate on anything."

"What difference does it make whether we get grades two weeks after exams end? I don't think it's important."

"Who's responsible for getting grades out?" (To this the "answers" include the dean of students, the dean of the faculty, and the president.)

"The real cause of the trouble is that they scheduled all the English exams on the last three days of the exam period. Somebody goofed, because those exams take longer to grade than any others."

"I heard the real reason is that a lot of the profs take off for Florida right after their last exam and mail their grades in."

"What do these people who are complaining mean by "late"? The last day of exams was January 31, and I got my grades at home on February 10. I don't think that's bad." (An informal poll of the council on this point shows that grades were received from 9 to 15 days after the end of the examination period.)

"There's no excuse for such lateness. They have 25,750 grades to record, and they should be able to get them processed and mailed two days after the students take their last exam."

"The trouble probably is that they do Evening Division grades first. Full-time undergraduates always come last at Quidnunc."

"I heard it was because they don't hire enough help. They've got five girls in the office, and they spend most of their time talking to students they know."

"I understand that the computer the school bought seven years ago, when the school's enrollment was half what it is now, is inadequate to handle the business it must now handle."

"The real headache from getting grades late is that a lot of us couldn't plan our second-semester courses until we knew whether we flunked something the first semester. I found out just this week that I flunked calculus and have to repeat it, so my whole schedule had to be changed."

"I heard that the registrar won't send out a single grade until they're sent out to all students."

The council president finally terminates the discussion by saying, "It looks as if we have a problem on which the student council should act. I'm therefore appointing Pat Boom to find out what causes it and to prepare a report or memo with recommendations we can send on to the college president. Let's have the written report for our meeting on April 10."

In your role of Pat Boom, you make the traditional response to all report-writing assignments by groaning. Nevertheless, this being the first such assignment you've ever done, you decide that you're going to learn as much as you can from the experience. To do so, you write across the top of the first page of your notebook THINGS TO REMEMBER ABOUT WRITING A REPORT.

PREPARING TO WRITE THE REPORT

Since you took no notes at the council meeting, forgot the exact words of the president's assignment, and had to ask the secretary and several other council members to reconstruct what had been said, you make your first entry in your notebook the next day:

TAKE ADEQUATE NOTES

You look over the reconstructed notes about the meeting, searching for clues as to the best method of getting material for your report. Wisely you decide that you will discard anything which doesn't relate to the purpose of your report. You decide that your purposes here are (1) to find out whether grades were late, and if so, why; and (2) to recommend ways in which lateness of grade reporting can be avoided in the future. You make your second entry in your notebook:

DECIDE ON THE PURPOSE OF YOUR REPORT AS SOON AS POSSIBLE

As you look at your own statement of purpose, it occurs to you that the word "late" was tossed around rather loosely in the council meeting. What exactly does it mean in the context of this problem? Some students were apparently completely satisfied with the timing of their grade reports; others considered them "late" or "very late." Into your notebook, because of the elusive word, goes another admonition:

DEFINE IMPORTANT WORDS OR TERMS

Finally, in glancing through the excerpts from the council meeting, you find comments like:

I heard the real reason grades are late is that the dean and registrar hate each other . . .

. . . the reason is a lot of profs take off for Florida after their last exam and mail their grades in.

> . . . the trouble is they scheduled all the English exams on the last three days, and they take longer to grade than any other subject.

> Who's responsible for getting the grades out?

You realize that the first two statements belong in the realm of opinion, hearsay, conjecture, assumption; the last two can be verified by investigation. *Were* all exams in English scheduled on the last three days? *Who* actually has final responsibility for getting grades out? One more injunction goes into your notebook:

SEPARATE FACT FROM OPINION, VERIFIABLE ASSUMPTIONS FROM SHEER CONJECTURE

Now, with these four bits of learning behind you, you start examining what you have thus far, what you need to find out, and how you will find out. You jot down the results:

> Forget all rumors about the dean and the registrar disliking each other; about English profs in Florida; about girls in the office gossiping with students.

> Find out these things:

> 1. Do other schools get grades out faster? How?

> 2. Is Quidnunc's computer adequate for the job it is being called upon to handle?

> 3. Does the scheduling by subject matter (i.e., English exams) affect the speed of reporting grades?

All of this, of course, adds up to one action—you must interview the official who is responsible for reporting grades and collect relevant facts from other sources.

GATHERING THE INFORMATION

Before you interview the registrar, who *is* responsible for recording, transmitting, and maintaining all academic records at Quidnunc, you use what you learned in an Elementary Logic course: in your subject for investigation you have a known *effect* (lateness of grade reporting), and you must reason your way back to the *cause(s)* which produced it. You list all the causes you can possibly think of:

> Lateness of reporting grades could be caused by:
> Insufficient help in the Recorder's Office?
> Faculty not reporting grades on time?
> An inadequate computer?
> Inefficient scheduling of final exams—English exam last?
> Grades for Evening Division interfering with efficient reporting of undergraduate grades?
> Any other causes?

You write each of these at the top of a 3×5 card and go off for your interview with the registrar prepared to take notes on what he says about these possible causes. You also carry another card on which you have written, "What do we mean by 'late'?" You wonder whether, because of his job, the registrar may not be a bit defensive and, perhaps, a rather prejudiced source of information; you write yourself one more admonition:

MAKE SURE SOURCES OF INFORMATION ARE UNBIASED

The registrar seems to be a model of an efficient administrator; his desk holds a four-foot shelf of black loose-leaf notebooks, carefully labeled, into which he seems to dive for answers to your questions. When you tell him about the council's investigation and the possibility that seniors will send a petition about late grades to the president, he merely laughs and says, "My name has always been Mudd"—which, incredibly, it is. From Mr. Mudd, you get the following information recorded on your cards:

> This year grades were mailed on Feb. 9; records going back to 1945 show the average time between the end of the examination period and students' receiving grades is eight days. This time interval is checked by Mr. Mudd, who inserts cards to 25 people, including himself, all of whom report when they receive them. He admits, however, that this past semester's grades arrived, on the average, ten days after the examination period ended. He wonders if the postal service could be slipping a bit.

> Mr. Mudd thinks the help in his office is adequate; this year, because two of his regular workers were ill, he brought in three temporary replacements.

> Grades for Evening Division students are sent out one week after all undergraduate grades have been mailed.

> An article in the *Bulletin* of the Association of University Registrars for February 1978 shows that "the average time for reporting grades in colleges of approximately 5,000 is seven days between the end of the examination period and the student receiving grades."

> This year English examinations *were* scheduled in the last three days, but this was done at the request of the head of the English department, who wanted to attend a meeting during the early part of the examination period. "If I had my way, I would never do it again," Mr. Mudd says. "But under college rules, I have to comply with the faculty's wishes wherever I can." Members of the English department were one day late in getting their grades to the registrar's office.

> Grades for students who fail one or more courses are sent by faculty members directly to the office of Dr. Leona E. Holcomb, Dean of the Faculty, so that a letter can be addressed to the student asking him or her to come in for an interview at a specific time. The names and grades of these students are then sent from the dean's office to the registrar's office. "It delays us about two days," Mr. Mudd says, "because normally about 550 to 650 students fail one or more courses."

Among the opinions expressed by Mr. Mudd were the following:

"The computer that we are now using is still adequate for the school's needs. It probably will, however, need to be replaced within the next five years if enrollments continue to increase."

"I believe all students should have their grades mailed at the same time. I don't favor putting senior examinations in the first five days and then mailing their grades out first. All they would do is go home the minute their last exam is finished. Furthermore, it's more efficient for my office to handle all grades at the same time. And the only fair way to treat students is for all freshmen, sophomores, juniors, and seniors to get grades simultaneously."

From your interview with Mr. Mudd, you go on to the office of Dr. Holcomb, the dean of the faculty, where you talk with Euclid Fourier, a teaching assistant in the mathematics department who spends half of his time assisting Dr. Holcomb with interviews. He tells you that neither Dr. Holcomb nor Mr. Mudd takes the student council's investigation of grade reporting very seriously because they believe that it reflects the views of only a small minority of students. He also tells you that no friction exists between the dean's and the registrar's offices, although Dean Holcomb would prefer to have senior grades sent first, grades of failures next (with a letter setting up an interview with the dean), and then grades of freshmen, sophomores, and juniors in that order. "Thus far the dean has deferred to Mr. Mudd's belief that it's faster and fairer to send out all grades at the same time," says Fourier. "The dean believes the registrar's office should use the sole criterion of efficiency, and for that reason she didn't approve of the English department having its exams placed last this year. Dr. Holcomb will give Mudd all the power he needs to schedule exams any way he wants to as long as it gets grades out more promptly."

With this mixture of fact, opinion, and authoritative evidence, you can at least eliminate such conjectures as "slowness in reporting grades is caused by inefficient help in the registrar's office" or by "friction between the dean and the registrar," or by "an inadequate computer." Now you must decide how to find answers to two nagging questions:

1. Do most students really believe that there is a problem of "late reporting" of grades, or do complaints to the student council represent a small minority, as Dean Holcomb and Mr. Mudd believe?

2. What criterion or definition for "late" can be used? Shall it be the seven-day average from the end of exams to students receiving grades, reported in the bulletin of the Association of University Registrars? Quidnunc's average of eight days from the end of exams to the grades being received? Or something different?

Wisely, you decide that if Quidnunc students think there is a problem, that very fact attests to the existence of a problem—although you realize that it may be a problem of a different nature, such as bad communication in informing students of the problems of reporting grades. The way to proceed, therefore, is to find out how many students think there is a problem and what most of them would consider "lateness" in reporting grades. To that end, you prepare a questionnaire to go to all Quidnunc students (see Chapter 7, Letters of Inquiry) which contains these three parts:

1. My class is (check one)

Freshman	_____
Sophomore	_____
Junior	_____
Senior	_____

2. Taking into account the practical necessities of recording grades, which of the following number of days *after the final day of examinations* would you reasonably expect to get your grades at your home address:

4–6 days	_____
6–8 days	_____
8–10 days	_____
10–12 days	_____
12–14 days	_____

3. If you have had any inconvenience or any problems because of what you considered slowness in grade recording and reporting, state what it was in the space below:

When the returns are in and tabulated, you have these results:

Percent of Class Answering		When Grades Are Expected
Fresh.	87	4–6 days (56% of those answering)
Soph.	46	10–12 days (60% of those answering)
Juniors	54	6–8 days (72% of those answering)
Seniors	92	6–8 days (90% of those answering)

Your third question, asking them to state inconvenience because of slowness in grade reporting, was apparently a poor one, because it brought forth a number of snide attempts at humor: "I suffered considerable inconvenience when my parents heard I'd flunked two subjects" and "My grades got there *too* fast—before I got home my parents had read them." Only seniors responded directly: 85 percent of them classified the inconvenience as needing transcripts for graduate school or for getting a job.

With this information you do three things for your report:

1. For the majority of students, "late" means receiving grades at home more than 8 days after the final day of examinations. This year they were received 10 days after that day.

2. The focus of the problem seems to be the senior class, where seniors need grades for a practical reason: to get records for admittance to graduate school

or for a job. Freshmen are eager to know grades but lack the practical need other than to satisfy their curiosity.

3. On the basis of your experience with question 3 of your questionnaire, you add another admonition to yourself:

> MAKE CERTAIN THAT ALL QUESTIONS ARE ACCURATELY PHRASED TO
> ASSURE A RELEVANT RESPONSE

ORGANIZING THE MATERIAL

The time has now come to take stock of the material you have, to start organizing it, and to prepare to write the report, which is due one week from now on April 10. You get a bit panicky at the deadline and add the warning that every report writer knows:

> NEXT TIME, ALLOW MORE TIME FOR ORGANIZING AND WRITING

As if to avoid noticing that big 10 which you have circled on the calendar for April, your mind drifts off to what might have been: I shouldn't have wasted so much time on that questionnaire. . . . Maybe I should have polled the faculty. . . . I ought to have gotten a lot more information. . . . I should have read a couple of books on how to do a report. . . . I should have told the student council at the March meeting that there isn't a problem. . . . I should have taken a lot more time. . . .

Abruptly, you say farewell to such wishful thinking about what-might-have-been, and you decide two things:

1. I've spent nearly six weeks on this subject, so I must know more about it than the other council members.

2. I'll have to use the material I've got, because a report has to be written, and I can't go on forever accumulating more information.

Then you go to work by writing out three questions:

1. Is there or is there not a problem of grades being reported late?

2. What causes the problem (if indeed it exists)?

3. What is the best way to solve it?

As you look back over your research and leaf through your notes, the answers to these questions *seem* to be:

1. There is a problem, but it's a different one from what the council thought. It's confined chiefly to seniors and freshmen. Seniors may, in fact, be experiencing real problems; freshmen are probably recalling the prompter reporting of

grades they experienced in high school. However, because these two groups *think* there is a problem, a problem exists and it requires solving.

2. The problem is caused by any or all of the following: (Here you decide to list every possibility you can think of and mark them "yes," "no," or "maybe" on the basis of what you have found out.)

> The dean and the registrar dislike each other and won't cooperate on getting grades out. (*No*)
>
> A lot of professors go off to Florida, and that's why grades are late. (*No*)
>
> The computer Quidnunc uses is now inadequate for the work it must handle. (*No*)
>
> All English exams were scheduled on the last three days. (*Yes*)
>
> Insufficient help to record grades. (*Maybe*)
>
> Delay in Dean Holcomb's office because she wants to have appointments with those who fail courses. (*Maybe,* but it affects only a minority of students.)
>
> Mr. Mudd's insistence that all grades be mailed at exactly the same time. (*Maybe*)
>
> Evening Division grades slow down reporting of undergraduate grades. (*No*)

3. Here are all the solutions you can think of to anything marked "yes" or "maybe":

> Schedule English exams first.
>
> Get more help, temporary or otherwise, to record grades.
>
> Dean Holcomb's office could just as well use carbon copies of flunkers' grades while the originals go direct from the registrar's office.
>
> Because graduating seniors encounter legitimate problems when grades are slow in reaching them, schedule their exams and mail out their grades first. This process could be made easier by sending out separate grade lists for such seniors in classes in which they are enrolled.

You now have what you consider a reasonable method of arranging your material into three parts:

> An *Introduction:* What the Problem Is
>
> A *Body:* Causes of the Problem
>
> A *Conclusion:* Recommended Solutions for the Problem

On these three pegs, you think you will be able to hang the various materials you have gathered.

WRITING THE REPORT

Mistakenly, you try to put your material into its final form at once. To your chagrin, you soon learn that you can't do an effective job of arranging all your material in logical sequence while you try at the same time to polish the way you express it. You give up on this attempt to do too many things at once and add this note to your list:

DON'T TRY TO WRITE THE FINAL VERSION OF THE REPORT IN YOUR FIRST ATTEMPT

Next day, you work up a rough outline and then put down all the facts, reasoning, explanations, and definitions in appropriate and logical sequence, paying minimum attention to the way they are expressed. Your sole purpose is *to get your ideas, facts, and conclusions down on paper* so that you can check to establish logical relationships among them. On the hunch—and it's a good one—that it will be easier to delete material than to add it during revisions, you include material whenever you are in doubt about it.

The following day you work on form and style, reading your first draft as if you had never seen it before. You find a paragraph or two which are so illogical in sequence that you wonder how you could have arranged them that way the day before. You find that by linking ideas and paragraphs you make your report more readable; and you realize what English teachers have told you for years, that paragraphing is the basic method of presenting information in readable units. When each paragraph develops your thought in a logical way and is linked to the paragraph preceding it or following it, smooth and readable writing results.

You find that this process of waiting, at least overnight, to do your revising makes it much easier to identify and correct the errors in the rough draft. You have learned three things by this process:

WORK UP SOME FORM OF OUTLINE

WRITE A FIRST DRAFT AND LET IT AGE AT LEAST OVERNIGHT

REVISE IT BY READING IT AS IF YOU, LIKE THE READER, HAVE NEVER SEEN IT BEFORE

THE REPORT

Here is "your" report, which you decide is not as good as you had hoped it would be—but that's a reaction all report writers share. Nonetheless, it does seem to you to be sufficiently factual and logical that the Quidnunc administration can take action on it, once the student council sends copies to the appropriate administrators. For you, therefore, the report has achieved its purpose.

(At the end of this chapter, the usual exercises have been supplemented by questions about the effectiveness of this report. Students should, therefore, read the report carefully to determine what changes they might make in it and whether the president and Dean Holcomb and Mr. Mudd, who are the responsible administrators, should act favorably on its recommendations after it is transmitted to them by the student council.)

A Report

on

The Reporting of Grades for Courses at Quidnunc College

Prepared

for

The Student Council

by

Pat Boom

April 10, 1978

BACKGROUND

At its meeting on February 24, 1978, the Student Council authorized a study of the procedures and practices related to the recording and sending out of semester grades. It instructed Pat Boom to report on the results of the study as the Council's representative in accordance with the Council's authorization to "bring student problems and possible solutions to the attention of the college administration. . . ."

The report which follows is based upon discussion with students, a questionnaire to all full-time students, and interviews with the registrar and representatives of the office of the dean of the faculty. (A copy of the questionnaire with the returns tabulated on it is attached to this report.) In every instance, the Council's representative received complete cooperation and interest from the representatives of the administration, all of whom were helpful in solving the problem under study.

STATEMENT OF THE PROBLEM

From the beginning of the investigation for this report, it has become very clear that considerable confusion exists among undergraduates at Quidnunc College as to the answers to the following questions:

Who is responsible for sending out final grades?

Does the system of reporting grades at Quidnunc operate as efficiently as that at other colleges?

Are grades reported late?

Student answers to the first two of these questions seem to be based on rumor and hearsay, rather than fact. For that reason, a very important byproduct of this report could be to have administrative officials provide factual answers to these questions in *The Quidnunc Student*. The Council makes this suggestion out of a conviction that a well-informed student body is a student body with high morale.

The final question, "Are grades reported late?" which is the focus of this study, requires definition. What is meant by "late"? According to the results of the questionnaire, grades are late when students do not receive them at their homes within 8 days after the close of final examinations. Here are the "expectations" of each of the four classes:

Freshmen	56% of 87%	answering expect grades in				4–6 days
Sophomores	60% of 46%	"	"	"	"	10–12 days
Juniors	72% of 54%	"	"	"	"	6–8 days
Seniors	90% of 92%	"	"	"	"	6–8 days

Since records provided by Mr. Mudd show that this semester's grades were received 10 days after the last examination on January 31, it may be concluded that the great majority of Quidnunc students other than sophomores considered their grades late in arriving. This fact is underscored by the undergraduates who are presumably most mature in their judgment and experience—the Juniors and Seniors—who expect grades within 8 days.

The Council considers it very important to record its belief that *if students think they have a problem, then a very real problem exists—and should be solved.* On that basis it believes that prompt action should be taken by appropriate administrative officials to ensure semester grades arriving at students' homes within 8 days after the close of examinations.

To maintain the long record of constructive approaches to student problems by both the administration and the Council, we urge that serious consideration be given to the next two sections of this report, which deal with the causes and solutions of the problem of lateness in reporting final grades.

CAUSES

Relevant to our earlier statement that student opinions are based on hearsay and rumor is our finding that many students ascribe lateness in reporting grades to such factors as:

Lack of cooperation between various segments of the college administration

Absenteeism among the faculty at grade-reporting time

Necessity of reporting Evening Division grades at the same time as undergraduates'

Inefficiency of employees in the registrar's office

Fortunately, our investigation shows that there is little or no basis for any of these so-called reasons.

A careful analysis does show, however, that one or more of the following causes may account for lateness in reporting grades:

1. Ineffective scheduling of such final exams as English, which require the longest time to grade. Last semester, all examinations for courses in English were held in the last three days. Certain members of the English department were therefore a day late in getting their grades to the registrar.

2. Grades of approximately 600 students were delayed because they had to be sent from the registrar's office to the dean of the faculty so that appointments could be made for those failing courses.

3. A prevailing policy of sending out all the grades of all students (except those who fail) at the same time. This policy stems from a belief that it is "more fair to send all grades at the same time."

It is significant to note that one or more of these causes is responsible for the fact that although a report by the American Association of College Registrars shows the average time for grades in students' hands is 7 days, Quidnunc's time is 10 days between the end of the examination period and the receipt of the grades.

We respectfully urge that the administration give serious consideration to putting into effect the actions endorsed by the Student Council and discussed in the final section of this report.

RECOMMENDATIONS

On the basis of this study, the Student Council of Quidnunc College recommends that the following actions be taken, as soon as feasible, to speed up the recording and transmitting of course grades:

1. Schedule examinations on the basis of which require the longest time for grading. For example, examinations in English, History, and Economics should be scheduled early; Mathematics, Statistics, and Physics later.

2. Send carbon copies of grades of students failing courses to the dean of the faculty's office so that originals may be sent directly from the registrar.

3. Establish a priority to replace the present policy of sending all grades of all students at the same time. This priority might well be as follows:
   a. Seniors, because they need semester grades for transcripts for graduate school and for job applications.
   b. Freshmen, who are receiving their first course grades at Quidnunc and are particularly eager to know how well they are doing in their first experience with the academic standards of the college.
   c. Sophomores and Juniors.

This priority should be incorporated in the examination schedule so that all senior exams are included in the first five days and all freshman exams in the first seven days, with sophomore and junior examinations being spread over the entire two weeks.

As soon as the examination schedule is completed by each of these classes, the registrar should start sending out grades.

The Student Council believes that these three recommendations, if put into effect, will clear up much of the confusion and tardiness which characterize the present method of reporting grades.

EXERCISES

1. The following questions concerning Pat Boom's report may be used for classroom discussion or for individual written critiques.
   a. What is the major purpose of the report? Is it just a fact-finding study, or does the Council desire action as a result of the facts? How might the order of the sections (background, problem statement, causes, and recommendations) vary depending on the report's major purpose? Do you think an order other than the one Pat used would be more effective? Why?
   b. Was Pat's use of a questionnaire a wise idea? Why? Do you think a report should usually contain some sort of survey results? What are some problems that can arise from undertaking a survey in connection with a report?
   c. Should the suggestion that administrative officials provide factual answers in the student newspaper to two rumor-based questions be included in the problem statement section? Or might this suggestion be more appropriate in the recommendations section? What should the problem statement section contain? What should it not?
   d. Do you agree with Pat Boom's statement that "if students think they have a problem, then a very real problem exists . . ."? How does this belief relate to the seriousness with which the administration will view the report?
   e. Was the last sentence of the problem statement section, "we urge that serious consideration be given to the next two sections of this report," necessary? Or the last sentence of the causes section, "We respectfully urge that the administration give serious consideration to putting into effect the actions . . ."? Can a well-written report result in serious consideration without the writer having to use such direct sentences? When might you use those kinds of statements?
   f. Reread the causes section. Is the report saying that one or more of the causes *may* account for lateness in reporting grades or that one or more of the causes *is* responsible? Would taking a definite position regarding causes lead to more serious consideration of the recommendations by Mr. Mudd and Dean Holcomb?
   g. Is the American Association of College Registrars' report given sufficient emphasis? If not, where and how would you incorporate it into Boom's report to make the report more forceful?
   h. Are the recommendations a logical conclusion to the ideas developed in the preceding sections of the report? Are they specific enough? Could the recommendations result in other problems, ones more serious than the lateness of grade reporting (particularly the recommendation that the exam schedule be based on grade level)?

i. Reread the sections in the chapter dealing with Mr. Mudd. Now put yourself in his place. What is your reaction to the report? Next assume you are Dean Holcomb— reread the information about her. Will your reaction be different from Mr. Mudd's? If the reactions are different, with one being more favorable than the other, what changes in the report would make it equally persuasive and appealing to both parties? If you feel you cannot make the report equally appealing, you will probably want to persuade the more influential person. Is this person Mr. Mudd or Dean Holcomb? In what ways will you change the report so that it will result in the action you desire by the more influential person?

2. Write a report for the following situation, using the steps in the report-writing process discussed in this chapter. After you have decided the purpose of your report, select what is appropriate for your situation from the material given. In addition, create any additional information desirable to produce a persuasive, cohesive report.

You are chairperson of the Student Activities Board of your college and are trying to persuade the governing commission for the five colleges in your state to allow student-controlled block booking of rock concerts at the various campuses. Presently, concerts at each individual college are booked by an agent at that college who is responsible for all musical and cultural events. These agents have not been very successful in booking popular rock acts appealing to the majority of the students. Further, the students have no input as to the acts they would like to see. In addition, profits from the few rock concerts that have been held have gone into a fund used to subsidize the less profitable musical and cultural affairs.

The five Student Activities Boards have formed a state-wide board; you have been asked to submit a report to the commission to promote the approval of a student-controlled block booking plan. Specifically, the proposal provides for the hiring of an experienced concert coordinator selected by the five board members and approved by the commission. Based on market research and recommendations from each of the five campuses, the concert coordinator will book acts for appearances at all or some of the five state colleges. Proceeds from the concerts will go into a special student activities fund to be used for concert booking and promotion fees. Also, if a concert is unprofitable, losses will be paid from this fund. After one year the coordinator, the state Student Activities Board, and the commission will determine what amount to leave in the fund to finance the next year's concerts. Any money beyond this amount will be divided among the five colleges to be used for local student activities. The proposal suggests that the plan be instituted on a two-year trial basis, with the concert coordinator being given a one-year contract. The plan will be evaluated during the last six months of the second year so that the board and the commission can decide whether to continue the student-controlled block booking arrangement.

Following is material you may wish to use in preparing your report. This material ranges from the relevant to the meaningless, from verifiable fact to prejudiced conjecture. Remember that you may supplement the material given with ideas of your own.

Musicians prefer block booking arrangements because they are performing several times in one state, thereby reducing their travel time and expenses.

Musicians' agents prefer block booking because it reduces the number of booking agents they must deal with.

Student input as to preferred acts will be solicited, thus increasing student participation in campus affairs.

Rock music and the lifestyle of rock musicians are detrimental to the morals of young people and should not be allowed on campus.

Block booking will enable the colleges to get more top-quality, popular groups.

Concert revenues will increase because groups the students want to see will be performing, and attendance will increase.

Although under the proposed plan the agents at each individual college will no longer be responsible for booking rock acts, they will still be needed to book other musical and cultural events. So they will be doing less but still receiving the same salary.

During an interview at one of the colleges, a booking agent explained, "I book about three events a year that I know will lose money but that I feel are important for the cultural literacy of the community. Popularity and true art are not necessarily the same thing. These unprofitable events could not be held if they were not subsidized by the profitable shows. Since the few rock concerts I do book are very profitable, removing the profits realized from them will mean the death of culture in our community."

Finding a qualified concert coordinator will be difficult.

The concert coordinator will be someone who knows the "right" people in the rock music world and will more easily be able to book top acts.

A student who had the proposed change in the handling of profits explained to him remarked, "Since it is mostly students who attend the concerts which produce the profits, these profits should eventually be used for other student activities. Why should students subsidize cultural events for the community? Additional money for student activities could help expand our intramural sports program, for example."

Hiring a special concert coordinator is foolish. Booking concerts couldn't possibly be a full-time job.

The college has a responsibility to the community to meet some of its needs, which includes cultural needs, even if a monetary profit will not result.

College students are not mature enough to get involved with personnel hiring, concert booking, and financial matters.

The commission should not be involved in the selection of the concert coordinator. They are old and stuffy and will be put off by the kind of person most likely to be the best qualified for the coordinator's position.

The idea of student input as to which groups to book sounds good but will not work. Students are too busy to respond to surveys. It is up to the activities board and the concert coordinator to know which groups are the most popular.

Block booking, with appearances in several cities in the same state, isn't necessary. If a group is popular enough, people will travel from one campus to another to see the show.

The division of profits among the five colleges will cause problems. Will the money be divided evenly, or will the division be based on a percentage of the net profit realized from each college?

Several professors have objected to the idea of an increase in the number of concerts. "Students aren't doing enough work now. They will do even less when there are a lot of concerts to attend."

A two-year trial period is necessary to get a complete picture of the plan. A shorter period might reflect unusual events and not general trends.

"I don't go to rock concerts. I object to having part of my student activities fee spent to put on that kind of entertainment."

The trial period should only be for one year. Three of the commission members' terms will expire in a year, and their replacements will not have been involved in the plan from its inception.

Students' musical tastes are so fickle that a group might be popular when booked but not so popular when the concert is held.

Because some of the students on the activities board are seniors, they will not be here during the evaluation period, the last six months of the second year.

The commission members do not like rock music, so even if the plan is adopted, they will hold unfavorable opinions and do their best to sabotage the plan. College is for studying. Concerts and other such things have no place there. Students should get as involved in their homework as they are in their music.

Is a one-year contract for the concert coordinator the usual length for such contracts?

A reliable source was said to have overheard one of the commission members saying, "Give the students some say in their entertainment and how the profits are used and the next thing you know they'll want to have a student member on the commission."

How will the plan be evaluated? This should be decided now.

Evaluation should be an ongoing process, not just during the last six months of the second year.

14
PLANNING
THE REPORT

In the preceding chapter we followed the entire process of producing a report by using a specific example. Implicit in Pat Boom's first attempt at report writing was a considerable waste of time and effort; inexperience resulted in a search of several blind alleys and wasted motion because a purpose was not established in the early stages of preparing the report.

As a matter of fact, students should recognize that no more disastrous "education" for report writing can be found than the way in which many students respond to assignments for term papers and long reports in college. All too often the customary procedure involves waiting until the night before the long paper is due and then, in a kind of frenzy matched by a last-minute Christmas shopper's desperation, attempting to transform scattered notes, miscellaneous clippings, and superficial "background material" into a report. This planless process results in thousands of words which fail to convey a single thought. Unfortunately, this same pattern of putting-off-to-the-last-minute prevails in business as well as in the academic community—but here it becomes not only a wasteful but also a very expensive process.

True professionals in any human activity—whether it be playing football, investing money, or building a home—know that at the outset *they must have a plan.* Similarly, experienced writers confronted with a report-writing situation know that their first step is to plan their time, their method, and their purpose before they do anything else. As the first step in writing a report, they should think their way through to the answers to four questions:

1. What is the purpose of this report?

2. How shall I define the problem?

3. How will I keep track of the material I collect for my report?

4. Who will read the report, and what use will be made of it?

We shall discuss each of these aspects of planning a report in the rest of this chapter.

PURPOSE IN REPORT WRITING

Time and time again, people in business complain that the reports they receive do not tell them what they need to be told. Sometimes the fault lies with the reader, who either has given misleading instructions or has simply failed to indicate what purpose the report is expected to serve. Generally, however, it is the writer's fault. If the instructions received are not clear, it is the writer's responsibility to go back for more. Before beginning work on a report, a writer should be absolutely clear about what the reader expects from it. In the next few pages we will discuss three purposes which readers often expect reports to serve.

1. Recommendation

Your reader may be expecting you to make a specific recommendation for a course of action. Let us take a situation where a company's sales manager has asked you for a report making a recommendation on whether or not to cut the price of a product. The sales manager, first of all, wants a specific recommendation. You must come up with a yes-or-no answer; and, presumably, if you come up with a yes answer, you must indicate the specific amount by which the price should be reduced.

This is only a beginning, however. What sort of reasoning or justification of your conclusion does the sales manager expect you to give? If you are experienced in your job and your boss trusts your judgment, you may not be expected to present much justification. On the other hand, if you are relatively inexperienced, and particularly if the sales manager has not yet begun to rely on you, you may be required to give considerable justification of your conclusion.

But even if you are experienced and the sales manager trusts your judgment, other factors may require you to include detailed reasoning and justification in your report. Your recommendation and your reasons for it may be passed on to a higher official in the company. Or, if your decision turns out to be a poor one, your sales manager may expect to be asked to produce the reasoning that lead to it. Hence, it would be best for you to have included such reasoning in the report. And you, for your own purposes, may wish to have on record the reasons for your conclusion, in case it is criticized or reviewed later.

Suppose you have determined, then, that the sales manager wants not only your conclusion but your reasoning. It may still be important to know just why. If you have reason to suspect that your recommendation may not be accepted without the reasoning, you will probably be wise to include the reasoning in the main body of the report. If, on the other hand, it appears that the reasoning is desired only as justification in case the decision is later criticized, you might present this reasoning as a sort of appendix or attachment to your report.

The reader of a report may, however, not be expecting a recommendation at all. Instead, you may be expected to present alternative courses of action in a report containing the significant data and reasoning which lead to a choice. The final decision, however, is left up to the reader. It is important to know whether you are expected to make the decision or to leave that to the reader. It is frustrating to a reader who expected a concrete recommendation to find only a series of possibilities, leaving the choice or decision up in the air.

If your report is to serve as the basis for someone else's decision, you are going to have to include a good deal of data and reasoning. Just how much you should include will depend on whether your reader expects you to work with the data and reduce the choice to a simple weighing of pros and cons, or to lay out all the data for a detailed analysis. The more precisely you can pin such factors down, the better your report will serve the reader's needs. If what's needed is a concise presentation of the major factors, a lengthy report that presents only masses of raw data won't do. On the other hand, if the reader likes to work with raw data and draw conclusions, a concise summary of the significant factors and no mention of the data that went into them is not likely to create the impact you desire.

2. Information

Your reader may simply ask for information, a deceptively simple request. But what purpose will the information serve? This is a crucial question, because the amount of information which you present and the form in which you present it must be tied to the use that is to be made of it.

Suppose, for example, that the same sales manager asks for sales information on a particular product. The information may serve as the basis for a decision as to whether the price should be cut and, if so, by how much. On the other hand, this information may be used to project future sales for the product so as to establish production schedules or inventory levels. Or the sales manager may want the information in order to pass it on to a superior who is endeavoring to establish the profitability of various company products. Obviously, the kinds of information wanted and the way in which the information should be presented are not the same for each of these purposes. If you work on the assumption that the sales manager wants your information in order to plan inventory levels, and it turns out that it is really wanted in order to determine whether the product is profitable, the sales manager is likely to be dissatisfied with your report.

3. Display of ability

In asking for a report, your reader may, quite frankly, be asking for an indication of your ability. This is particularly true in the case of a progress report. In fact, your report may even be passed on to your boss's superior as evidence of what your work unit is accomplishing. In the first case, you are demonstrating your own ability and accomplishment to your immediate superior. In the second case, you are indirectly displaying your own abilities while enabling your boss to demonstrate abilities and accomplishments to his or her superior. Again, it is essential that you be quite clear about the purpose before you begin to write.

Here are a few questions that may help you to establish the purposes of a written communication. These questions may not always be appropriate, and you may have to think of others yourself. They will, however, give you a start.

a. To whom am I addressing my communication? Who else may read it? (We will discuss this question in greater detail later in the chapter.)

b. If the communication was requested by the reader, have I been told specifically what is wanted? Should I ask for clarification? Are there any unstated purposes my reader probably wants the communication to serve—purposes I am not likely to be told about? If others may read the communication, what purposes will they expect it to serve?

c. If I am writing not in response to a request but on my own initiative, do I know exactly what I am trying to accomplish? What do I want the reader to do? to say? to believe?

d. Am I trying to persuade the reader? Am I attempting to change or strengthen convictions, or is the reader undecided? Am I sure what the reader's convictions are? Do I know the reasons for those convictions?

e. How important will my communication be to my reader? Will a long, detailed discussion be welcomed or impatiently received? Will brevity give the impression of a careless, skimpy job?

DEFINING THE PROBLEM

A particular aspect of the purpose of a report is to define the problem. In fact, one of the most useful questions you can ask yourself over and over again as you first plan your report, while you are doing your research, and finally when you write is: "What is the problem?" In asking this question you should maintain a flexible attitude, because your definition of the problem may change as you do your research. In this respect, it is worth noting that Pat Boom's "problem" of defining "lateness" could shift from deciding on a precise number of days to an attitude that "if students *think* there is a problem, there is one"; thus, the real problem was, in part, a communication problem to which the report pays little or no attention.

Suppose you work for a factory manager who is plagued with complaints that special orders—orders for unusual, custom-made products—are not being completed on time. Your boss says to you: "Find out why we can't keep track of these orders and get them out on time, and give me a report telling me what to do about it." At its broadest, your purpose or problem is clear: The manager wants to know how to get special orders out on time. But let's move on to a more specific, narrower definition of the problem. The manager implies that delay is due to a failure to keep track of special orders. Is this failure the real problem? You may not be so sure. There is little doubt that special orders are not being finished on time, but the reasons are not so clear. Could the real problem be faulty scheduling, poor judgment in promising deliveries too soon, or a system of priorities that always puts special orders after regular production? Until you investigate a little, it is probably unwise to select any of these, or the manager's suggestion, as *the* problem.

Suppose after some research you find the real source of delay is faulty scheduling. Too much time is allowed for some production operations, not enough is allowed for others. The result is that orders are sometimes set aside after an operation has been completed and yet are often not ready when another operation is supposed to begin. You now want to refine your definition of the problem even further. Why is the scheduling at fault? Is the problem carelessness among those responsible for scheduling? Are these people following a set policy that should be changed? Do they understand what operations must be performed and how much time is required to perform them? Or do they fail to take regular production into account and, therefore, fail to plan so that special orders can fit into the regular production schedule?

Again, investigation should reveal which of these is *the* problem. Eventually you should be able to determine the exact source of the trouble. You will have defined the problem as narrowly and specifically as possible, and you can get on with a solution.

In the example above we began with an obvious problem, in the form of an undesirable result, and then proceeded to trace this result to its source in an effort to reach a more specific definition of the problem. Sometimes the reverse is called for.

Suppose you work for the vice-president in charge of production in a shoe manufacturing company which produces both handmade and machine-made shoes. Demand for its products had led to a need for expansion. The vice-president, who views skilled hand workers as a very important part of the company's labor force, asks you for a report recommending a new plant location where the company will be assured of an adequate supply of skilled hand workers. As you try to formulate the problem you have been given to solve, you realize that adequacy of the supply of skilled hand workers is only a part of a larger problem: the number of hand workers needed. And this, in turn, is part of the larger problems of how big the new plant is to be and how much of its output will be handmade. And these questions lead back to the problems of how fast the company wishes to grow and what balance of hand- and machine-made shoes should be planned. Such problems may be beyond your jurisdiction. Some of them may be for the vice-president to solve, some for the president or the board of directors. But until you have answers to these questions, you cannot solve the narrow problem you have been given. The best you can do is to assume certain solutions to the larger problems and solve your problem on the basis of these assumptions.

We can summarize our observations on problem definition by saying that you must first understand the magnitude of the problem you are setting out to solve; you must be satisfied that you are not beginning with what is only part of a more fundamental problem and failing to deal with the fundamental problem itself. You must then identify the reasons for the existence of your problem; you must narrow down the definition of the problem until you reach the ultimate cause and can devise a solution.

KEEPING TRACK OF YOUR MATERIALS*

The scourge of the report writer is the lost fact—"I've got a note on that somewhere, but I can't put my finger on it." In anything but the simplest or briefest report, the method you use to assemble your material will determine the accuracy and effectiveness of your final product. As bad as the lost fact is the fact inadequately or inaccurately recorded.

While the gathering of material will be discussed in the next chapter of this book, you should at the very outset of your planning decide on the *method* you will use to record information. Most likely the major part of your research can be recorded simply—in a notebook (journal) or on note cards. (As you do further research, though, you will soon become acquainted with more sophisticated techniques—punched card, electronic tape, etc.) If you choose to keep your information in a notebook or journal, you will be entering your material in a chronological or serial fashion. This has the advantage of keeping the information together in prearranged order, and you need not fear losing one item.

Though the journal has its devotees (Edward Gibbon, the famous historian, was one), note cards are far more widely used. Here a piece of information is entered on a card or sheet of paper (many researchers advocate only one item per card), and the cards are then sorted into a scheme of classification.

In either method, though, the bywords are *system* and *consistency*. Use the top of your card or the margin of your journal for key words and phrases that allow you to classify and find information quickly. Date each piece if you use separate cards—probably at the top of the card. Be certain that you have accurate documentation. And do all these things consistently—*always* use the key words in the same way, *always* enter the date in the same place.

Treat each piece of information to the famous reportorial questions "Who? When? Where? How? Why?" Be precise and accurate, even though the material you will use in business research is often not like the "hard facts" of the exact sciences. If you are interviewing a fellow worker, be certain you quote the words accurately. Be precise about the name—it would be dangerous to attribute a statement you read to "Professor Rostow," for your reader will not have you there

* The material in this section is from *Business Research and Report Writing* by Robert L. Shurter, J. Peter Williamson, and Wayne Broehl. Copyright © by McGraw-Hill, Inc., 1965. Used with the permission of McGraw-Hill Book Company.

to ask whether it was Eugene Rostow of Yale or W. W. Rostow of Texas (or perhaps another Rostow altogether). The time—and embarrassment—that you will save by being careful and exact in your gathering of facts will pay off handsomely for you. Contrariwise, slipshod research is worse than no research at all, for it dignifies inaccuracy and misinformation.

If you plan it correctly, your process of keeping track of materials will soon become almost automatic. As you gain experience, you will develop certain refinements that will make your technique even more efficient. But only by starting with a plan—and sticking to it consistently—can you record what you need in the proper fashion, with no last-minute doubts about its accuracy. Any worthwhile report requires such planning.

KEEPING THE READER IN MIND

As we have said, a report is written for a purpose. It is also written for a person. Generally speaking, report writers have the advantage of knowing more about the person for whom they write than do letter writers. In addition, they often have the further advantage of being able to go back to the person requesting the report to clarify the assignment. When both the purpose and the person are known well, the business report can be a creative instrument for business accomplishment. Fortunate indeed, therefore, is the report writer who knows the precise answers to these questions:

Who will read my report?

What use will my reader make of it?

What questions does the reader want answered?

How much information does the reader need?

What is the best way to present the information?

Ideally, in the interpersonal relationships of a business enterprise, effective reports stem from an understanding of not only the boss but the boss's problems.

The size and complexity of today's corporate organizations, however, tend to place insulating layers between superior and subordinate, between writer and reader. Furthermore, reports written for one reader are frequently transmitted to others or get included in the larger package of the boss's report to his or her boss. Certainly a lot of wasted effort and unnecessary expense could be eliminated if forthright attempts were made to reduce the muffling, insulating barriers between those who ask for reports and those who read them. Even so, many situations would still prevail in which a writer has little guidance as to a reader's needs and preferences. What to do then?

An enlightening guide to many aspects of what readers want, even though they are unknown, can be found in these comments from representatives of top management:

My people who write reports always talk about the trouble they have writing the beginning of the report. They say that once they get started they can go along fine. My chief comment is that these same people, once they get started, don't seem to know how to stop.

Why can't they learn to highlight the main ideas or the chief points of their reports? I take a lot of reports home in my briefcase every weekend and I find myself wading through page after page looking for the main points. They waste their time and mine burying the very things I read for in a mass of unimportant details.

I'm always suspicious of sheer length, and most of our reports are far too long. After all, the navy commander who sent the message "Sighted sub, sank same" gave a pretty fair report of the essential facts of a situation. I keep telling my staff that I'm not impressed with sheer bulk, but they still keep on trying to "impress" me with the detail and the thoroughness of their investigations.

Too many of our reports sound as if no human ever had any part in writing them. In a day when magazines like *Fortune* know how to present facts vividly and accurately, why can't we adapt a few of these techniques to reports? Give them a little punch and some originality, and report readers won't have to pinch themselves to stay awake.

We employ hundreds of engineers, accountants, and research workers, and the chief basis on which we judge their activities and progress is the reports they send us. In too many instances, this is a disastrous judgment as far as their careers are concerned. The engineers send us elaborate accounts subtitled "apparatus," "calculations," "data," "procedure," "computations"; the accountants give us page after page of "financial exhibits" and explanatory (?) footnotes; and both of them write as if they had learned a special version of the English language. Isn't there some way these people can learn to write normal English? I think it was Boss Kettering who once said, "I've never seen a report that was too simple." Neither have I, but I've seen too many that are too complicated and specialized.

One final word needs to be said about keeping your reader in mind:

A report is always developed backwards.

This means that by the time you are ready to write, you generally know more about the subject than your reader knows—otherwise you wouldn't be writing the report. You must, therefore, plan to lead the reader into the report easily by asking yourself, "What does he or she need to know to understand this subject?" One means of doing this well is *to remember what you as a report writer knew when you began your investigation and to start your reader there.* In this respect, you are like the novelist who knows the conclusion of a tale but by exposition, description, and step-by-step narration leads the reader to the climax.

Thus, by the time you are ready to write (the presentation), you have already accumulated your facts and information (the research), and you should have thought your way through to the conclusions or recommendations you will present before you put a word on paper. Let's use an analogy from the process of building a skyscraper to make this plain. You will start with your foundation— *the research;* erect your structure's steel framework—*the organization;* and then finish your skyscraper—*the presentation*—from the top (the introduction) down to the first floor (the conclusion)—as some skyscrapers have actually been built— or starting with conclusions and working the other way, letting your reader "in on the first floor," so to speak, as many reports do. You will also want your structure to be functional (i.e., readable), economical (i.e., clear and concise), and in keeping with the best architectural standards (i.e., the rules of good writing). You will have, of course, a choice of many good architectural styles, of which you can always select the best by considering the preferences of your skyscraper-dwellers and the use to which they will put your edifice.

In succeeding chapters, we will discuss the three phases which are always involved in report writing:

1. Research: getting the facts and information (Chapter 15)

2. Organization: imposing a pattern on your material (Chapter 16)

3. Presentation: writing, using graphic methods or statistics to get your material across to your reader (Chapters 17 and 18)

But before we start our detailed discussion of these three phases of report writing, we cannot overemphasize the fact that for writers of reports, the process of digging for facts is a far more rewarding form of intellectual exercise than the process of jumping to conclusions. The report cannot stand on its rhetoric; it generally conveys opinions, recommendations, and conclusions from someone who has information and expert knowledge to someone who will have to act or decide. The report writer carries, therefore, a responsibility for seeing that the facts and information presented are accurate and that all conclusions and recommendations rest solidly upon them.

EXERCISES

1. You are office manager of a branch of the Marshall Insurance Company, a nationwide company. Reporting directly to you are five department heads, each in charge of a separate department: new policy processing, records management, billing, administrative support, and correspondence. The new-policy-processing department receives all initial communications from agents or directly from customers through the correspondence department. It then takes care of all the necessary paperwork and computer work to write and record the new policies. The correspondence department then prepares the letters to be sent to the new customers or the agents.

   The records management section is responsible for maintaining and updating all policy files. Inquiries from customers about their policies are transmitted to records management from the correspondence center; replies to the inquiries are sent from the correspondence department using the information provided by records management.

   The billing department, using data provided by records management, calculates premiums due and prepares the statements. Payments are likewise handled by the billing department.

The administrative support personnel serve as assistants to the various executives in the branch office. They do research, handle telephone calls, schedule appointments, prepare reports and correspondence, and perform a variety of other jobs that enable the executives to make better use of their own time for problem solving and decision making.

The correspondence department receives all mail and distributes it to the proper departments. Using data provided by the other departments, it is responsible for composing original letters and preparing correspondence from form paragraphs. Text-editing, visual-display word processing equipment is used for all work in the correspondence section, ensuring rapid turnaround and perfect copy. The other departments may also utilize the correspondence center for the typing of their reports—since revisions are easy with the word processing equipment, final reports can be made quickly from revised rough drafts. In-house memos may be typed either by the correspondence center or by the individual departments; outgoing correspondence is always prepared by the correspondence department.

Each of the five departments has separate functions, but all must be integrated and work together harmoniously for efficient, accurate operation of the branch. This was the case until about a month ago, when you perceived a change in the atmosphere of the office. Not only have you noticed friction among employees, less friendly banter, and fewer smiles, but inaccurate information is being sent from the office, correspondence is being mailed late, and the executives are complaining about the lack of cooperation and the lowered quality of work. Your superior, the administrative services manager, believes that the employees under your supervision need to develop better human relations skills or else have the skills they do possess revived. He has instructed you, the office manager, to prepare a report recommending a specific course of action. You recognize that he believes the present office situation is a result of poor interpersonal relations; he does not believe there are any other explanations.

a. Assume that the administrative services manager is correct in his analysis of the situation. Prepare a short report in which you reach a definite conclusion as to the preferred remedy.

b. Assume that he is correct in his analysis. Prepare a short report in which you present several alternative remedies, thereby leaving the final decision up to him.

c. You question the administrative services manager's assumption that the problem is simply a human relations one. What might be some other possible causes? Now prepare a report for the manager explaining some of these causes. After presenting the causes, you may choose either to make a specific recommendation of a solution or to present alternative courses of action.

2. Assume the same basic facts as in Exercise 1. However, in this instance the office is running smoothly, and interpersonal relations among all employees are excellent. Marshall is expanding its branch offices and wants your office to serve as a model for the newly created branches. The vice-president for administrative operations has asked you to prepare a report "to serve as guidelines for our new branches." That is all she has told you. Therefore, you need to answer the following questions before proceeding any further:

a. Who will read my report?

b. What specifically is wanted ? What use will the reader or readers make of it? Are there any unstated purposes the reader wants the report to serve?

c. Am I trying to persuade the reader in any way, am I merely giving information, or am I doing both?

d. What questions might I anticipate the reader having? Will I answer these in my report?

e. How much information is needed? Should I prepare a lengthy, detailed report or just give an overview of our operations?

f. What is the best way to present the information?

3. What do you consider the basic problem in the following situation to be? Assume that you are responsible for writing an action-getting report; prepare a one-paragraph statement of your purpose. Your report will be presented to the dean of student affairs and the owners of the town's movie theaters, and it will be printed in the campus newspaper.

One of the major activities of your college's cultural affairs board is the showing of movies on weekends. Depending on the movie, students either pay $1 or are admitted free. Recently, however, several movie theater owners in town have been raising serious complaints about "an institution which they support through taxes competing with and undercutting their private enter-prises."

The following statements have been made:

By Maria Sanchez, chairman of the cultural affairs board: "We show popular movies that are at least one year old and also old classic films such as Bogart, Bacall, Gable, and the Marx Brothers. Up until last year, the only place people could view these films was here at the college. Because local theater owners saw how popular such films were, they decided to get into the act and started showing some of the same films. There is no reason why we should abandon our program because profit-hungry people want to capitalize on our success."

By Ken Pulaski, a local theater owner: "One of the foundations of our free enterprise system is meeting a demand. Once the college film program established the fact that students would patronize older movies, I decided to help meet their entertainment desires. So I have booked such movies. My complaint is that the college is showing the same movies I am, except they are showing theirs a week or two after mine. Naturally if the students know they can see the same movie the next week for free, they will not pay $2 at my theater."

By Rita Eckhorn, a student: "I live on campus and do not have a car. Therefore, it's easier for me to see movies here at the college rather than find transportation into town."

By Nancy McDonald, another theater owner: "The college is in the teaching and research business, not the entertainment busi-ness. I don't offer free courses; why should the college offer free movies?"

By Mike Sidorak, a student: "The theater owners are right. They pay taxes which are being used to put them out of business. Is this the American way?"

By Chuck Rowan, a college professor: "Not everyone wants to see older movies. The theaters showing current movies are doing well. Perhaps the theaters in town should stick to those. However, if a theater wants to show older movies, perhaps its owner could coordinate his or her choice of films with those shown by the college. Surely there are enough older movies to go around."

4. Julie Tyler, the head of the customer service department of Action Sports, has been receiving a number of complaints from mail-order customers. These customers have ordered running shoes which they saw advertised by Action Sports in several sports magazines. But they have not received their shoes; some have been waiting for two months with no acknowledgment of their orders or explanations of the delay. Ms. Tyler was even told by one customer that she had called long distance to find out whether the shoes were in stock before she sent in her order and had been told that they were. Ms. Tyler has asked you, the mail-order supervisor, to "find out why we are so far behind in filling these orders so I can respond to the customers and so we can do something about this situation." You realize that Ms. Tyler is implying that the problem is a backlog of orders. You, however, are a person who looks beyond the assumed and the obvious. You realize that most often a general problem can be more narrowly defined, and that solution of a broad problem results from solving its subproblems.
   a. Therefore, what more specific problems do you think should be investigated?
   b. Does the identification of a subproblem often lead to the discovery of other issues stemming from the subproblem?
   c. List at least one related issue for each of the more specific subproblems you have identified.
   d. Since you have now looked beyond the general and the obvious, write a few sentences (1) describing the purpose of the report, and (2) defining the problem.

15
RESEARCH, DATA, AND REASONING

Today's business world is a world of research—and tomorrow's will be even more research-oriented. You do not need to be a scientist working in the company's laboratory to find yourself called upon to do research. Throughout the firm—in marketing, in finance, in production, in personnel administration—research forms the basis for management decision making. Old-time methods of operating by rule of thumb are practically extinct.

Clearly, therefore, you will need certain skills in research methods. Some of these can be learned only after close association and experience with the particular field of business you choose. But there are certain requirements common to all business research, and while this book is not intended to present a comprehensive treatment of all forms of research, we will cover the basic principles and methods applicable to report writing. It is worth noting, however, that the infinite variety of report-writing situations in business makes it impossible to provide specific instructions covering even a small fraction of the report-writing activities that involve research.

FINDING THE FACTS

A common mistake of inexperienced report writers is failing to take advantage of what is already known. It is true that much of the research required for reports in business involves material you get firsthand from the source—your own activities and experiences, questionnaires, work papers, and other materials from the company files or from conferences, interviews, and discussions with fellow employees. We will say more about these in a moment. But first, you should make certain that you do not needlessly repeat research that is already done.

Certain important business publications, directories, and indexes of publications serve as excellent starting points. The following are useful:

Overall Guides

A helpful place to begin is the comprehensive guide or bibliography of business sources, such as these:

HARVARD UNIVERSITY: GRADUATE SCHOOL OF BUSINESS ADMINISTRATION, BAKER LIBRARY. *Selected Reference Sources,* Boston, 1963.

JOHNSON, H. W. AND MC FARLAND, S. W. *How to Use the Business Library, with Sources of Business Information,* 4th ed, Cincinnati, South-Western Publishing Company, 1972.

DANIELS, LORNA. *Business Information Sources,* Berkeley, University of California Press, 1976.

WASSERMAN, PAUL (ed.). *Encyclopedia of Business Information Sources,* 3d ed, Detroit, Gale, 1976.

Indexes

There are many excellent indexes in the business field. The following are widely used:

a. Periodical Indexes
Business Periodicals Index, New York, The H. W. Wilson Company (monthly, with periodic cumulations).
    Note: See *Industrial Arts Index* for articles prior to 1958.
Public Affairs Information Service, New York, Public Affairs Information Service, Inc. (weekly, with periodic cumulations).
Readers' Guide to Periodical Literature, New York, The H. W. Wilson Company (semimonthly, with periodic cumulations).

b. Newspaper Indexes
New York Times Index (semimonthly, cumulated annually).
Wall Street Journal Index (monthly with annual cumulations).

Financial and Industrial Directories

These three general directories are widely used in business research:

DUN AND BRADSTREET. *Million Dollar Directory* (annual, with supplements). Identifies officers, products, annual sales, and numbers of employees for over 23,000 United States companies with a net worth of $1 million or more.

Poor's Register of Corporations, Directors, and Executives of the United States and Canada (annual, with quarterly cumulated supplements). Similar information as the above for about 29,000 corporations and for about 75,000 executives and directors.

Thomas' Register of American Manufacturers (5 volumes, annual). The first three volumes list manufacturers by product, the fourth is an alphabetical directory of companies, and the fifth a "product-finding guide."

Business and Financial Periodicals

A variety of periodicals are available in specialized business fields. These are also widely read for their general business information:

Barron's; National Business and Financial Weekly (weekly)

Business Week (weekly)

Commercial and Financial Chronicle (semiweekly)

Dun's Review and Modern Industry (monthly)

Fortune (monthly)

Harvard Business Review (bimonthly)

U.S. Board of Governors of the Federal Reserve System. *Federal Reserve Bulletin* (monthly)

U.S. Bureau of Labor Statistics. *Monthly Labor Review* (monthly)

U.S. Department of Commerce. *Survey of Current Business* (monthly)

Statistical Compendiums

The following contain statistics for business as a whole:

Economic Almanac. National Industrial Conference Board (annual).

Handbook of Basic Economic Statistics . . . A Manual of Basic Economic Data on Industry, Commerce, Labor, and Agriculture in the United States. Economic Statistics Bureau of Washington, D.C. (monthly, quarterly, and annually).

United Nations, Statistical Office. *Statistical Yearbook* (annual).

U.S. Bureau of the Census. *Historical Statistics of the United States.*

U.S. Bureau of the Census. *Statistical Abstract of the United States* (annual).

Computerized Search Services

As mentioned earlier, referring to the preceding guides, indexes, and directories can save a lot of time if we find that what we would like to do has been done before. Furthermore, discovering the "state of the art" of a subject of interest to us can be an exciting learning experience. Unfortunately, because of the time and legwork involved, it can also become a somewhat tedious process. However, a development of the last decade promises to reduce some of that tedium. That development is the increasing popularity of the various computerized search services available today. Two such services are ORBIT by SDC (Systems Development Corporation) and DIALOG by Lockheed. These services provide computerized storage and access to numerous data bases or abstracts in many fields. Some such data bases that might be of interest to business students are listed below:

ABI/INFORM (Abstracted Business Information)

ERIC (Educational Resources Information Center) Clearing House on Reading and Communication Skills

Psychological Abstracts

ASI (American Statistics Index)

AIM/ARM (for vocational and technical education)

NTIS (National Technical Information Service)

Accountants' Index

Where the computerized search services are offered, librarians are trained to help users search through whatever abstracts they might think useful. If, for example, you wanted to research a topic through a computerized service, a librarian would interview you to determine "key words" that might be used in references to that topic and the particular data bases or abstracts that might contain citations about that topic.

Once the librarian has established these preliminary items (the "key words" and the relevant data bases), he or she will obtain a list of citations from the computer. These citations might be a list of journal entries, or they might include abstracts of the articles. Which you would get depends upon the data base(s) you search through.

The cost of your computerized search may be less than $10, or it may be more. The cost will depend upon the amount of computer time you use and the number of citations you request of the computer. If you submitted three "key words," for example, the computer would tell you how many citations it could list that deal with each word and how many that deal with all three together. You could then choose to have it list only those citations that deal with all three. Thus, beyond a bare minimum fee, you, the user, control the ultimate expense of a computer search. So that this discussion doesn't end on a sour note, we should hasten to add that average user costs of computerized searches have declined and will further decline as these searches become more widely used.

GATHERING FIRSTHAND INFORMATION

A large part of the research required for reports in business involves, not published material from secondary sources, but primary material you gather from your own sources. In school or college, you came much closer to the actual kind of research used in business reports if you made an investigation of such subjects as "What Students at Blank College Think about the Peace Corps" or "The Salaries and Kinds of Jobs of Last Year's Senior Class" or "A Survey of the Cost of Room and Board in Our 23 Fraternities" or "What the Student Council Should Do about Representation on the Faculty's Student Affairs Committee." To report on these subjects you needed *primary sources,* materials that were directly available on your own campus. Though you may possibly have used secondary source materials in the library—for instance, you might have compared a senior class's jobs and salaries with those of other colleges' seniors—most of your investigation should have come from facts or opinions or ideas you got firsthand. What you did if you assembled the data, information, and calculations for a laboratory report probably came closest of all in technique to the research and investigation needed for business reports, though it was probably not so polished a job as you will now be expected to do.

Research that involves something other than the facilities of a library we can call *field research.* It presents some difficulties you do not encounter in *library research.* The card catalog in a library, provided you know how to use it, plus an assortment of bibliographies and indexes, will lead you to everything the library has to offer on your topic. There is no handy catalog for field research. You have to decide such things as: What information must I have? What would I like to have? What is probably available? Where? How do I go about getting it? How much will this cost? How much time will it take? How valuable will it be? And how can I implement the information—put it to work in solving my problem?

Types of Field Research

Although an almost infinite variety of research has been and is being conducted in business, most field research can be categorized as a variation or combination of one or more of three basic types: the survey, the observation, and the experiment.

The *survey* is the most popular method of collecting data in business. It is distinguished by the fact that data are collected by asking questions of people who are thought to have desired information. The questions may be asked in person, by phone, or through the mail. A formal list of such questions makes up a questionnaire. Since questionnaires may also be used in other methods of research, guidelines for their composition will be discussed in a section following the explanation and illustration of all three basic methods.

Surveys are usually designed to gain information about conditions, attitudes, or behavior patterns. A personnel manager, for example, may wish to assess employee receptivity to a new fringe benefits package or to a recently implemented suggestion system. In either case, a formal survey of the employees would provide indications of their receptivity. Marketing departments are probably the most prolific users of survey research. From the simple information cards appliance purchasers are asked to fill out to the more elaborate tests designed to gauge consumer acceptance of new products, marketers are forever attempting to stay abreast of newly emerging consumer needs as well as of their level of satisfaction with existing products. The survey plays an indispensable role in these information-gathering tasks.

An *experiment* might be defined as an attempt to assess the impact of one causal variable upon a resultant variable by holding all other causal variables constant. Most students tend to relate this type of primary research to that which is done by scientists or behavioral researchers in a laboratory. Actually, however, experiments have been used quite extensively in business. For example, companies have used them to gauge the reactions of consumers to new forms of advertising. Assuming other factors remain constant, the company might gauge such reactions by measuring sales before and during the campaign. The difference in sales levels (the resultant variable) would be interpreted as the effect of the advertising campaign (the causal variable).

There are numerous types of experiments available to researchers. The preceding illustration is an example of the simplest category, called the before-after experiment. A more involved type of experiment is the before-after-with-control-group experiment. As the name suggests, two groups are involved. The causal variable is introduced to one but not the other (the control group). After an appropriate time, changes in the resultant variable are measured in both groups. The *differences in the changes* are then thought to have been brought about by the causal variable. The company in the preceding illustration could have used this type of experiment by choosing two similar cities. In one, the new advertising campaign would be used; in the other, all sales efforts would be kept constant. If sales increased 5 percent in the control city and 15 percent in the experimental city, we could say that the advertising campaign was responsible for the additional 10 percent. The first 5 percent could be said to be due to "other factors" (e.g., the economy) that changed in both cities.

As we said earlier, there are many types of experiments available that can be adapted to the conditions under which research is being conducted. The preceding illustrations are examples of but two types. Since an involved review of all the categories available would be of questionable merit in our introductory discussion, suffice it to say that the experiment is a flexible and practicable tool of business research.

The *observation,* the third category of primary research we will discuss, is probably the least common of the three. As the name implies, in this form of research something is being observed. The person(s) being observed or the person(s) responsible for the thing(s) being observed is (are) not aware of the observation. Thus, the top management of a retail chain could use the observation to check the service or merchandising practices of its branches. Furthermore, it could be used to study the buying behavior of shoppers, or to gauge the quantity of traffic on a thoroughfare. As suggested by these illustrations, the major benefit of the observation is that the research is directly measuring some phenomenon (e.g., buying behavior) as opposed to being told about it (as would be the case if one surveyed buyers). The greater expense of the observation, however, is not always justified.

Sampling

In performing the types of primary research discussed in the preceding section, researchers, as likely as not, will be making inferences. In other words, they will be studying a small group of people or things so as to be able to transfer their findings to a larger group. Market researchers, for example, can rarely afford to survey the entire market for a product. They must be content to study a relatively small segment (sample), after which they transfer their findings to the larger population (the market).

The ultimate hope of researchers is that the findings from the smaller group are similar to those that would result from a study of the larger group. This similarity will theoretically be greater the larger the size of the sample, but there are usually practical limits on how large a sample one can draw. Consequently, researchers usually work with factors other than size alone to assure themselves that the sample is similar in makeup to the larger population. Thus, the findings would be similar. One of these factors is the sampling technique used.

Numerous techniques of sampling are used by researchers today. Some of the more popular ones are random sampling, stratified random sampling, systematic sampling, quota sampling, and area sampling. In *random sampling,* every member of a population has an equal chance of being selected. If a large enough number of names were selected (e.g., perhaps through names pulled from a hat), one could reason that the sample was like the larger population in character.

Stratified random sampling assures proportionate representation of categories of a larger population. If you wished to survey the reaction of your school's student body to a new administrative policy, you might consider using stratified random sampling. To do so you would randomly select from *each* of the rolls of the classes enough students so that your sample contained the same percentage of freshmen, sophomores, juniors, and seniors as the entire student body.

In *systematic sampling,* a researcher selects every *n*th name on a list. If you wanted your sample to be one-tenth the size of your population, you would select every 10th name on your list. This process still assures you that every member of the population has an equal chance of being selected because the first number is chosen randomly. In our example, a number from 1 to 10 would be chosen randomly. If it were 7, your sample would be made up of the 7th, 17th, 27th, etc., members of the list.

Quota sampling is a nonrandom method of sampling a population that assures a researcher that the sample will have the same breakdown of certain characteristics as the larger population. The goal is similar to that of stratified random sampling, but since more characteristics are involved, the process is more involved and, as mentioned before, nonrandom. Suppose, for example, you planned to distribute a product throughout a state and wished to assess people's likely reactions to it. Suppose you thought that such reactions might be influenced by the respondent's age, sex, marital status, family size, and income. To get an accurate idea of how the state's population would react, you would choose a sample that was similar in age, sex, marital status, family size, and income breakdowns to the entire state.

Area sampling is a random means of geographically breaking down a population into a sample. Of all the states in the nation, some would be randomly selected. Within those, some subdivisions, such as counties, might be randomly selected. Within the counties, some cities would be chosen. Applying the same process of subdivision and random selection, the researcher could ultimately work to some households on a block.

The preceding list of popular sampling techniques was not intended to make readers expert samplers. It was instead included to acquaint students with the variety of methods available. Before becoming involved with any major research effort, a student should become more intimately familiar with the subject of sampling through either statistics coursework or the wealth of library holdings on the subject.

Research Forms

With an appropriate method of sampling the population determined, the researcher is ready to approach the sample and collect the data needed. This data collection is usually facilitated by the use of some kind of research form. In the case of a survey, this form is called a questionnaire. Depending upon how this research form is worded and organized, the data collecting can be either a relatively smooth, unencumbered process or a tedious, hurdle-ridden task. To be more assured of the former case, if you are ever called upon to construct a research form, you would be wise to keep the following guidelines in mind.

First, determine specifically what information is needed. This guide may sound like a bit of an understatement. Indeed, this task would be part of the original statement of the problem that gets the research underway. But the guide bears repetition because of its importance. It would be impossible to design a thorough data collection form unless you were quite familiar with the types of information needed.

Second, seek one item of information per question. Seeking more than one item per question can overtax and confuse the respondent. The following example has that potential:

> Does the AYA machine operate at a satisfactory speed while minimizing the occurrence of errors?

Speed and the occurrence of errors are two separate items. As such, they deserve separate attention and should be handled in two different questions.

Third, ask only questions for which the respondent can logically be expected to have and remember the answers. Is the item sought in that person's experience? Is it logical to ask a person to rank a brand of cologne if you haven't established whether or not that person has ever used that brand of cologne? Can the respondent logically be expected to remember the information you seek? If you're asking about a recent event (What magazines did you read last week?) or one related to something very significant to the respondent (What make and model was the last car you purchased?), recall may be easy. Remember, however, that time plays havoc with most of the information and experiences to which people are exposed.

If a sample member is given choices of response, the choices can influence whether or not the respondent can answer. A simple "yes-no" option won't do if the respondent doesn't know the answer or doesn't have an opinion on the matter in question.

Fourth, think carefully about whether or not questions of a personal nature are really needed. People are naturally hesitant to talk of money matters, personal hygiene, family life, political beliefs, and religious beliefs. They will sometimes give what they consider an acceptable answer and sometimes just balk at such questions. If such items are considered necessary, a researcher might soften their impact in one of several ways. Guaranteed or apparent anonymity might encourage a response. Likewise, some personal information can be obtained indirectly. Income, for example, can be assessed from occupation or from neighborhood or house type. Any method of obtaining personal data, however, will have its drawbacks, and these drawbacks should be kept in mind when research results are analyzed.

Fifth, don't word questions in such a way as to suggest a certain response. One example of such "leading questions" is, "Is XYZ your favorite brand of detergent?" A person answering "yes" might have given a different choice if simply asked, "What is your favorite brand of detergent?" Similarly, if a question has a multiple-choice answer that doesn't cover all possible responses, be sure to include an "other" choice, with a blank for the identification of the other answer. Finally, keep in mind that questions may become "leading" by means other than the wording of the questions themselves. Companies conducting marketing research, for example, must be wary of identifying themselves in the cover letter or the envelope return address. Such a slip would probably predispose the respondents to react favorably to the company's product (in comparison with other products) and thus positively bias the results of the research.

Sixth and finally, plan the physical layout with response and tabulation in mind. First of all, save the toughest question for the last part of the form. To ask for personal information, or that which requires some effort, at the beginning of the form almost guarantees that it won't be answered. On the other hand, after a respondent has devoted a certain amount of time to answering most of the questions, he or she will be less likely to discard it over the last question or two. Another layout concern should be tabulation. Wherever possible you should arrange research forms so that the responses can be easily tabulated. When computer tabulation is used, the research form should be constructed so as to aid in the transfer of the data to computer code sheets.

Although the preceding guidelines should help a researcher to get the information desired, they cannot serve as a guarantee. To increase the likelihood that the research form will result in the data or opinions needed, a researcher should consider running a pretest. In other words, the form should be administered to a small number of respondents before it is given to the entire sample. In this way, problems can be spotted and corrected before the complete research project is conducted.

One final point of caution should be raised before we leave the topic of research forms. In recent years we have seen privacy and human rights become major issues of concern to the nation and its various levels of government. And the legislative tide stemming from concern over these issues does not promise to ebb any time soon. As a result, researchers must be very careful to make certain that it is legally permissible to ask the questions they present on data collection forms. Universities have established committees with just that purpose in mind regarding research conducted on people by students and faculty. Large businesses have their corporate staffs address the problem. Small businesses very often hire consultants on a retainer basis. How the problem is handled may vary with the circumstances, as illustrated above. The point is that these issues, privacy and human rights, are very real concerns that must be recognized and considered by every researcher of subjects concerning human beings.

REASONING

After you have decided on the method(s) of research you must use, after you have chosen the people (sample) with the facts and/or opinions you need, after you design the appropriate research form, and after you have collected the information you need—you still have quite a way to go. Now you must interpret and analyze what you've collected so as to reach a reasonable conclusion. How you reach a conclusion based on your primary product—the facts and opinions you have collected—can be described as part of a reasoning process. The four elements of this process are inference, analogy, assumption, and logic.

Inference

Suppose you observe the sales of two products, A and B, identical in all respects except name and price. Product A, which is priced below B, outsells B. In fact, in one day 10 units of A are sold for each 1 of B. So far we have discussed only facts: the nature of the products, their names, their prices, and their sales. Suppose you now conclude that A outsells B because it is cheaper. This is an inference. It is not a fact. It may be true or untrue; but until it is established as a fact or falsehood, it is an inference. Suppose that you have interviewed 600 purchasers of A and can present as a *fact* that 500 say they bought A because it was cheaper and 100 because they didn't notice B. (Notice that the reasons given are not facts but opinions, although the *giving* of the opinions is a fact.) This information would strengthen your inference. It becomes stronger as you find more facts or opinions to support it and as you investigate and prove groundless the objections to it. But it is still not as strong as a fact.

Inferences are important, at least as important as facts, but they must be evaluated. Facts can usually, although not always, be proved without much difficulty. You can ascertain that the price of product A is $14.95, and that is that. You may be very certain of your inference that A outsells B because of its lower price, you may be fairly certain, or you may not be certain at all. When you are trying to decide whether to recommend to the manufacturer of product B that the price be reduced to increase sales, the degree of your certainty becomes important. First, you must decide whether the inference is strong enough to justify a conclusion that the price should be reduced, and second, you must explain in your report how certain you are. If your inference is little better than a guess, but you can't do any better, you should say so. Don't pretend that you are sure. Make clear to the reader of your report which conclusions you are sure of and which you are not so sure of. In deciding what to do, the reader will then have a basis on which to evaluate the risks involved and cannot blame you for being misleading.

Many writers of business reports fail to appreciate the varying quality of inferences, and some are rather vague about the difference between fact, opinion, and inference. The result is that their analysis of a business problem is muddled and their reports do not make clear what can be relied on and what cannot, what is almost certain and what is only probable.

Here is an example of a test in which statements are classified as fact or inference, a "critical inference test." The example consists of a story followed by a series of statements based on the story. Each statement is to be classified as factually true or false, or as a strong or a weak opinion or inference. The classification is given in parentheses.

The firm of New Toys, Inc., owned by Carlton Wellman, manufactured the "Tot Walker," a device invented by Mr. Wellman to help babies learn to walk. During its first year the company sold 500 units to a large mail-order house at $3 each. The mail-order house offered them to the public at $4.50. Mr. Wellman believed the public would pay more than $4.50. He was confident that he could reduce his own price below $3 when his company began large-scale production.

1. *The "Tot Walker" was invented by Mr. Wellman.* (This is factually true, as stated in the story.)

2. *The "Tot Walker" was unique.* (This is not a fact, but an inference. The story does not say whether the device was unique. We know Mr. Wellman invented it, but others may have done the same. Whether you regard the inference as trustworthy or not will depend on whether you trust Mr. Wellman to have investigated to make sure there were no similar products available.)

3. *The public will pay more than $4.50 for the device.* (This is an opinion. We are in no position to evaluate it because the story tells us nothing about Mr. Wellman's reliability or about his qualifications for judging what the public will pay for his device.)

4. *New Toys, Inc., will be able to reduce its price below $3 per unit.* (This is opinion, and not a complete opinion at that. Mr. Wellman said he could reduce the price when his company began large-scale production. If you are willing to infer that the company will begin large-scale production, then you can treat this statement as Mr. Wellman's opinion. We still have no way of judging his reliability, but he has some qualifications which lend support to this opinion. He owns the company that has been manufacturing the "Tot Walker" and he invented the product, so he could be expected to have some expert knowledge of the cost of production.)

5. *The public will pay at least $4.50 for the "Tot Walker" because 500 were sold at this price.* (This is an inference. New Toys, Inc., sold 500 to a mail-order house. We do not know how many were resold and have no way of inferring the number. There is some support for the inference that the public will pay $4.50, because it is a fact that the buyer for the mail-order house, who is presumably an expert at this sort of thing, thought they would. In other words, this inference rests on an opinion that is not expressed in the story but which we can presume.)

Analogy

Analogy is a common method of reasoning. It consists of noting that two situations are similar in several respects and concluding that the similarity will hold for other respects.

Suppose you have observed that a much-advertised brand of fresh milk sold in grocery stores consistently sells at a higher price than a less advertised brand. You reason, therefore, that an advertising campaign could enable a sugar refiner to sell its sugar for more than its competitors, who do little advertising.

The first question to ask is whether the two situations are really analogous. You have a sound analogy only if the two situations have a sufficient number of *essential characteristics in common within the area of comparison* and if there are *no essential differences* within this area.

Several similarities are evident here: Both sugar and milk are grocery items, probably purchased by the same sort of person; both are staples; both are sold in large quantities at a fairly low price per unit. These similarities are certainly within the area of comparison—importance of price. Both are white, too, but this characteristic is irrelevant. We must next ask if there is any essential difference. One such difference will probably be enough to demolish the analogy. Most people would concede that sugar is sugar; there are no noticeable differences in quality. But milk may differ in freshness and in butterfat content, within legal limits, and purchasers may detect or think they detect quality differences. If customers consider quality differences in the case of milk but not in the case of sugar, then your analogy breaks down. No matter how many similarities you can find, that one essential difference prevents you from using the results of the milk case to decide the sugar case. This doesn't prove that advertising won't enable a sugar refiner to charge more than its competitors, but it means that your milk case does not support a conclusion that it will.

Analogies, like inferences, are rarely true or false. They range from poor or weak to good or strong. And, as in the case of inferences, you must evaluate them both for yourself and for your reader.

Assumption

An assumption differs from an inference. An inference is based on specific data— facts or opinions. In the example discussed above, we knew that product A outsold B, we knew A was cheaper, and we knew of no other reason why purchasers would prefer A. We inferred that product A outsold product B because of its lower price. Our conclusion that purchasers would prefer a low price to a high price, however, was an *assumption*. It seemed reasonable, but we had no data to justify it. Therefore, it was not an inference. It was based on general knowledge, on experience, on what most people would call "common sense." But it was a supposition, a taking for granted, and should be recognized as such. There are instances where this particular assumption does not hold. Purchasers of jewelry, for example, or perfume often prefer a high price to a low price because, even though they cannot perceive differences in quality, they believe that a high price in some way gives assurance of high quality.

There is nothing wrong with assumptions. We have to make them when factual data are not available and when no inferences can be drawn. In fact, we have to make assumptions about inferences. Frequently we have to assume that an inference is valid even though we are not really sure, in order to get on with research or a report. In order to discuss how large a cut in the price of product B would increase its sales to a profitable level, for example, we have to assume the validity of our inference that product A outsells it because of price. We can't set out to verify every inference as we go along. When we have reached a final conclusion, however, we may want to review the inferences on which it is based and decide whether some should be verified before action is taken.

It is important not to use assumptions when data are available and inferences can be drawn. When you know the price of A is $14.95 and the price of B is $16.95, it is foolish to assume a price difference of $3. And if you have actually interviewed purchasers and found they chose A over B because of the price difference, it is not necessary to assume that some purchasers chose A because of its lower price. A conclusion that *most* purchasers will behave this way, however, may involve an assumption that your interviews are a satisfactory measure of general purchaser opinion.

It is common for a business researcher to assume that his or her company wants to grow as fast as possible, that a new product will add to the company's profits, or that a reduction in price will increase sales, without bothering to use data at hand that might lead to quite opposite inferences. It is, unfortunately, always easier to assume than to work with data and infer.

Assumptions, like inferences and analogies, must be evaluated. An assumption must be consistent with the available data; it must have a reasonable possibility of being true. You can't assume no one will buy product B at a price of $16.95 when you know perfectly well that people are buying it.

It is especially important to label your assumptions. Be honest enough with the readers of your reports to tell them when you have no data and are relying on assumption, or when you are not certain of the validity of an inference but will assume it is valid for purposes of further discussion. Your readers may disagree with your assumptions: they may feel their experiences and general knowledge are a better guide than yours. At the same time, they may respect your inferences as being based on a familiarity with the data greater than their own. Give them the opportunity to sort out the assumptions from the inferences.

When you have completed a research project and reached a conclusion, it is important to review the inferences, analogies, and assumptions that went into it. You must judge the *importance* and the *validity* of each one. And, in the case of the inference, this involves judging the validity of data—facts and opinions. If an inference, analogy, or assumption is important, then you must be concerned about its validity. If you have inferred that an investment will earn 10 percent and you know that any return under 10 percent is not acceptable to your company, then you had better be sure of your inference before you recommend the investment. On the other hand, if the inference, analogy, or assumption is not very important, then you may not have to worry much about its validity. If you have assumed that a bank loan will cost 6 percent interest, but your conclusion would be no different even if the rate were 10 percent, probably you won't worry much about whether your assumption is a sound one.

When you write your report, perform the same service for your readers. That is, identify the important inferences, analogies, and assumptions. Assure readers of the relative validity of each, which means also warning them of unavoidable weaknesses. And point out which are unimportant, so they won't expect detailed evaluation of these.

Logic

There should be no need to stress the importance of logic in business research and business writing. Yet business reports all too frequently reveal the writer's failure to test statements on logical grounds.

 An example is quoted below. It is taken from a report on the subsidizing of scholarly books published by a university press. Subsidized books are not expected to sell well enough to reimburse the publisher for their cost. Sometimes the publisher expects to lose money on a book, and hence to subsidize it; sometimes other institutions—educational foundations or councils—will provide the funds (a collateral subsidy) to make a publication possible. It is often argued that if a foundation provides the money to subsidize a scholarly book which later proves to be profitable, the university press should refund the subsidy. The following paragraph from the report deals with this argument.

> It is occasionally suggested that a collateral subsidy should be "returnable" that is, that when the Press has recovered all its costs of publication, further proceeds, if any, should be applied to the reduction of the investment of the institution which provided the collateral subsidy. At first sight, this suggestion may seem to have merit, but in practice serious flaws appear. First, it will be noted that such a grant is not a genuine subsidy, but simply the provision of working capital, which may or may not be needed. Secondly, if the Press does not recover from sales its costs of publication above the amount of the collateral subsidy, its funds will be depleted—it is therefore risking an indefinite sum on its publishing judgment, and it should not speculate with the Subsidizing Fund on the basis that it will either be depleted or exactly reimbursed. Thirdly, the administrative cost of recording, computing, and returning proceeds in very small amounts is disproportionately high, and could even exceed possible returns. The situation is quite different if the institution providing the subsidy underwrites the entire cost; it is then assuming the whole publishing risk, and is entitled to all proceeds over and above the actual cost of handling sales.

 Let us look at the three "serious flaws." The first argument is that if a grant is repaid it is not a genuine subsidy. This is not a logical argument; it is a play on words. *Subsidy* is defined in Webster's dictionary as "any gift by way of financial aid." If the gift is returned, it is perhaps no longer a gift. But it really makes no difference to the foundation whether this money is called a gift, subsidy, or refundable advance.

 We can break the second argument down into three parts. First, the writer says that if the press does not recover its own costs of publication over the amount of the subsidy, its funds will be depleted. But this argument is fallacious, since the writer has already stated at the beginning of the paragraph that the suggestion being disputed is that the collateral subsidy be repaid only after the press has recovered all its costs of publication.

 The second portion of the second argument is that the press would be risking an indefinite sum on its publishing judgment if it returned a gift from another institution once a book had recovered its cost. It is hard to tell what the writer had in mind here. The risk was run when the book was published, when no one knew whether it would sell enough copies to repay its cost. Returning the gift after the book proved profitable could not increase this risk. Even so, the risk was never an indefinite one. The press knew how much money it was putting up to publish the book, and it knew that at most it could lose this amount.

The third portion of the second argument is that the press should not speculate with the funds available for subsidizing books in the expectation that these funds will be either depleted or exactly reimbursed. In other words, subsidizing funds should be used only when there is also a possibility of making money on a scholarly book. But the original suggestion seemed to be that a foundation's subsidy be returned to it only *after* the press had recovered all its costs and that *only* the subsidy be returned, so that profit would be kept by the press. Thus the statement that the result could only be depletion of funds or exact reimbursement is false. (It may be that the writer meant to discuss a suggestion that profits would go to the foundation; the first sentence in the paragraph quoted is ambiguous.)

The third argument may have some merit, but the amount of bookkeeping involved would probably be no greater than what is always necessary in order to compute an author's royalty.

The quoted example is an interesting one because, on superficial reading, it appears to make sense. You have to subject each of the writer's arguments to rather close scrutiny to discover that, on a logical basis, it falls apart.

This chapter cannot offer you a course in logic. But we have already discussed the use and misuse of inferences, analogies, and assumptions, and we will deal briefly with two classes of fallacious reasoning because they are so common in business reports. These are *begging the question* and the *non sequitur*.

Begging the Question

When a writer begs the question, he or she assumes what has yet to be proved and, therefore, simply substitutes one question for another. Here is an example:

> I have no hesitation in recommending this investment, because the return on it will be more than satisfactory.

In this sentence, the writer is *assuming* a satisfactory return in order to support a recommendation for investment. Whether the return will be satisfactory is the key question, the one that must be answered affirmatively before the recommendation can be justified. In other words, the question "Should I invest?" is not very different from "Will the return be satisfactory?" and you cannot logically answer the first by assuming an answer to the second. What the example above really says is, "I assume the investment should be made because I assume the return will be more than satisfactory." The recommendation is now shown for what it really is: a pure assumption, not a logical inference.

The *Non Sequitur*

Non sequitur, which means "it does not follow," is perhaps the most common fallacy in business reports. In a strict sense, every inference that is not justified by the data from which it is drawn is a *non sequitur.* The *non sequiturs* with which we are particularly concerned are conclusions drawn from irrelevant or quite insufficient data. For example:

> There are several communities within a 50-mile radius of our plant where we do not have stores. Most of our business is done with local customers; therefore, I believe that any stores opened in these towns would increase customers and sales.

The fact that most business is done with local as opposed to nonlocal customers does not justify the stated conclusion. The writer may have had some reason to think the premise was relevant to the conclusion, but that reason was not given to us. Here is another example:

> We are just breaking even at our present sales volume. Because of competition we cannot raise our prices; therefore, the only other way to make a profit is to lower costs.

The writer is concluding that there are only two ways to make a profit—raise prices or lower costs. And this conclusion is deduced, or appears to be deduced, from the fact that the company is breaking even. The conclusion simply does not follow. Why, for example, is an increase in sales volume not a way to make a profit?

If our discussion of reasoning and logic points to one thing, it is the need for care—for a study of every inference, analogy, assumption, and conclusion, to make sure that it makes sense logically. An absurdity can slip by with ease when thinking and reading are quick and superficial. This is shown by this gem from a book called *Sex and the Adolescent:*

> There are plenty of statistics which suggest how early is too early. Different studies come up with slightly varying figures but the conclusions drawn are quite similar. They indicate that about 60 percent of the husbands who were married between the ages of twenty-eight and thirty are happily adjusted whereas almost two-fifths of the boys who marry under twenty-one make poor marital adjustments.

We have covered a variety of topics in this chapter, and you may find the following summary helpful in remembering and applying them. The questions under each topic are designed to remind you of the discussion and give you a specific guide for testing your own research and reasoning.

1. *Defining the Problem.*   Have I isolated the fundamental problem facing me, or am I dealing with a problem that cannot be solved until others have been

solved? Have I narrowed down the scope of my problem so that I know exactly what are its causes?

2. *Research.* What information is necessary or desirable? Where can I obtain it? How difficult will this be? Will the information be worth its cost?

3. *Fact and Opinion.* Have I clearly differentiated between what is fact and what is opinion? Have I judged the reliability and qualifications of the sources of opinions I am relying on? Can I convince my reader of the value of these opinions?

4. *Inference.* What is the basis for the inferences I have drawn? How reliable are these inferences? How important are they to my conclusions? Have I made both their reliability and their importance clear to my reader?

5. *Analogy.* When I draw an analogy, am I comparing things that are essentially the same? Have I overlooked any essential difference?

6. *Assumption.* Are my assumptions necessary? Have I exhausted my resources of fact and inference? How reliable are my assumptions? How important are they? Have I clearly identified for my reader the assumptions I have made, and have I shown their reliability and importance?

7. *Begging the Question.* Have I pretended to reach a conclusion by logic when, really, I have simply assumed the conclusion?

8. *Non Sequitur.* Do my conclusions really follow from my reasoning? When I describe or imply a cause-and-effect relationship, does this relationship really exist?

EXERCISES

1. What information sources and what methods of obtaining data through field research, if appropriate, would you use if you were asked to write the following reports:
   a. To the personnel manager on the advantages and disadvantages of switching from Blue Cross/Blue Shield health insurance to a Health Maintenance Organization (HMO) plan. An HMO is a local clinic where most of a participant's preventive care, lab work, and treatment is conducted.
   b. To the same personnel manager on employees' satisfaction with the HMO six months after the company has joined.
   c. To the board of directors, who have expressed an interest in Management by Objectives and who need basic information about MBO.
   d. To the long-range planning committee, who remember that the *Wall Street Journal* ran a series of articles about trends in such areas as education, population, and transportation about a year or so ago.
   e. To the vice-president in charge of employee relations about transactional analysis as a management tool in preventing, diagnosing, and resolving conflicts between superiors and subordinates.
   f. To the marketing manager on the relationship between the distribution of free samples of a new mouthwash and the sales of that product.

g. To the advertising manager on the makes of cars driven by people attending the national drag racing finals

2. A local shoppers' newspaper, *Moneysaver*, contains advertisements of local merchants and personal ads from readers trying to buy and sell merchandise. *Moneysaver* is attempting to increase the number of local merchants who advertise in the weekly publication. What reasons might the newspaper use to persuade merchants to place advertisements? What data would be necessary to support these reasons? How might *Moneysaver* go about obtaining the data? What are some ways the newspaper might present its findings to the merchants?

3. Identify the purpose of each of the following statements, the type of reasoning used, and why the statement would or would not achieve its purpose.
   a. During the past five years, interest in solar energy has increased. Technical developments and breakthroughs have brought down the cost of heating one's home with solar energy. The reliability and dependability of the equipment and of the companies producing the equipment have further encouraged homeowners to look to the sun for some of their energy needs. And these satisfied homeowners are now searching for other energy requirements that can be met by solar energy. Here in Arizona, we use more energy for cooling than for heating. Doesn't it make sense, therefore, to investigate how solar energy can meet your cooling needs?
   b. A recent research study involving a group of business people and a group of educators indicated that businesses and schools have similar organizational characteristics. A valid and reliable instrument was used to compare the characteristics of leadership, motivation, communication, decisions, goals, and control. Statistical analysis of the data showed that there were no significant differences between the two groups. Therefore, the implementation of similar managerial approaches to the organizations should be investigated. If businesses and schools realized that they have much in common, they could learn from each other and share knowledge, research, and practical applications.
   c. With food prices skyrocketing, restaurant owners must look for ways to reduce expenses in order to operate at the same profit levels. The most effortless way to do this is to reduce the amount of food wasted. Since most restaurants have already adopted measures to ensure that food is not wasted during preparation, the next area of waste that needs attention is waste by the customers. Many customers do not eat all the food they are served. If they had not been served that amount, it would not have ended up in the garbage. Therefore, why not offer customers their choice of portion size? This would benefit both the restaurant and the customers, and not only the customers who waste food but also those who are hearty eaters.
   d. Projected sales for our new line of women's active sports clothes look bright. Since our clothes sell for about half the cost of Action's line and 30 percent below the cost of TNT's line, we should certainly be able to take almost half of Action's and nearly a third of TNT's. Action had sales of approximately $80,000 last year; TNT, $60,000. We can safely predict at least $60,000 in sales, therefore. And this amount can certainly be increased, depending on our marketing, promotion, and advertising strategies.

4. If you were the executive reading the reports in which the following statements were made, what supporting evidence or reasoning would you expect?

a. Our current policy of providing tuition reimbursement to our secretarial and clerical workers for skill improvement courses should be discontinued. Very few of these men and women are participating, and they have given me a number of reasons why they are not. Instead of the tuition reimbursement plan, we should develop in-house educational programs in which we can teach and update the shorthand, typing, transcription, language arts, and communication skills of our employees. Such a plan will be of more benefit to the workers and to the company.

b. The installation of our new minicomputer has greatly helped our company. The reduction in hours spent manually recording information and the resulting decrease in errors have enabled us to increase worker productivity and reduce expenses. Although there was some resistance to using computerized information storage and retrieval before the system was installed, this resistance is now becoming minimal, thanks to the efforts of our management team. Management decision making has also been facilitated by our new computer, and we expect the quality of decisions to improve.

c. Our forecasters and planners must look beyond short-term plans if our company is to maintain its position as one of the industry leaders. The scope of their study should also be increased. Much evidence suggests that we are moving toward a "global village" society; and the political, cultural, and economic aspects of the world in general, and specifically our company's relationship to these factors, must be examined. In addition, our planners must deal more with alternative plans than they do at present. As much of the recent business literature points out, the growing interdependence of internal and external environmental factors makes the formulation of only one strategic plan foolish. By developing a number of plans based on varying assumptions, a company is more able to make a quick change in actions should certain environmental factors change. The use of the computer in modeling these alternatives has proved to be successful, and we should investigate such usage in more detail.

d. Due to several factors, sales of our disposable flashlights have declined during the past two years. This decline has been significant enough to cause several of our executives to recommend discontinuation of this product. Our production facilities would be better utilized if we increased production of items that have proved to be good sellers. We should pay particular attention to those products for which the demand is greater than the current supply.

5. You have recently been hired as training director for Brunswick's, a 10-store chain of department stores. The president of the company has instructed you to "evaluate the strengths and weaknesses of our management training program and recommend necessary changes."

a. You decide that a survey of managers who went through the training program would be an appropriate data-gathering device. (1) Construct the questionnaire. (2) What sampling technique do you think would be best?

b. As a result of your research, you recommend that self-teaching learning packets be used to supplement regular classroom instruction. (1) Devise an experiment to test whether the students who use these packets learn more than those who do not use the self-teaching material. (2) What sampling technique do you think would be best?

c. What observation research might you undertake to complete your report for the president?

6. Find an article of interest to you in the *Wall Street Journal* or a business periodical such as *Business Week, Fortune,* or *Harvard Business Review.* The article should contain enough information so that you to can interpret it, analyze it, and draw conclusions. You may create any additional information you feel is necessary to produce a logical report with sound reasoning. Make a photocopy of the article to attach to your report.

   a. Write a short report (three to four paragraphs) utilizing the information contained in the article. Use either inference or analogy to reach your conclusions.

   b. If you find it necessary to state assumptions, be sure to identify them for your reader, and make the reliability and importance of the assumptions clear.

   c. Exchange your report and copy of the article with a classmate. Critique each other's reports in writing, answering questions 4 through 8 on page 290.

   d. Rewrite your report, using your classmate's suggestions where appropriate.

16
ORGANIZING THE MATERIAL

Now that you have collected the material for your report, you face the most difficult task of the report writer—organizing it so that your readers can easily follow the structure you have selected. The absence of such organization is easily detected by readers, although they may not be aware of precisely what is wrong. When business people complain that the reports they receive are badly written, yet they cannot explain exactly what is wrong, the chances are that the reports are poorly organized.

Organization involves imposing a pattern upon your material so that your readers can follow it easily and logically and so that it serves the purpose to which they will put your report. This task will be made much easier if your research methods follow our recommendation in Chapter 14 (*Keeping Track of Your Materials,* page 266) to use a consistent method of recording your research, because your cards can now be sorted into a skeleton outline for your report. In this process, you will have to eliminate extraneous ideas or irrelevant materials by using the criterion of whether they serve the reader's purpose. Particularly, you must avoid the temptation of inexperienced report writers to say: "I've done a lot of hard work to get this material, and I'm going to use it all even though some of it doesn't quite apply." This mental attitude will inevitably result in a report which confuses and overwhelms its readers with a mass of undigested facts. Remember that your job is to serve the readers' purpose, not to impress them with the amount of hard work you have done. If you have worked hard at both the research and the organization, the results will impress them without your being obvious about it.

Fundamentally—and we are speaking now in the broadest terms—there are three patterns by which material can be organized for reports. Each of them has innumerable adaptations and modifications depending upon purposes and readers, but a knowledge of these patterns is essential as you think about how to organize your report:

1. *The inductive pattern,* which proceeds from *specific* facts, statements, and examples to *general* conclusions, recommendations, or results based on them.

2. *The deductive pattern,* which starts with *general* material—conclusions, results, recommendations, effects—and moves on to *specific* information, i.e. facts, statistics, causes, opinions which support the general material.

3. *The step-by-step* or *time-sequence pattern,* which proceeds in the same order of events or the same sequence of time as the situation covered in the report.

You should keep these overall patterns clearly in mind not only because they are helpful to you but because you will want to *tell your reader how you have organized your material.* To do so is like providing signs along the highway—it makes it easy for people to follow their route to a destination. We shall discuss these three patterns in more detail in the following pages.

THE INDUCTIVE PATTERN

One of the oldest patterns of presenting thought can be paraphrased by saying, "Tell readers what you are going to do. Do it. Then sum up what you've done." In fact, this is so old that if we trace it back across the centuries we find ourselves back to Aristotle, who pointed out that "a whole is that which has a beginning, a middle, and an end." In the inductive report pattern these three parts are:

1. An introductory section in which you tell your reader what you are going to do and how you're going to do it

2. A central portion in which you report on what you have done in the way you said you would do it

3. A conclusion (or summary or recommendations or results) summing up what you have done (or indicating what should be done next)

It will help you to arrange reports in this inductive pattern if you raise the following questions:

Why was this work done?

What work was done?

What were the results?

What do the results mean?

What action should be taken because of these results?

This report goes from specific—facts, figures, material of research—to general—conclusions, summary, recommendations. Along with this, it uses the well-tested method of starting with introductory material and progressing through factual support to conclusions.

Psychologically this pattern of organization is particularly adapted to one type of reader and to one situation. Readers who like to examine all the evidence, who want to look the whole situation over carefully before they make up their minds, will usually welcome reports in this pattern. The situation in which it is psychologically sound to use this pattern occurs when you know that your readers may be surprised by or even hostile to your conclusions. By leading readers through an orderly presentation, you gently move them toward the unpleasant or surprising answer while preparing them along the way. Generally this will arouse less antagonism than would confronting them with what they consider disagreeable, unusual, or "unfounded" conclusions and recommendations at the outset of the report.

THE DEDUCTIVE PATTERN

This is by far the most widely used form of report organization in today's business world. It is often called the *executive* report, the *management* report, or the *action-getting* report. Whereas the inductive report can be thought of in terms of

Reason or reasons
therefore
Conclusion or conclusions

The deductive pattern follows this pattern:

Conclusion or conclusions
supported by
Reason or reasons

As they turn the pages of a report in the deductive pattern, readers go from the general to the specific, the more important to the less important. It tends to become more detailed or more specialized in its last pages because it is designed for a reader whose fundamental question is "What do I need to know to act or to decide?" and who wants the answer at the outset.

For such a reader, you must lead from your main point (or points). If it's a recommendation, you present that first and follow it with an analysis of the factors that led you to make the recommendation. If it's a summary, you start there, indicating that it is based on the factual or statistical information presented later in the report. Your reader wants to be told concisely what the facts are, what ought to be done, how it should be done, and if we do it that way, what the results will be.

In the deductive pattern, therefore, you have a special obligation to *think your way through to the central issue or main point*. That is where you have to start, and, in effect, you retrace your own thinking with your reader, starting from that central point as you go into successive pages of the report. Actually, your process here is close to that of newspaper reporters; they know their whole story when they start writing. But into their "lead" paragraph they put the major ideas, facts, or statements so that the reader can get a general idea of what it's all about. Successive paragraphs give more and more details and specific information so that these may be lopped off in later editions without serious loss to the reader's understanding.

The deductive pattern imposes one obligation on the writer—*to start on common ground with the reader.* Before you state your conclusions or recommendations, you must orient your reader by answering the natural question: "What is this about?" As a matter of fact, the chief complaint voiced by executives about deductive reports is that they seem to start in the middle without adequate explanation. Therefore, while your conclusions and recommendations say to your readers "Here's the story in a nutshell," you must always introduce them to this story by saying, "Here's what you must know to understand the story." You can do this by considering such questions as the following and providing answers to those which are relevant in a brief paragraph preceding the conclusions or recommendations:

> What is the report about?
>
> What relation does this report have to other problems, policies, research in the company?
>
> How is it organized? (Unless report forms are so standardized as to require no explanation.)
>
> How was the investigation done?
>
> How long did it take?
>
> What procedures, techniques, or materials were used?
>
> What persons were involved?
>
> Who authorized or requested the report? If it isn't authorized, why are you writing it?
>
> What is the reader supposed to do with it? Read it? Read it and route it to others? Keep it as part of a permanent record?

THE STEP-BY-STEP OR TIME-SEQUENCE PATTERN

Too many reports follow the step-by-step or time-sequence pattern because their writers are too lazy or too unaccustomed to think about their material. These patterns offer writers an easy way out by merely following the pattern the material itself offers—a sequence of time, a narration of steps involved, or a blow-by-blow description of how it all happened. This is effective when you aim at building to a climax, but the result is usually heavy on detail and light on emphasis. Furthermore, events or steps in an operation frequently follow one another in time, but they do not necessarily come to a conclusion or an end. The responsible report writer ought to look for causal relationships and logical developments in the material instead of merely recording chronological episodes.

Since the thesis of this book has been that by thinking you should impose an order on your material for your reader, we can hardly endorse a method which frequently avoids thought and allows the writer to say, "It happened in that order, and that's the way I'm going to tell it." Executives who read a lot of reports agree that this sequence-of-events pattern is used far too frequently. Young report writers will do well to use this pattern only when:

1. Time or the sequence of events are the most important factors in transmitting the facts of the report.

2. Readers express a definite preference for this pattern of organizing material.

Using the first of these criteria, you will generally find that a step-by-step pattern is well adapted to reports of manufacturing operations where a step-by-step analysis is essential; it is useful for reports about methods and procedures where you must follow through the responsibilities of individuals or departments so that a new procedure may be developed or an old one improved. Occasionally, this pattern is well suited to progress reports covering only a short period of time. Finally, some very specialized forms of report have to follow this pattern—for instance, claim reports on industrial accidents.

As to the second criterion, certain readers do prefer an analysis based upon a sequence of time or events. Often this preference is based upon an erroneous notion that such a pattern is the best way to present "all the background information." Such readers tend to be distrustful of attempts to summarize or to present the facts in brief. They prefer to have all the details, relevant or not, and occasionally they tend to lose sight of the forest because of all the trees. But if your readers prefer the blow-by-blow analysis, the step-by-step procedure, your reports should be patterned to these preferences.

The old cliché "first things first" does not really hold as a guide for writers, because the first event in time may not be the first in importance. To sort the inconsequential from the significant, the important from the trivial is the real function of effective report writing. To fall back on "it happened this way and I'm reporting it this way" is therefore an abdication of responsibility in most report-writing situations.

Nonetheless, there are situations in which the writer properly falls back upon the nature of the material being transmitted and upon the report's purpose to ascertain the best organizational pattern. For example, a report might be aimed at obtaining quick approval of a research project for which additional funding is needed. Tactically and psychologically the writer would err by beginning such a report with a blunt request for funds. Psychology and the content itself dictate that the request be garbed in an inductive pattern starting with the importance of the project, the possible benefits accruing, and similar matters before the request for money is made. Similarly, a report intended to recommend change in an involved manufacturing process is best broken into a step-by-step analysis of components so that the reader is not forced to comprehend it in totality.

MAKING ASSUMPTIONS ABOUT READERS AND PURPOSES

So far we have emphasized situations where readers and purposes are known. Unfortunately, this knowledge is not available in an increasing number of report-writing situations in today's business world. Complexity of organization often imposes layers of authority between executives requesting reports and those who write them. Frequently—with the best of intentions—intervening ranks try to "interpret" what is wanted; equally often, these interpretations are misleading or erroneous. Furthermore, since most large companies have facilities in different locations, sheer distance blurs what was formerly firsthand knowledge of readers' preferences and purposes. This lack of rapport is wasteful and costly, but it will doubtless persist until the specific cost of reports can be ascertained to reveal this inefficiency in terms of dollars and cents.

In such situations, the writer's only recourse is to make the best assumptions he or she can and proceed to organize and write the report on these assumptions. We can make this clear by showing how such assumptions will affect an actual report-writing situation. Suppose you get a request for a report from George Peters, the director of office services, whose office is located 500 miles from yours, saying, "I want to know whether we could save money on all our large mailings by typing the recipient's address on the envelope only, thus eliminating the duplication of an address on the letter itself."

The principal purpose of your report seems fairly clear: you assume that a decision must be made, and you collect the data necessary to make it. When you come to the writing of the report, however, you have to think through its purposes in more detail.

Let us look at one way in which you might organize your report:

Statement of Problem

Method of Getting the Information

1. You have sent out a questionnaire to 1,000 companies.

2. Here is how they were selected.

3. Here is the questionnaire sent.

Results of the Study

1. You have received replies from 490 companies, divided by size as follows:
   a. 79 replies from companies with fewer than 50 employees

    b. 153 from companies with 50 to 500 employees
    c. 81 from companies with more than 500 employees
    d. 177 from companies among the 1,000 largest in the United States

Conclusions

The study shows that:

1. A majority in all categories, except companies with fewer than 50 employees, pass mail on to individuals with the envelope unopened.

2. Even when the envelope is opened in the mail room or by other employees, the envelope is attached to the contents.

3. Of all firms answering, 87 percent—and, significantly, 95 percent of the largest companies, where mail could be misdirected more easily—either pass the mail on unopened or attach the envelopes to the contents.

You can, therefore, conclude that:

1. Your company need not go to the extra expense of double-addressing its direct mail.

2. However, it will have an added obligation to have the outside envelope in the most presentable form, since the great majority of recipients actually see it.

Notice the assumptions you have had to make in this situation. You are assuming that George Peters wants a recommendation, not merely information. You are assuming that he wants a systematic, fairly detailed presentation. If he wants only conclusions, your assumption was wrong, and he will find your report tedious. If he wants conclusions first, reasoning second, and the details supporting the reasoning last, you have made another wrong assumption, because you have probably organized your report backwards for him. Finally, you are assuming that he will want to read the questionnaire and the list of companies. If he doesn't, then this information should have been attached as an exhibit (or in an appendix) to indicate that it is optional reading.

    Only one person—George Peters—can say which of these assumptions are right and which are wrong. But speaking generally, we can guess with reasonable certainty that you were correct in your assumption about purpose and a systematic, detailed presentation, but that you were wrong in not presenting conclusions first and in not using an exhibit or appendix for the details.

ORGANIZING PARTS OF THE REPORT

The preceding pages have dealt with the overall organization of the entire report and the reasons for each of the alternative patterns available. Once you have decided on the general organization of your report, you will still have to make decisions about the methods you will use to further break down major parts of your report. These decisions will be especially noteworthy when your report is a long, formal one. Thus, the following pages will treat the ways in which you might organize the major subdivisions of your report.

The Introduction

Isn't it highly unlikely that you would ever take a perfect stranger into your boss's office and launch into a tirade of judgments about that person? If you ever did such a thing, wouldn't your boss have grounds for wondering about the tightness of the bolts in your upstairs anatomical compartment?

If you ever found yourself having to take a stranger into your boss's office, wouldn't there be certain facts you'd need to give your boss first off? You'd need to answer some questions: Who is this person? Why is this stranger here? What does this person do? What is the relevance of this individual's presence to your boss or your boss's work?

In much the same fashion, before expecting readers to comprehend the body of a report, there are certain introductory bases that have to be touched. In a relatively short memo, your introduction may not be more than a paragraph in length. In a long, formal report, the introduction could cover several pages and could be divided into several subsections. The following paragraphs describe subsections that might be found in long, formal reports.

An item often included in the introduction of long, formal reports is *authorization details.* As the title suggests, this section reviews facts about the origin of the report. Who authorized whom to do the research and the report? When, where, and how was it done? When a report contains such a section, it is typically the first subsection of the introduction. Often, however, this section is left out of short to intermediate-length reports because the information is presented in other parts of the report—the title page and the letter of transmittal (which will be discussed in the next chapter).

Every report you'll ever write, regardless of its length, should include a statement of the *purpose* of the report near the very beginning. Here you tell readers what the report is supposed to accomplish. Why was it written? What problem does it address? What is its value? Remember that reports will often have a very obvious primary value. They might also, however, have secondary values. As an example, suppose that you worked in the personnel department of an insurance company. Let's assume that your boss has asked you to conduct a study of agent background variables (age, marital status, number of dependents, education, etc.) to see if they relate to success at selling insurance. After thinking about your task, you would realize that your research and the report is to examine these variables and their relationship to degree of success with the ultimate goal of improving the selection process. What, however, might result from an improved selection process? If your company started hiring a higher percentage of potentially successful agents, your managers wouldn't have to spend as much time training new agents. Morale would probably be improved if the turnover rate were reduced. Also, if an improved selection process were able to weed out potential failures with some degree of reliability, your company would actually be doing these people a favor by not hiring them. All these outcomes might be considered secondary values to such a research project and report designed to improve the company's selection process.

Another important subject treated in the introduction to most reports is *sources and methods of data collection.* If your report is based upon library research, you'll tell your reader the types of references you consulted. If you did primary research, this section will be a bit more involved. You will need to describe the method by which you selected your sample. You will also have to describe how you gathered your information. In doing so, you will most likely note here that your research form is included as an appendix to your report. In deciding what to include in this introductory subsection, you might look to the following rule for guidance: Include whatever is necessary to allow your reader to judge the quality of your research efforts.

Although not all reports will require an introductory subsection on *historical background,* some will have been preceded by events of which readers should be made aware. Particularly will this be so when your topic has been previously researched in various ways. Graduate school theses, for example, usually devote an entire chapter to reviewing previously conducted research on the subject of the thesis. Likewise, if a number of events led up to the need for your research and report, you might want to briefly review the nature of those events in a subsection of your introduction.

The *scope* is an introductory subsection that defines the boundaries of your research efforts. Sometimes this subject is touched upon in the *purpose* subsection. At other times, it is of great enough significance to warrant separate treatment. Suppose, for example, that as an employee of a marketing research firm, you were asked to study the consumer profiles of three cities, using secondary data. Suppose further that you were asked to recommend one of these cities for the location of a restaurant that would cater to the elite of the community. Location studies usually involve much more than consumer profiles; thus your boundaries are narrower than would usually be the case. Furthermore, location studies often involve some primary research. Again, your research boundaries are likely to be affected by the instruction that you use only secondary data. Readers would need to be informed of these boundaries at the outset of the report.

The *limitations* introductory subsection would include mention of any factor that restricted the research or the report in any way. Time limits are one commonly mentioned example. Money also often serves to restrict research efforts. In the preceding example, you might very well have been instructed to use secondary sources of information because the authorizer of the report couldn't afford the cost of primary research. As this example suggests, sometimes various introductory subsections are very closely related. When this is the case, you might consider combining them.

If your report makes use of words possibly unfamiliar to your readers, you may want to include an introductory subsection on *definitions.* In this way, when readers come across these terms in the report, they'll know where to go if they need to review the definitions. If, however, you use an unfamiliar term only once in the report, an alternative way of handling it may be more convenient to readers. Consider defining it with a footnote at the bottom of the page on which it appears. This way your readers won't have to flip pages to find the definition.

In most medium-length to long reports, the last introductory subsection is the *preview* to the report. This subsection may be no more than a paragraph in length and is mainly a coherence device that helps to show readers the way through the report. It reviews the major topics covered in the body of the report, the order in which they are presented, and the logic for that order.

As was noted earlier, not all these subsections need to appear in every report you write. Sometimes two will be so closely related that you can combine them into one subsection. In determining what you need to include in your report's introduction, your guiding light should be your reader. You will be so familiar with your material that you may even be sick of looking at it. Your reader, on the other hand, will be seeing it for the first time when you submit your report. So, in the introduction, do give the reader whatever he or she needs to fully understand and appreciate the rest of the report.

The Body of the Report

The body of your report is the part in which you will present the information you have gathered and your analyses of that information. In most reports, especially in longer ones, the body will represent the bulk of the report. Because of the relative size of this part and because of the nature of the information conveyed in most business reports, it is crucially important that business report writers develop and follow a basic organization plan.

As we mentioned in Chapter 15, you may very well have had an organization plan in mind when you designed your research form. Thus, the groundwork may have already been established. But whether or not this groundwork has already been done, you cannot write a coherent report unless you have a clear picture of the subdivisions of the body of your report and the arrangement of those subdivisions. The following paragraphs will review the various available ways of dividing a report's body into logical subdivisions.

The most suitable method of dividing your report body into parts will be determined by the report's purpose and the nature of the information you have collected. If, for example, you were commissioned to write a progress report on the districts in your company, *place* would be a suitable basis for organizing your report body. In such a report, each district would represent a major part or subdivision of your report's body. One caution, however, is worthy of mention here. You may run across cases where place initially seems to be a suitable basis for major breakdowns of a report body when it actually isn't. Such a case would occur if your purpose were to compare several places according to certain specified concerns. To break down the body of your report by place would physically separate by several pages your treatment of each concern for each place.

In the preceding illustration, it would be far better to initially subdivide the body of your report according to *bases of comparison*. To illustrate, suppose you had to do research and write a report that would recommend one of four cities for the location of a manufacturing plant. Let's say that your primary concerns are availability of labor, nearness to markets, access to raw materials, and tax rates. To first subdivide your report by city would mean that you'd perhaps treat the availability of labor in the first city on page 2, that in the second perhaps on page 6, that in the third on page 10, and the availability of labor in the fourth city on perhaps page 14. The page numbers are of course hypothetical, but the point we are making is real. The information readers would need to compare would be pages apart, and this would cause them a great deal of inconvenience. A much better arrangement would be to initially subdivide the report body by basis of comparison and discuss the four cities' standings under each basis. A topic outline of such an arrangement appears below.

II. Availability of Labor

    A. Phoenix
    B. Los Angeles
    C. New Orleans
    D. Cleveland

III. Nearness to Markets

    A. New Orleans
    B. Los Angeles
    C. Cleveland
    D. Phoenix

IV. Access to Raw Materials

    A. Cleveland
    B. New Orleans
    C. Los Angeles
    D. Phoenix

V. Tax Rates

    A. New Orleans
    B. Cleveland
    C. Phoenix
    D. Los Angeles

Sometimes you won't have to spend very much time deciding on a breakdown for the body of the report. Sometimes the nature of the problem will dictate that certain *factors* or *logical subdivisions* of the larger problem be studied. These factors or logical subdivisions then might well serve as the basis upon which you break down the body of your report. For example, if you wanted to decide whether or not your company should enter into the production of a new product, there are certain factors you would need to consider. Among them would be production feasibility, availability of channels of distribution, consumer demand, existing competition, government regulation, capital requirements, and profit potential. Each of these factors might well serve as a major subdivision of your report's body.

One other method could be used to subdivide the body of a report if circumstances permit it. You may find that the nature of your problem and research is such that you are testing a number of *hypotheses,* perhaps possible answers to a question or possible explanations for a situation. If this is the case, you could organize your report body according to the hypotheses you are testing. As an example, imagine that you were working at the home office of a company made up of a chain of retail stores. Suppose sales at one of the stores had begun to decline in recent months. Let's say that your boss has asked you to investigate the decline and report your findings to her. Your approach might be to formulate certain hypotheses or possible explanations and test the validity of each one. Could the decline be due to a change in the local economy, increased competition in the area, some merchandising inadequacy, or some development at the store that might have affected morale? Your report body could then be organized according to these hypotheses. A section of the body could be devoted to your tests of and findings on each of the four hypotheses.

The Close

The close of your report may contain any of or all the following parts: a summary of the data in the report, a review of the conclusions you drew as you wrote the report, and/or one or more recommendations. If the purpose of your report is only to present the data you collected, your final section, or close, will be no more than a summary of the body of the report. If, on the other hand, you draw conclusions in the report, your close should also include a review of the report's major conclusions. If the person authorizing the report asked you to make recommendations, this last report section would be the place for you to make them.

The arrangement of the summary and conclusions parts typically resembles the way the subjects being summarized or concluded were arranged in the report body. The recommendations part of the closing section usually appears last. Using this organization for the closing section, the action part (the recommendations) points the way to the reader's next logical move *after* the reasons for that move have been reviewed.

EXERCISES

1. The consulting firm you work for has been hired by a national automobile manufacturer to investigate transportation alternatives to the gasoline-powered, internal-combustion automobile. Your particular part of the project was the investigation of electric autos. Your research shows that:

An electric car was built by Fred M. Kimball of Boston in 1888, but gasoline-powered automobiles were faster and had a greater range.

Rising fuel costs and growing concern about the pollution caused by internal-combustion engines are leading many people to reconsider the electric car.

In 1969 the Federal Highway Administration conducted an extensive study on the driving habits of Americans. Of all automobile trips, 54 percent were under five miles in length, and 95 percent were under 30 miles in length. Trips of 50 miles or more accounted for less than 2 percent of the total number of trips yearly.

You surveyed the driving patterns of 400 households in your city for two months and came up with similar figures: 56 percent of trips were under 5 miles, and 93 percent of trips were under 30 miles.

A government researcher, Harvey Schwartz, applied a mathematical formula to convert the 1969 figures into daily driving patterns and determined that an automobile with a range of 82 miles round trip would satisfy the driving needs of 95 percent of all urban car drivers.

New battery materials and car designs are expected to extend the range of electric cars within the next few years, but presently 82 miles is beyond the limits of electric cars.

The use of an electric vehicle as a second car specifically for short trips is possible now. Several families in town are using electric cars for these purposes and are satisfied with their performance.

In a discussion with an engineer, Alice Adams, she pointed out that electric vehicles should be judged on their own merits for their ability to perform certain specialized functions and should not be expected to match every performance feature of the internal-combustion car.

Developments foreseen by engineers and researchers for the near future include:

Electric cars for the handicapped. One such car has already been developed in France; it can be operated by a person in a wheelchair with no assistance from other people.

Electric service stations. A set of batteries needing recharging would be exchanged there for another set that was already charged. When the first set was recharged, it would be exchanged with another customer's set that needed recharging.

New patterns of driving behavior. Instead of our developing electric cars to match the habits of drivers, perhaps driving habits would change as a result of electric cars. Speed and power would be deemphasized and replaced by maximum efficiency and passenger convenience.

The United States Energy Research and Development Administration (ERDA) predicts that by 1982 family-sized electric cars will match the performance characteristics of today's internal-combustion cars and will be able to travel 200 or more miles without recharging.

The 1976 passage of the Electric and Hybrid Vehicle Act enabled ERDA to lease or purchase 2,500 electric vehicles in 1978. The performance of these vehicles is being assessed, and in 1981 the U.S. government will purchase 5,000 advanced electric vehicles if they meet ERDA's performance standards.

Although some of the electric cars are rather boxy and odd-shaped, some are similar in appearance to conventional cars.

Some scientists and engineers you interviewed stated that electricity will greatly increase in cost during the next few years; therefore, electric cars would not be more economical. They suggested that smaller internal-combustion cars should be developed, or more economical fuels for those internal-combustion cars should be invented.

You have been told that the executive of the auto manufacturing company who will first read your report is the kind of person who likes to examine all the evidence before he makes up his mind.
   a. Knowing this, what organizational pattern will probably be most effective for your report?
   b. Outline the report, being sure to include all parts necessary for the pattern you have chosen. From the data you have collected, draw conclusions and make recommendations about the feasibility of electric cars as a transportation alternative.
   c. You may create any additional data you feel will make your report clearer and stronger.

2. You have learned that the deductive pattern states the conclusions or recommendations and then gives the specific reasons for the conclusions and recommendations.
   a. Why should these conclusions and recommendations be preceded by an introductory paragraph?
   b. Using the material from Exercise 1, assume you are going to write the report in the deductive pattern. Write the introductory paragraph with which you would begin your report. Use the questions on page 298 as a guide. Create the additional information you will need for your introduction.

3. Find an article of interest to you in a current business periodical, such as the *Wall Street Journal, Business Week,* or *Fortune.* The article should contain data and conclusions.
   a. Outline the material so that you have it in easy-to-organize form.
   b. Arrange the outlined material into an inductive pattern.
   c. Write your report in the inductive pattern. You may have to draw your own conclusions and recommendations if they are not stated in the article.
   d. Arrange the outlined material from (*a*) into a deductive pattern.
   e. Write the report in the deductive pattern.
   f. Create any additional information you need to write the reports.

4. In many companies, reports are often team efforts and not the sole responsibility of one person. This exercise is good practice for such business assignments.
       As a class project, write a report in which you present research about the pattern of organization for reports preferred and used by business people in your area. The class as a whole should narrowly define the purpose of the report. Then the class should discuss the various specific aspects of the report-writing process and divide itself into

smaller teams, each to handle one of these specific aspects. Care should be taken to distribute the workload as equally as possible. Since not all teams will be working at the same time (for example, the writing team cannot begin until the research team has completed the data collection), a few weeks should be allowed for this exercise. Also, by the time the writing team is ready to do their part of the project, Chapter 17, *Writing the Report*, will have been covered.

5. The following report was written by a member of the research staff of Quandex, a medium-sized conglomerate which has grown quite rapidly during the past three years. Quandex is anticipating continued growth and is concerned not only with short-term planning but also with long-range future developments and opportunities. The head of the advertising department requested that the research staff investigate new communication forms; the following report is one of the reports prepared for the advertising department.
   a. Make an outline of the topics dealt with in the report and rearrange them in a more logical order.
   b. Explain why your order is an improvement over the original.
   c. Rewrite the report, using your outline as a guide and following the techniques presented in this chapter.

Development of the videodisc as a communication medium is something we should keep a close watch on. The technology to make the television program of tomorrow a 12-inch disc that is read through a person's TV set a possibility is here today, and the implications for communications and advertising in the future are unlimited.

The recent breakthrough which makes videodiscs a reality is a device that shines a thin beam of laser light onto a 12-inch aluminized plastic disc, then reads the signals encoded on the disc's surface in the form of tiny hills and depressions. The disc is played on phonographlike equipment that is hooked up to a television screen.

A show originating in the United States could be broadcast via satellite to Europe or Africa, converted into disc format, and distributed to homes or community centers the next day. Advertising on videodiscs could make the new medium self-supporting, just as commercials pay for most television programming today. Advertising on programs being seen outside the United States would have to be different from the advertising for domestic programs, and this could involve hiring specialists in the various cultures being broadcast to.

Each side of the disc can hold up to the equivalent of a half hour of broadcast television. In addition to the picture signal, there is room for two separate sound tracks. Also, pages of printed information or still photographs can be stored on the disc; one disc could take the place of 54,000 pages of business documents. Office filing space could be greatly reduced, and access to documents could be made faster and easier by adding a minicomputer to the playback equipment.

An advertising specialist recently stated that advertising on the videodiscs would also provide an incentive to develop a wide range of programs aimed at the particular needs and interests of people in developing nations, who before had to accept reruns or low-budget imitations of programs popular in developed nations. Again, emphasis must be given to the fact that if advertising in cultures other than our own is undertaken, this should be done carefully and by specialists in those cultures. Otherwise, we could end up offending, not selling.

Because the use of videodiscs will enable viewers to personalize their viewing, many programs with limited market appeal will be produced. Just as we currently have hundreds of special-interest magazines, we will in the future have many special-interest videodisc programs. This means our advertising market might be narrowly segmented.

Presently, videodisc systems are expensive, and several companies are manufacturing them. However, none of these systems is totally compatible with any other, which might cause potential buyers to delay their purchasing until the equipment is either more advanced or brand compatible.

Market segmentation has advantages and disadvantages for advertisers. If an advertiser knows exactly what type of person is watching the show, the product and the approach can be selected to appeal to that person; whereas when appealing to a general audience, an advertiser must be more general and perhaps not as effective. Also, specialized products that were not heavily advertised can now be. Of course, in specialized audiences, these people might tend to be more knowledgeable about the product and hence more critical of the advertisement. Also, foreign governments might be reluctant to have a foreign lifestyle presented via television as a model for their citizens. Opposition to international distribution of printed videodiscs might also be expected from private broadcasters and networks with large investments in conventional television equipment.

Paper-thin, lightweight discs which can be produced for about the same price as a newspaper and in small runs of 5,000 or 10,000 are also being developed. These inexpensive discs would be recyclable and could be considered as "newspapers" with general or special appeal. The advertising potential for these newspapers should certainly be investigated.

For the reasons presented in this report, videodisc technology should be watched closely, and our advertising department should start thinking of the implications and possibilities of videodisc advertising.

6. Your company encourages suggestions from employees and gives cash awards for each suggestion used. You are a member of the suggestion review committee and are evaluating the following suggestion from Vicki Miston:

We need to standardize our format for reports. There seem to be a number of ways reports are organized, and nobody seems to follow one style consistently. It all seems very haphazard, and much time could be saved if we all wrote our reports the same way. Some of the reports I receive don't even have an introduction, and some end so abruptly that I think the last page must have gotten lost. I suggest that a report-writing workshop be held for the employees in our main and branch offices who write reports. This could be one intensive session or several shorter sessions. If it's not possible to hold a workshop, then perhaps we could at least have a report-writing handbook written for us that would contain formats and guidelines to be followed.

The committee thinks Ms. Miston's suggestion has merit but wonders about the inflexibility that might arise from having just one report format. Also, the committee questions the practicality of holding a workshop for 350 employees. You have been asked by the committee to prepare a report evaluating Ms. Miston's suggestions and stating specific ways her ideas could be put into effect.

a. How would you go about getting information for your report?

b. What organization pattern would you use?

c. What methods would you suggest to achieve the results Ms. Miston wants?

7. For each of the following purposes for which a report is to be written, state the subdivisions which you think would be most appropriate and most convenient for your readers:

   a. A college student government association is investigating the necessity and feasibility of banning bicycle riding on the main mall of the campus weekdays between 8 A.M. and 3 P.M.

   b. A supervisor is evaluating five subordinates for promotion purposes.

   c. A college committee is making recommendations concerning the lack of student and faculty parking space.

   d. The Solar Energy Commission is comparing five cities to determine where to locate its research center.

   e. A production manager is attempting to discover the reason or reasons for the decrease in production during the past two months.

   f. An office manager is comparing four makes of text-editing typewriters to determine which to add to the company's present word processing system.

17
WRITING THE REPORT

When you have done your research and imposed a pattern on your material—and only then—you are ready to write. At this point, you may yearn to imitate the procedure of John Ruskin, the English essayist, to ensure the privacy you will need for your task. He sent out cards reading: "Mr. J. Ruskin is about to begin a work of great importance and therefore begs that in reference to calls and correspondence you will consider him dead for the next two months." You probably won't need to take such drastic measures, but at least you can try to find times when you will be uninterrupted.

STEPS IN WRITING THE REPORT

Here is a suggested sequence of steps in writing a report. They will help you to improve all aspects of your reports, but especially your organization.

1. *Plan your time* so that you are not forced to write your report at the last minute. Don't put off till today the report that is due tomorrow.

2. *Prepare an outline,* based on the structure you've selected and the notes you have arranged in groups, which shows your main points and the way the subpoints or subordinate detailed material relates to these main points. This not only will ensure that the discussion follows a logical sequence, but will keep you from inadvertently omitting points as you write.

3. *From your outline, write an entire first draft.* At this stage, you are attempting to get the whole report down on paper. Don't aim at perfection; it is hard enough to get down what you have to say without trying to say it perfectly.

4. *Put the completed rough draft away at least overnight and preferably for several days.* This aging step is important. When your subject is fresh in your mind, you cannot read your report as a stranger would. Your mind fills in the gaps in your exposition, and you are not aware of them. You are so aware of what you meant that you don't notice the points at which a reader may be confused.

5. *Then, come back to it and revise thoroughly.* At this point, you will have gained perspective, a more objective attitude toward your first draft. Generally speaking, it's always easier to edit someone else's writing. The lapse of time will help you to attain more of that impersonality, which is invaluable when you revise. Now you can look at the proportion of your whole presentation to see that you've given adequate space and treatment to your central ideas. You can insert transitions where you had left gaps. You can polish your writing— and you'll doubtless find that some of the phrases you thought highly of the day before aren't quite up to standard. And, beyond all else, you can read your report from the point of view of your reader, using the criterion of whether it serves its purpose. Many writers find it useful to have someone who is not familiar with the subject of the report read it, to pass judgment on it.

Don't be afraid, or too lazy, to tear your first draft apart. If your organization seems faulty, use scissors and paste to change it. Test each paragraph by asking, *How does this paragraph move the reader ahead toward my conclusion?* If the answer is that it doesn't, then delete or rewrite the paragraph.

Eliminate irrelevancies. No one likes to do a lot of research and get no recognition for it, and no one likes to cut well-written paragraphs out of a report. But if it turns out that the research results and the fine-sounding paragraphs are not essential, cut them out. They won't earn you any praise from a reader who recognizes their irrelevance.

You can't make these judgments until you have something concrete before you—that's why you need a first draft. You can't judge effectively while you are preparing the first draft, because you're too involved in the writing, too close to your material; that's why you should back off and let a little time elapse. Later, with your draft before you, you can apply your most rigorous standards and aim at perfection.

Is this procedure too cumbersome? too involved? Not at all. Even the greatest writers—poets, novelists, essayists, and journalists—have had to go through a similar process. We see only the final product and tend to forget the hard work, the rigid discipline of change and revision, that produced it. Except in the rarest instances, polished performance stems only from the grind of constant rehearsal, of endless attention to detail.

In the last analysis, the quality of your reports will depend on the standards you set for them. There will be times and occasions when you may not be able to follow through all the steps we have suggested, but your reports will show that you haven't. If you are convinced that the ability to write clear, accurate reports is of inestimable importance to your career—and all the evidence indicates that it is—you'll have to develop the capacity for taking pains which this procedure involves. The experience of others has proved that you'll save time and write better reports by doing them this way instead of trying to turn out the final product in one frantic rush before the deadline. In the rest of this chapter, we will discuss the more specific aspects involved in the five-step process of writing a report.

PREPARING AN OUTLINE

An outline is to a final report what a preliminary sketch is to a completed painting. It takes time, effort, and thought, but without it your report will lack coherence and logic. Just as you outline your reading to understand it completely, you outline your report material to help your reader grasp it in its final form. An outline helps in three ways: it enables you to spot gaps in your report, to test the relationships between parts of the report, and to see how the assertions, recommendations, or conclusions are validated. In summary, the process of outlining forces you to put your own thoughts in order so that you can put them before your reader in an orderly fashion.

For many students, outlining has been made to seem too formidable a task because of overfussy instruction in the mechanics of outlining. The important fact for report writers is that it doesn't matter what type of outline you use so long as it helps you. For short reports, a few major points jotted down in logical sequence will serve as a sufficient guide. Effective speakers learn this technique early, always noting their main points in relation to their thesis or their recommendation. Here's the way a brief report—oral or written—on metered mail might be arranged in what is called "jotted form," the simplest method of outlining:

> *Thesis: Our company should install postage meters for all departments*
> 1. Use of stamps is wasteful, inefficient
>   Have to be licked
>   Require frequent trips to post office
>   Employees frequently appropriate them for personal mail
> 2. Metered postage is more businesslike
>   Letters are dated, canceled, and postmarked before they go to post office;
>   hence, they get through post office faster
>   Provides place for small ad for business
>   Always gives right postage for letters and packages
>   No waiting in line at post office
>   Provides better appearance for letters

The great advantage of even such a simple outline is that it schedules ideas so that the writer is sure of the report's direction, certain of the relationship of its parts.

Probably the most useful form of outline for report writers is the topic outline, which expresses each point in single words or brief phrases or clauses and arranges material into heads and subheads, each rank in parallel phrasing.

The heads and subheads are marked by alternating numbers and letters in the following sequence: Roman numeral I, capital letter *A*, arabic 1, lowercase *a*, and finally (1) and (*a*). The mechanics are not important in themselves, but they are significant in revealing relationships, as for instance that *A*, *B*, and *C* are much more important than (1) and (2), and that *A* and *B* as well as (1) and (2) have the same *relative* importance. To illustrate the topic outline, let's assume that you have been commissioned to do a report on all forms of communication within your company and to recommend how economies can be effected. You have decided that a number of publications, reports, bulletins, and procedure manuals must be eliminated, but your first task is to show the large number and the diversity of readers prevailing at present. Here's how a topical outline of such material would look.

Thesis: Only by eliminating some of the large number of publications at Blankco can economy be achieved

I. Publications classified by readers:
   A. For stockholders
      1. Quarterly reports accompanying dividends
      2. The Annual Report in June
   B. For the general public
      1. "Research at Blankco—a Service to Society"
      2. "Free Enterprise"
   C. For Blankco employees
      1. To all employees
         a. Blankco Magazine
         b. "Your Pension Plan"
      2. To members of management only
         a. Six-month forecast
         b. Various manuals
            (1) Parts manuals for the repair department
            (2) The service manual for dealers
II. Criteria for judging these publications:
   A. ——————————
      1. —————— etc.

By making your headings grammatically parallel (i.e. using all nouns or all verbs for parallel topics instead of mixing phrases, nouns, sentences), you will underscore the relationship you are trying to develop in writing the report.

But the really important aspect of outlining is not such conventions and mechanics, *but what works for you*. You will develop your own efficient techniques with practice. Can you write a report without an outline? Perhaps—but unless you are very experienced and can comprehend and retain a maze of involved relationships in your head, the odds are against you. Actually, the best argument for outlining is that it saves time—one experienced writer estimates that every minute spent on outlining saves a half hour in writing.

BEGINNING THE REPORT

If you follow the method we recommend—writing a first draft and putting it aside for revision—the sometimes painful process of beginning the report is greatly simplified. At this stage, the important goal is to *start writing:* you will waste time if you wait for the perfect beginning to leap into your mind. There are several approaches that may be helpful when you start to write.

Many writers recommend, if you cannot think of the right beginning for your first draft, that you skip it and go on to something else. Start with some specific description or analysis. You will probably think of an appropriate beginning later—perhaps by the time you have written a paragraph or two, perhaps not until you have finished the whole report. It is usually much better to write up the material you feel able to handle and set the harder parts aside. It is easier to fill in the gaps than to struggle to produce a perfect document the first time through.

If you don't like leaving gaps, then simply write any sort of beginning, no matter how poor, and get on with the rest of the writing. You can then come back and think of a better beginning later. As a matter of fact, you are quite likely to find that you come up with an excellent beginning in the second, third, or fourth paragraph, or even later, and that all you have to do is transpose the material or discard your first paragraph or two.

Another way to get started is to imagine that the person you are writing to is sitting across from your desk. How would you begin a conversation about your topic? Use this as the beginning of your report. Remember that although you are quite familiar with the subject of your report, your reader is not. There are certain things that your reader will need to know before he or she can tackle the data and analyses in your report.

Chapter 16 covered some possible subdivisions or parts of report introductions. During the discussion of these parts, you were told that the nature of the report would dictate which subdivisions should be included. Regardless of how much of an introduction you write, however, and regardless of some writers' recommendations that you start writing where you feel like it, there is some justification for beginning to write your report at the beginning, at the introduction. That justification stems from the Aristotelian idea that that which is expressed is impressed. In other words, by writing the purpose, the scope, the limitations, and other parts of the introduction, you can assure yourself that you have these aspects of the report clearly in mind as you write the rest of the report.

When deciding what to include in the introduction to your report, consider also whether you are writing the entire report inductively or deductively. If you've decided upon a deductive organization, you'll want to state your conclusion(s) and recommendation(s) early in the report. You might want to include a separate section in your introduction to handle these subjects. If you wanted to be very direct, you could place this section immediately after the statement of the purpose of your report.

PARAGRAPHING THE REPORT

During the process of actual writing, the best way for the writer to view a report is as a number of paragraphs linked by logical relationships. For the paragraph is the basic unit in the organizing and writing of a report. It breaks the text into readable units; it groups sentences around a central idea or subject; it presents information in easily assimilated units because it clusters sentences around one central thought. This central thought is generally expressed in the *topic sentence,* and the accompanying sentences within the paragraph should expand, explain, define, contrast, exemplify, or support it. If you think of the topic sentence as providing a general label as to the contents of the paragraph, you can then make sure that the paragraph contains no extraneous or irrelevant sentences which cannot be classified under that label.

The ways of organizing and developing paragraphs are myriad. Because of the special functions and reading habits involved in reports, beginners will find it helpful to place the topic sentence either at the beginning or at the end of the paragraph. Later on you will learn other places for the topic sentence. But in your first reports, try to begin with a sentence which introduces the subject of the paragraph or to end with a sentence which summarizes its whole thought. By doing so, you learn to judge whether all the material in the paragraph is relevant to the topic sentence; you also help the reader who wants only your main ideas as well as the reader who prefers to be led through the detail.

You can generally support the statement in the topic sentence in three ways:

1. By giving reasons or facts

2. By providing examples or details which explain or clarify

3. By following a sequence of events or the steps in a process

Later, you can learn other methods to vary your paragraph organization; you can then use comparison, contrast, definition, restatement, and building to a climax.

No one can give dogmatic rules for developing paragraphs, but you will come very close to the essence of effective paragraphs if you ask two questions:

1. What is the central idea or main point in this paragraph?

2. What must I tell my reader to support or explain or clarify it?

We can illustrate this relationship between the topic sentence and the reader's expectation by a few examples of topic sentences from reports.

This policy of retaining canceled checks for six years needs revision.

Here the reader's natural question is, "*Why* does the policy need revision?" and the writer has an obligation to give reasons in the rest of the paragraph.

Several occurrences during the first quarter confirmed this opinion.

The reader logically expects specific instances which confirm the opinion.

> The modern manager ought to be a teacher too.

The reader expects an explanation to answer the question, "Why?"

Using the last topic sentence, we can show the difference between an organized, integrated, and logically developed paragraph and one which is thought-less:

> Modern managers ought to be teachers too. While college professors frequently lack business experience, they have had experience in teaching. Managers in business, however, do not normally think of themselves as teachers, but they are. Many young people starting their careers wish that their first supervisors had been better teachers. Their whole careers might have been different if only their supervisors had learned to train them properly. In fact, business wastes time, money, and future potential by not learning to teach.

(Notice the irrelevant comments on college professors, the shift in viewpoint to the opinions of young people in business, the jump to the last sentence.)

> Modern managers ought to be teachers too. In reality, they have two major functions—training understudies for their own jobs and helping young employees start careers effectively. In both these functions they are essentially teachers. By learning to instruct those they supervise, they can save time for themselves and money for the company. By training adequate understudies for themselves, they are actually preparing themselves for greater responsibilities in the future; by helping young people to start their careers properly, they are developing the potential human resources of the company.

(Notice the consistency of viewpoint, the logical analysis of the two functions of the manager, and the subsequent development of each of these functions.)

Vary the length of your paragraphs. When they appear too long and too unwieldy, break them up. Long paragraphs usually indicate that the thought expressed in your topic sentence is too complex or too inclusive; try breaking it down into smaller and simpler components. Test your paragraphs by these criteria:

1. What is the central idea or topic?

2. What does the reader need to support it or explain it?

3. Is there anything which does not relate to that idea or topic?

4. Are the sentences in logical sequence to explain or support the topic sentence?

LINKING THE PARAGRAPHS OF A REPORT

In the previous section we have urged you to consider the paragraph as the basic unit or building block of the report. In this section we will discuss how you can use paragraphs and sentences to give unity to your report by linking one part to another with a device which makes your reports readable—the transitional paragraph or sentence.

Now, take a careful look at the paragraph you have just read. It is called a *transitional paragraph;* it makes a transition between the material preceding it and the material which follows. The function of such a paragraph is to help the readers as they move along from one phase of the presentation to the next. It prods them to look back to where they have been and to look ahead to where they are going. The drawing at the top of page 321 illustrates how the paragraph bridges the gap as we move into a new phase.

Since many reports are long, complex documents, you should be particularly careful to insert such paragraphs of transition between the sections. You can place them either at the end of one section or, as we have done, at the beginning of the next one. The technique is simple—tell the readers briefly of the major points you have covered, or remind them of your earlier announcement of the overall plan of your report and point out what you are going to do next.

In linking your ideas as you go from paragraph to paragraph, you can employ this same technique, but here you will use transitional sentences instead of paragraphs. To do this skillfully, you must become aware that certain words and phrases make your readers look back and others make them look ahead. As your writing becomes more effective, you can do both in the same sentence. Notice how the underlined words in the illustrations on page 321 perform one or both of these functions.

By using such sentences, you can make your reports easy to follow because these transitions show your readers what material is coming next and how it relates to what they have already read. This is the mortar that holds chunks of ideas together. Make frequent use of words like *since, as a result, because of this* to show causal relationship; show purpose by *to* (*to* do this), *so that, with a view to.* Underscore added ideas by *also, in addition, furthermore.* Emphasize contrast by *and yet, on the other hand, in contrast to.* Give your reader a guide to the steps in your story by using *next, in the second place, the third step,* and *finally.*

USING HEADINGS

Some writers prefer to insert headings at the time of final revision; others find them useful guides for the rough draft. Regardless of the timing, headings are among the most useful devices in reports. They tell readers what is coming next; they break the text into readable units; and for business readers who are frequently interrupted when they read, they supply a convenient peg for emphasizing the section where the interruption occurred. Furthermore, headings clearly show the main divisions, subdivisions, and sub-subdivisions of your report, so that readers can see your outline at a glance and can easily locate the sections which are of special interest to them.

But don't rely on headings as a substitute for good organization. Many writers of business reports seem to think that any writing becomes adequately

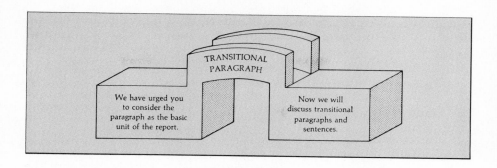

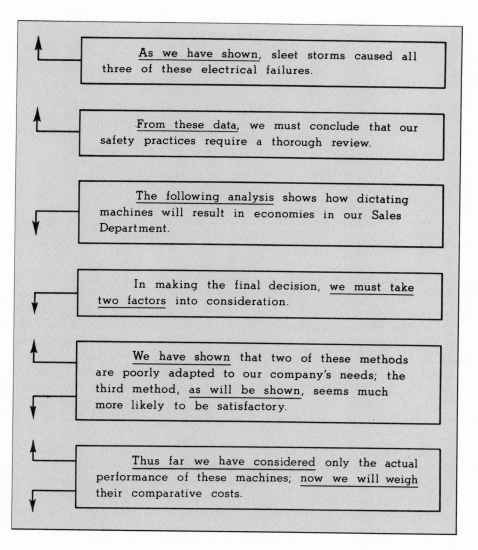

organized when headings are inserted. If your organization is bad, headings will either emphasize this or be inaccurate. In either case, your readers will not be pleased.

The Kinds of Headings

In a long, complex report, the position of the heading and the use of capitals or of underscoring help your reader to see the importance of the material as well as the subordinate relationship of the supporting material within the report. The best current practice is to indicate these headings and subheadings as follows:

<table>
<tr><td>1.</td><td align="center">TITLES or MAJOR DIVISIONS
(Center on the page; all capital letters; underscore each word.)</td></tr>
<tr><td>2.</td><td align="center">MAIN HEADINGS
(Center on the page; all capital letters.)</td></tr>
<tr><td>3.</td><td align="center">Subheadings
(Center on the page; begin each word with a capital letter;
underscore entire subheading.)</td></tr>
</table>

4. Marginal Headings

(Begin at the margin on a separate line with double space above and below; begin each important word with a capital letter; underscore each word.)

5. Paragraph Headings.   (Place these headings at the usual five-space paragraph indention; begin each important word with a capital letter; underscore each word. The entire heading is followed by a period, two spaces after which comes the first word of the paragraph.)

You will probably use all these headings and subheadings only in your longest reports, term papers, or theses. For shorter pieces of writing, you would have to adapt these headings to make them suitable to the material and useful to the reader. For instance, you would probably use only the marginal headings for short pieces of writing, such as two- or three-page reports. Your use of headings will require judgment on your part, since it is impossible to lay down any basic system of headings which will cover all kinds of reports; but remember that most reports use too few headings and present their material in large, eye-repelling chunks. By using headings judiciously, you can help your readers to locate the significant parts of your report and to see the relationship of one part to another.

You can also help them by the mechanical setup of the pages of your report. Since many reports are bound, you should take special care to see that the margins are wide, that the pages are numbered clearly—the most convenient place is the upper right-hand corner—and that you have left plenty of white space to let daylight into your copy. These are mechanical details, but they directly affect the impression your report makes.

THE STYLE OF THE REPORT

The way in which you express your thoughts and information is your style. When we come to the style of business reports, we run headlong into a convention or tradition which has straitjacketed the writing of generations of business writers. This tradition insists that the style of all reports should be impersonal, formal— and deadly dull reading. In grammatical terms, this convention insists on reports written in the third person, passive voice; it leads to such blurred pomposities as "In the case of the fourth experiment, however, a problem is presented which is very difficult," instead of "The fourth experiment, however, presents a difficult problem."

Here, for instance, is a statement from a book on report writing which was written about two decades ago and was used by many of today's business readers for their instruction in report writing:

> Good style is slightly formal; impersonality is the rule. Instead of "We completed the experiment," the preferable form is "The experiment was completed." All pronouns of the first and second person, colloquialisms such as "a lot of," and contractions such as "don't" are to be avoided. Yet, despite the professional tone, a successful report reflects its writer's personality.

The thoughtful reader of these instructions might well be a bit puzzled; he or she should also be a bit skeptical and ask *why* reports clothed in such style are effective and *how* "a successful report reflects its writer's personality" when these instructions can only lead to formality and impersonality.

In all fairness, we should point out that such rules governing the style of reports have grown up from many writers' laudable desire to be modest and to avoid injecting themselves into their reports. Commenting on this awkward style, *Fortune,* in an excellent article called "The Language of Business," examined the flaws of written and spoken English in today's business world:

> First, the written variety—and that infamous jargon, which for want of a better term, we'll call businessese. Almost invariably, "businessese" is marked by the heavy use of the passive construction. Nobody ever *does* anything. Things *happen*—and the author of the action is only barely implied. Thus, one does not refer to something, reference is made to; similarly, while prices may rise, nobody raises them.*

By now you have probably decided that in choosing a style for your reports you are between the devil and the deep blue sea. We have been saying that the style of a report follows a convention of being formal and impersonal—and we have been poking fun at the results. What's the answer for the person who wants to write reports in a style which is both effective and acceptable in business?

As always, the answer lies with the report reader. If your reader is of the

---

*Reprinted, by special permission, from *Fortune's* Communication Series, *Is Anybody Listening?* Copyright 1950 by Time, Inc.

older, more conservative school who learned the conventions of report writing from a textbook similar to the one we quoted, he or she will probably prefer a formalized, impersonal style. The number of such report readers has certainly diminished in the seventies, if only because ours is an era which strips aside artificial and conventional barriers to communication. For that reason, we can conclude that personalizing, simplicity and directness in language, and use of the active voice will increasingly characterize business reports. Here then are a few suggestions for transmitting your ideas in a clear, readable style for the majority of business readers, who are not so much concerned about a "special style" for report writing as they are about getting results from reports.

Make Every Word Count

Wordiness is without doubt the worst fault of all report-writing style; it results in needless expense and waste. The investment that business, industrial, and research organizations put annually into reports is impossible to calculate, but it is unquestionably a huge sum. To make your reports a sound investment, you will have to get rid of certain preconceived notions that have plagued report writers in business and industry. We can sum up the best ways to eliminate wordiness in reports by offering three suggestions: First, you will have to forget the concept of the formalized conventional style we have discussed. Second, you will have to get over the idea that a long report is somehow better or more impressive than a short one. Third, you must be willing to revise.

Keep Your Sentences Short

One of the barriers to good reports is the long, rambling, unorganized sentence, which we have already discussed in Chapter 3. We need only emphasize the general principle here—when you write reports, keep in mind that the short sentence is generally better than the long one. As you look over your first draft of your report, watch out for sentences that run on and on. Break up these long sentences into shorter ones.

In your preference for short sentences, you should avoid extremes; a series of short, choppy, uniform sentences can be as annoying to your reader as very long ones. Ideally, you should aim for variety in both the length and structure of your sentences. Here is an example of the writing of a student who thought that all he had to do to write well was to write short sentences. "There are two parts to the process. The first is the preparation of the sample. The second part is the actual test. The preparation of the sample requires three steps. The first step is the washing of the sample in dilute acid. The acid should be handled carefully." Such a series leaves your readers with a feeling that they are running in place; you can avoid this effect by tying your ideas together and varying your sentence patterns.

Avoid These Word Traps

We cannot make a comprehensive list of all the faults of report-writing style, since different writers will apply their own different devices to their writing. Certain forms of wordiness are, however, common to many reports, partly because writers are trying to be impersonal and partly because they pick up these "fuzzy" expressions from other reports. Notice how clear thinking cuts down the wordiness in the following sentences from actual reports:

> This appears to be particularly difficult in view of the fact that much of the detailed information required is not presently available until March of the following year.

By linking this causally, we can say: "Since much of the detailed information is not available until the following March, this will be difficult."

> Will you please get in touch with me at your earliest convenience in order that we can review this audit. We would also like to review with you at that time your final conclusions with respect to this situation.

When this concluding sentence of a report was discussed in a class of young business people, they agreed that "If it's the boss writing, he should use two words—*See me!*" If the relationship is the other way 'round, say "I'd like to review this audit with you, particularly the conclusions, whenever it's convenient."

> An extremely undesirable condition in the mismailing of invoices to customers is reported by our Accounts Receivable Department. This type of condition must not exist if we are to maintain satisfactory customer relationships. *(33 words)*

By tying ideas together: "To maintain satisfactory relationships with our customers, we must correct the mismailing of invoices which our Accounts Receivable Department has reported." *(21 words)*

> Another advantage of the prepunched form is that by reducing the time required to process a credit transaction, the next customers to be served will not be kept waiting as long as they normally would be. *(36 words)*

By eliminating unnecessary words: "The prepunched form will also reduce the time required to process a credit transaction so that the next customer can be served faster." *(23 words)*

> Bills were paid promptly thereby enabling us to take full advantage of any discounts which were offered to us by vendors. *(21 words)*

By making this direct and active: "By paying bills promptly, we took full advantage of vendors' discounts." *(11 words)*

We do not anticipate any difficulty in meeting the due date which we established, which is April 30, for this project. *(21 words)*

By eliminating the unnecessary clauses: "We expect no difficulty in meeting the established due date of April 30 for this project." *(16 words)*

Each of these men has instituted several changes during the last four weeks which have contributed toward the excellent operation of that section despite the temporary handicap due to the loss of a Control Clerk and a Supervisor as reported in last month's Summary of Operations. *(One sentence—46 words)*

By breaking it into separate sentences: "Both these men have made several changes which contributed to the section's excellent operation. They accomplished this despite the loss of a Control Clerk and a Supervisor, which was reported in last month's Summary of Operations." *(Two sentences—36 words)*

It is therefore necessary that a varitype production schedule be set up and maintained if this job is to be completed and in Minneapolis by April 30th. *(27 words)*

By cutting out the waste: "We must set up and maintain a production schedule to get this job completed and in Minneapolis by April 30." *(20 words)*

The mere counting of words saved by recasting these sentences is not primarily important except to demonstrate what can be accomplished. What is significant is the waste produced when such writing is multiplied throughout a long report—a waste of time in writing, in transcribing, and in reading. And, more important, these sentences *obscure* the line of communication by forcing readers to wade through vague, indefinite expressions to figure out relationships which the writer ought to point up for them. Such writers simply duck responsibility and, in effect, say to their readers. "Here it is—you figure it out and get to the essence. I'm too lazy, too tired, too busy, or too vague to think and to revise."

One Last Word about Your Style

In the final analysis, you should aim at a readable, unobtrusive style adapted to your reader. But get rid of any notions that you have to be pompous or dull. You can persuade or convince your reader more easily by being interesting than by being routine. Keep in mind the fact that reports you write in business may be passed up, or down, or across the organization to sales people, lawyers, accountants or personnel people and to representatives of advertising, operating, methods and procedures, or purchasing departments. The one quality all these people have in common—other than working for the same organization—is that they are all human beings. As one topflight executive said, "I don't care about anything else in reports as long as they are accurate, concise, and sound as if they had been written by one human being for another, which most of our reports don't!"

ENDING THE REPORT

Concluding paragraphs are generally easier to write than beginning paragraphs. When you reach your concluding paragraph, you know what your report is all about; you know what conclusions you have reached, which are important, and which are less important; you know which will be most useful to your readers and which less useful, which they will probably be pleased to read about and which they may not like so much. You are in a position to sum up what you have to say.

With the inductive pattern, a strong ending is easy because the whole structure builds from specific to general. With time or step sequence, you also have an order which often leads naturally to climax and effective conclusion. Even when you use the deductive pattern, don't just trail off into trivia the way some people let their voices drop off at the end of their sentences. Remember that different people may read different parts of your report for different purposes—and that you should end your detail section by a brief summary of its highlights. The deductive report may well have both an overall summary at the beginning for the management reader and a concluding statement at the end of the more detailed section for the technical reader. This arrangement may deny the old Danish proverb that "Everything has an end, except a sausage, which has two"— but it is nevertheless functional for the two types of reader. The really important instruction for ending a report is to stop when you've said what is necessary to your reader's understanding.

A helpful way to think about concluding paragraphs is in terms of their three basic functions—to give the reader a sense of completeness, to emphasize the things you want emphasized, and to indicate what your readers should be thinking about and what course of action they may follow.

In using the final paragraph for the first function, you should let your readers know that you have said all you need to say.

Consider the following example. It is the last paragraph of a report written in response to a request for an analysis and appraisal of a company's situation, with a recommendation for action.

> (1) The president of the company is in a state of poor health and there is some question as to the length of time that he will be able to remain as an active manager of the company. In early 1971, he was forced to retire from the active role of president for several months for reasons of poor health.

This paragraph gives the impression that the writer simply ran out of time, paper, or perhaps words. We expect something more: some explanation of the importance of this conclusion and some recommendation for action. Here is a similar example:

> (2) The credit terms given by this company may be too tight, since there have been no major bad debt losses for a long time. Tight credit, when the industry

trend is toward very liberal credit, could harm sales, as could a shortening of the discount period.

Again, we are led to expect that a topic will be discussed more fully, but the writer simply stops. Contrast examples (1) and (2) with the following:

> (3) I feel that this plan will enable your company to grow at a satisfactory rate. You may someday take your place as a national distributor, but you must grow into this stage gradually. I hope I have been of help in establishing the direction that you and your company should take in the future.

A second function of the concluding paragraph is to emphasize the things that you want to emphasize. You want to focus your reader's attention on the important matters and leave him or her with the proper perspective. Here is an example, again from a reply to a request for an analysis and appraisal and recommendations for action:

> (4) The president's selection of executives is further questioned, since there obviously is no one on the staff who can initiate ideas for new products, increased sales, or decreased costs. A vice-president maintains strict credit policies, whereas a more lenient policy might result in more dealers and increased sales.

This conclusion rounds out the report somewhat better than examples (1) and (2), although the second sentence seems to start a new train of thought. But example (4) does not provide any emphasis. It does not single out any particular problem or course of action with which the reader should be left.

Here is another example, one that appears to be better:

> (5) The company's basic difficulties lie in a lack of planning and a superficial analysis of their management, marketing, and production problems. Management concern should be centered on the company's overall strategy and its implementation in these general areas.

This paragraph is rather deceptive. It appears to be emphasizing the problem the writer feels is most important and suggesting the most important course of action to be followed. But if you read it closely, you will realize that it says very little. In extremely vague and general language, the writer directs the reader's attention to what looks like a major problem but turns out to be little more than a conclusion that the company should be better managed. Example (3) was much better, although more subtle: it quietly emphasized the need for *gradual* growth.

Finally, a concluding paragraph should provide a sense of direction. It should indicate what the reader ought to be thinking about and what course of action it is most important for him or her to follow. In some respects, this third function is not too different from the second. Consider this example:

(6) The company's problems are many and complex, but related; and one cannot be satisfactorily solved without depending upon the solution of another. The present condition of the company and the intensity of competition imply that continuance of the present management policy will make survival of the company increasingly difficult.

What is the reader supposed to do now?

Here is an even more extreme case:

(7) As a whole, your company has more bad points than good points.

Example (3) did a fairly good job of indicating direction. Here is a more specific example:

(8) The purpose of this study was to investigate and make recommendations. Because little useful data were available, I have concentrated on identification of the information you need to control your operation. I have then attempted to show what analyses should be made with this information. The data are not easy to obtain, and the analyses are not easy to make. Both require time and money. I feel the expenditure of both is necessary to maintain control over a rapidly expanding organization. I have tried to indicate exactly where and why money might be saved, and I believe the savings will more than offset the expenditures.

Notice how the writer has rounded out the report and has given a sense of completeness. What needed to be emphasized was indicated clearly and specifically. Also, this writer established, as specifically as possible within the limits of a single paragraph, just what the reader should do next. This is the kind of concluding paragraph that tells the reader that the writer has a confident grasp of the subject of the report.

EXERCISES

1. The president of your company said to you three weeks ago, "I just read an article in the Wall Street Journal about companies that have started stress-relief and exercise programs for their executives. I'd like to know more about these programs and if any companies in this area offer them. Then after I read your report, I might want some specific recommendations on whether we should start such a program. Please have your report ready in three weeks."

   a. What is the purpose of your report? (You may want to refer to Chapter 14.)

   b. What information sources will you use? Do you think some kind of field research would be appropriate?

   Here are some of the data you have collected:

   Some of the participants in the fitness programs are volunteers selected by the companies' medical departments as executives needing exercise to improve their hearts.

The Parker Company maintains an exercise room containing treadmills for the executives to run on. Television sets have been installed to relieve the boredom.

Two companies in your area have employed physical fitness directors to develop exercise and recreational programs for all employees. One of these companies, Cornerstone Insurance, has recently moved into a new building. The facilities include a swimming pool, an exercise room, and tennis and racquetball courts.

The health program personnel are encouraging, and in some cases pressuring, executives to reduce their smoking and drinking. Some of the executives you talked to resent this infringement by the company on their personal lives.

Some of the medical data you have collected indicate that managers tend to be healthier than others and more adaptable to stress; other data indicate that executives are more prone to heart attacks and stress.

The medical director of Reeves, Inc., estimates that health care and sick leave cost the company $30 million annually.

The director of health services programs at International Media stated that her company breaks even with its stress-relief program.

Programs are successful initially, but continued participation is a problem.

One stop-smoking program was less than 20 percent successful after four months.

Alcoholism programs have a greater success rate—60 percent in one company.

SRE Ltd. concentrates on identifying individual health problems through periodic voluntary physical examinations and then recommending specific programs, rather than using traditional health education programs aimed at all employees.

Some of the executives you interviewed spoke very favorably about the fitness programs.

Several companies store the personal information given by their executive volunteers in their computers. The confidentiality of the information was stressed by the people you spoke with at those companies.

c. Write an outline for the report you will prepare for the president, using the preceding data and any other information you believe will make your report complete. If you decided in (b) that some type of field research would be appropriate, be sure to include data from that research.

2. a. Prepare a written critique of the following paragraphs.
   b. Rewrite the paragraphs so that they are organized, integrated, and logically developed. Add any necessary information.
      (1) Communications ability is the most important quality looked for when personnel managers interview candidates for managerial positions. Colleges of business should do more to prepare their students to be better communicators. Many

graduates have difficulty writing simple business letters. Varis Associates, a management consulting firm with offices in six United States cities and in London, studied the importance of certain selected factors in evaluating applications for managerial positions. The least significant factor was the prestige of the college the applicant attended. Therefore, students should be encouraged to investigate the quality of the communication education offered by the colleges they are considering, and not just be taken in by a big name. Of the 350 key personnel people interviewed, 90 percent ranked communication skills as "very important," 10 percent as "important." Previous work experience was ranked as "very important" by 53 percent, "important" by 41 percent, and "of minor importance" by 6 percent of the respondents. Managers who feel their communications ability is lacking should seek additional training, particularly if they will be changing companies. The sample of personnel managers was taken from a diverse group of large and small companies representing a wide variety of organizations.

(2) Expense accounts are an accounting and cash-flow problem in many companies. A computer-controlled credit card can help alleviate some of the problems, although some executives who tend to abuse their expense accounts might not be agreeable to participating in the system. For a cost of $15 per card per year, International Express, one of the most widely used credit cards, will provide a monthly report analyzing in detail who spends how much, where, when, and for what. The printout will flag any charge of an unusual nature for special attention. Although the Internal Revenue Service is proposing stricter regulations for expense accounts, which may tend to decrease the number of abuses, the additional reporting to the IRS that may result could lead to this computer-controlled system being even more of a necessity. The printout gives a monthly and year-to-date summary in eight categories for each cardholder. The previously mentioned flagged charges can be programmed by the user based on individual and projected budgets, and different versions of the entire system are available to meet a variety of needs, since companies handle their accounting and budgeting in a variety of ways.

(3) The credibility of management and the integrity of executives are very much on the public's mind today. Seldom were these issues questioned in the past, but now they are, for several reasons. And the sometimes poor image that the general public holds of a company affects the employees, even if the poor image is based on fiction, not fact. A strong factor that contributes to the erosion of credibility is the "rotten apple" syndrome. This is where a chief executive is charged with lying and management does not dispel the rumors through clear, open communication. The newspapers and other media also use corporate "scandals" to sell their publications and do not investigate thoroughly enough the truth of their stories. The general public needs to become aware of the truth, and company employees can serve as excellent spreaders of the real truth. In a recent study of high school students, their opinions of business were extremely low. One way to stem the dangerous loss of credibility from the "rotten apple" syndrome is for company executives to be visible and to know and care about their audience, be it only their employees or the general public. People in an organization should know where the organization is headed, why it has chosen that path, and what their personal role in the new mission will be.

c. Exchange your paragraphs with a classmate. Critique each other's writing by answering in writing the four questions on page 319 for each paragraph.

3. How would you rewrite the following wordy sentences so that their ideas are presented clearly?

   a. So that all relevant and meaningful information is presented, in view of the problems and issues that now confront our company, I have found it advantageous and necessary first to examine the general problems of the industry as a whole and second to investigate and assess the specifics of our particular position.

   b. Your request has the possibility of being difficult to comply with, due to the fact that the information required for complete yielding to your requisition is not yet available and might even be considered confidential when it is communicated to us.

   c. You are to be applauded for the diplomatic and efficient handling of the Marlsbury situation, a situation which caused us much concern and worry for a substantial period of time. Congratulations on your settlement and on the approach you used to handle the matter are proffered to you from all of the executive staff.

   d. It is of imperative importance that you realize the urgency of making a decision by the due date which we agreed to, which is October 17, in order that we may either proceed with the original proposal or make alternative plans for other ways to expedite the affair.

4. The following paragraph was part of a first draft report a subordinate asked you to review.

   a. What do you feel is the paragraph's major shortcoming? What else could be improved?

   b. Assume you are the writer; make the suggested improvements.

   Flextime is where employees are allowed to arrange their work schedules. They arrange their schedules according to their individual needs. Flextime is becoming more common in companies. It relates well to the word processing environment. Often quick turnaround is needed at odd hours. The flextime word processing workers are available for a longer time range. Flextime has a positive effect on productivity. It helps reduce tardiness and absenteeism. Potential problems include additional record keeping. Increased indirect overhead costs are another problem. So is probable lack of supervision during part of the extended workday.

5. What changes would you make in the following opening paragraphs of reports?

   a. A large number of our executives travel to Europe, the Mideast, and Japan to conduct business. Our personnel department, which has as its prime interest the well-being of our employees, has recently become aware of apparent "jet lag" affecting many of these world travelers. The medical director was the first to notice the similarity of complaints reported to the health clinic from these travelers. She brought her findings to us here in the personnel department, and we in turn wrote a preliminary report for our company president, who has also reported some of the same symptoms. Now the president has requested us to recommend some remedies for the malady.

   b. Should we invest a substantial amount of money in building apartments? Only if apartments are in short supply. And they are. This report examines the reasons for this shortage. Among the major reasons are construction costs that are escalating, the inflated value of land, apartments being converted to condominiums, and fears of rent control. After the reasons have been detailed, the report goes on to explain what kind of financing is recommended, along with some warnings regarding zoning regulations and changes in the regulations that might be necessary for apartment building to be profitable.

c. This study was undertaken to investigate the veracity of the prediction by several labor analysts that if current trends in the computer industry continue, the cost of data processing personnel will reach alarming proportions. These analysts warned that the United States could become a nation of computer analysts and programmers. The present computer technology is presented and is contrasted with technology currently in the experimental stage and with developments predicted for the future. The findings indicate that personnel costs could reach a uncontrollable ratio, but that this is highly unlikely, for innovations aimed at correcting the problem will occur.

6. The following paragraphs appeared as the ending paragraphs for the reports begun in Exercise 5. What are the strong and weak points of each? Rewrite each paragraph to give the reader a sense of completeness, to emphasize what is important, and to indicate the recommended course of action. Add any other information you feel is necessary.

a. Jet lag is a real and generally inevitable affliction. Some travelers dispute that it is inevitable, but at any rate, there are a number of remedies for making it less of an affliction. These have been presented in detail in the body of this report, but I will summarize them here. On your first day of arrival, do only routine work; do not make any big decisions. Some travelers find that exercise like jogging or tennis when they arrive helps them adjust to the passage through the time zones. Abstain from drinking alcohol on the plane; drink plenty of water instead. If travel time exceeds 15 hours, split the trip by taking a one-night stopover. Another way of combating jet lag is to act as though no time changes have occurred, but this can be difficult for stays of several days. A few companies have formal policies on the subject of jet lag, and it is my recommendation that we develop some, too. We could print a booklet explaining jet lag and how to combat it.

b. In summary, we should give serious consideration to investing capital in apartment building. A real shortage of apartments exists in our tri-state area, with vacancies running an average of 2 percent, which is well below the 5 percent that government planners usually consider the shortage threshold. Along with careful analysis of all the financing options, we should give consideration to working with local governments to ease some of the land-use laws.

c. The purpose of this study was to determine whether personnel costs in the computer industry will continue their present trend and eventually become out of control. Approximately $20 billion is now spent each year in the United States to pay for programmers, systems analysts, and other computer personnel. This $20 billion is 55 percent of the total data processing outlay; the other 45 percent is spent on equipment and communications. This ratio will, however, be reversed within the next two decades, due to a number of innovations that are already helping or will be helping to reduce personnel costs. The people who made the original prediction of a continued rise in personnel costs were only using straight-line extrapolations and were not accounting for new developments. This is not to say that their incorrect warning is without value, however. For by being aware of what could happen, we can take steps to see that it does not happen.

7. Exercises 5 and 6 contained beginning and ending paragraphs of reports. Included in these paragraphs were summaries of ideas that were detailed in the bodies of the reports. Assume that you are now writing the body of each report and need a transitional paragraph between two of the ideas you have presented in depth.

    a. Write a transitional paragraph linking two paragraphs that explain remedies for jet lag. A number of remedies were suggested in the ending paragraph; create any additional information you need.

    b. Write a transitional paragraph linking two paragraphs that explain why apartments are in short supply. Several reasons were stated briefly in the opening paragraph; create any other data necessary.

    c. Exercises 5c and 6c dealt with personnel costs in the computer industry. These are some of the innovations referred to:

      (1) The use of "high-level" languages will enable computers to interact with humans in more intelligible ways. These languages will replace the very technical computer languages, which required highly trained, highly skilled programmers.

      (2) Computer systems will be more technically complex but simpler for the operator to use. The complexity will allow more efficient debugging (elimination of errors from programs).

      (3) More sophisticated units capable of editing and processing programs on the spot will become available, thus reducing the number of operators needed for programming.

      (4) Future systems, in addition to diagnosing and correcting their own problems, will require less installation and maintenance work. Fewer people will be needed for these functions, and their salaries will be lower because they will need a lower level of skills.

    Write a transitional paragraph linking paragraphs which elaborate on at least two of these innovations. Invent additional information if you need it.

8. You are preparing a report for the Vocational Education Division of the New Jersey State Department of Education in which you are presenting your ideas for a New Jersey Business-Industry-Education Council. You served for five years as a member of such a council in Arizona, a state which has been a leader in cooperative efforts of business, industry, and education. You presently own your own educational consulting firm and hope to be awarded a contract from the state of New Jersey to set up a council tailored to the needs of New Jersey. Here is what you know about the Arizona Business-Industry-Education Council (ABIEC):

    (1) The goals of the Council are to (1) develop awareness among students of career opportunities in business and industry; (2) encourage business and industry leaders to promote these careers; (3) expand the knowledge of educators about business careers and the qualifications necessary for such careers; (4) increase understanding among parents of the advantages of business career preparation; (5) make the resources and facilities of business and industry available to educators; (6) foster the principles of the American free enterprise system; (7) maintain a close and continuing relationship between education and business-industry in areas of mutual interest.

    (2) The Executive Advisory Board consists of a chairperson and 50 members. Of these, 30 are top corporate executives, 5 are retired corporate executives, 10 are collegiate and secondary school administrators, 2 are state legislators, and 1 is a retired United States senator. The mayor of Phoenix and the State Superintendent of Public Instruction are also members.

    (3) The Educational Advisory Board consists of 40 secondary school teachers, 6 community college teachers, 4 university professors, and 6 career education specialists.

(4) The Board of Directors consists of a president, vice-president (educational), vice-president (industrial), vice-president (public relations), secretary, treasurer, and executive director.

(5) There are 26 directors representing the Arizona Education Association, the State Department of Education, the Arizona Department of Economic Security, various school systems, newspapers and television, and large and small businesses.

(6) Career exploration programs for grades 7, 8, and 9 in which students gain "hands on" experiences in a variety of occupational clusters are supported by the ABIEC. These clusters include careers in manufacturing, construction, communication, power equipment, child care, offices, the fashion world, home economics, marketing, health, graphic arts, transportation, hospitality, and food services.

(7) The number of on-site visitations to businesses in the state increased by 52 percent over the previous year's totals. The number of students involved in these events increased by 41 percent.

(8) Figures from September through March of last year:
Speakers in schools—1,964. Students involved—130,480. On-site visits to businesses—1,463. Students involved—48,196.

(9) The ABIEC is also involved in school career days, student and teacher work exposure and work experience programs, and cooperative education.

(10) Ten members of the ABIEC Board of Directors and Educational Advisory Board participated in the United States Office of Education's National Conference on Career Education in Washington, D.C. last year.

(11) A business-student dialogue is held each year in which discussion groups consisting of business people and students talk about timely issues. Last year's topics were the social responsibility of business and energy conservation.

(12) The Work Education Council of the ABIEC consists of teacher-coordinators representing the various vocational on-the-job training programs throughout Arizona. Students in these programs attend school part time and work part time in supervised jobs. The council also operates a communications network for placing students in part-time jobs.

(13) A Business-Industry-Education Day is held yearly, with over a thousand business leaders, students, and teachers participating.

(14) The ABIEC cosponsors with the State Department of Education training workshops for teachers. In these workshops, teachers visit businesses, participate in group discussions, and develop curriculum materials for their particular teaching requirements.

(15) The ABIEC works with the state chapters of the Future Business Leaders of America (FBLA) and Distributive Education Clubs of America (DECA). ABIEC provides plaques for the winners in the competitive events at the annual FBLA and DECA state leadership conferences, and members of ABIEC serve as judges for the competitive events at the conferences. FBLA is a national vocational education organization for students interested in business and office careers; DECA is a national organization for students interested in marketing and management careers.

(16) The ABIEC also supports careers in technological fields by cooperating with the Arizona Council of Engineering and Scientific Associations (ACESA). ACESA supports educators and students who are interested in technical careers and also provides information and assistance to business, industry, and governmental agencies.

(17) The ABIEC is currently increasing its public visibility by sponsoring public-service newspaper and television advertisements about the American free enterprise system.

(18) Last year the ABIEC, in cooperation with the Valley of the Sun chapter of the American Society for Training and Development, conducted a research project which developed a system for informing students of the training and development opportunities available within the work world. Fifty companies in the metropolitan Phoenix area were involved in the project; the data were compiled in a booklet, printed by a local business as a public service, and distributed to all high schools in the state.

(19) The ABIEC is supported mostly by memberships from schools, businesses, and individuals.

   a. What is the purpose or purposes of your report?

   b. Who will read your report?

   c. Will you supplement your information with any additional research?

   d. Will you use the inductive or the deductive pattern?

   e. Prepare an outline for your report.

   f. Write a first draft.

   g. Exchange your first draft with a classmate. Using the information presented in Chapters 13, 14, 15, 16, and 17, prepare a written critique of your classmate's draft.

   h. Rewrite your first draft, making any of the suggested changes you feel are appropriate.

   i. Exchange your final report with the same classmate. Prepare a short written critique (you may make positive statements in a critique, remember). Rewrite your report if major revisions are still needed.

   j. Keep your report for use in Chapter 18 after your teacher has returned it to you.

18
CONVEYING
INFORMATION
GRAPHICALLY*

Charts and graphs can be a very useful adjunct to the written word for conveying information in reports. You should learn to use them where and when they are appropriate.

The test to apply in deciding when to use charts and other graphs is simple: Ask yourself whether your reader will understand the information better or more easily if it is presented graphically.

Graphic presentation has three major virtues—it is concise, dramatic, and revealing. Graphs condense a large amount of information into a small space; when well designed they are forceful and convincing; and they can be extremely effective in explaining and clarifying the information you wish to convey.

There are three principal forms of graphic presentation that are effective for business reports: charts, maps, and diagrams. Charts answer the question "how much," maps show "where," and diagrams show "how."

In executive reports, graphic presentation usually consists of charts. Maps or diagrams are sometimes called for, but not often. Of course, a report concerned with how something is distributed geographically may use only map illustrations; a report discussing the organizational makeup of a company or the flow of money or goods might rely on diagrams. But in general the kind of information contained in reports can be conveyed best in chart form; for that reason, the following discussion of graphic presentation deals primarily with charts.

In most charts used in management and administrative reports, the graphic part is geometrical rather than pictorial, making use of devices like circles and bars and lines rather than pictures. One reason for this is that many important kinds of comparisons cannot be shown effectively in pictorial form. Another is

* This material on charts and graphs was originally prepared by Kenneth W. Haemer, formerly Manager, Presentation Research, American Telephone and Telegraph Company.

that pictorial presentation is slower, is more costly, and generally requires much more space to present a given amount of information. Nevertheless, pictorial charts have their place. They are valuable for their popular appeal and are especially useful for presenting simple comparisons to audiences who are not familiar with conventional charts or who simply will not read them. They are used primarily in reports to customers, to employees, and to the general public; they are seldom appropriate in reports to management or administrative reports from management.

Charts used in business reports divide into two main groups: those using only one scale of measurement and those using two. (There are charts that make use of more than two scales, but they are specialized technical tools that are of no interest here.) In general, one-scale charts are much simpler and more limited than two-scale charts. However, you will find plenty of use for both types.

After discussing and illustrating the many, varied types of charts available to you, we will give some attention to a visual aid that is not really graphic. The table, although not graphic, can be used to convey a wealth of quantitative information in a relatively small amount of space. As will be demonstrated in our discussion at the chapter's end, tables can serve several purposes in business reports.

ONE-SCALE CHARTS

One-scale charts take two main forms: pie charts and bar charts.

A *pie chart* is a circle divided into wedge-shaped slices. Its purpose is to show how component parts add up to make a total. It is a good form for showing this sort of information because it so obviously adds up to 100 percent, and it has the additional virtue of looking simple and nontechnical. Figure 18-1 is an effective use of this type of presentation: notice particularly how the two parts of the largest component, North America, are held together by using the same shading pattern for both.

But pie charts can be used only for showing the components that make up a whole. They are of little or no use for comparing changes from time to time or for comparing a series of totals of different size. In general, pie charts have a very limited usefulness and are awkward to handle. You will soon find that most of the amount comparisons you want to put into graphic form are not quite simple enough for a pie chart, and that even when they are, another type of chart will usually do the job better.

Bar charts are made up of horizontal bars placed one above the other. In this form of chart the length of each bar shows the size or amount of some item under study. Thus a bar chart is a means of comparing the magnitude of a series of items. In Figure 18-2, the portion of the labor force unemployed in each of several Michigan cities is quickly seen and compared.

Remember that this type of chart has only one scale and that it measures horizontally; the vertical dimension is used only to list the items. The order of

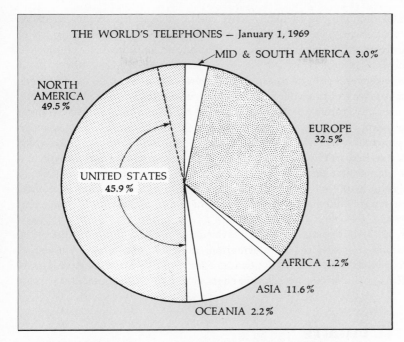

FIGURE 18-1 The pie chart shows the component parts that make up a total.

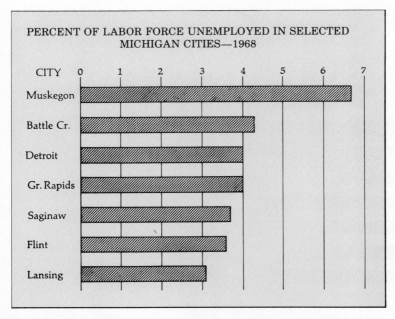

FIGURE 18-2 The simple bar chart compares different things at the same time.

items is flexible and may be varied in many useful ways. For example, items can be listed alphabetically, in order of size, importance, or in some arbitrary but established order, such as men, women, children, or shareholders, employees, customers.

There are several subtypes of bar chart, each of which can be used to bring out a different aspect of the information that is under study.

As shown in Figure 18-3, the bars can be subdivided to show the component parts of each item. The subdivided bar chart provides the same information as a series of pie charts, but in a more manageable and compact form. Subdivided bars can be handled in two ways: the components of each bar can add up to a total amount in dollars, carloads, customers, or some other absolute measure; or they can add up to 100 percent. In the 100 percent form, the bars are, of course, all the same length and show the *proportion* of the total that each component part contributes.

Figure 18-4 shows another useful variation of a simple bar chart; it is the result of adding a second set of information. It brings two simple bar charts together for comparison. Notice how shading the most important set of bars to set them off from the others makes this chart easier to understand.

TWO-SCALE CHARTS

The identifying feature of the second, larger family of charts is two scales placed at right angles, one measuring vertically, one horizontally. Thus each point drawn on the chart has a value on the vertical scale and a value on the horizontal, in the same way that the location of the New York Public Library has a value

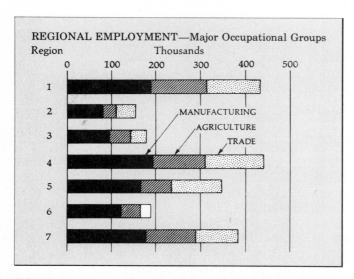

FIGURE 18-3 Subdivided bars show the component parts of several totals.

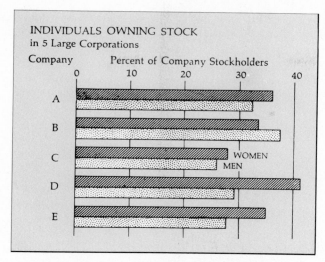

FIGURE 18-4 Grouped bars compare two different but related sets of data.

of 42 on the north and south (street) scale and a value of 5 on the east and west (avenue) scale. This two-scale arrangement permits you to picture all sorts of useful relationships that would be difficult to see in any other way.

Two-scale charts separate into three distinct yet related groups: line charts, surface charts, and column charts. Many of the varieties within each of these groups are matched by a corresponding variety in the other two groups. In fact, the same general kind of information can be shown in either line-chart, surface-chart, or column-chart form. However, these three forms aren't exact substitutes. As you will see, each provides a different emphasis; and usually one type is clearly more appropriate—for a specific set of data—than either of the others.

A *line chart* is well described by its name. It is made by joining a series of points with a line. Although this line is called a *curve* in chart language, it may vary from extremely smooth to extremely jagged, depending on the behavior of the data presented.

Figure 18-5 is a simple line chart showing how the quantity of something varied from one time to the next. It gives a clear, direct picture of how production dropped in the first few years and then increased rapidly, fell off again, then increased somewhat more slowly. In this type of chart—and most of the others that follow—the horizontal scale is used to measure *time,* the vertical scale to measure *number or quantity.*

Figure 18-6 is a somewhat more analytical chart: it shows a three-year span of data cut into yearly pieces and superimposed on a one-year chart. This form is especially useful for comparing each month this year with the same month in earlier years. It is widely used for such business data as production, sales, expenses, and earnings.

The next two illustrations are also examples of typical line charts. Figure

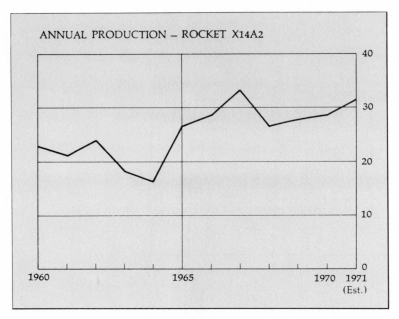

ANNUAL PRODUCTION – ROCKET X14A2

FIGURE 18-5   The simple line chart shows successive changes over a span of time.

18-7 compares the behavior of three measures of business activity, showing clearly that the leather and coal industries are not following the pattern of industrial activity in general. The type of chart illustrated by Figure 18-8 is somewhat more complex, but is still clear and informative. This example is adapted from a chart used in the Department of Defense to show progress and plans for purchases of a certain type of defense equipment.

There are many other kinds of line charts, each useful for a specific purpose. In fact, this basic type of chart is so versatile that it is used more than any other in the internal administration and operation of all businesses, whether private or governmental.

A *surface chart* looks like a shaded line chart, and in its simplest form it is exactly that. If you shade a simple line chart between the curve and the base, you get a simple surface chart; and the two are identical in meaning. The only difference is that the surface form is more striking. But shading other types of line chart changes the meaning. The reason is that in surface charts it is the distance *between* curves that is important, not the distance from each curve to the base.

The following examples illustrate the two most useful types of surface chart. They show the component parts of a total and how they change over a span of time. Figure 18-9 shows absolute amounts, such as dollars, tons, or employees; Figure 18-10 shows relative amounts, i.e., each component as a percentage of the total. The 100 percent version is especially valuable because it clearly shows changes in the *relative* distribution of the parts of a total—changes that are easily overlooked when the total is growing rapidly.

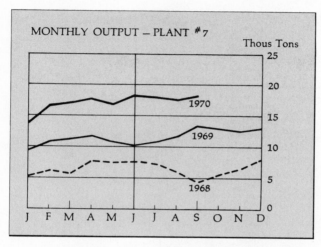

FIGURE 18-6 The repeated time scale compares changes during comparable periods of time.

Notice that in both cases the bottom layer is the only one that can be measured directly from the scale. The reader may, therefore, find it difficult to gauge the other layers with even approximate accuracy. Another weakness, from the reader's point of view, is that all surface charts are subject to an occupational disease—optical illusion. An irregular layer—one that moves up and down—makes all layers above it seem to move up and down also. The way to avoid this is to put irregular layers on top, if the order can be changed to do so. Another illusion occurs because a layer that moves along at the same level, then suddenly

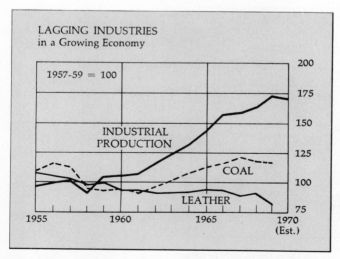

FIGURE 18-7 Multiple curves compare changes in two or more series of data.

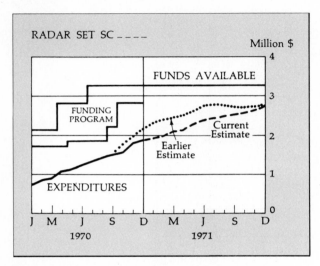

FIGURE 18-8 A combination of step curves and slope curves compares data that change abruptly and those that change gradually.

shoots up—or down—seems to be much thinner where it changes level than it really is.

The next four illustrations show a family of charts that are related to line charts but look like bar charts turned on end. These charts, called *column charts,* provide an entirely different kind of comparison than bar charts. Instead of comparing a number of different items at a given time, they compare a given item at different times, in the same general way that line or surface charts do.

Column charts are, in fact, first cousins to surface charts and are useful for

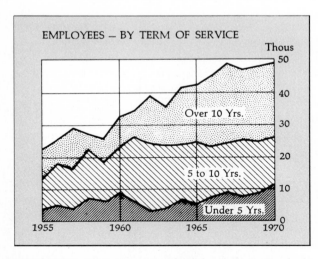

FIGURE 18-9 Subdivided surface shows the changes in the component parts of a total.

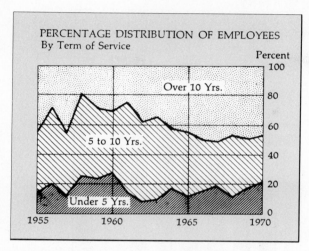

FIGURE 18-10   The 100 percent surface chart shows changes in the relative size of the components.

the same general purposes. But usually the nature of the information to be presented will suggest which to use. Surface charts are better when there are a large number of time periods to be shown, when the data do not move up and down very sharply, and when the nature of the information suggests a carryover from one period to the next (for example, average number of acres under cultivation each year). Column charts are better when only a few time periods are shown on the chart, when the data change level sharply, and when the information suggests a fresh start for each period (for example, number of acres added each year).

Figure 18-11 is a simple column chart showing the money spent for new construction by a large and growing company. It tells the story directly and forcefully, the separated columns emphasizing the size of each year's expenditures. Figure 18-12 uses the same kind of component-parts presentation that is used on the bar chart in Figure 18-3. Note that the columns are divided into four segments in this example. The use of more than four segments in such a chart is generally unwise, because the reader is given too many things to keep track of. Usually you can avoid too many divisions by combining some: either by using fewer but broader components, or by lumping several small components under "all other."

The next two examples show the result of combining two simple column charts and of presenting differences instead of totals. Figure 18-13 pictures gradually increasing farm income in a forceful way. You can easily see that this form is much better than a line chart would be for so few amounts. Figure 18-14 stresses the net gain or loss resulting from an "income" and an "outgo," in this case the difference between quantities put in and taken out of stock.

There are other families of two-scale charts, but most of these are too technical for management reports. Only one needs to be mentioned here: the so-called frequency chart. Frequency charts use a different set of scales than time-

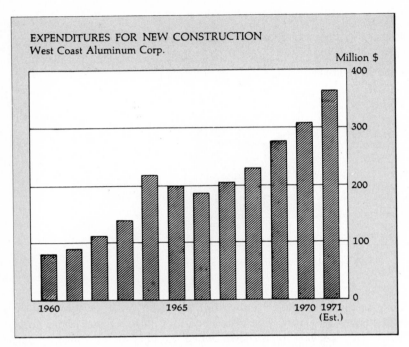

FIGURE 18-11 The simple column chart compares the same things at different times.

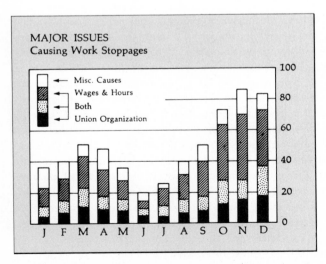

FIGURE 18-12 Subdivided columns show the component parts of a total at different times.

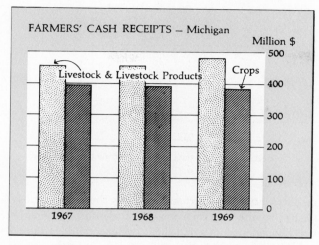

FIGURE 18-13 Grouped columns compare two related series of data over a span of time.

series charts. Instead of amount, the vertical scale measures frequency of occurrence; instead of time, the horizontal scale classifies size. A chart showing the number of employees (frequency measure) in each of several wage groups (size measure) is a typical frequency chart. In appearance they take the form of simple line or column charts.

As you can readily see, there is a wide variety of charts to choose from, each useful in its own way. Before deciding which kind to use, be sure you have a clear understanding of what the data mean and precisely what aspect of the

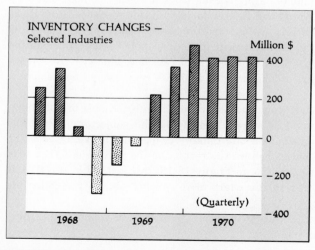

FIGURE 18-14 Net-gain-or-loss columns measure the difference between total income and outgo.

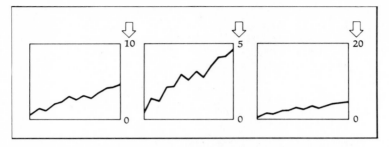

FIGURE 18-15 The importance of scale selection: The same data plotted on different amount scales.

data the chart is to focus on. No two types of chart serve exactly the same purpose, and so the type chosen should be the one that conveys the information most clearly, accurately, and forcefully. Be sure to avoid these two extremes; don't rely on one or two favorite types regardless of whether they suit the purpose or not; don't invent types that are so special and complex that no one else will understand them.

In designing charts, the most important thing is the choice of scale. As shown by the examples in Figure 18-15, the same information can be scaled to give widely different impressions. There is no rule for proper scaling: the correct scale is the one that produces the appropriate effect. What is appropriate will depend on the purpose of the report, the subject matter, the circumstances under which it is being studied, and your estimate of how important the changes or differences really are. For example, a million-dollar increase in the national debt is scarcely worth mentioning; a million-dollar increase in a manufacturing company's debt is quite a different matter.

Although charts are valuable mainly because they are graphic, note that they are meaningless without words and figures to explain and measure. How these words and figures are handled is just as important as how the graphic part of the chart is designed. In general, the same principles that apply to clear, informative writing apply equally to chart titles, labels, and captions, but with even more force. A single inept, foggy, or long-winded sentence may escape notice, but a poor chart title will not.

Chart titling is especially important because of the growing use of statement, or "narrative," titles. Instead of merely identifying the subject matter of the chart, this type of title tells what the chart shows. Sometimes it even goes a step further and explains the causes behind the results or the conclusions they lead to. As you can see from the example in Figure 18-16, this method is effective. It helps the reader to understand the chart more quickly and to remember its message more easily.

Although graphic presentation is excellent when it is appropriate, there are several cautions about using it:

1. *Don't use so many charts that they overwhelm the rest of the report.* The reader will either ignore everything else, or—if he or she doesn't like charts—ignore the entire report.

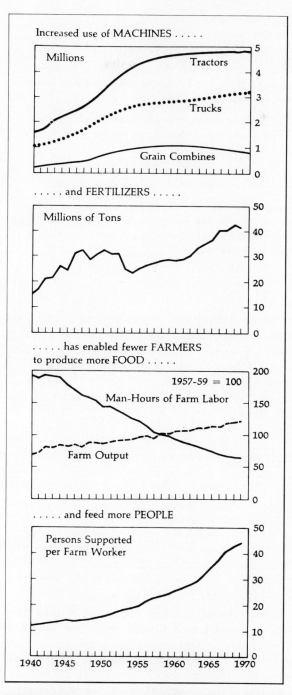

Increased use of MACHINES . . . . .

. . . . . and FERTILIZERS . . . . .

. . . . . has enabled fewer FARMERS to produce more FOOD . . . . .

. . . . . and feed more PEOPLE

FIGURE 18-16 "Narrative" charts: Related charts connected by titles that state the meaning of the data. This method of titling can be used also for single charts.

2. *Use charts to explain or support the major points in the report.* The fewer charts you use, the more attention each gets; so if you use only one or two, it is doubly important that they relate to the main facts you are trying to convey.

3. *Don't try to convey too much information on one chart.* If you do, it will be cluttered and hard to understand. It's better to put the information in two simple charts than to crowd it into one complex one.

4. *Design the chart to focus on the meaning you are trying to convey.* Don't merely convert figures into graphic form and expect this to tell readers what you want them to know.

5. *Keep it simple.* Leave out all unnecessary frills and trimmings. Don't add technical notes and other details that are not needed to *understand* the chart.

6. *Tie it in with your written presentation* by referring to it in the written text and by placing it as close as possible to the section of the text where you discuss it. This will spare your reader the annoyance of holding a thumb on page 4 when you refer to a chart on page 45.

TABLES

In addition to one-scale and two-scale charts, there is another type of visual aid that can be used to support, complement, and/or accent the text of a report. Though tables aren't graphic, they can be considered *visual aids* to a report writer faced with the job of transmitting a large amount of quantitative information.

A table might be defined as an organized presentation of numerical information in rows and columns. Table I is a relatively simple example that presents the population of three cities at five-year intervals.

Table I	CITY POPULATIONS AT FIVE-YEAR INTERVALS		
	Evergreen	*Oak Bridge*	*Pine Shadows*
1955	36,100	50,200	39,100
1960	42,600	53,400	44,300
1965	47,400	56,500	52,500
1970	53,000	61,200	61,400
1975	58,500	65,300	63,200
1980*	65,000	70,000	66,000

*Projected by the chambers of commerce.

There are several advantages to the use of tables in business reports. They are fairly easy to construct. Even a typist with limited experience can, with enough effort, put together a presentable table. Another advantage is their compactness. You can usually include a good deal more information in a table than in a graphic aid of the same size. Perhaps their most important advantage is reflected in the accompanying text of the report. When a group of numbers is included in a table, the writer is relieved of having to mention them all. Instead, he or she is free to note only the most important numbers, allowing the table to fill in the gaps for readers interested in more detail.

Besides their advantages, however, tables also have certain drawbacks that make charts a better choice for highlighting some collections of data. One disadvantage of tables is that they are not graphic. They don't visually depict the information in a way that helps readers to spot noteworthy comparisons or contrasts. Thus, they are not best for conveying information to a firm's publics: its stockholders, customers, employees, etc. Another disadvantage is that tables seem to intimidate some readers. They look at the wealth of data before them and realize that *they* are going to have to study it to make some sense out of it. Remember that some readers prefer not to be called upon to put forth very much effort to fully comprehend the content of a report. Just how much relevance this last disadvantage has will depend upon how committed your reader is to the subject and purpose of your report.

After you've studied the nature of the data you wish to transmit, and after you've thought about the reader-related advantages and disadvantages of the various types of visual aids available, you may still wish to use tables in your report. As you construct these tables, keep the following guidelines in mind:

1. Don't forget to include titles or captions for rows and columns.

2. Unless the numbers' meanings are clearly indicated by the table or column or row titles, specify them. *Bales* of cotton, for example, wouldn't be understood from the title *Cotton Production*. Also, if your numbers are expressed in hundreds or thousands, note that somewhere in the table.

3. Use "n.a." or a dash to indicate that a certain item of information is not available. Using a zero would be a definite misrepresentation, and leaving a blank space could suggest to readers that the value is zero.

4. If a number needs or deserves some explanation, use an asterisk (*), dagger (†), or double dagger (‡) to refer to your footnote explanation below the table. If you used numbers for footnote references, readers might mistake these numbers for part of the figures in the table.

A few final words of advice will end our discussion of visual aids. First, remember to give credit where credit is due. If you borrow a visual aid from another source, credit that source in a source reference below the aid.

Second, visual aids should enhance the appearance of your reports. Carelessly thrown together, sloppy, overcrowded tables and charts will detract from rather than enhance a report's appearance. To avoid a negative reader impression, you may have to do your aids two or more times. Resign yourself to this possibility, and plan enough time for putting the report together so that you won't have to rush through this final stage.

Finally, also for appearance, try to construct your visual aids within your normal page layout. Avoid having them awkwardly extend into what should be the margins of your page. If a visual aid is unusually wide or large (covering over half a page), consider using the *obverse technique*. Using this technique, you place the visual aid on the left page, the one that is blank in most typed, bound reports. The backside of the page containing the visual aid is left blank, with the exception of the page number and the word "obverse." This clues readers to the fact that there's a reason for their coming across a blank right page instead of the typing they would normally expect to see. The obverse technique has the additional advantage of allowing you to discuss a visual aid directly across from that aid, thus maximizing reader convenience.

Applying the preceding guidelines and suggestions should help you to create visual aids that assist your report in achieving its objective. But don't forget that the ultimate impression a visual aid makes is primarily a result of *your* planning, *your* thinking, and *your* conscientious, determined efforts. Combine all these ingredients in their proper proportions, and you're likely to produce visual material that actually complements, supports, and/or highlights the text of your report.

EXERCISES

1. Your marketing research firm has been hired by James Holbrook to prepare a report which will recommend one of three selected cities in which to open a gourmet restaurant. One section of your report will present a profile of the people in each of the three cities under consideration. To supplement your analysis and conclusions, you want to present the statistical information in chart form.
   a. Decide what type(s) of charts will convey the information most clearly.
   b. Can you combine some of the information in the nine categories into the same chart?
   c. Will you use both one-scale and two-scale charts?
   d. Might some other form of graphic aid be more appropriate than charts for some of the data?
   e. Prepare the charts and other graphic aids.
   The statistical information:
   (1) Populations: *Seadale:* 1970—60,000; 1972—64,000; 1974—63,000; 1976—61,500; 1978—62,200. *Landale:* 1970—25,000; 1972—26,300; 1974—28,000; 1976—29,-000; 1978—31,200. *Airdale:* 1970—10,000; 1972—12,800; 1974—23,000; 1976—25,000; 1978—29,000.
   (2) Male Percentage of Populations: *Seadale:* 1970, 1972, 1974, 1976, 1978—49.3; 49.3; 49.2; 49.2; 49.3. *Landale:* (for same years)—46.2; 46.2; 46.1; 46.0; 46.0. *Airdale:* (for same years)—41.0; 41.1; 44.2; 44.4; 45.0.
   (3) Average Number of People per Household (for same years as preceding): *Seadale:* 4.8; 4.7; 4.8; 4.8; 4.7. *Landale:* 4.6; 4.6; 4.6; 4.6; 4.6. *Airdale:* 5.3; 5.2; 4.8; 4.7; 4.7.
   (4) Unemployment Rates (for same years as preceding): *Seadale:* 6.2; 6.1; 6.0; 6.5; 6.0. *Landale:* 6.6; 6.5; 6.5; 6.8; 6.5. *Airdale:* 5.9; 5.9; 4.2; 4.5; 4.1.
   (5) Mobility Indicator, December of year reported—percentage of residents who had moved into the city during the year prior to the time surveyed (for same years as preceding): *Seadale:* 15; 16; 17; 15; 15. *Landale:* 18; 19; 19; 20; 21. *Airdale:* 5; 9; 26; 13; 12.
   (6) Age Distribution of Populations, rounded to the nearest percentage (for same years as preceding): *Seadale: 0–20:* 38; 37; 36; 35; 34. *21–40:* 24; 25; 25; 25; 25. *41–60:* 20; 20; 21; 22; 23. *Over 60:* 18; 18; 18; 18; 18. *Landale: 0–20:* 40; 41; 42; 42; 43. *21–40:* 25; 24; 23; 23; 23. *41–60:* 23; 23; 23; 23; 23. *Over 60:* 12; 12; 12; 12;

12. *Airdale: 0–20:* 30; 28; 33; 34; 34. *21–40:* 20; 20; 27; 28; 29. *41–60:* 25; 27; 29; 28; 27. *Over 60:* 25; 25; 11; 10; 10.

(7) Personal Disposable Income per Household—percentage of households in each income group (for same years as preceding): *Seadale: $0,000–5,999:* 35; 33; 33; 31; 30. *6,000–13,999:* 37; 38; 38; 36; 34. *14,000–21,999:* 16; 17; 18; 19; 21. *22,000 and up:* 12; 12; 14; 14; 15. *Landale: $0,000–5,999:* 32; 31; 28; 26; 25. *6,000–13,999:* 36; 36; 35; 34; 32. *14,000–21,999:* 18; 19; 20; 22; 23. *22,000 and up:* 14; 14; 17; 18; 20. *Airdale: $0,000–5,999:* 41; 40; 34; 32; 30. *6,000–13,999:* 39; 38; 34; 32; 31. *14,000–21,999:* 14; 15; 22; 24; 26. *22,000 and up:* 6; 7; 10; 12; 13.

(8) Education—average number of years of formal education completed by employed adults surveyed (for same years as preceding): *Seadale:* 11.3; 11.5; 11.7; 12.0; 12.2. *Landale:* 12.6; 12.9; 13.5; 13.8; 14.6. *Airdale:* 10.7; 10.9; 11.8; 12.6; 12.9.

(9) Percentage of Total Retail Sales Spent in Eating and Drinking Establishments (for same years as preceding): *Seadale:* 4.8; 4.9; 5.1; 5.1; 5.4. *Landale:* 5.5; 5.7; 5.8; 5.8; 6.0. *Airdale:* 4.1; 4.3; 5.4; 5.5; 5.7.

2. You are preparing a report about the effectiveness of your company's employee suggestion program, in which cash awards are given for suggestions judged worthy of implementation. You distributed a questionnaire to all employees to learn their perceptions of the suggestion program and have received the following information from 339 of the 580 employees:

(1) Age breakdown of the respondents and their answers: *Under 25:* 17 responded "Effective," 41 "Ineffective," 10 "Undecided." *25–35:* 45 "Effective," 31 "Ineffective," 10 "Undecided." *36–45:* 54 "Effective," 25 "Ineffective," 14 "Undecided." *46–55:* 30 "Effective," 22 "Ineffective," 9 "Undecided." *Over 55:* 10 "Effective," 13 "Ineffective," 8 "Undecided."

(2) Sex of the respondents: *Male:* 88 "Effective," 92 "Ineffective," 33 "Undecided." *Female:* 68 "Effective," 40 "Ineffective," 18 "Undecided."

(3) Years with Company: *0–5:* 58 "Effective," 66 "Ineffective," 22 "Undecided." *6–10:* 44 "Effective," 37 "Ineffective," 6 "Undecided." *11–15:* 28 "Effective," 24 "Ineffective," 10 "Undecided." *16–20:* 17 "Effective," 3 "Ineffective," 10 "Undecided." *Over 20:* 9 "Effective," 2 "Ineffective," 3 "Undecided."

(4) Job Classification: *Labor:* 77 "Effective," 62 "Ineffective," 13 "Undecided." *Supervisory:* 48 "Effective," 4 "Ineffective," 9 "Undecided." *Clerical:* 19 "Effective," 40 "Ineffective," 19 "Undecided." *Sales:* 12 "Effective," 26 "Ineffective," 10 "Undecided."

(5) System Usage and Results: *Used and rewarded:* 57 "Effective," 6 "Ineffective," 0 "Undecided." *Used, not rewarded:* 46 "Effective," 78 "Ineffective," 14 "Undecided." *Had not used:* 53 "Effective," 48 "Ineffective," 37 "Undecided."

(6) Totals: 156 "Effective," 132 "Ineffective," 51 "Undecided."

The monthly activity of the plan since its inception has been:

	Suggestions	*Accepted*	*Prizes*
January	119	21	$312
February	88	6	109
March	43	4	123
April	62	7	141
May	71	9	146
June	80	7	191
July	63	5	66
August	59	5	62
September	71	4	60
October	82	4	58

a. Based on the responses, do the employees perceive the program to be effective?

b. What other conclusions can you draw from the data?

c. What recommendations might you make?

d. What graphic aids will you use in your report to present your findings and to best support your conclusions and recommendations?

e. Prepare these graphic aids.

3. Refer to the report you wrote for Exercise 17-8.

a. Where could you have used graphic aids to make your proposal a stronger, more persuasive one?

b. Prepare two graphic aids for the report. Create any information you need if you feel the report doesn't contain enough data from which to prepare meaningful charts or tables.

19

THE FORMAL REPORT AND THE MEMORANDUM

In Part 1 of this book, we called attention to the fact that many details of form and style in business writing vary from company to company and can only be learned on the job. This is particularly true of formal reports and memorandums, for which many companies have worked out detailed forms; if you go to work for one of these companies, you will have to learn its forms. Yet it is possible to generalize about memos and formal reports so that general principles can be applied to specific on-the-job requirements.

THE MEMORANDUM

As we indicated in the introduction to Part 3, the line between the short report and the memorandum is thin. We can come close to the function and definition of a memorandum by thinking of it as an *internal letter,* as contrasted with letters going outside the organization, and as shorter and less formal than the average report. In fact, some companies call memorandums *interoffice letters* or *intraorganization reports*. Generally speaking, the memorandum performs three functions:

1. It maintains a flow of information *across* the levels or ranks of an organization, as when an employee in one department sends a memorandum to a counterpart in another department or office.

2. It conveys information and policy procedures both *up* and *down* within the organization, as when a subordinate writes a memorandum to a superior or when a vice-president notifies the staff of a policy change or sends information on to subordinates.

3. It serves as a reminder and maintains a permanent record of discussions, meetings, activities, changes, procedures, or policies. Said Lewis Carroll in *Through the Looking Glass:*

"The horror of that moment," the King went on, "I shall never, never forget!"

"You will, though," the Queen said, "if you don't make a memorandum of it."

The memorandum is generally written under pressure of time. The great majority of memos are undoubtedly written under conditions that add up to instructions to "do this right away." The department head, the section chief, or the top executive usually couches directions in such terms as, "Send out a reminder of that meeting tomorrow," or "Give me a memo on last month's employment figures so that I can have them for today's conference," or "Let me have a summary of the meeting I missed before we discuss it tomorrow." As a matter of fact, it is precisely because the memo is so well adapted to such urgent conditions that business people have made it their most frequently used medium of exchange *within the organization.*

That there are other reasons than sheer adaptability for the proliferation of memos is neatly shown by Theodore Irwin's satirical "Memo on Memos (Six Copies, Please)" in the *New York Times Magazine* (November 17, 1963)*:

Consider, particularly, the Memo. How to succeed in business through memos is preoccupying the get-ahead-fast organization man. In the classic ploy, "You spend half your time doing your job and half your time telling your boss how good a job you're doing." Thus, as management consultants observe him, the chronic memo-writer falls into two main categories:

(1) The reputation-builder. The more memos he pours out, the more executives will hear about him.

(2) The alibi-fixer. Generally he produces defensive memos to protect himself and prove he is right if anyone should question him. ("You see I didn't want to do it; he forced me to.")

Mr. Irwin concludes his article by describing a humorous method of disposing of the mountains of memos produced in business:

Today, despite the herculean efforts of systems-and-procedures doctors, American businessmen continue to battle their paperwork with a ferocity akin to Don Quixote's tilting at windmills—and with pretty much the same result. One possible answer may have been discovered in the Lake Maracaibo, Venezuela, branch office of a New York oil company. There the staff was being plagued by wild goats in the area.

"When we receive a memo from New York," the branch manager complained, "before we get a chance to read it, a goat sticks his head through the window and eats it."

Perhaps what the U.S. economy needs is more goats.

*© 1963 by The New York Times Company. Reprinted by permission.

Nonetheless, the memo is the workhorse of written communications inside the organization because it provides a medium for quick response when information, recommendations, or background are needed. It provides no time generally for "fancy" writing or prolonged revision. These factors place a heavy premium on memo writers' ability to analyze a situation quickly and to state it concisely. In this process they must do three things:

1. Decide on the central idea or main purpose of the memorandum.

2. Subordinate every fact or idea to this central idea or main purpose and show how these facts or ideas are related logically to the central theme.

3. Reject any material which is superfluous, irrelevant, or unnecessary for the reader's understanding of the central idea.

In many memos, you will not have to lead your reader into the subject by telling him or her what it's about—the time interval may be short, and the form of the memorandum takes care of this. But regardless of the circumstances, the process of preparing a memorandum follows the same steps we have analyzed for the more complex report—getting the facts, imposing a pattern on them, and writing to serve a reader's purpose.

We can illustrate this process best by a specific example which occurs frequently in business. Suppose that your superior has sent you to New York to attend a three-day meeting on the problems of modern management and has asked you to send her a memo about the meetings when you return. You could conceivably begin your memorandum this way:

> As you requested, I attended the three-day meeting in New York on "The Problems of Modern Management."
>
> After a rather rough flight which got me there 45 minutes late, I tried to get a room at the hotel where the meetings were held, but there was apparently a mix-up in reservations. I then had to spend another hour locating a room and finally arrived at the meeting at the end of the president's address of welcome. Incidentally, a friend told me later that I hadn't missed anything.
>
> On Monday morning, I heard talks on "The Obligations of Modern Management" and "Changing Concepts of Today's Executive." That afternoon, I heard an excellent presentation by Mr. Fred W. Becker on a specific program for "Evaluating and Preparing Tomorrow's Executive" which the Blank Company has carried on during the past year. This program consists of . . .

Ridiculous? Not at all; this memorandum typifies too much memo writing with its irrelevant detail and rambling style. Above all else, it illustrates the worst faults of the step-by-step pattern of organization discussed in a previous chapter of this book. The result is a tiresome, detailed, blow-by-blow account which irks the reader and makes her lose patience.

Suppose, instead, that you had asked yourself two questions after you had assembled your material:

1. What does my supervisor want to learn from my visit to the meetings?

2. How can I best tell her?

From such thinking, you could probably draw two conclusions—the supervisor wants to know what you learned that might be useful to the company and wants you to sort out all the information so that it will be presented in readable form to stress only the essentials. Elementary as it seems, this is the essence of good organization. The result might be a memorandum which starts this way:

> This memorandum summarizes those meetings on "The Problems of Modern Management" which I thought were especially applicable to our own problems. Of all the discussions listed on the attached program, the following three seemed worth consideration since they concern problems which we have been thinking about:
>
> **1.** Mr. Fred W. Becker of the Blank Company described his company's experience with a one-year training program to select and prepare personnel for executive responsibilities. This company has spent almost two years developing a method of evaluating management personnel; they now have an elaborate rating sheet by which every member of management is rated by *(a)* his or her immediate superior, *(b)* two members of the executive staff, and *(c)* five subordinates. At my request, Mr. Becker will send you a copy of this rating sheet, which I think might help us to develop one of our own.

Notice what has been accomplished in about the same number of words as the first example used for mere rambling. You tell your reader the following things:

1. What the memo concerns (a report on the meetings)

2. The method of selection (information most applicable to the organization's problems)

3. The method of rejection (the attached program gives all the unimportant details)

4. The organization (three meetings are described in detail because they are most useful to the reader)

Most companies have developed specific printed forms for their memos in an attempt to reduce all details to a standard pattern. The ultimate purpose of any such form should be to help the writer get on with the message as soon as possible and to place at the top of the first page, where it is readily accessible in the files, all the information about who wrote it, to whom it was sent, when it was written, and what was its subject. These topics should be arranged for maximum efficiency in typing and easy reading, as in the following typical example:

THE BLANK ELECTRIC COMPANY
MEMORANDUM

TO Members of FROM   C. W. Black DATE May 17, 1970
Management PHONE 757
Committee   SUBJECT Advanced Management Program

The individual elements of such a form will, of course, depend on the size, diversity, and location of the business. Companies with plants or buildings in various places usually have *Location* or *Plant* or *Building* in place of the phone extension. Businesses with a large number of offices in the same building frequently include *Room* or *Office* or *Department* under *To* and *From* so that internal mail can be delivered easily. Small concerns often reduce the elements to *To, From, Subject,* and *Date.* Practice varies considerably on whether titles are used, either as part of the printed form or the typed information; for example, the use of such titles as

TO: Ms. Florence E. Virden, Director of Personnel

FROM: Mr. Charles W. Black, Manager of Personnel
      Evaluation

should be cut to a minimum unless a very good reason exists for their use. Generally speaking, the larger the company, the more information is needed; but even here, every element on the memo form should be carefully scrutinized to see whether it is absolutely necessary. In an attempt to take care of every contingency, some companies have developed such cumbersome memo forms that they defeat the main purpose of having such forms printed—namely, to reduce details to a standardized form, easily typed, read, and filed. The classic four W's which a good newspaper reporter should answer in the lead still constitute the best guide for material to be included on a memo form—Who? What? When? Where?

EXAMPLES OF SHORT MEMORANDUMS

Memorandum Giving Information

This will remind you that we agreed in our last management meeting to extend our discussions for three additional sessions. We have now scheduled these as follows:

    March 27—Speaker: Dr. Heinz Weihrich, Arizona State Univer-
                   sity
            Subject: "Transactional Analysis and Management
                   by Objectives"

      April   24—Speaker: Dr. Keith Davis, Arizona State University
               Subject: "The Office Grapevine"

      May   21—Speaker: Dr. Leon Megginson, Louisiana State University
               Subject: "Management Compensation"

All sessions will start at 9:30 A.M. in Conference Room C. If you *cannot* attend any of these meetings, please let me know before March 20.

Memorandum Giving Policy and Procedure

As you know, the Company has designated certain organizations in which we will pay one-half the membership fees. To assure uniform procedure in all departments, we request that you follow these instructions:

1. Each employee wishing to join or renew membership in such an organization should first obtain the approval of the department head.

2. The employee will then make his or her own arrangements for joining, pay the full amount of the fees, and obtain a receipt showing the amount and the period covered.

3. The employee will then prepare a petty-expense voucher, Form H-3, for one-half the amount of the fees.

4. The department head will then sign the voucher, which the employee may take to the Cashier's Office, Room 107, to receive a check for reimbursement.

If you have any questions about our policy or procedure in this matter, I will be glad to discuss them with you. We, of course, want to be as generous as possible in helping employees with these memberships; at the same time, I urge you to scrutinize each application carefully to see that it will be of practical benefit to the Company.

Memorandum Asking for Recommendations

During the last two months, we have had approximately 3,000 requests for the pamphlet "A Giant Conserves Its Resources," which we issued for our twenty-fifth anniversary. I would like your recommendation as to whether we should reissue this pamphlet, which is out of print.

FACTORS TO CONSIDER

Mr. C. M. Eckman has reported the following facts, which I hope you will consider carefully in your recommendation:

1. The cost of reprinting 5,000 copies is approximately $3,250.

2. An analysis of the requests we now have shows that 1,731 came from high school and college students, 339 from other industries, and 891 from individuals.

3. Our previous printing of 10,000 copies was sent to all shareholders, employees, and key industrial and educational leaders in the area we serve.

4. Pages 12 to 15 of the pamphlet should probably be revised, since we now have more up-to-date sales figures and more accurate analyses of costs.

RECOMMENDATIONS

Since I am sending this request to 47 members of management, I will greatly appreciate your making your recommendation in the form of answers to the following questions so that we may tabulate the results easily:

1. Do you think we should reprint 5,000 copies of the pamphlet?

2. What, in your opinion, was the chief value of this publication?

3. Could it be improved in any way to get across our message that modern industry is interested in conserving natural resources?

May I have your answers by May 21?

Example of a Long Memorandum

This memo covers the general characteristics our company should aim at in our audit reports. It results from a two-week survey by the procedures group at the request of Mr. C. F. Smith, Controller.

IMPORTANCE AND SCOPE OF AUDIT REPORTS

Since our audit reports are the principal means of recording our work, they greatly influence the judgments made about our activities and our personnel. Furthermore, they go to people who have many demands on their time and who are primarily interested in results.

For these readers, audit reports should be short, concise, and factual. Usually they should include the following:

1. What was covered in the audit

2. What was revealed that should be called to the manager's attention

3. What is the effect of the variance, if there is one

4. What you recommend to correct the situation

While we do not want reports which follow a rigid pattern, we can reduce both writing and reading time by following these topics.

GENERAL ARRANGEMENT
AND ORGANIZATION

Audit reports should generally include:

1. A letter of transmittal which serves as a guide to tell the reader what really significant information the report contains.

2. The main section of the report, covering the scope, findings, and recommendations.

3. The schedules and exhibits which present documentary evidence to support a finding or a recommendation. In the Quarterly Audit Reports, this should be labeled "Exhibit Section" with the exhibits clearly separated into three classifications:
    a. Information furnished the previous month to all managers who will read the report
    b. Material previously furnished to some, but not all, district supervisors
    c. Material which the auditor creates and which does not duplicate previous monthly reports

As a general rule, we should limit material to what is necessary for a complete understanding of the audit, being careful always to include enough to avoid any possible misinterpretation.

REVIEW WITH LOCAL
MANAGEMENT PERSONNEL

Wherever possible, discuss your findings with the local management *before* you prepare the final report. This review is intended to do three things:

1. Assure the examining auditor that his or her data and opinions are correct and factual.

2. Minimize any feeling in the local office that the audit is an undercover operation.

3. Provide the local manager with advance information on the report so that she or he can take corrective action immediately or recommend changes which lie outside his or her authority.

ANALYSIS OF PRESENT REPORTS

Our survey covering the entire Auditing Division showed that we can improve reports by:

1. Putting all facts in a general context. For instance, if the auditor says, "Ten errors were discovered," it is difficult for the reader to evaluate the situation. How many items were examined? What was the ratio of errors? Is this ratio within our generally accepted standards or is it too high?

2. Making all statements clear-cut and forthright. Many comments in our present reports seem to hedge. They force the reader to read between the

lines. Where an honest difference of opinion exists between the auditor and the local manager, say so clearly. If possible, give the reasons for both opinions so that the reader can pass factual judgment rather than guessing.

3. Ending with a definite conclusion. When everything reviewed complies with established policies, say so. If you believe policies should be changed, say so, giving your reasons and the benefits which may result from the change.

CONCLUSION

Our sole aim is to make our audit reports effective instruments for telling management whether action is needed, and, if so, what action should be taken. Remember that you write for readers who dislike technical terms, detailed analyses, and repetitious statements. Give them adequate information for making judgments; present your recommendations clearly; review your report thoroughly. By doing so, you can help us make our reports an effective management tool.

THE FORMAL REPORT

Some day you may be asked to write what is called a *formal report,* although less use is being made of this form in today's business. These reports are generally written by people who through years of experience have acquired an expert knowledge of some field and are asked to apply that knowledge to solving a complex problem. Nevertheless, you ought to know the components of a formal report and, if possible, get some actual practice in writing one. These reports usually contain the following elements:

1. A *title page,* which includes the title of the report, the names of the author (or authors) and the report recipient with their titles, company affiliations, and addresses, and the date when the report is submitted.

2. A *letter of transmittal,* discussed later in this section.

3. A *table of contents,* designed to give an outline of the main topics in the report and make them easy to refer to.

4. A *synopsis,* or *summary,* which gives the reader the most significant information contained in the report without his or her having to read the entire document.

5. The *body of the report,* which is, of course, the main part of the report, telling what you did, how you did it, what you found, and what conclusions or recommendations you have drawn.

6. The *appendix,* which might be called the department of miscellaneous, but very essential, information. Its purpose is to keep the rest of your report unencumbered by a lot of detail. Here you can put tabulations, data sheets, work papers, calculations, samples of forms, questionnaires, records, and

anything else that is relevant to the text of your report. If it isn't relevant, perform a partial appendectomy.

7. An *index,* which provides easy, alphabetically arranged reference to specific subjects in the report. This is generally needed only in long and highly complex reports.

8. A *bibliography,* listing books or articles cited in the report or relevant to it, is particularly useful in technical or highly specialized formal reports.

The order of these elements may be changed by local conventions and the reader's preference—for instance, the letter of transmittal sometimes follows the table of contents. But the basic principles of investigation and organization which we have discussed apply just as much—and probably more—to the formal report as to any other report form.

The new element in the formal report is the letter of transmittal; and since you may be asked to include such a letter with even your shortest reports—certain companies insist on this—you should know its pattern. While practice varies considerably, this letter usually contains the following information:

1. A reference to the person or agency who authorized the report

2. A general statement of the purpose and scope of the report

3. A reference to the time spent in the investigation

4. Any comments that may help the reader to understand and use the report

5. Any appropriate statements of appreciation or acknowledgment of assistance

The letter of transmittal, like the answer to an inquiry accompanying printed material, may also refer to specific parts of the report without duplicating them. However, if the material is included in a foreword, the letter of transmittal is not needed. The following is a good example of a letter of transmittal:

Gentlemen and Ladies:

Here is the report on our study of possible reorganization plans, which your Board of Directors authorized on February 16.

Mr. E. C. Jacobs, Ms. J. W. Greene, and Mr. C. E. Wilcox spent six months visiting your seven production plants and thirteen distributing centers and interviewing all members of your management. Their information was then analyzed by our planning committee. Since your instructions were to find the best plan for centralizing authority, we have incorporated this policy in the charts shown on pages 11 and 12. Our central purpose in the report and the charts is to adapt to the actual conditions and personalities the best method of organization.

I want to express our appreciation for the frankness and cooperation of all your employees whom we interviewed, and particularly to Mr.

C. W. Winne, who was of invaluable assistance as a liaison person. I shall, of course, be glad to go over any parts of the report with you in detail or to answer any questions you may have.

Respectfully yours,

EXERCISES

1. You are in charge of the mail room and handle all incoming and outgoing mail, as well as the distribution of internal correspondence, for the corporate headquarters of the ABC Corporation. Over 500 ABC employees work on six floors of a 15-story building. One of the top executives, Beverly Simmons, has noticed, however, that many employees are delivering their own internal correspondence instead of relying on the services of the mail room. Ms. Simmons explains to you that the mail room assumed responsibility for distributing internal correspondence two years ago as a result of an efficiency study conducted by an outside consultant. Ms. Simmons asks you to "write a memo under your signature to all employees reminding them that the mail room has responsibility for internal correspondence."
   a. What is the main purpose of your memo?
   b. Are any other purposes related to this main purpose?
   c. Write the memo. Create any information you need such as hours of operation, pickup schedules, rush delivery procedures, etc.

2. Assume now that you are Beverly Simmons, the executive in Exercise 1. Although a month has passed since the memorandum from the mail room was sent to all employees, you have observed that some employees are still wandering around delivering their own mail. You even asked a few why they were distributing the mail, and their answers were rather feeble: "Oh, I needed to come to this floor anyway"; "Charlie needed this right away"; "I was afraid this would get lost."
   a. How will you reemphasize that the mail room is to handle all internal correspondence distribution? Will you write a memo, hold meetings, or use some other strategy? List at least one advantage and one disadvantage for each suggestion.
   b. Assume that you have chosen to write a memo about the mail room. To whom will you send it—to all employees, to supervisors, to those you have seen delivering their own mail?
   c. What is the purpose of your memo?
   d. Will you use the inductive or the deductive pattern? Why?
   e. Write the memo.

3. Exchange the two memos you wrote for Exercises 1 and 2 with a classmate. Answer the following questions in writing:
   a. Assume you are an employee who has been using the mail room for internal distribution of mail. Read the memo from Exercise 1. What is your reaction to it? Read the memo from Exercise 2. What is your reaction?
   b. Assume you are an employee who has not been using the mail room. Read the memo from Exercise 1. What is your reaction? As a result of the memo, will you use the mail room from now on?

c. Assume that even after receiving memo 1, you still continue to deliver your own internal mail. You have just received memo 2. Will you now follow established policy? Why or why not?

4. As part of its continuing program to improve interpersonal communication among employees, your company is holding a three-hour workshop on "Transactional Analysis as a Communication Tool." The workshop will be held on Wednesday, March 19, in conference room A, starting at 3:30 P.M. Since the regular day is from 8:30 to 4:30, employees attending the workshop are being given an hour of company time. A half-hour break with refreshments will be taken from 5 to 5:30, and the session will run until 7 P.M. Write the memorandum inviting and encouraging the 120 employees to attend the workshop.

5. You are assistant personnel director of Absco International and are presently involved in evaluating the services available to the 400 Absco employees at corporate head-quarters. One of the major services is medical care, provided by the health clinic. The clinic is staffed by two doctors and four nurses and is involved not only with treatment of illnesses but also with preventive screening, education, and care. You have statistics about the number of employees using the clinic but are interested in getting information directly from the employees. You want to know whether they have used the clinic, what they liked or disliked about it, and what recommendations for improvement or for additional health services they might have. Write a memorandum to the employees requesting this information; particularly encourage them to make recommendations for improvement.

6. You are office manager of the Meridian Company, whose president, Roger Rackham, is very active in community affairs. Roger has just informed you that he has offered the services of Meridian's office staff to the United Fund's final fund-raising campaign of the year. At least 10 employees will be needed on Saturday to type letters and reports, make telephone calls, and perform other office tasks. The volunteers will not be paid for their work on Saturday, but they will receive a day off with pay next month. Today is Tuesday; write the memorandum to your office staff requesting volunteers for this community service project.

7. Your boss, a very conservation-minded person, has just said to you, "I'm concerned about the amount of paper wasted in this office. I know we use more paper than we need to—much of it ends up unused in the trash basket. Write me a memo assessing the situation. Observe the paper usage habits of the office staff for a week without anyone knowing. Then let me know what measures we can take to reduce the waste." Prepare the memo for your boss, reporting on your observations and stating your recommendations.

8. Write a brief memorandum for each of the following purposes. Either use actual experiences of your own as a basis for the memos or create appropriate information. Be sure to indicate to whom the memorandum is written.
   a. To report to your coworkers on a professional meeting you attended.
   b. To recommend a change in a specific college or company policy.
   c. To explain to subordinates why you made certain recommendations to top management.

d. To announce the promotion of an employee you supervise.

e. To request something of a subordinate.

f. To request something of a superior.

g. To announce a company social function.

h. To explain a problem to subordinates and solicit their solutions.

i. To remind someone that you requested information from him or her two weeks ago.

j. To report the major achievements of your department during the past month.

9. a. Find an article in a business periodical reporting on a trend or new development in some aspect of business. This article may be strictly informational or may include recommendations. Make a copy of the article.

  b. Exchange your article with a classmate. From the article you have been given, write a long, well-organized memorandum presenting either a recommendation or a warning. The type of business you assume you are in will depend on the specifics of the article. Create any additional information you need.

  c. Return the article and memorandum to your classmate. Prepare a written critique of the memo in which you answer these questions:

  (1) What is the main purpose of the memo?

  (2) Is every fact or idea in the memo related logically to the central theme? Cite specific examples.

  (3) Does the memo contain any irrelevant or unnecessary material, information which adds nothing to the reader's understanding of the central purpose? Give specific examples.

  (4) Has the memo achieved its purpose? Are you convinced of the value of the recommendation or warning? If you are not convinced, do you at least understand why the writer believes as he or she does?

10. Write the letter of transmittal for a report on electronic mail, which was requested by the vice-president of communications of your company, the Centrex Corporation, on April 4. The first part of the report explains what electronic mail is, how it operates, what is present status is, and what its probable and possible futures are. The second portion of the report presents first-hand accounts of electronic mail usage. You and an assistant visited businesses in various parts of the country which were using electronic mail in varying degrees. The third section of the report makes specific recommendations for electronic mail applications, both present and future, for Centrex.

FOUR
NONWRITTEN
ASPECTS OF
WRITTEN
COMMUNICATION

Previous parts of this book have dealt solely with the most common forms of written communication in business. The express purpose of these previous parts was improving the quality of the written messages you'll formulate throughout your career. If you've taken this book's many suggestions and guidelines to heart thus far, you should already be seeing evidence of improved quality in your writing. Furthermore, other people familiar with your writing should also be able to see that evidence.

A fringe benefit of your efforts to improve your written communication could be the improvement of your oral communication. The organization, word choice, sentence construction, conciseness, coherence, and tone of your conversations or oral presentations should improve if you apply the guidelines and suggestions you've seen here to your oral exchanges. And this transfer of methods from written to oral communication will become easier as applying these guidelines and suggestions to your writing becomes a habit.

Even though your oral communication may benefit from your studious efforts to write well, there are still some nonwritten aspects of written communication that you should give some specific attention to if you wish to become a better business communicator. Those aspects are dictation, the oral presentation of reports, and communication reception.

It's been said that far too many letters are being sent to today's word processing centers in handwritten form. In other words, too many executives are still reluctant to use dictating machines. Whatever their reasons, this reluctance is one big reason why word processing isn't always fully realizing its cost-saving potential. Chapter 20 is thus devoted to helping you to become a better dictator. If you're the boss's son or daughter and you're lucky enough to get a private secretary with your first job, this chapter should help you to dictate to that secretary. If you're not so lucky, the chances are good that your letters and memos will be typed at a word processing center. If this is the case, you'll find that the guidelines presented in Chapter 20 can be very important aids in your efforts to become a better machine dictator.

In Chapter 21 we'll consider the possibility that your written reports may have to be orally presented. We'll look at the steps you'll want to take to prepare for oral presentations: researching the subject and the audience, organizing your presentation, picking the most suitable props, and making the right assumptions about the audience. We'll also study what should be your major concerns regarding the actual delivery of your talk: projecting interest in the subject, using "content uppers," choosing the right type of delivery, being aware of your body language, and cleanly concluding your talk.

Chapter 22 concentrates on the general subject of communication reception because we spend a large part of our time receiving messages as well as sending them. The subject of reading is reviewed first, with the intent of stimulating your interest in reading and providing you with ways of improving your reading abilities. Listening is the next topic treated in this chapter. Specifically, five guides to more effective listening are discussed. If applied, these guides should assure you of getting much more out of the oral presentations you are required to attend. Finally, nonverbal communication, as it specifically pertains to business meetings, is studied. Agendas, space preparation, nonword vocal cues, and body language are treated as means of communicating messages that support or contradict our words to others attending the meeting.

The fact that this part of the book contains only three of twenty-two chapters does not mean that they are relatively insignificant. The fact that this book has always dealt with written communication meant that this had to be given primary emphasis. Also, as you should fully realize by now, improving written communication is not an overnight job. Writing is a multifaceted task, and improving your writing takes considerable effort. Furthermore, demonstrating how you might do so requires considerable space and attention in any textbook that professes to do so. The importance of the nonwritten aspects of written communication is, however, gaining recognition. In all likelihood, these subjects will be given more and more attention in the future.

20
DICTATION

Within the last ten years, people in business have observed the growing popularity of something called word processing. *Word processing* is defined by the Word Processing Institute as "the combination of procedures, personnel, and equipment to accomplish the transformation of ideas to printed form."

In trying to give a more detailed description of what word processing is, some people focus on the new equipment or technology used in word processing. They talk of magnetic keyboards, timesharing systems, text-editing display systems, communicating terminals, high-speed copiers and facsimile machines, advanced dictating systems, minicomputers, microfilm, and electronic mail. Because most of you reading this text are unlikely to have to master these new technologies, a detailed review of them is considered beyond the scope of this discussion.

What will concern us is the reasons for word processing's growing popularity and the likely impact of word processing upon readers of this book. The reasons why word processing has made the strides it has made can be summed up in one word—efficiency. The greater specialization of personnel and the equipment and procedures used all result in greater output at lower per-unit costs.

The major implication of word processing for readers of this text relates directly to the subject of this chapter—dictation. It is in your dictating that you will come into contact with whatever word processing procedures, personnel, and equipment your company has. Whenever word processing is used in a company, only the top executives retain their private secretaries. Everyone else gets his or her words turned into print through some form of machine dictation. Thus, in the early years of your career, you are most likely to be dictating to a machine. Although the guidelines presented in this chapter are important when you are dictating personally to a stenographer, they are crucial to effective machine dictation. Feedback from the word processor is time consuming and costly when machine dictation isn't handled carefully.

Whether you are dictating to a machine or to a secretary, you can analyze your task and improve your performance by viewing the process of dictation in four phases:

1. Preparing to dictate

2. Dictating

3. Transcribing

4. Signing the materials dictated

Admittedly, this functional analysis may appear to make a comparatively simple process unnecessarily complex, but by following it through step by step, we can analyze the problems which arise in dictation.

PREPARING TO DICTATE

To the long list of signs and slogans—THINK, Do it TODAY, and Better Service at Lower Cost—which adorn the desks and offices of business people, we might profitably borrow from Scouts a special admonition for dictators, *Be Prepared*. Without question, the worst qualities of most dictated material are a rambling, disorganized style and unnecessary repetition; both stem from the dictator's failure to take time to think before dictating. In earlier chapters of this book we have stressed the importance of thinking before you write—and this applies especially to dictation. Until correspondents abandon the foolish idea that they can "dash off" a dictated answer to a letter or memo, there is little hope for improving business communications. In fact, if secretaries appeared for the dictation session as ill-prepared as many of their bosses are, they would arrive without notebook, pencil, and knowledge of shorthand. Here's the way unprepared dictators sound:

> Take a letter, Pat, to the-uh . . . oh yes, the Brown Swidget Company . . . you've got the address somewhere . . . I sorta remember writing to them the first of the year or maybe it was last year . . . make it to the attention of E.Z. or something Brown . . . get the initials from your correspondence files . . . Dear Mr. Brown . . . no, change that to Gentlemen . . . We are-uh in receipt of your letter of the fifteenth in which you inquired about . . . now what was it he wanted to know? Oh, here it is . . . whether in the event you send us your remittance in 10 days after the invoice our terms don't permit a cash discount of 2 percent for payment within 10 days . . . Certainly, I wanted you to take that down, Pat. On second thought, maybe that sentence is too long. Let's start all over. Dear Mr. Brown . . . I mean, Gentlemen.

This word-juggling process costs money because it occupies the time of two people. Let's see how we can cut the high overhead of such dictation. In a few minutes of advance preparation, the dictator should:

1. Assemble all the materials needed for dictation. This includes copies of letters or memos to answer as well as any previous correspondence or information relevant to his or her needs.

2. Read over carefully the letters to be answered, checking important points or questions.

3. Make a mental note or write marginal notes on the actual correspondence or the material to be covered.

4. Decide what is the most important function of the letter or memo and organize the material to achieve that function.

5. Select as the starting point something which is close to the reader's interest by answering a question the reader has raised, by stating what the letter is about, by agreeing with him or her, or by any of the other methods which have been discussed as appropriate for letters, reports, and memorandums in the previous chapters of this book.

When you dictate, try to visualize your reader so that *you can talk directly to that reader* instead of merely uttering words to be transcribed on paper. Montgomery Ward, for example, instructs its correspondents to imagine they have a television set before them and to talk their messages to the image on the screen. Artificial? Perhaps—but not nearly so artificial as the letter dictated without any mental picture of the reader. If you have this picture, you'll ask yourself before you dictate:

What does the reader want to know?

Have I enough information to answer all relevant questions, to be convincing, or to interest him or her?

What is the best way to approach the reader?

What do I want him or her to do or to think?

And if you follow the steps we have outlined in preparation for dictation, keeping your reader always in mind, you're bound to be prepared.

DICTATING

The legend of American business is heavy with the "howlers," the "boners," and the hilarious mistakes which occur in the process of transcribing sounds into typed words. Among these classics is the tale of the insurance agent, a native of Alabama, who dictated to his Iowa-born secretary, "We are gravely concerned by the report about Mr. Blank's heart murmur" and got back a typed version of concern about "Mr. Blank's hot mama." Another one concerns the district manager's memo in the central office that "Miss Brown has asked us to do something about the bare inner office," which emerged as Miss Brown's startling request to do something about "the bear in her office."

These footnotes to the folklore of modern business underscore the prime function of dictation—to produce in type the exact words of the dictator. In this process, dictators are completely responsible for getting their words across to transcribers exactly as they utter them; transcribers are equally obligated to ask questions if there are things they don't understand or if the meaning seems confused. Most of the difficulties of dictation can be eliminated if dictators will follow five simple principles:

1. Relax and dictate in a clear, natural tone of voice.

2. Enunciate clearly.

3. Spell out any names or words that sound similar to other names or words.

4. Dictate only periods, paragraphs, and unusual punctuation. Leave normal punctuation to the transcriber.

5. Ask the transcriber to read back—or if it is machine dictation, play back—any parts of the message which may not be clear.

An analysis of each of these principles may help start youthful dictators on the road to good dictation or guide "experienced" dictators back to the shortest path.

Relax and Dictate Clearly, Naturally

You doubtless remember the pompous, classic poses assumed by the political dictators of the twentieth century—Hitler, strutting and prancing; Mussolini, with jutting jaw and arm raised in Fascist salute; Stalin, cold and expressionless in a pose he must have considered appropriate for a man of steel. Many dictators in business unconsciously assume similar pompous poses during the dictation period. Some become orators, making the walls of the office—and their secretary's ears—ring with their words. Others affect a special form of speech, an expressionless monotone which seems to arise from a feeling that any expression will hinder the transcriber's ability to get the words down. Still others belong on the raceways, since they cover 10 paces for each word uttered. Some day, the Society for the Prevention of Cruelty to Secretaries will draw up bills of indictment against these offenders with the appropriate punishment that they be forced to listen to or watch themselves in action.

When you dictate, relax. Think of yourself as *talking* directly to your reader, and do it in a natural tone of voice without affectation, without posing. This concept of *talking* to your reader in dictation is vitally important, because the pompous affectations we have described are almost invariably accompanied by pompous, stilted, artificial language. Regard your dictation session as simple, natural talk and you'll go far toward unaffected, direct language in your letters, reports, and memos. If you freeze up, as many dictators do, you'll cover up by using mannerisms which really aren't you at all.

Listen to yourself occasionally when you dictate, or, better still, listen to a recording of your dictation. If you want to profit from good human relations, ask your secretary or transcriber how you are doing occasionally. After all, you are missing a chance to improve if you don't find out how the signals are getting across to the other half of the team.

Enunciate Clearly

Among the notable characteristics of the English language is the fact that words which sound alike can be poles apart in meaning; some of these words are listed under the next point to be discussed. In certain instances, the only recourse is to spell out the word. But in general, your best assurance of getting an accurate transcription is to enunciate clearly when you dictate. The difference between words like *receive* and *received,* between the sound of *m* and *n,* between *f* and *v* is often hard to get by ear unless considerable emphasis is placed on their pronunciation. If you slur your speech, "this sort of machine" can sound very much like "the sorter machine" or "this order machine."

You can check your own enunciation quite easily. If people have difficulty understanding you in conversation and, particularly, on the telephone, you're probably not enunciating clearly. Here, too, listening to a playback of your dictation will prove helpful. Most important of all, become conscious of the way you enunciate; listen to find out whether you have a tendency to slur your words together, to drop syllables (for example, saying "incidently" instead of *incidentally* or "finely" instead of *finally*), to ignore the final *g* (as in "writin' new copy," which can emerge as "write a new copy"). Slovenly speech is frequently just one indication of a lot of other sloppy habits; avoid it in dictation and then let your good practices there carry over into all your speech.

Spell Out Words and Names That May Be Strange or Confusing

Even the most precise enunciation will not clear up confusion between words with identical sounds. For instance, *cite, sight, site; know, no; coarse, course; through, threw;* and a host of other words are identical. Here, of course, a transcriber's intelligent appraisal of the context will help, although a realtor, for example, can just as logically be describing a beautiful sight as a beautiful site and examples can be both cited and sighted. In such instances, dictators should remember that whatever admirable traits their secretaries have, being mind readers is not among them. Good dictators spell out technical terms, unfamiliar words, strange names; if they don't, their stenographers should ask—and then, like Ko-Ko, the Lord High Executioner in *The Mikado,* should keep "a little list" of these terms, words, and names so that they will know them the next time they occur. Here is another little list of words which cause confusion:

accede, exceed	forth, fourth
accept, except	incidence, incidents
access, excess	its, it's
addition, edition	legislator, legislature
affect, effect	loose, lose
allusion, illusion	maybe, may be
already, all ready	miner, minor
altogether, all together	no, know
anyone, any one	new, knew
assistance, assistants	ordinance, ordnance
bare, bear	passed, past
brake, break	personal, personnel
capital, capitol	practical, practicable
cease, seize	precedence, precedents
coarse, course	principal, principle
cite, sight, site	residence, residents
complement, compliment	respectfully, respectively
correspondence, correspondents	rite, right, write
council, counsel, consul	some one, someone
decent, descent, dissent	stationary, stationery
deference, difference	their, there, they're
disapprove, disprove	therefore, therefor
eligible, illegible	through, threw
era, error	waive, wave
everyone, every one	whose, who's
finally, finely	your, you're
formally, formerly	

Dictators should take particular care to see that names are properly spelled. The most efficient way is to give secretaries the letters or memos which are being answered at the end of the dictation; they can then check names, addresses, and dates carefully with the written information before them when they transcribe. Since people are most sensitive to the spelling of their own names, special care should be taken by both dictator and transcriber to see that names like Stewart or Stuart, O'Neill or O'Neal, Schwartz or Swarts are accurately typed. The same care should, of course, prevail with names of companies, partnerships, titles, or anything else where errors may occur.

Dictate Only the Major or Unusual Marks of Punctuation

One of the most annoying habits that you as a dictator can develop is to include every mark of punctuation in your dictation. Not only does this interrupt your own thinking, which should be focused on the content rather than the mechanics of the material, it also distracts the secretary or transcriber from his or her main task of getting your words down exactly. This habit implies that you don't trust the transcriber to punctuate properly and that you know more about it than he or she does. Perhaps you do, but the best way to find out and to maintain the teamwork we have advocated is to let the transcriber try. If you're not satisfied with the results, maybe you need a new secretary—or maybe, since this habit reflects considerable ego, you should take a course in shorthand so that you can be dictator, secretary, punctuator, and transcriber, all in one.

Basically, only three situations require punctuation by the dictator:

1. Punctuation at the end of the sentence—say "period," "question mark," "exclamation point."

2. The end of a paragraph—say "new paragraph." Your transcriber can help you a great deal with paragraphing if you ask for suggestions. Even the most experienced dictators occasionally lose sight of how much material or how many sentences they incorporate in a paragraph.

3. Unusual punctuation marks—a dash for emphasis, an exclamation point, or quotation marks.

The only other mechanical aspects of the letter, memo, or report that should concern you in dictation are the number of carbon copies to be made, to whom they must go, and what enclosures or attachments are to go with the dictated material. Occasionally, you should tell the transcriber how you want material set up in special situations; for instance, where you have dictated a list of comments numbered 1, 2, 3, 4 which are to be indented within the margin of the text of a letter, you can help by saying at the end of the list, "This goes back to the original margin." But remember that you and your typist, secretary, or transcriber are both specialists. Give that person as much freedom in his or her specialty as experience warrants. After all, you still hold a veto power which you can exercise when the time comes to sign the letter, memo, or report.

Reading or Playing the Material Back

Even the best-prepared dictator will want to make changes in wording or phraseology during dictation. By having the secretary read back or the machine play back your dictation, you are doing exactly what you do when you revise your written material. The sole difference is that you can't pencil in the changes yourself; for that reason, your instructions for changing dictated material must be unusually explicit and clear. Say, "Let's change that 'arbitrary decision' in the second sentence to 'final opinion' " or "Omit the 'very' before 'delighted' in the last paragraph." Be sure that your transcriber understands the changes you want.

One aspect of dictation which worries the inexperienced is how fast to go. In the early stages, you will be wise to slow down your normal rate of speech a bit until you find by experience the speed of your transcriber. Then you can go at a pace which produces the best results, under the principle that in this division of labor, it is the transcriber's responsibility to keep up with you rather than yours to slow your words down to his or her shorthand or typing.

At the beginning of this chapter, we stressed dictation as a tool to produce better results more quickly and economically. Like every tool, it has its merits and limitations. Dictation is most useful for writing a large number of shorthand letters or memos. Unless you are very unusual, you should not try to dictate the final draft of a long report or a complex memo. If you do, you will find that you are merely pouring words into the microphone or the secretary's notebook and wasting two people's time in the process.

TRANSCRIBING

From transcribers, dictators should expect one result—an exact transcript of their words, set up in appropriate form, without errors in typing, division of words, spelling, or punctuation. If transcribers find errors in grammar in the dictation, they should always suggest a correction, on the general principle that the company doesn't want such mistakes recorded permanently in type.

SIGNING THE MATERIALS DICTATED

Read over all dictated material before you sign your name because your signature means that you are assuming final responsibility for everything in the letter, memo, or report. For that reason, the humor or annoyance that many dictators express about "my secretary's carelessness in making that error" only reflects their own carelessness in not catching the error when they signed the material. By insisting on accuracy and excellence at the time you sign, you are also establishing the high standards of performance you expect from your transcriber.

MACHINE DICTATION

To increase efficiency in producing written communications, more and more companies are installing dictation machines to facilitate the processing of their correspondents' words. The greatest advantage of machine dictation is its saving in time, since it eliminates the need to tie up dictators and transcribers at the same time. The machines are always there for dictators to use at their convenience and to fit their dictation into their schedule. Furthermore, modern electronic and mechanical dictating equipment is so flexible and adaptable that all the objections which used to be raised about the difficulties of making changes in dictated materials have been removed. The actual fact is that almost all the failures of machine dictation arise from the human element rather than the machine. Because of their reluctance to change, to adopt new and efficient methods, many executives are handicapped by their inability or lack of familiarity in using dictating equipment.

As noted in the beginning of this chapter, everything that we have said about dictation to a secretary applies in even greater degree to machine dictation. Because the transcriber cannot ask questions directly, machine dictation demands even greater preparation, clarity, and enunciation on the part of the dictator. One of the greatest faults of the novice at machine dictation is a tendency to shout. The sensitivity of modern equipment is so great that this merely distorts the message. Another fault of the novice is to hesitate and to leave long pauses in the dictation. This stems partly from lack of preparation and partly from a mild form of microphone fright or fear of the unfamiliar. Anyone who wants to learn to dictate efficiently to a machine should follow these guiding principles:

1. *Hold the microphone or speaking tube in the position recommended by the manufacturer. Don't* wave it around, don't shift it from one position to another.

2. *Speak in a normal conversational tone. Don't* shout and don't drop your voice.

3. *Talk steadily and at a little slower rate than normal,* unless you are a very slow speaker. *Don't* fluctuate by rushing occasional phrases or by hesitating for long intervals.

4. *Take special care to enunciate clearly,* to speak distinctly, and to pronounce unusual words with unusual care. If there is any doubt, always spell the words out. *Don't* mumble.

5. *Dictate paragraphs and uncommon punctuation:* semicolons, colons, dashes, parentheses. Voice inflections as in normal conversation will indicate commas and other conventional punctuation.

6. *Dictate figures by digits.* Spell names and unusual words unless they appear in the correspondence which you send on to the transcriber.

7. *Make all corrections carefully* in accordance with the directions for the type of equipment you are using. Many a transcriber, confronted with a dictator who either neglects to indicate corrections or indicates them on a following cylinder or record which requires retyping the material, might vent feelings in the famous words from the *Rubáiyát* of Omar Khayyám:

   The moving finger writes; and, having writ,
   Moves on; nor all your piety or wit
   Shall lure it back to cancel half a line
   Nor all your tears wash out a word of it.

   Don't force the transcriber to guess at corrections or to retype material because the corrections are not clearly indicated at the appropriate place.

8. *Attach all necessary forms,* guide sheets, cards, or all other information to the cylinder or records. *Don't* force the transcriber to call you or to ask you for additional information which you should have sent.

9. *Start the machine before you begin dictating and stop it after you have finished. Don't* clip your words at the beginning or chop off the end of your dictation.

The best test of the effectiveness of your techniques of machine dictation is the transcriber. For that reason, many companies ask transcribers to analyze the effectiveness of individual dictators at regular intervals. Such an analysis is recommended as a practical device for securing good teamwork between dictators and transcribers of machine dictation.

The following is a simple illustration of the actual procedure used in dictating, with the instructions to the transcriber italicized, the dictation to be transcribed in regular type.

Operator this is to be a letter with two carbons   Indicate that one carbon copy goes to Edward C Borton our dealer in Middletown   Letter to Charles M *as in Mary* Kohn *K as in kick o-h-n as in November* 2739 Broadway Middletown New York 12760 Dear Mr Kohn We appreciate your telling us of your interest in our air *hyphen* conditioning units as advertised in Life *period Operator underline Life Paragraph* Our dealer Mr Edward C Barton *correction* Borton will call on you to discuss the various Breezie units in which you expressed an interest *period* Since we regard every installation as an individual engineering project we want you to have the opportunity to discuss your needs with Mr Borton so that he can work out the best and most economical solution *period Paragraph* You will be interested I know in reading the three brochures I am enclosing *colon   Operator please indent and list the following items* 1 What Breezie Air Conditioners Can Do 2 A Survey of the Effects of Air Conditioning on Retail Sales by Professor R. O. Fidel *F as in Frank i as in island d as in door e as in eat l as in lot* and 3 We Cite *Operator that's c-i-t-e* These Results with Pride *Operator return to the original margin* Thank you for giving us the opportunity to discuss our units with you *period* I am sure that one of our units will suit your needs and that air conditioning will mean better business for you *period Operator underline you* Sincerely yours Sue Wind Customer Service Agent *Mark the letter for three enclosures and pick up the brochures listed from Ms Gompert at the reception desk That's all*

SOME OTHER SUGGESTIONS

Now that we have analyzed the process of dictation from predictation preparation through to the signing of materials, here are a few other suggestions to help you when you get into business and dictate frequently:

1. If possible, set up a regular period for dictation. Try to arrange your dictation schedule so that you can take care of answering an average day's mail the same day it comes in.

2. Without being officious or pompous about it, let it be known that you don't want to be interrupted when you are dictating. There will, of course, be important exceptions to this, but you'll do your best work if you can arrange to concentrate on your dictation and go straight through from beginning to end. Many companies insist on this in the interest of efficiency and set up specific dictation periods when, by mutual agreement, all telephone calls

between departments stop and outside calls are handled by one person in each department.

3. Your relations with your transcriber will improve—and so will your typed material—if you'll avoid the frictions generated by the following situations:

  a. Don't habitually locate "one more important letter" that has to be dictated at 5 P.M. and mailed that day. Remember that stenographers have lives of their own to lead.

  b. Don't mark up typing which can easily be corrected or draw ink lines across a whole letter because one word is misspelled. Indicate changes by light pencil checks or by telling the typist what you want corrected.

In this chapter we have outlined the four aspects of dictation, all of which contribute to the final result. While it is impossible to assign accurate equivalents to each phase of dictation, the checklist following arbitrarily rates each phase of dictation as equally important. If you can answer "yes" to these questions, you are indeed a good dictator.

A CHECKLIST FOR DICTATION

Preparing

Do you have all the previous correspondence and other information you need to dictate efficiently?

Have you read through the material you are answering and made notes of the points you want to cover?

Have you decided on the main point of your letter or memo and how best to get it across to your reader?

Do you visualize the kind of reader you are dictating to and how you can approach him or her?

25

Dictating

Do you have a mental picture of your reader as an actual human being to whom you are talking when you dictate?

Are you dictating naturally without affectation?

Are you enunciating clearly?

Do you spell out names or words that may be strange or confusing to your transcriber?

Are you dictating only the major and unusual marks of punctuation?

Are you revising by having the secretary read back or the machine play back, and are you indicating your revisions clearly?

Are you dictating at a rate which is efficient for both you and the   25
transcriber?

Transcribing

Is the material transcribed in a form you approve?

Have you been consulted about any changes?

Is it accurate and without errors in spelling, punctuation, and grammar?

When your transcriber generally does a good job, have you told him or her   25
so occasionally?

Signing

Have you read over the transcript carefully before you signed?

If it does not meet the standards set up under *Transcribing,* do you insist
that it be corrected or done over?

Do you habitually establish high standards of performance which you   25
expect from your transcriber?   100

EXERCISES

1. The following exercises give students information they can use as they practice their
   business letter dictation skills. The specifics of the dictation practice will vary depending
   on the equipment available and the teacher's preferences. Some suggestions are:
   a. Have the business communications class and a shorthand or transcription class work
      as a team. A communications student could dictate live to a secretarial student, who
      would then transcribe the letter and return it for review and signature. Or the
      communications student could use a dictation machine or cassette recorder, and the
      secretarial student would transcribe from that medium. The appropriate parts of
      the checklist on pages 381 and 382 should be used by both the dictators and the
      transcribers for self-evaluation and evaluation of each other's work.
   b. Have the communications students dictate on tape, using either college equipment
      or their own personal tape or cassette recorders. After the student has dictated a
      letter, he or she should use the checklist on pages 381 and 382 to evaluate the
      dictation. Then the student should dictate the letter again, concentrating on improving
      the weak points in the first dictation.
   c. Have the communications students dictate the letters on tape and then exchange
      their tapes with a partner. The partner should evaluate the dictation using the
      checklist. For further dictation practice, a memo could be dictated to the partner in
      which the evaluation of the letter dictation was discussed.
   d. If no recording equipment is available, the students could practice dictating to each
      other. They could try to write as much of the dictation as possible in longhand. Or
      the students could dictate to each other over the telephone, thus simulating one type
      of machine dictation.

2. You have seen an advertisement in *Business Week* about ZYX's new line of word-processing equipment. Dictate a letter of inquiry requesting additional information about this equipment; the name of the dealer in your area; and, if possible, a demonstration.

3. You are the customer service representative at ZYX and have received the letter dictated in Exercise 2. Create the information needed and dictate your reply. Also mention that you are holding a special demonstration of the new equipment in that person's city next month, and invite him or her to attend. Be sure to state the date and place for the demonstration and be very encouraging in your invitation.

4. Order a book from Dow Jones, Box 245, Princeton, New Jersey 08536. You don't recall the specific title, but the book deals with trends in certain aspects of our society, such as population, communications, energy, transportation, education, and medicine, and the implications of these trends for business. Excerpts from the book appeared in the *Wall Street Journal* about two months ago. Request that you be billed for the book.

5. Dictate an answer to the letter in Exercise 4. The name of the book is *Business in a Changing World*. The cost is $10.95 plus $1.50 postage and handling, and payment must accompany all orders. Enclose a copy of your book list with the letter so that the customer will be aware of all the books Dow Jones has published.

6. You have received the following letter:

Dear Credit Manager:

I have been a charge customer of Lorbach's for five years and have always paid my account within the 30-day payment period. Therefore, I was puzzled three months ago when my payment of $78.40 did not appear as a credit to my account. Instead, an interest charge of 50 cents was added to the claimed outstanding balance of $78.40 and the $32.75 in purchases during that month.

I contacted your office, and the clerk explained that some error must have been made and that it would be corrected on the next bill. However, this was not done—the $78.40 appeared as an overdue amount; and another 50 cents interest charge was added.

I again talked to your office, and the clerk assured me that this would be cleared up immediately. Today I received my bill. The $78.40 has now shown up as a credit, but I am still being billed for the $1 interest.

Would you please see to it personally that this incorrect charge is removed. I am losing patience with your credit system.

> Lee Nilson
> 7498 MacNeil Terrace
> Schenectady, NY 19088

Dictate a reply in which you not only provide an explanation of the action you have taken but also attempt to ease the customer's annoyance.

7. You are manager of the branch of Jear's, a nationwide department store, in your town. Dictate a memo to all 120 employees explaining the new vacation procedures decided upon by the Board of Directors at their January meeting. The main points of their decision are that employees must apply for their vacation at least one month ahead of the time they want off, that requests for the same time off by members of the same department will be handled on a seniority basis, that approval of the requested time is the store manager's decision, and that the requested vacation date is only a request and *not* a right. Also, the paid time off is now:

1–2 years employed	1 week vacation
3–5 years employed	2 weeks vacation
6–11 years employed	3 weeks vacation
12 and up	4 weeks vacation

Unpaid vacation time allowed is now:

1–5 years	1 week
6 and up	2 weeks

This guaranteed unpaid time off allows employees to take longer vacations if they wish. Dictate this memo so that each of the points covered is set up as an enumeration (as a numbered sentence or sentences). Add any information you think is necessary. Present the new policy in whatever order and words you think best suited to your readers.

8. Dictate a memo to your department head asking for the 14th of next month off so that you can attend a time management seminar presented by the Center for Executive Development at the local university. In addition to the paid day off, request that the company pay the seminar fee of $85; be sure to justify your request.

9. You have received the memo in Exercise 8. Answer it however you wish, and send a carbon copy of your reply to the personnel department.

10. You are personnel director for your county and have received a letter from the business club of the local high school asking you to speak at their meeting on March 18. Dictate a letter to the club's president, Pat Kuriski, declining the invitation because you will be attending a national conference in Denver the week of the 18th.

11. You have just been hired as the credit manager of Soleri's, a locally owned department store. You don't like the form letter which is sent to all new charge customers, so one of your first tasks is to compose a new one. Although the letter is a form letter, it is typed on word processing equipment, and each letter looks like an original. Dictate this welcoming letter to new customers, remembering what you learned about credit letters in Chapter 9.

21
ORAL
PRESENTATION
OF REPORTS

One of the certainties of a business career is that someday someone will tell you to prepare a report on some topic for oral delivery to some group. How you react to this assignment will depend upon a number of factors, but your personality, experience, and knowledge of the subject are probably the most important.

People with different personalities approach the task of public speaking in distinctly different ways. Extroverts, or outgoing individuals, generally love the spotlight of the speaker's podium. They tend to thrive upon being the center of attention and welcome the opportunity to show their stuff, so to speak. On the other hand, introverts are reserved and somewhat withdrawn and don't relish the idea of being in the spotlight. To them the task of making a formal oral presentation can be quite traumatic. Most people fall somewhere between these two extreme personality types. We may not cringe with horror at the thought of making a speech, but we normally have at least some apprehension about it.

The degree of apprehension people experience when given a speaking assignment differs. These differences in degree are, in most cases, directly related to the amount of experience in public speaking the individuals have had. Regardless of personality, most people do improve their public speaking as they gain experience at it. Practice may not make perfect, but it does make better.

Another determinant of people's reactions to public speaking assignments is their knowledge of the subject being discussed. In most cases speakers know a great deal more about the topic than the audience does; however, not all speakers can be easily convinced of this edge. Some tend to be unduly concerned about the person who knows enough to ask that embarrassing question. Only more experience at speaking can convince such people that audiences are not "out to get the speaker." The most constructive approach to handling this aspect of public speaking is to know as much as you possibly can about the subject.

Regardless of your personality, experience, and knowledge of the subject, the importance of your speaking ability cannot be overstated. Evidence of the relationship between communicating abilities and success in business is published almost daily. One such study rated "oral persuasiveness" as the most important of five qualities most successful managers share.[1] Because of public speaking's well-acclaimed importance, the remainder of this chapter will be devoted to tips aimed at helping you improve your ability to present reports orally.

BE FULLY PREPARED

Nothing will help your presentation of a report like being adequately prepared. Admittedly, the formality of the presentation will dictate the time and effort you put into your preparation, but for most oral presentations getting prepared will involve at least the following steps.

Research the Subject and the Audience

As already mentioned, knowledge of the subject you're discussing is a major determinant of the attitude with which you approach the task of making a speech. If you know your subject well and feel confident that you can handle any questions your audience might ask, you've probably taken a big step toward delivering the comfortable kind of oral presentation that people enjoy hearing. Do keep in mind, however, that if someone asks a question for which you don't have an answer, all is not lost. Most people will take a simple "I don't know" or "I'll have to check into that" much better than a bluff.

Studying the subject is not the only research you'll have to do before you make a talk. How well you know the audience can also make or break you as a public speaker. If at all possible, try to find out as much as you can about your audience. What is their general level of education? How much do they already know about your subject? Listening to a talk delivered far above or below one's level of understanding can be a pretty boring and/or frustrating experience. And the reaction the speaker is likely to get from the audience in such cases doesn't do much for that speaker's ego.

Researching the audience's level of understanding is important, but another audience characteristic may be even more important. That characteristic is the audience's attitude toward the subject and what you'll be saying about it. Do they consider the subject dry and boring or exciting and dynamic? The former attitude, of course, presents a much greater challenge to the speaker. Also, how are they likely to react to what you'll be saying about the subject? If you expect to encounter some resistance, you might want to organize your talk indirectly and give a lot of factual support before you present your conclusions. Presenting

[1]John Costello, "What You Need to Climb the Business Ladder," *Nation's Business*, June 1976, p. 6.

a controversial conclusion at the beginning of your speech just might condemn your credibility to the gallows for the rest of your presentation.

Organize Your Presentation

The first step in organizing your presentation will be deciding what or how much you want to say. Unless you're talking about a very exciting subject to an extremely interested and alert audience, you'll find there's a limit to how much meat you can cram into an oral presentation. You will usually have to be content with making three or four significant points. The rest of your talk will be made up of support for those points.

Although your audience's attention span and powers of recall are limited, there are ways in which you can reduce those limitations and increase the number of significant points you can make. Using appropriate props is one of those ways. Since we'll discuss props later in the chapter, we won't say much about them here. However, you should keep in mind that handouts and visual aids can enhance the interest value of your talk, help listeners follow the plan of your presentation, and help them to recall your talk after it is over.

After you've decided what you want to say, you'll need to determine the order in which you want to say it. At this point you may wish to refer to Chapter 16, because the steps used in organizing an oral report are similar to those used in organizing a written report. Whether you organize your whole talk or parts of it deductively or inductively, and whether you organize the meat of your talk according to place, time sequence, bases of comparison, factors, or hypotheses will depend upon the nature of your material and the people to whom you are presenting that material.

As you decide what you're going to say and the order in which you are going to say it, do make an effort to tie your talk together so that you develop a coherent end product. Try to make certain that, during your talk, your audience knows where you've been, where you are, and where you're going. You might wish to review the material on transition in Chapter 4. It is even more important in speaking than in writing to signal changes or continuations in thought. An audience usually can't relisten to part of your talk if they lose your trend of thought. Give them whatever signposts are necessary to "show them the way" through your presentation.

Pick Suitable Props

While you are organizing your presentation and afterward, give some thought to the props you'll be using during your talk. If you decide to write on a chalkboard, use posters, or use a projector and screen, make certain that what you write, post, or project is clearly visible to all the members of your audience.

If you decide to use a handout, be careful not to give too many details in it. An outline of major subjects to be covered can help the audience see your overall organization plan. But including too many details of your discussion might create several problems. Some folks might think that listening to what you've got to say is unnecessary because they think they've got all the details on the handout. Others might choose to read ahead and miss most of what you have to say. Thus, the handout could become more of a distraction and a hindrance than a help.

If you decide to use a podium, be careful not to overrely on it. With few exceptions, you should try to maintain fairly consistent eye contact with your audience. You can't very well do this if you're staring at the podium. Remember, the podium can't hear you, and it's not the podium that will be expressing pleasure or displeasure at the impact of your talk.

Take the Proper Head Trip

The final step in preparing to give a talk is to develop the proper frame of mind about your audience. Although you don't want to be so calm that you appear listless, you also don't want to be a "bundle of nerves." Most good speakers would admit to having a touch of the jitters before addressing a group. Unfortunately, many speakers, especially inexperienced ones, get much more than a touch of the jitters; they get something more akin to a one-two punch of the stuff. In many of these cases where the butterflies in the tummy seem to be multiplying like rabbits, the problem can be traced to false assumptions about the audience.

If you get very nervous before addressing a group, ask yourself a few questions about your attitude toward your audience. Do you think that there are some ornery people out there who are likely to be searching for an embarrassing question to ask you? Do you think that your credibility with the entire audience will be shot to Hades if you can't answer that question? Then ask yourself how true these assumptions are likely to be.

In actuality, most audiences prefer to be supportive of speakers. Furthermore, most audiences include people who have been in the speaker's position. They can empathize with a touch of nerves. Also, most audiences know that speakers are human; thus, they realize that speakers are usually neither omnipotent nor infallible. What the preceding discussion boils down to is this: Relax, you're among friends. At least at the start of your talk, the audience is in your corner.

One final element of speech preparation must be mentioned before we talk about the actual delivery of a talk. That element also relates to your attitude toward your audience. Regardless of the circumstances, audiences are very sensitive to being spoken up to or down to. The speaker who effusively praises the audience or has a fawning demeanor is saying this: I don't know if you'll like or get any use out of what I have to say, so I'll try to get in your good graces by telling you how much I like you.

Equally if not more offensive is the speaker who talks down to the audience.

Such a speaker appears to see himself or herself as the expert on the subject who is condescending to impart some of his or her expertise to a group of real dummies. Needless to say, that attitude doesn't usually strike a positive note with the audience.

Much more constructive and much better received than either of the preceding attitudes is one of equality and mutuality. The most appropriate attitude for a speaker to have results in the image of one mature adult with some information of which the other mature adults in the audience may be unaware. This view portrays the speaker as a source of useful information—not a master or a servant, but a resource. It suggests neither subservience nor condescension and usually results in a positive rapport between the speaker and the audience.

DELIVER WITH DELIBERATION

For some people, completing the preceding preparatory steps, means that more than half the battle has been won. These fortunate individuals find public speaking easy. They perform with what appears to be a natural grace. For some, that grace may in fact be natural. For others, the graceful delivery may be the result of years of experience at public speaking.

Not all public speakers are as fortunate or as polished as the ones discussed above. Those readers who haven't as yet developed that natural grace or style may find the following guidelines useful for avoiding the pitfalls that beset the inexperienced speaker.

Project an Interest in Your Subject

Interest is contagious. It's much easier for an audience to get worked up about a subject if the speaker appears to be worked up. At the other end of the spectrum, nothing will convince an audience that a subject is dry and dull faster than a monotonous, boring discussion by the speaker.

The best and safest way to project an interest in your subject is to *really be interested* in it. If you are given the option, choose a subject that does in fact get your adrenalin going. Usually, you'll find that the audience responds well to your enthusiasm—provided, of course, that you haven't picked a topic to which they would naturally respond negatively. Most American veterans, for example, would react unfavorably to a discussion of the virtues of communism, regardless of how enthusiastically the talk was delivered.

Suppose, however, you are not given a choice of subject, and suppose you are not initially greatly interested in the assigned topic. To a certain extent, a good speaker can project a higher degree of interest than he or she actually possesses. A conversational tone, voice inflections, good eye contact, and suitable gestures are a few of the ways in which a good speaker can keep an audience from straying.

Another way of handling the problem of speaking about a topic that doesn't initially "turn you on" is to give the topic a second chance. Dig into it. Research it thoroughly. Most subjects have at least a few interesting aspects. Your job is to uncover them. To illustrate, many students of management find the scientific school of management thought relatively dry because of its somewhat mechanistic approach. The principles of scientific management are relatively dry, but the people behind those principles aren't. A speaker on this subject could liven up his or her talk appreciably by concentrating on people like Frederick Taylor or Frank and Lilian Gilbreth (*Cheaper by the Dozen*) and their personal, as well as professional, lives.

G. K. Chesterton once said, "There is no such thing as an uninteresting subject; there are only uninterested people." Your job as a speaker is to present the subject in such a way as to minimize the number of uninterested people. And however you choose to look at it, the job starts with you, the speaker.

Give Your Audience a "Content Upper" Here and There

Even though you are enthusiastic about your subject, and even though your audience may be genuinely interested in what you have to say, you had better keep human frailties in mind. There are limits to the span of attention people can devote to listening to points, principles, and conclusions. They need an occasional boost to keep them moving along with you, rather than giving into distractions when tempted. Jokes, stories, audience-involvement exercises, quotes, and impressive facts can give a talk that occasional boost.

Humor can go a long way toward getting audience acceptance and attention. It can shed sunlight upon an otherwise overcast presentation. Jokes, when related to the discussion, are especially effective as openers and closers for talks. Remember that the beginnings and endings of presentations, whether written or oral, carry the most emphasis. Also, keep in mind that people form impressions or make judgments about others shortly after initial contact. Within a few minutes of the time you begin a talk, your audience will have made some judgments about you and your subject. If you can cause those judgments to be favorable by using a little humor, do so. You just might clinch their attention for the rest of your talk.

Stories, like jokes, can help a talk. They suggest a plot and climax and thus can reach out and grab an audience's attention. When closely related to your discussion, they can paint vivid pictures that lend concrete support to what you are saying. In fact, after any relatively long talk, the stories and jokes are the first things the audience is likely to recall. Most speakers would hope, however, that recollection of the points they were making would closely follow the recollection of the jokes and stories.

Audience-involvement exercises are another way of boosting attention. Questionnaires and other such instruments can be effective tools for impressing upon the audience the personal relevance of your subject. They can also be used at the start of your talk to indicate to the listeners how little they actually know about your subject. Role playing is another audience-involvement exercise that can spice up a talk. In role playing, participants actually act out aspects of your subject. This acting, of course, demands the complete involvement of the actors and gives the observers a pleasant break in the routine of the talk, as well as some practical insight into your subject.

Finally, quotes by important people and impressive facts are two other ways of pepping up a discussion. Relevant quotes by significant people can lend heavy support to your theme. They also might suggest that you are well read, which usually won't hurt your credibility. Impressive facts can serve a similar purpose. The weight of fact can sometimes be awesome, but don't overuse this technique. A few facts in a speech can impress an audience, but a seemingly endless stream of statistics can put that audience to sleep.

However you choose to liven up your talk, remember that spice is an essential ingredient in any recipe. A speech devoid of any of the preceding "ingredients" is likely to be as bland as an unseasoned boiled chicken.

Choose the Most Appropriate Type of Delivery

Different types of talks, talkers, and audiences will call for different types of deliveries. Perhaps the type of delivery least popular with audiences is the reading of a speech. When the speaker is a widely recognized, very busy person (like a U.S. President), or when the speech is very long and/or technical, the audience may *put up* with a talk that is read. Unless one or more of the preceding conditions prevail, however, the audience is likely to feel no compulsion to listen and is likely to hunt for the slightest distraction to while away the time.

Akin to the read speech is the memorized talk. It has the important advantage of allowing a speaker to move from the podium and maintain eye contact with the audience. Furthermore, if well practiced and spoken with a natural tone, the memorized delivery can come across well. Unfortunately, many memorized speeches are delivered by people who are primarily concerned with which sentence comes next. Gestures and voice inflection take a back seat to remembering the words that are to be regurgitated. The significance that such speakers assign to saying words in their proper order gives rise to the major disadvantage of the memorized speech. That disadvantage is the mind-shattering possibility that the speaker will forget a line. When this possibility becomes a reality, the speaker and audience are usually subjected to a period of very awkward silence. Even when the speaker remembers the line or is coached from the side, the prevailing mood will not be the same. The speaker's confidence is often noticeably dented, and he or she wobbles through the rest of the speech like a three-legged dog.

Probably the most popular and most commonly used form of oral presentation is delivery from an outline. This outline may be formally prepared and placed on the podium or, if brief, may be stored in the speaker's mind. This form of delivery has several advantages. First, to be outlined, a speech must have a basic organization, and the speaker must be aware of that organization. Because of these requirements, the from-an-outline delivery can bring to a talk an order that might not otherwise be there. Second, the speaker has the security of knowing that certain bases have to be touched. The brief outline in the speaker's mind or the more involved one on the podium gives assurance that all will not be lost if a point is forgotten. Third, the outlined presentation can be most effective from the audience's point of view. Although speakers may plan their most significant word choices, this form of delivery still allows them to look like they are speaking conversationally *to* the audience, rather than delivering an impersonal canned presentation. An audience is thus more likely to stay attentive because it looks as if the speaker will know if they are not.

As stated earlier, different circumstances may suggest different forms of delivery. Choose the one that is most appropriate for you, your subject, and your audience.

Be Alert to What Your Body Is Doing while Your Mouth Is Moving

Nonverbal communication experts tell us that people form impressions about us within four minutes after meeting us in any social situation. Furthermore, these impressions are based largely upon the nonverbal aspects of our behavior.

The very first impression we make will be influenced by the way we are groomed and attired. Not everyone attributes monumental importance to these aspects of our nonverbal communication, but some folks do get slightly disturbed if we are not dressed and groomed to their expectations. Without becoming paranoid about this aspect of behavior, it wouldn't hurt to give some thought to audience norms and the formality of the event when you dress and groom yourself for a speaking engagement.

Another aspect of nonverbal communication that you should consider when giving a talk is eye contact. The degree of eye contact you maintain with your audience can be crucial to the success of your presentation. An audience will be attentive to you and your discussion in direct proportion to the extent to which you attend to them. The personal relevance of your subject will, of course, affect the attention your talk gets. Beyond that, however, you should be attentive to your audience *while* you are speaking. Do they appear to understand? Do they have any questions? Are you going too fast or too slow? Are you using enough "content uppers"? You can't determine the answers to these questions and respond to them unless you are maintaining appropriate eye contact. And you can't maintain appropriate eye contact if you're reading too much of your talk or just staring at the podium.

Two forms of nonverbal communication or body language that can help or hinder a talk are gesturing and walking. "Degree" is an important word to keep in mind when you consider these aspects of speech behavior. Pointing, finger raising, extending the arms, head movement, and walking to props or to different parts of the stage when addressing a large audience are all acceptable forms of speech-related body language—when not overdone. They can support and/or give emphasis to what you are saying, when used in appropriate doses. When used to extremes, however, these nonverbal messages can upstage your verbal message and actually distract the audience from what you are trying to say.

Convey a Clean Conclusion

The last aspect of the actual presentation of an oral report is the ending. Make sure that your talks have one. Truly anticlimactic to an audience is the decent speech that is left dangling without a clear moral or conclusion. It's like being brought to the peak of a roller coaster track and left there.

If you introduce the purpose of your presentation at the start of your talk, you should construct your conclusion in such a way as to point out and emphasize how your presentation has accomplished that purpose. Your listeners should be left impressed at how you have done so.

PATROL PRACTITIONERS AND PROFIT FROM WHAT IS PREACHED

This chapter was written with the express purpose of offering guidelines for the effective presentation of oral reports. If you examine your attitude toward public speaking, prepare adequately for the task, and deliver your talks with enthusiasm, conviction, and an appropriate repertoire of "content uppers" and nonverbal behaviors, you should become a better public speaker.

Beyond the hopefully helpful hints already presented in this chapter, one other suggestion will be offered to you. That suggestion is, take advantage of opportunities to listen to other speakers. Listen and observe with educated ears and eyes. Note what the speakers do, and note the audiences' reactions. Then, in your own talks, eliminate what you've seen produce unfavorable reactions, and try to incorporate what you've seen produce favorable reactions. In other words, practice what you've seen preached with success.

EXERCISES

1. Your boss is pleased with your ability to write good business letters and has just told you, "Many of our employees seem to lack any understanding of how to write a clear, concise letter. I would like you to present a talk covering the basics of business letter writing at next week's staff meeting. If this general presentation goes well, we might deal with specific kinds of letters in future meetings." About 15 of your coworkers will be in attendance at your presentation; most of you are at the same organizational level, with a few one level higher or lower.
   a. What thoughts enter your mind about researching the subject and the audience?
   b. Organize your presentation; prepare a written outline.

     c. Will you use any props or handouts? If so, prepare sketches of the props and copies of the handouts.

Optional:

     d. If equipment is available, record your presentation on cassette or tape; imagine that your audience is present.

2. Pick a topic you are familiar with and create a business situation (who, what, where, when, why) which requires you to speak for five minutes on the subject.
   a. What is the situation you have created?
   b. How can you find out more about your audience?
   c. Prepare a written outline of your presentation.
   d. Present your talk to the class. Let them know the details of the situation you have created before you begin.

Optional:

     e. If videotape equipment is available, you should tape your presentation and then privately view it for self-analysis.

3. Choose an article of interest to you from a current business periodical. Assume that your boss has asked you to give an oral report about the article to a group of five or six of your coworkers.
   a. Prepare your presentation; be sure to follow the guidelines given in this chapter.
   b. Form a group with four or five of your classmates. Take turns presenting your talks.
   c. After each talk has been given, group members should evaluate the speaker, covering these points:
        (1) What was the general topic?
        (2) What specific points do I remember the speaker stating (at least two)?
        (3) Was I initially interested in the subject?
        (4) Did I gain or lose interest as the talk progressed?
        (5) What were the speaker's strong points?
        (6) What were the speaker's weak points?
        Spend a maximum of five minutes on these anonymous evaluations; be sure that everyone receives his or her evaluations at the end of the class period.

4. You are sales manager of the Avco Corporation, a sporting goods distributor. The Board of Directors is interested in the results you are achieving in the Southwest territory since the hiring of a representative for that area two months ago. Before that representative was hired, stores did not have personal contact with a company salesperson—business was transacted by mail or telephone. The Board is interested not only in whether sales have now increased in the Southwest, but also in how Southwest sales compare with those of the other territories (Pacific Northwest, California, and Southeast).
   a. Create the necessary sales figures for your presentation. You may be either positive or negative in your report.
   b. What additional information would make your presentation thorough, to the point, and interesting? Research or create this information.
   c. What should you know about your audience? How will this affect your presentation?
   d. Prepare an outline of your report. Prepare props and handouts.
   e. Form a group with several of your classmates, preferably not the same ones you worked with before. Role-play part of a Board of Directors meeting, with each group

member serving once as chairperson of the board (to lead the meeting) and once as sales manager (to present the report). During the report, directors should play their roles and ask questions, make comments, etc. This will probably require the sales manager to create additional information on the spot.

5. Not all the oral presentations you will be asked to give will be of great interest to you. Nevertheless, you must still try to make them interesting to your audience.

   a. Think of a rather boring business topic. It should be one that can easily be researched—you are not concerned with obscurity, only boredom.

   b. Exchange your boring topic with a partner, one who also thinks the topic is uninteresting.

   c. Prepare a five-minute presentation on the topic your partner has given you. Your task is to uncover a few interesting aspects of the subject. Be creative, perhaps a bit zany!

   d. Present your report either to the entire class or to a small group. Afterward, write a one-paragraph evaluation of your presentation, focusing on your perception of the audience's interest.

   e. Each audience member should also write a short anonymous evaluation of each presentation so that the speaker can compare his or her perceptions with the actual audience reactions.

6. Attend some kind of oral presentation other than a classroom lecture, such as a club meeting, a public lecture, a committee meeting, or an event on campus, where you can have the opportunity to hear a public speaker. Evaluate the talk, using the main points in this chapter as your guide. You might find it helpful to make a checklist of these main points for immediate reference and evaluation during the presentation. Then afterward, when you have more thinking time, you can expand your initial criticisms and comments to produce a detailed written critique.

7. You have read in this chapter about four aspects of nonverbal communication which can help or hinder the effectiveness of your presentation—dress, eye contact, gesturing, and walking. Prepare an oral presentation which gives more information about nonverbal communication and public speaking. Submit a written outline of your report to your instructor. Use at least two periodical articles or one book as your information sources, and cite these fully in your presentation. In addition to conveying the information verbally in your class presentation, do so nonverbally. For example, if you were talking about eye contact, you could purposely avoid looking at the audience, thus enabling them to experience the effect of poor eye contact. Try to deal with aspects of nonverbal communication other than the four discussed in this chapter. If possible, have your presentation videotaped for later self-analysis.

22
COMMUNICATION RECEPTION: READING, LISTENING, AND NONVERBAL COMMUNICATION

Up to this point this book has been devoted to helping you to become a better initiator of messages, written and oral. But we can't ignore the fact that you will also receive many messages in business. This last chapter, therefore, is aimed at helping you to become a better receiver of written and oral communications.

The first part concentrates on the value of reading and presents some instructions designed to improve your reading abilities. It is followed by three bibliographies compiled to broaden your reading horizons in business and communication.

The next part attends to the function of listening. This section gives you five tips that, if followed, will make you a more effective listener and a more highly valued employee.

The last part of this chapter examines the subject of nonverbal communication. This examination has the primary purpose of helping you to better interpret the full meaning of the oral messages you receive. It also, however, has a secondary purpose. You'll find that as you study the messages of nonverbal behavior, you can't help but become more sensitive to what you are communicating nonverbally.

READING

One of the soundest generalizations that can be made about good writing is that it always stems from a broad background of reading. Almost unconsciously, reading will help you develop techniques of style, of word usage, and of organization which you can carry over into your own writing. But beyond these techniques, reading gives you the inestimable benefit of learning from other people's experience. Notice what C. B. Larrabee has to say in the following editorial from *Printers' Ink* (May 28, 1954, p. 13):

START WHERE THE LAST MAN LEFT OFF

FROM A GENERAL ELECTRIC advertisement, by way of *Mill & Factory News,* this quotation:

"Edison, to explain his incessant and tireless reading of scientific journals . . . said he read to avoid useless repetition of old experiments. 'I start where the last man left off.' "

That seems to me to be the best answer to the man who says, "I don't have time to read."

The "don't-have-time-to-read" people usually want to leave you with the impression that they are so busy gaining practical experience that they can't waste any precious minutes on magazines, newspapers or books. They are the "school of experience" boys, who fail to realize that even their favorite school operates a lot better with a library.

I think it is significant that most of the great leaders in almost every business activity have been students. Oh, yes, I know of cases of the hardbitten self-made man who never got farther than the third grade and eventually became head of a great steel company. The only reading he ever did was supposed to be financial reports.

Somehow when they write the lives of those people, they neglect to point out in almost every case they were surrounded by some pretty smart lads who were not afraid to crack a book—or even look into a business paper.

Civilizations are built on the ability of today's man to start where yesterday's man left off. And there are only two ways to do this. You either work with the other man, or with someone who did, or you read about what he did.

One of the most expensive wastes in business is caused by the unnecessary duplication of effort. Every time a man in a laboratory does as an original experiment something that's been done by somebody before him and written down, he has wasted time. Every time a businessman tries out a plan that has been tried out and failed before, he is wasting time and money.

That is why reading is so essential to the modern businessman. And that is also why you can be pretty sure that the successful businessman who says, "I don't have time to read," is either lying or is surrounded by a lot of people who do have time.

Don't fall back on the worn-out alibis which Mr. Larrabee mentions; what these statements really mean is "I don't want to read" or "I don't know how to read"—and that is exactly where you must start by:

1. Making up your mind that reading will give you the breadth of interests, the

personal development, the added experience, and the fun that confirmed readers know it does.

2. Learning how to read so that you can at least use this tool at your highest efficiency.

No one except you can make the first decision. Your college career may already have developed your interest in reading; if so, you should make every effort to continue a good habit. If not—and a college education is no guarantee that you will read—you should consciously make the effort. The best way to begin is by getting a book that interests you; more personal reading programs have been stopped short by dull books than by any other cause. Select your book carefully, and choose one outside your field of business or professional interest; it's always a good measure of a person to learn what he or she knows *outside* a field of specialization. Reading is the one key to unlock the doors which will otherwise hold you within the narrow confines of specialization.

But whether you read for general breadth and pleasure or for professional advancement, you can at least learn how to read well. By now, you probably want to protest "Of course I can read. I've been reading ever since I was in the second grade." But the chances are good that you aren't reading efficiently and that you are plodding along at about the same rate you used in the fifth grade. For studies show that the average adult reads about 250 words a minute; that with normal vision, this person can increase this rate by 50 to 100 percent; that in doing so, he or she will suffer no loss of comprehension, the old saw of "I'm a slow reader but I really remember what I read" having been disproved time and again. Hence, you have the opportunity to acquire a skill which will help you read from one and a half to twice as much material in the same amount of time with just as much, and probably more, comprehension. How?

Depending on your job and location, you have two possibilities: to get professional guidance or to do it on your own. If you are in a college or university or metropolitan area which offers the facilities of a reading clinic—many business organizations have set up their own—by all means take advantage of this opportunity. In six to twelve sessions you can learn the basic principles and can work with the reading accelerators, tachistoscopes, and reading films which such clinics have.

If this opportunity is not available, you can still accomplish a great deal in improving your reading on your own by following these instructions:

1. *Start by finding out what your present speed is.* You can do this by reading the next pages of this book or anything else you select for exactly three minutes. Read with the purpose of comprehending, since speed alone is useless if you don't know what you've read. At the end of three minutes, determine your rate each minute by getting an average of the number of words a line, multiplying by the number of lines you have read, and dividing by three. This book, for example, averages about 12 words a line, 42 lines a page.

2. *Before reading, take an overall survey of the material to be covered.* This will

give you a general idea of what the material contains, what the main ideas and details are. Look for clues in boldface type, headings and subheadings, and the other devices which we have emphasized as helps to your reader when you write.

3. *Keep forcing yourself to move ahead.* The more regressions (moving back) you make, the slower your reading. If passages seem vague or hazy in meaning, move on; they may be clarified later, or you may come back to them at the end after you have the general meaning. When you start this technique, your comprehension will suffer a bit, but when the habit of moving forward constantly is firmly established, you'll gain.

4. *Learn to group words into thought units instead of proceeding word by word.* To the word-by-word reader the following sentence goes like this:

The / office / boy / put / the / mail / on / the / desk.

Learn to break it into units of thought like this:

The office boy / put the mail / on the desk.

Your eyes should move along in a definite rhythm, stopping (called a *fixation*) about the same number of times on each line, pausing about the same length of time at each fixation, and swinging back to the next line like the carriage on a typewriter. (Here is where the devices of the reading clinics are especially helpful; but if you want to get a rough check on your eye movements, you can have someone sit across from you and count your eye movements or you can place a mirror on the page opposite from the one you are reading and have the person counting stand behind you.) Usually you should make three or four fixations for each line to read efficiently.

5. *Postpone looking up the unfamiliar words until you are finished.* Jumping back and forth from dictionary to reading interrupts your comprehension. Check the unfamiliar words and look them up later.

This reading technique involves getting rid of old habits and learning new ones. For that reason, you will have to *practice* it, making periodic checks of your reading speed to ascertain your progress. But no matter how fast you now read, you can still improve if you are willing to work at it; and increased efficiency in reading is important to you and your company. A survey of 200 employees, ranging from supervisor to top management, shows that they averaged four and one-half hours of daily reading. Their average speed was 250 words a minute. By doubling their reading speed, they could save themselves and their companies 450 work-hours a day!

FOR FURTHER READING

"Knowledge is of two kinds," said Samuel Johnson. "We know a subject ourselves, or we know where we can find information upon it." This selected bibliography is intended to help you with the second kind of knowledge. Since there are hundreds of books and articles dealing with the principles and problems of communication, it seems best to focus on a few which are recent, readable, and useful. These books will lead you to other sources of information. But you should remember that all reading can help you—and novels, biographies, and articles of general interest will help you to become a better writer just as the books on communication do.

The words of Francis Bacon have been repeated so often that we perhaps lose sight of their significance. Nonetheless, it is true that for the twentieth-century citizen whose career is oriented toward business, the words of this seventeenth-century genius hold profound meaning: "Reading maketh a full man, conference a ready man, and writing an exact man." In a technological society which has made inexpensive paperbacks available to every citizen, there is little or no excuse for not broadening one's horizons through reading—no excuse, that is, other than the age-old ones of laziness, indifference, and lack of intellectual curiosity.

As part of your program of self-development as a writer in business, you should become a regular reader of such periodicals as *The Wall Street Journal, Business Week, Fortune, U.S. News & World Report, Direct Marketing,* and *Saturday Review.* All of these magazines are themselves good examples of communication, and you can learn a great deal by studying the techniques they use to get information across. But you will be wrong if you limit your reading exclusively to books and periodicals dealing with business and communication; in fact, there are business executives who recommend staying away from the specialized subject matter of one's career. Business in the seventies has been heavily influenced by such things as a national report on pollution or a widely read study of crime or a bestseller dealing with the civil rights movement. Read as widely as you can, therefore, because in the interdependent society of the United States almost every social movement or trend directly affects business people and their careers.

The following books are intended to suggest the wide variety of interesting, provocative, and informative treatments of the topic of communication in its various facets:

BARNLUND, DEAN C. (ed.). *Interpersonal Communication: Survey and Studies,* Boston, Houghton Mifflin Company, 1968.
A useful anthology containing 37 articles about what the social sciences can offer to improve communication.

BERNSTEIN, THEODORE M. *Dos, Don'ts & Maybes of English Usage,* New York, New York Times Books, 1977.
A well-known editor of *The New York Times* wittily attacks awkward constructions and distortions of language in a book which contains more than 2,000 alphabetically arranged entries.

FLESCH, RUDOLPH. *The Art of Readable Writing,* 2d ed., New York, Harper & Row, Publishers, Incorporated, 1974.

This 25th-anniversary edition of his 1949 book presents his readability formula (pages 247 to 251) and some still sound advice concerning the principles of clear writing.

FOLLETT, WILSON. *Modern American Usage,* New York, Hill & Wang, Inc., 1966. Edited and completed by Jacques Barzun in collaboration with several distinguished scholars, this authoritative book presents a sensible approach to problems of usage.

FOWLER, HENRY WATSON. *A Dictionary of Modern English Usage* (2d ed. revised and edited by Sir Ernest Gowers), New York, Oxford University Press, 1965. This classic, which first appeared in 1926, has now been revised and updated. A mixture of dictionary, style book, and arbiter of good taste in writing, Fowler's book offers bright and amusing comments on such topics as "Battered Ornaments," "Elegant Variations," and "Hackneyed Phrases."

HANEY, WILLIAM V. *Communication and Organizational Behavior,* 3d ed., Homewood, Ill., Richard D. Irwin, Inc., 1973.
This is one of the increasing number of studies centering on the important relationship between organizational patterns and communication.

HARRIS, THOMAS. *I'm OK—You're OK,* New York, Harper & Row, Publishers, Incorporated, 1969.
This extremely well-written best seller presents transactional analysis as a very useful tool for understanding our interactions with others and leading better lives.

HODGSON, RICHARD. *The Dartnell Direct Mail and Mail Order Handbook,* 2d ed., Chicago, Dartnell Corp., 1974.
Hodgson, a man of vast experience in the field, presents a very comprehensive variety of methods, techniques, approaches, thought-starters, and formulas for designing direct-mail strategies.

JOHNSON, H. WEBSTER. *How to Use the Business Library,* 3d ed., Cincinnati, South-Western Publishing Company, Incorporated, 1968.
A useful reference and guide to the handbooks, directories, business services, government publications, and trade reports which can be found in a library.

LAIRD, CHARLTON. *The Miracle of Language,* Cleveland, The World Publishing Company, 1953.
This is an exception to the characteristic dullness of books about our language. It achieves its purpose of answering "the most important questions about our language" in a very readable fashion.

MOCKRIDGE, NORTON. *Fractured English,* Garden City, N.Y., Doubleday & Company, Inc., 1966.
Mockridge takes aim at today's malapropisms and tortured language and uses hilarious examples and illustrations to hit his targets.

REDDING, W. CHARLES, and GEORGE A. SANBORN. *Business and industrial Communication: A Source Book,* New York, Harper & Row, Publishers, Incorporated, 1964.
Although it is intended primarily as a college text, this collection of readings makes readily available to business people and others 44 important articles dealing with all aspects of business communication.

SHIDLE, NORMAN G. *The Art of Successful Communication,* New York, McGraw-Hill Book Company, 1965.
An original approach to the subject of business communication, this book contains two chapters which are especially valuable—"Barriers to Communication: In the Writer" and "Barriers to Communication: In the Reader."

STRUNK, WILLIAM, JR., and E. B. WHITE. *The Elements of Style,* New York, The Macmillan Company, 1972.
This brief book is probably the best treatment of style written in the past 20 years.

THAYER, LEE O. *Communication and Communication Systems,* Homewood, Ill., Richard D. Irwin, Inc. 1968.
Basing his book on the premise that better understanding of communication theory leads to better practice of communication, Thayer offers a mind-stretching analysis of communications concepts.

VARDAMAN, GEORGE T., and CAROLL C. HALTERMAN. *Managerial Control through Communications,* New York, John Wiley & Sons, Inc., 1968.
A difficult book requiring serious study, but it achieves its authors' aim "to provide the means by which managers can improve personal and organizational operations" and to present "useful theories, concepts, and principles which the manager can translate into action on the job."

WILLIAMS, FREDERIC. *Reasoning with Statistics: Simplified Examples in Communication Research,* New York, Holt, Rinehart and Winston, Inc., 1968.
On the assumption that readers have no expertness in statistics, this book fulfills its promise of explaining basic statistical methods in understandable and nonmathematical terms.

The following articles provide considerable information on various aspects of communication; they will also serve as excellent sources for classroom reports and discussions.

ANONYMOUS. "Caveat Emptor: Many Americans Complain about the Quality of Goods," *The Wall Street Journal,* June 26, 1969, pp. 1, 15.
This survey by the staff of the *Wall Street Journal* provides excellent background on the situations which lead to claim and adjustment letters.

ANONYMOUS. "Grooming Executives for the Spotlight," *Business Week,* Oct. 5, 1974, pp. 57–61.

This article reveals how many companies are having top executives trained at seminars to deal with questions on touchy issues asked by TV interviewers.

ANONYMOUS. "Psyching Them Out," *The Wall Street Journal,* Nov. 20, 1972, p1.
This article shows how psychology can be used to make a product's design appeal to deep-rooted emotions and feelings in customers.

ANONYMOUS. "The Growing Threat to Computer Security," *Business Week,* Aug. 1, 1977, pp. 44–45.
This article talks about the growing problem of unauthorized people getting access to computers and what some companies are doing about it.

ANONYMOUS. "Turning Federalese into Plain English," *Business Week,* May 9, 1977, p. 58.
This article reviews President Carter's efforts to get government officials to speak plain English rather than their special bureaucratic version of the language.

ACKOFF, RUSSELL L. "Management Misinformation Systems," *Journal of the Institute of Management Sciences,* December 1967, pp. 146–156.
An expert examines some of the ways in which the systems approach to communication may go astray.

BROWN, DAVID S. "Shaping the Organization to Fit People," *Management of Personnel Quarterly,* Summer 1966, pp. 12–16.
A brief look at the increasingly important relationship between the structure of the organization and its communication.

COE, ROBERT K., and IRWIN WEINSTOCK. "Publication Policies of Major Business Journals," *The Southern Journal of Business,* January 1968, pp. 7–9.
A useful summary of publication practices for those who consider submitting material to business publications.

DAVIS, KEITH. "The Care and Cultivation of the Corporate Grapevine," *Dun's Review,* July 1973, pp. 44–47.
This insightful discussion of the grapevine treats its significance and how a manager can turn it into a valuable feedback device.

FITZGERALD, STEPHEN E. "Literature by the Slide Rule," *Saturday Review,* Feb. 14, 1953, pp. 15–16, 53–54.
Written shortly after the formulation of Flesch's Readability Formula and Gunning's Fog Index, this article protests the principles and techniques of what the author calls "the readability boys and their word-counting machines." It raises excellent questions for discussion of whether readability can be reduced to formulas.

GEHMAN, BETSY HOLLAND. "Junk Mail," *This Week,* March 6, 1966, p. 11.
A humorous account of the various methods "second-class" citizens have used to get their names removed from mailing lists.

GENERAL ELECTRIC COMPANY, Public and Employee Relations Services. "Letters to Employes' Homes; the Techniques of Employe Communication," New York, no date.
A practical discussion of the role of letters in employee communications and how to write them. Sample letters to individuals and groups are included.

GREENBAUM, HOWARD. "The Audit of Organizational Communication," *Academy of Management Journal,* December 1974, pp. 739–751.
A broad but detailed overview of what is necessary to examine and control communications processes in organizations.

GREER, ALLEN. "All You Have to Do Is Get a List," *Direct Mail,* Summer 1968, pp. 25–27.
Useful background on the general subject of mailing lists, how to test them, and what may reasonably be expected from their use.

IRWIN, THEODORE. "About Mailing Lists," *The New York Times Magazine,* March 22, 1964.
A comprehensive view of the methods used in compiling lists, how lists are classified, and what problems are involved in getting a name removed from a mailing list.

KNAPPER, ARNO. "Good Writing—A Shared Responsibility," *The Journal of Business Communication,* Winter 1978, pp. 23–27.
This article argues that writing must be stressed over and over again in a student's college career. All faculty members must share commitment and responsibility for improving the quality of writing of their students.

KRUK, LEONARD B. "Word Processing and Its Implications for Business Communications Courses," *The Journal of Business Communication,* Spring 1978, pp. 9–18.
This article suggests that machine dictation be taught in business communications courses because the present reluctance of executives to dictate by machine is one of the factors holding back full achievement of the cost-saving potential of word processing.

KRUTCH, JOSEPH WOOD. "Who Says It's Proper English?" *Saturday Review,* Oct. 14, 1967, pp. 19–21, 132ff.
A well-known scholar and writer presents a thoughtful analysis of the age-old problem of "correctness" in language.

MERRILL, PAUL W. "The Principles of Poor Writing," *Scientific Monthly,* January 1947, pp. 72–74.
This article, written by a staff member of Mount Wilson Observatory, has been so widely reprinted as to become a classic. Dr. Merrill starts by asking "Where can you find sound, practical advice on how to write poorly?" By giving that advice, he provides sound counsel on how to write well.

MCLEAN, ED. "How to Write a Profitable Letter," *Direct Mail,* Summer 1968, pp. 37–40.

An executive in a firm of direct mail consultants provides 10 practical rules for writing effective sales letters.

MINTZ, HAROLD K. "How to Write Better Memos," *Chemical Engineering,* Jan. 26, 1970, pp. 136–139.
A good, concise discussion of the importance, organization, and stylistic qualities of the memorandum in today's business and scientific world.

MORRIS, JOE ALEX. "What Credit Bureaus Know About You," *Reader's Digest,* November 1967, pp. 85–89.
Useful background on the methods by which information is obtained and exchanged whenever credit is granted.

MORRIS, M. D. "Why Engineers Don't Write," *Engineer,* September–October 1969, pp. 15–19.
Despite its title, this article applies not only to engineers but to all technical specialists who are struggling to express technical content in readable English.

NEWMAN, RUTH. "The Case of the Questionable Communiqués," *Harvard Business Review,* November–December 1975, pp. 26–40+.
A general manager's touchy problem of how to tell employees of a textile mill that they are not going to get a raise he thinks they expect.

PEI, MARIO. "A Loss for Words," *Saturday Review,* Nov. 14, 1964, pp. 82–84.
An eminent linguist takes a look at the debate between "the Advocates of Usage" and "the Custodians of the Language." This is an eminently sensible approach to the heated discussions which followed the publication of Merriam-Webster's *Third International Dictionary* in 1961.

ROSS, BRUCE E., and JOHN WHITE. "The Computer and Direct Mail," *Pharmaceutical Marketing and Media,* May 1968, unpaged.
This article provides specific examples in a very specialized medium of how the computer can team with direct mail to provide new and more sophisticated marketing techniques.

SCHAFFER, RICHARD. "Easy Access," *The Wall Street Journal,* March 27, 1978, pp. 1, 20.
This article describes how computers that use plain English can have vast new applications.

SESSER, STANFORD N. "How Credit Bureaus Collect and Use Data on Millions of Persons," *The Wall Street Journal,* Feb. 5, 1968, pp. 1, 14.
This feature story presents data and background excellent for credit and collection correspondents and for students who want to find out how the credit system works.

SHAH, DIANE K. "What Does It Take to Make You Happy at Work?" *The National Observer,* Jan. 8, 1977, p. 6.

This article talks of "career anchors" as values, suggesting five types of needs that are of prime importance to five different types of people.

SPENDER, STEPHEN. "The Age of Overwrite and Underthink," *Saturday Review*, March 12, 1966, pp. 21–23, 132–133.
Poet Spender doesn't even mention business writing, but he does present a brilliant analysis of the role of language in the famous controversy about two cultures with his statement, "If there truly is a gulf between the literary and the scientific culture, it cannot be bridged by science but only by language."

TANNENBAUM, JEFFREY. "Selective Service," *The Wall Street Journal*, Feb. 19, 1974, pp. 1, 23.
Describes how mailing list brokers collect and sell more than names on their lists and how these data help advertisers spot especially hot prospects for their products.

TOBIN, RICHARD L. "Like Your Cigarette Should," *Saturday Review,* May 14, 1966, pp. 59–60.
The communications editor of *Saturday Review* takes a conservative view of the advertising for Winston cigarettes, concluding that "talking English and writing English are two different forms of language and that certain colloquialisms acceptable in casual, regional conversation are still unacceptable on the formal printed page." Readers' reactions in subsequent issues of *Saturday Review* make an excellent subject for student reports.

WEEKS, FRANCIS W. "Current Issues in the Practice of Business Communication in the USA," *The Journal of Business Communication,* Spring 1976, pp. 61–68. In his address to the Japanese Business English Association, the Executive Director of the American Business Communication Association talks of new developments and age-old problems in the practice of business communications.

WEIHRICH, HEINZ. "MBO: Appraisal with Transactional Analysis," *Personnel Journal,* April 1976, pp. 173–176.
Transactional analysis is here shown to be a workable tool for handling problems of superior-subordinate interaction in MBO programs.

WITKOVICH, CARL. "Neither Rain, nor Snow, nor ZIP Code . . ." *The Columbia University Forum,* Spring 1968, pp. 46–48.
A good account of how and why Zip numbers were set up and some of the idiosyncrasies of the system.

Throughout our discussion of reading, we have stressed the desirability of selecting books and articles which provide a broad background for business or a general knowledge of people. It is interesting to note, for example, that three of the best-selling books of the past dozen years have dealt satirically with one or another aspect of the business community or the business organization—C. Northcote Parkinson's *Parkinson's Law and Other Studies in Administration,* Lawrence J. Peter and Raymond Hull's *The Peter Principle,* which remained on best-seller lists for more than 50 weeks in 1969 and 1970, and Robert Townsend's *Up the Organization*. Students and those who make careers in business would do well to keep up with all facets of writing concerned with the business community— from Ralph Nader's *Unsafe at Any Speed* (1965) and James Bishop and Henry W. Hubbard's *Let the Seller Beware* (1970) to William Rodgers' *Think: A Biography of the Watsons and I.B.M.* (1969) and William Cahn's *Out of the Cracker Barrel* (1970), a history of the National Biscuit Company. All reading is grist to the writer's mill, and books about business are especially valuable for those who intend to write in business.

Nevertheless, you may want to refer occasionally to books which deal with the specific aspects of writing reports and letters and the other technical aspects of writing in business. To the production of such works there seems no end, but here is a representative sample:

ANONYMOUS. *Writing Reports That Work: A Programmed Instruction Course,* prepared and published by the American Management Association, New York, 1969.

AURNER, ROBERT R., and MORRIS P. WOLF. *Effective Communication in Business,* 6th ed., Cincinnati, South-Western Publishing Company, Incorporated, 1974.

BERLO, DAVID K. *The Process of Communication: An Introduction to Theory and Practice,* New York, Holt, Rinehart and Winston, Inc., 1960.

BLUMENTHAL, LASSOR A. *The Complete Book of Personal Letter Writing and Modern Correspondence,* Garden City, N.Y., Doubleday & Company, Inc., 1969.

BROMAGE, MARY C. *Writing for Business,* Ann Arbor, Mich., The University of Michigan Press, 1965.

BROWN, LELAND. *Effective Business Report Writing,* 3d ed., Englewood Cliffs, N.J., Prentice-Hall, Inc. 1973.

BROWN, LELAND. *Communicating Facts and Ideas in Business,* 2d ed., Englewood Cliffs, N.J., Prentice-Hall, Inc., 1970.

BRUSAW, CHARLES T., GERALD J. ALRED, and WALTER E. OLIU. *The Business Writer's Handbook,* New York, St. Martin's Press, Inc., 1976.

CLOKE, MARIJANE, and ROBERT WALLACE. *The Modern Business Letter Writer's Manual,* Garden City, N.Y., Doubleday & Company, Inc., 1969.

COMER, DAVID B., and RALPH SPILLMAN. *Modern Technical and Industrial Reports,* New York, G. P. Putman's Sons, 1962.

COYLE, WILLIAM. *Research Papers,* 4th ed., New York, The Odyssey Press, Inc., 1976.

DAMERST, WILLIAM A. *Resourceful Business Communication,* New York, Harcourt, Brace & World, Inc., 1966.

DAWE, JESSAMON. *Writing Business and Economic Papers: Theses and Dissertations,* Totowa, N.J., Littlefield, Adams & Co., 1965.

DAWE, JESSAMON, and WILLIAM JACK LORD. *Functional Business Communication,* 2d ed., Englewood Cliffs, N.J., Prentice-Hall, Inc., 1974.

DAWSON, PRESLEY C. *Business Writing: A Situational Approach,* Belmont, Calif., Dickenson Publishing Company, Inc., 1969.

DEVERELL, C. S. *The Techniques of Communication in Business,* London, Gee & Co. Ltd., 1964.

GALLAGHER, WILLIAM J. *Report Writing for Management,* Reading, Mass., Addison-Wesley Publishing Company, Inc., 1969.

GRAVES, H. F., and L. S. S. HOFFMAN. *Report Writing,* 4th ed., Englewood Cliffs, N.J., Prentice-Hall, Inc., 1965.

HATCH, RICHARD. *Communicating in Business,* Chicago, Science Research Associates, Inc., 1977.

HAY, ROBERT D. *Written Communication for Business Administration,* New York, Holt, Rinehart and Winston, Inc., 1965.

HICKS, T. G. *Writing for Engineering and Science,* New York, McGraw-Hill Book Company, 1961.

HIMSTREET, WILLIAM C., and WAYNE M. BATY. *Business Communications: Principles and Methods,* 5th ed., Belmont, Calif., Wadsworth Publishing Company, Inc., 1977.

HOUP, KENNETH W., and THOMAS E. PEARSALL. *Reporting Technical Information,* 3d ed., Beverly Hills, Calif., The Glencoe Press, 1977.

JOHNSON, THOMAS P. *Analytical Writing: A Handbook for Business and Technical Writers,* New York, Harper & Row, Publishers, Incorporated, 1966.

KREY, ISABELLE A., and BERNADETTE V. METZLER. *Effective Business Communication,* 2d ed., New York, Harcourt Brace Jovanovich Inc., 1976.

LAMB, MARION M., and EUGENE H. HUGHES. *Business Letters, Memorandums, and Reports,* New York, Harper & Row, Publishers, Incorporated, 1967.

LAMBUTH, DAVID. *The Golden Book on Writing,* New York, Viking Press, 1964.

LESIKAR, RAYMOND V. *Business Communication: Theory and Application,* 3d ed., Homewood, Ill., Richard D. Irwin, Inc., 1976.

LESIKAR, RAYMOND V. *Report Writing for Business,* 5th ed., Homewood, Ill., Richard D. Irwin, Inc., 1977.

LEWIS, LESLIE LLEWELYN. *The Business-Letter Deskbook,* Chicago, The Dartnell Corporation, 1969.

McCRIMMON, JAMES M. *Writing with a Purpose,* 6th ed., Boston, Houghton Mifflin Company, 1976.

McLUHAN, MARSHAL. *The Medium Is the Massage,* New York: Bantam Books, Inc., 1967.

———. *Understanding Media: The Extensions of Man,* 2d ed., New York, Signet Books, 1966.

MAMBERT, W. A. *Presenting Technical Ideas: A Guide to Audience Communication,* New York, John Wiley & Sons, Inc., 1968.

MENNING, J. H., C. W. WILKINSON, and PETER CLARK. *Communicating through Letters and Reports,* 6th ed. Homewood, Ill., Richard D. Irwin, Inc., 1977.

MILLER, LYLE L. *Increasing Reading Efficiency,* 3d ed., New York, Holt, Rinehart and Winston, Inc., 1970.

MITCHELL, J. *A First Course in Technical Writing,* London, Chapman & Hall, 1967.

MORRIS, JOHN O. *Make Yourself Clear,* New York, McGraw-Hill Book Company, 1972.

MURPHY, HERTA, and CHARLES E. PECK. *Effective Business Communications,* 2d ed., New York, McGraw-Hill Book Company, 1976.

NEEDLEMAN, MORRISS H. *Handbook for Practical Composition,* New York, McGraw-Hill Book Company, 1968.

New York Times Manual of Style & Usage, 2d ed., New York, Quadrangle/ McGraw-Hill Book Company, 1976.

OTTE, FRANK R. *Complete Book of Extraordinary Collection Letters,* Englewood Cliffs, N.J., Prentice-Hall, Inc., 1965.

PUGH, GRIFFITH T. *Guide to Research Writing,* 3d ed., Boston, Houghton Mifflin Company, 1968.

REID, JAMES M., JR., and ROBERT M. WENDLINGER. *Effective Letters: A Program for Self-instruction,* New York, McGraw-Hill Book Company, 1964.

ROBINSON, DAVID M. *Writing Reports for Management,* Columbus, Ohio, Charles E. Merrill Books, Inc., 1969.

SHERMAN, THEODORE A. *Modern Technical Writing,* 2d ed., Englewood Cliffs, N.J., Prentice-Hall, Inc. 1966.

SCHNEIDER, ARNOLD, WILLIAM C. DONAGHY, and PAMELA JANE NEWMAN. *Organizational Communication,* New York, McGraw-Hill Book Company, 1975.

SHIDLE, NORMAN G. *The Art of Successful Communication,* New York, McGraw-Hill Book Company, 1965.

SHURTER, ROBERT L. *Effective Letters in Business,* New York, McGraw-Hill Book Company, 1954. [Paperbound edition, 1963.]

——. *Handy Grammar Reference,* New York, McGraw-Hill Book Company, 1959. [Paperbound edition.]

—— and JOHN R. PIERCE. *Critical Thinking,* New York, McGraw-Hill Book Company, 1966.

—— and JAMES M. REID, JR. *A Program for Effective Writing,* New York, Appleton-Century-Crofts, Inc., 1966.

——, J. PETER WILLIAMSON, and WAYNE G. BROEHL, JR. *Business Research and Report Writing,* New York, McGraw-Hill Book Company, 1965.

SIGBAND, NORMAN B. *Communication for Management,* 2d ed., Glenview, Ill., Scott, Foresman and Company, 1976.

TICHY, H. J. *Effective Writing: For Engineers, Managers, and Scientists,* New York, John Wiley & Sons, Inc., 1966.

WALTON, THOMAS F. *Technical Manual Writing and Administration,* New York, McGraw-Hill Book Company, 1968.

WARD, RITCHIE R. *Practical Technical Writing,* New York, Alfred A. Knopf, Inc., 1968.

WEEKS, FRANCIS W. (ed.). *Readings in Communication from Fortune,* New York, Holt, Rinehart and Winston, Inc., 1961.

WEISMAN, HERMAN M. *Basic Technical Writing,* 2d ed., Columbus, Ohio, Charles E. Merrill Books, Inc., 1968.

WELLS, WALTER. *Communications in Business,* 2d ed., Belmont, Calif., Wadsworth Publishing Company, Inc., 1977.

WILCOX, ROGER P. *Communication at Work: Writing and Speaking,* Boston, Houghton Mifflin Company, 1977.

WILLIAMS, CECIL B. and F. GLENN GRIFFIN. *Effective Business Communication,* 3d ed., New York, The Ronald Press Company, 1966.

WILLIAMS, FREDERICK. *Reasoning with Statistics,* New York, Holt, Rinehart and Winston, 1968.

YECK, JOHN D., and JOHN T. MAGUIRE. *Planning and Creating Better Direct Mail,* New York, McGraw-Hill Book Company, 1961.

Finally, anyone who becomes deeply involved with business communication should read the invaluable *Journal* and *Bulletin* of the American Business Communication Association, published four times a year at the University of Illinois, Urbana, Illinois, 61810. Their issues provide one of the best means of keeping up with changing attitudes, methods, and principles in business writing. Similarly, publications and proceedings emerging from the annual institutes on technical and organizational communication at Colorado State University, Fort Collins, Colorado and on technical writing at Rensselaer Polytechnic Institute, Troy, New York constitute valuable sources for staying up to date with the experts in communication.

LISTENING

At one time or another in your life, you have probably accused others of not listening. Whether the nonlisteners were parents, children, teachers, students, bosses, subordinates, coworkers, sales clerks, or service people, the indictment was the same: "They just won't listen to me!" If you can recall an instance where you made such a statement, you can probably also recall that the overall experience was pretty frustrating.

In your business career you will probably encounter similar instances where people won't be predisposed to give you their full attention. Chapter 21 provided you tools for presenting reports orally. By applying these tools conscientiously, you should develop the knack of delivering talks that obtain the attention of even your more resistant listeners.

But what about the times when you'll be assuming the role of listener? In your business career, isn't it likely that you'll be called upon to listen to more talks or oral reports than you'll be called upon to give? And isn't it likely that, from time to time, you'll be tempted to "turn off" a speaker? If you're human, the answer to that last question will have to be "yes."

Since you have just concentrated on the role of speaker in Chapter 21, ask yourself if this tendency is fair to the speaker. Furthermore, ask yourself if giving in to the temptation not to listen is the most constructive approach for an audience member to take. Isn't it likely that the oral report is being delivered with a purpose—a purpose that obviously involves you in some way? Isn't there a distinct possibility that the speaker is distributing information that might be of some value to you?

Having acknowledged the significant probability that you'll have to listen to many oral reports in your business lifetime, and having agreed that it would probably be wiser and would definitely be more courteous to listen than not to listen, let's look at some tips aimed at helping you to become a better listener.

Accept Your Responsibility as a Listener

Psychologists talk of an adjustment mechanism called *projection* whereby a person focuses his or her own weaknesses or feelings upon another. For example, "It's not that I don't like him; it's just that *he* doesn't like me." Or how about this: "I failed that class because the teacher didn't like me" or "because the teacher wasn't fair." One more: "My car broke down because it was cheaply made, not because I failed to take care of it."

You could probably come up with your own examples that you've observed or acted out. The point is that people do sometimes excuse or draw attention from their own guilt or failure to accept partial responsibility for something by dwelling upon the real or supposed faults of others. It's a human condition. Some people do it very seldom. Others seem to be addicted to the tendency to project.

Your first step in becoming a better listener is to accept your responsibility as a listener. You are a member of the audience for a reason. Something is to be gained by your attendance and attention. If you don't gain that something, there's a good chance that you are at least partially responsible. Don't project your complicity in the talk's failure entirely upon the speaker. Consider whether you did or did not play your part.

As a member of the audience, did you really make a serious effort to stay attuned to what the speaker was saying? Did you really try to resist any distractions that presented themselves? Did your posture suggest that you were listening? Were you sitting erect, perhaps tilted slightly forward? Did you nod in agreement when appropriate? Did you look at the speaker during most of the talk?

There's an important fringe benefit to accepting your responsibility as a listener and sending the right nonverbal messages to a speaker. By saying nonverbally that you are interested in what the speaker has to say, you are likely to get a better presentation. Most speakers prefer to talk to people who are interested in the subject. They deliver more enthusiastic talks to this kind of audience. Thus, by listening, you increase the likelihood that you will hear a stimulating presentation.

Critique What Is Said, Not How It Is Said

Related to the adjustment mechanism of projection discussed in the preceding section is the tendency of some people to concentrate upon a speaker's delivery. You'll hear them coming away from presentations saying things like, "Boy, was that guy ever a lousy speaker!" or "Did you hear how many 'uh's' she said?" or "Because he read his speech, I just about went to sleep."

Try to resist the temptation to be so judgmental. Remember instead that you are in the audience for a purpose. This speaker apparently has something to tell you. Concentrate upon what is being said and whether or not it can be useful to you. Remember also that if enough members of the audience do likewise, you might have an indirect influence upon improving the quality of the speaker's delivery.

Try to Keep Your Emotions in Check

Even though you may consider yourself a very calm, rational person, if you are human you'll have to admit to having your emotional side. Deep within your feelings and sensitivities is a little trigger. This trigger can be pulled by situations or messages that spark those feelings and sensitivities.

If a speaker appears to be telling you that you're doing something wrong or thinking incorrectly, or if that speaker appears to be identifying with a concept or group that you don't like, watch out. Your mind has the potential for engaging in many different kinds of activities that could make you an ineffective listener.

Perhaps the least harmful, although still undesirable, mental activity is to turn the turkey off. "After all, how dare that person enter the private domain of one of my most cherished views!" you reason. Thus, you inwardly turn his or her volume down and think about other things, arguing that the speaker can't have anything worthwhile to say after having made *that* statement. Needless to say, you gain little from the rest of the presentation.

A more harmful and even less desirable form of mental activity is the establishment of a contest between you and the speaker. If you resort to this type of activity when a speaker touches one of your sore spots, you almost automatically begin calculating when and how to ask the question that will destroy the speaker's credibility. By dwelling on these calculations, you miss the rest of the speaker's message.

Neither of the preceding reactions is worthwhile primarily because *you lose.* You miss the bulk of what the speaker has to say because of your response to a very small part of what that person said. To become a more effective listener, you need to recognize the extent to which you are inclined to react emotionally to speakers. Then, become determined to change. Count to ten when tempted. Think about what you might miss if you slipped back into your old habits. Give the speaker a second chance.

Listen for Major Themes, Not Just Minor Details

Most of you have probably known of a case where despite dedication and effort, you or another student faired poorly in a course. It may have seemed inexplicable at the time. If it happened to you, you may have lamented that you paid close attention in class, you took notes feverishly, and you studied for the tests. What else could you have done?

If this experience is in fact familiar, ask yourself whether you ever considered the possibility that you weren't listening properly. As was mentioned in Chapter 21, most talks have several major points surrounded by supporting detail. Is it possible that you were so busy getting down the supporting detail that you missed the major points or themes?

This tendency to concentrate on details may be quite natural because the supporting details are usually more concrete and vivid than the major themes. Recognize this tendency and become determined to counteract it. Force yourself to stay alert to the major themes of presentations, and don't give undue emphasis to lesser details.

Usefully Occupy Your Excess Thinking Time

Humans are thought to be capable of thinking at a rate four times faster than they are capable of speaking. What this comparison suggests is that you will have excess thinking time when you are listening to oral presentations. What you choose to do with that excess thinking time can be very important to your goal of being an effective listener.

If you are like many people, you might use that thinking time to entertain thoughts unrelated to the presentation. You might go off on tangents, thinking about the people seated around you or things that are happening in the room. You might even stray further by thinking about problems facing you at home or at work.

The real risk is that one of these little side excursions could turn into an extended mental cruise. When this happens and you eventually wake up to what the speaker is saying, you find that you've lost the trend of thought in the presentation. The big temptation then is to forget the talk and return to your cruise.

One good way of eliminating this obstacle to effective listening is to occupy your excess thinking time usefully. Think about the presentation itself. Every now and then, summarize what the speaker has said. You could also try to second-guess what the speaker is going to say. Another way you could usefully occupy your thinking time is to carefully consider the value of the speaker's supporting details. What sources is he or she using? Are they reliable? Finally, you could devote some time to getting the full meaning of what is being said. Consider the speaker's nonverbal communication. Is he or she sending nonverbal messages that support or contradict the verbal message? Do you sense any meanings being delivered between the lines?

If you occupy your excess thinking time in the ways suggested above, it's unlikely that you'll have time to entertain any major distractions. And you'll find that you get a great deal more from oral presentations when you listen to them in this determined, involved manner.

If you accept your responsibility as a listener, if you try not to be too nit-picky about the speaker's delivery, if you keep your emotions in check, if you concentrate on major themes, and if you occupy your excess thinking time usefully, you'll find that the value of your attendance at oral presentations will improve greatly.

NONVERBAL COMMUNICATION

The study of nonverbal communication has truly blossomed in the last decade. The studies conducted and books written on the subject are multitudinous. In fact, because of the pervasive impact of nonverbal communication upon our daily lives and because of the public appeal of many of the books written on the subject (like Julian Fast's *Body Language*), it would not be stretching the truth to say that the subject has caught the entire nation's attention.

Before proceeding further, however, we might do well to offer a definition of nonverbal communication. For our purposes, we'll regard it as any facet of our behavior or surroundings that might convey to receivers something other than the words we speak. We'll see that these nonverbal messages can be conveyed by room arrangement, space between speaker and listener, various aspects of a person's voice, posture, facial expressions, and body gestures. Furthermore, there is a good chance that occasionally our nonverbal messages will actually contradict our verbal messages. And when such contradictions occur, observers are often prone to believe the nonverbal message rather than the verbal message.

To say that nonverbal communication is significant to our interactions with others is really an understatement. If you've ever visited a discotheque, you know that hints of interest are signaled and those hints acknowledged or rejected without a single word being spoken. On the lighter side, think about your reactions to sales people who smile when helping you, as opposed to those who frown or look bothered by you.

To give even a surface treatment of all the research done and theories proposed on the subject of nonverbal communication would be a monumental task indeed. Rather than attempt such a task and fall short of the mark, we shall concentrate our attention on the implications of nonverbal communication for conducting and attending meetings in business. Although some of those implications were discussed in Chapter 21 and in the preceding section on listening, our scope will be expanded in this section.

Although business people frequently moan about the number and quality of meetings they must attend, the fact remains that meetings and committees are becoming more and more prevalent in business today. Admittedly, the verbal messages delivered at many meetings could be improved. In fact, many of the principles presented throughout this book, if applied, could improve those verbal messages a good deal. But the nonverbal messages also influence whether points are made or missed at meetings, and so they deserve considerable attention also.

Before we discuss specific types of nonverbal communication at meetings, let us recognize that meetings may differ greatly in formality and purpose. Because of these differences, forms of nonverbal communication that are suitable at one meeting may be inappropriate at another. With this situational awareness in mind, let's look at the various types of nonverbal messages that may be sent and received at meetings.

Agenda Preparation, Distribution, and Follow-up

Many business people complain that they don't receive an agenda before the meeting or, if they receive one, it isn't followed. As a result, either they have little idea what the meeting will be about, or they come prepared to discuss subjects that aren't covered. Both of these unfortunate circumstances can cause these people a great deal of frustration.

If you're ever called upon to organize and conduct a meeting, do carefully consider developing an agenda. Only in the most simple, informal circumstances will one not be necessary. If you decide to prepare one, distribute it to those who will attend the meeting at least a day or two before. This will give the impression that you are well organized, with specific, valid purposes in mind.

Whether or not that impression lasts depends upon what happens at the meeting. If you stick fairly closely to the agenda, you will reinforce the impression of orderliness and validity of purpose. If, on the other hand, you allow some of the more vocal people there to steer the discussion off on tangents, your earlier favorable impression will deteriorate.

A good meeting leader has to accept responsibility for guiding members through the discussion of predetermined subjects. This guidance often takes the form of questions aimed at returning people to the right track. Forming and posing these questions in an unthreatening, tactful manner takes a certain skill. Developing that skill may take some practice, but the effort will be worth your while.

When you prepare a good, legitimate agenda and distribute it in advance, and when you closely follow it at the meeting, your reputation will spread. People attending your meetings will be more likely to regard them as necessary and useful activities. If, on the other hand, you don't prepare and follow an agenda, you run the risk of having people regard your meetings with dread and disdain.

Space Preparation

Another aspect of meeting preparation that communicates something about your orderliness is the extent to which you recognize the importance of space. A very basic part of this recognition is providing enough space for the people you expect. Is the room large enough so that all in attendance can be seated comfortably? This requirement may seem so basic as to be undeserving of mention. It is, nonetheless, worthy of special attention because of the seriousness of overlooking it.

People are said to exist in a kind of private bubble, sometimes called their personal space. They, in effect, lay claim to a certain area immediately around them and don't appreciate people encroaching upon this spatial territory. In fact, their displeasure is sometimes as strong as that of Archie Bunker when someone has had the audacity to sit in his chair. At a minimum, the displeasure will manifest itself in a fashion akin to the discomfort that most people experience in crowded elevators.

Because of this phenomenon of personal space and because of people's reactions to encroachments upon their personal space, it is especially important that your meeting room be adequate for the number of people expected. If not, the resultant cramped conditions could jeopardize the atmosphere of cooperation and interest that should prevail.

Another facet of space preparation that you should consider is the arrangement of chairs and tables in the room. It is here that meeting formality and purpose most clearly influence your choices. If the meeting is to be a rather large, formal gathering at which you are to make a report or deliver some kind of news or decision, you would probably arrange the room in a fairly traditional fashion. You would probably stand at a podium before a seated, probably rectangularly arranged audience. This type of arrangement may not encourage feedback or discussion; but if the purpose of the meeting suggests clear, authoritative, one-way communication, it may be justified.

If, on the other hand, your meeting is to be a small, informal gathering at which you hope to generate a good deal of discussion, your arrangement should be different from that of the preceding example. You might consider seating the group at an oval or round table with no apparent head. Nonverbal communication authorities feel that this type of arrangement suggests a more democratic or participative atmosphere and is more likely to generate discussion among the group members.

We might point out here that the significance of nonverbal communication must always be weighed in the context of the verbal communication taking place. For example, the informal room arrangement just discussed would not result in participation if the leader made it clear in some other way that he or she didn't want feedback.

Nonword Vocal Cues

Specialists in nonverbal communication talk of *paralanguage* as the manner in which words are spoken. They suggest that the way you utter words can sometimes be more influential in communicating your attitude than the words themselves. Before we discuss paralanguage, one important point should be made. Whenever we consider our own nonverbal communication or that of others, we should be careful not to overgeneralize. Although nonverbal communication is a subject worthy of study, it is not a science yet. Much more research needs to be done before we can talk of laws or principles of nonverbal communication. What we shall be discussing in the rest of this section, therefore, will be the educated observations and generalizations of people working to develop the discipline of nonverbal communication.

Paralanguage actually takes in a number of different voice characteristics.[1] The general *quality* of your voice is one such characteristic. The pitch, volume, rate, and rhythm at which you speak become associated with you by others. Of special importance here is that a change in one of these qualities signals things to listeners. A higher volume might suggest anger. A faster rate might indicate that you are nervous or impatient.

Vocal *characterizers* are voice factors that often convey rather obvious emotional meaning. Crying, for example, suggests sadness; laughing, the opposite. Sighing might indicate frustration and anxiety. In fact, authorities who have studied cases of executive stress warn that executives who begin to sigh quite frequently may be indicating to anyone who'll listen that the stress is becoming too great to handle.

Another subarea of the field of paralanguage is that of vocal *qualifiers*. These are the momentary variations in pitch and volume we use while speaking. Giving special emphasis or accent to a certain word in a sentence is one example. To illustrate, suppose the board of directors of your company was grappling with a controversial decision. Let's further suppose that at a meeting with your subordinates, you were asked to comment about a rumor suggesting the likelihood of a certain decision by the board. You might answer, "I wouldn't make any guesses." Depending upon how you said that sentence, it could have several meanings. If you put no special accent on any word, it would seem to say that you don't think the board has any special leanings. If you accented the "I," you would appear to say, "*I* wouldn't guess, but *you* may—and perhaps correctly." If you accented the word "guesses," you would suggest that the rumor is probably wrong.

The category of paralanguage that most closely borders on words is called vocal *segregates*. These include the "ah's" and "uh's" and silent pauses in our speech patterns. Speech teachers usually try to get their students to eliminate "ah's" and "uh's" from their public speaking because these sounds suggest nervousness and lack of preparation and can be distracting. Pauses, on the other hand, when strategically placed, can suggest that something very important has just been or is about to be said.

As stated earlier, paralanguage is not an exact science. But evidence does suggest that people do get messages from the manner in which we say what we say. We should, therefore, at least make some effort to make sure that our voices are not conveying a message that contradicts the words we are saying.

[1] G. L. Trager, "Paralanguage: A First Approximation," *Studies in Linguistics,* 13 (1958), pp. 1–12.

Body Language

Since body language was given some attention in Chapter 21, only a few additional points will be made here. These points will relate to the subjects of posture, facial expressions and gestures.

Posture can be an important aspect of our nonverbal communication in a group setting. For example, assuming the posture that prevails in a group might suggest a desire to identify with the group. Leaning toward someone who is speaking is likely to indicate interest in what that person is saying. A rigid posture, depending upon the setting, could suggest dislike for others or could suggest recognition of the higher status of the person being addressed. A slouched position could convey disdain or contempt for the person speaking or the subject being discussed. As mentioned before, this aspect of nonverbal communication (like other aspects) must be examined in the context of the overall communications setting.

Facial expressions can play an extremely important part in determining whether or not you communicate what you want to communicate in a group setting. As stated before, eye contact is important, whether you are speaking or listening. Furthermore, a pleasant, unthreatening facial expression will usually include an occasional smile.

Finally, remember that gestures can help a person to clarify and reinforce what is said and can help command the attention of others. But they can only do so when the speaker's body interacts naturally with what he or she feels and says. Inhibited people may have to work at becoming more expressive with their bodies. Outgoing people, on the other hand, may have to work at not being overactive with their gestures. The ultimate goal is to develop a natural interaction between body and mouth so that the gestures don't distract listeners from what is being said.

WHERE TO FROM HERE?

Doing more reading and becoming a better reader, applying this chapter's guides to effective listening, and becoming more sensitive to the importance of nonverbal communication may not get you your company's presidency overnight. But it should make you a more effective communicator and a more highly valued employee.

Business people continue to lament the fact that their employees can't communicate and productivity is dropping. These two aspects of business life are not just casual acquaintances; they're blood relatives. By giving attention to developing your ability to send and receive clear and complete messages, you can become a more productive member of your organization. The choice is yours. In this age, when mediocrity is becoming a ceiling of performance, if *you* make the right choice and put forth a determined effort, *you* can stand tall.

EXERCISES

1. Pick a book that you will read every day for the next two weeks—either a textbook or one of your own choosing.
   a. Find out what your present reading rate is by following the instructions in Item 1 on page 399.
   b. Spend at least one-half hour a day reading your chosen book. Concentrate on practicing the techniques explained on pages 399–400. Check your reading speed as you did in *a* at least twice a week.
   c. Record your progress on a chart similar to this:

Day	1	2	3	4	5	6	7	8	9	10	11	12	13	14
Time spent.*														
Utilize techniques?†														
Reading rate.‡														

* Refers to how much time you spent practicing reading.
† Yes or no—the truth!
‡ From new material in your book—at least twice a week.

   d. You may want to continue this exercise for another few weeks until the reading techniques become habit.

2. Read two of the articles cited in this chapter. Using the good writing techniques you have learned this semester, prepare a one-page reaction paper for each article. Your paper should not be simply a summary of the article; rather, you should state your opinions about the ideas presented.

3. The adjustment mechanism of projection was discussed in this chapter. For the next three days, be conscious of your use of projection; keep a list of these instances. You may be reluctant or unwilling to admit to some of them; but if you enter into this activity with an open mind, you are taking the first step toward becoming a better listener.

4. Observe for the next three days instances where other people are using projection; compile a list of these examples. What were your reactions when the individuals made these statements?

5. Analyze your role as a listener during a lecture given in one of your classes by answering the following questions. Write the analysis as soon after the lecture as possible so that your impressions are fresh.
   a. (Write this down before the lecture begins.) What is your reason for listening? What do you hope to learn?
   b. Did you accept your responsibility as a listener by making a serious effort to stay attuned, by resisting distractions, and by showing interest nonverbally? Give specific examples of your successes and failures in accepting responsibility.
   c. To what extent did you concentrate upon the speaker's delivery, rather than the content?
   d. Which of your emotions were you conscious of during the lecture? How did you handle them?
   e. What was the major theme of the presentation?
   f. Were you aware of excess thinking time during the lecture? If so, what did you do with that time?

6. Using the format given in Exercise 5, analyze a nonclassroom oral presentation, such as a public lecture, television talk show appearance, or keynote address at a meeting or dinner.

7. **a.** The class as a whole should select several controversial topics on which a majority of the members favor one side.

   b. Each person is to prepare a five-minute oral presentation which favors the unpopular viewpoint. The presentation must be based on at least one article or book as well as the speaker's own thoughts.

   c. The oral presentations can be given to the entire class or to small groups which contain one speaker for each topic.

   d. When you are the speaker, practice what you learned from Chapter 21.

   e. When you are the listener, concentrate on keeping your emotions in check, since the speaker is presenting a viewpoint with which you do not agree. Answer in writing the following questions for each presentation:

   (1) Which of my emotions was I aware of?

   (2) Was I tempted to turn the speaker off? Did I? If not, how did I keep from doing so?

   f. Write one or two clear, concise paragraphs explaining the value of listening to a speaker who threatens your beliefs or presents viewpoints you do not agree with.

8. You work for Information Resources, Inc., a 100-employee firm involved in the development and dissemination of information technology. You are chairperson of a committee of eight coworkers which was formed for the purpose of studying motivational techniques. The committee has divided itself into two-person teams to investigate the following areas: the philosophy of motivation, the psychology of motivation, motivation in specific business organizations, and the need for motivational approaches and programs at Information Resources. Today is Monday; you have called a meeting for next Wednesday at which each team will report its findings. Then, based on the research presented, the committee is to design a motivation plan for the organization. The plan might include small and large group seminars and an ongoing educational program, for example. The committee may be able to design the plan at the Wednesday meeting, or it may need to conduct further research and then meet again to make final plans.

   a. Prepare the agenda you will distribute to each committee member. Create any information you feel is necessary to supplement the information in the preceding paragraph.

   b. When will you distribute the agenda?

   c. What space arrangement do you think would be best for the meeting?

9. Study the paralanguage of one of your professors, giving particular attention to the characteristics discussed in this chapter. Write a one- to two-page report of your findings. You may want to observe the professor over a period of several days to discover any speech patterns.

10. Supplement the material on body language in the chapter by reading at least one article on the subject. The *Reader's Guide* in the library is probably your best source for locating the articles. Use what you have read in the articles and in this chapter to observe the body language of people in the college cafeteria, student union, or a public restaurant. Pay particular attention to posture, facial expressions, and gestures. Write a report explaining where and what you observed, and cite the articles you read.

CASES

The cases in the following section are intended to confront you with actual problems of written communication as they occur in business. They are designed to counteract the erroneous notion that the sole problem in business writing is to produce one letter or one memorandum or one report. In reality, communication in modern business frequently involves a specific situation from which a whole series of related and interrelated memos, letters, and reports flow. These communications often encompass different departments within the company, people outside the company, and messages up, down, and across the organizational pattern. They emerge as the result of conferences, committee meetings, and instructions from supervisors and frequently require the preparation of written material for other people's approval or signature.

Each case begins with a general statement of the situation or problem from which the various communications arise. In some instances, this situation or problem changes as the result of the communications or because of the lapse of time—and this, too, is realistic in view of the dynamic rather than static nature of business communication. *It is important, therefore, that you read through the entire case before writing any of the specific letters, memos, or reports involved.*

Because *people,* as readers, as supervisors, as customers, are the essence of communication, their preferences—even their whims or their prejudices—are of salient importance. For that reason, certain cases include oral statements by key people who make assignments, request information, or state policies. These statements should be read carefully as clues to the purpose of the communication and to the best choice of appeal and organization for the specific memo, report, or letter.

The cases are arranged in order of difficulty and complexity with the simpler ones first. At the discretion of your instructor, several of them can be used as the basis for classroom discussion and for role playing by students. In certain instances, it will be easy to add other examples of communication to the total case; in others, your instructor may want to select certain problems from those which are suggested within the case. The first cases can be carried out by a single student, while the later ones may be assigned to a team of students, depending, of course, upon the judgment of the instructor.

TO LIE OR NOT TO LIE

As personnel director for Lawn Care, Ltd., a large manufacturer of lawn care equipment, you have just read an article in your local newspaper that has you a bit disturbed. The article reviews a speech delivered by James Quarter, head of a large Chicago executive placement agency.

In his speech to a group of personnel directors from the Chicago area, Mr. Quarter contended that job seekers must engage in outright lying if they wish to become employed. Furthermore, he used some rather ridiculous examples of what he viewed as the truth to support his contentions. Here are some excerpts from the article about Mr. Quarter's talk:

"The business lie has become institutionalized. The person who lies is usually rewarded, while the totally honest candidate significantly diminishes his or her chances of being hired," Quarter said.

"Sad but typical, most résumés read like balance sheets—without any liabilities."

Quarter said most employers actually prefer distortions, and he offered these examples of painfully truthful résumés.

—"Graduated with a B average for my three years, placing me second in my class. (However, it should be noted that there were only six students in my class.)"

—"Minnesota Mining and Manufacturing was the beginning of my career. With some regrets I look back on those very successful and pleasant years and wonder why I ever left."

—"Desperately need income! Will work if necessary. I will sit for an interview in good faith with anyone of any sex, race, color, or creed."

—"Goals: I would like to be a meteorologist. Because of either the law or my incompetence, employment should probably be sought in accounting or other fields at present."

"Those people certainly told the truth," Quarter said. "But would you hire them?"

As someone who has worked in personnel for 10 years, you can't accept his views. Furthermore, you feel you have an obligation to express a contrasting view to your community and to its youth. Write a letter to your editor suggesting that honesty is still the best policy to follow when applying for a job.

A COLLEGE SENIOR'S ENGLISH

The senior who won the Albert J. Schlemmer Commencement Award of $500 for "demonstrating outstanding campus citizenship" sent the following letter to Mr. Schlemmer:

Dear Sir,

I want to extend may sincerest thanks for the 1978 Schlimmer Award. As for deserrving it, I am granting to myself the benefit of the doubt; who am I to question.

The award itself came at a time of particular want and will be appreciated a second time in that sense. My only regret is the work of the other fellows which never seems to gain significant recognition, but then they will get their's.

I hope that someday I will be able to thank those responsible in person. In any event

Sincerely,

Peter M. Roberts

Peter M. Roberts

Mr. Schlemmer has sent an angry note with a copy of Roberts' letter to the Development Office, which persuaded him to set up the prize in the first place with the hope that he would eventually make substantial contributions to the university. Here are excerpts from Mr. Schlemmer's letter:

> It seems to me that the one mark of anyone graduating from your college ought to be the ability to speak and write good English. This letter from Roberts is a disgrace. He doesn't know what to say and he doesn't know how to say it. I would like to know how the college can justify letting such a person graduate when he can't spell or write a clear sentence.

Using this situation, you are to write the following:

1. The letter you would write to Mr. Schlemmer if you had won the Schlemmer Award.

2. The letter you would write to answer Mr. Schlemmer's comments on Roberts' letter if you were a member of the staff of the Development Office of the college.

3. After a meeting of the whole staff, the Development Office has decided to use this situation as a way to get Mr. Schlemmer to give an *additional* award next year—The Albert J. Schlemmer Commencement Award of $1,000 for "demonstrated excellence in speaking and writing." Write the letter. (This is not a substitute for question 2.)

AN EXPLANATION OF A STATEMENT OF POLICY

The following policy statement concerning vacations has been posted on every bulletin board in the offices and production facilities of your Company:

> The vacation period shall be from January 1, 1979 to December 31, 1979, and vacations will be granted as follows:
>
> Employees with less than 1 year's service—none
> Employees with more than 1 year's service but less than 5—one week
> Employees with more than 5 years' service but less than 10—two weeks

Employees with more than 10 years' service but less than 15—three weeks
Employees with more than 15 years' service—one month

All 1979 vacations must be completed by December 31, 1979.

The time which is lost by an employee for a period of at least one payroll week during the vacation period due to the exigency of the company needing to reduce its work personnel, or due to bona fide sickness or accident on the company's premises or injury, or due to leave of absence (granted under the customary terms affecting such leaves of absence) may be applied to any vacation time to which such employee is entitled but with the direct stipulation that it must be at the request of said employee.

It is the intent and purpose and implication of the company vacation plan that all individual employees shall receive the benefit of a relief from work, a relaxation from normal rigid scheduling, and an opportunity for a change of environment or normal activities. However, the employee who is required or given the privilege to work in lieu of seizing the opportunities presented by vacations shall be entitled to receive vacation pay in addition to and over and above regular pay, providing that employee has not lost time as described applied to all the vacation time to which that employee is entitled.

The employee shall take vacation time as scheduled by management and in the amount to which he or she is entitled as indicated above, provided the employee has not had time lost as described applied to all vacation time to which he or she is entitled. The employee's wishes as to time off or vacation pay insofar as he or she decides to continue employment rather than to exercise the vacation benefit will be considered, but such scheduling shall, in the final analysis, be based upon and/or decided upon by the operating requirements of the company.

Here are some of the questions that have come in from employees:

"I want to start my two-week vacation on January 1, which is a holiday. Do I get just two weeks or do I get 15 days?"

"This thing says I've got to work on my vacation if you want me to. When am I going to know? I want to plan right now."

"I started work on July 5, 1974 and I want to start my vacation on July 1, 1979. Are you going to tell me I get only one week when, if I wait four days—one of which is a holiday—I'm going to get two weeks?"

"I'm going to work on my new house during my vacation. Is that what the statement means by 'a change of environment'?"

"I took a leave of absence to go to summer school. Does that time get deducted from my length of service?"

"Can I start my vacation the day before Christmas and carry it over into 1979?"

"I'd like to keep on working here during vacation to earn more money. What must I do to be sure I can?"

"I was sick for three months in 1978, but I've been here seven years. How much vacation do I get? Or does that three months wipe out my vacation?"

There has been such confusion about this statement, which was drawn up by a committee representing the management of the company and the company union, that both the union and management recognize the need for clarifying the statement.

Keeping in mind the questions that have been raised, you are now to write out a statement which will (1) answer these questions and (2) meet the need—subscribed to by both management and the union leaders—for "a clear, simple statement which tells employees how much vacation they can have, what it's based on, when they can take it and who makes the decision, and what happens if they want to or have to work during vacation."

Write such a statement.

THE ELUSIVE SUCCESSFUL INSURANCE AGENT

You are a research assistant to Mr. Rigby Hawthorne, Director of Ordinary Agencies for the Western Home Office of the Megalaharlitan Life Insurance Company of America. Your company is plagued by the same problem that faces other life insurance companies—high turnover of agents. Its retention rate has been averaging about 11 percent for agents remaining with the company for over three years.

A consulting firm recently approached Mr. Hawthorne, offering to do a multivariate analysis of personal background factors related to the success or failure of his agents. Although Mr. Hawthorne feels that such a study might have some value, he is leery of spending the money the consulting firm would charge without doing some preliminary research.

He has therefore asked you to do a study on the importance of certain factors to the eventual success or failure of life insurance agents. Typically, the industry has recognized three major influences upon the productivity of such agents: the selection process, training, and supervision. It is the first of these upon which Mr. Hawthorne expects you to concentrate.

He knows that the 26 agency managers in his region have been assigning different degrees of importance to factors like age and education of applicants when they made hiring decisions. What he was interested in determining was whether such factors did or did not seem to have any relevance to the eventual success or failure of agents hired.

The other two areas, training and supervision, are to be held constant in the following ways. All agents in your sample will have been exposed to the same precontract orientation (i.e., training program). To minimize the effect of supervision, the retention rates of the supervisors of your sample agents will be studied. Agents supervised by managers with either extremely high or extremely low retention rates will be eliminated from your study.

Other restrictions placed upon your sample will be as follows: All agents will be male Caucasians who have had no previous experience selling life insurance. Also, all of them will have been contracted under the same financing arrangements. These restrictions are designed to help assure you of as homogeneous a sample as possible.

You and Mr. Hawthorne jointly decide upon the criteria to be used to decide whether an agent is to be considered a success or a failure. A success has remained with the company and has either reached his sales quota for the first two years or been promoted to a supervisory position. A failure has either left the industry or failed to reach his preassigned quota during both of his first two years with the company. Agents who have joined another insurance company and those who reached their quota during only one of their first two years are excluded from the sample.

Through further consultation with Mr. Hawthorne, you and he decide that you'll be able to collect data on the following factors: age, marital status, living quarters, education, life insurance owned, assets, indebtedness, monthly income from last job, employment status, and number of full-time jobs held in the 10 years prior to being hired by Megalaharlitan. The information that you collect would pertain to the agents at the time of their application. Mr. Hawthorne estimates that you will be able to gather data from a sample of 800 to 1200 agents.

1. Write a memo to Mr. Hawthorne accepting what you perceive to be the assignment he has given you.

Now assume that you have gathered data on 932 agents hired by your home office from January 1, 1975, to December 31, 1976. According to the criteria that you and Mr. Hawthorne developed, 168 have proven successful, while 764 have failed. The information you collected is presented below:

		Number hired	Number successful
AGE			
	Under 25	373	47
	25–29	280	38
	30–35	93	36
	36–40	46	17
	41–45	75	15
	over 45	65	15
MARITAL STATUS			
	Single	186	23
	Married	522	109
	Divorced or separated	168	25
	Widowed	56	11
LIVING QUARTERS			
	Rent furnished rooms	93	17
	Rent apartment	205	34
	Rent house	186	28
	Own home (mortgaged)	298	55
	Own home (clear)	103	29
	Other	47	5

	Number hired	Number successful
EDUCATION		
Less than high school graduate	0	0
High school graduate	65	10
Some college	280	45
College graduate	447	96
Graduate training	140	17
LIFE INSURANCE OWNED		
$ 0–10,000	392	59
10,001–20,000	149	27
20,001–30,000	140	22
30,001–40,000	130	27
40,001 & over	121	33
ASSETS (excluding life insurance)		
LESS AMOUNT OWED		
$ 0– 5,000	261	47
5,001–10,000	112	18
10,001–15,000	177	30
15,001–20,000	186	32
20,001 & over	196	41
INDEBTEDNESS		
$ 0– 1,000	252	45
1,001– 5,000	261	55
5,001–10,000	233	40
10,001 & over	186	28
MONTHLY INCOME FROM LAST JOB		
Under $500	140	27
$500–599	186	33
600–699	280	46
700–799	121	21
800 & over	205	41
EMPLOYMENT STATUS		
Student	177	28
Self-employed	56	11
Unemployed	364	51
Employed full time	270	58
Other and part-time job	65	10
NUMBER OF FULL-TIME JOBS HELD		
IN THE 10 YEARS PRIOR TO BEING		
HIRED BY MEGALAHARLITAN		
0	261	39
1	140	25
2	308	69
3	130	22
4 or more	93	13

2. Analyze this information. Then write a report that transmits and interprets the data to Mr. Hawthorne in a clear, complete, concise, coherent, and lively manner.

BY WORD OF WHOSE MOUTH?

You were recently hired to work in the Training and Communications Department of the Second Republican Bank of Arizona. As you understood your orientation procedure, you were to work with the various units of this department over the next few months to familiarize yourself with the workings of each unit. The units include the American Institute of Banking liaison unit, the new employee orientation unit, the communications analysis unit, and the staff of the *Second Republican Letter*. The last unit composed monthly letters to employees, quarterly letters to customers, and semiannual letters to stockholders. At least, that was your understanding of the orientation procedure until this morning.

This morning John Eaton, your department head, called you into his office. He was quite enthusiastic about an article in *Business Week* which he had just read. This article listed the virtues of using TV to compete with the office grapevine. Mr. Eaton was a bitter opponent of the grapevine and "its potential for disseminating damaging, incorrect gossip." He saw this article as someone's brainstorm of a way to completely eliminate the informal communications networks at the home office and branch banks.

Since your bank has used closed-circuit TV in its training program for several years, he pointed out, it would not be very expensive to start broadcasting company news through this medium. He noted the similar cost advantage experienced by Ashland Oil Company, Exxon, Travelers Insurance Company, and American Telephone and Telegraph.

He also had to admit, however, that not all the 10 or 15-minute daily or weekly programs attempted had met with success. Pacific Telephone, Aerojet, and Citibank were among the companies that had dropped their news shows for various reasons.

Mr. Eaton was, nonetheless, interested in pursuing the idea of a company news program for the Second Republican Bank of Arizona. Furthermore, he wanted you to accept this research task as a special assignment.

1. Write two separate letters to the two groups of companies listed above asking about the benefits and drawbacks they experienced in producing in-house newscasts.

Assume that you receive the following comments in response to your letters:

"It allows us to get the corporate image to employees."

"The medium has a special impact not shared by the printed word."

"Since we already had the equipment, the program is very cost-effective. We get to our employees for about a dollar a head."

"The medium is very timely, and it has built-in credibility."

"We can call special attention to national news items that directly affect the company."

Also included in the comments received were warnings of drawbacks:

"We simply ran out of good stores."

"We had major problems finding places to set up monitors, places that were heavily trafficked but wouldn't intrude on employees or customers."

"In a survey our employees ranked it lowest among the company's internal communications media."

"You'll never eliminate the grapevine regardless of what you do."

2. In view of these comments, develop a questionnaire designed to gauge the reactions of a sample of the bank's employees to the idea of in-house newscasts.

3. Considering what you know about your department's equipment and personnel, considering the responses you received to your letters, and assuming a generally favorable or unfavorable response to your questionnaire, write a memo that either supports or rejects the idea of news broadcasts at Second Republican Bank of Arizona.

NATIONAL, REGIONAL, AND LOCAL M.B.A. SUPPLY AND DEMAND

As assistant to the marketing manager of an employment agency in Los Angeles, you have observed the increasing numbers of M.B.A. degree holders in your area, but you haven't seen very many of these graduates registering with your agency. If you could get more of them to do so, you know your company would profit because they are commanding some pretty good salaries.

You personally feel that your firm hasn't made enough of an effort to contact them and communicate with them. Thus, M.B.A.s are not aware that you could be of some real assistance to them in their job-hunting process. Also, there's a good chance that M.B.A.s approaching graduation feel that the demand for them is so high that they can easily get jobs through their career placement offices on campus. Unfortunately for these graduates, these offices aren't always the best contacts with industry. They range in quality from excellent on some campuses to inexcusably unaggressive on others.

You have an idea that might increase your firm's involvement in M.B.A. placement. Each year you could put together a brochure reviewing M.B.A. supply and demand at the national, regional, and local levels. Such a brochure would suggest that you have a grasp of the market these graduates are entering. Then you could mail these brochures to M.B.A. students in the Los Angeles area as a complimentary introduction to the services your agency can provide. Along with the brochure would go a sales letter describing those services in greater detail.

As the firm builds a track record in M.B.A. placement, you can give more attention to your proven performance.

1. Write a memo to your boss selling her on the merits of your ideas.

2. Assume that your boss accepts your ideas as having some merit. Assume also that she would like to see a sample of the brochure (or report) that would be sent to M.B.A. students. From the following information, put together a brochure (in report form) that would grab and hold the attention of its readers.

   a. Comments of an authority addressing the Graduate Management Admissions Council:

   Regular M.B.A. enrollments should hold up well for a few more years, probably rising gradually into the early or mid-1980s. But the bloom is off the rose. Enrollments will be restricted by

   (1) The gradually declining money value of the M.B.A.

   (2) Aside from money, the growing realization that all M.B.A.s cannot become chief executive officers, that they will not climb the managerial ladder as fast as in the past, which may discourage some from pursuing the degree.

   (3) The slower rate of growth in the economy.

   (4) The reduced rate of introduction of new M.B.A. programs.

   (5) Reduced financial support.

   Part-time M.B.A. enrollments will continue to expand for at least another decade *if* the schools offering such programs can improve the quality of the programs with better teachers and better library, computer, audiovisual, etc., facilities, and if they are able to adapt their methods of instruction to the needs of older students who are already employed.

   If schools of business want to maintain and expand their total postbaccalaureate programs, they would do well to gear themselves up for continuing education for the over-30 group. Some of these will be M.B.A. candidates, but many will not.

   b. Findings from a national survey of 200 well-known companies asking them about their hiring practices last year and intentions this year:

Table 1 M.B.A. EMPLOYMENT LAST YEAR AND HIRING EXPECTATIONS THIS YEAR

	Last year		This year	
	No. of companies	No. of graduates	No. of companies	No. of graduates
M.B.A. with technical B.S.	32	279	37	299*
M.B.A. with nontechnical B.S.	64	615	63	643†

* Represents a 7.2% increase.
† Represents a 4.6% increase.

Table 2 AVERAGE STARTING SALARIES FOR M.B.A.s LAST YEAR AND THIS YEAR

	Last year	This year	Increase
M.B.A. with technical B.S.	1,604	1,710	6.6%
M.B.A. with nontechnical B.S.	1,519	1,606	5.7%

c. Figures from a recent *M.B.A. Employment Guide* representing the increase in demand for upper and middle management executives last year over the preceding year, by region:

Northeast	50 percent
Midwest	66 percent
Southeast	38 percent
Southwest	102 percent
West	103 percent
International	22 percent

d. The *AMBA Executive*'s report of executives' satisfaction with the various regions of the country:

Table 3 REGIONAL RATINGS BY EXECUTIVES

	Very good/Excellent	Good	Fair/Poor
West	77%	20%	3%
Mountain	82	16	2
West North Central	65	33	2
East North Central	60	34	6
West South Central	71	25	4
East South Central	45	46	9
Southern Atlantic	58	33	9
Middle Atlantic	54	41	5
New England	69	31	0

e. Results of a survey of last year's M.B.A. hiring practices and this year's hiring intentions of 100 large firms in the L.A. area:

Table 4 M.B.A. EMPLOYMENT LAST YEAR AND HIRING EXPECTATIONS THIS YEAR OF FIRMS IN THE L.A. AREA

	Last year		This year	
	No. of companies	No. of graduates	No. of companies	No. of graduates
M.B.A. with technical B.S.	29	198	37	209*
M.B.A. with nontechnical B.S.	58	463	66	487†

* Represents a 5.6% increase.
† Represents a 5.2% increase.

Table 5 AVERAGE STARTING SALARIES FOR M.B.A.s LAST YEAR AND THIS
YEAR IN THE L.A. AREA

	Last year	This year	Increase
M.B.A. with technical B.S.	1,622	1,731	6.7%
M.B.A. with nontechnical B.S.	1,504	1,598	6.3%

f. Upon contacting several universities in the L.A. area, you find that enrollments in M.B.A. programs this year are up 15 percent over last year.

3. Let's further assume that your boss is impressed by your first draft of the brochure. Now, write the sales letter that would accompany it. You can make up statistics about things like numbers of registrations with your agency, numbers of business and industrial contacts, and percentages of placements.

BUILDING A COMPANY'S IMAGE

You work in the public relations department of a large manufacturing company whose director of engineering, Eric M. Halvorsen, is a very able, very articulate, and very opinionated individual who boasts that he had little formal education. He insists that the only useful function of the public relations department is "to keep my name and the company's name out of the paper when I want it out and to get it on the front page when I want it there."

At a recent Chamber of Commerce panel discussion, Mr. Halvorsen launched into an unexpected attack on today's colleges as being "irrelevant to today's specialized needs and too theoretical." To prove his second point, he cites what he calls "illiterates with B.A.s and graduates with all the letters after their name who can't write a letter."

The following are excerpts from his remarks:

Just to show you how they preach all this theory and then forget it, I've got a collection of letters from our university here. They're nice and dignified—and they belong back in the nineteenth century.

So I went out and talked to the head of the business communication department and I asked him if he knew how to save money on letters and reports. He did—he knew all about simplified letters; he knew about enclosing what we call a "courtesy carbon" so the reader can just write his answer on the carbon of our letter and send it back to us; he knew about using window envelopes and cutting out all the guff about "Dear Mrs. Smith" and "Yours truly"—but *not one letter from that university reflected what he knew.*

And so, gentlemen, I say to you that if our universities really know about management techniques, about political techniques, and especially about communication techniques, it's time they put their own house in order by using what they know!

That night's paper carries a headline:

LOCAL EXEC FIRES AT COLLEGE HYPOCRISY

Halvorsen is furious both at the headline and because public relations didn't "keep it out of the paper." Professor Wilcox, head of the business communication department at the university, says in an interview that "I was never asked for any advice about the letters and reports that go out from the university." Your boss, John Minshall, head of public relations, says, "This is real trouble. We've got to salvage whatever we possibly can because no modern business can go around attacking education."

From this situation, you are to write any of the following:

1. A statement that supports the viewpoint expressed by Eric M. Halvorsen.

2. A memo which includes a specific set of recommendations to the university concerning its techniques and methods of written communication based on the premise that "they should use what they know."

3. A letter defending the university's conservative attitude toward its own communications.

4. A statement which will fit in with Minshall's attempt to "salvage what we can." (This will involve "translating" Mr. Halvorsen's statement and viewpoint into less blunt language.)

5. A brief report that might be sent to the university concerning its practice in communication with the purpose of "making it as modern as today."

6. A memorandum to Mr. Halvorsen from the public relations department recommending "certain ways in which he can be helpful in projecting the best image for the company in the future."

THE BUSINESS READERS' SERVICE

Two months before your graduation, Professor Howard C. Neal, head of the business administration department of your college, has informed you that there is a position open at Bluestone, Knox, and White, a well-known firm of management consultants who specialize in services to small business. They want a young graduate who knows various forms of business communication, especially reports and letters; who can write well; and who has ambition and imagination.

1. Write an application letter for this position

As a result of your letter, you are interviewed by Mr. Warren Bluestone, president of the company. When he finally decides to employ you, he says: "Your advancement will depend on how many ideas you can come up with. The field of management consulting is very competitive, and Bluestone, Knox, and White have to stay ahead of the pack. We want you to have ideas about how we can do things better and we want you to be able to sell those ideas to us in writing. The report is the backbone of our business, and we judge our employees on their ability to sell us and to convince us in their reports."

Your first assignment is in the research department, where a librarian, seven other research workers, and four typists work at assembling business statistics, analyzing business trends, and digesting books and articles of interest to key employees of Bluestone, Knox, and White. The library contains a complete collection of books and magazines on business subjects. The annual budget for staff, books, and magazines is $93,500, and the librarian has told you that the three partners in the firm have been looking for some method of reducing the cost of this operation.

One day an idea strikes you—if this work of digesting books and articles, compiling abstracts and bibliographies is useful at Bluestone, Knox, and White, why wouldn't it be helpful to the small businesses who are clients? The firm could get out a 12-page newsletter every month calling their attention to things they ought to read. That way the costs of operating the department could be covered by putting it on a paying basis. In your mind you go over the other reasons for venturing on this project: you've just seen a report showing that the average businessperson reads about three and one-half hours a day and still can't keep up with all the available material; the small businessperson usually can't afford to maintain a library or research staff to provide information; the library contains a list of 12,500 companies that could potentially be interested in the other management services of Bluestone, Knox, and White; most of the work necessary for such a newsletter is already being done, and therefore little additional staff will be needed.

You go to Mr. Bluestone with your idea. He is somewhat skeptical but admits that your plan has some possibilities. "We could charge $100 a year for such a service, and if we got 1,000 subscribers, it would carry the costs of the research department. But you'll have to convince Mr. Knox and Mr. White and me—as partners we make all policy decisions. I'm interested in cutting costs; Mr. Knox likes anything that gets our name out before people—he might like this as a method of getting new clients for our other services; Mr. White wants as much diversification in our services as we can get. You think this thing through and then give us a complete report on why Bluestone, Knox, and White should go into it. Or maybe you'd better emphasize what will appeal to each of us in a separate report prepared differently for each partner. I'll leave that to you; you're supposed to know about written communication."

2. Write one report to go to all three partners or three reports angled to the individual interests of each partner. Choose the method you think will be more effective in this situation.

A week later, Mr. Bluestone informs you that your proposal has been tentatively approved. The three partners have agreed that the service must sell for $100, but that an offer can be made to those who subscribe and apply for the service in advance to obtain it for $75; others will be billed for $100 at the end of a three months' trial period. Mr. Bluestone tells you: "Mr. Knox and Mr. White are greatly concerned about the way we sell this service. We've been in business for 21 years, our reputation is excellent, and we want to maintain it. Both my partners and I want you to prepare a sales letter, for our approval, which will be dignified and yet get results."

3. Prepare a sales letter for the partners' approval, assuming that it will go eventually to the 12,500 companies on the list of those who may be potentially interested.

Assume, now, that the project has complete approval and the first issue of *Business Readers' Service* will appear in three months. Two problems immediately arise. The librarian, who, of course, will be in charge of all printed and source materials, has expressed some fear that certain books and magazines may not now be in the library of Bluestone, Knox, and White. "We ought to send out a letter of inquiry asking publishers about their important books in the field of business and making sure that we get all their announcements of new books in the future. I think they ought to see that it is to every publisher's advantage to have publications represented in our service, since we intend to list the publisher's name and the price of the publication with every item we mention."

4. Write such a letter of inquiry to go to publishers.

The other problem concerns human relations within the company. Rumors of this project hang heavy on the office grapevine; strong feelings have been expressed that this new service is outside the scope of the normal professional activities of management consultants, that the firm will lose professional standing, that "we are going into the publishing business."

5. Prepare a memorandum for the 16 department heads to use as a basis for discussions with the members of their departments. Explain in the most tactful way you can why the decision has been made and why it will enhance rather than diminish the prestige of Bluestone, Knox, and White.

Business Readers' Service has now sent out its first three issues to 1,107 subscribers—803 of whom paid $75 in advance, the other 304 to be billed for $100 at the end of three months. Since you need every subscriber you can get, Mr. Bluestone has authorized you to send out a letter which will offer to send the next 12 issues of your service to these 304 for $100; in effect, you are, therefore, giving them the first three issues if they pay the $100 fee for the next 12 issues within three weeks.

6. Write a combination collection-and-sales letter to be sent to the 304 companies which have already received the first three issues.

In the fourth issue, just when you want most to impress readers with your service, through a mistake at the printer's in assembling pages, approximately

400 copies go to subscribers with the same four pages of copy repeated three times. These readers are, therefore, short eight pages that they should have received. Since you don't know which subscribers have received the garbled copies, except for 34 who have written in to complain, you have to reissue the material to all 1,107 subscribers.

   7. Write a claim letter to Mr. Morgan C. Newell, The Blank Printing Company, explaining this situation and insisting that he bear the expense of reissuing and mailing complete copies to all your subscribers.

   8. Write a letter of explanation to the 34 subscribers who have written in to register a complaint.

   In the twelfth issue of *Business Readers' Service* you are to include a questionnaire which has two purposes: first, to get reactions from subscribers as to the general usefulness of the service, what they would like included (such as, more complete synopses of books and articles; coverage of specialized areas like accounting, finance, and sales; or carefully selected short lists of the most important books and articles); second, to get statements from subscribers which you can use as testimonials for a sales letter you expect to send out to get new subscribers.

   9. Prepare this questionnaire.

   The readers' response to the questionnaire shows that they have found *Business Readers' Service* very useful. Among the suggestions they have made for changes are the following:

   Pay more attention to articles in the better-known and easily accessible magazines. Our company library does not contain a number of the highly specialized magazines you refer to, so this aspect of *Business Readers' Service* is useless to us.

   We wish that you would select *one* important article or book each month and really highlight it. Continue the lists of magazines and books, but add this useful feature.

   We'd prefer that you pay more attention to general articles and books on the skills and techniques of management. Some of the specialized articles on accounting, operations analysis, and automation don't fit our needs.

Among the statements from subscribers that you can use as testimonials are the following:

   Your service has been invaluable because we have used it as a guide in building up a small collection of carefully selected books and magazines. It has paid for itself many times over.

                          C. V. Smith, President
                          The Standard Company

One article mentioned in *Business Readers' Service*, which we wouldn't have known about under ordinary circumstances, enabled us to save $1,200 on a phase of our operations. You can imagine that we feel we made a good investment when we subscribed.

> E. J. Baird, Vice-President
> Baird and Jones, Inc.

You've helped me immeasurably. For the first time I feel that I can keep up with developments in our field. I no longer waste time reading a lot of material that is irrelevant, and I can concentrate on the most significant published materials.

> N. M. Wilson, Superintendent
> White and Company

Assume that *Business Readers' Service* will, in its forthcoming issues, incorporate the suggestions made by the readers and that you can use the statements from Mr. Smith, Mr. Baird, and Mr. Wilson.

10. Write a sales letter to go to potential new subscribers for the service at $100 a year.

PROBLEMS IN THE COMMUNICATIONS AND EDUCATION SECTION

You have just been employed by the personnel department of the New Utility Company and have been assigned to the section called C & E, meaning Communications and Education. The functions of this section, as indicated by the title, are (1) to edit the company's magazine; (2) to run the in-service training programs in what is called the Employees Educational Program, conducted by the company in its own classroom facilities and taught partly by company employees and partly by teachers brought in from outside; and (3) to arrange for company employees to take courses at two local universities, where the company will pay 50 percent of the tuition "provided the education or training can be shown to be directly related to the job the employee is doing within the company."

Ms. Fewsmith, head of the whole personnel department, has talked to you on your first day on the job and told you, "We've been having some problems in the C & E Section, and I hope you'll be able to help us out since you're close to your own education. Mr. Washington, the section head, is going to retire in a few months, and he's lost interest in planning next September's educational program. So I'm going to ask you to do some things in which you report directly to me. But there's one thing you have to remember—in the New Utility Company, the C & E section is by definition a service function. That means that we supply the in-service courses or the communication services which are needed, but we don't initiate them. We serve the needs of the various department heads and executives—so, for example, if Mr. Casey as head of the accounting group thinks his people need a course in programming a computer, or writing accounting reports, it's our job to get the best teacher available and to take over all the mechanics of getting the course set up the way Mr. Casey wants it. If it doesn't work out the way Casey expected it to, we hear from him—and fast."

At this point Ms. Fewsmith starts thumbing through a number of reports and memos on her desk. "Well, we might as well get started," she says. "Now I understand that you don't know the forms and methods we use yet, and I can't expect you to. But if you can just put something down in writing about each of these—and I'll tell you who to talk to about them and you can say I told you to get the information—it'll give me a good idea of where we can use you best, and you'll get a good chance to get your feet wet on some of our problems. Now I'll go through each of these memos or letters with you, and you make notes on it about what's to be done when I hand it to you."

Here are brief summaries of the messages, plus the background Ms. Fewsmith provides you with, plus what you have found out by your own subsequent investigation and what Ms. Fewsmith wants you to do. For convenience they are divided into (a) the message to be answered, (b) the background provided by Ms. Fewsmith or by your own investigation, and (c) the assignment given you by Ms. Fewsmith.

1. **a.** A letter from Mr. J. S. True of the accounting department complaining that the New Utility Company pays only 50 percent of employees' tuition at the University, whereas four other local companies pay 100 percent.

   b. "He's wrong. Two of them pay 100 percent, the other two pay 100 percent if the employee gets a grade of A—otherwise it's 50 percent. The theory of our educational committee is that employee education is more meaningful if the employee puts a little stake in it. But the committee would change policy if they saw good reason to do so because they've talked it over several times.

   c. *Write* for Ms. Fewsmith a draft of the message she might send to Mr. True.
      Write what Ms. Fewsmith has described as "a clear-cut presentation for the educational committee stating all the pros and cons of this tuition plan." (Last year 57 employees were enrolled in approved courses at various universities at a cost of $8,500 to the company and an equal amount to the employees.)

2. **a.** Mrs. Tillie Jones, with 18 years of service on the maintenance staff, writes, "I feel that if you would let me take a course in eurhythmic dancing I would be in better condition to perform my duties on the maintenance staff, and I am hereby requesting you pay half my tuition for a year, which will cost the company $150."

   b. "We have to be awfully careful here. Tillie's a good worker, but she sulks and tells her problems to everybody in the place. Besides, if we don't stick to our policy of insisting the course be directly related to the job, we'll have everybody in the place taking all kinds of stuff from basket weaving to stamp collecting. But treat Tillie very carefully."

c. *Write* the response to Tillie.

Write to the educational committee telling why you think the policy of job-related courses should be modified and state in specific language the new policy. (You have found that there is some resentment among a number of employees that the policy has been so rigidly enforced.)

3. a. Five members of the in-service course in economic theory complain, "This is nothing but company propaganda saying the services and charges of the company are always right. Why don't they bring in a labor leader, a Communist, and a member of a regulating committee to give different viewpoints so we can hear all sides?"

b. Ms. Fewsmith groaned when she read this one to you. "We've got a president and several directors who already think we shouldn't be in the education business when our job and our revenue involve providing cheap power. I can imagine what they'd say if they read this request. I'd rather keep what we have as an educational program than run the risk of having the whole thing canceled. Maybe we ought to cancel the economic theory course—it's been a headache every time we offer it." She pauses for a moment. "Incidentally, why does a young person like you think we *should* offer our own in-service educational program—or do you think we shouldn't?"

c. *Write* an answer to the five members of the course in economic theory.

Write a formal statement presenting your answer to Ms. Fewsmith's last question, and do it in such a way that she can transmit it to the educational committee without any change.

4. a. The company magazine committed a horrible blunder in announcing as winners of the company bowling league championship the team of the auditing department rather than the customers' service department, and displaying a picture of the auditing department's team on the front page of last month's issue. "Sometimes I think we should give up this bowling competition. You have no idea of how seriously they take it. We've had about thirty phone calls and notes complaining about that wrong picture."

b. You find that the editor of *The Utilitarian* left the front page to the photographer, thinking that he knew which department won the bowling championship, and then an assistant, seeing the cover layout, wrote a long complimentary article congratulating the auditing department.

c. *Write* down the steps you would take to correct this error. (The next issue of *The Utilitarian* appears in three weeks.)

Write recommendations to Ms. Fewsmith to set up a procedure to minimize the possibility of such errors in the future.

Write what you think *The Utilitarian* should carry concerning this situation in the next issue.

5. a. Twenty members of the advertising department have signed a request for a course in creative writing to be included in the Employee Educational Program's offerings in September and sent the request directly to Ms. Fewsmith without any approval by John Stark, the department head.

b. "I know why," Fewsmith tells you. "Stark won't sign if they ask him to. He thinks they're all going to write novels and short stories on company time. This puts me right in the middle because I won't authorize anything without department-head approval. On the other hand, when we've had that many requests for a course in the past, we've always given it."

c. *Write* out a statement which Ms. Fewsmith can transmit to Mr. Stark, explaining why you think the request for such a course should be rejected (or granted).

On the assumption that the request was rejected by Stark, *write* a memo which will be sent to the 20 members of the advertising department announcing the reasons for the decision.

6. a. Six employees who were urged by their department heads to take a course in business law at the university have, at Ms. Fewsmith's request, submitted an appraisal of the course so that she will have information to give to other department heads for the coming year's offerings. The gist of the six employees' comments is: "It was a waste of my evenings"; "For the most part it was unstructured and disorganized"; "Even though I paid only half my tuition, I wasted my money"; "I should have stayed home and read a good textbook—I would have learned a lot more."

b. The reason underlying these comments is that although business law, taught by Professor Jack Kirksteen, is one of the best courses in the university, during the past year Professor Kirksteen has been doing a great deal of consulting—occasionally for the New Utility Company—and a lot of speechmaking, so that the course was for the most part handled by Kirksteen's graduate students.

"We have to tread lightly in dealing with this one," Fewsmith says. "Our president's on the university's board of trustees, and we've made generous contributions to support their educational program every year. But if Jack Kirksteen isn't going to teach a course, the catalog should say so. Instead, he's listed as teaching this course, and that's why the department heads urged our employees to take it.

"Actually what the university needs is one official who can serve as the liaison with business and industry. Every time I have any dealings with them, I get shunted from one provost or academic vice-president or dean or director of this-or-that to another, until I decide it's useless. They could use the help of our specialists in management organization for a few weeks."

c. *Write* any of the following on the assumption that you graduated from the university and know its organization and personnel reasonably well:

(1) A memo to the six employees who took the course in business law. Ms. Fewsmith hopes to send six more employees to take the course next year, if it is taught by Professor Kirksteen.

(2) A letter to Professor Kirksteen, whom you know, to get his assurance that he will actually teach the course next year.

(3) A letter to be signed by Ms. Fewsmith suggesting to the provost in charge of education that the university should appoint one person to deal with the educational problems of business and industry.

(4) A report which Ms. Fewsmith can transmit to the president of your company urging that the university and industry would mutually benefit if the university were to use qualified people from business to advise on problems of organization and to teach some of the courses dealing with management problems.

(5) A response in writing to this note from Ms. Fewsmith: "The president is very much annoyed by the attached editorial from *The Record,* the students' daily newspaper. Give me your best thinking as to how this company should respond to it so that our goal of establishing a partnership between the university and the business community is clearly stated."

The following excerpts are typical of the editorial:

This University's problems are compounded by a kind of false notion that we must serve business and industry, we must do research for the industrial-military complex, and we must forget teaching in favor of consulting, publishing-or-perishing, and being all things to all agencies in society.

Let us now—this minute—start a policy by which every administrator, every faculty member puts first things first. And that means that every one in the administration and on the faculty will right now decide that the first obligation is to the students enrolled here and that he or she will give up every other obligation (however lucrative) in favor of that primary obligation.

This means no courses for business people at night, it means no research for government agencies, it means that every resource of everyone in this community will be directed toward teaching the full-time students who spend their time and money to benefit from great teaching, which they don't get now.

REFERENCE SECTION

WRITING CORRECTLY

PARTS OF SPEECH

THE SENTENCE

PUNCTUATION

MECHANICS

LETTER FORM AND MECHANICS

As the reader is well aware, there is an endless debate between those who are permissive about language usage and those who are restrictive or conservative about rules and "what is correct." On the following pages we attempt to present sensible answers to the specific usage problems encountered by writers in business. The rules are given as a refresher for those who want to brush up on principles or as a reference section for business writers to consult for guidance on specific problems.

In using these principles, students should remember certain specific conditions that affect business writing. In the first place, the force of tradition is strong in the communications of business. In the second place, much business writing reflects not only the writer but the company or organization for which he or she works. In the third place, probably no other type of writing so directly forms the basis of judgment about the writer's future career—promotion, transfer to new assignments, assignment of new responsibilities. For these reasons, most business writers realistically decide to "play it safe" with a conservative approach to linguistic innovation and a healthy respect for generally accepted standards and rules.

It is worth noting, for example, that a great corporation, the General Electric Company, issued thousands of copies of a pamphlet called "Why Study English." This pamphlet, designed to stress the importance of writing correctly and effectively, says, among other things: "Every day in your future you will be called upon to speak and write, and when you open your mouth, or write a letter or report, you will be advertising your progress and your potential worth."

Errors in grammar and spelling call attention to themselves and thus distract the reader's mind from the message. And in that moment of distraction, the reader will probably make this harsh comment about the writer, "He or she doesn't know any better."

As a minimum standard for business writing, we can certainly expect correctness in grammar, spelling, and punctuation. Although errors in grammar do not always result in a lack of clarity—for example, so far as clearness is concerned, it makes no difference whether a writer says, "It don't matter to us" or "It doesn't matter to us"—students should remember that the grammatical rules of our language generally incorporate the most logical means of expression. Grammar involves not an artificial and arbitrary set of rules but a logical system of expressing our thoughts clearly and exactly. We should follow these rules not—as so many students seem to think—because they are the annoying whims of English teachers, but because good grammar is the easiest, most logical form of construction and because certain usages have become conventional. To the writer in business, a knowledge of correct English usage is a basic and minimum skill. Not only do grammatical errors distract the reader, but ignorance of correct usage interferes constantly with the task of writing. For if the writer has to stop continually to think about whether the verb should be singular or plural or whether pronouns should be subjective or objective case, he or she cannot concentrate full attention on the message. Effective writers have learned to use correct language in the same way that good drivers instinctively use the mechanical equipment of their cars without stopping to decide whether they should step on the accelerator or the brake.

In using these principles, students should remember that many of them incorporate logical relationships, and many reflect mere custom or tradition. The danger in printing such rules is a real one because they appear so final, so dogmatic, whereas serious students of the language now think that there are several levels of usage, or "cultural levels" of language, appropriate to different uses or functions. Since most business writing tends to be semipermanent and somewhat formal, these principles incorporate the rules of language suitable to these functions and the cultural level of the educated or professional person, characterized by precision, good taste, and logic. For such people, certain conventions are important, particularly when they write; these conventions are the essence of the following pages. They are not final and absolute dogma, and many good writers have violated them when the occasion demanded it; but to be realistic, we should also add that the demands of such occasions on young writers in business will be rare.

WRITING CORRECTLY

Attitudes toward correctness in writing run the gamut. At one extreme is the famous comment of Will Rogers: "A lot of people who don't say 'ain't,' ain't eating." At the other are the well-known advertisements with a gentleman pointing an ominous finger and asking: "Do *you* make these mistakes in English— mistakes which can be ruinous to your career?" Between these two extremes we can probably find agreement that correctness is important to business writers if it is not extended to the slavish worship of rules that marks the pedant.

Nonetheless, one has to face up to the fact that the past five or ten years have brought a more profound change in American manners, morals, and methods than any previous era—and certainly our standards of expression have been greatly affected by this rapid evolution. We could quote the ominous words of Ralph Waldo Emerson ("The corruption of man is followed by the corruption of language") to draw some pessimistic conclusions about what has been termed the breakdown of linguistic standards. There are those who believe sincerely that we approach linguistic anarchy if we proceed any farther down the road of denying that there are "right" and "wrong" ways of speaking and writing.

At the other extreme are those— and they have a great deal of scholarly support from linguists and lexicographers—who insist that correctness rests on usage and that today's linguistic innovations will be tomorrow's accepted standards, endorsed in textbooks and recorded in dictionaries. Unquestionably, much merit rests with the argument that language usage is a dynamic, changing pattern, that flexibility and vigor will be lost if rules become inflexible and restrictive.

The key to this debate rests with the word "usage"—but usage *by whom?* By advertisers with "Me and my Winston, we got a real good thing"? By activists with the four-letter words of the so-called "free speech movement"? By the purist at the switchboard haughtily inquiring, "To whom did you wish to speak?" By the *New York Times,* or the hastily mimeographed underground newspaper? Here we get into the most difficult of human value judgments—*good taste,* a term which is practically undefinable and which, says the Latin adage, "there can be no disputing about."

Fortunately, the answer to these questions of usage and taste is relatively clear for writers in business. Except for those employed in advertising, most skilled business writers adopt a wait-and-see attitude toward rapid linguistic change. Their viewpoint seems to reflect a conviction that fundamental changes in linguistic etiquette benefit from evolution rather than revolution. Since their writing almost invariably represents a company or partnership or corporation, they tend for the most part to be conservative about infractions of "rules" and to make haste quite slowly toward more permissiveness.

One of the curious characteristics of discussions of "good English" and "correct grammar" in business is that such discussions provoke the strongest opinions and emotions from those who, as students, considered grammar "the driest subject I ever studied." It would be helpful if we could argue from a premise that correctness is always a method of achieving clarity—but this is not always true. "I ain't got my pay yet" is perfectly clear, but you wouldn't try using it in a letter or report as an effective representative of your company's writing. On the other hand, the incorrect "After eating lunch, the bus went its way" is a logical absurdity. There are two good reasons for avoiding incorrect writing: first, it annoys readers who recognize such mistakes, and, second, it presents a poor impression of the company or firm for which you write. For these two reasons, no one planning a career in business should accept sloppy or substandard English, or accept excuses for his or her own or others' deficiencies in the use of English. Instead, such people should subscribe to the viewpoint expressed in this reference section: *Certain standards of usage are generally accepted by the business community in letters, reports, and memos, and competent writers follow these standards.*

The danger here is that in emphasizing standards we become too *prescriptive,* the opposite of the "permissive" attitude toward usage. You can go too far in following rules. This is the mark of the purist, the office pest. He or she insists on observing rules that are becoming obsolete. Rules follow usage by what used to be called "cultivated people," not the other way around. About six hundred years ago Geoffrey Chaucer quite properly used triple negatives, as in "There was never no man nowhere so virtuous," but subsequent changes in usage have made this form of expression obsolete and ungrammatical. What you should aim at is the standard of best usage in business writing *today.* That usage is being affected enormously by increased casualness and informality, by the diminishing gap between our oral and written expression, and above all else by the impact of mass media, particularly television. Yesterday's bad grammar may be today's most widely used phrase and tomorrow's archaic or obsolete form in the long perspective of linguistic change. As you read the rest of this section, therefore, you should temper the heavy boldface print of the rules with the wisdom of these five concepts, which have the endorsement of the National Council of Teachers of English:

1. Language changes constantly.

2. Change is normal.

3. Spoken language is *the* language.

4. Correctness rests on usage.

5. All usage is relative.

The best policy is to try to stay up to date with regard to current usage, and you can begin to do so by forgetting two "rules" that for some reason seem to be stamped indelibly in the mind of almost everyone who has taken courses in English. The first is that you should try *to never split* an infinitive. The second is nicely stated in the following bit of verse:

The grammar has a rule absurd
Which I would call an outworn myth:
A preposition is a word
You mustn't end a sentence with!

These "rules" have a purpose: to avoid the lack of emphasis of a sentence ending on a minor note, such as a preposition; and to avoid the awkwardness of putting unnecessary words between *to* and the verb form of the infinitive. But there are times when you'll find it less awkward to end with prepositions and to split infinitives. Said Sir Winston Churchill in an ironic comment on this overprissiness, "This is arrant pedantry up with which I will not put." The late Carl Van Doren, a great teacher and writer, used to tell a story to end all stories about prepositions. A father was asked by his small boy, who was sick in bed upstairs, to read from the boy's favorite book. He selected the wrong book and was greeted by, "What didya bring that book I don't want to be read to out of up for?" You'll have to try very hard to achieve such awkwardness, but try to avoid splitting the infinitive in the following sentence without changing the meaning:

He will try to more than justify the cost of an assistant.

("Try to justify more than the cost" and "try more than to justify the cost" do not convey the meaning of the statement. *More than* must be located so that it clearly refers to *justify*.)

Where split infinitives and concluding prepositions are less awkward, use them; where they can be avoided without unnaturally warping the word order of the sentence, avoid them. There are far more important things to remember in achieving correct English than these minor points, which have somehow attained a significance far beyond their worth.

The rest of this section attempts to do three things to help you meet the generally accepted standards of correctness in business writing:

1. *It states 10 principles which will help you to avoid the most frequent and most important errors in business writing.* This will give you a starting point, just as when you begin collecting classical records it is helpful to have a list of "the 10 classical records every music library must have." You may later decide you don't agree with the selection; they may not agree with your standards or with what you consider to be the standards of the business community. But, together with the topics discussed in Chapters 2 and 3, they will get you started.

2. *It attempts to reduce grammatical terminology to a minimum or to translate it, wherever possible, into other terms.* Nonetheless, a certain amount of grammatical shop talk cannot be avoided.

3. *It gives you an opportunity to test your knowledge of correct usage.* On pages 461 to 466 you will find 100 sentences taken from business letters, reports, and memos. If you think this part is not for you, skip over to the test. If you can correct the errors and explain the principles, that is, the reasons the examples are incorrect, in 85 of them, your skepticism is justified, and you need not start in again right here.

Later in this reference section you will find a more conventional and comprehensive statement of rules, including those given here. It serves three purposes: an instructor may want to refer you to them when you write in college; or, more important, you may want to keep them for reference when you are writing, either in college or in your business career; and, finally, it relieves your author of having to say, "Consult a good handbook of grammar or composition for details." You will be urged frequently to consult a good dictionary, you have already encountered a list of recommended readings on the subject of word choice, and you will find enough grammatical principles in the reference section to solve most of your problems in business writing. You are especially encouraged to read the sections on punctuation and on letter form and mechanics, which have not been discussed previously.

TEN MAJOR PRINCIPLES

Subjects and Verbs

Since you express yourself in sentences, and since you can't write a sentence without a *subject* and a *verb,* these words are a good place to begin. If you're an adult, you don't say "we is," "he are," or "you wasn't," although you may be guilty of "it don't," which means *it do not*. The rule—and it's a hard and fast one—states that *verbs must agree with their subjects in number* ("singular," meaning *one*; or "plural," meaning *more than one*) and *person* ("first person," *I, we*; "second person," *you*; or "third person," *he, she, it, they*).

The rule is simple. The difficulties arise when you are not sure whether the subject of a verb is plural or singular, or when you aren't sure even what the subject is. Principles 1 through 4 following are designed to help you in these situations.

Principle 1   Words intervening between subject and verb do not affect the number of the verb.

Correct examples:

The manufacturing *processes,* which are under the direct control of the vice-president in charge of production at the head office, *are* extremely complex.

Particularly when you're dictating, you'll have a natural tendency to forget just what the subject of your sentence was and to think of intervening words—here, *control, production,* and *head office*—as affecting the number of the verb. They don't; and you should follow the same advice in handling this construction as the counsel given to speakers: *Keep your mind on the subject.*

Improvements in the annealing and cleaning process *were* a basic factor in this increased efficiency.

Here the subject, *improvements,* is plural and the intervening words are singular; the businessperson who originally wrote it succumbed to a tendency to let the last words affect the verb and used *was*.

Principle 2   Words linked to the subject by expressions such as *together with, as well as, along with, including, and not,* and *in addition to* do not affect the number of the verb.

This, too, is an easy trap for dictators to fall into because of the tendency to lose sight of the subject.

Correct examples:

The office *manager,* as well as her two assistants and the three supervisors, *writes* concise reports.

This *example,* together with the ones cited in our last three reports, *shows* how important it is to correct this situation.

The *vice-president,* and not his reporting department head, *was* charged with this responsibility in the Procedures Manual.

The *statement* of policy, in addition to its general provisions, clauses, and applications, *is* wordy.

Principle 3   When the subject is any of the following words or is limited (modified) by them—*each, everybody, anybody, nobody, every, a person,* and *either*—the verb must be singular. When the subject is *neither* or *none,* the verb is almost always singular.

Correct examples:

Each of these men *has* instituted several changes during the last month.

Everybody in this office *is* permitted to take a 15-minute coffee break at 10 o'clock.

Neither of us *wants* that to happen.

Current usage is recognizing plural verbs after *neither,* and you will find constructions using *neither* to link plural nouns. In the latter case, a plural verb is demanded:

Neither the men nor their wives *want* to stay.

A plural verb after *none* is well accepted in constructions such as this:

None of our employees *are* so incompetent as the people in her department.

You might note, incidentally, that the indefinite *it* always takes a singular verb:

It is the workers who join unions.

Principle 4   When the subject is a collective noun, a word which by its meaning collects a lot of people or things—such as *committee, staff, company, crowd,* and *group*—the meaning you wish to convey should determine whether the subject is singular or plural.

When you are thinking of the parts, units, or individuals comprised in the collective, make your verb plural; when you are thinking of the collective as a whole, make your verb singular. You will use the singular more frequently, as:

The *group was* interested in investing in new plant facilities.

The *staff is* holding a monthly meeting to discuss sales forecasts.

Occasionally, you will want to emphasize the individuals, as in:

The executive *staff are* listed on page 42 of the annual report.

The *committee were* evenly divided in supporting the two policies.

Verbs

The verb is a remarkably versatile part of speech: It describes action or situation, tells time (by its *tense*), and provides a general background of assumptions (by its *mood*). It can describe reality (in the *indicative mood*), give commands (in the *imperative*), or express certain assumptions or statements that are not true (in the *subjunctive*). Besides all this, it adapts itself to performing the functions of other parts of speech. When *-ing* is added, the verb can function as a noun (a *gerund*) or remain a verb (a *participle*). This versatility adds importance to the need to know just which role the verb is playing.

In the next section, under "Danglers and Squinters," we will take a look at the participial form of verbs. Here we will discuss tenses, an aspect of verbs that often seems to leave business writers tied in knots. Later, under V3*a*, you will find the major tenses of the verb *prepare*. Look these over and be sure you know what the tenses of a verb look like. Then observe the rule:

Principle 5 **Tenses of verbs in a sentence should accurately indicate the correct sequence of actions; the verb in a subordinate clause should therefore take a tense consistent with the verb in the main clause.**

If your sentence describes actions at different times, you must sort out the proper time sequence, decide what tense you want for the main clause, and then make the other clauses relate logically. For example:

> When the machine *stopped,* the supervisor *realized* that no one *had oiled* it.

The main clause is *the supervisor realized,* and it is in the past tense. We imply that the stopping came simultaneously with the realizing. (If we wanted to make clear that the stopping came before the realizing, we would use *had stopped* rather than *stopped,* and *after* in place of *when.*) The second subordinate clause *no one had oiled it* describes an action that clearly preceded both the stopping and the realizing. Since we have chosen to put the realizing in the past, we must put the oiling in the "past perfect."

Here are two incorrect examples:

> When she *oiled* the machine, it *was ready* for service again. (The main clause is in the past tense, but the oiling had to take place before the machine was ready. The correct form is *had oiled.*)

> When he *retires* this month, the supervisor *will complete* ten years of work for the company and *will train* over a thousand men during those years.

We have a specific point of time in mind here—the supervisor's retirement date. As of that time he will be able to look back on a training job completed: He *will have trained* over a thousand men. As it stands, the clause means he will train the men on his retirement day. We might quibble over *complete,* too, and argue that it should be *will have completed.* Does the supervisor complete ten years of work the moment he retires or the moment before? The point doesn't seem important.

Frequently, words like *after* and *before* and even *since, therefore,* and *because* clarify time relationships and eliminate reliance on tense to show sequence. Compare the following examples:

> When he came, I had left.
>
> After he came, I left.
>
> Before he came, I left.
>
> Because he came, I left.

The time sequence is quite clear in each sentence.

Danglers and Squinters

A dangling phrase is one that ought to refer to something in the sentence, but doesn't. Most dangling phrases are participial phrases; hence the common term "dangling participle."

By adding *-ing* (as in writ*ing*) to a verb, or by placing *being* or *having* before it (as in *being seen* or *having done*), we form participles. When such forms function as nouns (as in "*writing* is hard work" or "*having* the work *done* was a source of satisfaction to him"), they are called *gerunds* or *gerundives.* Since participles get heavy use in letters and reports, you should watch them to see that they follow this rule:

Principle 6 **When a participle is used in a phrase (such as** *"referring* **to your letter," or** *"reviewing* **these results"), there must be something appropriate for the phrase to modify, to cling to or depend on.**

Here is an example of a dangling participle:

> While watching the Browns on TV recently, an argument broke out.

Even if you change the word order, an argument cannot watch the Browns. This is clearly nonsensical, but you are being equally illogical when you use the following constructions in your letters and reports:

> Referring to your letter of March 25, the situation is being investigated.
>
> Reviewing the results of the Greenpoint Plant, the same conclusions were reached.

It is only fair to point out that the meaning of these two sentences is probably clear, despite the dangling participles. For this reason, many business writers will defend the sentences as they stand and regard our criticism as characteristic of the "office pest." It may be that dangling participles will come to be accepted when there is no doubt as to what the reader means, but you are on safer ground when you avoid them. And unless you make a habit of avoiding them, you may find yourself using them to create unclear or even humorous statements, like the following example from a London newspaper's description of a race won by a horse from the royal stables:

> Sired by the Royal Stallion, the Queen could not but feel satisfaction at the result.

Usually the dangling participle results from the use of the passive voice. One method of correcting the construction is to make the doer of the action in the participle serve as the subject of the sentence (ask yourself *who* is referring to the letter) and eliminate the passive voice:

> Referring to your letter of March 25, *we* are investigating the situation.

> Reviewing the results of the Greenpoint Plant, *the committee* reached the same conclusions.

A second method of correcting the dangling construction is to change the phrase containing the participle to a clause (by giving it a subject and verb) and eliminate the participle.

> *While we were watching the Browns on TV,* an argument broke out.

> *After the committee reviewed the results of the Greenpoint Plant,* the same conclusions were reached.

Sometimes a phrase which refers to something in the sentence, and is therefore not a dangler, is so located that the reader is prevented from seeing the reference clearly. For example:

> The testimonial dinner will be held in the grand ballroom of the hotel *consisting of the regular banquet fare.*

The italicized participial phrase modifies *dinner* and should be placed next to it in accordance with this simple rule:

Principle 7   Modifiers must be located so that it is clear what they modify.

We have already discussed the matter of logical location of the parts of a sentence in Chapter 3, so we won't deal with it any further here except to note the special problem of the "squinter." A squinter is a modifier located so that it might refer to more than one element in the sentence; the reader doesn't know which. For example:

> Even though it will take six years for the machines to pay for themselves, if conditions do not bring about a change in prices, the investment is decidedly attractive over the long run.

Does the *if* clause refer to *it will take six years* or to *the investment is attractive?*

Pronouns

If verbs and nouns play leading roles, pronouns may be called *stand-ins.* They take the place of nouns and serve the highly useful function of giving variety to such monotonous repetitions as this:

> Mr. Smith wrote a report in which Mr. Smith summed up the observations Mr. Smith made based on Mr. Smith's six months' stay at the Brookside Plant.

Troublesome as pronouns may be at times, this sentence should make you thankful that you can use them in your cast of characters. And their function as substitutes or stand-ins gives you the clue to why they are troublesome. Basically, your problem is to notify your reader without a shadow of doubt for *whom* or *what* your pronoun is substituting.

> When Mr. Smith reported the matter to the proper department head, he told him he would take action.

This is as bad a business sentence as you will ever see, because it fails to do what business communication must do: tell the reader clearly and unmistakably what the actual situation is. Who told whom? Who will take action? The reader doesn't know. Worse than ungrammatical, awkward, and nonstandard forms of English—bad as they are—is ambiguous English in business; and a large amount of this ambiguity derives from careless use of pronouns.'

Reference of Pronouns

A pronoun stands for a noun; the noun for which it stands is called its *antecedent.* Your prime responsibility when you use *he, she, it, they, who, which, this, that,* and other pronouns is to see that they refer unmistakably to their antecedents. There are certain exceptions. We can use *it,* for example, in an indefinite sense: "it rains," "it becomes more difficult," "it was felt," etc. But then we must be sure we don't create confusion by mixing an indefinite *it* with one intended to refer to something specific.

It (indefinite) is the responsibility of the management to see that *it* (supposed to refer to *management*) gets reports promptly; to do this, *it* (indefinite) is necessary to have *its* (management's?) report writers properly prepared.

The principle to keep in mind is this:

Principle 8   Pronouns must refer unmistakably to their antecedents, and relative pronouns—such as *who, which, that—* **must be placed as close as possible to their antecedents.**

Here are some incorrect examples:

We are sending you a check for the defective part which we hope will prove satisfactory. (Not the defective part, we hope, which has already proved unsatisfactory.)

During the second half of the discussion of Mr. Green's report, it was decided that it would be unnecessary to continue it. (Continue the report, the discussion?)

She had already informed the typist that she would be responsible for the general form of letters. (Who is responsible?)

Our economy of operation, achieved through an intensive work-simplification program, has eliminated the former high cost of production. This we can now pass on to our customers. (A new method of losing customers by handing them high costs.)

The supervisor told the young accountant that his statement was incorrect. (Whose statement?)

Selling has always been this young man's major interest, and that is why he is looking for employment as one in your company. (One what?)

We can correct these statements in this way:

We are sending you a check for the defective part, and we hope this adjustment is satisfactory to you.

During the second half of the discussion of Mr. Green's report, the committee decided that he need not continue the report (*or* decided that further discussion of the report was unnecessary).

The supervisor, who was responsible for the general form of letters, had already told the typist of this responsibility.

By getting rid of high production costs through an intensive work-simplification program, we have achieved greater economy of operation. The savings we can now hand on to our customers.

The young accountant's statement was incorrect, the supervisor told him.

Selling has always been this young man's major interest; that is why he wants to be a salesperson in your company.

These examples show what you can do to clear up vague pronoun references. Occasionally you will have to repeat words, but repetition is better than ambiguity. Sometimes you will have to recast the whole sentence or break it into two sentences.

Case of Pronouns

In their role as stand-ins for nouns, English pronouns have the troublesome trait of changing their garb when they perform different functions of the same role. If you think you have troubles as an English producer, though, you should be thankful that you aren't in charge of a language production in German or Latin, where four or six such changes are possible, or, to take an extreme, in Finnish, which has no less than fifteen cases! This functional change of garb is called *case*. When English nouns change case, they affect only one minor costume change. You can use *letter* as subject, as in "The letter was written," or as object, as in "He wrote the letter." The word remains the same. The only alteration is in the possessive, as in "The letter's style is objectionable." Your major attention to case, therefore, can be concentrated on certain pronouns. The terms used to describe the three cases illustrate their functions—*subjective, possessive, objective.* Here are the changes of case you ought to keep an eye on:

Subjective	I	you	he	she	it	we	they	who	whoever
Possessive	my	your	his	her	its*	our	their	whose	whosever
Objective	me	you	him	her	it	us	them	whom	whomever

*Not *it's*, which means "it is."

This is not an overwhelming list, and you are well advised to keep it in mind and to place special emphasis on *who, whose,* and *whom,* which particularly plague business writers.

Principle 9   The form (case) of pronouns must suit their function, as follows:

a. *A pronoun as the object of a preposition must always take the objective case.* (Prepositions relate nouns or pronouns to some other word in the sentence. Among the most frequently used prepositions are *at, by, in, for, from, with, to, on, between, except, below, above,* and *under.*)

   b. *A pronoun modifying a gerund uses the possessive case.* (A gerund is a verb used as a noun: *"Swimming* is good exercise.")

   c. *A pronoun used to explain, to give in detail what is covered by another word* (this is called *apposition*), *takes the same case as the word which it explains.*

Here are examples. You might note that your intuition is especially likely to let you down here and lead you to incorrect constructions.

   a. Between you and *me,* this must remain strictly confidential. (*Me* is object of the preposition *between.*)

   This report did not agree with the previous one submitted by Mr. Jones and *her.* (*Her* is object of the preposition *by.*)

   Copies were sent only to the executive staff and *him* as secretary. (*Him* is object of the preposition *to.*)

   He has been a capable employee with *whom* I have worked closely. (*Whom* is object of the preposition *with.*)

   No one from our company attended except Mr. Jones and *us.* (*Us* is object of the preposition *except.*)

   b. We appreciated *your* writing us frankly. (*Writing* is a gerund; *your* is possessive.)

   We did not learn about *his* being in the city until too late. (*Being* is a gerund; *his* is possessive.)

   c. Only three employees could be located when the accident occurred—Mr. Smith, Mr. Henry, and *I.* (*I* is in apposition with *employees,* which is subjective case.)

   There was some question as to whose responsibility it was—*his* or *mine.* (*Whose* is possessive; *his* and *mine* must be in the same case.)

You know that pronouns used as subjects of verbs are subjective case, and objects of verbs are objective case. Here are some situations affecting *who* and *whom* which cause difficulty:

He is one of the people *who,* I think, should be considered for the position. (The difficulty here arises from *I think,* which actually is a parenthetical comment injected into the middle of the sentence. *Who* is the subject of *should be considered* and must be subjective case.)

He is the man *who,* you will remember, was interviewed last year. (This is like the previous sentence, with *you will remember* as the interjected parenthetical comment.)

On November 12, Mr. Smith, our representative, questioned the dealer as to *who* was responsible for this misunderstanding. (This type of involved sentence causes confusion because many writers think they must use *whom* as the object of the preposition *to.* Actually, your primary obligation is to provide a subject for the verb *was responsible.* This situation arises from the fact that an expression such as "the person" or "the individual" is understood, but not expressed, immediately before *who*. By saying this more simply, you can avoid all the confusion: "Mr. Smith questioned the dealer to find out who was responsible for the misunderstanding.")

We would appreciate your letting us know *whom* you addressed your reply to. (This usage shows some signs of breaking down, but in formal communication, like letters and reports, you will do well to stick to the objective *whom* as object of the preposition *to*. The sentence could be improved and the case of *whom* made more obvious by moving the concluding preposition: "We would appreciate your letting us know to whom you addressed your reply.")

Our receptionist is instructed to jot down this information: *Who* called? *Whom* did he or she ask for? (*Whom* is objective after the preposition *for*. The best method of analyzing grammatical problems in interrogative sentences is either to turn them around: "He or she did ask for *whom*," or to relocate the concluding preposition: "For *whom* did he or she ask?" As in the previous example, this usage is breaking down. In speech we say "Who did he or she ask for?" but it is just as well to observe the rule in written communication.)

Principle 10   The spelling of all words should be correct; where there is any doubt, a good dictionary should be checked.

Admittedly, in an era of atomic fission and lunar exploration, the ability to spell does not rate as one of our highest skills. Nonetheless, it *is* assumed to be an acquisition of educated citizens who are motivated by a desire to follow accepted usage. You can test these generalities best by noting your own reaction if you were to receive a letter or report in which these errors occurred:

> We recieved your request and it occured to us that you would get prompter delivery if we sent the heaviest items seperately by freight.

Quite properly, the reader would conclude that such a writer is either uneducated or contemptuous of correct usage.

Admittedly, too, certain words are difficult to spell. (You can win bets with your friends, most of whom will be unable to spell these five words: desiccate, rarefy, vilify, supersede, inoculate—but they are hardly expressions used frequently in business writing.) The solution to your spelling problems is fairly obvious: learn to spell the words you use frequently, and use a good dictionary to find out the proper spelling for the others. To assist you, we have included in the Reference Section under "Mechanics" first of all a helpful list of the 25 words most frequently misspelled and then a list of 300 words frequently misspelled in business writing. Both lists make an excellent place for you to begin if you want to check your ability to spell correctly.

In this section we have presented 10 principles which should help you to attain correct usage in your letters, reports, and memos. By committing them to memory, you can learn to avoid the oft-repeated errors of much business writing. By applying them constantly, you will find that you are improving your efficiency as a writer because through practice you will soon learn to concentrate on *what* you want to say instead of *how* to say it correctly. These 10 principles will not, of course, solve all your problems of correctness in writing; but they will carry you a long way because they are based on an analysis of the actual errors that occur most frequently in business writing. (In the following pages you will find a much more detailed analysis of grammar, punctuation, and spelling.) You can have a little fun in the process of going through the following tongue-in-cheek "instructions" by Marie Longyear, manager of editing services at McGraw-Hill Book Company:

> Subject and verb always has to agree.
>
> Being bad grammar, the writer will not use dangling participles.
>
> Parallel construction with coordinate conjunctions is not only an aid to clarity but also is the mark of a good writer.
>
> Do not use a foreign term when there is an adequate English *quid pro quo*.
>
> If you must use a foreign term, it is *de rigor* to use it correctly.
>
> It behooves the writer to avoid archaic expressions.
>
> Do not use hyperbole; not one writer in a million can use it effectively.
>
> Avoid clichés like the plague.
>
> Mixed metaphors are a pain in the neck and ought to be thrown out the window.
>
> In scholarly writing, don't use contractions.
>
> A truly good writer is always especially careful to practically eliminate the too-frequent use of adverbs.
>
> Use a comma before nonrestrictive clauses which are a common source of difficulty.
>
> Placing a comma between subject and predicate, is not correct.
>
> Parenthetical words however should be enclosed in commas.
>
> Consult the dictionary frequently to avoid mispelling.*

A Test of Correctness in Business Writing

In a more serious vein, you can test yourself with the following 100 sentences containing many of the most frequent errors in business writing. A few of the sentences contain more than one error. You ought to be able to correct the error and to state the general principle it violates.

*Reprinted by permission of the author.

1. Upon reviewing your credit references, a decision to open an account was made.

2. Since our products are only available through dealers, we have asked Mr. Jones to immediately get in touch with you.

3. We are making every effort to find out as to whom was responsible for this oversight; in the meantime, we want you to know that we appreciate your calling this matter to our attention.

4. This was one of those errors which is particularly unfortunate when it happens to an old customer like you.

5. These advantages in addition to the clear presentation and simple style makes this a book you will want for your office.

6. The increase in sales as well as economies of operation and recent wage adjustments make an optimistic forecast possible for the next six months.

7. We only use the finest materials and most skilled craftsmen.

8. He had sent one of those letters which is usually better thrown into the wastebasket.

9. Three representatives were asked to be present—Mr. Smith, Ms. Jones, and myself. With the purpose of insisting that all kinds of businesses be represented to give a cross section of Blanktown's industry.

10. When the letter you sent to the Main Office was not forwarded, there was naturally some confusion between their accounting division and I.

11. Neither of these possibilities were explained in your letter to us.

12. These facts are simply background material, and if they are to be included at all should have been condensed into a paragraph or two.

13. Every one of our 48 inspectors have been trained at the factory before they are given a territory.

14. We were pleased to learn that the crowd at your opening were so enthusiastic about the new models.

15. She is one of those people who I suppose we should consider.

16. I own a car that the brakes don't work.

17. I wish I was there when the report was presented.

18. Referring to your request of October 22, the brochure on "How Sales Affect Production" is out of print, and I am very sorry that we cannot send you a copy for that reason.

19. This is a growing company. Their sales have increased steadily in the past and I think they will continue to do so.

20. The personnel policy which had been submitted to all the administrative staff and to the department heads were then issued.

21. Neither of these machines can be used at speeds which are beyond their capacities. Which are listed on the metal tags attached to the base.

22. A consistent policy and not the trivial amounts of these discounts are our first concern.

23. If anyone else was in his place, they would do the same thing.

24. She as well as our thousands of other representatives have learned that selling Blanko Products in spare hours pays big dividends.

25. Among the services we intend to provide is constant supervision of the product and prompt replacement of parts.

26. I certainly agree that I would not expect this mistake to be repeated and if I was in your place, I would expect an adjustment.

27. The dealer who had sent three orders and two requests for window displays were visited by our representative.

28. Neither of these letters contain information about the exact model number or the date when you purchased the equipment.

29. If we do not hear from you in five days, we shall have to turn your account over to our collection agency which, I am sure, neither of us wants.

30. Beginning work on a Monday, he found he was not paid until the following week.

31. This product not only has years of tested experience behind it but also a reputation for efficiency established by those who have used it.

32. We should have asked them to have stayed.

33. The writer of the report and not the three accountants who supplied the facts and cost estimates believe the change is necessary.

34. Each of our representatives have told us of your interest in Blanko Products. A report by which we are highly gratified.

35. In this assortment is contained a wide variety of toys for children of all ages and a set of dolls in authentic historical costumes.

36. To everyone who worked so hard on this sales campaign and to our sales manager especially go our appreciation for a job well done.

37. He notified the new employee that he would see the office manager about his office that day.

38. Her income depends on rents which is less stable than income from bonds.

39. When the machine stopped we realized it had not been oiled and since then we oiled it daily.

40. Enclosed with this letter was a signed affidavit and a carbon copy of her request to our main office.

41. A question has arisen as to whose territory Belleville is—Mr. Smith or me.

42. Neither of us want to see your credit reputation jeopardized by only an amount of $72.19.

43. He has been a conscientious employee who I have enjoyed working with and who I will miss.

44. She presented a great many reasons why she did not approve them going to lunch at the earlier period.

45. Your last order as well as the two previous ones were sent, as you instructed, by truck.

46. This campaign was conducted to reduce the number of accidents at the end of the year which was successful.

47. In my letter of August 4, I said that we would send our technical expert to call as to who was the person to see.

48. Along with this offer goes a money-back guarantee and a six-month supply of detergent to make your wash days easy.

49. A loss of morale could be caused among workers kept underground by officious supervisors.

50. Employing such communication media as newspapers, posters and employee meetings, the financial position of the firm was presented.

51. Neither of our field representatives were able to get to the factory on such short notice.

52. I would gladly grant this request if it was possible for me to do so; but we have a policy of keeping such information confidential.

53. This was one of those situations which is unfortunate but which are almost inevitable in sending out large mailings.

54. I don't believe anyone besides the president checks the treasurer's report as carefully as himself.

55. We are hoping to find a man for this job that he gets along well with other people.

56. The departmental staff were planning to attend the local Community Chest Luncheon at which the results of our company giving was to be announced.

57. Your signature as well as those of two members of your Board of Directors are required to complete the document.

58. We must reward every worker to raise our production standards to meet those our competitors who is trying hard.

59. Included in the group invited to attend the sales conference were three dealers—Mr. Smith, you, and me.

60. The group were agreed in inviting you to be the speaker.

61. She is one of those rare people whom I think are never at a loss for words.

62. The Annual Report together with our last two quarterly reports to shareholders are being sent to you by our Public Relations Department.

63. We are sending you this check to compensate you for the loss of time which we hope you will use for something you want.

64. We certainly appreciate you writing us as one of the 15 companies which was selected.

65. I expect that salary increases this year that will please us all.

66. Referring to your letter of April 23, in which you requested information about our Model U Home Air Conditioning Unit.

67. Trends in consumer buying and the individual's preference for one brand name affects the situation.

68. To the best of our knowledge, this company is well known for their excellent working conditions.

69. It is apparent that it was her responsibility to remove the hazard; since she didn't carry it out, she should at least have reported it.

70. He only does what he is told and that is done none too well.

71. Being unaccustomed to long reports, this one has been kept brief.

72. A person like you who pays their bill promptly is the backbone of American business.

73. Every one of her references speak highly of her business abilities; this will, of course, affect her chance of getting a position here.

74. The committee members disagreed and has to meet again.

75. In this invoice is included the charges for the past month.

76. Our sales are falling, but we hope they can be reversed next year.

77. She has sent us this information too late on the sales increase which was unfortunate.

78. The board of directors meets this week and are going to debate the question of whether to expand.

79. Referring to our telephone conversation yesterday, the materials you asked for are enclosed.

80. The accountants give us reports that are in such technical language that we can't understand always.

81. Neither the file copies nor the original, which was sent on March 12, were found; we appreciate your waiting so patiently for this information.

82. Included in our last letter was the statement of terms, a signature card, and an air mail envelope, none of which has yet been received.

83. Concluding that this customer was a poor risk, the question was submitted to the Central Office for decision.

84. This is only one of the many problems which confronts the writer in business and which this service will help you to solve.

85. With our granting of this credit goes our best wishes for continued success in the expansion of your marketing facilities.

86. A smaller staff might be appropriate for handling the regular volume of clerical work but not a larger one.

87. Either of these products are ideally suited for the purpose you mentioned in your letter of February 2.

88. Will you please let us know who you sent your original request to since it apparently was not received at this office.

89. We will try to replace the machinery that the cost of operation is too high, this year.

90. They urged that he was considered for the position.

91. Necessary to complete this agreement is your signature on the contract and three references from firms with whom you have done business.

92. Attached to this letter is an employment form and three sheets which your references should fill out.

93. Everybody in our office want to express their appreciation to you for your thoughtfulness.

94. As analyses such as was requested in your report constitute an important source of executive decision, I will attempt to give you some helpful suggestions.

95. The supervisor could help the new employee to increase her output without much difficulty.

96. After taking all the factors into consideration and analyzing the potential sales in your area, your best course seems to us to be buying on a cash basis for the next six months.

97. To make up for the noise and dirt employees who work in the foundry we offer extra pay and shorter hours.

98. If a delay was to occur we can ship by truck but we will never have had to do it yet.

99. The supervisor puts his name on the notice board to humiliate him every time an employee is late.

100. The store in Lee, Massachusetts, is doing very well and its population is only 5,271.

PARTS OF SPEECH

If in our communication we had only to consider words as individual units of thought, writing the English language would be comparatively simple. To be sure, English words change form in what is called *inflection;* but basically, most problems arise from the relationship of words or word groups to one another within the sentence. This branch of grammar is called *syntax;* the branch of grammar devoted to the study of the eight parts of speech and their inflections is known as *morphology.*

But these are academic definitions. What the writer in business usually needs is the answer to such questions as: Should that verb be singular or plural? Should it be *I* or *me?* Should I say *was* or *were?* How do I punctuate that clause? These are questions which business people might appropriately label "matters of procedure"; for answers, modern management would ask "What is the policy?" or if there is none, they would formulate one.

Grammatical policy is rather clearly formulated, though it is not nearly as rigid as many college students think. In the following pages, you will find the policy statements which apply to the parts of speech; when you're in doubt about writing procedure, you'll find it good business to consult this policy manual, which is not intended to be complete but to refresh your mind on the major points of syntax. All this derives from the fundamental principle that all parts of a sentence must fit together or must *agree* in the working relationship of the sentence. Since you cannot write a sentence without a subject and a verb, we will start with the verb and then go on to the other parts of speech which make up the sentence:

Nouns and pronouns

Adjectives and adverbs

Prepositions and conjunctions

These are, of course, seven parts of speech; *interjections* (Hello there! Alas! Wonderful! How about that! and similar exclamations), the eighth, present no grammatical problems, so we can ignore them. Following the parts of speech, we will analyze the sentence, modifiers, and problems of logic and consistency in writing.

Verbs

Verbs are the words or word groups used to make an assertion (she *leaves* tomorrow) or to express a state or condition (business *is* good). The properties of verbs are discussed in the rules which follow. Since no complete sentence can be written without a verb, writers in business ought to take special care that their sentences always contain verbs. Verbless sentences, known as *incomplete thoughts,* are discussed in the section on the sentence, but they occur frequently enough in business writing to justify emphasis here. Only by making sure that every sentence has a verb can business writers avoid such often repeated errors as the following:

Not: Referring to your letter of August 16, in which you requested our latest catalogue.

But: Thank you for your letter of August 16, in which you requested our latest catalogue.

Not: This being the decision and the final business of the committee.

But: This decision was the final business of the committee.

Not: To accomplish this efficiently and with a minimum of confusion resulting from the transfer of machinery.

But: To accomplish this efficiently and with a minimum of confusion, we must plan the transfer of machinery carefully.

Not: No word as yet as to when the typist will return.

But: We have received no word yet as to when the typist will return.

Agreement of Subject and Verb

V1 *A verb always agrees with its subject in number and person.*

This rule is basic and universal. When we say that a verb *agrees* with its subject, we mean that they have the same *person* (first, second, or third) and *number* (singular or plural). Since English verbs (except *to be*) have just one form for singular and plural and for all persons (except the third person singular—I *write*; he *writes*), this basic rule would seem to be easy to apply. The real difficulty in applying it arises from certain specific situations where the subject is hard to identify or where its number or person may seem confusing. These specific situations are explained in the following rules.

V1a *The number of the verb is not affected by words intervening between the subject and the verb.*

When business writers dictate their letters or reports, they frequently lose sight of the subject. Because intervening words may be of different number, they tend to "sound" as if they governed the verb. Notice how easily this could happen if you were speaking the following sentences:

Incorrect: The decision to add 11 new sales people and to conduct intensive advertising campaigns in industrial areas *were made* at the monthly meeting.

Correct: The *decision* to add 11 new sales people and to conduct intensive advertising campaigns in industrial areas *was made* at the monthly meeting.

Incorrect: One of the new models sent for exhibition purposes *were lost* in transit.

Correct: *One* of the new models sent for exhibition purposes *was lost* in transit.

Incorrect: These improvements in the filter and in the motor *makes* it our outstanding buy.

Correct: *These improvements* in the filter and in the motor *make* it our outstanding buy.

The best time to correct such errors is when you revise reports, when you sign letters or memos. Read them over *carefully* to see that verbs and subjects agree.

V1b *The number of the verb is not affected by such phrases, joined to the subject, as* as well as, together with, along with, in addition to, including, *and and not.*

Not: The department head together with his three assistants *report* weekly to the head of the division.

But: The *department head* together with his three assistants *reports* weekly to the head of the division.

Not: The clean-cut lines as well as the noiseless operation *makes* this an attractive addition for your kitchen.

But: The *clean-cut lines* as well as the noiseless operation *make* this an attractive addition for your kitchen.

Not: Your promptness in meeting your obligations as well as your unfailing cooperation and courtesy *have made* our relationship a pleasant one.

But: Your *promptness* in meeting your obligations as well as your unfailing cooperation and courtesy *has made* our relationship a pleasant one.

V1c *When any of the following words is the subject of the sentence or modifies the subject, the verb is always singular:* each, everybody, anybody, nobody, every, a person, either, *and* neither.

Not: Everybody in the entire organization *are* responsible.

But: *Everybody* in the entire organization *is* responsible.

Not: Neither of them *were* qualified for that position.

But: *Neither* of them *was* qualified for that position.

Not: Every man and woman in our company *are* factory-trained to service these machines.

But: *Every* man and woman in our company *is* factory-trained to service these machines.

Not: Either of those decisions *are* difficult at best.

But: *Either* of those decisions *is* difficult at best.

Be especially careful to distinguish this use of *either* and *neither* as pronouns from *either . . . or, neither . . . nor* as correlative conjunctions.

V1d   *Collective nouns (words like* company, group, staff, committee, crowd, *and certain expressions of money, time, or distance) are singular when they are thought of as a unit; they are plural when the individuals or individual elements are thought of. For the most part, business writing properly treats the great majority of such words as singular in number.*

Correct: The committee *has* sent in *its* report.

The group *is* in a meeting.

Twenty-five years *is* a long time for a company to stay in business.

A thousand dollars *is* a lot of money to save on just one process.

This company *has* an excellent reputation.

In such sentences as the following, where the individuals or individual elements are stressed, the collective noun can be considered plural:

Correct: The committee *were* unable to agree.

The board *are listed* individually on the inside cover of the Annual Report.

V1e *Subjects joined by* and *require a plural verb.*

Correct: The report and the accompanying letter *are* being sent.

The chief accountant and I *have* been invited.

This is so obvious as to require no special emphasis. Only one situation can cause confusion; when the *and* connects two titles or designations which apply to the same person, the verb is singular:

Correct: Our comptroller and treasurer *is* the person for this assignment.

The vice-president and director of services *informs* us of this.

V1f *When the subject contains singular and plural words linked by* either . . . or, neither . . . nor, *the verb agrees with the subject closer to it.*

Correct: Either the method used or the *principles* involved in this investigation *were* wrong.

Neither the chief accountants nor the financial *vice-president was* able to attend.

V1g *When the normal order of words in the sentence is shifted so that the subject comes after the verb, the verb agrees with the word which is actually the subject.*

This shift in the normal pattern of sentences is a good device for varying sentence patterns, but don't lose sight of your subject in the shuffle.

Correct: Included in this offer *are* a six months' guarantee, a complete set of instructions, and one free inspection of the equipment. (To locate subjects in this inverted order, find the verb—*is included? are included?*—then ask *what* is included? Here, the subject is *guarantee, set of instructions, free inspection;* hence the verb must be *are included.*)

Among the items on the bill *were* an overcharge of $2.19 and an omission of the credit for my last payment.

To these and to the others who cooperated on this venture *go* our congratulations and best wishes.

V1h *When the sentence begins with* there is *or* there are, *the verb agrees with the subject which follows it.*

Correct: There *is* little time for long-range planning. (Subject is *time,* singular.)

There *are* many reasons for doing this.

There *are* so many communications needed to conduct business today.

V1i *The verb agrees with the subject and not with the predicate complement with which it is sometimes confused.*

Not: His chief concern *are* his many coworkers.

But: His chief concern *is* his many coworkers.

Not: The most important sales feature *are* the three new elements in the design.

But: The most important sales feature *is* the three new elements in the design.

Careful writers will note that even the correct versions of this construction are awkward and can be greatly improved by recasting the sentence.

The welfare of his many coworkers is his chief concern.

The three new elements in the design comprise the most important sales feature.

V1j *Certain nouns though plural in form are singular in meaning and, therefore, take singular verbs.*

Usually singular: *news, economics, ethics, mathematics, whereabouts.*

Correct: The news *is* good.

The ethics of business *prevents* that conduct.

Her whereabouts *is* unknown.

Other words with similar form, like *tactics* and *acoustics,* are usually plural. The best guide as to whether a specific word is singular or plural is a good dictionary.

Verbs—Mood

V2 *Use the correct mood of the verb to indicate whether the statement is a fact, a command, or a wish or unreality. The English language has three moods, the indicative, the imperative, and the subjunctive.*

Indicative is the mood of actuality, reality. This you use about 99 percent of the time.

Imperative is the mood of command. "Bring your textbook to class next time." The "polite imperative" occurs frequently in letters and may be used without a question mark in such expressions as "Will you please let us know if there is anything else we can do."

Subjunctive is the mood of unreality, improbability, and, finally, high desirability in formal motions or strong necessity or insistence, as in collection letters.

V2a *Use the subjunctive mood in verbs when you make statements that are contrary to fact, highly improbable, or expressive of formal wishes, as in parliamentary procedure, nominating, or electing.*

Since the verb *to be* causes most subjunctive troubles, all you need to remember is that:

> *a.* The present tense uses *were* in all persons.

> *b.* As an auxiliary form (that is, part of other verbs), *be* is used after verbs like *ask, urge, insist, require, vote, move,* etc.

Here are correct uses of the subjunctive as it occurs commonly in business writing:

> If I *were* you, I would call on him again. (Contrary to fact, since I am not you.)

> If that *were* to occur, we would have to cut production in half. (A highly improbable supposition.)

> She moved that the meeting *be adjourned.* (Following a formal expression of wish; note the *be* as auxiliary form.)

> I, therefore, urge that this *be reconsidered.*

> We must insist that this payment *be made* within three days.

> He strongly urged that all violations *be reported* within twenty-four hours.

> If she *were* to do that, we would cancel the contract.

> We are, therefore, requesting that your check *be sent* immediately.

> He insisted that he *be given* one more chance.

> If I *were* in her place, I would take the following action.

> I wish this report *were* more simple and less technical.

> He then ordered that all requisitions *be signed* by department heads.

> I wish it *were* possible to comply with your request.

> Even if that *were* to happen, we have a big backlog of orders.

Verbs—Tense

V3 *Use the correct tense of the verb to express time accurately.*

To express various times and their relationships accurately, the English language has six tenses—present, past, future, present perfect, past perfect, and future perfect. The keys to forming all these tenses are the *principal parts*—the present, the past, and the past participle—*employ, employed, employed. Employ* is a regular verb because it maintains its basic form and adds *-ed, -ed* to form past tense and participle. Irregular English verbs change these forms—*write, wrote, written; sing, sang, sung; lie, lay, lain.* The best guide to whether a verb is regular or irregular is the dictionary; but note carefully that if the verb is regular, *only one form is given,* i.e., *employ,* but where it is irregular, all three forms are given, i.e., *sing, sang, sung.*

Formation of Tenses

V3a *Learn how to form the tenses of regular verbs.*

Here are the major tenses of the verb *prepare*—principal parts, *prepare, prepared, prepared;* infinitive forms *to prepare, to have prepared, to be prepared, to have been prepared;* participles, *preparing, having prepared, being prepared,* and *having been prepared.*

INDICATIVE MOOD

Present tense

Active

I prepare	we prepare
you prepare	you prepare
he (she, it) prepares	they prepare

Passive

I am prepared	we are prepared
you are prepared	you are prepared
he (she, it) is prepared	they are prepared

Past tense

Active

I prepared	we prepared
you prepared	you prepared
he (she, it) prepared	they prepared

Passive

I was prepared	we were prepared
you were prepared	you were prepared
he (she, it) was prepared	they were prepared

Future tense

Active

I shall prepare	we shall prepare
you will prepare	you will prepare
he (she, it) will prepare	they will prepare

Passive

I shall be prepared	we shall be prepared
you will be prepared	you will be prepared
he (she, it) will be prepared	they will be prepared

Present perfect tense	Active	
	Active	
	I have prepared	we have prepared
	you have prepared	you have prepared
	he (she, it) has prepared	they have prepared
	Passive	
	I have been prepared	we have been prepared
	you have been prepared	you have been prepared
	he (she, it) has been prepared	they have been prepared

Past perfect tense

Active
I had prepared	we had prepared
you had prepared	you had prepared
he (she, it) had prepared	they had prepared

Passive
I had been prepared	we had been prepared
you had been prepared	you had been prepared
he (she, it) had been prepared	they had been prepared

Future perfect tense

Active
I shall have prepared	we shall have prepared
you will have prepared	you will have prepared
he (she, it) will have prepared	they will have prepared

Passive
I shall have been prepared	we shall have been prepared
you will have been prepared	you will have been prepared
he (she, it) will have been prepared	they will have been prepared

As one student once commented, "This is an awe-inspiring mess of tenses." But you need not let it worry you, because in actual writing you might have to contrive some highly ingenious time sequences before you used certain of these forms. What you need to know is the basic pattern of how the tenses are formed, the proper sequence of tenses, and the difference between the use of active and passive voice.

V3b *Learn the principal parts of irregular verbs.*

To help you with the formation of tenses of certain irregular verbs which are widely used in business, here are the principal parts of those that cause difficulty:

Present	Past	Past Participle
arise	arose	arisen
begin	began	begun
bid	bid	bid *(to make an offer)*
break	broke	broken

Present	*Past*	*Past Participle*
choose	chose	chosen
deal	dealt	dealt
dive	dived	dived
get	got	got *or* gotten
lay	laid	laid
lead	led	led
lend	lent	lent
lie	lay	lain (*to recline; to be situated*)
lie	lied	lied (*to tell an untruth*)
loose	loosed	loosed
lose	lost	lost
pay	paid	paid
prove	proved	proved
raise	raised	raised (*to cause to rise, as salaries*)
rise	rose	risen (*to get up of its own power*)
set	set	set
sit	sat	sat
write	wrote	written

Proper Sequence of Tenses

V3c *Use each tense to express the time of the action accurately and to show its relationship to other verbs in the sentence.*

1. Use the present tense:
    a. To express present time:

    I interview, I am interviewing, etc.

    b. To express actions which take place habitually or ideas which are permanently true:

    Every day he *opens* the store at 9 o'clock.

    She always *tells* her employees that she believes in them.

    In her speech she emphasized her conviction that honesty *is* the best policy. (Not "honesty *was* the best policy"; presumably, this is a permanent truth.)

    He had been taught that concise writing *is* the best writing.

2. Use the past tense to express action completed in the past.

    I *wrote* to her yesterday.

    He *told* me in his weekly conference.

The only difficulty here is with irregular verbs, where the second principal part (*the past*) and the third principal part (*the past participle*) are confused. Hence result such illiteracies as:

> *I swum* for *I swam; I drunk* for *I drank; I laid in the hammock* for *I lay in the hammock.*

3. Use the future tense to indicate that an action or condition will take place in the future.

> I *shall write* to him.
>
> You *will be attending* the convention next week.

V3d *In the more formal types of business writing, distinguish between the use of* shall *and* will.

Perhaps no phase of English has been the subject of greater dispute than the distinction between *shall* and *will.* (The only other candidate within recent years would be the famous "This is *me,* Winston Churchill, speaking.") In speech, most of us get around the whole subject easily by saying *I'll, we'll, they'll;* or we express futurity by *going to* or *about to* as "He is going to do it Tuesday." Many writers still have strong convictions that the only correct way to express simple future in formal writing is:

> I shall do it   we shall do it
>
> you will do it   you will do it
>
> he will do it   they will do it

and that strong determination can only be expressed through:

> I will do it   we will do it
>
> you shall do it   you shall do it
>
> he shall do it   they shall do it

There is little question that this distinction is breaking down; many business writers use *shall* and *will* almost interchangeably. The extent of this change is illustrated by a story widely current some 25 years ago. It seems that a group of English professors were walking along a lake when an unusually obtuse freshman shouted from the lake, "I will drown; nobody shall help me!"— and the professors let him drown. Recently, another professor told this story, without explanation, to a group of students, and none saw the point.

Because the lines of distinction between *shall* and *will* have become greatly blurred, you will have to use your common sense in such sentences as:

> We *shall* insist on payment. (Would your insistence be stronger with *will?* Probably not.)

Will you make an address at our annual meeting? [This sentence illustrates why the distinction breaks down, because *will* here is in the sense of "are you willing to." Some purists insist that such a question should anticipate the answer ("I shall") and use the same form in the question. This kind of hairsplitting has probably been a major cause of the breakdown in distinguishing between *shall* and *will*.]

We *will* be glad to ship the order as you directed. We *shall* be pleased to follow instructions. I *will* be there next week. I *shall* send the instructions you asked. (The distinction in sentences such as these has largely passed away. Use whichever form seems comfortable and less artificial *unless* you feel better with an absolute rule to follow—then you can follow the conjugation given.)

V3e *Use* should *and* would *carefully.*

Should and *would* similarly have tended to follow patterns of meaning rather than standards of arbitrary usage. *Should* chiefly implies obligation in the sense of "ought to"; *would* expresses a customary action with all three persons.

I *should* urge you to keep this policy. (Ought to)

You *should* do everything possible to protect your credit reputation. (Ought to)

Every day he *would* answer his letters as soon as he finished reading the incoming mail. (Habitual action)

I *would* always advise a careful revision before signing. (Habitual action)

They *would* take a coffee break every morning at 10.

V3f *Use the perfect tenses to express time relationships precisely.*

The perfect tenses, for the most part, are used to indicate time relationships with regard to other times expressed or implied.

By the first of the month, we *will have completed* our quota for the year if the present sales rate continues. (Notice the use of future perfect to look back on something from a point in the future.)

Last month she reported she *had met* her sales quota. (The main verb *reported* is past tense; to indicate action prior to that, we use the past perfect.)

The action was taken by the time all the facts *had been assembled*.

By next year, *we will have been* in business a quarter of a century.

Of the three perfect tenses, the present perfect is probably the most frequently misused in business writing. This results from a misunderstanding of the meanings of the three basic ways the English language has of indicating action in the past. A simple way to think of these three methods of expressing past actions is:

Past tense: Action begun and completed in the past. Example: I *wrote* to him yesterday.

Past perfect: Action begun and completed in the past prior to some other stated or implied time. Example: I *had not heard* (past perfect) from him before I *wrote* (past) to him yesterday.

Present perfect: Action begun in the past and completed at any moment up to the present. Example: Up until today, I *have written* him every day this month.

Taking the present as the line at the right, the sequence of these tenses in their relationship to one another may be indicated thus:

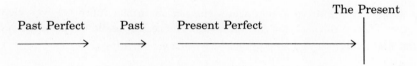

Hence in correctly using the present perfect tense, business writers should avoid such statements as:

Wrong: So far this month I *sold* 11 refrigerators. (Misuse of past for present perfect.)

Right: So far this month I *have sold* 11 refrigerators.

Inaccurate: She left the first of the month and I since *completed* her assignment. (Notice that there is no discrimination between two past tenses here; actually the completion of the assignment occurred after her leaving, as the sentence indicates.)

More precise: She left the first of the month, and I *have* since *completed* her assignment.

Inaccurate: We read your comments with great interest, but lack of information *prevented* a complete reply until today.

More exact: We read your comments with great interest, but lack of information *has prevented* a complete reply until today.

Inaccurate: The Chicago office *corresponded* with him ever since it happened.

More exact: The Chicago office *has corresponded* with him ever since it happened.

As a general principle, be careful to use the tense that exactly expresses the time you want indicated in the verb, particularly when these verbs show a relationship to other verbs or implied times in the same sentence. Do not shift back and forth from one tense to another without reason.

V3g *Use the present infinitive to express all times except when the infinitive represents action clearly completed before the time of the main verb.*

One other aspect of tenses plagues business writers—the use of the infinitive. Shall we say:

> I hoped *to see* you before the meeting.

> I hoped *to have seen* you before the meeting.

> We were pleased *to see* you at our quarterly meeting.

> We were pleased *to have seen* you at our quarterly meeting.

Use a present infinitive except when the action in the infinitive was clearly completed *before* the action of the main verb. Hence, *seeing* did not precede *hoping* in the first sentence, and the correct form is:

> I hoped *to see* you before the meeting.

In the second illustration, the correct form is:

> We were pleased *to see* you at our quarterly meeting.

Thus, the following infinitives are correct:

> We intended *to be* at the meeting. (Not *to have been* because the action of intending preceded being there.)

> He was expected *to report* in Waco by the first of the month.

> *To have reported* this to her superior would have caused her all kinds of trouble. (Note that the *reporting* comes prior to the *causing trouble;* hence the past infinitive.)

Verbs—Voice

Besides tense and mood, verbs have *voice,* a grammatical term which indicates whether the subject of the sentence is performing the action or being acted upon. In the *active voice,* somebody or something does something.

> He *wrote* the report.

> The typewriter *fell* to the floor.

In the *passive voice,* something is done to or by somebody or something.

> The report *was written* by the new employee.

> The typewriter *was knocked* off the desk by the secretary.

(The complete conjugation of all tenses of the verb *to prepare* in the passive voice is shown on pages 474 and 475.)

V4 *Use the active voice for direct, personalized expression; the passive for indirect, impersonal expression.*

In this book, we have stressed concise, direct, and personalized writing for business purposes. For achieving such qualities, the active voice is most appropriate. But students should recall that we have also stressed the primary factors of all writing—the purpose for which it is written and the reader. These are the criteria which determine our use of the active or passive voice according to these principles:

> Use the active voice when direct and natural expression suits the purpose and the reader.

> Use the passive voice when impersonal expression is appropriate to the subject matter and to the reader.

Because so much business writing is couched *unnecessarily* in the passive voice, authors of books such as this belabor the construction as if it were incorrect or ungrammatical. It is neither, and it has its uses. When you want to make a suggestion, many readers will accept it as less harsh, less blunt, if you write:

> It is suggested that this method be tried by the Marketing Group. (passive)

instead of:

> I suggest that you try this method. (active)

You can test your own reaction to the following ways of expressing ideas in active and passive voice:

> *Passive:* It is suggested by the Executive Staff that only one coffee break a day be taken by employees.

> *Active:* We suggest that employees take only one coffee break a day.

> *Passive:* Members of the department are urged to contribute as much as possible to this worthwhile cause.

> *Active:* I urge you to contribute as much as possible to this worthwhile cause.

Passive: When the business day is ended, the totals should be phoned to the Central Office, Extension 6533.

Active: At the close of business, you should phone the totals to the Central Office, Extension 6533.

Many readers—particularly older ones who were trained to write in an impersonal style—prefer the passive for suggestions, instructions, and recommendations. But don't use the passive merely to avoid the use of *I* or *we;* if you are writing about yourself or your company, *I* or *we* is the natural and unaffected method of expression.

Instead of: It is the belief of the undersigned that prices will be increased.

Say: I think prices will increase.

Instead of: It is the opinion of our management that a stock participation plan will be helpful to employee morale.

Say: We think a stock participation plan will help employee morale.

In short, use the active for direct, forthright, personalized—*and concise*—writing; use the passive for impersonal and indirect expression.

V4a *Do not shift unnecessarily from active to passive or from passive to active.*

Indefinite: We began our investigation and the report was written later. (This is accurate if "we" did not write the report or if you want to leave your reader in the dark as to who wrote it.)

More accurate: We began our investigation and later wrote our report.

Unnecessary shift: We have a fine selection of the latest books and records, and a complete stock of sporting goods is being displayed for our customers this week.

More direct: We have a fine selection of the latest books and records, and we feature a complete display of our sporting goods this week.

Awkward: We use adding machines at the tellers' windows; the electronic computers are used by the Central Office.

Improved: We use adding machines at the tellers' windows; the Central Office uses electronic computers.

More concise: We use adding machines at the tellers' windows and electronic computers at the Central Office.

Nouns and Pronouns

In grammatical handbooks, nouns are properly treated as well-behaved parts of speech—and can, therefore, be ignored. Pronouns, as the troublemakers, properly receive the major share of attention because they change form, called *case,* as they perform various functions (see the discussion on the following pages). A pronoun is a word which stands in place of a noun; the noun for which it stands is called its *antecedent.*

P1 *A pronoun should agree with its antecedent in number, person, and gender.*

Number means, of course, singular or plural: *I* or *we; he* or *they,* etc.

    Person means whether it is first person, *I,* as the speaker; second person, *you,* as the person spoken to; or third person, *he, it, she, they,* as the persons or things spoken about.

    Gender means classification by sex—masculine, *he;* feminine, *she;* neuter, *it;* and common, *they.* All changes in grammatical form affecting gender have disappeared in English.

P1a *When a pronoun has as its antecedent such singular words as* every, each, anybody, either, neither, nobody, a person, *etc., use a singular pronoun in the third person. Traditionally, writers would use third person masculine when they were not certain of the gender of the antecedent. However, feminists who want equal time and recognition have caused the following types of pronoun references. Writers who get tired of seeing* he or she *should give some thought to recasting sentences in the plural so that the common* they *could be used.*

Each of these employees should check *his or her* list of responsibilities.

Neither one of these men was sure of *his* exact time of arrival.

Everybody in the office should report to *his or her* supervisor on Monday at 10.

Every department head is requested to sign *his or her* own requisition slips.

A person who is not sure of *his or her* writing should study grammar.

Nobody should authorize changes which affect summer employees in *his or her* department.

    Similarly, business writers frequently use such expressions as "one of those situations which," "one of those problems that," "one of those people who." Should these be followed by singular or plural verbs? Your best rule of thumb is to regard the word closer to the pronoun as its antecedent; so "instead of one of those situations which is annoying," you will follow this practice:

> She described one of those situations which *are* annoying to secretaries.
>
> This is one of those problems that *are* constantly coming up in business.
>
> He is one of those people who *annoy* everyone in the office.

Case refers to the change in form of nouns and pronouns to show their relation to other words in the sentence. Since English nouns have only one change of form—the *'s* to indicate possession—it is pronouns which cause most difficulty. Here are the changes in the three cases—subjective, possessive, and objective:

Subjective	I	you	he	she	it	we	they	who	whoever
Possessive	my	your	his	her	its	our	their	whose	whosever
Objective	me	you	him	her	it	us	them	whom	whomever

P2 *The case of a pronoun is determined by its function in the sentence.*

Applying the basic principle that the case of the pronoun depends upon its use, we get the following specific rules:

P2a *Use the subjective case of the pronoun as the subject of a verb and as predicate nominative.*

The first part of this rule is so obvious as to call for no explanation; sheer habit should require you to say "We write" not "Us write." After forms of the verb *to be*, formal writing requires the use of the subjective case in what is called a predicate nominative. While "It is *me*" and "That was *him*" are acceptable colloquialisms in speech, business writers use the following subjective cases in letters and reports:

> It was *we* who first sent the report on that subject.
>
> That was *he* who sent this suggestion.

Notice that these sentences are wordy and awkward and that you can avoid the whole difficulty by more incisive writing: "We first sent the report on that subject" and "He sent this suggestion."

P2b *Use the possessive case of the pronoun to indicate possession and to modify a gerund.*

Again, only the second half of this rule calls for explanation. A gerund is a verb form used as a noun—*"Writing* is fun"; *"Having accomplished* that is a record in itself." Pronouns modifying gerunds should be put in the possessive case. To the person saying, "Do you mind me making a suggestion?" the following response in doggerel is appropriate:

> *Please don't think I'm too aggressive*
> *By suggesting your participle needs possessive*

Not: We appreciated *you* sending this information promptly.

But: We appreciated *your* sending this information promptly.

Not: We must insist on *you* paying this bill.

But: We must insist on *your* paying this bill.

Not: She did not object to *us* collaborating on reports.

But: She did not object to *our* collaborating on reports.

P2c *Use the objective case of the pronoun as the object of a verb, the object of a preposition, and the subject of an infinitive.*

The chief source of trouble here is the pronoun as object of a preposition, and usually it is the pronoun linked to another pronoun by *and* which causes the incorrect construction.

Wrong: We found it impossible for him and *I.*

Right: We found it impossible for him and *me.*

Wrong: Between you and *I,* that is correct.

Right: Between you and *me,* that is correct.

Wrong: Copies had been sent to the members of the executive staff, the secretary of the committee, and *she.*

Right: Copies had been sent to the members of the executive staff, the secretary of the committee, and *her.*

But notice that when the pronoun is the subject of an infinitive (*to* plus a *verb*), it is objective case too.

Wrong: He instructed Mr. Smith and *I* to decide that problem.

Right: He instructed Mr. Smith and *me* to decide that problem.

P2d *Pronouns in apposition take the same case as the word with which they are in apposition. (A word in apposition explains or gives in detail whatever is comprised in another word in the sentence.)*

Not: The three sales representatives—Smith, Jones, and *me*—were sent.

But: The three sales representatives—Smith, Jones, and *I*—were sent. (Smith, Jones, and I are in apposition with representatives, which is subjective case.)

Not: There was some problem of deciding whose service was better—*him* or *me.*

But: There was some problem of deciding whose service was better—*his* or *mine.*

Not: She informed the three of them—Smith, Jones, and *he*—that they would be transferred to the new plant.

But: She informed the three of them—Smith, Jones, and *him*—that they would be transferred to the new plant.

Not: Among the employees affected, principally Ms. Smith, Ms. Jones, and *she,* the only one to refuse the transfer was Ms. Jones.

But: Among the employees affected, principally Ms. Smith, Ms. Jones, and *her,* the only one to refuse the transfer was Ms. Jones.

P2e *In an elliptical clause in which the verb is omitted, the pronoun takes the case which would be required if the verb were expressed.*

We have been in business longer then *they* [have].

They have had a better sales volume than *we* [have had].

Their company makes greater use of mechanical equipment than *we* [do].

You are as good a student as *she* [is].

While the informalities of speech occasionally make the use of the objective case permissible, careful writers regard pronouns as the subject of the understood verb and, hence, use the subjective case as in the examples given above.

P3 Myself, yourself, himself, ourselves, themselves, *and other reflexive pronouns require as reference a personal pronoun or the person's name in the same sentence.*

He hurt *himself.* (Reflexive)

She washes *herself.* (Reflexive)

This would become a minor grammatical error were it not for the widespread use business people make of these *self* words, which are also called *intensive pronouns:*

> I bought *myself* a new coat. (Intensive)
>
> He will do it *himself*. (Intensive)
>
> We *ourselves* did not understand the meaning. (Intensive)

You can avoid such frequent misuses as the following by inserting a personal pronoun.

> He and *myself* are members of the committee. (Replace with "I.")
>
> Mr. Jones and *yourself* are to attend. (Say "you.")
>
> She addressed her remarks to her own staff and *ourselves*. ("Us")

You can generally get along very well without these *self* words by using the personal pronoun. When you really want to emphasize or intensify your meaning, use the *self* words but only after the appropriate pronoun.

P4 *In using the relative pronouns* who, which, *and* that *in formal writing, remember that* who *refers only to people,* which *refers only to things, and* that *refers to people and things.*

> *Not:* He sent me to the chief correspondent, *which* I finally found.
>
> *But:* He sent me to the chief correspondent, *whom* I finally found.

Adjectives and Adverbs

These are the words that put color and size and shape and manner of doing things into our language—and, fortunately, they cause little grammatical difficulty.

A1 *Adjectives modify nouns or pronouns and may be used to describe, to tell number, and to show specific identity or quantity.*

> The *large* desk   A *few* books   The *last* day of the month

A2 *Adverbs modify verbs, adjectives, or other adverbs and, in general terms, describe how, where, when, why, and to what extent.*

> Type *quickly*   *Very* quickly done   A *gratifyingly* large response

Many adverbs end in *ly*, but this is not an infallible means of identification, since a number of adverbs are indistinguishable from adjectives. For example, the long-standing debate of motorists as to whether it is correct for roadside signs to read "Drive slow" is grammatically inconclusive since slow is *both* an adverb and an adjective.

A2a *Do not substitute an adjective for an adverb to modify a verb.*

> *Wrong:* He certainly treats her *different* from the rest of us.
>
> *Right:* He certainly treats her *differently* from the rest of us.
>
> *Wrong:* They want information *quick.*
>
> *Right:* They want information *quickly.*

(Although *quick* is sometimes used conversationally as an adverb, *quickly* is the much more common adverbial usage.)

A2b *Be careful in the use of such adverbs as* scarcely *and* hardly *to avoid double negatives.*

Scarcely and *hardly* are negative in meaning, as "I have scarcely any ambition" or "I hardly have a chance." They should not be used in combination with *not* or *no* because they form a double negative. Omit either the adverb or the negative in such sentences as these:

> *Wrong:* We could *not hardly* be expected to accept these items for credit.
>
> *Right:* We could *hardly* be expected (or: We could *not* be expected) to accept these items for credit.
>
> *Wrong:* That is the kind of error that can*not scarcely* occur twice.
>
> *Right:* That is the kind of error that can scarcely occur twice (or: cannot occur twice).

A3 *Use an adjective with verbs of the five senses* (taste, smell, feel, sound, appear, look, *and* be, *etc.*) *when the subject is referred to, an adverb when the verb is referred to.*

Notice the distinction in the following sentence:

> He looks *ridiculous.* (*Adjective* describing *he.*)
>
> He looks *intently* about him. (*Adverb* describing *looks.*)

It sounds *loud*. (*Adjective* modifying *it*.)

It sounds *carefully* planned. (*Adverb* modifying *planned*.)

She appears *strong*. (*Adjective* modifying *she*.)

She appears *rarely* at her office. (*Adverb* modifying verb *appear*.)

A4 *Comparison is the change in the forms of adjectives and adverbs to show a greater or smaller degree of the quality they indicate. There are three degrees of comparison—positive, comparative, superlative.*

Most adjectives and adverbs may be compared by adding *er* or *more* or *less* and *est* or *most* or *least* to the regular, or positive, form.

Positive	Comparative	Superlative
efficient	more efficient	most efficient
quick	quicker	quickest
capable	more capable	most capable
simple	less simple	least simple
able	abler	ablest
constructive	more constructive	most constructive

Some adjectives and adverbs are compared irregularly:

Positive	Comparative	Superlative
bad (adj.)	worse	worst
good (adj.)	better	best
well (adv.)	better	best

A4a *Use the comparative degree in comparing two things, persons, or actions, the superlative for three or more.*

On the informal level, we frequently say, "That's the best team on the field today" or "He was by far the best of the two speakers." In writing, however, accuracy demands a more logical use of these degrees. Hence we write:

Of the two men, he seemed to us to be the *more* qualified. (Not *most*)

This was the *most* difficult of all my assignments.

Of the two suggestions, we thought yours was the *better*.

This is the *best* of all the suggestions submitted by employees.

A4b *Use* other *following* than *in making comparisons with adjectives or adverbs.*

He is more efficient *than any* man in the office.

This is a sensible statement only if the "he" is not a member of the office staff; otherwise, the comparison should logically be:

He is more efficient *than any other man* in the office.

> *Wrong:* This improvement makes our product better *than any.* (This construction, widely used in advertising, is logically absurd, since it cannot be better than itself.)

> *Right:* This improvement makes our product better *than any other.* (This construction emphasizes what sales personnel want emphasized— your product is better than your competitor's products.)

Conjunctions and Prepositions

Conjunctions and prepositions are our joining words, the mortar which holds sentence parts together. In themselves, they offer no particular grammatical problems; but they are important in two major aspects of writing—the methods of punctuation and the principles of coordinating and subordinating sentence elements.

C1 *A conjunction links words, phrases, or clauses to other parts of the sentence and shows the relations between them.*

Conjunctions differ from prepositions in that they may introduce whole clauses (a group of words with subject and verb) and may indicate relative importance of ideas. Used properly, conjunctions may show that two ideas are of equal importance or that one is less important than the other.

C1a *Coordinating conjunctions join words or groups of words of equal importance. The most commonly used coordinating conjunctions are* and, but, for, or, *and* nor.

C1b *Subordinating conjunctions join to the sentence clauses of unequal importance:* since, because, if, although, when, where, how *are examples of subordinating conjunctions.*

C1c *Conjunctive adverbs are adverbs used as connectives. Examples are:* therefore, moreover, however, nevertheless, hence, thus.

C2 *Use coordinating and subordinating conjunctions to convey meanings and establish relationships precisely.*

By definition, conjunctions establish relationships of ideas. They should be used, therefore, with precision to be effective. There is nothing grammatically incorrect, for example, in a sentence like:

> This machine incorporates a revolutionary new principle, *and* it is based on three years of research.

This writer has two things to say about the machine, and ties them together with a coordinating conjunction. Such a sentence indicates a slovenly process of thought because the two statements are probably not equally important. By subordinating conjunctions, we can show this relationship more precisely.

> *Because* we spent three years on research, this machine incorporates a revolutionary new principle.

> *So that* this machine could incorporate a revolutionary new principle, we spent three years on research.

Quite obviously, the circumstances will dictate which of these or other methods of expressing two facts is used. If the two ideas *are* of equal importance, the use of the coordinating conjunction would be correct.

C2a *Conjunctions usually indicate relationships of cause, comparison, condition, time, sequence, and contrast.*

To show a cause-and-effect relationship—*since, because, hence, thus, therefore, inasmuch as, so that, for that reason.*

To make comparison—*than, as if, as well as, similarly, although.*

To state conditions—*if, unless, except, provided that, under these circumstances, accordingly, or else.*

To show time sequence—*before, after, earlier, later, following, since, when, while, preceding, subsequent to.*

To show a sequence of ideas or facts—*first, second, finally, in conclusion, primarily, furthermore, moreover.*

To sum up—*thus far, up to now, hence, accordingly, finally.*

To show contrast—*however, on the contrary, on the other hand, by contrast, furthermore, not to mention, still less, still more.*

This is an elementary list; you can doubtless think of hundreds of other ways to express such relationships. The important principle is to see that your connectives express these relationships and your meaning as precisely as possible.

No teacher or reader of business writing needs to be told what is one of the chief faults of letters, reports, and memos. It is an endless succession of *and's, but's,* and *for's* reflecting an utter lack of subtle relationships or discrimination.

Ask a child what he or she has been doing all day, and you expect an answer like "I got up and I had my breakfast and then I got on the school bus and we shouted and sang and cheered and then we got to school . . ." and so on.

To avoid this monotonous level, learn to use conjunctions and conjunctive adverbs precisely to show shadings of thought and relative importance of facts and ideas. Study those which have been cited previously and use them in your writing when you are overworking *and* and *but* and *for*.

C3 *A preposition links a noun or pronoun to show its relationship to some other word in the sentence. Examples:* with, by, for, to, in, of, before, after, *etc. Prepositions also combine with other parts of speech in hundreds of idiomatic expressions like* comply with, desirous of, different from, agreeable to, *etc.*

C4 *In formal writing, use* like *as a preposition or a verb, not as a conjunction.*

Many people use *like* as a conjunction in speech (He acts *like* he knows everything), but avoid its use in formal writing. Perhaps *like* will one day attain the status of *as,* a conjunction; at present, its use as a conjunction will grate on the nerves of many. It is interesting to note that Robert Gunning's *The Technique of Clear Writing* has a chapter titled "Write Like You Talk"; on the jacket of the book, the publishers have changed this to "Write As You Talk." Young writers in business will similarly play safe by using the preferred form below:

> *Not:* He always talks *like* he knows more than anyone else in the office.

> *Preferred:* He always talks *as if* he knows more than anyone else in the office.

> *Not:* She writes her reports in the impersonal style *like* she was instructed to do.

> *Preferred:* She writes her reports in the impersonal style *as* she was instructed to do.

You can test these easily by noting whether *like* introduces a group of words with subject and verb; if so, substitute *as* or *as if.* Notice that *like* is properly used as a preposition in these sentences:

> I did not know he would talk *like that.*

> She writes reports *like those* we recommend to our employees.

THE SENTENCE

By definition the sentence is a group of words that must express at least *one complete thought* or two or more *closely related thoughts.* The sentence is capable of standing alone and "making sense"; grammatically, this means that the sentence has a verb and its subject, expressed or understood.

Frequently, in conversation especially, we can convey thought without sentences:

> "Who will do the final report?"
> "Smith."
> "Your department?"
> "No. Elwyn Smith in Sales."

Furthermore, experienced business writers have learned to use sentence fragments or *elliptical statements,* as they are called, to good effect, particularly in sales letters and advertising copy:

> You know the wonderful feeling that comes when you've finally completed a tough job? A sense of achievement. An air of satisfaction. A feeling of well-being.

> All under one roof . . . Research. Art. Planning. Engineering. Construction.

> Everything for one complete service. And all backed by 27 years of service. An organization of 213 professional people with creative ideas. To serve YOU.

This elliptical or fragmentary writing is effective for packing a number of facts or ideas in short space. It gives punch and forward movement, particularly in sales writing; but in the more formal types of business communication, fragmentary writing is undesirable and incorrect.

Structure

S1 *Avoid writing part of a sentence as if it were a complete thought or statement (the period fault).*

This is an important rule for writers in business, particularly for those who dictate. Some use their opening "sentences" as a warm-up period and dictate a clause or a phrase as if it were a complete idea; others merely add an incomplete thought in the form of a phrase or subordinate clause to what has been said before. These fragments can be corrected in two ways:

1. By connecting them to the preceding or following sentence if they logically belong there.

2. By recasting them to make complete sentences, usually by supplying a main subject or verb.

Notice how the following examples correct these faults:

> *Wrong:* Referring to your letter of March 21. We will notify our dealer in Covington.

Right: Referring to your letter of March 21, we will notify our dealer in Covington. (Connecting the fragment to the following sentence; but see the discussion of this participial construction on pages 454 to 455.)

Wrong: As we agreed over the phone yesterday.

Right: As we agreed over the phone yesterday, the campaign will begin April 10.

Wrong: To confirm our agreement on November 12 at the Hotel Grandview.

Right: This letter will confirm our agreement on November 12 at the Hotel Grandview. (Supplying a subject and verb)

Wrong: *During* the sales period from Labor Day to Thanksgiving, we will introduce five new models. Each of these adaptable to color.

Right: During the sales period from Labor Day to Thanksgiving, we will introduce five new models, all of them adaptable to color.

Wrong: She had spent most of the month on the report evaluating personnel problems for the next five years. Which her supervisor thought good enough to transmit to the vice-president.

Right: She had spent most of the month on the report evaluating personnel problems for the next five years. Her supervisor thought it was good enough to transmit to the vice-president.

Will it stand alone and make sense? This is the final test of the sentence. If not, correct the fragment by one of the two methods suggested.

S2 *Avoid putting two or more unrelated thoughts in the same sentence (the comma splice).*

This construction stems from sheer carelessness or lack of logic. It consists of connecting two unrelated sentences with a comma; correct it by replacing the comma with a period. If a logical relationship can be established between the thoughts, then the appropriate conjunction and punctuation should be used.

Wrong: The department had had a high accident rate, this was caused by several inexperienced employees who had not had their safety indoctrination.

Recast the whole statement to show a logical relationship:

Right: Because several inexperienced employees had not had their safety indoctrination, the department had had a high accident rate.

Wrong: Our employees stay with us over the years, the new stock purchase plan is an added incentive.

Right: Our employees stay with us over the years. The new stock purchase plan is an added incentive.

Wrong: As you requested, I forwarded the report to the Dallas office, the word then came back that the manager agreed with our conclusions.

Right: As you requested, I forwarded the report to the Dallas office. The word then came back that the manager agreed with our conclusions.

S3 *Avoid breaking ideas up into short, choppy sentences.*

Occasionally, this style can be used by skillful writers to obtain an effect:

> He read our invitation. He visited the exhibit. He saw for himself the efficiency of the new design. And he ordered a year's supply then and there!

More frequently, these sentences sound choppy, childish, and thoughtless because they result from the writer's failure to organize closely related ideas into sentence units. Correct such constructions by putting ideas which logically belong together in the same sentence.

Choppy: At that time, I first called it to your attention. You asked me to keep you informed. I wrote you again in March. The auditor arrived on April 2. The employee was found responsible. He was replaced on April 15.

Improved: When I first called this to your attention, you asked me to keep you informed and so I wrote you again in March. After the auditor arrived on April 2, the employee was found responsible and was replaced on April 15.

S4 *Avoid long, rambling sentences with too many qualifying clauses and phrases.*

Such sentences frequently occur in reports. Often, they stem from an admirable trait of mind—the desire to avoid saying something which is not always true and hence packing all kinds of qualifying phrases and clauses into one statement. This tendency can be corrected by putting the general statement into one sentence, the qualifers or exceptions into successive sentences. Frequently these sentences stem from less admirable traits—mental laziness and inability to organize; here, the only cure is to think about grouping ideas as logical sentence units which readers can grasp.

Unorganized: We have made special efforts during April to bring our fleet of cars up to summer conditioning, which includes cleaning and painting, where that is necessary, but as you are aware, the heavy rains of late April have overcome some of these efforts, and furthermore we had an unusually heavy number of road calls, totaling 87, for the month and this too hampered our efforts. (From the report of a transportation department)

Improved: During April, we have made special efforts to bring our fleet of cars up to summer conditioning, which includes cleaning and painting wherever necessary. As you know, the heavy rains of late April hampered some of these efforts. Furthermore, an unusually heavy number of road calls—87 in all—limited our conditioning work.

Rambling: The number of new unemployment claims, which, of course, definitely affect consumer buying power, dropped 400 in the municipal area from the previous week and in the suburbs dropped 211 from the high of 1,453 the previous two weeks, although the suburban high was affected by certain unusual conditions, and it would now appear, unless some very unexpected conditions arise which are not in this forecast, that the peak of unemployment claims for the first six months was reached during the week ending April 17. (From a market analysis report)

Improved: New unemployment claims dropped 400 in the municipal area from the previous week and 211 from a high of 1,453 in the suburbs the previous two weeks. The suburban high was affected by unusual conditions. Unless unexpected circumstances arise, the forecast is that the peak of unemployment claims for the first six months was reached during the week ending April 17. This will, of course, have definite—and beneficial—effects on consumer buying power.

Rambling: We try to supply our customers with the best merchandise and most economical service that is possible and this includes all brands of nationally advertised sporting goods, garden supplies, and hardware and a discount of 2 percent for cash payments within 10 days.

Improved: Our customers get the best in merchandise—nationally advertised brands of sporting goods, garden supplies, and hardware. And they get the most economical service, with added savings of 2 percent by paying cash within 10 days.

S5 *Avoid monotony and dullness for your reader by varying your sentence structure*

Sentences can be classified as simple, complex, compound, and compound-complex according to their parts, or a loose, periodic, and balanced according to their overall structure. It is not within the province of this book to go into a detailed analysis of all these classifications. What is important is that business writers become conscious of the pattern of their sentences; if they tend to express most of their ideas in one monotonous pattern, a change of pattern will add to the reader's interest. Remember that you have three kinds of sentences to add variety to your style—loose, periodic, and balanced. Each of these is analyzed in the following three sections.

S5a *The loose sentence*

Actually, most business writing consists of "loose" sentences. This is no derogatory term; it merely means that the sentence is organized in a normal pattern of subject, verb, and modifiers and that its essential meaning is disclosed before the end of the sentence. But because the loose sentence is so common, it lacks emphasis and strength.

> We sent the order on August 12 by Railway Express as you had instructed.
>
> The total seniority rating of each employee will then be posted in the department where the rating applies.
>
> This report covers the operations of the purchasing department from August 1 to September 1, the first month of its activity under the plan of reorganization, which went into effect on July 15.

This is the normal pattern of sentence organization, and the great majority of sentences in almost any report, letter, or memorandum will necessarily be loose—subject, verb, modifiers. But when all your writing falls into this pattern, the result is dullness, monotony, and lack of interest.

S5b *The periodic sentence*

Change this basic pattern of the loose sentence by occasionally pushing a clause or phrase ahead of the main subject and verb.

> In accordance with the plan of reorganization effective July 15, this is my first report as head of the purchasing department.
>
> Unless a careful check is maintained at all times, these records of seniority ratings can cause difficulty and considerable discussion.

With this shift from normal loose order to a different arrangement, we force our reader to keep certain ideas in mind until the entire meaning is complete. Actually, without the reader recognizing it, we force attention by holding him or her in suspense until the final meaning is clear. This is *the periodic sentence,* an arrangement which suspends meaning and builds to completion at the final word or group of words. Used judiciously, it adds considerable variety to style; readers of *Time,* the news magazine, will recognize it as *"Time* style":

> Last week, as it must to all men, to Joe Doakes of Koakesville, came death.

The periodic sentence is an effective method of breaking up the monotonous regularity of loose sentences. Business writers should learn to intersperse such sentence patterns occasionally. The technique is to hold back the main subject and verb until the end of the sentence, pushing the modifying clauses and phrases forward to the beginning. Notice that you have to read these sentences through to the last word before the meaning is complete.

> Thus at month's end, even though we discount most favorable factors and emphasize the few unfavorable ones, the immediate future looks good.

> To the good looks, attractive design, and low cost of this unit, add our 31 years of experience.

> For those who do not face the realities of this situation, a danger of surplus exists.

S5c *The balanced sentence*

And finally, you can learn to write one other sentence pattern—the balanced sentence. This pattern should be used infrequently for emphasis because it has a contrived air which calls attention to itself. For most twentieth-century writers who seek a casual, informal style, the balanced sentence is a bit artificial. If you write advertising copy, however, this sentence pattern can be very useful. The balanced sentence uses a symmetrical arrangement of corresponding parts. Many of the world's most famous sayings have come in the form of the balanced sentence, a pattern which has made them memorable.

> I came; I saw; I conquered. (*Caesar*)

> Reading maketh a full man, conference a ready man, and writing an exact man. (*Bacon*)

> If I could save the Union without freeing any slave, I would do it; and if I could do it by freeing all the slaves, I would do it; and if I could save it by freeing some and leaving others alone, I would also do that. (*Lincoln*)

Notice the advertisers:

> Eye it; try it; buy it.

> Fasten it better and faster with Bostitch.

> How magical its refreshment, how welcome its sparkling goodness, how perfectly it goes with other foods.

> Better things for better living . . . through chemistry.

This is the essence of balanced sentences—putting parallel parts in balanced, symmetrical form. For the unusual occasion, for highlighting an idea—such as the summary statement of a report or memo—for the sales letter or advertisement, it is a useful variant.

> The greater our efficiency, the lower the cost to you.

> By nature, he is carefree; by disposition, he is cheerful.

Logic and Consistency

L1   *Express parallel ideas in parallel form.*

This principle of parallelism can be applied to both the simplest and the most intricate forms of expression. It is both a logical and a stylistic device to help a reader. In its most elementary form, this principle is unnecessarily violated in such a sentence as:

> We are wholesalers for clothing for men, women, and *those who are under eighteen years of age.*

This is both sloppy expression and haphazard logic; in parallel form these elements would be expressed:

> We are wholesalers for clothing for men, women, teen-agers, and children.

To apply this principle, you should generally pair nouns with nouns, adjectives with adjectives, phrases with phrases, and clauses with clauses.

> *Not:* This new product offers ease of operation, economy and *it is easily available.*
>
> *But:* This new product offers ease of operation, economy, and *availability.*
>
> *Not:* The manual gives instructions for operating the machine and *to adjust it.*
>
> *But:* The manual gives instructions for operating the machine and *for adjusting it.*
>
> *Not:* We will send you advertising material for increasing sales and *to acquaint your customers with our new products.*
>
> *But:* We will send you advertising material for increasing sales and *for acquainting* your customers with our new products.

L1a   *Repeat necessary words (article, conjunction, preposition, pronoun, auxiliary verb, etc.) when repetition is needed to make parallel structure clear.*

> *Not:* We received a large order from her in September *and which* was increased in October.
>
> *But:* We received a large order from her *which* she sent us in September *and which* she increased in October.

Whenever you use *and which, and who, and that,* you are linking two parts of a sentence which should be in parallel form. The best rule of thumb to apply to such expressions is to use *and which, and who, and that* only when they are preceded by another *which, who,* or *that* to which they are logically parallel. Notice the changes in the following sentences:

Not: This bill includes all charges through August 25 *and which* are subject to 2 percent discount within 10 days.

But: This bill includes all charges *which* were made through August 25 *and which* are subject to 2 percent discount within 10 days.

Not: The report reflects a great deal of research *and which* is all too rare.

But: This report reflects a great deal of research, *which* is all too rare.

Not: We found him a reliable employee *and who* has a high sense of integrity.

But: We found him to be a man *who* is a reliable employee *and who* has a high sense of integrity.

Not: This is a service of considerable value to typists *and that* many supervisors of stenographic departments have used.

But: This is a service *that* is of considerable value to typists *and that* many supervisors of stenographic departments have used.

L1b *Make certain that listed items which are parallel in thought are also parallel in form. Because lists are so widely used in business writing, particularly in reports, this principle should be scrupulously applied.*

Not: In this kind of analysis, three steps are always involved:
1. Scrutinize all the details carefully.
2. Eliminate all the unnecessary details.
3. A chart showing the flow of work should then be made.

But: In this kind of analysis, three steps are always involved:
1. Scrutinize all the details carefully.
2. Eliminate all the unnecessary details.
3. Make a chart showing the flow of work.

Not: When we wrote you previously, we requested you to send us the following:
1. A financial statement
2. A list of credit references
3. You were to obtain a letter of credit from a wholesale firm with which you have done business

But: When we wrote you previously, we requested you to send us the following:
1. A financial statement
2. A list of credit references
3. A letter of credit from a wholesale firm with which you have done business

Not: We appreciate your promptness in sending us the three items we requested—the questionnaire, the personnel evaluation blank, and *you are to be complimented* on the copy of Mr. Handy's speech.

But: We appreciate your promptness in sending us the three items we requested—the questionnaire, the personnel evaluation blank, and the copy of Mr. Handy's speech, on which you are to be complimented.

L2   *Do not unnecessarily shift the point of view within the sentence.*

When you express thoughts, facts, or information in sentence form, you necessarily take a *point of view*—that is, a relative position from which you view the events or from which you consider the subject discussed. You should therefore, maintain one point of view in your writing unless there is good reason for change. This principle particularly applies within the individual sentence. We have already discussed unnecessary change of voice and tense (see verbs) as a major form of inconsistency. This construction occurs in such sentences as:

Inconsistent: The *writer* of this letter was educated in Texas and *New York City* has been his place of employment ever since. (Note the unnecessary shift of subject in the two clauses.)

Consistent: The writer of this letter was educated in Texas and has been employed in New York City ever since.

Inconsistent: When *one* does a thorough job of gathering facts, *you* find that time passes rapidly. (Note the needless shift of person in the pronouns. *One* is third person, *you,* second person. This shift is a bad habit of inexperienced writers.)

Consistent: When *you* do a thorough job of gathering facts, *you* find that time passes rapidly.

or

Consistent and more formal: When *one* does a thorough job of gathering facts, *he or she* finds that time passes rapidly.

Inconsistent: We *received* this notification on April 2 and on April 4 we *arrive* there to find the plant shut down. (This shift in tense from past to present occurs chiefly in narratives and reports of accidents, safety accounts taken on the scene, and similar business communications.)

Consistent: We *received* this notification on April 2 and on April 4 *arrived* there to find the plant shut down.

Inconsistent: It was the opinion of the group that this should be done and I agreed. (This is unnecessary shifting from impersonal passive style to personalized active.)

Consistent: The group thought this should be done, and I agreed.

Modifiers

Within the sentence, any word or phrase or clause which limits or qualifies the meaning of other parts of the sentence is a *modifier*. The rule governing all such elements can be stated simply:

M1 *Every modifier must have a word to modify and should be placed so that it is logically and naturally connected with the word it modifies.*

This principle points to the two central problems arising from modifiers: sometimes they have nothing to modify; sometimes they are placed too far from the element they modify to be recognizable as modifiers. The result can be ambiguity or absurdity.

> A man bumped into me upon getting off the elevator. (Who is getting off?)

> Upon getting off the elevator, the newsstand may be seen. (Does the newsstand get off the elevator?)

> These are the methods used to correct mistakes which we think are good policy. (Methods or mistakes are good policy?)

> You ought to have the knowledge which this reference book offers you at your fingertips. (Do you read Braille?)

M2 *Verbal phrases (participial, infinitive, gerund) or elliptical clauses which do not logically refer to some word in the sentence are said to "dangle."*

> Coming around the curve, the schoolhouse was seen.

Even if you change the word order, the schoolhouse is still coming around the curve. This is nonsensical; but you are being equally illogical when you use any of the following constructions in your letters and reports:

> Submitting these reviews of operations, the matter was referred elsewhere.

> Referring to your letter of March 25, the situation is being investigated.

> Reviewing the results of the Greenpoint Plant, the same conclusions were reached.

Writers of business letters, memos, and reports should be particularly careful about dangling modifiers. "Confirming your telephone conversation," "Referring to your memorandum of February 16," and "Thanking you for your cooperation" are constructions that are frequently encountered in business writing. In an earlier chapter, we have pointed out that these are weak expressions, ill-adapted for the beginning or ending of letters and memos. They can be avoided entirely in most instances; but since they are so deeply intrenched in the business vocabulary, we can at least make them grammatically correct.

M2a *Correct dangling participles or infinitives (1) by making the doer of the action in the phrase the subject of the thought that follows or (2) by changing the phrase to a subordinate clause.*

Not: Having shipped the order yesterday, our thanks are due you for your patience during this unavoidable delay.

But: Having shipped the order yesterday, we want to thank you for your patience during this unavoidable delay.

Not: To issue reports promptly, the duplicating group should be called.

But: To issue reports promptly, you should call the duplicating group.

When you want reports issued promptly, the duplicating group should be called.

Not: To obtain the utmost in comfort, the house should be insulated.

But: To obtain the utmost in comfort, you should insulate the house.

If you want to obtain the utmost in comfort, the house should be insulated.

M2b *Correct elliptical clauses by supplying the omitted words (subject or verb) or by supplying a subject which the elliptical clause can modify.*

Misleading: When ordered in large amounts, the transportation charges mount rapidly.

Correct: When this merchandise is ordered in large amounts, the transportation charges mount rapidly.

Misleading: While climbing the pole, the electricity was shut off.

Correct: While climbing the pole, the lineman shut off the electricity. While the lineman was climbing the pole, the electricity was shut off.

Misleading: When three years old, the move to larger quarters occurred.

Correct: When the company was three years old, it moved to larger quarters.

Misleading: When announced, the public will be urged to visit local dealers.

Correct: When the new prices are announced, the public will be urged to visit local dealers.

M3 *Place adverbs such as* only, almost, nearly, merely, also, scarcely, *and* even *near the word they modify.*

The idiom of popular speech has blurred much of the preciseness of meaning in such statements as:

> He only won the fifth prize in the sales contest.

> She only wanted to take her vacation in August. (Did she want to take her vacation only in August, or is this *only* in the sense of an excuse of her action?)

These statements are perfectly appropriate in conversation where explanations can be made as needed. But careful business writers will watch the position of these words to see that a precise meaning is conveyed. It makes considerable difference, for instance, whether you say:

> Our dealer is only open on Friday in the evening.
> *or*
> Our dealer is open in the evening only on Friday.

> He had an accident in a company car almost at the township line.
> *or*
> He almost had an accident in a company car at the township line.

In these sentences, your meaning will determine the proper position of the modifier. If your dealer is open once during the week, he or she is "only open on Friday"; if, instead, the dealer opens the store one evening a week, he or she opens "in the evening only on Friday."

Note the different connotations when these words are placed to modify different elements.

> She even reported that there was a chance of malfeasance.

> She reported that there was even a chance of malfeasance.

> They just called about the conference which had finished.

> They called about the conference which had just finished.

These are *merely* a few illustrations of how one word can affect your meaning in business writing; they also illustrate how *just* one word can change your meaning. *Only by placing such words properly can you convey your precise meaning when you write.*

M4 *Avoid placing a modifier so that it seems to modify either the words preceding it or those following it.*

This construction, known as the *squinting modifier,* can sometimes be corrected by punctuation; more frequently, however, a recasting of the sentence is needed.

> *Ambiguous:* Since we accumulated more information by this method *in two weeks* we finished the report.

Clear: Since we accumulated more information by this method, we finished the report in two weeks.

Ambiguous: The machine she had been running *noisily* fell off the desk.
Clear: The machine she had been running fell off the desk with a great deal of noise.

Ambiguous: While he gained this experience *off and on* he went to night school.
Clear: While he gained this experience, he went to night school occasionally.

M5 *Avoid putting words between* to *and* the *verb form of an infinitive unless greater clarity and more natural expression result from doing so.*

This is the highly publicized "split infinitive" construction on which we commented earlier. It is actually a problem of misplaced modifiers. Common sense and the meaning to be conveyed should govern such constructions as these:

Not: We tried to quickly and economically issue reports.

Say: We tried to issue reports quickly and economically.

Not: To never own one is to completely miss one of life's satisfactions.

Say: Never to own one is to miss one of life's satisfactions completely.

PUNCTUATION

Over the years, a marked decrease has occurred in the amount of punctuation used in business writing, as in other forms. One survey of the punctuation used in the editorial pages of *The New York Times* shows that the number of commas decreased almost 50 percent in 60 years. In letters, closed punctuation, which puts commas at the end of the lines and a period at the conclusion of the inside address, is now practically obsolete. It has been replaced by what is known as the *open form of punctuation*. The modern trend is to omit punctuation wherever it is not necessary for clarity; from that principle, open punctuation may be considered the most up-to-date method.

How far to extend this functional approach to punctuating business letters is still a problem, however, since usage has not completely crystallized. Business writers will find it helpful to think of punctuation as an aid to the reader rather than as marks to be strewn more or less at random. Punctuation has a functional use—making material more readable. Read these sentences:

When the car is in the garage doors should be shut.

On the day following the report was sent on to the manager.

To get their meaning, you'll have to read them at least twice and even then it will be very awkward. But suppose we insert one punctuation mark:

> When the car is in, the garage doors should be shut.
>
> On the day following, the report was sent on to the manager.

This is punctuation for clarity. There is also a lot of punctuation which is simply conventional—a colon after the salutation of a business letter, but a comma after the salutation of a friendly letter; a period after Mr.; a comma after a complimentary close. But conventional uses of punctuation make material more readable too, if only because readers have become accustomed to certain of these conventions.

You'll have to exercise judgment in punctuating reports and letters and memos, but your judgment will be better if you remember the following general tendencies:

1. Long sentences or long elements (like clauses or phrases) tend to require more punctuation than short ones.

2. Elements which interrupt the flow of a sentence require punctuation.

> You knew that he was going. (Normal sentence order with no punctuation)
>
> You knew—did you not?—that he was going.
>
> You knew, of course, that he was going.

3. Elements which are out of the natural order of a sentence require punctuation. Natural order of the sentence consists of subject and modifiers—object or predicate noun and modifiers. Notice that the following sentences are identical except for the order of parts and that the second sentence requires punctuation for that reason.

> We will take action when the report is turned in to the committee.
>
> When the report is turned in to the committee, we will take action.

In addition to these general tendencies, each of the major marks of punctuation indicates certain relationships and performs certain functions which should be kept in mind. These relationships and functions are explained in the rules which follow.

PU1 *The comma marks a rather close connection of parts, a slight pause for the reader. The most frequent uses of the comma are as follows:*

PU1a *Use a comma to separate two independent clauses connected by a coordinating conjunction* (and, but, for, *or* not).

We greatly appreciate the interest you have shown in our methods, and we certainly wish we could comply with your request of October 15.

The fact that the users of our products take the time to write us of their experiencies is a source of gratification to us, *for* through such reports we get a valuable indication of how our appliances perform under conditions of everyday use.

Our investigation showed that the Internal Auditing Section had recommended essentially the same changes, *and* we have collaborated with that section in making a joint recommendation to the executive vice-president.

When the two clauses are short and closely connected, the comma may be omitted.

This is your responsibility and you must accept it as such.

We appreciate your inquiry and you will see a demonstration of this equipment next Tuesday.

PU1b *Use a comma to separate words, phrases, or clauses in series.*

This plan is designed to give you *more profit, easier payments, and wider selection of merchandise.*

You will find him to be *cooperative, likable,* and *intelligent.*

Increasingly business writers omit the last comma, between the next to the last and the last elements, in such series when the meaning is unmistakably clear.

We have it available in small, medium and large sizes.

These reports are submitted on the last day of the week, month and quarter.

When there is any doubt that the meaning is clear, the comma should be placed before the conjunction. Notice the confusion that can result, particularly when the reader is unfamiliar with the subject, by dropping this last comma:

We received inquiries about this research from Smith and Jones, Johnson and Cohen and Black.

Is it Johnson and Cohen or Cohen and Black? Only proper placement of the final comma will indicate this unmistakably.

The comma is not necessary when each member of the series is joined to the others by a conjunction.

We sent the desks *and* the chairs *and* the files by express.

This applies to memos *and* reports *and* all forms of internal communication.

He will send the originals *or* the carbons *or* the new authorizations today.

PU1c *Use a comma to set off lengthy dependent elements preceding the main subject and verb.*

When you have seen all the features of this latest model, you will certainly want one.

At the time when we had originally scheduled the annual sales conference, a drop in consumers' purchasing power had occurred.

Since our offer of an adjustment did not seem satisfactory to you, we should like you to tell us just what you would regard as a fair settlement.

Where the elements are brief and closely connected to the rest of the sentence, the comma may be ommitted.

Naturally you should expect better mileage.

In this instance no action is necessary.

By sheer coincidence both reports arrived in the same mail.

PU1d *Use commas to set off nonrestrictive clauses, introduced usually by* who, which, that, *or* where.

This rule requires careful differentiation between nonrestrictive clauses using commas and restrictive clauses requiring no commas. The simplest method is to read the sentence *without the clause;* if the meaning is changed radically, the clause is restrictive and needs no punctuation. Restrictive clauses limit or restrict meaning or pin down whatever they modify to a specific thing or things; nonrestrictive clauses usually supply an additional piece of information or add a comment about whatever they modify. Notice how the meaning is changed in the first sentence but not in the second when you read them without the clause:

A refrigerator *that gives 15 years of service* is properly designed. (Not *any* refrigerator but "a refrigerator that gives 15 years of service"; this is restrictive and requires no punctuation.)

A refrigerator, *which is a necessity to American housewives,* is a luxury in most parts of the world. (The clause here adds a comment or an additional piece of information but it does not limit or restrict the meaning of "a refrigerator.")

Notice that commas setting off nonrestrictive clauses *always come in pairs,* except when the clause ends the sentence. Many writers make the mistake of putting one comma at the beginning and none at the end of the clause. The following nonrestrictive clauses are correctly punctuated:

> Ms. Gray, *who has been with us many years,* has earned an enviable reputation in our personnel department.

> Our largest plant, *which is located in Columbus,* will be open for inspection this spring.

> Our annual convention is held in New York City, *where our sales offices are located.*

Notice that the following clauses require no punctuation because they are clearly restrictive:

> The man *who sold me this merchandise* is no longer associated with your company.

> The order *that we received on October 15* was shipped on October 17.

> Memos *which are sent to the stenographic department* must be received before 3:00 P.M. of the day they are to be typed.

PU1e *Use commas to set off parenthetical expressions and appositives.*

Many writers use commas as a kind of light parenthesis which gives less emphasis or marks a less abrupt interruption than the dash or parentheses themselves. Parenthetical expressions such as *of course, however, as you know,* and numerous others, when placed so that they interrupt the normal flow of a sentence, require two commas to set them off. Notice that here, too, the commas always come in pairs:

> We knew, *of course,* that these prices would not prevail for a very long period.

> On June 5 we reported, *as you will recall,* that this situation would call for careful handling.

> The general conditions of the market, *as you will undoutedly realize,* imposed definite limits on production.

The appositive can be informally defined as *another way of saying the same thing,* as in giving a person's title or citing accomplishments briefly. It actually is a nonrestrictive element, as many teachers call it, and like the nonrestrictive clause requires commas. Because of the habitual use of titles, business writing requires an unusually large number of appositives.

> We are sending Ms. Roberta Evans, *our chief engineer,* to assist you.

Mr. Alexander Smith, *Director of Personnel of the Blank Company,* will conduct a seminar on "How to Evaluate Personnel."

The Executive Staff, *composed of Mr. E. C. Smith, Mr. P. W. Jones, and Ms. L.I. Johnson,* asked me to send these minutes of their meeting.

Our latest model, *the finest and most economical we have ever produced,* will be announced immediately after Labor Day.

PU1f   *Use commas to punctuate the following conventional or routine situations.*

1. Following the complimentary close of a business letter (optional):

> Cordially yours,
> Sincerely yours,
> Yours very truly,

2. Separating geographical names, dates, and elements in addresses:

> Our nearest dealer is in Springfield, Missouri.
>
> This occurred on Friday, February 17, 1978.
>
> Please send it to Mr. John Chapman, 275 Park Drive, Cleveland, Ohio 44124.
>
> We will appreciate your forwarding this information to the Standard Development Corporation, Kingston, N.Y. 12401. (Notice that no comma is used before the postal delivery zone: New York 10036, Omaha, Nebraska 68103.)

3. Separating initials or titles following a person's name:

> This report was then sent on to Adams, F. W., Adams, T. H., and Baldwin.
>
> The certificate in the name of Frank X. Park, Jr., is listed as Frank X. Park, Sr., on our stock records.
>
> You might write to L. M. Bole, M.D., their industrial physician.
>
> Our alphabetical list of dealers shows him as Cohn, A. C., instead of Kohn, A. T.

4. To separate the name of a person who is directly addressed, from the rest of the sentence:

> Then, Mr. Reynolds, you can look forward to years of relaxation.
>
> By June 20, Mrs. Holland, you should receive your new luggage.

PU2 *The semicolon can be regarded almost as a period within the sentence. It marks the end of one thought which is somewhat closely connected to the thought which follows. The most frequent uses of the semicolon are as follows:*

PU2a *Use a semicolon to separate two independent clauses not connected by a coordinating conjunction.*

We shall send your merchandise on March 25; it should arrive in ample time for your Easter sale.

This new camera is not intended for novices; it was designed primarily for those whose knowledge and experience enable them to appreciate its greater versatility and finer craftsmanship.

The report was submitted on time; the resulting action corrected the difficulty.

PU2b *Use a semicolon to separate two independent clauses connected by conjunctive adverbs, such as* however, thus, hence, therefore, otherwise, consequently, moreover, *and similar words. (Notice that a comma follows these conjunctive adverbs.)*

We know that you like this new design; however, you may return any of this merchandise within 30 days.

By placing your order now, you can be certain of delivery within 30 days; thus, you can assure your customers of an adequate supply of antifreeze this winter.

We believe that this problem should be prevented in the future; therefore, we recommend that a thorough study of the causes be made.

These words are also frequently used as parenthetical expressions requiring pairs of commas; writers should carefully distinguish between this parenthetical function and their function as connectives joining independent clauses.

We knew, *however,* that he would not complete the assignment. (parenthetical)

We knew that he would not complete the assignment; *however,* he was the only person who could start it by supplying the background. (conjunctive adverb)

She concluded, *therefore,* that you were not interested. (parenthetical)

She concluded that you were not interested; *therefore,* she looked elsewhere. (conjunctive adverb)

PU2c *Use a semicolon to separate two long or involved independent clauses with internal marks of punctuation.*

Even though such independent clauses are connected by coordinating conjunctions and would ordinarily require commas (PU1a), careful writers distinguish between the commas *within* clauses by using a heavier separator *between* the clauses.

> This department wrote a series of 10 small advertisements, prepared slides, and drew graphs for the sales campaign; as suggested, we have placed heavy emphasis on electric fans, air-conditioning units, and water coolers in preparing this campaign.

> When these changes are made, their cumulative effect will be to reduce our staff, our labor costs already being too high; and this reduction, which I mentioned to you last week, constitutes a major economy in this department.

PU2d *Use a semicolon to separate elements in a series when the elements contain commas.*

> The sales quotas are, for John, 10,000; for Mark, 12,000; and for Jane, 14,000.

> Our greatest promotional efforts were directed at Phoenix, Arizona; New Orleans, Louisiana; and Canton, Ohio.

PU3 *The colon marks a very close connection of parts; it notifies the reader that a list, an explanation, or closely related material will follow. The most frequent uses of the colon are as follows:*

PU3a *Use a colon to introduce a formal list when the introduction is a complete thought.*

> There are three steps in this procedure:
>
> **1.** Analyze the job carefully.
>
> **2.** Eliminate unnecessary details.
>
> **3.** Reduce operations to routine wherever possible.

> These restrictions can be changed in any of the following instances: (1) required jury duty; (2) death in the immediate family of the employee; (3) illness of the employee; and (4) military service, such as the State Guard.

> Three models will be shipped to you for display: 6W9—Portable, 17E2—Console, and 21N4—Commercial.

PU3b *Use a colon to introduce further explanation.*

> We should like to make a suggestion to help you: ship the damaged part to your nearest dealer, notify us when you have done this, and we will send a factory-trained expert to your dealer to make the necessary repairs.

The analysis shows that suburban buying habits are changing with the new housing: more land means increased demand for gardening equipment, functional architecture brings a trend to do-it-yourself merchandise, and greater distances make a second car a family necessity.

We have it available in five colors: charcoal gray, maroon, off-white, dark green, and navy blue.

PU3c *Use a colon to punctuate certain routine or conventional situations.*

1. After the salutation of a business letter (optional):

> Gentlemen and Ladies:

> Dear Mr. Flemming:

2. Between hours and minutes in time:

> Employees must report at 8:30.

3. In introducing a formal quotation:

> We call your attention to the statement in your policy:
> This provision will remain valid under all conditions except military service, self-inflicted injuries, atomic attacks, or as is specified later, Act of God.

This use of the colon depends on the degree of formality and the length of the quotation. Many writers use a rule of thumb that quotations of more than four or five lines or about fifty words should be introduced by colons and be dropped down and indented to a new margin. Where the quotation is shorter, the writing more informal, a comma is used.

> He summed up his whole practice of human relations by saying, "Always talk to the guy."

> Maybe you've said to yourself, "I wish I could afford that kind of vacation." Well, now you can!

PU4 *The apostrophe indicates the possessive case of nouns and of indefinite pronouns* (anybody's, everybody's) *and tells the reader the precise point in a contraction where a letter or letters have been omitted. The most frequent uses of the apostrophe are as follows:*

PU4a *Use an apostrophe to indicate the omission of letters in contractions.*

Can't, didn't, don't, we'll, you'll, I'd, '54

PU4b   *Use an apostrophe to show possession.*

> A company's location   A customer's statement   Companies' locations
> Customers' statements

PU4c   *Place the apostrophe properly.*

The real problem business writers face is not when to use the apostrophe to indicate possession but where to place it properly. The following principles should, therefore, be strictly observed:

1. Add an *'s* to form the possessive singular.

> A child's book   A company's location   A customer's statement

2. Add an *'s* to form the possessive plural of words which *do not* end in *s* in their plural form.

> Women's clothes   Children's books   Men's suits

3. Add only the apostrophe to plural nouns ending in *s*.

> The creditors' meeting   The directors' report   Three days' pay

4. Indicate possession in company names by placing *'s* after the last word or name only.

> Johnson and Johnson's new location
>
> The Universal Casting Company's products
>
> Green, Black, and White's service

5. Proper names ending in *s* or *z* add *'s* if the name is of one syllable; if it is a two-syllable name ending in *s* or *z*, only the apostrophe is required.

> One-syllable names ending in *s* or *z:*

> Keats's poems   Schwartz's clothes   Jones's report

> Two-syllable names ending in *s* or *z:*

> Dickens' novels   Landis' ideas   Hopkins' appointment

6. Personal pronouns require no apostrophe in the possessive. It should be noted, however, that the form *it's* is a contraction for *it is*.

> The book is hers (yours, theirs, ours, etc.).

PU5 *Quotation marks are used to enclose direct quotations, and to indicate borrowed material, and words or phrases used in a special sense. Their most frequent uses are:*

PU5a *Enclosing direct quotations.*

> At that time you wired us, "Send the goods immediately by express; John C. Worden, your city, will furnish credit information."

> Your letter of November 23 notified me of this change and said, "I will send you a payment by December 10."

PU5b *Placing quotation marks properly.*

Notice that commas and periods are always placed inside the final quotation marks. Other marks of punctuation, like question marks and exclamation points, are placed inside the quotations when they pertain only to the quoted matter; outside when they belong to the whole sentence.

> At that time, I thought you said, "Can you maintain production at this rate over a long period?" (The question is asked here *within* the quoted material; hence, the question mark is inside the quotes.)

> What did you think when we wrote, "We have maintained our side of this contract"? The question is asked in the material *outside* the quotes; hence, the question mark is outside.)

An increasing practice in reports, letters, and memos is to indent quoted material inside the margins of the text. If this is done, *no quotation marks* are needed. When reports, letters, or memos are double spaced, these quotations should be single spaced. (See PU3c for use of the comma or colon in introducing such quotations.)

We were, therefore, greatly interested in the following

statement he made about the jargon that mars too much business

writing:

> The very fact that business has become conscious of jargon is a hopeful sign. But much remains to be done. In business writing, an amazing collection of strange, meaningless, trite, and pompous expressions has persisted chiefly because untrained writers sit down to write with only the incoming correspondence and the hackneyed reports in the files to guide them.

PU5c *Use quotation marks to indicate special usage of a word or phrase or to enclose slang or technical words.*

This function of quotation marks is frequently abused by inexperienced writers in a quest for emphasis or humorous effect. Underlining the word or phrase is increasingly used in place of the quotes. Whichever practice is followed—quotes or underlining—use it sparingly and do it only at the first appearance of the word or phrase; after that no special treatment is required.

> In the ratings, we think of this as "factual information"; actually, a very large element of human judgment and possible error enters this factual information.

> Our search for the material was like those "who-dun-its."

> She was so proud of her first letter until the supervisor called her attention to "Respectively yours."

> In this sense, has he really "learned" anything?

PU6 *Use the end mark (period, question mark, or exclamation point) appropriate to the major intent and meaning of the sentence.*

PU6a *The period marks the end of a complete thought and a definite pause for the reader. It is used after ordinary declarative or imperative statements which are not intended to express strong feelings.*

> Send the report as soon as possible.

> She declared her intention to buy.

PU6b *The question mark is used at the end of a sentence intended as a direct question. Notice that questions can also consist of a single word.*

> When did you say the report is due? Tomorrow?

> Why did he write so tactlessly?

Do not use the question mark after an indirect quotation.

> *Not:* He asked whether I would go?

> *But:* He asked whether I would go.

The omission of question marks where they are required is generally caused by carelessness in rereading or revising written material. Since this mark of punctuation radically changes the meaning of a sentence, special care should be taken to see that it is used properly. Notice the difference in meaning in the following sentences, identical except for punctuation:

> She wrote that report.
>
> She wrote that report?

In so-called polite questions, there is an increasing tendency to omit the question mark in business writing. One way to distinguish the polite question from a regular one is that the polite question typically asks for action, while the regular question asks for an answer of some kind.

> Will you please send the signed copy as soon as possible.
>
> Won't you please notify us of your change of address.

PU6c *The exclamation point is used to express surprise, strong emotion, command, or emphasis.*

> Do it today!
>
> Indeed I wish I could grant your request!
>
> Let's start our planning at once!

In business writing, the exclamation point should not be overused. Particularly to be avoided are attempts to label humor or irony by the exclamation point, as in these examples:

> We told you we would get there firstest with the bestest line of merchandise!
>
> If it weren't for people, we'd never make mistakes!

PU7 *Dashes, brackets, and parentheses may be used to set off certain types of parenthetical material.*

Since good business writing should reflect careful planning and organization, business writers should avoid overusing these marks of punctuation; by their very definition, these marks indicate afterthoughts and, occasionally, irrelevant comments.

PU7a *The dash marks an abrupt shift; it tells the reader, "This is an afterthought, or this doesn't really belong here, or this requires special emphasis," the last being its most useful function in business writing. The chief uses of the dash are:*

1. To emphasize or contrast a short phrase or word.

> This new device they have developed is designed well, constructed sturdily— and priced far too high.

He said that smoking was a useless, expensive, time-consuming habit—to which he was completely addicted.

Report writers who report to readers with the same educational background are fortunate because their readers—and notice this phrase—speak the same language.

2. To indicate an interruption or an afterthought.

We are writing the customer—and we should have said this in our previous letter—that the guarantee cannot be interpreted that way.

The difficulty—as I think I reported to you—lies in the shortage of personnel.

This man—you must remember him—would make an excellent reference to use for such a position.

PU7b *Brackets are generally used to set off inserted material which is extraneous or incidental to the text. Such insertions may be comments, explanations, or editorial corrections.*

She reported that her research had preceded [Note] at a rapid rate.

Be careful to write it re-creation [to distinguish it from recreation].

Parentheses ( ) and brackets [ ] are often confused. Since most standard typewriters carry parentheses but not brackets, brackets must generally be inked in.

PU7c *Parentheses are generally used to enclose explanatory material or comments which may be helpful but are not absolutely essential to the reader's understanding.*

The discussion of accounting (see Book 2) was most helpful.

If you have these in stock (they must be available now), please send them immediately.

The practice of enclosing figures in parentheses to repeat for accuracy is used infrequently in letters and reports today. Unless there is a special reason for doing so, do not write "He sent eleven dollars ($11.00)." Instead, write "He sent $11."

PU8 *The hyphen is a device which indicates that words or parts of a word belong together. Technically, it is more nearly a mark of spelling than of punctuation.*

Among the problems that plague business writers and typists is whether to use the hyphen in certain compound words and where to place it when an individual word is broken at the end of a line. In both situations, a good dictionary should be consulted, although even the best dictionaries differ about certain words. The status of compound words changes; *nevertheless,* for instance, has evolved from *never the less* through *never-the-less* to its present form. The following rules for the use of the hyphen are particularly useful for business writers:

PU8a *Use a hyphen to join words which form a compound adjective before a noun.*

We say "He is well known" but "He is a well-known man." (Well-known is here a compound adjective modifying a noun.) While this rule is not always strictly followed, precise writing such as technical reports, specifications, contracts, or procedures should follow it to the letter. Here are a few examples.

a 21-inch screen	longer-life wire
up-to-date merchandise	right-of-way statements
well-planned campaign	designed-for-comfort construction
better-than-average performance	copper-coated pipe
150-watt lamps	house-to-house survey
a middle-of-the-road policy	

PU8b *Use a hyphen to indicate the division of syllables in a word at the end of a line of typed or printed matter.*

Here, the dictionary is your only complete guide. But remember that words of one syllable (bought, sold) cannot be divided, that hyphenated words should be divided only at the hyphen (long-delayed *not* long-de-layed), and that it is pointless to divide a word just to set off one or two letters at the beginning or end of a word (divid-ed, e-lude).

PU8c *Use a hyphen to separate words or syllables in certain conventional situations.*

1. With the prefixes *ex* and *self:* ex-president, ex-officer, self-focusing, self-determining.

2. When awkward doubling of vowels or tripling of consonants would result or when an awkward word would result:

semi-independence	stall-less
re-elect	pre-empt
wall-like	re-enlist
re-educate	anti-intellectual
pre-engineered	anti-inflation

co-worker (to avoid the awkward word *coworker*)

3. With compound numbers from twenty-one to ninety-nine.

> Forty-seven people were sent.
>
> Twenty-seven dollars and seventy-three cents.

4. With words where repetition is avoided by indicating to the reader that the first word is incomplete.

> time- and labor-saving methods
>
> medium- and low-income groups
>
> upper- and middle-management categories

MECHANICS

Numbers

Like many other aspects of business writing, the practice of writing numbers has not been standardized. This is particularly unfortunate because numbers are so frequently used in letters, reports, and memorandums; and considerable savings could be effected if certain general principles were adopted to replace the haphazard methods now prevailing. The most authoritative attempt to achieve standarization is a Committee Report (Robert D. Hay, chairman) of the American Business Writing Association (December, 1952) titled "Standardization of Rules for Writing Numbers"; the following rules are based on this report, which recommends, as a general rule, that all numbers be expressed in figures when there are several numbers in a paragraph, a letter, or a report. To this general rule, the committee recommended the following modifications for readability and clarity in the use of numbers:

NU1 *Use the "rule of ten" and write out single numbers of ten or below and numbers divisible by ten up to one hundred. Hence*

We employed *nine* stenographers last year.

They invited *sixty* guests.

NU2 *If a sentence begins with a number, the number should be expressed in words.*

Forty people attended.

When this number is awkward to express in words, recast the sentence so that it begins with some other word.

Not: Three hundred and nineteen requests for the pamphlet were received.

But: We received 319 requests for the pamphlet.

NU2a *When numbers are expressed in words, as at the beginning of a sentence, use a hyphen to join compound numbers.*

Correct: Twenty-three, seventy-one, ninety-four.

NU2b *When a number standing first in the sentence is followed by another number to form an approximation, both numbers should be expressed in words.*

Not: Twenty or 25 days will be sufficient.

But: Twenty or twenty-five days will be sufficient.

NU3 *Use a consistent method to express numbers in a connected series or in related groups.*

NU3a *When a sentence contains one series of numbers, all numbers of the series should be expressed in figures.*

We have 9 dealers in Chicago, 11 in Detroit, and 23 in New York.

NU3b *When a sentence contains two series of numbers, the numbers in one series should be expressed in words and the numbers in the other series should be expressed in figures.*

Five students scored 95 points; seventeen students scored 80 points; and eleven scored 75 points.

Two stocks moved to $115; seven went to $100; and four dropped to $87.50.

NU3c *Use a tabulation when more than two series of numbers are involved.*

Name of accountant	Daily rate	Number of working days	Total earnings
Barlow, Helen	$50	3	$150
Dickson, A. J.	$35	2	$70
Oman, Charles	$40	1	$40

NU4 *When one number immediately precedes another number of different context, one number should be expressed in words, the other in figures.*

He ordered twenty-five 10 by 12 prints.

The specifications call for four 3-inch bolts.

You requested 350 two-way sockets.

NU5 *Amounts of money, generally speaking, should be expressed in figures.*

This is particularly true when a sentence, a paragraph, a letter, or a report mentions several different amounts of money. However, some questions invariably arise on how to use numbers in money amounts. The following practices are recommended.

1. When several amounts are written close together, all should be expressed in figures.

   Correct: The assets were $17,000; the liabilities were $3,000; and the net worth was $14,000.

2. When an amount of money consists of dollars and cents, the amount should always be expressed in figures. The dollar sign should precede the amount (unless in a tabulated column).

   Correct: The invoice total was $50.51.

   Correct: The bonds were sold at $999.50 each.

3. When an amount of money consists only of dollars, it should not be followed by a decimal point and a double zero. The double zero is not necessary unless the amount is tabulated in a column which includes both dollars and cents.

   Correct: The invoice total was $150.

   Correct: $ 250.80
                  200.00
                  312.70
                  286.50
             $1,050.00

When a series of money amounts contains mixed figures, all even figures should include the double zero for consistency.

   Correct: The committee raised amounts of $15.00, $33.75, and $75.00 in the three rummage sales.

4. An amount should not be written in both figures and words. This procedure is acceptable only in legal documents and financial documents.

Correct: The check was for $57.

Correct: The total assets are $23,000.

5. An isolated amount of money of more than ten cents but less than one dollar should be expressed in figures.

Correct: The piggy bank yielded $.57.

Correct: The piggy bank yielded 57¢.

Correct: The piggy bank yielded 57 cents.

Correct: The piggy bank yielded nine cents.

6. An isolated amount of money in even dollars should be written in figures. When the even amount is ten dollars or less, it should be written in words.

Correct: The check was for $57.

Correct: The other check was for five dollars. (Assuming an isolated amount.)

7. When amounts of money are to be tabulated, care should be taken to align the numbers correctly. The right-hand digit of the largest amount governs the tabulation. All decimals, commas, and dollar signs should be aligned properly. A dollar sign should be used both at the beginning of a column and at the end of a column after the underline. It should be set far enough to the left to take care of the longest amount.

Correct:		*Correct:*	
$	50.00		$1,000.50
	100.90	$5,000.00	
	1,100.10	475.00	
	10,133.10		5,475.50
	$11,384.10		$6,475.50
			1.00
			35.00
			$6,511.50

NU6   *Miscellaneous. The following numbers should be expressed in figures:*

1. Dates:

Correct: October 10, 1968   10 Oct 68 (Military)
             10th of October   Your letter of October 10 was most welcome.
             tenth of October

2. Street numbers:

Correct: 1503 Garland Street

3. Numerical names of streets:

    Correct: 110 First Street (All numerical street names under ten should be spelled out in accordance with the general rule of ten.)

    Correct: 110 69th Street

    Correct: 110 110th Street

    Correct: 110 110 Street

4. Numbered items such as page numbers, chapter numbers, figure numbers, table numbers, chart numbers, serial numbers, and telephone numbers:

Correct:	*Correct:*
Page 10	Chart X
Chapter 10	Service Serial No. 01845283
Chapter X	Policy No. V9109815
Figure 8	Policy #V9109815
Fig.8	Claim No. 13189756
Table X	File No. 2716
Table 10	Telephone CA-7175
Chart 10	Model No. 3223

5. Decimals:

    Correct: 10.25
                 3.1414
                 0.3535

6. Dimensions:

Correct:	*Correct:*
8½ × 11 in.	2 × 4 in.
8½ by 11 in.	2 by 4 in.

7. Time:

Correct:	*Correct:*
7 P.M.	7:35 P.M.
7 a.m.	7:35 p.m.
seven o'clock	seven in the morning

8. Percentages:

Correct:	*Correct:*
35%	6%
99.99%	6 percent
0.09%	six percent ("isolated" figure only)

9. Fractions:

Correct:		
$1/32$	one-half	$110^{1/5}$ or 110.2
$8/64$	two-thirds	
$25/64$	one-fourth	
$25/100$ or 0.25	three-fourths	

Capitalization

Inexperienced writers generally use too many capitals. A good general principle is to capitalize only when some specific convention requires it. The following rules indicate the conventional uses of capitalization which business writers should follow:

CA1 *Capitalize the first word of the salutation and of the complimentary close in the business letter.*

Gentlemen and Ladies:	Sincerely yours,
Dear Ms. Smith:	Yours very truly,
My dear Mr. Smith:	Cordially yours,

CA2 *Capitalize the first word and all other important words in titles of books, reports, or business documents.*

The term *important words* is generally interpreted to mean all words except articles (*a, an, the*), prepositions, and conjunctions.

A Report on the Last Quarterly Sales Conference

An Analysis of Plant Operations for the Executive Committee

The Man in the Gray Flannel Suit

CA3 *Capitalize proper names used to identify specific organizations, places, buildings, and the like.*

the Warren Company	the Washington Monument
the Chrysler Building	the Standard Corporation
Times Square	the Modern Language Association

CA4 *Capitalize the first word of the following structural units:*

1. Complete sentences.

2. Fragments intended as units of expression.

What beauty! What economy!

3. Quotations, but only if the quotation is a complete statement.

Your letter of August 25 said, "Send the replacement part by air express."

Your letter of August 25 said "good wishes for success" in a most gracious way.

4. Complete statements following a colon.

This experience has raised one major question: How can we cut these costs?

Do not use capital letters in the following instances:

1. *North, east, south,* and *west* except when they refer to a specific section.

He traveled west.

We have relocated in the South and the Middle West.

2. General terms which do not identify a specific person, place, or thing.

a doctor (but Doctor C. E. Jones)

our president (but President C. E. Smith)

a high school education (but East High School)

a professor (but Professor Brown)

the city coucil (but the Centerville City Council)

his company (but the White Company)

my uncle (but my Uncle John)

3. The names of the seasons.

spring, winter, summer, fall, midwinter

4. Nouns used with numbers or figures.

page 57, type A, method 3

Exceptions to this are capitals in expressions like Table 3 and Figure 3 within a report, which may be used for emphasis; model numbers used within the company—Model 26; and trademarks—Brillo, Verifax, and Anacin.

5. The first word of an indirect quotation.

Not: He reported that *He* would attend.

But: He reported that *he* would attend.

6. The names of studies when they are not used in the sense of specific courses.

history, calculus, engineering, accounting, forestry, agriculture, nursing

Use capitals when referring to specific courses.

History 101   Calculus 263

Remember, however, that names of nationality and language require capitals. Hence,

He studied history, English, calculus, and French.

Italics

Since many typewriters do not have italic type, the most common practice is to underline typewritten words which would be italicized in printed material.

IT1 *Use italics to indicate titles of books, newspapers, magazines, and reports.*

She sent a copy of *A Report on Management Methods.*

You will be interested in his book *Modern Communication in Business.*

The advertisement appeared originally in *The New York Times.* (Note that this is the correct title—not the New York *Times.* Use titles exactly as they are given, and if the articles *the, a,* or *an* are part of the title, italicize them.)

IT2 *Use italics to indicate foreign words or phrases.*

Her sales policy can best be described by the words *caveat emptor.*

Noblesse oblige can be said to apply to the modern businessperson.

IT3 *Use italics for a word, a letter, or a number referred to as such.*

You should note the difference between *its* and *it's.*

Because the *3's* and *5's* looked so much alike, we unfortunately misread the order.

He never seemed to learn that there are three *l's* in *parallel.*

IT4 *Use italics to give special emphasis to a word or a group of words.*

For most business writers this statement about use of italics should be followed by a note of caution, for the tendency is to overuse italics and, hence, to diminish their effectiveness as a device for emphasis. In sales letters and sales material, however, italicized words and phrases can underscore key ideas if the underlining is used judiciously and sparingly.

> You can continue to have this service and *at the same low price.*

> Won't you call our dealer for a *free* estimate?

> This book is authoritative, complete, and above all, *easy to understand.*

> His deadline for the report was June 4, but I did not receive it until *July 17.*

Footnotes and References

Many business writers shy away from the use of footnotes either because they do not know the proper form or because they think of them as being too pedantic or scholarly. Admittedly, footnotes are not used as frequently in business writing as in scholarly papers. One easy way for business writers to make reference to source materials is to incorporate the reference in the text itself by one of the following methods:

> As Stuart Chase says in *Power of Words* (New York, 1954), p. 173, "Good listening aids us in sizing up a person, a meeting, a line of argument."

or

> Stuart Chase in *Power of Words* (p. 178) comments, "A study of the remarkable communicating ability of honey bees shows that humans are not alone in possessing elaborate systems."*

How much reference there should be to publication dates, places, pages, and publishers' names should be governed entirely by the purpose and the reader. If a bibliography is attached, the reference in the text can appropriately be cut to a mere mention of the author and title. As for the mechanics of setting up such references, a good rule of thumb is that quotations of less than four lines are spaced exactly like the rest of the text, with the same margins, and are enclosed in double quotation marks. Longer quotations are single-spaced, set off from the text by double spacing at top and bottom, and indented from the left-hand margin.

In long, formal reports and complex business documents, footnotes should be used, generally, for three purposes:

1. To cite the authority and evidence for statements, opinions, or quotations in the text

2. To make acknowledgments for assistance given or research done by others

3. To provide a place to define a term used in the text, to give additional

* Both quotations from Stuart Chase's *Power of Words* are reprinted by permission of the author and Harcourt, Brace & World, Inc.

information that does not fit into the text, or to explain in greater detail what has been referred to in the text

While practice varies considerably in different fields, the most common usage is to place footnotes at the bottom of the page on which the reference occurs. Hence, the typist must gauge the spacing carefully to provide room for the same number of footnotes as there are reference numbers within the text of that page. Footnotes should be single-spaced. They should be numbered *consecutively* throughout the report or document; in other words, they should not be numbered 1, 2, 3 on page 4 and start 1, 2 on page 5. They may be set off from the text by a solid line from margin to margin, although this is not mandatory.

F1 *Place footnotes properly and consistently in the text.*

In the text, the footnote should *follow* the passage to which it refers; for example, if the passage is a quotation, the reference should be placed at the end of the quotation, not after the author's name or the title of the book. The place in the text at which the footnote is introduced is marked by an Arabic numeral (1, 2, 3); Roman numerals (I, II, III) are not used for this purpose. In typed material, the footnote number is elevated slightly above the line but is never a full space above it. While usage in business reports and documents has not completely crystallized, the most general practice now is to leave the number[1] without punctuation. The older practice of following it with a period[1.] or surrounding it with parentheses[(1)] or[(1.)] is not recommended. Whichever form is used, it should be used consistently throughout the document and in the references within the text as well as in the reference numbers at the bottom of the page.

Writers who prepare reports or articles for publication should always look at the magazine or journal to which they intend to submit their material and follow that publication's practice concerning the form and placement of footnotes. If you are in doubt about any of the many highly specialized problems which arise about footnotes, consult *The Modern Language Association Style Sheet* (you can obtain a copy from the Materials Center, MLA, 62 Fifth Avenue, New York, N.Y. 10011) or Kate L. Turabian's *A Manual for Writers of Term Papers, Theses, and Dissertations* (The University of Chicago Press). While these definitive works tend to emphasize a more formal and scholarly pattern of footnoting than that customarily employed in business reports and documents, they can be relied on as completely authoritative.

F2 *Adopt a standard form of footnote style and be consistent in its use. Remember that a footnote is used to give the source of information.*

In writing footnotes, use the title page of the book you are citing as the source for the information contained. There is no need to repeat in the footnote any items, such as the author's name or the title, which have been supplied in the text. If you remember the purpose your report or document will serve and the kind of reader or readers, you can then select the appropriate items from the following list and arrange them in this order:

1. The name of the author in its normal order—not last name first—followed by a comma. If the author's name is unknown, begin with the title; Anon. or Anonymous is not necessary except in alphabetical listings in bibliographies.

2. The title of the book, underlined or in capital letters if not underlined, followed by a comma.

3. What edition of the book you are citing, if it is not the first edition—for example, 4th ed.

4. These facts about the book, grouped within parentheses:
    a. The place of publication, followed by a comma.
    b. The year of publication, the last element within parentheses, so there is no punctuation. Place a comma outside the parenthesis.

5. The page number or numbers which you are citing, followed by a period—for example, p. 142. or pp. 147–148.

Typical footnotes would be arranged as follows:

Robert Gunning, *The Technique of Clear Writing,* 2d ed., (New York, 1968), p. 74.

Raymond Lesikar, *Report Writing for Business,* 4th ed., (Homewood, Ill., 1973), p. 25.

If the book has two or three authors, begin the footnote:

Gordon H. Mills and John A. Walter, *Technical Writing,* etc.

Glenn Leggett, C. David Mead, and William Charvat, *Prentice-Hall Handbook for Writers,* etc.

When the book contains a collection of articles, reports, or documents by different authors but edited by one individual:

Eldridge Peterson (ed.), *Advertiser's Annual,* etc.

When you refer to a report with no author given:

Annual Report of the American Management Association for the Year Ending December 31, 1978.

or

American Management Association *Annual Report for the Year Ending December 31, 1978.*

When you refer to articles in magazines, use the following form for the footnote:

1. The name of the author followed by a comma. The title comes first if the author's name is unknown.

2. The title of the article placed within quotation marks and with a comma *inside* the final quotation mark.

3. The name of the periodical, underlined and followed by a comma.

4. The date of the magazine—December 5, 1978—if it is comparatively recent; if it is a few years back, give the volume number in capital Roman numerals or Arabic numbers—XXV, February 16, 1974. Many magazines have abandoned the clumsy system of numbering volumes in Roman numerals; if you refer to such a magazine, your reference is vol. 25. The date of the magazine is followed by a comma.

5. The page number or numbers, followed by a period.

The footnote referring to a magazine article will conform to one of these examples:

> Walter McQuade, "There's a Saving Grace in the New Office Lighting," *Fortune,* December 1977, p. 152.

If no author is given:

> "Colleges Learn the Hard Sell," *Business Week,* February 14, 1977, p. 93.

When you list the volume number of the periodical:

> Robert M. Wendlinger, "Improving Upward Communication," *Journal of Business Communication,* vol. 10, no. 4, Summer 1974, 18. (Notice that you can delete the p. or pp. when you include the volume number in the reference.)

References to newspapers are made as follows:

> *Cleveland Plain Dealer,* November 27, 1978, p. 13.
>
> *The New York Times,* October 2, 1978, p. 42.
>
> *The Times* (London), October 2, 1978, p. 12.

Notice that the name of the city is italicized when it is part of the title of the newspaper; otherwise, the place (London) is put in parentheses to avoid confusion with other newspapers of similar name.

References to letters, reports, minutes of committee meetings in company or individual files should contain names, title, file numbers, dates, addresses, or any other information which is sufficient to identify them:

Minutes of the Monthly Meeting of the Cost Reduction Committee, October 22, 1978 (in the files of John C. Dunn, Secretary).

Letter from Mr. C. E. Woodley, 3907 East Auburn Street, Minneapolis, Minn. 55440 to N. M. Boland, Sales Manager, February 4, 1978.

Quarterly Report of the Personnel Department, July 10, 1978, p. 6 (in the files of the Department).

While they are not written materials, interviews constitute sources for many reports and formal documents in business. References to them are properly made in this form:

Interview with Charles F. Springer, Director of Business Information, The Los Angeles Chamber of Commerce, May 9, 1978.

Interview with Dr. Thomas Gresham, Coordinator of Research, The Blank Chemical Company, Warrington, West Virginia, June 10, 1978.

When sources are referred to more than once in the document or report, the footnotes following the first reference can be shortened. Two devices are then used:

Ibid. (for *ibidem*—"in the same place"). Use this when you refer to a source which is *the same as that in the footnote immediately preceding. Ibid.* is always underlined and followed by a period; it is capitalized only when it is the first word in the entry.

Op. cit. (for *opere citato*—"in the work cited"). Use this when you refer to a book or article already mentioned in a previous footnote *but when there are other references intervening. Op. cit.* replaces the title and facts of publication cited in the previous reference; it does not replace the author's name, since its meaning is "in the work cited."

These two useful devices are illustrated in the following:

[1]Graham Kemp, *The Company Speaks* (London, 1973), p. 32.

[2]Robert D. Ross, *The Management of Public Relations* (New York, 1977), p. 82.

[3]*Ibid.,* p. 44.

[4]Kemp, *op. cit.,* p. 51.

F3 *Use a consistent system in listing bibliographic entries, including sufficient information to serve your reader's purpose.*

Many reports and business documents require a list of sources used in their preparation. This bibliography, of course, contains an entry for each different source referred to in the footnotes as well as any other sources which may help the reader. Entries in the bibliography are arranged alphabetically by the author's last name or (where no author is given) by the first word of the title, disregarding the articles *the, a, an* (hence "The Cost of Planning" is alphabetized under *c*). For very long or complex reports and documents, bibliographic entries are sometimes classified according to type: books, magazine articles, business reports, and the like. When this classification is used, a separate heading—Books, Articles, Periodicals—should be supplied for each section of the bibliography, and the items are then alphabetized within each section.

The first line of each entry is not indented; additional lines are indented the number of spaces used in paragraph indention throughout the report or document. Single spacing is used within each entry, double spacing between entries. The entry contains the same information as is used in the footnote except that it omits page references for books. Many report writers omit references to publishers in their footnotes and add this information to the other facts in the bibliography. Notice the arrangement in the following section of bibliography containing books, articles, and a newspaper reference.

Brown, Ralph J., and James D. Somerville, "Evaluation of Management Development Programs . . . An Innovative Approach," *Personnel,* July-August 1977, pp. 28–46.

"B-school Buzzword: Creativity," *Business Week,* August 8, 1977, p. 66.

Gallese, Liz, "Transferred Executives Learn It's Not so Easy to Find a New Home," *The Wall Street Journal,* June 14, 1978, pp. 1 & 27.

Hitchings, Bradley (ed.), "New Twists in Adult Education," *Business Week,* July 14, 1977, pp. 61–62.

Huseman, Richard C., Cal M. Logue, and Dwight L. Freshley, *Readings in Interpersonal and Organizational Communication,* Boston: Holbrook Press, Inc., 1977.

Joslin, Edward O., "Career Management: How to Make It Work," *Personnel,* July-August 1977, pp. 65–72.

Marlowe, Leigh, *Social Psychology,* Boston: Holbrook Press, Inc., 1975.

Philips, Madison, "Developing Healthy Attitudes for Dealing with a Union," *Personnel,* September-October 1977, pp. 68–71.

"The Pressure to Compromise Personal Ethics," *Business Week,* January 31, 1977, p. 107.

"Stonewalling Plant Democracy," *Business Week,* March 28, 1977, pp. 78–82.

Spelling

Most teachers have heard all the alibis pertaining to bad spelling. These excuses run the gamut from the optimistic "I'll have a secretary to correct any mis-spellings" to the fatalistic "I'm a hereditary bad speller and nobody can do anything about it." Perhaps too much emphasis has been placed on the horrors of poor spelling—although many "modern" schools seem to be offsetting this tendency by giving it no emphasis at all. Certainly there are more serious flaws in writing than misspellings; unclear, ambiguous, or meaningless constructions are far worse. But a misspelled word is something definite, something tangible for all who read to see. They may conclude that the error results from ignorance, from carelessness, or from inattention to detail. None of these conclusions will aid the business writer in his or her career or enhance the reputation of the company for which he or she works; and that is why misspelling should be avoided in memos, reports, and letters.

Correcting Errors in Spelling

How can this be done? First, you'll have to make up your mind that a working knowledge of correct spelling is important to your business career. Second, you can do these things:

1. Observe the arrangement of letters in words carefully. (When you don't, you write words like *thier, Britian, fourty, buisness* and *similiar.*)

2. Watch your pronunciation. If you mispronounce a word, you will probably misspell it. (This produces *accidently* for *accidentally; maintainance* for *maintenance; dispite* for *despite; suprise* for *surprise.*)

3. Proofread your work carefully. Whether you submit written work to an instructor in college or sign material which you have dictated in business, you have a responsibility to see that it represents you at your best.

These instructions really add up to one—*use your dictionary constantly.* For anyone who writes, it is the one indispensable tool; for those who are unsure of their spelling, it is the only satisfactory answer, since the "rules" of English spelling frequently have so many exceptions. You will do well, therefore, to look up each word about which you are uncertain and to keep a list of these words on which you can concentrate.

Twenty-five Words Most Frequently Misspelled

An exceedingly helpful and significant study made by Dean Thomas Clark Pollock of New York University, as reported in *College English* for November 1954 (volume 16, pages 102 to 109), sheds considerable light on actual spelling errors. Dean Pollock collected reports from 599 college teachers of English in 52 colleges and universities on the 50 words these teachers found misspelled most frequently by college students. His analysis of these data shows that the majority of misspellings occur with a comparatively small number of words or word groups; in fact, 9 percent of the different words or word groups in the study account for over half of all the misspellings of the total of 4,482 words or word groups the college teachers submitted to him. The conclusion which can logically be drawn from this exhaustive study is that college students can greatly improve their spelling by concentrating on a relatively small number of words or word groups.

Here are the 25 words and word groups which Dean Pollock's study revealed as being most frequently misspelled, along with specific suggestions for spelling them correctly or for using the proper form in the proper place:

1. *Their, they're, there*
   Their—possessive case of the pronoun *they.*
   They're—contraction for *they are.*
   There—an adverb meaning *in or at that place,* as "We sent the order *there* rather than delay delivery." Used also in sentences in which the verb comes before the subject: *"There* is hope of a quick solution."

2. *Too, to, two*
   Too—an adverb meaning *in addition* or *to an excessive extent or degree.*

   > He *too* had difficulty organizing his reports.

   > She used *too* many words.

   To—a preposition expressing motion or direction toward something.

   > He sent it *to* the New York Office.

   > We expressed our thanks *to* her.

   Two—a number: *two* people.

3. *Receive, receiving*
   Remember the rule: *i* before *e* except after *c.* Not all English words with *ei* or *ie* follow the rule, but rece*i*ve and rece*i*ving do.

4. *Exist, existence, existent*
   Memorize the exact sequence of letters in *exist* and remember that the other two forms are formed with *e*—exist*e*nce, not exist*a*nce; exist*e*nt, not exist*a*nt.

5. *Occur, occurred, occurring, occurrence*
   Remember the basic form *occur* and that any suffix added requires that the final *r* be doubled.

6. *Definite, definitely, definition, define*
   There is no *a* in any of these words and only one *f* in each of them. Most misspellings result from an attempt to spell the basic form as de*fin*ate. Pronounce it carefully and use the *i* before the *t* of the first three forms.

7. *Separate, separation*
   Remember the *a* (not *e*) which always follows *p* in these words.

8. *Believe, belief*
   These words also follow the *i* before *e* rule.

9. *Occasion*
Two *c*'s and one *s*

10. *Lose, losing*
Memorize *lose* and remember that the *e* drops out to form *losing*. These words should not be confused with *loose, loosing,* whose general meaning is *to free from bonds* or *not firm*, as "He got his hands loose" or "The loose papers in her briefcase."

11. *Write, writing, writer*
The long *i* sound requires just one *t;* note the difference in pronunciation of wri*t*er and wri*tt*en.

12. *Description, describe*
Always an *e* in the first syllable.

13. *Benefit, benefited, beneficial*
Bene is Latin for "well" and your reader will regard you benevolently if you rigidly adhere to the Latin. *Benefited* is a bit tricky in requiring only one *t*.

14. *Precede*
Misspellings of this word result from confusion with *proceed*, meaning *to move forward* to *to carry on an action*. *Precede* means *to go before in time or rank or importance*. You'll simply have to learn these spellings and meanings and then commit to memory the fact that *procedure*, a word used frequently in business writing, is a maverick in its spelling.

15. *Referring*
Refer ends with one *r*, but the participle doubles the *r*. Since *referring* occurs frequently in business reports, letters, and memos, you should learn its spelling.

16. *Success, succeed, succession*
Keep your attention on the two *c*'s, which cause most of the trouble in spelling these words.

17. *Its, it's*
Its—the possessive case of the pronoun *it*.

> That report has proved *its* worth.

> The machine was delivered without *its* fixtures.

It's—a contraction of *it is*.

> *It's* a pleasure to serve you.

> Contrary to written expressions of opinion by generations of college students, there is no word spelled *its'!*

18. *Privilege*
The *i* before the *l* and the *e* after it are the trouble spots in this word.

19. *Environment*

Careless pronunciation causes most misspellings of this word—*enviorment* being the most frequent misspelling. Sound the word carefully, syllable by syllable—*en-vi-ron-ment*—and you can eliminate the major danger of misspelling.

20. *Personal, personnel*

Your *personal* hopes for attaining a career in business will probably start on the road to reality in a *personnel* office. Note that these two words are pronounced and spelled differently.

21. *Than, then*

Than—a conjunction used after an adjective or adverb in the comparative degree.

> This is a better report *than* last year's was.

Occasionally it is a preposition followed by a noun or pronoun:

> I joined the company earlier *than* John.

But as either part of speech, *than* always indicates some kind of comparison. Then—an adverb indicating *at that time* or *soon afterward*.

> She did not know *then* what she knows now.

> We had to stop our research for a time and *then* we began again.

22. *Principle, principal*

These two words are really *three* in their functions, and to use them correctly you must know their functions and meanings.
Principle—can be used *only as a noun* meaning *an accepted or professed rule of action or conduct.*

> These *principles* have been an integral part of our company's conduct of business.

> He is a man of good *principles.*

Principal—can be used as an *adjective* or *as a noun.* As a noun, principal means *a governing official* such as the *principal* of a high school or *a capital sum* such as

> She drew 5 percent interest on her *principal.*

As an adjective, principal means *chief, most important, first in rank, foremost.*

> The *principal* parts of a verb.

The *principal* reason for the action

Remember that only *principal* can be used as an adjective, that *principle* can be used only as a noun.

23. *Choose, chose, choice*
    Choose is the present tense, *chose* is the past tense, and *choice* is a noun or adjective:

    I hope you will *choose* our products.

    He *chose* to take his vacation at Christmas.

    She had a clear *choice*. (noun)

    We sell *choice* merchandise. (adjective)

24. *Perform, performance*
    Careful pronunciation will eliminate much of the possibility of error here. The word is not "*pre*form" but "*per*form."

25. *Similar*
    Here, too, exact pronunciation will help; the most frequent misspelling is *similiar* which would have to be pronounced "sim-il-yar." The word is properly pronounced "sim-i-ler"—but remember, the last vowel is an *a*.

Three Hundred Words Frequently Misspelled in Business Writing

Use this list to check the accuracy of your spelling and keep a list of the words you misspell.

absence	analysis	calendar
acceptable	apologize	canceled
accessories	appreciation	cancellation
accidentally	appropriate	carburetor
accommodate	approval	career
accompanying	argument	cashier
accustom	arrangement	changeable
achievement	assurance	chargeable
acknowledge	athletic	chiefly
address	attendance	Cincinnati
addressed	authorize	clientele
adequate	auxiliary	collectible
adjustment	balance	column
admirable	bargain	commission
advisable	believing	commitment
allotted	beneficial	committed
all ready	bookkeeper	committee
all right	bulletin	commodities
already	bureau	comparative

competence
competitive
complementary
complimentary
concede
concession
conducive
confer
conference
congratulate
conscientious
consensus
controlled
convenience
correspondence
correspondents
corroborate
counsel
courteous
courtesy
creditor
criticism
criticize
decision
deductible
deferred
deficient
deficit
depreciation
desirable
despite
development
disappointment
discrepancy
dissatisfied
distributor
eligible
embarrass
enforceable
equipped
equitable
equivalent
erroneous
evidently
exaggerate
exceed
exceptionally
exchangeable
exorbitant

expenses
experience
explanation
extension
extraordinary
familiar
feasible
February
financial
flexible
forcible
foreign
forfeit
formally
formerly
forty
fulfill
fundamental
government
grievance
guarantee
guaranty
guidance
handicapped
helpful
hesitancy
hindrance
humorous
hurriedly
illegible
immediately
inadequate
inaugurate
incidentally
inconvenience
independent
indispensable
inducement
initiative
inquiries
insolvency
insurance
intelligible
intentionally
intercede
interchangeable
interruption
installation
invariable

irrelevant
jeopardize
judgment
justifiable
labeled
laboratory
legible
liable
license
liquidation
livelihood
maintain
maintenance
manageable
manufacturer
mediocre
mercantile
merchandise
miniature
miscellaneous
misspell
mortgage
naturally
necessary
negligible
neighbor
nineteenth
ninety
ninth
noticeable
obsolete
occasionally
offered
official
omission
omitted
opportunity
optimistic
originate
pamphlet
parallel
parliamentary
particularly
permanent
permissible
permitting
perseverance
persistence
planned

possession	remittance	transferable
precedence	repetition	transferred
predominant	representative	treasurer
preferable	requisition	truly
preference	retroactive	twelfth
preferred	salable	typical
prejudice	satisfactory	unanimous
preparation	scarcity	unbelievable
prevalent	schedule	unconscious
procedure	secretary	uncontrollable
proceedings	seize	undoubtedly
profited	serviceable	unforeseen
progress	significance	unnecessary
promissory	specifically	until
proportionate	stationary	usage
purchasing	stationery	using
quantity	statute	usually
questionnaire	subsidiary	vacancy
readjustment	substantiate	variety
receipt	substitute	versatile
receivable	successful	vicinity
recipient	superintendent	visible
recommend	supersede	volume
reconcile	supervisor	warehouse
reducible	supplementary	warranted
reference	systematic	Wednesday
referred	tactfulness	welfare
register	technique	wholly
regrettable	temperament	witnessed
reimbursement	temporarily	writing
relief	tendency	written
relieve	thoroughly	yield

LETTER FORM AND MECHANICS

Suppose you received the following letter from your insurance company in response to your request for some policy changes. The letter would appear on a 3 × 6 piece of stationery designed to be mailed in a window envelope. What would be your reaction?

This letter's form is that of the *simplified letter*. It is associated with achieving maximum efficiency in the typing of a business letter. The smaller stationery is thought to discourage excess verbiage. The window envelope means the typist won't have to retype the receiver's name and address. Notice also that the salutation and complimentary close have been eliminated. Proponents of this form consider them unnecessary and antiquated. Finally, observe how the recipient's name and address are typed in reverse order, just as the post office would read them.

From — The Blank Ins. Co. R. M. Smith Vice–president
49201, Michigan, Jackson, 27 Wildwood Avenue

June 10, 1978

To — 40124
Ohio, Cleveland
Union Commerce Bldg. 1313
Ms. A. E. Staley

Thank you so much for sending us the information
concerning what you want done with your policy.

We shall make these changes as you wanted them and will
let you know as soon as possible how much the new premium
will be.

R. M. Smith

R. M. Smith

This type of letter represents a significant change in the practices of traditional business communicators. That change would save senders of such letters a considerable amount of time and money. The relevant question is, how far and how fast ought we to proceed with such changes? The answer really lies in how rapidly readers will accept changes from the more conventional letter forms to which long usage has accustomed them. Again, consider how you might react if you received the preceding letter. Would you resent it as too impersonal in an already impersonal society? Or would you applaud it as a meritorious attempt to streamline communication? Do you, for instance, associate window envelopes with bills? Efficiency with coldness and impersonality? Does the abruptness of the message make you long for the conventional greeting and farewell of the traditional letter? If so, such a letter may save money but antagonize you—and other readers.

No one can say authoritatively that one specific letter form is the correct form. But before we fly in the face of custom, we do well to fall back on what is generally considered acceptable usage and to expect a *gradual* change. For instance, the past two decades have seen growing acceptance by readers and correspondents of a semiformal style. This style incorporates greater efficiency but retains warmth and personality by replacing the inside address and salutation with a mention of the recipient's name in the first line of the letter (see the illustration on page 544).

One way of studying how fast letter form can be changed is for students and correspondents to try out the several modes in which they can clothe their message and to select the most appropriate form. In many instances, this choice will be governed by the practice of the company they work for. That practice will undoubtedly be based on one of the forms discussed next.

LETTER FORMS

The Block Form

This is probably the most widely used form today (see the illustration on page 545). With its two variants—the semiblock and the complete block—it seems to have more reader acceptance than any other format. The block form takes its name from the fact that the inside address, the salutation, and the paragraphs of the letter are arranged in blocks without indention. Divisions between the inside address and the salutation, between the salutation and the body of the letter, and between the paragraphs in the body of the letter are indicated by spacing, with double spaces *between* the units (i.e., between the inside address, the salutation, and the body of the letter) and single spacing *within* the units (i.e., within the inside address and the individual paragraphs). The open form of punctuation should always accompany the block form (see the illustration on page 544).

The block form offers two definite advantages: it saves stenographic time because each part of the letter except the date, the complimentary close, and the signature is aligned with the left margin, so that no time is consumed by indention, and, second, its current wide acceptance offers assurance that the letter arranged in block form is correct and modern.

The Semiblock Form

This form is exactly like the block form except for the indention of paragraphs, which appeals to those who are accustomed to seeing paragraphs indented in type and print. The most common practice is to indent the first word of each paragraph five spaces from the left margin, although you will find occasional variations. The semiblock form is illustrated on page 546.

The Complete-block Form

Another variation of the block form is the complete or full block (see the illustration on page 547). The basic principle of this letter form is to bring all the elements of the letter out to the left-hand margin. Hence no changes of margin are required of the typist, and this form can be said to carry the basic premises of the block form to their logical conclusion. Some correspondents still object to the full-block form because it appears to be unbalanced and heavy on the left side. It is, nonetheless, becoming more and more popular because of the time it saves the typist.

The Simplified Letter

The simplified letter, originally advocated by the National Office Management Association (now the Administrative Management Society), is being increasingly used in all kinds of variants for logical reasons. It is efficient; it reduces typing time and consequently costs. Although a variation of this form was illustrated earlier, another example is included on page 548. Notice that this example is written on regular-size stationery. Firms using the simplified letter would stock several sizes of stationery for messages of different lengths.

MECHANICS OF THE BUSINESS LETTER

While the physical setup of the letter is usually the primary responsibility of typists and secretaries, many companies have general policies, set forth sometimes in letter-writing manuals, which govern the mechanical or routine aspects of the letter. Speaking generally, it is desirable for all letters emanating from a company to be uniform both in form (block, semiblock, etc.) and in the arrangement of parts within the letter itself. Since these practices vary from company to company, students should familiarize themselves with the different methods which may be used in setting up the letter and in handling such parts as the salutation and the complimentary close. This section on letter mechanics is intended as a guide to today's widely used practices; but students should remember that change affects all aspects of the letter and that, therefore, these practices are not permanent or rigid.

1.   Arrange and center the letter on the page for symmetry and balanced appearance.

Whichever letter form is used, the correspondent should remember that the first impression of a letter results from the arrangement of text on the page. The arrangement is the most noticeable feature of the letter and can interest or prejudice the reader at a glance. A letter's first appeal is to the reader's eye by means of attractive display, balance, and proportion. Lopsided letters, top-heavy letters, or letters running off the bottoms of pages indicate inefficiency and carelessness and reflect unfavorably on the sender. The text should be centered on the page, with wide margins on both sides and top and bottom. The usual procedure is to leave a margin of 20 spaces at the left. If the message is very brief, double spacing may be used. The letter should be symmetrical and balanced in appearance; if it is unattractively arranged, it should be retyped, unless the correspondent is willing to have the reader conclude that he or she is careless and inefficient.

2.   Select letterhead and stationery on the basis of simplicity of design and quality.

Business people are becoming increasingly conscious of stationery and letterheads, partly because manufacturers have educated them to appraise other companies by their letterheads and stationery. Whether rightly or wrongly, a snap judgment may be passed on a company as the result of the impression made by its letterhead and stationery. Those who use cheap stationery run the risk of being judged

JENNINGS & JENNINGS
MANAGEMENT CONSULTANTS
116 EAST BOULEVARD
TOLEDO, OHIO 43614

October 15, 1978

Thank you, Mr. Jones . . .

. . . for your interest in why we use this form for our letters.

Actually, we adopted it five years ago because we wanted our
letters to look modern but not freakish and because we felt
that other letter forms contained a great deal of excess
baggage like stereotyped salutations and closes.

Our clients like it too because it gets off to a direct start;
they learn to use the broken construction of the first sentence
very quickly, and it can be arranged in a wide variety of ways,
but always with the reader's name mentioned.

Finally, this form forces the correspondent to stop without the
conventional "gobbledygook" of complimentary endings. In short,
we think this form reflects the modern, efficient approach to
management problems we use every day.

George C. Demarest

George C. Demarest
Vice-President

Mr. Chauncy E. Jones
3876 Sunset Drive
Long Beach, California 90805

JOHNSON & JOHNSON SECRETARIAL SERVICE

1111 EAST STREET
TARRYTOWN, NEW YORK 10591

March 5, 1978

Mr. J. C. Cummings
347 East Oak Street
Council Bluffs, Iowa 51501

Dear Mr. Cummings:

This letter illustrates the block form of letter dress, which
has become one of the most widely used methods of arranging
letters.

It takes its name from the fact that the inside address, the
salutation, and the paragraphs of the letter itself are
arranged in blocks without indention. The block form offers two
distinct advantages: it saves stenographic time and reduces
the number of margins. Its wide acceptance at the present
time offers assurance that the letter arranged in block form
is correct and modern.

If you desire your letters to be attractive in appearance,
modern, and economical with regard to stenographic time, I
heartily recommend the block form as the most suitable for
the needs of your office.

Sincerely yours,

Geraldine A. Fisher

Geraldine A. Fisher
Correspondence Supervisor

GAF:GWC

C. L. DREW & CO.

STENOGRAPHERS · TYPISTS · DUPLICATING

100 BROADWAY

NEW YORK, N.Y. 10005

March 5, 1978

Ms. Roberta C. Vanderlyn
2202 Middlebury Road
Winchester, Maine 21873

Dear Ms. Vanderlyn:

　　I appreciate your interest in my reasons for recommending the type of letter arrangement which our company uses in its correspondence.

　　After careful consideration, I recommended the semiblock form as the most effective for our company. This recommendation was based on my belief that this form combined most of the advantages of the block and the indented forms.

　　The block arrangement of the inside address appeals to me as symmetrical and economical of secretarial time; furthermore, open punctuation is modern and efficient. Perhaps it is no more than a whim on my part, but I prefer to have the paragraphs of the actual message indented as they are in books, newspapers, and magazines.

　　The semiblock form meets all these requirements; it has proved effective and is well liked by our staff of correspondents and secretaries after six years of use.

Sincerely yours,

John H. Porter

John H. Porter
Correspondence Supervisor

JHP:CPA

BAUMGARTNER & JONES

MANAGEMENT CONSULTANTS
4 RIVER STREET
CHICAGO, ILL. 60656

March 5, 1978

Mr. Donald E. Woodbury
3126 Westview Road
Seattle, Washington 98119

Dear Mr. Woodbury:

Your comments about the form of our letters interested me
greatly. As you pointed out, letters do reflect the personality
of the firm which sends them, and that fact played a large part
in our decision to adopt the complete— or, as it is sometimes
called, the full-block form.

As management consultants, we felt that our letters should
exemplify the same standards of efficiency and the modern
methods we advocate in industry. For that reason, we saw no
sound reason for retaining a letter form which requires changes
of margins and unnecessary stenographic time.

The salient features of the full-block form are illustrated
in this letter. You will be interested to know that we have
received a number of favorable comments about our letter form and
that our Stenographic Department likes it very much.

Sincerely yours,

E. J. Baumgartner

E. J. Baumgartner,
Partner

EJB:mo

FRY'S OFFICE HELPERS

490 175TH PLACE

WESTBERRY. N.Y. 10603

March 5, 1978

Ms. Office Secretary
Better Business Letters, Inc.
1 Main Street
Busytown, U.S.A.

HAD YOU HEARD?

There's a new movement under way to take some of the monotony
out of letters given you to type. The movement is
symbolized by the Simplified Letter being sponsored by NOMA.

What is it? You're reading a sample.

Notice the left block format and the general positioning of the
letter. We didn't write "Dear Ms. _____," nor will we
write "Yours truly" or "Sincerely yours." Are they really
important? We feel just as friendly to you without them.

Notice the following points:

1   Date location
2   The address
3   The subject
4   The name of the writer

Now take a look at the Suggestions prepared for you. Talk them
over with your boss. But don't form a final opinion until you've
really tried out The Letter. That's what our Secretary did.
As a matter of fact, she finally wrote most of the Suggestions
herself.

She says she's sold—and hopes you'll have good luck with better
(Simplified) letters.

Vaughn Fry

VAUGHN FRY

parsimonious and careless. While undue importance should not be placed on the letter's physical appearance, an attractive letterhead certainly has great value. Like a well-tailored suit, it makes a good impression; and since the cost of this "suit" is a very minor part of letter costs, it should be custom tailored to your needs.

A standard size and good quality of stationery is, therefore, a good investment. Although there has been a trend to various colors of stationery, white or some conservative color is preferable to anything that might give an impression of gaudiness.

The letterhead should be as simple as possible, but it may be considered inadequate unless it answers the following questions?

1. Does it tell who you are?

2. Does it tell what you do? When the company name is not sufficiently descriptive of the type of business, a line should be added to do this.

3. Does it tell where you are located and how you may be reached by telephone, cable, or both?

4. Can it be read easily at a glance?

5. Does it represent your company in a dignified and effective way?

Any symbol or emblem associated with a business may be included as a part of the letterhead. Many companies include the date of their founding and names of company officials, but long lists of agencies, products, or personnel should never be a part of the letterhead because they give the whole letter a cluttered appearance. The worst fault of most letterheads is the attempt to pack too much information in them, with a resulting complexity and cluttered appearance. If simplicity of design and quality are the criteria used in selecting the letterhead and stationery, the result will be in good taste.

3. In the salutation and complimentary close, capitalize only the first letter of the first word, except for proper names and titles.

A. Except for proper names and titles (President, Mr., Sir, Dr., etc.), capitalize only the first letter of the first word of the salutation.

Dear Mr. Davidson:

My dear Mr. Davidson:

My dear Sir:

B. Capitalize only the first letter of the first word of the complimentary close.

Your very truly,

Very truly yours,

Sincerely yours,

Cordially yours,

C. When no salutation or complimentary close is used, as in the less formal or simplified letter forms, the first paragraph with its mention of the recipient's name may be arranged in a variety of ways:

You know, Ms. McCleod, that we are having our spring sale this week.

Did you remember, Mr. Jones . . .
. . . that your premium was due last week?

Thank you so much, Ms. Smith, for calling this matter to our attention.

Since these letter forms call for no complimentary close, only a signature above the typed name (and title, if appropriate) is needed:

We do appreciate your cooperation in this matter.

James C. Jones

James C. Jones
Vice-president

The typed name is usually three spaces below the last line.

4. The salutation and the complimentary close should agree in tone.

As we have seen, much of the verbiage of business letters is now somewhat meaningless and the result of outworn tradition; however, certain degrees of formality or acquaintanceship can be expressed in the choice of the salutation and the complimentary close. These two parts should agree in tone, since it is obviously inconsistent to begin with a highly formal salutation and to close in an informal or even friendly fashion. The following groups show the various salutations and closes that may appropriately be used together:

Rather Formal

My dear Mr. Smith: Yours very truly,
My dear Sir or   Very sincerely yours,
Madam:

Less Formal

Dear Sir or Madam: Sincerely yours,
Dear Mr. Smith: Sincerely,
Gentlemen and La-   Yours truly,
dies:

Cordially yours usually implies acquaintanceship or long business relationship; *Respectfully yours* is generally used in letters to those older or of higher rank than the letter writer. *Dear Sirs* as a salutation is obsolete. As mentioned before, some correspondents would completely eliminate salutations and complimentary closes if they could. Traditionalists, on the other hand, would insist that they be retained and used properly so as to suggest the relationship that exists between the writer and reader. If these two warring camps were ever to approach a bargaining table, an arbitrator might encourage them to accept something like the following alternative middle ground.

With proper respect for tradition and due regard for the goals of efficiency and contemporary usage, how about retaining *but simplifying* salutations and complimentary closes? How about just *Dear Mr. Jones* or just *Mr. Jones?* And how about just *Sincerely* or *Respectfully* or *Cordially?* Why does a writer have to be *yours?*

5. Punctuate the salutation with a colon and the complimentary close with a comma.

Usage in punctuating the business letter has not completely crystallized. The general tendency to reduce punctuation has affected the letter as well as other forms of writing; more and more companies, for example, no longer use the colon after the salutation and the comma after the complimentary close. Letter writers, therefore, have to choose how far they want to go toward an absolute minimum in punctuating the major parts of the letter; if they follow the more traditional practice, the date, salutation, and complimentary close will be punctuated as shown in these examples.

Ms. Jane McDowell
15 East Main Street
Ann Arbor, Michigan 48103

Dear Ms. McDowell:

                                        Sincerely yours,

The Eastside Corporation
2900 Amsterdam Avenue
New York, N.Y. 10047

Gentlemen and Ladies:

                                        Yours truly,

Within the letter itself, the accepted rules of punctuation should, of course, be followed. See the appropriate pages of the other parts of the reference section for the major rules of punctuation.

6. Company policy should determine the signature.

The signature of the letter should be several spaces directly below the complimentary close; the stenographer customarily leaves sufficient space between the complimentary close (or, if there is none, the last line of the letter) and the typed name and title of the writer for the actual signature, as in the following example:

Sincerely yours,

James Adams

James Adams
Sales Manager
The Green Company

Company policy will determine whether the typed name, title, and company name should follow the pattern of the preceding example or whether the company name comes first, as in the following example:

Sincerely yours,
THE GREEN COMPANY

James Adams

Sales Manager

There is no hard and fast rule on whether the individual's signature or the typed company name is the better practice. A survey by *Printers' Ink* indicates that the use of the company name is somewhat affected by the subject of the letter. Where the message tends to be more personal in tone or is addressed to an individual known to the writer, the great majority of letters surveyed carried the personal signature followed by the typed name and title. On the other hand, when the subject is more general or the correspondents do not know one another, the company name is likely to be used as part of the signature.

Another guide to whether the company or individual form of signature should be used is whether the letter is written in terms of "I" or "we." The use of "we" exclusively in such expressions as "We have looked into the record" and "We want to extend our best wishes for a prosperous year" often gives the letter a rather pompous air. On the other hand, frequent shifts from "I" to "we" within one letter are likely to confuse the reader. Here again practice is not fixed; many companies set up their own policies governing this phase of letter style.

7. A woman should sign her full name.

If the correspondent is a woman, that fact should be clearly indicated. Such a practice would eliminate the possibility of Agatha Winters being addressed as Mr. A. Winters. Although the current use of *Ms.* has minimized the importance of a woman's marital status, women still have the option of using Miss or Mrs. The final choice, of course, is up to the writer.

8. Signatures should be legible.

The widespread use of the typewriter has fortunately decreased the need for handwriting. This boon to the business world has not altered the fact that too many correspondents still sign their names in indecipherable scrawls and too many typists fail to type the correspondent's name beneath the signature. Particularly in companies that deal with handwritten letters from the general public, the cry is still heard, "Why on earth don't you sign your name so I can read it?" People who have received such letters will enjoy the opinions expressed by Thomas Bailey Aldrich in the following letter to Professor Edward S. Morse:

> It was very pleasant to me to get a letter from you the other day. Perhaps I should have found it pleasanter if I had been able to decipher it.
>
> I don't think I have mastered anything beyond the date (which I knew) and the signature (which I guessed at). There's a singular and a perpetual charm in a letter of yours; it never grows old, it never loses its novelty.
>
> Other letters are read and thrown away and forgotten, but yours are kept forever—unread. One of them will last a reasonable man a lifetime.

Since the signature is an integral and important part of the business letter, it should be legible, placed correctly in the space provided for it, and put on an even keel. Many correspondents erroneously think that a distinctive touch is added by slanting the signature or, what is worse, by writing over the typed name.

9.   The date is usually written in the upper right-hand section.

Unless the letterhead is of a design that makes a different place preferable or unless the simplified letter form is used with the date at the left-hand margin, the date should be placed in the upper right-hand section of the letter and at least two spaces above the first line of the inside address. The day of the month should always be set off from the year by a comma:

> February 24, 1971
>
> December 5, 1970

Such abbreviations as 6/7/71 should be avoided because they cause confusion; and there is no necessity for writing *th, nd, rd* after numerals in the date (September 15th, May 2nd, July 3rd)—write September 15, May 2, July 3). Military usage requires that dates be written 20 August 1978. While some business writers have adopted this usage, there seems to be little justification for changing from the traditional order of month, day, year—August 20, 1978.

10.   Use the address shown on the letterhead.

The correct address to use in writing to any company or individual is exactly that which the company or individual uses on its stationery or advertising. When street names using numerals, such as Fifth Avenue, East 116th Street, Second Avenue, are part of the address, the best procedure is to write them out if they are numbers from one to ten or if they can be expressed in one word; if they are more complex, use numerals:

79 Fifth Avenue

2719 East 116th Street

3019 102nd Street

With the establishment of the ZIP code (for Zone Improvement Plan), it may be only a matter of time before all big mailers will be using addresses such as:

Mr. Robert Sterling
291 Middle Street
45202

when they want speedy delivery to Cincinnati, Ohio. The system divides the country into areas east to west (there are exceptions), starting with 00601 (Puerto Rico) and ending with 99929 (Wrangell, Alaska). The first digit identifies one of ten basic geographical areas; the next two mark a major city or section center; the last two focus on specific mailing areas. Contrary to general opinion, the real savings of the Zone Improvement Plan result from the fact that large mailings of so-called "promotional" materials and the like are sorted according to Zip numbers before being taken to the post office. (An indispensable reference for all businesses is the *National ZIP Code Directory,* which contains the Zip codes for every mailing address in the United States and its territories. It may be ordered from the Superintendent of Documents, U.S. Government Printing Office, Washington, D.C. 20402.)

In using the Zip code, correspondents should remember the following:

1. Always use a Zip number, if you know it.

2. If you are certain of the number, you need use no state or city identification, as in the example for Mr. Sterling.

3. If you use city, state, *and* Zip number, the best practice is to use no punctuation between the state name and the Zip number other than the punctuation required for the state abbreviation:

Bloomington, Ill. 61701

Bloomington, Illinois 61701

4. The Zip number is customarily placed on the same line as the city and state names, but with short addresses it is sometimes placed on the last line by itself:

Mr. James Jones
Acra, New York
12740

Company policy and your own judgment must determine when it is appropriate
to make the change and drop city and state completely:

Mr. Jon Smith
517 Oak Street
61701

11. The salutation should agree with the first line of the inside address.

The most widely used salutations are *Gentlemen* (for companies or organizations)
and *Dear Mr. Smith* (for an individual). *Gentlemen* has largely supplanted the
former use of *Dear Sirs.* Careful writers feel that mentioning the individual by
name in the salutation—as *Dear Mr. Doe*—gives more warmth and a more
personal touch to the letter; for that reason *Dear Sir* has come to be considered
as too impersonal.

    The salutation should always agree with the first line of the inside address;
if that line is plural (a partnership, a company, a firm name), the salutation
should be plural. If the first line is feminine (a firm composed entirely of women),
the salutation should be feminine. Even though the letter is directed to the
attention of an individual, if the first line of the address is the company name,
the salutation should be plural. The following examples illustrate these points:

Williams, Clement, Constant, and Williams, Inc.
1410 Broadway Building
Cleveland, Ohio 44106

Gentlemen and Ladies:

Most American correspondents gag a bit over using *Mesdames;* consequently, *Dear Ladies* or the following can be used:

The Three Sisters Dress Shop
3914 East Third Street
Seattle, Washington 93071

Ladies:

Note the difference in the salutation when the *Attention* device is used:

Mr. Arnold Lehman, Sales Manager
The Viking Air Conditioning Company
3133 Constitution Avenue
Omaha, Nebraska 69717

Dear Mr. Lehman:

but

The Viking Air Conditioning Company
3133 Constitution Avenue
Omaha, Nebraska 69717

Attention: Mr. Arnold Lehman, Sales Manager

Gentlemen and Ladies:

When addressing a post-office box, a newspaper number, or a reader whose identity is unknown, use *Gentlemen and Ladies* as the proper salutation:

B14978, *The New York Times*
Times Square
New York, New York 10036

Gentlemen and Ladies:

12.   To direct the letter to the attention of an individual within the company, add an "Attention" line two spaces below the inside address.

Frequently it is desirable to direct letters which concern the business of a whole firm or corporation to the attention of an individual within the company with whom one has had previous correspondence or who is familiar with the specific problem at hand. The word *of* after *Attention* has come to be regarded as superfluous, and practice varies as to using the colon after *Attention*. The *Attention* line should be placed two spaces directly below the last line of the inside address and with the same margin. The earlier practice of centering the *Attention* line is no longer followed, because that space is customarily used to indicate the subject of the letter.

The Black Company
1419 Broad Street
Winchester, Massachusetts 01890

Attention Mr. Michael Cunningham

Gentlemen and Ladies:

Mention of file numbers, policy numbers, or other aids in identifying the business at hand may be made in a similar manner.

The Worthy and White Company
2789 Canal Street
Kingston, New York 12749

Your file No. 71698

Gentlemen and Ladies:

In accordance with the principle that salutations should agree with the first line of the inside address, the following are the forms most frequently used:

Inside address	*Salutation*
Mr. John C. Smith 3194 Blank Avenue Middletown, Conn. 06547	Dear Mr. Smith:
The John C. Smith Company 4978 Center Street Centerville, Idaho 83610	Gentlemen and Ladies:
The John C. Smith Company 4978 Center Street Centerville, Idaho 83610 Attention Ms. E. D. White	Gentlemen and Ladies:
Ms. E. D. White The John C. Smith Company 4978 Center Street Centerville, Idaho 83610	Dear Ms. White:
The Lakewood Women's Club 130 Fourth Avenue Lakewood, New Jersey 08701	Ladies:

13. The second page of the letter should not be on letterhead paper and should be clearly numbered.

When letters are more than one page in length, the additional pages should be on stationery to match the first sheet but without the letterhead. These pages may be headed in any of the following ways, although the first form is most frequently used because it is most suitable for filing:

Mr. Cunningham　　　　　-2-　　　　July 7, 1978

Page 2
Mr. Cunningham　　　(the addressee)

14. The initials of the dictator and the stenographer and a reference to any enclosures should be indicated at the bottom of the letter.

Numerous methods of indicating the initials of the dictator of the letter and the stenographer are in common use. This information should be placed at the left margin of the letter and at least two spaces lower on the paper than the last line of the signature.

FJP/KRS

FLT:CMJ

DJL/mag

W:m

Whenever there are enclosures, notation of that fact should be made as follows:

FJP:KRS

Encl.

Enclosures should be arranged in back of the letter in the order of their importance or in the sequence in which they are mentioned in the letter. With the exception of checks or drafts, enclosures should never be placed on top of a letter.

15. Envelopes should give the complete address.

The complete address should always be given on the envelope, and if one of the letter forms with an inside address is used, the address on the envelope should be identical with that on the letter. As section 10 indicates, a name, street and number, and Zip code could be considered a "complete" address if company policy permits. While it seems somewhat gratuitous to say so, a number of correspondents have discovered to their chagrin that a great deal of confusion and embarrassment can be avoided by placing the proper letter in the proper envelope!

16. The signer of the letter has final responsibility for it.

Since the finished letter is, in a very real sense, *your* representative, take care to make it correct in every detail. In today's business world, the best letters are those which are the result of careful thought by *both* dictator and transcriber. Ultimately, the final responsibility for every aspect of the letter rests completely on the person who signs it, but the best results occur when the dictator and transcriber work as a team. The transcriber should proofread carefully for errors in spelling, punctuation, grammar, or typing and should see that all initials, names, dates, and addresses are accurate. The correspondent should then read the letter carefully for the same purposes and to see that it effectively does what it is intended to do. By signing a letter without reading it—as too many correspondents do—the correspondent is shirking a fundamental obligation to see that every letter mailed is as nearly perfect as the correspondent and the typist can make it.

INDEX